Frommer's®

EUROPEAN CRUISES

AND PORTS OF CALL

Here's what the critics say about Frommer's:

"Amazingly easy to use. Very portable, very complete."

—*Booklist*

♦

"The only mainstream guide to list specific prices. The Walter Cronkite of guidebooks—with all that implies."

—*Travel & Leisure*

♦

"Complete, concise, and filled with useful information."

—*New York Daily News*

♦

"The best series for travelers who want one easy-to-use guidebook."

—*U.S. Air Magazine*

Other Great Guides for Your Trip:

Frommer's England

Frommer's Europe

Frommer's France

Frommer's Germany

Frommer's Greece

Frommer's Greek Islands

Frommer's Ireland

Frommer's Italy

Frommer's Portugal

Frommer's Scandinavia

Frommer's Scotland

Frommer's Spain

and other great city, regional, and budget guides

Other Great Frommer's Cruise Guides:

Frommer's Alaska Cruises and Ports of Call

Frommer's Caribbean Cruises and Ports of Call

Frommer's®

1st Edition

EUROPEAN CRUISES
AND PORTS OF CALL

by Fran Wenograd Golden

IDG Books Worldwide, Inc.
An International Data Group Company
Foster City, CA • Chicago, IL • Indianapolis, IN • New York, NY

About the Author

Fran Wenograd Golden is the editor of the first-time cruisers pages on cruisemates.com and the cruise columnist at concierge.com and is coauthor of *Frommer's Alaska Cruises and Ports of Call,* a contributor to *Frommer's Greece,* and author of *TVacations: A Fun Guide to the Sites, The Stars and the Inside Stories Behind Your Favorite TV Shows.* She lives north of Boston with her husband, Ed, and their two kids.

IDG Books Worldwide, Inc.

An International Data Group Company
919 E. Hillsdale Blvd.
Suite 400
Foster City, CA 94404

Find us online at **www.frommers.com**

ISBN 0-02-863489-6
ISSN 1527-1641

Editor: Matt Hannafin
Production Editor: Christina Van Camp
Design by Michele Laseau
Digital Cartography by John Decamillis and Hans G. Andersson
Page creation by Melissa Auciello-Brogan, Kendra Span, John Bitter, Angel Perez, Carl Pierce, and Linda Quigley
Cruise review format developed by Heidi Sarna and Matt Hannafin

Special Sales

For general information on IDG Books Worldwide's books in the U.S., please call our Consumer Customer Service department at 1-800-762-2974. For reseller information, including discounts and premium sales, please call our Reseller Customer Service department at 1-800-434-3422.

Manufactured in the United States of America

5 4 3 2 1

Contents

4 The Cruise Experience 45

Part 2: The Cruise Lines & Their Ships

5 The Ratings (and How to Read Them) 63

6 The American Mainstream Lines 68

7 The European Lines 119

Part 3: The Ports of Call

List of Maps

Acknowledgments

Special thanks to Heidi Sarna, author of *Frommer's Caribbean Cruises and Ports of Call,* from which portions of chapters 4 through 9 have been adapted. Thanks, too, to the other writers who contributed to this book: Ted Scull, Jonathan Siskin, Vivian Fancher, Arthur Harris, David Mott, Matt Hannafin, Laura Dennis, Carla Hunt, and Jerry Brown. Special thanks as well to the land programs department at Silversea Cruises; the public relations departments of all the cruise lines; Cruise Europe; The Association of Mediterranean Cruise Ports; the Cruise Lines International Association; and to Anne Kalosh and Carla Hunt for their help.

This book would not have happened without the hard work of editor Matt Hannafin or the loving support of my family and friends. Big hugs especially to Ed, Erin, and Eli.

An Invitation to the Reader

In researching this book, we discovered many wonderful places—hotels, restaurants, shops, and more. We're sure you'll find others. Please tell us about them, so we can share the information with your fellow travelers in upcoming editions. If you were disappointed with a recommendation, we'd love to know that, too. Please write to:

Frommer's European Cruises and Ports of Call, 1st Edition
IDG Travel
1633 Broadway
New York, NY 10019

An Additional Note

Please be advised that travel information is subject to change at any time—and this is especially true of prices. We therefore suggest that you write or call ahead for confirmation when making your travel plans. The authors, editors, and publisher cannot be held responsible for the experiences of readers while traveling. Your safety is important to us, however, so we encourage you to stay alert and be aware of your surroundings. Keep a close eye on cameras, purses, and wallets, all favorite targets of thieves and pickpockets.

What the Symbols Mean

✪ Frommer's Favorites

Our favorite places and experiences—outstanding for quality, value, or both.

The following abbreviations are used for credit cards:

AE	American Express	EURO	Eurocard
CB	Carte Blanche	JCB	Japan Credit Bank
DC	Diners Club	MC	MasterCard
DISC	Discover	V	Visa
ER	EnRoute		

Find Frommer's Online

www.frommers.com offers up-to-the-minute listings on almost 200 cities around the globe—including the latest bargains and candid, personal articles updated daily by Arthur Frommer himself. No other Web site offers such comprehensive and timely coverage of the world of travel.

Europe

Norwegian Sea
North Atlantic Ocean
Bergen
NORWAY
Aberdeen
SCOTLAND
Perth
Edinburgh
North Sea
DENMARK
Belfast
IRELAND
Dublin
Liverpool
Cork
U. K.
THE NETHERLANDS
Hamburg
Bath
Oxford
London
Salisbury
Amsterdam
Rotterdam
Antwerp
BELGIUM
GERMANY
English Channel
Brussels
Liège
Bonn
Le Havre
Frankfurt
LUX.
Rothenburg ob der Tauber
Paris
Strasbourg
Augsburg
LOIRE VALLE
Munich
Bern
Innsbruck
FRANCE
SWITZERLAND
Bay of Biscay
Geneva
Bordeaux
Milan
Bilbao
Arles
PROVENCE
MONACO
Portofino
Marseille
Nice
Florence
Porto
St-Tropez
Côte d'Azur
ANDORRA
Livorno
Cannes
PORTUGAL
Madrid
Barcelona
CORSICA
Lisbon
SPAIN
Córdoba
Valencia
ALGARVE
Seville
ANDALUSIA
MALLORCA
SARDINIA
Granada
Cádiz
Málaga
Cagliari
Costa del Sol
Mediterranean Sea
Gibraltar (U.K.)
0
150 Mi
0
150 Km
N
E-0001

SWEDEN
Trondheim
Sundsvall
Gulf of Bothnia
FINLAND
Tampere
Helsinki
Petersburg
Gävle
Oslo
Stockholm
Tallinn
ESTONIA
RUSSIA
Göteborg
Riga
LATVIA
Baltic Sea
Copenhagen
LITHUANIA
Vilnius
Tver
Minsk
Gdansk
Warnemünde & Rostock
BELARUS
Poznan
Warsaw
Berlin
POLAND
Kyiv
UKRAINE
Karlovy Vary (Carlsbad)
Prague
CZECH REPUBLIC
Krakow
Lvov
Mariánské Lázně (Marienbad)
Danube River
SLOVAKIA
Vienna
Bratislava
MOLDOVA
DANUBE VALLEY
Budapest
Chisinau
Odessa
Salzburg
AUSTRIA
HUNGARY
Cluj-Napoca
Lake Balaton
Ljubljana
SLOVENIA
Zagreb
CROATIA
ROMANIA
Venice
Black Sea
Constanta
Bucharest
BOSNIA
Sarajevo
Belgrade
SERBIA
Varna
Adriatic Sea
BULGARIA
ITALY
Dubrovnik
MONTENEGRO
Sofiya
Rome
Titograd
Skopje
MACEDONIA
Istanbul
Naples
Tirana
ALBANIA
POMPEII
Sorrento
TURKEY
Tyrrhenian Sea
GREECE
Aegean Sea
Delphi
Ionian Sea
Kusadasi
Palermo
Athens
MYKONOS
PELOPONNESE
SICILY
RHODES
SANTORINI
MALTA
CRETE

Introduction

I first cruised in Europe—or, more exactly, *to* Europe—in 1959 when I was 3 years old and my mother, brother, and I traveled transatlantic from New York to Southampton on the old *United States.* I remember nothing of the trip by sea, but obviously something stuck since I love to visit Europe, I love to cruise, and I find it great fun to combine the two.

Cruising in Europe can be a wonderful experience, whether you are a first-time visitor to the region or are returning to see countries you've visited before from a new ocean-view perspective (many European cities were, in fact, built to be seen from the sea) and a different pace.

The ports in Europe hold treasures of antiquities and natural beauty, fascinating history (you'll quickly realize how young 1776 is in the scheme of things), and enchanting cultural experiences.

From your ship, depending on the route you choose, you will have easy access to such delights as the ancient cities of Pompeii and Ephesus; Europe's historic and cultural capitals, including London, Paris, and Rome; modern port cities; gorgeous islands; scenic fjords; rugged coastlines; and glamorous resorts.

You can visit museums, cathedrals, palaces, and monuments and learn everything you always wanted to know about the region's history. Or you can concentrate on the Europe of today, checking out the latest trends in food and fashion before they hit the shores of the U.S.

WHY A CRUISE?

Europe is a popular cruising region, second only to the Caribbean (and followed in third place by Alaska), and it's really a no-brainer to see why. The region truly offers something for everyone: great sights, shopping, beaches, museums, a diversity of cultural and natural attractions, and a decent climate.

The **ports** are close together, meaning you can visit several in a limited period of time; the seas relatively calm; the opportunities interesting and diverse. Europe has a seafaring tradition that goes back to ancient times—you can even choose an itinerary that follows the same exact route as the ancient mariners—so is it any wonder a European cruise sounds so exciting and romantic?

A cruise is also one of the most practical, comfortable, and economical ways to see Europe. You only have to unpack once, your floating hotel takes you to different ports in different countries, and you don't have to deal with the hassle and expense of getting around Europe by plane or train.

On a cruise you are fed, pampered, and taken care of in a stress-free environment. You don't have to worry about things like currency fluctuations and their effect on your hotel, entertainment, and meal costs, since all of these are included in your cruise fare. Food offerings will be familiar—you can even sip a piña colada while viewing, say, St. Petersburg—and you don't have to deal with potential language problems, since there will be personnel on the ship who speak English.

A downside to cruising is you might not have as much time as you'd like in port to experience the local culture, although some lines overnight in cities like Venice, Monte Carlo, and Istanbul, and smaller ships may overnight in smaller cities. The cruise lines do their best, through their organized shore excursions, to get passengers to the major sights. And if you'd rather sit at a cafe and check out the local scene than do an organized tour, you can just head off on your own.

I've found when cruising in Europe, it's best to think of your cruise as a **sampler package.** If you fall in love with a city, plan on visiting again later.

EUROPEAN CRUISING 2000

Cruise lines—including major American lines like Princess, Holland America, Royal Caribbean, Norwegian Cruise Line, and Celebrity—have steadily been increasing their presence in Europe, and they offer all sorts of itinerary options and a variety of ships to suit everyone's tastes. The season has even expanded from April to October to March to November, and there are even cruises offered now in the winter, mostly in the Mediterranean.

North American fleet capacity in Europe, according to G. P. Wild (International) Ltd., a cruise-industry analyst, grew from 774,149 bed-days in 1989 to 3,714,437 bed-days in 1998, an increase of almost fivefold. And the numbers continue to rise, despite current events: A couple years ago the cruise lines were predicting that 1999 would be the biggest year for Europe cruising ever, but the conflict in Kosovo caused those hopes to fizzle. The cruise lines ended up rerouting and canceling some sailings, and some passengers decided 1999 was not the year to visit after all (although the conflict was resolved early enough in the season to allow most cruise lines to recover without major losses). The lines are now pinning their hopes on Europe 2000, which they say will *really* be the biggest year ever, barring any new conflict in Eastern Europe or the Middle East.

The fleet will expand this year with new and additional ships. Holland America Line, for instance, will for the first time have three ships in Europe for the season; Orient Lines is adding a second ship; and Celebrity will introduce its brand new megaship *Millennium* in Europe this season. You can see Europe on a giant floating **American resort ship** with Las Vegas–style entertainment, a lavish casino and spa, and a mostly American clientele; choose a ship that's more like a **floating European hotel** where multiple languages will be spoken, Americans will be the minority, and meals will be a form of entertainment; or pick a small, **casual ship** where you can jump off a platform at the stern for a swim.

And you can choose **itineraries** as diverse as the Rivieras, where the sun shines on cafes and beaches in places like St-Tropez or the Norwegian fjords, where the midnight sun may shine all day and night, but you'll use that light to spot whales and reindeer rather than the rich and famous in their skimpy bikinis.

You can easily extend whatever itinerary you choose with a **land stay,** which the cruise lines can arrange for you, usually at reasonable rates, or which you can arrange on your own.

The lines are also expanding into different cruise regions in Europe and introducing ore 1-week options in addition to more traditional 10- and 12-day Europe itinerar-. For instance, Royal Olympic's new high-speed *Olympic Voyager* will introduce a

1-week itinerary that combines the Greek Isles with Egypt and Israel; and Holland America will join Costa Cruises in offering 1-week Baltic sailings.

Cruising in Europe has been a rather big-ticket item in the past, but various recent specials offered by the cruise lines are bringing **prices** down, making it more affordable. And while Europe has traditionally drawn a senior crowd, the cruise lines, through shorter itineraries and a greater diversity of product, have done a good job of late in attracting families, younger couples, singles, and honeymooners. (A Greek Isles cruise is a particularly good romantic choice!)

BON VOYAGE!

Just the fact that you've bought the book means you've got a hankering to cruise; now it's my job to find the cruise that's just right for you from among the huge selection of ships and cruise experiences in the market. In the following chapters, I'll detail the various and diverse itinerary options in Europe and the types of ships that can take you there. And I give you a taste of what you can expect from your European cruise experience.

Whichever cruise option you choose, I'm sure your Europe cruise will be an enlightening experience that will leave you wanting to come back again for more.

Frommer's Favorites

Whether you're looking for pampering and resort amenities or an off-the-beaten track experience, cruise ships offer it in Europe. To make it easier for you to see what's what, I've put together a list of Frommer's Favorites—my picks for the best cruise experiences and offerings. You'll find full details on the ships in Part 2, and full details on ports in Part 3.

1 Best Ships for Luxury

- **Seabourn:** Small and intimate, Seabourn's sleek modern ships are floating pleasure palaces bathing all who enter in doting service and the finest cuisine at sea. You'll luxuriate in unprecedented amounts of onboard space and an almost 1 to 1 passenger/staff ratio, with service worthy of the grand hotels of Europe.
- **Silversea:** A little less high-brow than Seabourn, and operating slightly larger ships (carrying about 200 passengers against Seabourn's 89 to 140), Silversea still offers one of the most luxurious experiences around.
- **Crystal:** Crystal's dream ships offer the best of two worlds: pampering service and scrumptious cuisine on ships large enough to offer lots of outdoor deck space, generous fitness facilities, four restaurants, and over half a dozen bars and entertainment venues. Crystal's California ethic tends to keep things more mingly and chatty than aboard the more staid Seabourn.

2 Best Mainstream Ships

- **Celebrity:** While everyone's new ships are beautiful, Celebrity has proved itself above the norm and I have no reason to doubt the line's newest ship, *Millennium,* debuting in Europe this year, will carry on the tradition. I particularly like the fact that these ships have cutting-edge art collections. The dining rooms are stunning and feature wonderful French-inspired cuisine, and there are plenty of plush getaway areas including cigar and champagne bars.
- **Holland America Line:** Another top pick would have to be Holland America Line's flagship *Rotterdam,* which offers everything a new ship should while not forgetting its seafaring tradition.

3 Best Small Alternative Ships

- **Classical Cruises' *Clelia II:*** The *Clelia II* is an all-suite vessel that offers a very comfortable, educationally focused small-ship experience generally attracting an older clientele.
- **Clipper Cruise Line's *Clipper Adventurer:*** The *Clipper Adventurer* is another solid contender in this category—again, usually attracting an older crowd.
- **Zeus Tours' *Galileo Sun:*** For the younger crowd, a fun small-ship experience that's not too shabby can be had on Zeus's *Galileo Sun.*

4 Best Ships for Families

- **Princess's *Grand Princess:*** Nothing beats the giant *Grand Princess* in this category. The 109,000-ton vessel has a spacious children's playroom, a fenced-in outside deck area designated as kids' space (with a kiddie pool and a fleet of red tricycles), and for older kids a teen center complete with computers, video games, a sound system, and even a teens-only hot tub and sunbathing area. Supervised activities are offered for those ages 2 to 17, and the ship also has amenities designed to please adults and kids alike, including a pizzeria, basketball and volleyball courts, and a virtual-reality game room (including a motion-simulator ride).
- **Classical Cruises:** Also worth a mention in this category is Classical Cruises, which while it tends to attract an older crowd, once a year offers a special antiquities itinerary specifically designed for families.

5 Best European Ships

- **Costa:** Italian line Costa does the best overall package with interesting entertainment, fun activities, comfortable surroundings, and wonderful itineraries. The line's affiliation with Carnival Corp. (which owns a major stake in the company) hasn't hurt it one bit.
- **P&O:** The British P&O—parent company of Princess Cruises—has a fleet of classy, beautiful ships sailing interesting itineraries. Entertainment is high quality, the onboard atmosphere is generally low-key, and dining is more varied than you'd expect, owing to infusions from the cuisines of Britain's former colonies (curries from India, for example).
- **Fred. Olsen:** British Fred. Olsen caters to a professional and/or early retired class of mostly British Europeans and offers a friendly atmosphere, fairly priced, aboard a couple of older ocean liner–style ships.
- **Swan Hellenic:** Swan Hellenic provides one of the strongest enrichment programs on the high seas, with four or five lecturers giving talks aboard, dining with the passengers, and accompanying them ashore. The non-repeating itineraries, generally lasting 2 weeks, attract a very loyal and generally well-educated British clientele for whom a standard cruise would never do. Good manners and a quiet approach to life reign.

6 Most Romantic Ships

- **Windstar:** Got to go with the sails here. Windstar's large sailing ships offer a product that's hard to beat for romance. You can snuggle in your comfy cabin watching movies on the VCR or on the deck, enjoy a romantic dinner for two in the open-seating restaurant, and go off hand-in-hand to explore the lovely ports.

- **Sea Cloud:** The gorgeous, historic sailing yacht *Sea Cloud* offers some of the most lavish fantasy-suites at sea.

7 Best Value

- **Orient Lines:** Orient Lines' product is solid, port-focused, and popular with an older clientele. Pre- and/or post-cruise hotel stays, airfare, sightseeing, and transfers are all included in the price.
- **Renaissance Cruises:** Renaissance, which advertises aggressively through direct mail and on the Internet, is gaining fans with its extraordinary values. As with Orient, pre- and/or post-cruise hotel stays, airfare, sightseeing, and transfers are all included in the price, but be aware that there may be hidden costs, such as recommended crew tips that are double the industry norm.
- **Norwegian Coastal Voyage:** Norwegian Coastal Voyage gives passengers a close-up view of Norway on working ships (they also carry cargo and vehicles) that are both comfortable and budget-priced.

8 Best Ships for Pampering

- **Crystal Cruises:** Crystal pampers all around, including in its nice spas.
- **Celebrity Cruises:** Celebrity's ships, including the new *Millennium,* offer AquaSpas with indoor thalassotherapy pools and a wealth of soothing and beautifying treatments that are hard to beat.
- **Royal Caribbean:** The *Splendour* and *Legend of the Seas* offer wonderful, soothing ShipShape spas with adjacent spacious solarium pool areas.
- **Princess's *Grand Princess:*** The *Grand Princess* reserves a good portion of the Sun Deck for pampering.
- **First European Cruises *Mistral:*** First European's new *Mistral* offers an unusual outdoor thalassotherapy pool.

9 Best Ships for Entertainment

- **Royal Caribbean:** The Las Vegas–style shows are well-produced, with music provided by a big live band. You'll also find headliners, a variety of cabaret and lounge acts, and even classical music presentations.
- **Celebrity:** Aboard Celebrity's elegant modern ships you'll find well-produced musical reviews of the Broadway-show-tune variety, interactive entertainment like a magician who does card tricks at your table, and good cabaret acts.
- **Holland America:** At Holland America you'll find some of the glitziest costumes afloat (in the show lounge), as well as a variety of cabaret acts including magicians, comedians, and illusionists. An added bonus is the crew talent show, which usually features folk song and dance from the Philippines and Indonesia.
- **Norwegian:** Ambitious Vegas-style show productions, comedians, and juggling acts are the regular offerings, and excellent local entertainers, including folk dance troupes, come on board in some ports.
- **Princess:** The Las Vegas–style show productions are well-executed and the cabaret singers excellent (sometimes including known performers). There are also quiet delights like pianists and jazz performers and fun acts like puppeteers and hypnotists.
- **Costa:** Show lounge presentations are creative and include attempts at modern ballet, plus lots of nighttime participatory activities like dance contests, a carnival, and even a Mr. Universe competition.

10 Best Cuisine

- **Crystal:** Crystal's cuisine is well-prepared and creative in the dining rooms and at buffets, but the very best is served in the alternative Asian restaurant, where the offerings include sushi. There's also a specialty Italian restaurant.
- **Seabourn:** The culinary experience on these ships— creative, flavorful, and well-presented—rivals any fine dining you can find on land and is absolutely the best you can find at sea.
- **Silversea:** Silversea offers excellent dining, not only in the main dining room but also at the informal buffets and in theme dinners like Italian, Chinese, and Southwestern.
- **Radisson:** The *Radisson Diamond* has one of the nicest dining rooms afloat and fine cuisine to match, with an emphasis on the regions where the ship is cruising.
- **Windstar:** Renowned Los Angeles chef Joachim Splichal advises on Windstar's creative "California cuisine" menus and wonderful presentation.
- **Celebrity:** Though it's of not quite the same caliber as the luxury lines, Celebrity, with its cuisine overseen by celebrity French chef Michel Roux, is certainly tops among the mainstream lines, offering elegant French-inspired dishes.
- **The French river barges:** The closest many of us can come to having a private chef, the French-trained chefs aboard these barges have the advantage of being able to incorporate great local ingredients in their menus.

11 Best Itinerary

- **HAL's *Rotterdam:*** For a comprehensive tour of Europe, I've got to go with the 38-day itinerary offered on Holland America Line's *Rotterdam* from Copenhagen to Athens. Included are port calls in Estonia, Russia, Finland, Sweden, Germany, Denmark, Norway, Iceland, Ireland, Spain, Monaco, Italy, Greece, Cyprus, and Turkey, as well as Egypt and Israel. You can also take the cruise in a 19-day portion, either Copenhagen to Dublin or Dublin to Athens.

12 Best Adventure Itineraries

- **Special Expeditions:** Europe is not traditionally an adventure destination, but Special Expeditions has made inroads, including its offer of a soft-adventure experience in the British Isles.
- **Norwegian Coastal Voyage:** Norwegian Coastal Voyage's ships sail as semi-cruise/semi-ferry ships between Bergen and Kirkenes, visiting no fewer than 35 ports (though sometimes the stops are incredibly short). Bergen Line, a related company, also sails *really* adventurous itineraries to Spitsbergen, an archipelago lying 360 miles north of Norway, in the Arctic.
- **OdessAmerica:** For something truly different, OdessAmerica offers river cruises in Siberia, including one down the Lena River to the Arctic Sea. See chapter 10.

13 Best Ports

- **Overall:** There are so many great ports in Europe it's hard to choose, but my personal favorite is **Venice,** a city where every view is museum-quality.
- **For Ancient History:** You can't top Athens or Rome and the ancient cities of Ephesus in Turkey and Pompeii in Italy.
- **For Shopping:** I head to the French Riviera (Nice, Cannes, and Monaco) or ports in Italy (including Venice).

- **For Fun:** The French Riviera offers great art museums and, of course, beaches. Fun times can be had in Copenhagen, home of the famous Tivoli Gardens amusement park, and Amsterdam, a youthful city and happening place.
- **For Quaintness:** For quaintness, it's hard to beat Portofino, Italy.
- **For Drama:** The most dramatic port scene has to be Santorini, Greece.
- **Other Faves:** Barcelona is looking awful spiffy since it was fixed up for the Olympic Games; Lisbon is a perpetual favorite; and Istanbul's exotic (yet crowded) ambiance always impresses. Bergen, Norway, is a surprise with its excellent museums and historic waterfront, and Edinburgh and Dublin offer the best of the British Isles.

14 Best Shore Excursions

- **Medieval walled cities:** St-Paul-de-Vence or Eze (France), Lindos on Rhodes (Greece), and Mdina (Malta) all offer medieval walled cities with cobblestone streets and quaint homes located on hilltops with gorgeous ocean views—and art galleries and other shopping options to boot.
- **City tours:** If you are at one of the ports close to London, Paris, Berlin, Rome, or Florence, take the shore excursion (or at the very least the bus transfer) to explore the city.
- **Ephesus, Turkey:** For ancient history, nothing beats Ephesus, the ancient city found under a mountain near Kusadasi, Turkey.
- **Pompeii, Italy:** Tour this once-prosperous ancient city of 20,000, which was buried when Vesuvius erupted in A.D. 79. Today, nearly two-thirds of the city has been excavated and the ruins are amazing.
- **Excursions from St. Petersburg, Russia:** In Russia, you can't tour without a visa unless you book a shore excursion. The best are the summer palaces of Peterhof or Pushkin, or the Hermitage (Winter Palace).
- **Zeeland and the Delta, the Netherlands:** For something totally different, Zeeland and the Delta give you a look at how the Netherlands has developed water management techniques, with a massive project of dams, canals, and dikes.
- **Nordkapp, Norway:** The excursion to the North Cape (Nordkapp), Norway, gives you the chance to see the northernmost accessible point in Europe.

Part 1

Planning, Booking & Preparing for Your Cruise

With advice on choosing and booking your ideal cruise and tips on getting ready for the cruise experience.

Choosing Your Ideal Cruise

1

There are many things you should consider before plunking down big bucks for the perfect European cruise. What kind of itinerary are you looking for and when do you want to go? What size ship will make you most comfortable and will its age matter? What special things should you know if you are a family traveler, a honeymooner, or handicapped? European cruises come in all different styles to suit all different tastes, so the first step in ensuring you'll have the best possible vacation is matching your expectations to the appropriate itinerary and ship. In this chapter, I'll explore the differences between your various European cruise options.

1 The European Cruise Season

The European cruise season is generally considered to be April to November, although some lines operate in the Mediterranean year-round. April, early May, and November are considered shoulder season, and lower fares are usually offered during these months. High season is the summer months.

If you are considering traveling in the shoulder season, keep in mind that some visitor facilities will operate during more limited hours, and some—say, in the Greek Isles—may not be open at all. The least expensive cruises are typically the first and last runs of the season, though these have their own charm: specifically, you'll avoid the big tourist crush, which can really make a difference in some port towns. During the high season in Venice, for instance, you can't swing a stick without hitting a family from Duluth.

WEATHER

Europe is a continent of distinct seasons, but, just as in the U.S., there can be great variations in temperature from one part to another. The warmest months are July and August. August is the month many Europeans go on vacation, and is when beaches and other resort facilities will be particularly packed.

Here's the typical summer weather you can expect to encounter by region:

- **Britain & Ireland:** Average temperatures in the low- to mid-60s (may be milder in Ireland). August, September, and October tend to be the sunniest months.

What Time Is It?

Want to know what time it is at home? Based on U.S. eastern standard time, Britain, Ireland, and Portugal are 5 hours ahead, Greece and Estonia are 7 hours ahead, and western Russia is 8. The rest of the countries in this book are 6 hours ahead. The European countries observe daylight saving time, but not necessarily on the same day or in the same month as in the U.S.

- **Scandinavia:** Average temperatures above the Arctic Circle in the mid-50s; in the south, in the 70s (Denmark tends to be the mildest). It may be rainy in the fjords.
- **Holland & Belgium:** Average temperatures in the high 60s in Holland and Germany (may be rainy in May); in the low 70s in Belgium (sunniest in July and August).
- **France:** Average temperatures in the mid-70s in Paris; can be hot in the Riviera (high 80s or above).
- **The Baltics:** Average temperatures in the 70s (the best weather is late summer).
- **Italy, Greece, Spain, Portugal & Turkey:** Temperatures in the high 80s or higher, but there may be nice breezes along the coast. Portugal tends to be cooler (more like mid-70s), but also rainier. Greece and Turkey are the hottest, and if you're not a hot weather buff you're best off visiting these countries in mid-April to June or mid-September to the end of October.

2 European Cruise Itineraries

So where in Europe do you want to cruise? There's really no such thing as a standard European itinerary. Instead, the cruises focus on specific regions (sometimes more than one region). And there are many variations on each theme. A cruise of the Norwegian fjords, for instance, may depart from Bergen, Norway. Or it may depart from London or Copenhagen.

TYPICAL CRUISE ITINERARIES

The Greek Isles/Eastern Mediterranean The Aegean Sea and sometimes the Adriatic as well, with port calls in the Greek islands (Rhodes, Santorini, Mykonos, etc.), in Athens, in Kusadasi, Turkey, and sometimes in Istanbul. Some of the cruises also visit Dubrovnik or other ports in Croatia.

Western Mediterranean The area from Barcelona or Lisbon to Rome and including port calls in Spain, France, and Italy.

The Rivieras The French Riviera (with ports such as St-Tropez), Monte Carlo, and small Italian Riviera ports (such as Portofino). May also include Rome.

Scandinavia & Russia The Baltic Sea; Copenhagen, Denmark; Stockholm, Sweden; Helsinki, Finland; Tallinn, Estonia; and St. Petersburg, Russia. May also include Oslo.

The British Isles England, Scotland, Wales, and Ireland, and sometimes France; sailing in the North Sea, Irish Sea, and English Channel.

Norway & the Fjords Norway from Bergen up to Honningsvag and the North Cape.

The Black Sea The area from Athens or Istanbul to Yalta, with port calls in Bulgaria, Romania, and the Ukraine. May be combined with the Red Sea (Egypt and Israel).

SPECIAL ITINERARIES

The Best of Europe One of the best ways to see Europe if you've never been here before is on one of the 2-week cruises that visit the major cities. These cruises tend to combine aspects of the above itineraries to give passengers a comprehensive look at

Europe. A typical 2-week cruise—for instance, as offered by Holland America—might take you from Barcelona to Stockholm, with port calls in or near Lisbon, Paris, London, Antwerp, Oslo, and Copenhagen. You can extend your vacation with a night or two in Barcelona or Stockholm or both.

Some offerings combine eastern and western Mediterranean highlights, such as Princess Cruises' sailings from Istanbul to Barcelona, with port calls that might include Athens (Greece), Kusadasi (Turkey), Venice, Naples, Florence/Pisa, and Livorno (Italy), and Monte Carlo.

And there are cruises that explore major cities in Scandinavia and the Baltics; for instance, Costa's 10-day sailing from Amsterdam, with port calls in Gdansk, Poland; Tallinn, Estonia; St. Petersburg, Russia; Stockholm, Sweden; and Copenhagen, Denmark.

River Cruises Europe's inland waterways offer a wealth of cruise opportunities on smaller vessels specifically designed for river and canal travel, including luxurious barges that ply the waterways of inland France, Holland, Belgium, and England, offering a close-up view of the local culture.

There are also larger river ships in France, Holland, Belgium, Germany, Austria, and the former Soviet counties, as well as in Italy and Portugal.

COMPARING ITINERARIES

LENGTH OF CRUISE

In choosing a region or regions to visit, you will obviously have to consider the length of cruise you want to take. Itineraries in Europe range from 3 to 38 days. The shortest cruises, **3- and 4-day offerings,** can be found in the Greek Isles and on in-land waterways. P&O offers a 4-day itinerary from Southampton that visits Holland and Belgium; Bergen does 5- and 6-day cruises in Norway; and Club Med offers occasional 3- and 4-day Italy and France sailings. **One-week cruises** are regularly offered in the Greek Isles/Eastern Mediterranean, Western Mediterranean, British Isles, Norway, French and Italian Rivieras, and on Europe's inland waterways. There are also 1-week sailings in the Baltics and other regions. But more common in most parts of Europe are **10- and 12-day cruises.** The longest cruises include several different regions. Holland America's 38-day cruise (which can also be booked in 19-day segments) includes the Baltic and Scandinavia, Norway, the British Isles, the western Mediterranean, and the Greek Isles (as well as Egypt and Israel).

TIME IN PORT & TIME AT SEA

It's important when comparing the various itineraries to make sure there will be enough time in port to see what you came to see and do what you came to do. Some ships even overnight in key ports such as Venice, Monte Carlo, or Istanbul to give you time to both explore and enjoy the local nightlife. Alternative ships may spend most evenings in port.

Keep in mind that visiting a port a day in an exciting region like Greece, where there are so many ancient sites to see, can be exhausting. And some of the ships make more than one port call a day. Experienced cruisers will know some of the most relaxing times to be had on ships are lazy days at sea, and consequently often choose an itinerary that spends a day or two without a port call.

MATCHING YOUR HABITS TO YOUR DESTINATION

Some ports are better for certain things than others. Here's a short run-down (see part 3, "The Ports of Call," for more detailed information).

Ports for Shoppers

London, Paris, Rome, and all the other major cities; Nice and Cannes, France; Venice, Italy.

> **Indulging Your Obsessions at Sea: Theme Cruises**
>
> Theme cruises are becoming more and more popular, as lines look for more ways to attract passengers with unique onboard activities. There are sailings focused on cooking and wine; and cruises focused on golf. **Crystal,** for instance, features an annual series of food and wine cruises where well-known chefs and sommeliers are on board to conduct demonstrations and tastings, and for Europe 2000 will offer cruises themed on opera, art and architecture, golf, and health & fitness. **Fred. Olsen**'s ships host sailings themed on wine, bridge, photography, golf, and other topics. **Silversea** offers golf-themed cruises, with play at courses throughout Europe. **Seabourn** also has some golf-themed offerings. **Holland America** does an annual Big Band cruise in Europe.

Ports for Beach Lovers

Cannes and St-Tropez, France; Mykonos and Rhodes, Greece; Málaga and Palma, Spain

Ports for Antiquities

Kusadasi, Turkey (Ephesus); Sorrento (Pompeii); Athens (the Parthenon); Rome (the Colosseum et al).

Ports for Nature Buffs

Norway (especially above the Arctic Circle); British coastal areas

Shore Excursions: The What, Why & How

No matter what size ship you're on or what its itinerary is, you can choose from a variety of shore excursions at any given port, ranging in price from around $30 to more than $200 per person. The most popular are city tours, which typically highlight the historic and scenic attractions in each port city. Other, pricier tours take you beyond the port city to inland attractions.

I enjoy exploring port cities on my own and take only those tours that go further inland, but that's just me. It's a personal choice.

On the big ships, excursions can sell out quickly, so don't dawdle if you know what you want; sign up before the trip (if the cruise line allows you to do so), or the first or second day of the cruise. Because of the large numbers of passengers on large ships, be prepared for some waiting around as each jumbo-sized tour group is herded from the ship to the waiting army of buses or minivans.

On smaller ships, there's usually room on the excursions to accommodate all passengers on board, and the excursions may even be included in your cruise fare (in which case 100% attendance is not uncommon). The whole process is saner, and group sizes are most likely smaller.

Whatever the size of the ship, the attraction itself, quality of the tour guide, and execution of the tour are what determine whether you have an enjoyable time.

In chapter 2, I list the pros and cons of taking shore excursions, and in chapters 12 and 13 I list both the best shore excursions and the top sights you can see on your own.

3 Choosing Your Ship

After choosing your itinerary, picking the right ship is the number-one factor in ensuring you get the vacation you're looking for. Cruise ships operating in Europe range from **small alternative-type vessels** to **resort-like megaships,** with the cruise experience varying widely depending on the type of ship you select. There are casual cruises and luxury cruises; educational cruises where you attend lectures; soft adventure cruises that explore remote areas and offer watersports opportunities; and resortlike cruises where massages and Las Vegas–style shows are the order of the day.

You'll need to decide what overall cruise experience you want. Type of cruise is even more important than price. After all, what kind of bargain is a party cruise if what you're looking for is a quiet time? Your fantasy vacation may be someone else's nightmare, and vice versa.

BIG SHIP OR SMALL?

Unlike the Caribbean, which usually attracts people looking for fun in the sun, visitors to Europe generally have a different goal: They want to experience Europe's history and culture. The cruise lines recognize this, so almost any option you choose will allow you opportunities to see what you've come for. The main question, then, is *how* you want to see those sights.

When comparing ship sizes, think the difference between a small New England inn and a big resort hotel in Miami. The difference is major. A ship's size, like that of a hotel, greatly determines its personality and the kind of vacation you'll have. Big ships tend to be busy, exciting affairs, while the smaller ships are most often low-key retreats with unique personalities.

THE BIG SHIPS

Big ships operating in Europe vary in size and scope, and include everything from classic cruise ships to really, really big and really, really new megaships. They all offer a comfortable cruising experience, with virtual armies of service employees overseeing your well-being and ship stabilizers assuring smooth sailing. And all have plenty of deck space from which you can take in the coastal sights.

Due to their deeper drafts (the amount of ship below the waterline), the biggest of the big ships can't get to some of the islands and small ports smaller ships may visit. However, the more powerful engines on these ships allow them to visit more ports during each trip, and shore excursions allow you to more closely explore different aspects of the port's history and culture. The itineraries of these ships tend to be the tried-and-true routes sailed by many other vessels.

Due to the number of people getting off the ship, disembarkation can be a lengthy process.

The classic-style ships (some of which are really mid-sized in today's market) embrace their nautical history and don't look as much like floating Hyatt hotels as the bigger megaships (see below). Classic-style ships may be older vessels (and some tattered ones at that) or they may be modern ships designed to appeal to those who don't want everything really big and really glitzy. These ships range from luxurious down to budget. Some are European-operated while others are operated by American firms. On the more expensive of these ships, the crowd will be older and more refined, and take formal nights seriously. On the more moderately priced ships in Europe you'll find lots of middle-class Europeans and family travelers (as well as value-conscious Americans) and a generally more casual atmosphere.

Megaships are newer, bigger (the biggest cruising in Europe holds more than 2,500 passengers), and offer the latest and greatest. They're glitzy American-style floating resorts and, with the exception of those operated by Costa, attract more Americans than Europeans. The atmosphere is casual during the day, with a few formal nights so you can really put on the ritz.

Both the classic-style ships and the megaships have all the facilities you can imagine on a cruise ship. There are swimming pools, health clubs, spas (of various sizes), nightclubs, movie theaters, shops, casinos, bars, and children's playrooms. In some

Ship Size Comparisons

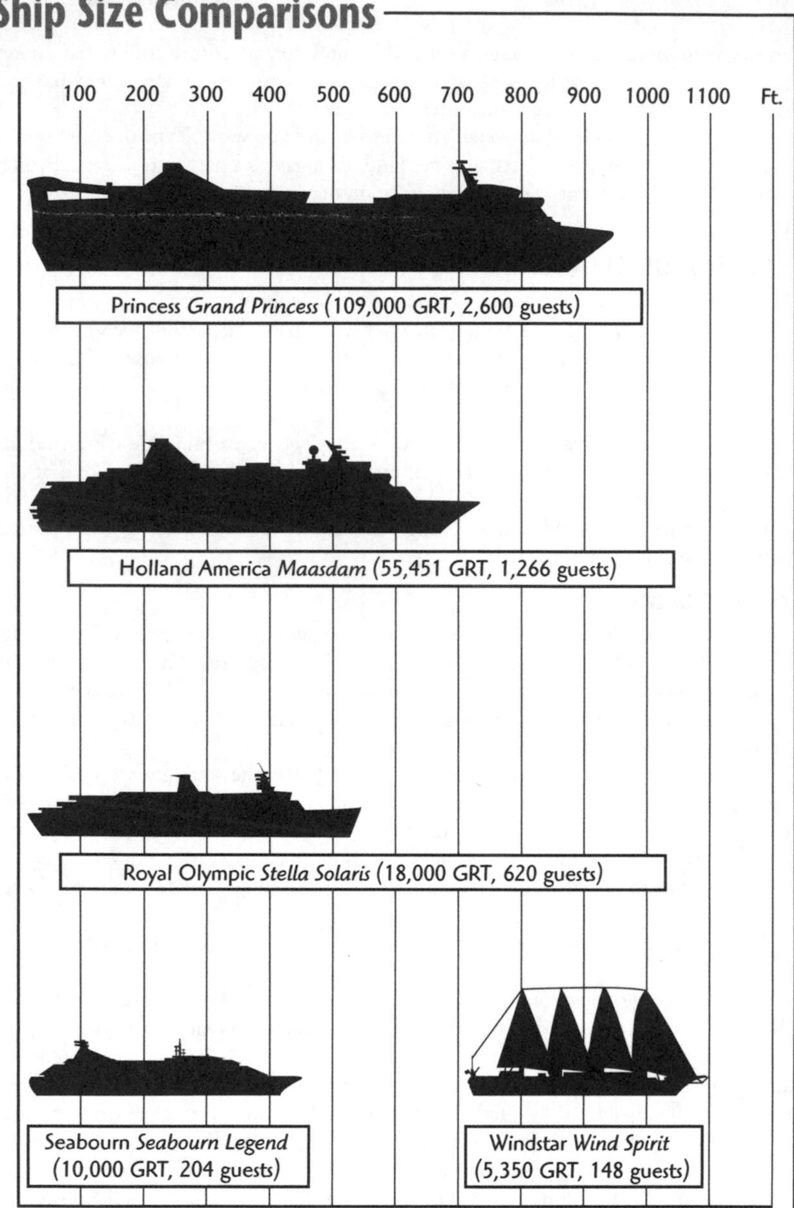

Ships selected for this chart are representative of the various size vessels sailing in Europe for 2000. See the specifications tables accompanying every ship review in chapters 6–9 to see the approximate comparative size of all the ships not shown here. (GRT = gross register tons, a measure that takes into account interior space used to produce revenue on a vessel. One GRT = 100 cubic feet of enclosed, revenue-generating space.)

cases—especially on the megaships—you'll also find sports decks, virtual golf, computer rooms, and cigar clubs, as well as quiet spaces where you can get away from it all. There are so many rooms you won't likely feel claustrophobic.

These ships have big dining rooms and buffet areas serving more food with more variety and at more times (including midnight) than you can possibly think about, much less eat. There might also be additional eating venues such as pizzerias, hamburger grills, ice-cream parlors, alternative restaurants, wine bars, champagne bars, caviar bars, and patisseries.

In most cases, these ships have lots of onboard activities to keep you occupied when you're not in port, including games and contests, classes, children's programs, and lectures (possibly by archaeologists and historians). The activities are somewhat lower key than they would be in, say, the Caribbean, where the crowd is more party-hearty. These ships also offer a variety of entertainment options that might even include celebrity headline acts, and usually include stage show productions, some quite sophisticated (particularly on ships run by American companies).

Cabins, in many cases, offer modern comforts such as TVs and telephones, and some even have personal safes and minibars. The cabins themselves might be cubbyholes or large suites, depending on the ship and the cabin level you book. On most of these ships, options will include picture windows and private verandas.

These ships carry a lot of people, and as such can at times feel crowded—and there may occasionally be lines at the buffets and in other public areas. On the other hand, you aren't stuck with the same faces for your whole cruise.

The Small & Alternative Ships

Just as big cruise ships are mostly for people who want every resort amenity, small or alternative ships are best suited for people who prefer a casual, crowd-free cruise experience that gives them a chance to get up-close-and-personal with Europe's coastal offerings.

Thanks to their smaller size, these ships can offer a yacht-like experience (some of them even have sails) and can go places that larger ships can't, such as islands and smaller ports that cater mostly to yachts and small fishing vessels. The decks on these ships are closer to the waterline, too, giving passengers a more intimate view than from the high decks of the large cruise ships. These ships tend to hug the coast, and in Europe they usually visit a port a day (although some spend a day or two at sea exploring areas of natural beauty).

The alternative ship experience comes with a sense of adventure, although it's usually adventure of a soft rather than rugged sort, and offers a generally casual cruise experience: There are usually no dress-up nights, the food may be rather simply prepared, and because there are so few public areas to choose from—usually only one or two small lounges—camaraderie tends to develop more quickly between passengers on these ships than aboard larger vessels, which can be as anonymous as a big city.

Cabins don't usually offer TVs or telephones and tend to be very small, and in some cases downright spartan. Meals are generally served in a single open seating, and dress codes are usually nonexistent.

Instead of aerobics and pool games like on the big ships, these ships may offer a brisk walk around the deck or, on some ships, the opportunity to enjoy watersports right from the ship. And the alternative ships more frequently feature expert lectures on archaeology, history, and other intellectual pursuits.

There are no stabilizers on most of these smaller ships, and the ride can be bumpy in open water. There are also often no elevators, making cruises on most of these ships a bit difficult for travelers with disabilities. And the alternative ship lines do not offer

Leading Web Sites for Cruise Planning

When it comes to getting cruise info on the Web, you have a mixed deal. While some of the cruise line sites are amazing, giving you everything from their ships' itineraries and prices (the site for Peter Dielmann EuropeAmerica Cruises is particularly impressive in this regard) to virtual tours (the Holland America site, for instance, at www.hollandamerica.com), that's mostly all they do: give you information. Unlike airline and hotel sites that allow you to book your trip or stay directly through the Web, hardly any cruise line is prepared to anger the travel agent community by taking this step, as agents are responsible for the overwhelming percentage of cruise bookings.

All this aside, the cruise line sites (listed in chapters 6 through 10 in the individual cruise line reviews) will give you some great visual reference points, and the following independent sites can provide other valuable information as you plan your cruise.

- www.cdc.gov/nceh/programs/sanit/vsp/scores/scores.htm
  Twice each year, the Centers for Disease Control's Vessel Sanitation Program rates sanitary conditions aboard all ships that have foreign itineraries and carry 13 or more passengers. Access this link for the latest test results. (Note: Since the CDC is a U.S. agency, some ships in this book won't be rated in their listings.)
- www.cruising.org
  Cruise Lines International Association (CLIA), the U.S. cruise industry's marketing arm, maintains a Web site that lists CLIA-affiliated travel agencies and more.
- www.cruise-news.com
  Cruise News gives news on seasonal and themed cruises and information about upcoming launches of new ships. You'll also find links to agents who specialize in selling cruise vacations.
- www.cruisemates.com
  The Cruisemates site contains ship reviews, information for first-time cruisers, and lots of opportunities to chat with other cruise aficionados.

specific activities or facilities for children, although you still may find a few families on some of these vessels.

4 Matching the Cruise to Your Needs

CRUISES FOR FAMILIES

More parents are taking their kids with them on vacation, and cruises to Europe have become increasingly popular with families, including intergenerational gatherings: parents traveling with their kids and the grandparents too. The lines are responding with youth counselors and supervised programs, fancy playrooms, and even video game rooms to keep the kids entertained while their parents relax. At night, most ships offer baby-sitting (for an extra charge). Some lines offer reduced rates for kids. It's important to note that most lines discourage people from bringing infants.

ACTIVITIES It's important to ask whether a supervised program will be offered when you plan to cruise, as sometimes the programs are only operated if there are a certain number of kids on board. Depending on the program, the youngest children may frolic

- www.reply.net/clients/cruise/news.html
  Cruise News Daily provides a matter-of-fact daily update on cruise news, such as delays on a cruise line unveiling a new ship or special deals on off-peak cruises. You can sign up for a weekly e-mail dispatch or check the Web site daily for news items.
- www.cruiseopinion.com
  The most valuable part of CruiseOpinion.com is the section of passenger reviews. Most people who comment include their age, occupation, and number of cruises they've taken, and some add their e-mail address so you can send follow-up questions. This site is a fine example of travelers getting online to help one another.
- www.travel.org/CruiseTravel
  The Web site of *Cruise Travel,* a cruise-lovers' magazine, offers in-depth, well-researched articles on ships and all facets of cruising.
- www.cruise-week.com
  Cruise Week News posts a concise roundup of the week's cruise news each Wednesday. You can also have this dispatch delivered via e-mail.
- www.dialysis-at-sea.com
  This site lists all ships outfitted to care for dialysis patients. Also see ADA Vacations Plus (www.vacations-plus.com).
- www.porthole.com
  The Web site of *Porthole* cruise magazine offers light feature articles on cruising and a great list of cruise links.
- www.sealetter.com
  The well-stocked Web site Sealetter, managed by a husband-and-wife travel agent team, features a lot of reader ship reviews, cruise tips, and loads of great cruise links.
- www.steinerleisure.com
  Steiner runs most of the onboard spas in the cruise industry. Via their site, you can get a preview of the spa treatments you'll find aboard ship.

in toy- and game-stocked playrooms, listen to stories, and go on treasure hunts; older kids can do things like arts and crafts, computer games, lip-synch competitions, pool games, and volleyball; and teenagers can mingle at teen parties or hang out at the video arcade. The megas have large playrooms with computer stations and video games as well as shelves of toys. There's usually a TV showing movies throughout the day and, for the younger ones, there are ball bins and plastic jungle gyms to crawl around in. Many megaships have shallow kiddie pools, sometimes sequestered on an isolated patch of deck.

BABY-SITTING Baby-sitting is offered on most large cruise ships from around 8pm to 2am. Group baby-sitting is about $4 to $5 per hour per child and, if available, private in-cabin baby-sitting by a crew member is a steep $8 to $10 per hour per child, plus generally a dollar or two more for a sibling.

FAMILY-FRIENDLY CABINS A family of four can share a cabin that has bunk-style third and fourth berths, which pull out of the walls just above the pair of regular beds (some even have a fifth berth), but there's no two ways to slice it: A standard cabin with four people in it will be cramped. However, when you consider how little time you'll spend in the cabin, it's do-able. The incentive to share one cabin is the price—whether children or adults, the rates for third and fourth people sharing a cabin with two full-fare (or even heavily discounted) passengers are usually about half of the lowest regular rates. On occasion there are special deals and further discounts. Norwegian Cruise Line and Royal Olympic Cruises allow children under 2 to sail for free. If you can afford it, and if space equals sanity in your book, consider booking a suite, many of which have a pull-out couch in the living room. Families with older kids can always consider booking two separate cabins with interconnecting doors. Lots of ships, big and small, have them. You'll be close to each other, but separate.

TAKING THE KIDS ON SMALL SHIPS While there's no doubting the big new ships are best prepared for families, if your children are at least 10 or 12, some of the casual, alternative cruises can be loads of fun and educational to boot. While you won't find a kids' playroom stuffed with toys, the experience of visiting a culturally rich port of call every day will help keep you and the kids from going stir crazy on board.

FAMILY CRUISING TIPS Here are some suggestions for smoother sailing on your family cruise.

- Ask about children's amenities. Check in advance with the cruise line to make sure the ship you're sailing offers things your child might need. Are cribs available? Children's menus?
- Pack some basic first-aid supplies plus any medications your doctor may suggest, and even a thermometer. Cruise lines have limited supplies of these items (and charge for them, too) and can quickly run out if the ship has many families aboard. If an accident should happen aboard, virtually every ship afloat has its own infirmary staffed by doctors and/or nurses. Keep in mind, first aid can usually be summoned more readily aboard ship than in port.
- Warn younger children about the danger of falling overboard and make sure they know not to play on the railings.
- When in port, prearrange a meeting spot. If your child is old enough to go off on his or her own, prearrange a meeting spot either on board or on land, and meet there well before the ship is scheduled to depart to make sure no one is still ashore.
- Make sure your kids know their cabin number and what deck it's on. The endless corridors and doors on the megas look exactly alike.
- Prepare kids for TV letdown. If your kids are TV addicts, you might want to make sure your cabin will have a TV and VCR. And even if it does, they should be prepared for a little bit of withdrawal, since televisions on ships just don't have 200 channels of cable—you'll be lucky to get five or eight channels. On the bright side, big ships are likely to have nightly movies and a video arcade.

CRUISES FOR SINGLE TRAVELERS

A nice thing about cruises is you needn't worry about dining alone, since you'll be seated with other guests (if you don't want to be, seek a ship with alternative dining options). You also needn't worry much about finding people to talk to, since the general atmosphere on nearly all ships is very congenial and allows you to easily find conversation, especially during group activities. And the ship may even host a party to give singles a chance to get to know one another and/or offer social hosts as dance partners.

The downside is that you may have to pay more for the cruise experience than those sharing a room. Since cruise line rates are based on two people per cabin, some lines charge a "single supplement" rate (which sounds like a deal, but it's *you* who pays the supplement) that ranges from 110% to an outrageous 200% of the per-person, double-occupancy fare. As a single person, you have two choices: find a line with a reasonable single supplement rate or ask if the line has a cabin-share program, under which the line will pair you with another single so you can get a lower fare. You may not be able to get much information about your roommate before the sailing, although all lines match gender and most also try to match age. Some lines also offer a single guarantee program, which means if they can't find you a roommate, they'll book you in a cabin alone but still honor the shared rate. On some older ships (including the *QE2* and *Caronia*) and a few small ships, there are special cabins designated for single travelers, and in some cases they carry no additional charge. But keep in mind that these cabins, originally designed on the older ships for nannies or maids accompanying passengers, are really really small, and that they tend to sell out fast.

CRUISES FOR TRAVELERS WITH DISABILITIES

If you are a traveler with a disability, it is important to let the cruise line know your special needs when you make your booking. If you use a wheelchair, you'll need to know if wheelchair-accessible cabins are available (and how they're equipped), as well as whether public rooms are accessible and can be reached by elevator, and whether the cruise line has any special policy regarding travelers with disabilities—for instance, some require that you be accompanied by an able-bodied companion. I've noted all this information in the cabin sections of the ship reviews in chapters 6 to 10. Note that newer ships tend to have the largest number of wheelchair-accessible cabins. Old ships and small ships may be very difficult to maneuver.

Travelers with disabilities should inquire when they're booking whether the ship docks at ports or uses tenders (small boats) to go ashore. Tenders cannot always accommodate wheelchairs. Also, once on board, travelers with disabilities will want to seek the advice of the tour staff before choosing shore excursions, as not all will be wheelchair-friendly.

If you have a chronic health problem, we advise you to check with your doctor before booking the cruise, and, if you have any specific needs, to notify the cruise line in advance. This will ensure that the medical team on the ship is properly prepared to offer assistance.

A handful of experienced travel agencies specialize in booking cruises and tours for disabled travelers. Accessible Journeys, 35 W. Sellers Ave., Ridley Park, PA 19078 (☎ 800/846-4537), can even provide licensed health-care professionals to accompany those who require aid. **Flying Wheels Travel,** 143 W. Bridge St., Owatonna, MN 55060 (☎ **800/535-6790**), is another option.

CRUISES FOR GAY & LESBIAN TRAVELERS

There are a number of gay-friendly cruises and special chartered sailings for gay men and lesbians. For details, contact these specialists:

- **RSVP Cruises,** 2800 University Ave. SE, Minneapolis, MN 55414 (☎ **800/328-7787** or 612/379-4697).
- **Pied Piper Travel,** 330 W. 42nd St., Ste. 1804, New York, NY 10036 (☎ **800/TRIP-312** or 212/239-2412).
- **Olivia Cruises and Resorts,** 4400 Market St., Oakland, CA 94608 (☎ **800/631-6277** or 510/655-0364); caters specifically to lesbians.

You can also contact the **International Gay Travel Association,** 4331 N. Federal Hwy., Ste. 304, Fort Lauderdale, FL 33308 (☎ **800/448-8550**), which has over 1,000 travel industry members. You might want to check out ***Frommer's Gay & Lesbian Europe,*** the well-known ***Out & About*** travel newsletter ($49 a year for 10 issues; to subscribe, call ☎ **212/645-6922** or 800/929-2268), or ***Our World*** travel magazine

($35 a year for 10 issues; call ☎ **904/441-5367** to subscribe) for articles, tips, and listings on gay and lesbian travel.

CRUISES FOR HONEYMOONERS

Most 1-week cruises depart on either Saturday or Sunday, although there are some exceptions. You'll want to look carefully at sailing times as you plan your wedding weekend. You will also want to make sure that the ship offers double, queen-, or king-size beds, and you may want to book a cabin with a tub or Jacuzzi. Rooms with private verandas are particularly romantic. You can take in the sights in privacy, and even enjoy a private meal, assuming the veranda is big enough for a table and chairs (some are not) and that the weather doesn't turn chilly. If you want to dine alone each night, make sure the dining room offers tables for two and/or that the ship offers room service (your travel agent can fill you in on these matters). You may also want to inquire as to the likelihood that there will be other honeymooners your age on the ship. Some ships—among them those of Princess, Royal Caribbean, Costa, Celebrity, and Holland America—offer add-on honeymoon packages that provide champagne, a fruit basket, and the like. Most lines will offer special perks, like an invitation to a private honeymooners' cocktail party, if you let them know in advance that you will be celebrating your special event on the ship.

High-end lines, such as Windstar, Radisson Seven Seas, Seabourn, Cunard, and Crystal, don't offer special cocktail parties and the like, but their ultra-deluxe amenities are especially pleasing to honeymooners. From terry-cloth bathrobes and slippers that await you in walk-in closets to whirlpool bathtubs, five-course dinners served in your cabin, stocked minibars, and high crew-to-passenger ratios (meaning more personalized service), extra-special touches are business as usual on these upscale lines.

2

Booking Your Cruise & Getting the Best Price

Cruise prices are not always the easiest things to figure out, and cruises in Europe can run you big bucks, but the first important rule to remember is that **few people pay full price.** The retail price, or the rate in the brochure, is the optimum price the cruise line hopes to get for the cruise—like the sticker price on a new car—rather than the price it really *expects* to get. Demand for the European cruise product is expected to be intense this year (especially since a lot of people cancelled plans last year due to the situation in Kosovo), but there are all sorts of deals and discounts out there, and virtually all the lines offer early-booking discounts that generally amount to 10% to 50% off if you book at least 3 months in advance of your sailing date. The best way to find the best deals is through an experienced cruise travel agent.

In this chapter, I'll point you in the right direction on finding the best fare, keeping costs down, and choosing a good agent, and clue you in on what's included in your "all-inclusive" fare and what's not. I'll also help you through those sticky areas of choosing a cabin and dining-room seating time.

1 The Scoop on Cruise Fares

FINDING THE BEST FARE

The best way to save on a European cruise is to **book in advance.** Cruise itineraries are usually printed 10 to 12 months ahead of the season, and the cruise lines offer early-bird rates ranging from discounts of about 10% on up to 50%. Policies for the rates also vary, but generally you have a good chance of qualifying for the rates (which are offered in limited numbers on a first-come, first-served basis) by booking at least 3 months in advance (some cabin categories may even sell out 6 to 9 months in advance). If cabins aren't selling, the lines may even extend the early-booking deadlines closer in to the sailing dates.

Booking early gives you the advantage of getting first pick on cabins (the cheapest and most expensive ones tend to sell out first). And, if you are booking your own air, you have a better chance of getting a deal from the airlines.

If cabins are still not filled up as the season begins, the cruise lines will start marketing **last-minute deals,** usually through their top-producing travel agents. Last year, with the conflict in Kosovo in full swing at the beginning of the European cruise season, the discounts got into absurd territory. One couple I heard about booked a last-minute 12-day cruise for $700 (for two!). Keep in mind, though, that last-minute

Price Protection

It's a little-known fact that if the price of your cabin category goes down after you've booked it, most cruise lines will make up the difference, in effect giving you the lowest rates. The cruise lines, of course, won't call to tell you this. But if you have a good travel agent he or she will monitor the rates and call the cruise line for you if the rates go down.

deals require a certain amount of flexibility. Your desired sailing date may sell out, and even if it doesn't, you will have to take whatever cabin is still available. Also, you may have trouble getting a good last-minute deal on your airfare. And most last-minute deals are completely nonrefundable.

You can also save by booking a cruise in the **shoulder months** of April, early May, and November, when pricing is usually less than in the summer peak season.

And keep in mind that the lines also tend to offer cut rates when they are **introducing a new ship** or **new itinerary** in a market. So it pays to keep track of what's happening in the industry—or to have your agent do so. You should be aware, though, that several new ships have experienced construction delays and have had to cancel their maiden voyages and inaugural sailings, sometimes only weeks ahead of time. Of course passengers on those cancelled sailings were well-compensated with refunds, big discounts on their rebooked cruise, and the like, but if you want to try a brand-new ship, some flexibility may be required.

Discounts for Third & Fourth Passengers

Most ships offer standard discounts for third and/or fourth passengers sharing a cabin with two full-fare passengers. These discounts are designed for families and others who don't mind the closeness sharing a cabin brings. Generally, the first two in a cabin are booked at a regular fare, with the third and fourth passengers booked at a highly discounted rate. You can add the four rates together and then divide by four to get your per-person fare.

Some lines offer **special rates for kids,** usually on a seasonal or select-sailings basis, that may include free or discounted airfare. Those under age 2 generally cruise free.

Group Rates

One of the best ways to get a cruise deal is to book as a group, so you may want to get a family reunion together or convince your friends or colleagues they need a vacation, too. A group is generally at least 16 people in at least eight cabins. The savings include not only a discounted rate, but at least the cruise portion of the 16th ticket will be free (on some upscale ships you can negotiate a free ticket for groups of eight or more). The gang can split the proceeds from the free ticket, or, just for the fun of it, hold a drawing for the ticket, maybe at a cocktail party on the first night. If your group is large enough you may be able to get that cocktail party—or perhaps some other onboard amenities—for free as well.

Buying on Time

If you're worried about how you're going to pay for your trip, you might want to consider taking out a **cruise loan.** Princess Cruises offers its customers special loans, which are repayable in 24, 36, or 48 months. These are approved on an instant basis after you review your credit information on the phone with the participating bank. Princess's loan program is aptly called the **Love Boat Loan** and offers rates that can vary from 14.99% to 26.99%, depending on your credit history. Call ☎ **800/Princess** for details.

SENIOR-CITIZEN DISCOUNTS

Senior citizens may be able to get extra savings on their cruise. Some lines will take 5% off the top for those 55 and up, and the senior rate applies even if the second person in the cabin is younger. Membership in groups such as AARP (American Association of Retired Persons) is not required, but such membership may bring additional savings.

Tour operators who sell cruise packages to senior citizens may book blocks of cabins and offer group discounts. One well-known operator is **Grand Circle Travel,** 347 Congress St., Boston, MA 02210 (☎ **800/221-2610** or 617/350-7500). You can write to them for a free booklet called "101 Tips for the Mature Traveler."

REPEAT-PASSENGER PROGRAMS

If you've been on a cruise before and are traveling with the same line, you may qualify for a repeat-passenger discount or other perks. Policies vary by line, but repeat passenger discounts generally range from 5% to 20% (you may have to take several cruises to qualify) and repeaters might also get invitations to private shipboard cocktail parties, priority check-in, and cabin upgrades (and nearly every line sends its repeaters enticing direct mail pieces).

OTHER DEALS

Cruise lines market Europe cruises with **free hotel stays** and, in some cases, **free airfare** offers. You may also see **two-for-one** deals or offers that tack a few **free days** on to a cruise (such as 14 days for the price of 12). All of these should be evaluated carefully. Add up the total amount you would spend with the line for your cruise, hotel, and airfare and compare it to that offered by competing lines. Make sure you are comparing apples and apples and not apples and oranges.

Repositioning cruises, such as when a ship repositions from the western Mediterranean to the Greek Isles, may be value priced. But keep in mind since these cruises tend to cover greater distances than standard cruises they usually offer more days at sea and tend to be for more than 1 week (but you get to see more than one region, which is a particular advantage to those trying to see as much of Europe as possible).

Some of the more upscale lines will reward customers willing to **pay their full fare in advance** (thus giving the cruise line cash in hand). The discounts—sometimes as much as 15%—are significant enough that it could pay to go this route rather than putting a comparable sum in a CD.

GOOD DEALS FOR THOSE WHO CAN'T GET ENOUGH

You can usually get a good deal, if you want to visit more than one region, by booking two cruises **back-to-back** (you stay on the ship for more than one sailing).

If you like your European cruise so much you decide you want to vacation here again, consider **booking another cruise on the ship.** Cruise lines have gotten savvy about the fact that when you're on a ship you're a captive audience, so they may pitch you to make your future vacation plans onboard, with discounts—usually 5%—part of the pitch. Before you sign on the dotted line, though, *make sure the on-the-spot discount can be combined with other offers you might find later.* Keep in mind if you do choose to book onboard you can still do the reconfirmation and ticketing through your travel agent by giving the cruise line his or her name.

AIRFARE & PRE- AND POST-CRUISE OFFERINGS

Your cruise package might include airfare, but if not, you will be offered an air add-on. As a general rule, if you are offered air transportation from the cruise line, it's best to take it. Why? First of all, as big customers of the airlines, the cruise lines tend to get very good (if not the best) discounted airfare rates, which they pass on to their customers.

Secondly, booking air with the cruise line also allows the line to keep track of you. If your plane is late, for instance, they might even hold the boat. And most cruise lines include **transfers** from the airport to the ship, saving you the hassle of getting a cab. (If you do book on your own, you may still be able to get the transfers separately—ask your agent about this.)

The only time it may pay to book your own air transportation is if you are using frequent-flyer miles and can get the air for free. Or if you are fussy about which carrier you fly or route you take (you are more or less at the mercy of the cruise line to make these choices if you take their air offers, and may end up on chartered aircraft).

Some lines offer special **deviation programs** which allow you to request specific airlines and routing for an extra fee. The deadline for these requests is usually 60 days prior to the sailing date or the day your cruise reservation is made if you book later.

Be aware that once the ticket is issued by the cruise line, you will be charged a fee if any changes are made.

If you choose not to book your air transportation with the cruise line, and said airfare is part of the cruise deal, you will be refunded the air portion of the fare.

If you are not booking airfare through the cruise line, make sure to allow several hours between the plane's arrival and when you need to get on the ship. It may be best, in terms of reducing anxiety, to come in a day before and spend the night in a hotel.

Pre- & Post-Cruise Packages

All sorts of add-on programs are offered by the cruise lines in Europe, and most people will want to stretch their cruise vacation by adding a hotel stay in a port city. These hotel stays are typically booked at the same time you book your cruise, to create what's known as a pre-cruise offering (before the cruise) or post-cruise offering (after the cruise).

Just like air add-ons, the cruise lines negotiate **special deals with hotels** at port cities. An advantage to coming in a day or two early is that you don't have to worry if your flight is running late. Plus, the extra evening gives you time to recover from jet lag before your cruise begins.

Some lines, including Renaissance and Orient Lines, include a hotel package in the cruise fare.

When evaluating a cruise line's hotel offering, make sure you review carefully to see what's included. See if the line offers a transfer from the airport to the hotel and from the hotel to the cruise ship; make sure the line offers a hotel that you will be happy with in terms of type of hotel and location; and inquire if any escorted tours, car-rental deals, or meals are included.

Cruisetours

Most of the cruise lines also offer some **escorted land tours,** usually in major cities like London, Paris, Madrid, Lisbon, Venice, Athens, or Istanbul, that can complement (and stretch) your cruise vacation.

The land portion is typically 4 to 6 nights, and may be offered before or after the cruise. The package usually includes hotel accommodations, sightseeing, admission to attractions, and some meals, as well as ground transportation (usually by bus) and all transfers (between the airport, hotel or hotels, and the ship).

Extra Costs to Consider

While your cruise will include accommodations on the ship, meals and snacks, activities, and entertainment, it's important when figuring out what your cruise will cost to also look at what extras are not included in your cruise fare. Before your trip you may want to make a tentative budget. Areas that should be included in your planning are shore excursions, bar drinks, dry cleaning and laundry (some ships have coin-operated machines for passenger use), phone calls, massage and other spa services, beauty parlor services, photos taken by the ship's photographer, wine at dinner, souvenirs, and crew tips. Such extras can easily add up to $50 to $60 per person per day, and if you really indulge, can sometimes rocket up much higher.

Shore Excursions

The most expensive addition to your cruise fare in Europe will likely be shore excursions. Ranging from about $32 for a 4-hour city tour to more than $200 for a long excursion to a city far from the port, these sightseeing tours are designed to help cruise passengers make the most of their time at the ports the ship visits, but they can add a hefty sum to your vacation costs. Sometimes, you'll actually be in port long enough to take more than one excursion.

My advice? Don't discount the excursions on the basis of cost. Think about it this way: You probably don't get to Europe very often, so it would be a shame to limit your experience just to save a few bucks.

I've highlighted the best of these tours in chapters 12 and 13, described them, and provided their approximate prices to help you in your planning.

In general, you get the most bang for your buck by taking tours that go beyond the port city (in many cases, it's easy to walk around the port city on your own).

Shore excursions are generally booked on board, not in advance, and you will have an opportunity on board to ask questions of the ship's tour staff, who will even offer lectures on the subject, before you make your decision. Keep in mind that popular tours sell out fast.

Gratuities

You'll want to add to your calculations tips for the ship's crew. Of course, tipping is at your own discretion—Holland America even makes a point of this, with their "no tipping required" policy—but with the cruise lines being so forthcoming with their tipping advice (they even have special envelopes and cheat sheets prepared to help you out), you'll feel like a crumb for not obliging.

Tipping is usually paid at the end of the cruise, and passengers should reserve at least $9 per person, per day, or $63 a week, for tips for the room steward, waiter, and busboy (in practice, people to tend to nudge it up to $10 or $12).

Additional tips to other personnel, such as the head waiter or maitre d', are at your discretion. Most lines automatically add 15% to bar bills, so you don't have to tip your bartender, though some people will slip a bartender they really like a few bucks at the end of the cruise anyway. You aren't asked to tip crew members who bring you room service, or bring back your clean laundry, but you can if you want to (having a few dollar bills on hand is useful). On some European and small-ship lines, the crew pools tips, with the recommended contribution $10 to $15 per person, per day. Other lines suggest you pay your tip based on a percentage of what you paid for your cruise (usually 5%). Some luxury lines, including Radisson and Silversea, include tips in the cruise fare.

See Appendix A, "Wrapping Up Your Cruise—Debarkation Concerns," for more on tipping.

Booze

Most ships charge extra for alcoholic beverages (including wine at dinner) and for soda. Nonbubbly soft drinks such as lemonade and iced tea are typically included in your cruise fare.

What's Not Included in Your Cruise Fare

To help you calculate what you'll need to cover onboard costs, I've put together this little chart:

Baby-sitting (per hour, for two kids)	
Private	$10
Group	$6
Bar drinks	
Soda	$1–$1.50
Mixed drinks	$2.95 & up
Beauty services (shampoo and haircut)	$15 & up
Cruise line logo souvenirs	$3 & up
Dry cleaning (per item)	$2.50 & up
Phone calls (per minute)	$12 & up
Photos	$6 & up
Wine at dinner (per bottle)	$14–$200

Port Charges & Other Fees

Port charges, taxes, and other fees are usually included in your cruise fare but not always, and these charges can add as much as $200 per person onto the price of a European cruise. I've noted in the cruise reviews when ships do not include port charges and taxes in their rates.

Phone Calls from the Ship

Making phone calls from any ship is extremely expensive (up to $18 a minute), so you're much better off waiting until you're at a port. However, making calls from a port in Europe can also be tricky. You should bring along an AT&T, Sprint, or other **phone service card** from home, and make sure you know the local access number for the card in advance (you can call your phone service for the numbers for each country you will be visiting).

On some pay phones in Europe you can drop in a coin (in the local currency) to connect to your local access number, but others require the use of prepaid phone cards (not coins). In either case, you usually can't just pick up the receiver and dial the local number for your phone service, even if that number is toll-free. If the phone requires a prepaid card, you can buy one at a newsstand or tobacco shop. If you are using the prepaid card just to connect to your phone service's local number, buy the card in the smallest denomination available.

If you don't want to hassle with the prepaid cards or figuring out local coinage, I've found most hotels will let you use a phone to call AT&T or your other phone service if you walk in and ask nicely (looking lost helps). They may charge a small fee.

Other Onboard Costs

Cruise lines make a substantial amount of their revenue on board, meaning you'll find enticements at every turn (especially on the big ships), from the friendly bar staff offering the Drink of the Day (the largest source of onboard revenue for the cruise lines is drinks), to the roving photographer snapping that must-have photo, to the glass snow globe with the cruise ship inside.

There may be additional extras as well, depending on the ship, such as extra-charge caviar at the champagne bar (if your ship has one), or cigars at the cigar bar (if your ship has one). Some ships charge extra for afternoon ice cream sundaes. All ships that offer baby-sitting (as opposed to the organized kids' programs) charge for it.

You'll also pay extra for such activities as golf simulators or mini-golf, and video games. And some lines charge a small service fee for dinner in the ship's alternative restaurant (Princess even charges extra at its Häagen-Dazs ice cream stands).

Don't underestimate in your budget planning the lure of items in the gift shop. The shops offer frequent sales, and are especially attractive during days at sea (when you can't shop in port). Also, don't think you won't be tempted by the photos snapped onboard by the ship's photographer. Even if you're a reluctant poser they'll get you, and you'll find them offered the next day not only in regular pictures but also as key chains and other nifty souvenirs.

2 Booking Through a Travel Agent

Booking a cruise is a complicated process, with lots of nuances. That's why more than 95% of cruise passengers book through agents. The cruise lines are happy with the system, have only small reservations staffs themselves (unlike the airlines), and actually discourage direct sales. Even if you do try to call a cruise line to book yourself, you may be advised to contact an agent in your area (the cruise line may even offer you a name from its list of preferred agencies).

A good travel agent can save you both time and money. If you're reluctant to use an agent, consider this: Would you represent yourself in court? Perform surgery on your own abdomen? Tackle complicated IRS forms without seeking help? You may be the rare type that doesn't need a travel agent. But most of us are better off working with one.

A good agent can save you both time and money, and can often provide additional information about cruise lines you're interested in. You don't have to hassle with calling cruise lines for brochures; agencies have them in stock. Plus, agents usually work for you *for free* (the bulk of their fee is paid by the cruise lines). Your agent will also help you make decisions on the type of **cabin** best suited for your needs, and help you arrange your dining-room seating preference and travel insurance.

Your agent will discuss with you optional **airfare programs** offered by the lines, **transfers** from the airport to the pier, and any pre- or post-cruise **hotel or tour programs.** Some lines also let you purchase **shore excursions** in advance (for more on shore excursions, see above). And there may also be pre-bookable spa packages available.

There are really no advantages to booking a cruise yourself, even on the Internet, and consider this: If you do try to book your cruise yourself and make a mistake, who are you going to blame? Unless you're a total control freak, working with an agent is really the way to go.

If you don't have a good travel agent, try to find one through your friends, preferably those who have cruised before. For the most personal service, look for an agent in your local area, and for the most knowledgeable service, look for an agent who has cruised him- or herself, preferably on one of the lines you're considering. It's perfectly okay to ask an agent questions about their experience, such as whether they have ever cruised in Europe.

It really doesn't matter whether your agent is at a small agency or works for a large national agency. And it's a personal choice whether you prefer to work with an agent face-to-face or over the phone. What is important is that the agent gets to know you and understands your vacation desires. He or she should ask you questions about your lifestyle and past vacation experiences (if the agent doesn't ask you such questions, be wary of using him or her).

It is important to realize that **not all agents represent all cruise lines.** In order to be experts on what they sell, and to maximize the commissions the lines pay them (they're paid more based on volume of sales), some agents may limit their product to, say, one luxury line, one mid-priced line, one mass-market line, etc. If you have your sights set on a particular line or have it narrowed down between a couple, you'll have to find an agent who handles your choices. As I mentioned above, you can call the lines themselves to get the name of an agent near you.

It's perfectly okay to **shop around,** calling a few different agents to compare rates. Some agents will even offer perks to keep your business (such as a free cabin upgrade or a bottle of champagne).

CONSOLIDATORS & DISCOUNTERS

You'll find these high-volume operators advertising with low come-on rates in the Sunday newspaper and over the Internet. They might have tempting offers, but be aware they also tend to deal more in price than service (their personnel are usually trained more as order-takers than advice-givers). Their deals may sound good, and may in fact *be* good, but they tend to be last-minute offers with only limited departure dates and cabin types available (the ads tend to feature the very lowest cabin category), and the rates tend not to include port charges and taxes and may not come with any sort of discounted airfare. I recommend working with these operators only if you either know very specifically what you want or are very flexible with your travel plans.

CRUISE AGENCIES & CRUISE SPECIALISTS

The easiest way to ensure the agent is experienced in booking cruises is to work with an agent at a **cruise-only agency** (meaning that the whole agency specializes in cruises) or to find an agent who is a **cruise specialist** (meaning the agent him- or herself specializes in cruises). If you call a **full-service agency** (an agency that handles all types of travel), ask to speak to someone on that agency's **cruise desk.**

The easiest way to find reputable cruise agents is to check the membership rosters of the **Cruise Lines International Association (CLIA)** (☎ **212/921-0066,** www.cruising.org) or the **National Association of Cruise Oriented Agencies (NACOA)** (☎ **305/663-5626,** www.nacoa.com). Members of both groups are cruise specialists.

Membership in the **American Society of Travel Agents (ASTA)** (☎ **800/275-2782,** www.asta.net.com) ensures the agency is monitored for ethical practices, although it does not in itself designate cruise experience.

You may also run across cruise specialists with the **Certified Travel Counselor (CTC)** designation. This means they have completed a professional-skills course offered by the Institute of Certified Travel Agents (ICTA, ☎ **781/237-0280,** www.icta.com), and is another guarantor of in-depth knowledge of the travel industry.

In the past few years, several top U.S. cruise agencies have been combined to form **The Travel Company,** a company that now handles something like 10% of all cruise bookings worldwide. Unlike your local Mom and Pop agency, The Travel Company conducts most of its business through the telephone. For more information, call ☎ **800/242-9000** or see their Web site at www.travelco.com.

GETTING EXTRA-SPECIAL DEALS THROUGH AGENTS

Agents, especially those who specialize in cruises, are in frequent contact with the cruise lines, and are alerted by the lines, either by e-mail or fax, about the latest and greatest deals and **special offers.** The cruise lines tend to communicate such deals and offers to their top agents first, before the general public, and some of these will never appear in your local newspaper.

Keeping an Open Hot Line to Your Agent

Since you'll be traveling on Europe time, it's particularly important to make sure your agent has some sort of 24-hour service in case you run into any problems. Many agencies contract with outside firms for this coverage, which is perfectly okay. The bottom line is, you want someone you can call for assistance no matter what time it is back home.

Depending on the agency you choose, you may run across additional incentives for booking through an agent.

- **Newsletters:** To keep their clients alert to specials, agencies may offer newsletters or have other means of communication, such as postcards, e-mail, or posting the specials on their Internet sites.
- **Group Rates:** Some agencies buy big blocks of space on a ship in advance and offer it to their clients at a group price only available through that agency. These are called group rates, although "group" in this case means savings, not that you have to hang around with the other people booking through the agency.
- **Rebates and Incentives:** Some agencies are willing to give back to the client a portion of their commissions from the cruise line in order to close a sale, in what is known as rebates or incentives. This percentage may be monetary, or it may take the form of a perk such as a free bottle of champagne or a cabin upgrade.

ROUNDING UP ADDITIONAL INFORMATION

The **glossy brochures** produced by all the cruise lines are basically advertisements, but they do contain valuable information that'll help you when selecting and booking your cruise—such as deck layouts and schematics (and sometimes photos) of the different cabin categories. Of course, the verbiage in these brochures may not be all that straightforward. For instance, "comfortable cabins" can be another way of saying "small." The lines put a lot of money into these brochures, and they all show off their ships in a beautiful light. Rarely are lower-end cabins shown, for instance.

In addition to brochures, many lines offer **videos** of their products. While the videos always feature the same kind of utopian view you see in the brochures, they may give you a better idea than print pieces about the ship's size, space, and other offerings. Your travel agent may have videos you can borrow, or you may be able to order one directly from the cruise line. You can also place an order with **Vacations on Video** (**☎ 602/483-1551**), a major distributor that offers videos for virtually all the major lines. The videos vary in length and go for an average price of $7.95, plus shipping charges.

The **Internet** is another good source for gathering information on cruises. Most major lines have their own sites, which typically offer information on cabin configurations and public rooms, and sometimes feature a virtual tour of the ships. The industry marketing group Cruise Lines International Association (CLIA) site (www.cruising.org) has information on CLIA-approved travel agents. Most of the cruise lines' sites also have links to that line's preferred agents.

Only a few sites offer on-line booking capability. You may find sporadic **special deals** at the sites, but these are usually the same deals your travel agent can get for you. An exception is Renaissance Cruises, which offers both Web discounts and direct-mail discounts not available through agents.

For a listing of cruise line sites and other sites that will be valuable in researching and planning your trip, see "Leading Web Sites for Cruise Planning" in chapter 1.

Watch Out for Scams

The travel business tends to attract more than its share of scam operators trying to lure consumers with incredible come-ons. If you get a solicitation that just doesn't sound right, or if you are uneasy about an agent you're dealing with, call your state consumer protection agency or local office of the Better Business Bureau. Or you can check with the cruise line to see if they've ever heard of the agency in question.

The American Society of Travel Agents also offers the following recommendations for how to avoid the bad apples in the crop:

1. **Be extremely skeptical about postcard and phone solicitations** (and e-mail come-ons) that say you've been selected to receive a fabulous vacation.
2. **Never give out your credit card number** unless you initiate the transaction and you are confident about the company with whom you are doing business.
3. **Get everything in writing.** You should receive complete details in writing about any trip prior to payment. These details should include the total price and any applicable cancellation and change penalties. They should also include specific information about all components of the package.
4. **900 numbers aren't toll-free.** If you call a 900 number in response to a travel solicitation, understand that there are charges and know the risks.
5. **Walk away from high-pressure sales presentations** that don't allow you time to evaluate the offer, or that require you to disclose your income.
6. **Be suspicious** of companies that require you wait at least 60 days to take your trip.

3 Choosing Your Cabin

Once you've got an idea of the cruise line you're interested in and you've talked over your options with your travel agent, a big decision you'll have to make is what type of cabin best suits your needs.

The cruise lines have improved things a bit since Charles Dickens referred to his stateroom as a coffin, but cramped, windowless spaces can still be found. On the other hand, so can penthouse-size suites with expansive verandas, Jacuzzis, and hot and cold running butler service.

What kind of cabin is right for you? Price will likely be a big factor here, but so should the vacation style you prefer. If, for instance, you plan to spend a lot of quiet time in your cabin, you should probably consider booking the biggest room you can afford, and you should also consider taking a cabin with a picture window or a private veranda. If, conversely, you plan to be off on tours or out and about the ship's public areas and will only be using your cabin to change clothes and collapse in at the end of the day, you might be just as happy with a smaller (and cheaper) cabin.

Most cabins on cruise ships today have a private bathroom with a shower and twin beds that are convertible to queen-size (you can request which configuration you want). Some cabins have bunk beds that are obviously not convertible. Some ships also have a limited number of double beds.

Many ships have cabins designed for three or four people that will include bunks. In some, it is possible to put in a fifth, portable bed. Some lines offer special cabins designed for families. Families may also be able to book connecting cabins (although they'll have to pay for two cabins to do so).

Model Cabin Layouts

Typical Outside Cabin Configurations

- Twin beds (can often be pushed together)
- Upper berths for extra passengers fold into walls
- Bathrooms usually have showers only (no tub)
- Usually (but not always) have TVs and radios
- May have portholes or picture windows

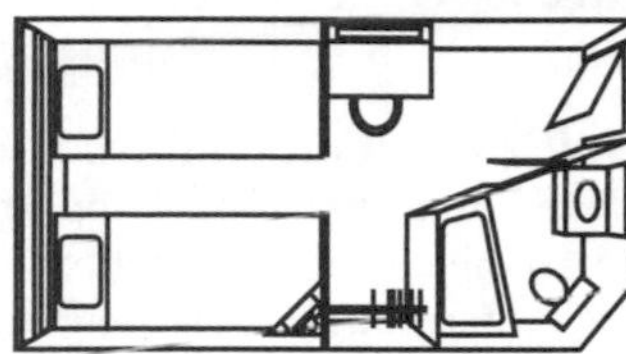

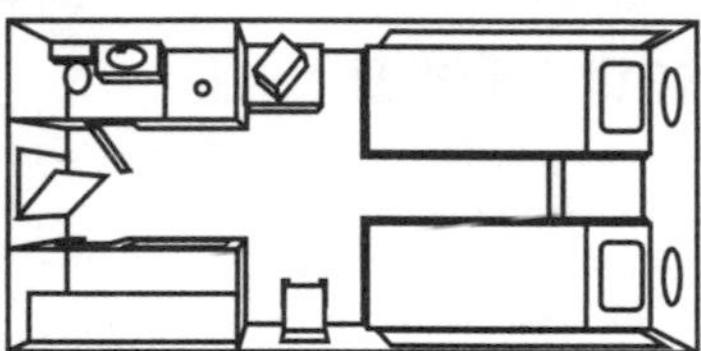

Typical Suite Configurations

- Queen-size or double beds
- Sitting areas (sometimes with sofa beds for extra passengers)
- Large bathrooms, usually with tub
- Refrigerators (sometimes stocked, sometimes not)
- Stereos and TVs with VCRs are common
- Large closets
- Large windows or outside verandas

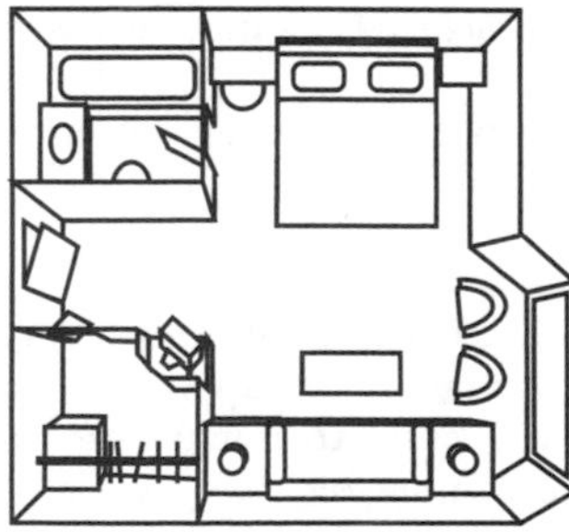

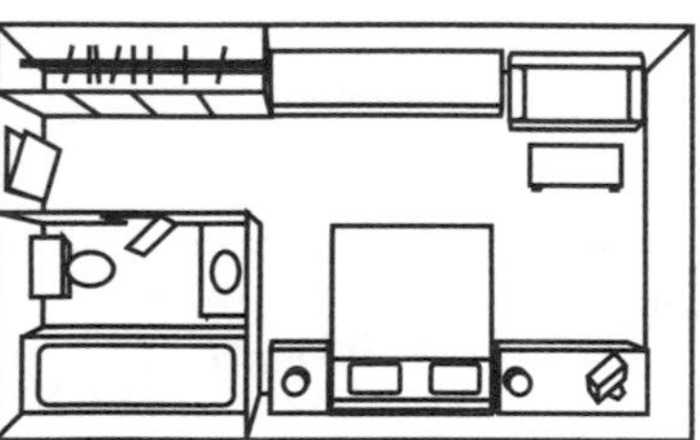

Some cabins have televisions. Some also have such extra amenities as safes, mini-refrigerators, VCRs, bathrobes, and hair dryers. A bathtub is considered a luxury on ships and will usually only be offered in more expensive rooms.

CABIN TYPES

The typical ship offers several types of cabins, as outlined by floor plans in the cruise line's brochure. The cabins are usually described by **price** (highest to lowest), **category** (suite, deluxe, superior, standard, economy, and others), and **furniture configuration** ("sitting area with two lower beds," for example). Diagrams of the various cabin types are typically included. See "Model Cabin Layouts" above for a sample.

The cabins will also be described as being **inside** (without windows or portholes) or **outside** (with). Outside cabins are more expensive since windows allow natural light into the cabin and may allow ocean views—though some may be obstructed (usually by a lifeboat) or look out onto a public area, which will be an issue if you crave privacy. An experienced travel agent should be able to advise you on these matters.

THE SOUNDS OF SILENCE

Noise can be a factor that may influence your cabin choice. Consider that if you take a cabin on a lower deck you may hear engine noises; in the front of the ship, anchor noises; and in the back of the ship, thruster noises. A cabin near an elevator may bring door-opening and -closing sounds. Cabins on the Promenade Deck may sound great, but you may hear passengers walking or talking outside or even peeking into your cabin. And a cabin above or below the disco may pulse until all hours of the night. If noise is a problem for you, make your cabin choice accordingly. A ship's deck plan can clue you in to potential problems.

On the big ships, the more deluxe outside cabins may also come with **verandas** that give you private outdoor space to enjoy sea breezes. But the verandas vary in size, so if you're looking to do more than stand on your balcony, make sure the outdoor space is big enough to accommodate deck chairs, a table, or whatever else you require.

Usually, the higher on the ship (by deck) the cabin is located, the more expensive and nicer the cabin is. This is true even if there are cabins of the same size on lower decks (the decor changes).

Luxury suites are usually on upper decks, but a quirky thing about cabin pricing is that the most stable cabins during rough seas are those in the middle and lower parts of the ship.

On **small ships,** cabins can run to the truly spartan, though some can also give the big-ship cabins a run for their money. Generally, the difference lies in the orientation of the line: Those promising a real adventure experience tend to feature somewhat utilitarian cabins.

Aboard both large and small ships, keep in mind the most expensive and least expensive cabins tend to sell out first.

CABIN SIZES

The size of a cabin is described in terms of square feet. This number may not mean a lot unless you want to mark it out on your floor at home. But to give you an idea: 120 square feet and under is low-end and cramped, 180 square feet is mid-range (and the minimum for people with claustrophobia), and 250 square feet and up is suite-size.

A FEW CABIN-CHOOSING TIPS

Make sure the **beds** in the cabin can be configured the way you want. Not all cabins offer double or queen-sized beds. If you want a **bathtub** or **television,** make sure you choose a cabin that has one. If you are in a **wheelchair,** make sure the cabin and

What Is Luxury?

Cruise lines freely use terms like *deluxe* and *luxury,* but these terms vary greatly from line to line. They are, therefore, virtually meaningless. You are better off evaluating cabins based on size and amenities offered.

bathroom door is wide enough to accommodate your chair. **Book early for first-choice of cabins** (the cheapest and most expensive tend to sell out first).

4 Choosing Your Dining Options

In addition to choosing your cabin, you can also choose your preferred meal seating time. Smaller ships usually serve dinner in one sitting, at an open seating, allowing you to sit at any table you want, so if you plan to sail one of these lines you don't have to read this section at all. But because most dining rooms on larger ships are not large enough to accommodate all passengers at once, these ships typically offer two seatings, or sittings, especially for dinner. All table space is on a reserved basis. Early or main seating is typically at 6pm. Late seating at 8:30pm.

There are advantages and disadvantages to both times, and it basically comes down to personal choice. **Early seating** is usually less crowded and is the preferred time for families and seniors. The dining experience can be a bit more rushed (the staff needs to make way for the next wave), but food items may be fresher since they haven't had to wait under warmers. You can see a show right after dinner, and have first dibs on other nighttime venues as well. And you just may be hungry again in time for the **midnight buffet.**

Late seating, on the other hand, allows you time for a good long nap or late spa appointments before dining. Dinner is not rushed at all. You can sit as long as you want enjoying after-dinner drinks—unless, that is, you choose to rush off to catch the 10pm show. You probably won't be hungry again at midnight, but you can go and laugh at all those who are.

If you choose to also eat **breakfast and lunch** in the dining room as opposed to at the more casual venues on the ship, theoretically you are also supposed to eat at assigned times as well. I've found, though, that most ships aren't hard-and-fast on this. Crowds in the dining room are typically only an issue at dinner (a lot of people eat lunch in the ports). If you show up other than at your assigned time for breakfast or lunch and your assigned table is full, the staff will probably just seat you elsewhere.

Typical meal times for breakfast are 7 or 8am for the early seating and 8:30 or 9am for the late. For lunch, it's usually noon for the early seating and 1:30pm or so for the late.

SPECIAL DIETARY OR MENU REQUESTS

Though many cruise lines these days offer vegetarian and low-fat meals as a standard feature, you should still arrange any special dietary needs through your travel agent at the time you make your reservation. Some lines offer kosher menus, and all will have vegetarian, low-fat, low-salt, and sugar-free options available.

Also let the cruise line know of any birthday or anniversary that will occur during the cruise so they can plan to help you celebrate accordingly.

TABLE SIZES

Do you mind sitting with strangers? Are you looking to make new friends? Your dinner companions can make or break your cruise experience. Most ships offer tables configured for two to 12 people. For singles or couples who want to socialize, generally a table of six to eight seats allows enough variety so you don't get bored and also allows you the ability to steer clear of any one individual you don't particularly care for (tables are assigned, not seats). Couples may choose to sit on their own, but singles may find the ship reluctant to offer a table for one. A family of four may want to choose a table for four, or request to sit with another family at a table for eight.

You need to state your preference in advance, but don't worry if you change your mind once you're on board. You'll probably be able to move around. Just tell the dining room maitre d' and he'll review the seating charts for an opening (greasing his palm will probably help).

Many ships now feature **smoke-free dining rooms,** but if smoking is a particular concern to you, check this out with your travel agent. If the room isn't nonsmoking, you can request a nonsmoking table. Vice versa for smokers.

5 Deposits & Cancellation Policies

DEPOSITS

You'll be asked by your travel agent to make a deposit, either of a fixed amount (usually $300 to $1,000) or at some percentage of your total cruise cost (Renaissance requires full payment up front). You'll be asked to pay the remaining fare usually 60 to 90 days before your departure date. Make sure before making any payment that you carefully review the line's refund policy. You'll find the policy listed in the back of the cruise line's brochure.

Cancellation penalties vary by line. Before paying a dime you should make sure you understand the payment schedule that you're agreeing to by putting down your deposit.

If at all possible, make your payment with a credit card. This gives you an additional avenue of recourse should you encounter any problems.

CANCELLATIONS

Cruise lines have varying policies regarding cancellations, and it's important to look at the fine print in the line's brochure to make sure you understand the policy. Most lines, but not all, allow you to cancel for a full refund on your deposit and payment anytime up to 76 days before the sailing, after which you have to pay a penalty that increases as you get closer to your sailing date. If you cancel a month before the sailing, for instance, you might have to pay 50% of your fare as a penalty. If you cancel at the last minute, you may not be refunded any of what you've paid.

6 Your Cruise Documents

About 1 month before your cruise and no later than 1 week before, you should receive your cruise documents, including your **airline tickets** (if you purchased them from the cruise line), a **boarding document** with your cabin and sometimes dining choices on it, boarding forms to fill out, **luggage tags,** and your prearranged **bus transfer vouchers** and **hotel vouchers** (if applicable). There will also be information on shore excursions and additional material detailing things you need to know before you sail.

Read all of this carefully. Make sure your cabin category and dining preferences are as you requested and that your airline flight and arrival times are what you were told. If there are problems, call your agent immediately. Make sure there is enough time so you can arrive at the port no later than an hour before departure time.

You will be required to have a **passport** for your trip (see chapter 3 for more on this). You won't likely have to have a visa, but you can consult with your travel agent in this regard based on your specific itinerary.

I recommend you **confirm your flight** 3 days before departure. Also, before you leave for the airport, tag your bags with the tags provided by the cruise line, and fill in your boarding cards. This will save you time when you arrive at the ship.

7 Travel Insurance

You can buy trip-cancellation insurance (TCI) to protect yourself if for some reason you're not able to take your cruise, or in case your trip is interrupted. You can also get coverage to handle the expense of any medical emergencies not covered by your regular health insurance.

Travel insurance is not a bargain, however—some would say it's downright overpriced—and you should be wary of buying too much. The insurance is either based on a percentage of your cruise fare or offered at a fixed rate (usually $200 to $300 per person for a basic policy). When evaluating insurance policies, check to see that they cover the following situations:

- **Trip cancellation.** Caused by you or a member of your immediate family getting sick or dying, not limited to those who cruise. If you are traveling with a non–family member, make sure the policy covers you if you need to cancel the cruise because that person cannot cruise.
- **Pre-existing medical conditions.** The policy should include a pre-existing sickness exclusion rider—critical if you or any family member has a pre-existing medical condition.
- **Medical expenses.** Should cover expenses on board or in port, and should include any necessary medical evacuation from the ship or port of call.
- **Emergency air travel home.** Your transportation should be taken care of in the event of a family medical emergency or death.
- **Trip delay.** Your policy should have interruption protection should you encounter problems such as weather that prevent you from getting to your cruise on time.
- **Accident coverage.** Should include getting to and from the ship.
- **Baggage protection.** Should include loss, damage, and late arrival.
- **Bankruptcy or default of cruise line.** Not the most common occurrence, but hey, who knows?

Coverage for your **jewelry** and other valuables usually falls under your homeowner's policy. Jewels should be kept in the safe on the ship when you're not wearing them (or better yet, just bring fakes).

WHERE TO BUY INSURANCE

Several firms offer coverage that combines TCI with medical insurance, and some cruise companies (and a few large travel agencies, too) offer their own plans (although these are not usually as comprehensive as the insurance companies' offerings). Your travel agent should be able to guide you through the various offerings.

Two of the top firms are **Access America,** 6600 W. Broad St., Richmond, VA 23230 (☎ **800/284-8300** or 804/285-3300), and **Travel Guard International,** 1145 Clark St., Stevens Point, WI 54481 (☎ **800/826-1300** or 715/345-0505).

3 Things to Know Before You Go

You've bought your ticket and you're getting ready to cruise. Here are a few nuts and bolts, odds and ends, FYIs, and helpful hints to consider before you go.

1 Passports & Visas

Citizens of non-EU countries need a **passport** to enter any European country. You should keep your passport in a safe place (don't pack it in your check-in luggage) and keep a photocopy in a separate place, just for backup. On some ships, you are required to turn your passport in to the purser's office for the duration of your cruise.

APPLYING FOR A NEW PASSPORT

U.S. CITIZENS If you do not have a passport, you will have to apply for one in person at one of the 13 passport offices throughout the U.S., or at a federal or state court, probate court, or major post office. You need to bring a certified birth certificate as proof of citizenship; bringing along your driver's license, state or military ID, or social security card is also wise. You also need two identical passport-sized photos (2" × 2"), taken at a photo shop or special passport photo venue (strip photos from photo machines are not acceptable).

For those over age 15, a passport is valid for 10 years and costs $60 ($45 plus a $15 handling fee); for those 15 and under, a passport is valid for 5 years and costs $40.

If you are replacing an expired passport that was issued within the past 12 years, you can renew it by mail and bypass the handling fee.

Make sure to allow plenty of time before your trip to apply, as processing takes about 3 weeks (but can take longer during busy periods). You may be able to expedite things by paying extra for FedEx delivery. For more information, contact the **National Passport Information Center** at ☎ **900/225-5674.** On the Web, check out www.travel.state.gov.

CANADIAN CITIZENS You can pick up a passport application at one of the 28 regional passport offices or most travel agencies. Passports are valid for 5 years and cost $60. Children under 16 may be included on a parent's passport, but they need their own passport to travel unaccompanied by the parent. Applications must be accompanied by two identical passport-sized photos and proof of Canadian citizenship. Processing takes 5 to 10 days if you apply in person; or about 3 weeks by mail.

What to Do if You Lose Your Passport

If you lose your passport, notify the ship's purser. He or she will help you arrange a visit to the nearest consulate of your home country as soon as possible to have the passport replaced.

For more information, contact the central **Passport Office,** Department of Foreign Affairs and International Trade in Ottawa (☎ **800/567-6868**). On the Web, check out www.dfait-maeci.gc.ca/passport.

U.K. CITIZENS For passport information, call the **London Passport Office** (☎ **0171/271-3000**); or check out www.open.gov.uk/ukpass/ukpass.htm.

AUSTRALIAN CITIZENS You can apply for a passport at your local post office or passport office, or call ☎ **131-232** (www.dfat.gov.au/passports/pp_home.html) for more information.

NEW ZEALAND CITIZENS You can pick up a passport application at any travel agency or Link Centre. For information, contact the **Passport Office** (☎ **800/225-050;** inform.dia.govt.nz/internal_affairs/businesses/doni_pro/pports_home.html).

VISAS

Your cruise line will advise you if any visas are needed for the countries you will visit (if in doubt, call the line or ask your travel agent). In most cases, a visa is not required if you are visiting a country for a limited amount of time (less than 24 hours). If you are visiting Russia, you do not need a visa to take a shore excursion, but you will need one to head off on your own. Visas need to be applied for well in advance of your trip. The easiest place to apply is through a **visa service,** and your travel agent can guide you to one in your area. A small fee is charged for the service. You can also apply by contacting the embassy of the country you will be visiting.

2 Money Matters

You have already paid the lion's share of your cruise vacation, but you will still need a credit card, traveler's checks, or cash to handle your onboard expenses such as drinks, shore excursions, photos by the ship's photographer, spa services, gift shop purchases, and so forth. Some ships (but not all) will take a personal check.

You will want cash for taxis, drinks, small purchases, and tips for guides in port. You may also need cash to pay crew tips at the end of the cruise, although some lines allow you to charge tips. And you'll want a few dollars on hand in case you want to tip a crew member for room service or laundry delivery.

ABOARD SHIP

Cruise ships themselves operate on a cashless basis. Basically, this means you keep a running tab. You sign for virtually everything you want to buy all week long—drinks at the bar, shore excursions, and gift shop purchases—and pay up at the end of the cruise with cash or a credit card (you can use cash in the casino). Very, very convenient, yes—and also very, very easy to spend more than you would if you were doling out cash each time you needed to pay for something.

On some European ships, the onboard items are priced in European currency such as Italian lira, so you may want to bring a calculator with you to figure out what you are really spending for that nifty T-shirt with the ship's logo or that special drink of the day. First European Cruises, on its new *Mistral,* was the first to use the euro to price onboard items (which is helpful to Europeans but not necessarily to Americans). Fortunately, the line also gives out calculators as an onboard amenity.

I've included a chart in chapter 11 showing relative currency values of the major European currencies at press time. For up-to-the-minute conversions, see CNN's currency converter at **www.cnn.com/travel/currency**.

Shortly before or after embarkation, a purser or check-in clerk in the terminal or on board will request an imprint of one of your credit cards. (If you want to pay in cash or by traveler's check, you will be asked to leave a deposit, usually $250 for a 1-week sailing.) Larger ships will then issue you an **identification card** that you show whenever you get back on the ship after spending the day in port and that you also use when you sign for something. On the newest ships, this same ID card often serves as your room key. Smaller and older ships may not use these ID cards, and still issue regular room keys.

On the last day of your cruise, an **itemized account** of all you've charged throughout the cruise is slipped beneath your cabin door. If you agree with the charges, they are automatically billed to your credit card account. If you are paying in cash or if you dispute any charge, then you need to stop by the ship's cashier or purser's office, where there's usually a long line.

I suggest you keep careful track of your onboard expenses to avoid an unpleasant surprise at the end of your cruise. Some ships make this tracking particularly easy by offering interactive TV. By pushing the right buttons you can check your account from the comfort of your own stateroom. On others, you have to go to the purser's or guest relations desk to review your account. You can do so as often as you choose, but you may encounter lines of others doing the same.

IN PORT

The cashless system works just fine on board, but you will need some dough in port. Of course, you can put any shore excursions you sign up for on your room tab, and credit cards are accepted at most port shops (as are traveler's checks), but I do recommend having some real cash on you, ideally in small denominations, for any taxi rides, snacks, and street-side souvenir vendors.

It is more expensive to exchange your money for foreign currency in your own country than it is once you've reached your destination. But it's a good idea to arrive in Europe with a bit of local currency, enough at least to buy a cup of coffee and a newspaper between flights or to get you to your hotel or ship. About $30 to $50 should do it.

Many of the larger ships operating in Europe offer **exchange services** where you can exchange your currency for the local currency of the country you're visiting. This is usually accomplished by a local bank official coming on board at the port. Some ships, including Princess's *Grand Princess,* have special ATMs that do currency exchange (for a fee). Most ships do not offer exchange services at the purser's desk.

Your ship, if it's an American line, may also have an ATM that delivers greenbacks (usually for a hefty fee). Some lines will also cash personal checks up to a set amount (usually around $200).

See chapter 11 for an exchange table giving rates from U.S., Canadian, U.K., Australian, and New Zealand currencies into all the local currencies you'll use in port.

ATMs IN EUROPE

In nearly every town in Europe (even the tiny ones) you can find an **ATM** that will give you local currency (but not dollars) from your ATM or PIN-enabled Visa or MasterCard (contact the issuing bank to enable this feature and get a PIN). PLUS and Cirrus cards work on many ATMs in Europe and present what is really the fastest and easiest way to exchange your money. You get a good rate (better than banks or exchange services) and unless your home bank charges you for using a nonproprietary ATM you don't have to pay a fee or commission (which you usually do at banks and exchange services). I usually rely on ATMs, but I also find it's a good idea to have some cash or traveler's checks just in case of emergency (or in case the bank computer lines are down).

Before you leave home, make sure the PINs on your bank- and credit cards will work in Europe; you usually need a four-digit code (six digits may not work in Europe). And keep in mind you can only access your checking account (not savings) from ATMs abroad. Both the **Cirrus** (☎ **800/424-7787**) and **PLUS** (☎ **800/843-7587**) networks have automated ATM locators that list the banks in each country that will accept your card.

American Express card cash advances are usually only available from AMEX offices, which you'll find in every major European city.

Exchanging Money

If you are not using ATMs, then try to exchange your money at a bank rather than the exchange services you will see in busy tourist areas or at your hotel. The rate of exchange is usually higher at banks, and the fee charged for the service less.

Using Credit Cards

Most restaurants, shops, and hotels in Europe accept major credit cards such as American Express, Diners Club, MasterCard, and Visa (but not Discover). The most widely accepted cards are Visa and MasterCard.

Using Traveler's Checks

Most banks in the U.S. sell traveler's checks, charging fees of 1% to 2% of the value of the checks. AAA members can buy American Express traveler's checks commission-free. The checks offer great insurance since, if you lose them—and have kept a list of the numbers and a record of which ones you cashed—you can get them replaced at no charge. Be aware, though, that you won't get as high a rate when you go to exchange them for foreign currency as you will for cash. Personal checks are pretty much useless in Europe, except as accepted on your ship (check your ship's policy before relying on this method of payment).

American Express (☎ **800/221-7282**) is one of the largest issuers of traveler's checks, and its are widely accepted. **Thomas Cook** (☎ **800/223-7373** in the U.S. or Canada, 0171/480-7226 in London) issues MasterCard traveler's checks. **Citicorp** (☎ **800/645-6556**) and other banks issue checks under their own name or under MasterCard or Visa. Checks issued in dollar amounts (as opposed to, say, French francs or Italian lira) are the most widely accepted in the world.

Value-Added Tax (VAT)

All European countries charge a Value-Added Tax (VAT) of 15% to 35% on goods and services, which is already included in the price you see. Rates vary from country to country, although most are moving toward a 15% rate. Citizens of non-EU countries can get back most of the tax on purchases (but not on services) if they spend a designated amount (usually between $50 and $200) in a single store.

Regulations vary by country (you should check when you get there or with your ship's purser), but generally you can collect your refund for goods purchased in any EU country at the airport as you leave Europe, or have it mailed to you. To do this, you will be required to have forms and receipts from the store where your purchases were made (make sure to ask for the forms), and may be required to show the items purchased to a VAT official at the airport. Allow an extra 30 minutes at the airport to get through the process (if you've spent a lot, the wait will be worth it).

3 Health & Safety

It's a good rule of thumb to check with the **Centers for Disease Control** in Atlanta (☎ **800/311-3435** or 404/639-3534; www.cdc.gov/travel/) or your physician to see if there are any health precautions you should take before your trip. In the past, for instance, tetanus-diphtheria boosters have been recommended for travel in St. Petersburg, Russia.

The CDC also publishes a green sheet of cruise ship sanitation scores. If the ship you are considering regularly visits U.S. ports, you will be able to check the vessel's sanitation rating. You can access the latest sanitation report at the Web site above, or call for more information (☎ **305/536-4307**).

TRAVELERS' ADVISORIES

The U.S. State Department issues advisories on areas travelers should be concerned about visiting (Kosovo was one of these areas in 1999). You can look up the advisories on the State Department's Web site (http://travel.state.gov) or call ☎ **202/647-5225** for recorded information.

4 Packing

The great thing about packing for a cruise is once you're aboard the ship, you only have to unpack once. The downside is you don't always get all that much storage space.

People (including myself on some occasions) tend to overpack for cruises, but you don't have to. A cruise vacation is no different from any other, except that you will want to change your clothes for dinner, and there may be a formal night or two.

CLOTHING

Check your cruise documents for specifics on the types of nighttime dress codes (see more on these below) and to see if there are any theme nights you may want to dress specifically for (Greek night on Greek ships, for instance, means wear blue and white, the national colors). The daily bulletin delivered to your cabin each day will advise you on the proper dress for the evening.

Obviously what you pack will be determined by when you plan to travel (summer is hotter than spring and fall) and where (Northern Europe and Scandinavia are cooler than the Mediterranean). Consult chapter 1 for average temperatures. The type of ship you are on also has some bearing on what you pack—some alternative ships are totally casual.

As a general rule, you are best off packing loose and comfortable cotton or other **lightweight fabrics.** If you are traveling in Northern Europe, bring clothing you can layer. Comfortable **walking shoes** are a must in Europe as many tours involve walking on cobblestones and other uneven surfaces.

You'll want to pack a swimsuit, a sun hat, sunglasses, and plenty of sunscreen (the sun reflects off the water and can be quite bright). And you'll want to have a raincoat and umbrella, as well as a sweater (even in warm climates you'll want some protection against overactive air-conditioning).

If you plan on hitting the gym, don't forget sneakers and your workout clothes.

I recommend you leave the family jewels home and stick with costume. But if you must bring the real thing, be careful. If you're not wearing it, leave it either in your in-room safe (if there is one) or with the purser.

If you wear glasses or contact lenses, bring an extra pair. And remember to pack whatever toiletries you require (you probably won't be able to find your preferred brand in Europe if you forget).

Cruise Tip: Tuxedo Rentals

If you don't own a tux or don't want to bother lugging one along, you can often arrange a rental through your travel agent for about $75. In some cases, a rental offer arrives with your cruise tickets. If you choose this option, your suit will be waiting for you in your cabin when you arrive.

DAYTIME CLOTHES

Across the board, daytime wear is the same as casual resort wear, meaning T-shirts, polo shirts, bathing suits, jeans, khakis, jogging suits, and sundresses. Remember to bring a cover-up and sandals if you want to go right from your deck chair to lunch in one of the restaurants or to some activity being held in a public room. Many ships ban swimsuits and tank tops from the dining room. When in port, the same dress code generally works. But keep in mind that some religious sites prohibit shorts and sleeveless shirts and require women to wear knee-length skirts. Also be aware of the local culture of the port you are visiting (at some, parading around in short shorts and a bathing suit top is simply not acceptable). And don't forget to wear comfortable shoes!

EVENING CLOTHES

When it comes to evening attire on all ships, except on the casual alternative ships described in chapter 9, you'll want to pack some dressy duds. Most ships have casual, informal, and formal nights. What the cruise line means by these terms will be explained in your documents package, but as a general rule **casual** means men can wear slacks (jeans may be banned) and shirts with collars, women slacks, skirts, and sundresses. **Informal** (or semiformal) means men wear a jacket (but not necessarily a tie), and women wear something slightly fancier than a sundress. **Formal** means bring out the tuxes and dark suits for the men and cocktail dresses, gowns, or other fancy wear for women. At night, as a woman, I find the best approach is simple outfits you can dress up or down with scarves or other accessories. And if you stick to one or two colors, you don't have to pack as many shoes.

In spite of the suggested dress codes, which are usually described in the back of a cruise line's brochure, you'll still find a wide variety of outfits being worn. Invariably, one person's "formal" is quite different from another's. So, like hemlines and everything else these days, to a large extent, anything goes.

SUNDRIES

Like hotels, many ships (especially the newest and the high-end ones) come equipped with hair dryers and supply bathroom amenities such as shampoo, conditioner, lotion, and soap, although you might still want to bring your own products. If you bring your hair dryer, electric razor, curling iron, or laptop, you might want to bring an adapter, since not all ships in Europe run on 110 (the cruise line will provide you with this information).

No need to pack a **beach towel** as they're almost always supplied on board. Bird watchers will want their **binoculars** and manuals, golfers their clubs (although they can always be rented), and snorkelers their gear (which can also be rented).

If you forget to pack a personal effect or two, don't worry. Most ships offer items like razor blades, toothbrushes, sunscreen, and film on board (but you'll pay a premium price).

Most ships have **laundry service** and some offer **dry-cleaning** service as well (there will be a price list in your cabin). Some ships also offer **self-service laundry rooms** (you'll find them on Royal Caribbean, Crystal, and Holland America, among others) so you can wash, dry, and iron your own clothes.

If you like reading but don't want to lug three or four hefty novels on board, there are options. Most ships of all sizes have **libraries** stocked with books and magazines. Some libraries are more extensive than others, of course; the *QE2*'s is huge, for example. Also, most ships stock paperback best-sellers in their shops.

LUGGAGE RESTRICTIONS

Keep in mind there may be limitations on the number of bags you can take on the plane (usually two checked bags and one carry-on per person). Checked baggage should not weigh more than 70 pounds. It's a good idea to make sure your baggage is sturdy. Before you use it, make sure there are no rips and the handles are still firmly attached.

You should plan on bringing a piece of **hand luggage** in which you should pack all valuables, prescription and over-the-counter medication, and your cruise documents, passport, and air tickets. You should also keep in your hand luggage your credit cards, house and car keys, and claim checks for airport parking, as well as a change of clothes, chewing gum, and reading materials.

With all the tempting things for sale in Europe, it's important to remember to **save room in your luggage for your souvenirs.** You may even want to pack an extra foldable suitcase for your treasured finds.

The Cruise Experience

4

Unlike their more utilitarian ancestors, today's cruise ships aren't just about transportation. Rather, they're attraction-filled destinations themselves, bustling resorts at sea where there are countless things to do, people to meet, good food and drink, entertainment, and nonstop activities.

While the cruise experience varies from ship to ship, the common denominator is choice. You can run from an aerobics class to an art auction, and then play bingo, all before lunch, or you can choose to watch the seascape from a quiet deck chair. Whether you like to do it all or do nothing at all, cruising is a convenient and leisurely way of traveling from one exotic port to another. While ports may be the focus for most of us on European cruises, you'll have plenty of time to sample shipboard life as well.

In the pages that follow, I'll give you a taste of that shipboard life, starting with a little history . . .

1 A Brief History Lesson

What we today think of as the leisure-cruise industry has its roots in the early 1840s in Europe.

Among the earliest "cruise" passengers was Charles Dickens, who booked passage in 1842, along with 86 fellow travelers, on a mail ship called *Britannia,* operated by Canadian Samuel Cunard, founder of the **Cunard line.** Writing in *American Notes* about his journey from Liverpool to Halifax, Nova Scotia, and Boston, Dickens described cramped quarters (the lounge, he says, was "not unlike a gigantic hearse with windows in the sides"), coffinlike cabins, and passengers, including himself, getting seasick (although he claims that he just got woozy).

Things had improved by the time Mark Twain took a transatlantic voyage on the steamship *Quaker City* in 1867. At least he didn't get sick. In *The Innocents Abroad,* Twain wrote, "If there is one thing in the world that will make a man peculiarly and insufferably self-conceited, it is to have his stomach behave himself, the first day at sea, when nearly all his comrades are seasick."

But at least the shipboard accommodations had improved. Twain described his cabin as having "room to turn around in, but not to swing a cat in, at least with entire security to the cat."

Okay, so Dickens and Twain probably weren't quoted much in early cruise promotions. But despite the bad press, passenger cruise ships became increasingly popular. Author William Makepeace Thackeray traveled in 1844 on a series of ships operated by **P&O** (the parent company of today's Princess Cruises) to Malta, Greece, Constantinople, the Holy Land, and Egypt. In his *From Cornhill to Grand Cairo,* he describes his "delightful Mediterranean cruise." But, like the other early cruise writers, he also writes of people getting seasick.

Hamburg, Germany, claims to be the place where cruising on a ship dedicated to cruising (as opposed to transporting cargo) was invented. In 1845, the Sloman Shipping Line placed an ad in a Hamburg newspaper saying, "A fully rigged ship is to go on a voyage of the world which will not have as its aim any mercantile purposes, but the ship's whole facilities and accommodation, the fixing of the times of sojourn in the towns and countries to be visited, the overriding aim of the whole voyage will only be consideration for the security, comfort, entertainment and information of the travelers." The ad further stated that the cruise was only for people "of good reputation and education—preferably scientifically educated."

In the late 19th century, P&O introduced *Ceylon,* a vessel powered by both steam and sail, that was converted to a cruising yacht for carrying wealthy, adventurous guests on world cruises in lavish style. A few years later, in 1887, North of Scotland, Orkney & Shetland Steam Navigation's *St. Sunniva* was launched as the first steamer built expressly for cruising. And more cruise ships followed.

The **Hamburg-American Line** in 1901 introduced its 4,400-gross-ton *Prinzessin Victoria Luise,* the first ship to offer bathrooms in every passenger cabin. The luxurious early cruise offered pleasure cruises to ports in the Canary Islands, the Caribbean, Scandinavia, and the Mediterranean.

But before World War I, cruising still took a backseat to the more lucrative trade of transporting both well-off travelers and immigrants across the Atlantic. The competition was fierce among the famous shipping lines such as Cunard, White Star, Hamburg America, the French Line, North German Lloyd, **Holland America,** and Red Star Line, all of whom sought to attract customers by trying to build the fastest, largest, or most luxurious new ships. It was an era for ships of rich wood paneling, chandeliers, grand ballrooms and smoking lounges, and huge gilded suites with antiques, art, and servant's quarters. The ships featured three classes of service: first class, second (or cabin class), and steerage (tourist class). When these ships did do pleasure cruises, generally only first-class accommodations were sold and the other cabin classes were shut down until the transatlantic schedules were resumed; it wasn't until the late 1960s that the multi-class system was pretty much eliminated.

THE SHIP YOU ALL KNOW (AND A FEW OTHERS) Soon after Cunard launched its popular 2,165-passenger ***Mauretania*** and ***Lusitania*** in 1906, J. Bruce Ismay, son of White Star Cruise Line founder Thomas Ismay, envisioned a trio of the largest and most luxurious vessels in the transatlantic service to appeal to the rich American industrialists then crossing regularly. By 1911, the first of these three sisters, the 2,584-passenger, 46,000-ton *Olympic,* was in service, with the ***Titanic*** (yes, that one) scheduled for an April 1912 maiden voyage. (The third sister, originally planned as the *Gigantic,* was on the drawing boards to follow *Titanic.*)

Touted as the world's greatest ship, the *Olympic*'s maiden voyage in June 1911 was a grand, much-heralded affair. In fact, the launch of *Titanic* was not greeted as nearly as important; then, as we all know, tragically, the *Titanic* never made it to New York. The *Olympic* sailed on, doing time as a hospital ship in World War I, and the third of Ismay's planned trio, launched in 1914 as the *Britannic,* had a short life as a hospital ship in the Mediterranean before hitting a land mine and sinking in 1916.

Right up until World War I, the Brits and Germans continued building bigger and bigger ships, exceeding 50,000 tons. During the war, practically any seaworthy ship was requisitioned to carry soldiers, supplies, and weaponry to the troops in Europe. Many grand ships were lost in the war, including Cunard's *Lusitania.*

CRUISING BETWEEN THE WARS After World War I, the popularity of pleasure cruising increased tremendously. During the winter months, when transatlantic travel was slow, more and more ships were rerouted to sunnier climes in the Caribbean and Mediterranean for long and expensive cruises geared to the well heeled. For instance, Cunard's *Mauretania* and her new running mate, the *Aquitania,* were yanked off the Atlantic for a millionaire's romp through the Mediterranean, carrying as few as 200 pampered passengers in the lap of luxury. In the 1920s, Cunard introduced five ships—the *Scythia, Samaria, Laconia, Franconia,* and *Carinthia*—which offered a variety of cruising options worldwide, including Bali, Bangkok, Saigon, Athens, and the Holy Land, as well as the Caribbean and Scandinavia.

By the 1930s, shipboard activities and amenities were becoming much more sophisticated all around, with morning concerts, horse racing, quoits, shuffleboard, bridge, Ping-Pong, motion pictures, and the first "swimming baths" (as pools were called in the early years) appearing on board. Often no more than burlap or canvas slung over wooden supports, the first permanent outdoor pools appeared in the 1920s on the Italian transatlantic ships the *Roma* and the *Augustus.* In the '30s, the large outdoor pool on the *Rex* actually included a patch of sand to evoke the Lido Beach of Venice. When the great French liner *Normandie* made its maiden voyage in 1935, it boasted the cruising world's first air-conditioning system in its first-class dining room.

WORLD WAR II When World War II began, the great liners were again called into service, and many never made it back to civilian life. The *Normandie* burned and capsized at her pier while under conversion in New York to become a troopship. Cunard's *Carinthia* and *Laconia* didn't survive either. A few, however, did complete distinguished wartime service, like the United States Line's *America,* Cunard's *Queen Elizabeth* and *Queen Mary,* and Holland America's *Nieuw Amsterdam.*

THE POSTWAR YEARS When the war ended and with the economy in great shape, cruising boomed in the '50s and for the first time became accessible to the growing middle class. More than ever before, cruising was both transportation and a pleasurable vacation experience, with onboard life enhanced by activities like pool games, bingo, art classes, dance lessons, singles' parties, and midnight buffets—all aspects of cruising that still exist today. In the '50s, New York became one of the biggest and most important cruise ship ports in the world, offering short runs to Bermuda and serving as the home port for longer world cruises.

In 1958, a sea change occurred when Pan Am flew the first nonstop jet flight from New York to Paris. Cruise travel as transportation was rendered somewhat obsolete. People now had a viable and quicker transportation option.

But the concept of cruises as a vacation option remained. And in 1966, Ted Arison, who would later form Carnival Cruise Lines, and Knut Kloster, who would later form Norwegian Cruise Line, introduced the *Sunward,* a converted car/passenger ferry that debuted as a Caribbean cruise ship. The *Sunward* began offering 3- and 4-day cruises that traveled from Florida to the Caribbean and back again, and the success of the venture quickly drew other competitors and laid the foundation for what would become an unprecedented leisure cruise marketplace.

In the years that followed, Carnival (the industry's biggest success story with its "fun ship" theme) would do much to further the idea of the cruise ship as a vacation destination, and the Caribbean would become and remain—even to this day—cruising's top destination. (Europe is number 2 and Alaska number 3.)

The vacation cruise ships did away with the liners' multi-class system and focused solely on offering a fun-in-the-sun party at sea for all. (Cunard's ***QE2,*** built in 1969 for both crossings and cruising, is one of the last ships with a multi-class system.)

Soon, the Caribbean cruise trade exploded. **Royal Caribbean Cruise Line** was formed in January 1969, and in the late '60s and early '70s, **Royal Viking, Carnival, Princess, Costa,** and **Holland America** joined the lucrative circuit as well. It was in 1968, on board Costa's *Carla C.* (at the time chartered to Princess and doing Mexican Riviera and Panama Canal cruises from Los Angeles), that American writer Jeraldine Saunders was inspired to write the novel *The Love Boat,* from which the popular television series was born.

THE LOVE BOAT The TV show, introduced in 1977, helped the industry truly become a mass-market phenomenon. Using the real Princess Cruises ship *Island Princess* and its twin, *Pacific Princess,* as well as other vessels as floating sets, *The Love Boat*—produced by Aaron Spelling *(Beverly Hills 90210* and *Melrose Place)* and Douglas Cramer *(Love, American Style)*—was virtually a weekly 1-hour prime-time commercial for the cruise industry.

The Love Boat's weekly vignettes about love and romance nearly always had a happy ending. And that didn't hurt the image of the cruise industry. Neither did the fact that some of the show's interior scenes were shot on a Hollywood set, including shots of pretend cabins that were much larger than those on the actual ships.

The Love Boat ran on ABC from September 1977 to September 1986 and was broadcast in 29 languages to 93 countries. Suddenly, everybody wanted to cruise, including major stars who signed on for guest shots on the show, attracted by the on-ship filming schedule. Princess Cruises made the most of the exposure by signing on actor Gavin MacLeod (Capt. Merrill Stubing) as its pitchman and adapting "The Love Boat" as its nickname. Even today, if you sail on a Princess ship, you'll hear a lounge-lizard rendering of *The Love Boat* theme song ("the Luuuuuve Boat . . .") blaring out of speakers as the ship embarks.

CRUISING TODAY The cruise product has changed radically in the last 30 years, and it seems like a new and often gargantuan vessel is being launched every other month. In fact, more than 40 new ships are scheduled to debut over the next several years.

The biggest among the new ships are really big. For example, Royal Caribbean's *Voyager of the Seas,* introduced in late 1999, is 142,000 tons, and carries more than 3,000 passengers. It's double the size of the 1969-built *QE2!*

At the same time that the ships have been growing, the cruise experience in general has been going up the evolutionary ladder and, in the process, has gotten more diverse. A lot of the change has come as a result of cruise companies realizing that they're not just competing against other cruise companies but against land-based vacations. The lines have taken steps accordingly, and you can now find on cruise ships most offerings you would find at land-based resorts, including golf (sometimes via high-tech simulated machines, other times on real shipboard mini-greens, and other times as shore excursion options). On the *Voyager of the Seas* (which only sails in the Caribbean) there's even ice-skating.

Consumer input has led to changes in ship design, with big trends today including cabins with private verandas, expanded spa areas, a focus on families and kids' facilities, and alternative dining choices (for those who don't want a formal dinner in the dining room every night).

While some traditionalists may disdain the fact that today's cruise ships retain few vestiges of ocean travel's golden age, time does move on. Casual, active, and geared to the masses, today's passenger ship industry is bigger, bolder, and more successful than ever before.

2 Checking In & Boarding

AIRPORT CHECK-IN

Now to some practical matters. It's a good idea to confirm your flight a few days before your trip. Call the airline and say you'd like to confirm the time and that you have a seat reserved. The day of your trip, call the airline again to make sure your flight is on time. No sense arriving at the airport for a long wait if you don't have to.

Since you are flying to Europe, you should get to the airport $1^1/_2$ to 2 hours before your scheduled flight time. This will give you time to check in your bags, get your seat assignments, and pick up a magazine for the long flight.

Make sure your bags are tagged properly with your name and address, and that the airport check-in person puts the tags on for the correct airport destination. If you are checking your bags through to the ship or a hotel booked through the cruise line, make sure your bags are also appropriately tagged with the tags provided by the cruise line.

Remember to bring in your carry-on any valuables (including jewelry and camera equipment), your cruise documents, airline tickets and passport, claim checks for airport parking, house and car keys, eyeglasses, all prescription medications, and any other items you can't do without. It's also a good idea to pack a change of clothes so you can freshen up when you get to the ship or hotel, even if your bags haven't yet arrived. You may also want to pack gum, a snack, a book, a magazine, and Dramamine (in case it's a bumpy flight).

WHAT TO DO IF YOUR FLIGHT IS DELAYED

If your flight is delayed, and you are sailing that day, tell airline personnel. They may be able to get you onto another flight. Also call the cruise line to advise the ship of your delay (there should be an emergency number in your cruise documents). Keep in mind that you may not be the only passenger delayed, and the line might just hold the ship until you arrive. If your ship does leave without you, you'll be flown or driven to the next port, and if you booked your air through the cruise line you will not be charged for this service (if you booked air on your own you may have to pay).

ARRIVAL

Assuming you booked air and transfer through the cruise line, you will be met at the airport, after you clear Customs and Immigration, by a cruise line representative. You will probably have to identify your luggage in the baggage area before your bags are transferred to the ship (you won't see them again until they are delivered to your cabin). You will then be escorted to buses to take you to the cruise terminal (or your hotel if you've booked a pre-cruise hotel stay).

If you booked air on your own, you will have to claim your bags and arrange your own transportation to the hotel or ship (you may have to negotiate with a cab driver for a good rate). Make sure you find out in advance exactly which terminal the ship is departing from, since some ports are quite busy and your cab driver may not know exactly where to go. If you need a porter at the terminal, tip him $1 per bag (U.S. dollars will be gladly accepted).

CHECKING IN

What happens as you enter the terminal depends on the cruise line and the size of the ship, but generally at this point you can expect to wait in line. Despite the best efforts of the cruise line, the scene at the pier may be zoolike.

You will not be able to board the ship before the scheduled embarkation time, usually about 3 or 4 hours before sailing. That's because the ship has likely had to disembark passengers from the previous cruise earlier that day, and the crew needs time to clean and prepare and take care of the various paperwork and Customs documents that need to be completed. If you fly in on an early flight on the day of departure, the ship may let you board early and wait in a lounge or restaurant until your cabin is ready.

European ships are very strict about boarding times. If it says the last boarding is at 5pm, you better be there by 5pm, even if the ship doesn't leave the dock until 6pm. You have up until a half hour (on some ships it's 1 hour) before departure to board, but there are some advantages to boarding earlier, like getting first dibs on prime dining room tables (if you haven't been assigned a table in advance) and spa treatment times. Plus, if you get on early enough you can eat lunch on the ship (depending on the ship and departure time, lunch may be served until 3pm or even 4pm the first day).

Either right before or right after you get to the check-in desk, you will likely have to pass through an x-ray machine like those at the airport.

During check-in, your **boarding documents** will be checked and your passport will likely be taken for immigration processing. You will get it back sometime during the cruise (you might want to carry a photocopy as backup). If you have booked a suite you may get priority boarding at a special desk. Special-needs passengers may also be processed separately.

Depending on the cruise line, you may establish your **onboard credit account** at this point by turning over a major credit card to be swiped or by making a deposit in cash or traveler's checks (usually $250). On other ships you need to report to the purser's office once on board to establish your onboard credit account. You may also be given your cabin key at check-in (in some cases your onboard credit card doubles as your room key and boarding card), though on some ships your cabin key will be waiting for you at your cabin.

Protocol for establishing your **dining room table assignment** also varies by ship. You may be given your assignment in advance of your sailing (on your tickets), or advised of your table number as you check in. Or a card with your table number may be waiting for you in your stateroom. If you do not receive an assignment by the time you get to your stateroom, you will be directed to a maitre d's desk set up in a convenient spot on board. This is also the place to go to make any changes if your assignment does not meet with your approval.

Make sure your seating time (early or late) and table size are as you requested and that you are in the smoking or nonsmoking section you requested (where applicable). Special dietary requests can also be confirmed at this time.

A bevy of cruise line employees will be on hand to make sure your check-in goes smoothly. Don't be afraid to ask them questions.

After you clear the check-in area, you will likely be corralled into posing for the ship's photographer. These pictures sell for about $5 to $8, and will be displayed later for your perusal at the ship's photography shop. You are under no obligation to buy them. Ditto for any drinks you may be offered as you board.

STEPPING ABOARD

As you exit the gangplank, a crew member will escort you to your cabin, probably offering to help carry your hand luggage. No tip is required, but would be accepted.

Either immediately or a short time later your steward, the person responsible for the upkeep of your cabin, will stop by to introduce him or herself. He or she will point out the various cabin amenities and controls, such as air-conditioning and light switches, advise you on how they can be reached when you need them (usually by phone or buzzer), and answer any immediate questions you have. The steward will also make you aware of the ship's safety drill procedures (see below) and advise you of the location of your muster (assembly) station for the drill.

> **English Comes Second**
>
> Even aboard American-owned ships, some crew members—especially cabin stewards, who come from all over the world—may have limited English language skills, so you might want to brush up on your non-verbal communication skills. Crew members have to know a modicum of English to be hired, but sometimes it seems less rather than more, and you might run into some frustrating moments trying to communicate. Remember, these folks are very hardworking employees who are sending most of their wages home to their families, and it won't kill you to speak slower and more simply if need be.

You'll have plenty of time to talk to this person later in your voyage, and now is not the time to quiz this person about where they are from and so forth because they probably have to do this cabin tour for some 20-odd other cabins too.

It's important to alert the steward immediately if the beds are not configured to your liking or if there are any other problems you can see. If the cabin itself is not what you thought you booked, go right to the hotel manager with your complaint.

You can also make the steward aware of any special needs you might have, such as a preference for foam as opposed to feather pillows (extra pillows and blankets should already be in your closet).

In your cabin you will find a **daily program** detailing the day's events, meal times, and so forth, as well as important information on the ship's safety rituals.

There may also be a hotel-like **menu of services** notebook, including room service options, and a phone directory. Your room should also be outfitted with a DO NOT DISTURB sign (important for nappers), order forms for room service breakfast (if offered), and forms and bags for dry cleaning and laundry services.

You may want to try the TV, safe, and other gadgets to see how they work, check out the bathroom, etc. The loud whoosh of the toilet is normal (most ships use a vacuum system). Note that you are not supposed to put any objects other than paper in the bowl.

There may be bottles of water provided in your cabin (although the water on most ships is perfectly drinkable). Just because the bottles are there doesn't mean they are free. If you don't know, ask before you open them. Items in the minibar are not free.

There should be directions near the phone advising you how to make calls to other passengers on the ship and to ship personnel, as well as how to request wake-up calls. There should also be directions on dialing outside. Note the cost of outside calls, which can be really expensive (as much as $18 a minute).

Your **luggage** probably won't have arrived yet, but if it has, go ahead and unpack. If not, after you've exhausted your tour of your room, I recommend checking out the rest of the ship.

Before you do this, though, don't forget to put your cash, ID, air tickets, and other valuables in the **cabin safe.** If there is no safe in your room, take this all down to the purser's office where there will be one available. Don't forget to take your shipboard credit card (in case you want to buy a drink) and key with you.

You may find a **deck map** of the ship in your cabin. If not, you should be able to get one at the purser's office, so find your way there. There are usually deck plans and directional signs at main stairways and elevators. You probably won't need the map after the first day (part of the fun of being on a big ship is getting lost, anyway), but it's a good way to establish the layout in your mind.

What Happens if Your Bags Get Lost?

Before you start to panic, keep in mind that on big ships, some 4,000 bags need to be loaded and distributed. But if you're hours into the sailing and getting concerned, don't hesitate to call the guest relations desk (or purser's office). If your luggage really is lost, the cruise line customer relations folks are supposed to spring into immediate action. They, not you, will contact the airline and ground operators to see what's what.

Usually, missing bags will arrive at the ship the next day. They will be either driven or flown to the first port-of-call.

If your baggage is lost, the cruise line will likely provide an overnight kit with such items as a toothbrush and toothpaste. The first night of a cruise is always casual dress, so you don't have to worry about wearing what you have on in the dining room.

If the baggage is still lost the next day, your baggage insurance, if you purchased any, will kick in and you get to go shopping in the ship's shops for proper attire. If you do not have insurance, the line may, at its discretion, offer you cash compensation—usually $50 a day.

If the second night is a formal night, the line may be able to provide a tux for a man and may also have a small selection of clothes available that a woman can borrow.

Begin your tour on the top deck and work your way down, checking out the main public rooms. That way, you can stop at the beginning of your tour at the **"welcome aboard" buffet,** which is usually set up in the casual dining area, near the pool deck.

If you plan to use the spa services, stop by and make appointments so you can get your preferred times (the best times go fast, and some popular treatments sell out). The staff may be offering an introductory **spa tour.** Also stop by at the gym, especially if you plan on taking fitness classes. The fitness staff will likely be on hand to hand out schedules and answer any questions you might have.

Note the ship's casino and shops are always closed when the ship is in port. While in the port, the swimming pool(s) will also likely be tarped. They will be filled with either fresh or salt water after the ship sets sail.

Some ships offer **escorted tours** of the public rooms. If you aren't comfortable roaming on your own, check the daily program in your cabin for details.

LIFEBOAT/SAFETY DRILL

In your room you will find, either waiting on your bed or in the closet or a drawer, bright orange **life jackets.** If you are traveling with kids there should be special jackets for them (if not, alert your steward). Ships are required by law to conduct safety drills within the first 24 hours. Most do it either right before the ship sails or shortly thereafter. Attendance is mandatory. A notice on the back of your cabin door will list the procedures and advise as to your assigned **muster station** and how to get there. You will also find directions to the muster station in the hallway. You will be alerted as to the time in both the daily program and in repeated public announcements (and probably by your steward as well).

To start the drill, the ship will broadcast its emergency signal. At this time you will be required to return to your cabin, grab your life jacket, and report to your assigned muster station (this will be in a lounge, the casino, or another public room). Some drills last only a few minutes, while others are quite detailed. At the muster station, a crew member will review how to put on your life vest. He or she will also point out the features of the vest, including the whistle to call for help (don't try it out here!) and the light that turns on when it hits the water. The drill may also include a visit to the **lifeboats** and even a discussion of how to jump into the water.

In some cases guests will be required to put on the life jacket so a crew member can check and make sure it's being worn correctly. But other ships don't even encourage guests to put on the life jacket; you just bring it with you.

The crew is supposed to take attendance to make sure everyone attends the drill. After the drill, return to your cabin and put your life jacket back in its place.

If you have additional questions about safety procedures, you can address them to a crew member or officer at this time. On some ships, in addition to the drill, a safety video will also be broadcast on the TV in your cabin.

3 An Introduction to Onboard Activities

Of course, in Europe, you will want to spend most of your time exploring the ports. But from morning till night, most big ships also offer an extensive schedule of onboard activities, especially during days at sea (when the ship isn't visiting a port). All the contests, lessons, and classes will be listed in the ship's **daily program,** which is placed in your cabin the previous evening, usually while you're at dinner. A **cruise director** and his or her staff are in charge of the festivities and do their best to ensure a good time is had by all. Smaller ships offer activities, too, but often with less hoopla; there may be wine-tastings, port talks by the cruise director and captain, and maybe presentations by guest lecturers.

JOINING THE FUN

Many lines encourage passengers to let their hair down. Hence you will find Family Feud and other group contests, bingo, shipboard horse racing, pool games, and the like.

If you're a performer at heart, volunteer for the weekly **passenger talent show** or head to the nightclub one evening for **karaoke.** Brainy types can sign up for trivia quizzes, and there will also likely be chess, checkers, bridge, or backgammon tournaments.

Winners of any of the above get prizes like champagne, T-shirts, mugs, or key chains, maybe even a massage from the spa, all of which make joining in a worthwhile proposition.

SHIPBOARD CASINOS

For all you high-rollers out there, all but the smallest, adventure-oriented ships have casinos. Not surprisingly, the megas have the biggest, flashiest, Vegas-style casinos, full of neon, with literally hundreds of slot machines and dozens of blackjack, poker, and craps tables as well as roulette. Smaller ship lines, like Windstar, Seabourn, and Cunard, have casinos as well, albeit scaled-down ones, with maybe a dozen slots and a couple of blackjack and poker tables. European ships tend to have smaller casinos than American ships (it's a cultural thing). Stakes aboard most ships are relatively low, with maximum bets rarely exceeding $200. Average minimum bets at blackjack and poker tables are generally $5; the minimum at roulette is typically 50¢ or $1. Children are not allowed in onboard casinos.

CLASSES, LESSONS & DEMONSTRATIONS

There are plenty of learning opportunities available on ships in Europe. Most feature a lecturer, usually a university professor, author, or museum curator well versed in the art, architecture, and history of the regions you will be visiting.

For those seeking less cerebral pursuits, there are likely to be **line dancing and ballroom dancing lessons** held a few times a week on big ships in the main show lounge, and taught by one of the onboard entertainers. There may also be informative **seminars** on subjects like cooking, bartending, arts and crafts, and wine tasting; there is usually a $5 to $15 charge for the wine tasting and sometimes there's a cost for arts and crafts materials. There may even be classes on intriguing topics such as **personal investing** or **handwriting analysis.**

The chef might do a food-decorating demonstration and share tips on how to carve flowers and animals out of fruits and vegetables. Demonstrations by the salon and spa staff on hair and skin care are common too (and are a ruse for getting passengers to sign up for the not-so-cheap spa treatments).

QUIET DIVERSIONS

For those seeking quieter times, there is always the option of planting yourself in a deck chair with a good book. Many ships have **libraries** (some are nice plush retreats) stocked with classic books and new releases. Some of the libraries also have chairs specially equipped with CD players and headphones and a collection of CDs. Some ships also have **video libraries** (you can take the movie back to your cabin to play on your VCR) and/or offer both standard TV movies and pay-per-view first-run movies on in-cabin TVs. **Cinemas** on some ships also show classic and first-run movies. Some ships offer **computers** preprogrammed with both reference materials and games. Usually adjacent to the library you'll find the **card room,** which is designed to be a nice quiet place to play (usually with bridge as the top attraction). Here you'll often also find board games like Monopoly, Backgammon, and Scrabble.

ART AUCTIONS

Many large ships offer art auctions, which are fun and entertaining but not necessarily guaranteed to give you a bargain price. Outside concessionaires with really entertaining salespeople run the auctions, with the artwork fetching anywhere from $50 to $85,000 or more. The auctions are big business on ships these days, and you'll see a lot of pieces sold.

The auctions are held several times during the cruise in a lounge, with the salesperson briefly discussing each painting before opening the floor up to bids. The offerings will include some big names like Peter Max, Marc Chagall, Joan Miró, Walt Disney, and Salvador Dalí, plus some absolute schlock. They're usually sold duty-free, with or without frames, and can be packed and mailed home to the winner for an additional fee (it will take several weeks to arrive).

On Princess ships, you can also bid on some of the art that's displayed aboard the ship if something really catches your eye.

ONBOARD SPORTS & FITNESS OPTIONS

If you're into sports, the megaships pack the most punch. In addition to well-equipped gyms rivaling those on shore, they boast outdoor volleyball, basketball, and paddle tennis courts as well as outdoor jogging tracks and several pools for water polo, volleyball, aquaaerobics, and swimming.

WATERSPORTS

For watersports enthusiasts, small ships are the best equipped. Windstar, Radisson Seven Seas, Cunard, Club Med, and Seabourn have retractable watersports platforms that, weather permitting, can be lowered from the stern into calm waters when the ship is anchored, allowing passengers to almost step right from their cabins to snorkel, windsurf, kayak, sail, water-ski, go on banana boat rides, and swim.

GOLF

If you're a golfaholic, you'll be happy to find that more and more cruises are offering the opportunity to tee off, both on board and on shore. For the casual golfer, a few ships—Royal Caribbean's *Splendour* and *Legend* and Princess's *Grand Princess*—have **miniature golf courses** on board. For the more serious swingers, the new, technologically advanced ships like Celebrity's *Millennium* and Princess's *Grand Princess* have **golf simulators.** These state-of-the-art virtual-reality machines allow you to play the great courses of the world without ever leaving the ship (for about $20 per half-hour). Full-sized clubs are used and a virtual-reality video screen allows players to watch the electronic path of a ball they've actually hit soar high over the greens or land flat in a sand trap.

Many more lines, including Norwegian, Crystal, Princess, Radisson Seven Seas, and Cunard, have **outdoor golf cages,** areas enclosed in netting where you can swing, putt, and whack at real golf balls.

More and more lines are offering **golf programs** that include instruction and tips by golf pros who sail on board, videotaping lessons and going over technique with passengers. Half-hour lessons are about $30 to $40, and hour-long lessons are $60 to $70. In port, Silversea, Crystal, and Seabourn are among lines that offer **golf excursions** to well-known courses.

SPORTS FOR COUCH POTATOES

No need for those sports-loving couch potatoes out there to be deprived. NCL's *Norwegian Dream* and Princess's *Grand Princess* are among the vessels that, in Europe, have dedicated sports bars with large-screen televisions broadcasting ESPN International (which features a lot of soccer). On some ships, you may also be able to watch ESPN International on your in-cabin TV.

4 An Introduction to Onboard Entertainment

The cruise lines offer a vast repertoire of exciting entertainment. As you'd expect, the biggest ships offer the most variety, from Vegas-style cabaret to magicians, soloists, pianists, dance bands, quartets, jugglers, DJs, puppeteers, and comedians.

ENTERTAINMENT ON THE MEGASHIPS

Entertainment is a big part of the cruise experience on the biggest ships, particularly those in the fleets of Royal Caribbean, Celebrity, Costa, Princess, Norwegian Cruise Line, and Holland America. Not surprisingly, they have an extensive variety of options throughout the day. Afternoons, you can dance the day away on deck with the **live dance band.** Or get your waltzing shoes on and head inside to one of the lounges for some big-band-style dancing; lines like Holland America, Cunard, and NCL often feature a Glenn Miller–style group playing a set or two of 1940s dance tunes.

By about 5pm, before the first-seating dinner (and again at 7pm before the late seating begins), the entertainment choices really kick in. Head to the piano bar for a cocktail or do some pre-dinner dancing.

After both the early and the late dinner seating, 2 or more nights during your cruise, the main show lounge will feature **Vegas-style musicals,** where a flamboyant troupe of anywhere from 4 to 16 male and female dancers decked out in feather boas, sequins, and top hats slide and kick their way across the stage (and lip-synch to the songs' choruses) as a soloist or two belts out show tunes. You'll hear favorites from *Phantom of the Opera, Cats, Hair, Grease, A Chorus Line,* and all the classic Gershwin and Rodgers and Hammerstein greats. Elaborate stage sets and frequent costume changes on the biggest ships make these exciting shows the entertainment highlight of the week. On some of the European ships, these shows can be downright amateurish, but are no less amusing.

When the Broadway show stuff isn't scheduled, entertainment may be a **magic show,** complete with sawing in half scantily clad assistants and pulling rabbits from hats, **acrobatic acts** (always a big hit), and **headlining soloists** (some are quite good). In Europe some ships bring on **local performers** at ports for special performances (held in the afternoon or evening) usually of the folkloric variety. You might, for instance, be entertained by flamenco performers, or an Irish stepping group.

The **disco** will probably get going around 9pm or 10pm (later on European ships) and goes until 2 or 3am or later. Shake your booty to the best of '70s, '80s, '90s, and Y2K pop and rock music; often a live band plays until about midnight, when a DJ takes over until the wee hours.

An alternative to the disco or the main show might be a **1950s sock hop,** held in another lounge or a **jazz trio** in yet another romantic nightspot. Show-offs, or those who just like to embarrass themselves, will probably be able to find a karaoke lounge.

ENTERTAINMENT ON THE SMALL SHIPS

Ships carrying 100 to 400 passengers have fewer entertainment options, but are no less appealing if you like things mellow. On the high-end lines, there may be a quartet or pianist performing before dinner and maybe afterward, a small-scale **Broadway dance revue,** and dancing in a quiet lounge. The more casual small ships might have taped music or a synth-piano player before and after dinner; or no entertainment at all (you can go off to a club at a port for that). Expect a crew and passenger **talent show** to be scheduled during the cruise, too. While in port, small-ship lines like Windstar and Star Clippers might bring **local performers** on board for an afternoon or evening of entertainment. Some small ships also offer movie evenings when a movie is shown in a lounge.

5 Shipboard Gyms & Spas

If your idea of a perfect vacation includes a run on a treadmill or a relaxing seaweed facial, the newest big ships have the biggest and best-equipped fitness and spa facilities. Since the early 1990s, cruise lines have prioritized their spa and fitness areas, moving them out of windowless corners of bottom decks and into prime top-deck positions with oodles of space and lots of glass for soothing views of the ocean. They offer **state-of-the art workout machines** and a host of **spa treatments.**

GYMS: AN ANTIDOTE TO THE MIDNIGHT BUFFET

The well-equipped fitness centers on the megaships may feature a dozen treadmills and just as many stationary bikes, step machines, upper- and lower-body machines, and free weights.

The roomy **aerobics studios** on ships like the *Grand Princess* and on Holland America's post-1990 ships are like the kind you have at your gym back home, with mirrors and special flooring. There are at least a couple of aerobics and stretch classes per day. Certified instructors teach the classes, which usually range from the traditional to the trendy—high- and low-impact, funk, step, body sculpting, stretch and tone, and abdominals.

Older ships, usually those built before 1990, often do not devote nearly as much space and resources to sports and fitness. The gyms are generally smaller and more spartan, but on all but the smallest alternative ships you'll find at least a couple of treadmills and a stationary bike or step machine or two, plus some free weights. On ships with limited gym facilities, aerobics classes tend to be held out on deck or in a lounge.

ONBOARD SPAS: TAKING RELAXATION ONE STEP FURTHER

If your idea of a heavenly vacation is spending half of it under a towel being massaged and kneaded with some soothing mystery oil, choose a cruise ship with a well-equipped spa.

Shipboard spas are big business. On big ships built in the past 10 years, they've been given spacious quarters on top decks. The largest spas have eight or 10 treatment rooms, a sauna and a steam room or two, and full locker rooms with showers. On ships built pre-1990 the spas, like the gyms, are generally going to be small; the large spa on the *QE2* is an exception. Even most of the smaller upscale ships have some semblance of a spa and a beauty salon. Windstar Cruises' *Wind Surf* carries only 300 passengers, but boasts a particularly big spa facility (not so on the other Windstar ships, though). As with gyms, you won't find spas at all on the smaller alternative ships.

Some of the best spas and fitness facilities at sea are on board **Celebrity Cruises'** vessels. Called the AquaSpa, these spacious health meccas are as pleasing to the eye as they are functional. The focal point is a 115,000-gallon **thalassotherapy pool,** a bubbling cauldron of warm, soothing seawater that's a great place to relax before a massage.

Other impressive spas include the Pompeii Spa on **Costa Cruise Lines'** *CostaVictoria,* which features accoutrements such as tile mosaics, rattan lounge chairs, and a small plunge pool. And First European's new *Mistral* offers outdoor thalassotherapy.

Spa treatments range in price from about $15 to over $150, plus the 10% to 15% tip that's expected (some lines add this on automatically) and can be charged to your onboard account. Celebrity and Windstar allow you to **pre-book spa packages** with your travel agent, but appointment times cannot be reserved until you board the ship.

6 An Introduction to Shipboard Dining

Food takes on Fellini-esque proportions on cruise ships. With meals a major part of the cruise experience, they are served with much pomp and circumstance, particularly on the bigger ships.

Forget your standard breakfast, lunch, and dinner. You will be offered, on a daily basis, an early-riser's continental breakfast, choice of breakfast in the dining room or a lavish breakfast buffet, a mid-morning snack, lunch in the dining room or a lavish luncheon buffet, afternoon tea, dinner in the dining room or in an alternative venue such as an intimate, reservations-only restaurant or more casual Lido restaurant, and an unbelievable midnight buffet or trays of late-night snacks.

And if that's not enough, some ships also have pizza parlors, poolside grills, 24-hour room service, and specialty food venues such as caviar bars, ice cream parlors, and gourmet coffee shops. And you may even be offered fresh fruit daily in your cabin.

DINNER IS SERVED

The nighttime meal on most ships is one of the main social events of the day. The table setup is quite formal, with china, silver, fresh flowers, and starched linens, and serving will be at a leisurely pace. You will likely sit with other passengers (tables for two are hard to come by) and should enjoy some lively conversation which no doubt will center on some of the sights you have visited that day.

On most ships, you'll find at least five courses, with three to six options for each course, and you can choose from a wide array of international fare like escargot, vichyssoise, veal scaloppini, poached salmon, prime rib, and pastas. There will also likely be **vegetarian choices** as well as **healthier entrees** that are lower in fat, calories, cholesterol, and sodium.

The Ubiquitous Steiner

The spas and hair salons on most ships (over 90 of them) are staffed and operated by a firm called Steiner, a London-based company with a hands-down corner on the market. You'll find most of the prices are steep—for instance, a 55-minute facial is $69, and a 55-minute massage is $70 (and that's right now; prices are due to increase this year). Rates are standardized across most ships, except on the *Seaboard Legend, Sun, Spirit,* and *Goddesses,* and the Holland America and Radisson Seven Seas fleets, where they are about 10% higher.

The young women, mostly Brits, who do the massages, facials, manicures, pedicures, reflexology, and other services are professional and charming, but they don't always deliver consistent service. A best bet is the massages, which are nearly always well executed. The manicures, pedicures, and facials can be disappointing. And you can't usually get your nails done unless you also submit to a pricy hand (or foot) softening and massaging treatment.

Be aware that Steiner isn't shy about pushing its extensive and expensive collection of creams, exfoliants, moisturizers, toners, and masks, either. Get a facial and you'll wind up with an itemized list of four or five products, easily adding up to over $200, that they recommend you buy to get the same effect at home (of course you can just say no). The shameless promotion of the fancy ointments on some ships, which occurs just as you're coming out of your semi-conscious post-massage trance, certainly brings you back to reality. That said, people rave about the quality of the products.

It's considered good etiquette to arrive at the dining room on time, to show up dressed correctly according to the dress code of the day, and to wait until everyone at your table has arrived before you order.

You are not required to order every course. Conversely, if two appetizers or main courses catch your fancy, you can order both. If you do not like something you ordered, send it back and ask for another selection.

DINNER TABLE DIVORCES

If you get stuck with a couple of yahoos who seem to offend every bone in your body or there just isn't any chemistry, no need to suffer in silence. It's best to explain to the maitre d' as courteously and as soon as possible that your table assignment simply won't do, and request a change. You will usually be accommodated (a greasing of the palm will help).

SPECIAL DIETS

If you follow any special diet, inform the cruise line as early as possible, preferably when booking your cruise. **Vegetarian dishes** and **kosher food** are commonly available, and almost all cruise lines now feature a selection of healthier, **lighter meals,** labeled as such on the menu. On all but the most cost-conscious cruise lines, the kitchen usually tries to satisfy reasonable culinary requests.

CASUAL DINING

If you'd rather skip the formality of the main dining room, all but the tiniest ships serve breakfast and lunch in a casual **buffet-style cafe restaurant.** Usually located on the Lido Deck, with indoor and outdoor poolside seating, these restaurants serve an extensive spread of both hot and cold food items. On the mega ships, nearby may be a **grill** where at lunch you can get hamburgers, hot dogs, and often chicken. Veggie burgers are also showing up regularly at the grills these days. On most ships, **breakfast and lunch buffets** are generally served for a 3- to 4-hour period, so guests can stroll in and out whenever they desire. Princess Cruises has the Lido cafe open around the clock on its newest ships.

If you're not in the mood for the fuss of formal dining in the evening, either, many big ships now offer dinner as well in the casual Lido restaurant (sometimes not every night). Most serve casual dinner buffet-style, but some do a combination of sit-down service and buffet. Wear what you want, stroll in when you please, and, in most cases, sit where you please (most are open seating). After soup and salad, two or three entrees are offered, like prime rib, salmon, or stir-fry, followed by dessert.

If you do want the fine dining and formality, but with fewer fellow diners in tow, lines (in recent years) have added intimate, **reservations-only restaurants** seating less than 100. Some examples: the *Crystal Harmony* has an Asian and an Italian restaurant; the *Radisson Diamond,* Italian; *Grand Princess,* Tex-Mex and Italian ($3.50 per person cover charge); *Seabourn Legend, Spirit, Pride,* and *Sun,* French and Italian; Cunard's *Vistafjord,* Italian.

7 Onboard Shopping Opportunities

Even the smallest ships have at least a small shop on board selling T-shirts, sweatshirts, baseball caps, and the like bearing the cruise line's logo. The big new megaships, though, have the most extensive onboard shopping. Like mini malls, there may be as many as 10 different stores selling everything from **toiletries and sundries** like film, toothpaste, candy, and paperback books (and even condoms) to totes, T-shirts, mugs, toys, key chains, and other **cruise line logo souvenirs.** You'll find **formalwear** like sequined dresses and jackets, silk dresses and scarves, purses, satin shoes, cummerbunds, ties, and tuxedo shirts, as well as **perfume, cosmetics, jewelry** (costume and the real stuff), and **porcelain figurines.**

All merchandise sold on board while a ship is at sea is tax-free, and to maintain that tax-free status, the shops are closed whenever a ship is in port. Though tax-free, prices aren't always deals, though some good deals can be had on alcohol, and by mid-cruise there are often good sales on a selection of T-shirts, tote bags, and jewelry as well. Some ships stock **local arts and crafts items** at great prices. Things that usually cost you more on board than off are disposal cameras, sunscreen, and candy and snack foods. Prices on clothing and good jewelry vary.

8 Sundry Shipboard Services & Facilities

RELIGIOUS SERVICES

Some ships, including those in the Costa fleet, have priests on board who lead Catholic Mass. Most ships have a nondenominational service on Sunday and a Friday-night Jewish Sabbath service, usually run by a passenger. On holidays, whether Jewish or Christian, clergy is typically aboard large ships to lead services. The services are usually held in a library or conference room, although some ships have chapels, and the *QE2* has its own synagogue.

MEDICAL CARE

Unless you're on a very small ship, your vessel will have a medical facility staffed by a doctor and a nurse, ready to handle any medical emergencies that may arise at sea. Some

Seasickness; or, How to Avoid Getting Green Around the Gills

Unless you're particularly prone to seasickness, you probably don't need to worry much if you're on a big ship (small ships can be bumpier). But if you are, there are medications that can help, including Dramamine and Bonine (although it's recommended that if you use either medication, you not drink alcohol; Dramamine, in particular, can make you drowsy). Both can be bought over the counter, and most ships have supplies available onboard—the purser's office may even give them out free. Another option is the Transderm patch, available by prescription only, which goes behind your ear and time-releases medication. The patch can be worn for up to 3 days, but comes with a slew of side-effect warnings. Some people have also had success in curbing seasickness by using ginger capsules available at health-food stores, and with the acupressure wristbands available at most pharmacies.

are quite elaborate. The *Grand Princess,* for instance, has high-tech medical equipment that, using cameras and a live video system, links the ship's medical team to doctors at Cedars-Sinai Medical Center in Los Angeles. The medical center will typically be open during set office hours, with the medical team available on a 24-hour basis to deal with emergencies (on some ships, the doctor can handle everything up to and including an appendectomy, but more typically, he or she dispenses seasickness shots and antibiotics and treats sprained muscles). If there is a major medical emergency, the passenger will be taken off the ship either at the nearest port or by helicopter.

If you have a chronic health problem, it's best to check with your doctor before booking your cruise, and if you have any specific needs, to notify the cruise line in advance. This will ensure the ship's medical team is properly prepared to meet your needs.

GETTING THE NEWS

Newshounds don't have to be out of touch just because they're on a ship. Most newer ships offer **CNN International** on their in-room TVs, and nearly every ship will post the latest news from the wire services outside the purser's office. Some lines even excerpt information from leading newspapers and each day deliver the printouts to your cabin.

STAYING IN TOUCH

In addition to the **telephone** in your cabin (which will cost you big bucks if you use it), you may be able to send **faxes** home via your ship's business center. You may even be able to send **e-mail.** Crystal Cruises offers a computer center where you can create an e-mail account for use while you're on the ship (you can send and receive messages, but you cannot check your e-mail at home). Norwegian Cruise Line last year introduced an Internet cafe on its new *Norwegian Sky* (also planned for its other ships) that lets you hook into the Internet and check your e-mail back home. The ship was also the first to introduce satellite modem links in cabins so you can use your own laptop. Royal Caribbean is also introducing a new service fleetwide that gives passengers direct communications to the Internet from a shipboard computer center (so you will be able to tap into your e-mail back home). All of these services are available for a fee, of course.

For those into more traditional modes of communications, the purser's office on your ship should have **postcards,** local stamps (U.S. stamps don't work in Europe), and a mailbox that is emptied at each port of call.

Part 2

The Cruise Lines & Their Ships

Detailed, in-depth reviews of all the cruise lines in Europe, with discussions of the experiences they offer and the lowdown on their ships.

5 The Ratings (and How to Read Them)

Okay, here's where you get to decide which ship is going to be your home-away-from-home as you explore Europe. All ships are not created equal. Some are big, some are small, and some are very big while others are very small. Some are floating resorts with glitter and fluff; others resemble summer camps with watersports. In the following section, I'll fill you in on what's what and who's who to help you decide which ship is the right one for you.

1 Cruise Line Categories

To make your selection easier (and to make sure you're not comparing apples and oranges), I've divided the cruise lines into five distinct categories and given each category a chapter of its own. The categories are as follows:

THE AMERICAN MAINSTREAM LINES (chapter 6) These U.S.-based lines are the most prominent players in the industry, catering primarily to American passengers and providing a cruise experience designed to suit most tastes. **Lines reviewed:** Celebrity Cruises, Holland America Line, Norwegian Cruise Line, Orient Lines, Princess Cruises, Renaissance Cruises, and Royal Caribbean International.

THE EUROPEAN LINES (chapter 7) Want to see Europe with Europeans? Here's the place. The lines in this chapter tend to pack in plenty of good times, with a special focus on the ports of call. While some operate ships that are as big and up-to-date as many of the American mainstream lines, others have older, smaller vessels. The common denominator is that the cultural experience you'll have on board is distinctly European. **Lines reviewed:** Costa Cruises, First European, Fred. Olsen, Mediterranean Shipping Cruises, Norwegian Coastal Voyage, P&O, Royal Olympic, and Swan Hellenic.

THE ULTRA-LUXURY LINES (chapter 8) Got some big bucks and want superior service, cuisine, and accommodations? These are the ships for you. Some of these finely appointed vessels are really quite tony, while others offer casual elegance. Think Ritz Carlton and Four Seasons. **Lines reviewed:** Crystal Cruises, Cunard, Radisson Seven Seas Cruises, Seabourn Cruise Line, Silversea, and Windstar Cruises.

THE ALTERNATIVE LINES (chapter 9) And now for something completely different. If you're not sure the razzmatazz of a bigger ship is for you, head to this chapter, where you'll find sailing ships and other small vessels, some where a good book or intellectual discussion is the order of the day; others that are more like going to summer camp. **Lines reviewed:** Classical Cruises, Clipper Cruise Line, Club Med Cruises, Sea Cloud, Special Expeditions, Star Clippers, Zeus Tours.

RIVER CRUISES (chapter 10) Cruising on Europe's rivers, canals, and lakes affords a pleasant alternative that allows you to see a good deal of each country you visit. The main types of inland cruises are on river ships and on small converted commercial barges. On both, the pace is leisurely and the ambiance generally informal. Unlike cruise ships, river ships and barges are often privately owned and are marketed through a number of brokers, who may handle dozens of vessels. I've provided details on 15 of these brokers.

2 Structure of the Cruise Line & Ship Reviews

Each cruise line's review begins with **The Line in a Nutshell** (a quick word about the line in general) and **The Experience,** which is a short summation of the kind of cruise experience you can expect to have aboard that line. Following that is a description of fleetwide dining, entertainment, activities offerings, and service levels, as well as a discussion of the fleet and some background about each line.

HOW TO READ THE RATINGS

The cruise industry today offers such a profusion of experiences that it makes comparing all lines and ships by the same set of criteria completely impossible.

Think about it: Would you compare a Mercedes-Benz to a sport utility vehicle? A jumbo jet to a hang glider? No, you wouldn't. For the same reason, the typical, across-the-board ratings used by most cruise guidebooks don't give you, the reader, the kind of comparisons you need to make your decision. For that reason, our "Frommer's Ratings" system, based on the classic customer satisfaction survey, judges the cruise lines on the following important considerations, rating them either *poor, fair, good, excellent,* or *outstanding.*

- Enjoyment Factor
- Dining
- Activities
- Children's Program
- Entertainment
- Service
- Overall Value

Again, though, you can't compare the experiences you'll have aboard an ultra-luxury line like Seabourn, an exploratory alternative line like Special Expeditions, and a megaship line like Royal Caribbean. They're different animals, catering to different kinds of travelers seeking different kinds of experiences. For that reason, **we've graded the cruise lines on a sliding scale,** comparing ships *only with the other ships in their category*—mainstream with mainstream, luxury with luxury, alternative with alternative. So, for example, if you see in the "Alternative Lines" chapter that Sea Cloud achieves an "outstanding" rating for its dining experience, that means that among the lines in that chapter, Sea Cloud has the best cuisine. It may not be up to the level of, say, the ultra-luxurious Seabourn, but if you're looking for an adventurous cruise with great food, this is your best bet. (Note: Since many of the European lines described in chapter 7 are comparable in terms of amenities with their American mainstream counterparts described in chapter 6, the ratings between those two chapters will be comparable.)

Note that since the river ships and barges described in chapter 10 are marketed through brokers rather than cruise lines that strive to present a consistent product identity, categorical ratings for these vessels are not possible.

Frommer's Cruise Line Ratings at a Glance

1 = poor **2** = fair **3** = good **4** = excellent **5** = outstanding

Cruise Line	Enjoyment Factor	Dining	Activities	Children's Program	Entertainment	Service	Overall Value
The American Mainstream Lines							
Celebrity	5	5	4	3	4	5	5
Holland America	5	4	4	2	3	4	5
Norwegian	4	2	5	3	4	2	3
Orient Lines	5	4	4	N/A	3	4	5
Princess	5	3	4	4	4	4	4
Renaissance	4	4	2	N/A	3	4	5
Royal Caribbean	5	3	4	4	5	3	4
The European Lines							
Costa Cruises	4	2	4	3	3	3	3
First European Cruises	4	4	3	3	2	2	3
Fred. Olsen Cruises	4	2	3	2	2	2	5
Mediterranean Shipping Cruises	4	2	2	2	2	3	3
Norwegian Coastal Voyage	5	3	N/A	N/A	N/A	3	4
P&O	4	4	3	4	4	4	4
Royal Olympic Cruises	4	4	3	2	2	4	4
Swan Hellenic	5	4	5	N/A	3	3	5
The Ultra-Luxury Lines							
Crystal	5	5	5	5	5	4	5
Cunard	5	4	4	4	4	3	4
Radisson Seven Seas	5	5	2	N/A	3	4	4
Seabourn	5	5	2	N/A	3	5	4
Silversea	5	5	3	N/A	4	5	5
Windstar	5	5	2	N/A	2	4	4
The Alternative Lines							
Classical	4	3	5	N/A	2	2	4
Clipper	4	4	4	N/A	3	4	4
Club Med	4	4	5	1	4	4	3
Sea Cloud	5	5	3	N/A	3	4	4
Special Expeditions	4	3	4	N/A	N/A	3	4
Star Clippers	5	5	4	N/A	5	5	5
Zeus Tours and Yacht Cruises	4	3	2	N/A	N/A	2	3

NOTE: Cruise lines have been graded on a sliding scale that compares them only with other lines within their category. See "How to Read the Ratings" in this chapter for a detailed explanation of ratings methodology. Ratings marked N/A indicate that the line does not offer anything in the designated category.

THE SHIP REVIEWS

The individual ship reviews that follow give you details on the ships' accommodations, facilities, amenities, comfort level, and upkeep. It's a fact that people bond with the ships they sail on. They find themselves in the gift shop, loading up on T-shirts with the ship's name emblazoned on front. They get to port and the first question they ask other cruisers they meet is "Which ship are you sailing on?" and then engage in a friendly comparison, each walking away knowing in his heart that *his* ship is the best. There are people who have sailed the same ship a dozen times or more, and feel as warmly about it as though it were their own summer cottage. That's why, when looking at the reviews, you want to look for a ship that says "you."

I've listed some of the ships' vital statistics—ship size, year built and most recently refurbished, number of cabins, number of officers and crew—to help you compare, then rated such things as cabin comfort, decor, itinerary, etc., on a scale of 1 to 5, which you can read just like the Frommer's Ratings at the beginning of each line review (i.e., 1 = poor, 2 = fair, 3 = good, 4 = excellent, 5 = outstanding).

Size is listed in tons. Note that these are not actual measures of weight, but **gross register tons (GRTs),** which is a measure of the interior space used to produce revenue on a ship. One GRT equals 100 cubic feet of enclosed, revenue-generating space.

Among the crew/officers statistics, an important one is the **passenger/crew ratio,** which tells you approximately how many passengers each crew member is expected to serve.

ITINERARIES

Each cruise line review includes a chart showing a sampling of itineraries for each ship the line is operating in Europe for 2000. Because some of the ships in Europe sail many different itineraries through the course of the season (some change their itinerary almost weekly), I could not always provide exact port-by-port lists of the destinations visited, in these cases listing a sampling of ports. Consult your travel agent or the cruise lines' Web sites for exact ports of call and sailing dates.

3 Evaluating & Comparing the Listed Cruise Prices

Figuring out the price of a cruise is rarely a simple task. As I discussed in chapter 2, "Booking Your Cruise & Getting the Best Price," rates listed in the cruise line brochures are inflated and, with the exception of holidays, you can expect to pay anywhere from 10 to 50% less if you book your cruise early (which generally means 3 to 6 months in advance). The rates listed in this book are the starting rates listed in the cruise line's brochures. I have not added in any discounts that may be applied.

In each ship review, I've calculated **per diem prices** (the cruise price broken down to represent the rate paid per person, per day) for the following three basic types of accommodations:

- inside cabins (without windows)
- outside cabins (with windows)
- suites

Remember that cruise ships generally have several different categories of cabins within each of these three basic divisions, all priced differently, and that *the prices I've listed represent the lowest categories* for inside and outside cabins and suites. If you're interested in booking a roomier, higher-level cabin in any category, you'll find the price will be higher. In general, the cost of a top-level inside cabin will probably be very close to the rate for a low-level outside cabin, and the cost of a top-level outside may be very close to the rate for a low-level suite.

Rates listed include port charges and taxes unless otherwise noted. Other extras that are included, such as airfare and hotel stays, are also noted.

Cruise lines have various ways of expressing the number of days or nights of the itinerary. When calculating the number of days, I have eliminated the disembarkation day, since you usually leave the ship in the morning. So when I describe an itinerary as 7-day, that means you spend 7 nights on the ship.

6 The American Mainstream Lines

The American mainstream ships offer a little something for almost everyone—all ages, backgrounds, and interests. The more elegant and refined of the lot are commonly referred to as **premium,** a notch up from **mass-market** in the sophistication department. Of the ships we review below, Celebrity, Holland America, Princess, and Renaissance are premium lines, while Norwegian and Royal Caribbean are mass-market lines and Costa and Orient fall somewhere in between.

Since the mainstream category is the most popular, it's the one that's seen the most growth, innovation, and investment in recent years. This is the category where the **megaships** reside, those hulking floating resorts that offer the widest variety of activities and entertainment.

The mainstream ships as a whole offer a broad range of different cabins—outside (with windows), inside (no windows), suites, and cabins with private verandas. They have both formal and informal dining options, a wide array of entertainment (heavy on the Vegas-style stuff), and more activities than you can possibly squeeze into 1 day. Overall, the atmosphere is very social and passengers tend to enjoy mingling.

Even the smaller mainstream ships, like those of Renaissance and Orient Lines' *Marco Polo,* offer lots of choice in accommodations, dining venues, activities, and entertainment. Offering variety to make your onboard experience as pleasant as possible is what these ships are really about.

When these ships visit ports, especially with the larger of the lot, their presence does not go unnoticed, and since these ships mean so much to the local economy of the ports they are visiting, they are sometimes greeted with much pomp and circumstance, including marching bands and onlookers waving from the shore. It's often a festive affair for both passengers and locals.

DRESS CODES On week-long cruises aboard mass-market and premium ships, there are 2 formal nights calling for dark suits or tuxedos for men and cocktail dresses, sequined numbers, or fancy pantsuits for women. The other 5 nights are some combination of semi-formal and casual, and call for suits or sport jackets and slacks for men, and dresses, pantsuits, or skirts and tops for women. Guests are asked not to wear shorts and T-shirts in the formal dining rooms. Daytime is casual.

Cruise Lines Reviewed in This Chapter

- Celebrity Cruises
- Holland America Line
- Norwegian Cruise Line
- Orient Lines
- Princess Cruises
- Renaissance Cruises
- Royal Caribbean International

Celebrity Cruises

SHIPS IN EUROPE Millennium (preview)

1050 Caribbean Way, Miami, FL 33132. ☎ **800/327-6700** or 305/539-6000. Fax 800/722-5329. www.celebrity-cruises.com.

THE LINE IN A NUTSHELL Celebrity is simply the best of the American mainstream lines, offering pampering, an elegant environment, and fine food at a price normal people can afford.

THE EXPERIENCE With the most elegant mainstream ships in the industry, Celebrity offers the best of both worlds: a refined cruise experience, yet one that is affordable and fun. Each of the line's ships is spacious, glamorous, and comfortable, mixing sleekly modern and updated classic styles, and throwing in astoundingly cutting-edge art collections to boot. Celebrity hires a team of renowned international designers to create an effect that is dramatic and at the same time friendly.

The genteel service onboard is exceptional for a mainstream product. Cabin stewards, waiters, sommeliers, bartenders, and other staff members are exceedingly polite and professional, and contribute greatly to the elegant shipboard mood. Dining-wise, Celebrity shines, offering innovative cuisine with a French influence that's a cut above what's offered by all the other mainstream lines.

There's plenty to do on Celebrity ships, but the focus is on mellower, more relaxing pursuits. Innovative programming helps set the line apart from the pack. Niceties such as roving a cappella bands and magicians who sidle up to your table to entertain during pre- and post-dinner drinks lend a warmly personal touch.

Celebrity gets the "best of" nod in a lot of categories: The AquaSpas, with their indoor thalassotherapy pools, are the best at sea; the art collections the most compelling; the cigar bars the most plush; and the onboard activities among the most varied. Cabins are good-sized (there is really not a bad cabin in the house) and Celebrity pampers suite guests with butler service. Guests in any cabin can get in-cabin pizza delivery.

Pros

- **Spectacular spas and gyms.** Beautiful to look at and well-stocked, the spas and gyms are the best at sea today.
- **Fabulous food.** Consistently high-rated cuisine is tops among mainstream ships.
- **Innovative everything.** Entertainment, art, cigar bars, service, spas, and cuisine are some of the most innovative in the industry.

Cons

- **Sort-of-private verandas.** Most of the huge private verandas are exposed to the public outside decks above (keep that robe on!).

Frommer's Ratings: Celebrity Cruises

	Poor	Fair	Good	Excellent	Outstanding
Enjoyment Factor					✓
Dining					✓
Activities				✓	
Children's Program			✓		
Entertainment				✓	
Service					✓
Overall Value					✓

CELEBRITY: THE BEST OF TWO WORLDS

Celebrity is one of those rare companies that lives up to its advertising: As the song in its commercial says, it's "simply the best" for moderately priced cruises that feel like they should cost a lot more.

Celebrity's roots go back to the powerful Greek shipping family Chandris, whose patriarch, John D. Chandris, founded a cargo shipping company in 1915. The family expanded into the cruise business in the 1960s with the down-market Fantasy Cruises, a line that served mostly the European market, and in 1989 pushed into the Caribbean marketplace in a big, big way by creating Celebrity Cruises. The company's rise to prominence was so rapid and so successful that in 1997 it was courted and acquired by Royal Caribbean Cruises, Ltd., which now operates Celebrity as a sister line to Royal Caribbean International. So far it's been a fortuitous marriage: Reservations, bookkeeping, maintenance, and provisioning were merged, but Celebrity has maintained its own very fine identity, offering a product that's among the best in the cruise industry.

THE FLEET

With their crisp navy-blue and white hulls and rakishly angled funnel decorated with a giant *X* (actually the Greek letter for *ch,* as in *Chandris,* the line's founding family), the profiles of Celebrity's ships rank among the industry's most distinctive. Especially striking are the design of their rear decks, tiered in dramatically rising increments upward and forward, like the terraces in a formal garden, and their bows, steeply pitched toward the water and flowing smoothly up into the ships' superstructures, suggesting both speed and grace. Inside, the ships are just as innovative and modern, offering, among other things, the most impressive and striking art collections at sea, featuring works by artists including Robert Rauschenberg, Damien Hirst, Jasper Johns, David Hockney, Pablo Picasso, Andy Warhol, Sol LeWitt, and Helen Frankenthaler.

As the line never tires of pointing out, it has among the youngest fleets in the industry—all of its ships having been built since 1990. The oldest ships are the 1,354-guest *Horizon* and the twin 1,375-guest *Zenith,* both of which look practically as modern and innovative today as they did when they were introduced. The megaships that followed, the 1,750-guest *Century* and the 1,870-guest *Galaxy* and *Mercury,* retain many of the same design features as the *Horizon* and *Zenith,* as will the new 2,000-passenger ***Millennium,*** Celebrity's largest ship at 91,000 tons and the only one of the line's vessels that will be in Europe for 2000. With their distinctive exteriors, large cabins, innovative spas, and fine dining, there's no mistaking which line these ships sail for.

There are three siblings to the *Millennium* in the works, due in January 2001, August 2001, and April 2002. The ships are being built at the Chantiers de l'Atlantique shipyard in St. Nazaire, France.

PASSENGER PROFILE

Celebrity vessels attract a wide range of ages and backgrounds, although the common denominator among passengers is that they want a toned-down, elegant brand of fun cruise, with activities and a glamorous, exciting atmosphere but without the wild or nutty atmosphere you get aboard some other megaships. The line focuses on middle- to upper-middle-income cruisers, although a handful of discreetly wealthy patrons might be on any given cruise or, conversely, a small business owner, school teacher, police officer, or restaurant manager.

Celebrity entered the Europe market just last year with the *Century,* attracting mostly Americans but some European passengers as well. This year, the brand-new *Millennium* is the line's major presence in Europe.

DINING

Celebrity has poured lots of time and money into creating a culinary format that consistently provides well-orchestrated, well-presented, and good-tasting meals.

In the mid-1990s, the line signed on as its culinary consultant internationally known chef **Michel Roux,** whose most visible successes were his direction of Le Gavroche, one of London's best restaurants, and the Waterside Inn (in Bray, Berkshire), which has attracted the attention of well-heeled European foodies—including the Queen of England—for many years. While some people consider Roux's cuisine a bit overrated and only slightly better than that of other mainstream lines, I personally find it quite tasty.

A dinner menu is likely to feature something along the lines of escargots à la bourguignonne, pheasant mousseline with blueberry vinaigrette, pan-fried salmon with parslied potatoes, pad Thai (noodles and veggies in a peanut sauce), tournedos Rossini with foie gras and Madeira sauce, or a well-seasoned slab of prime rib with horseradish and baked potato. At every meal, Celebrity also offers **lighter "spa" fare,** like a seafood medley in saffron sauce or oven-roasted rack of veal with steamed veggies (calories, fat, cholesterol, and sodium are listed on the back of the menu), and **vegetarian entrees** such as curried Indian vegetables or linguini with shiitake mushrooms and herbs.

An **alternative casual dining venue** is available in the Lido restaurant, where those who don't want to dress up can get a simple five-course meal, with a choice of main entrees like salmon, steak, pasta, and chicken. Serving dinner between 6:30 and 8:30 by reservation only, it's a good place to bring the kids, and a good option if you want to skip the hustle and bustle (and formality) of the main restaurant. It's open every night but formal nights. The menu features options such as fresh fruit cocktail, soup du jour, salad, and entrees like pasta, broiled salmon steak, spit-roasted chicken, and grilled sirloin steak, as well as pizza and dessert selections. The *Millennium* will also feature a **specialty restaurant** that will incorporate hand-carved wall panels from the RMS *Olympic,* sister ship to the *Titanic.* In this ornate, nostalgic setting, guests will be able to experience something of the elegance of early–20th-century luxury liners.

Lunch buffets feature all-American favorites like salads and stir fries, grilled hamburgers and hot dogs, fish and chips, cheeses and breads, omelets, pizza, smoked salmon, shrimp cocktail, and French onion soup.

A nice touch that appears on all formal nights is a late-night culinary soirée known as **Gourmet Bites,** where a series of upscale canapés and hors d'oeuvres are served by waiters in the ship's public lounges between midnight and 1am. On other nights, themed **midnight buffets** might offer up Oriental, Italian, Tex-Mex, or tropical smorgasbords, with a spread of fancifully carved fruits.

On the *Millennium,* buffets are served in the massive (25,000-square foot) AquaDome.

Wine-wise, Chef Roux's choices are offered in a wide price range to suit every budget. Interestingly, a few of the wines featured on board are produced by French vineyards with which Roux has a direct link and, in some cases, of which he is the owner.

Room service is available 24 hours a day and offers a limited menu with hot and cold sandwiches, pizzas, salads, desserts, and beverages. **Gourmet pizzas** are available from room service from 3 to 7pm and 10pm to 1am.

ACTIVITIES

On Celebrity, there's a lot to do and a lot not to do, and the ships offer opportunities for both.

If you like to stay busy, activities during days at sea are fairly standardized across the fleet, and may include one of the fascinating **enrichment lectures** often offered by experts on topics such as personal investing, handwriting analysis, and body language. There are also the tried-and-true wine tastings, horse racing, bingo, art auctions, trivia games, arts and crafts, spa and salon demonstrations, and line-dancing lessons. During days at sea, a live pop band plays a couple of sets on the Pool Deck.

If you prefer curling up with a good book in some quiet nook, you'll have no problem finding one. On the *Millennium,* you can grab in a lounge chair at the spa's thalassotherapy pool or duck into one of the many lounges, including the quiet, clubbish Michael's Club cigar bar, which offers the atmosphere of a British men's club—for both sexes, of course.

Although managed by Steiner like the spas on most other ships, Celebrity **spas** offer more exotic treatments than most—for example, mud packs, herbal steam baths, and a variety of water-based treatments involving jet massages and "aquameditation," in which you're caressed by light, whirling showers while lying on a soft mat. Certain procedures are offered in a partner arrangement, whereby you and your significant other can apply medicinal muds to each other and share an herbal steam bath. The whole shebang ends with a warm shower and the application of an aromatic "potion" to the skin. Exotic, huh?

Children's Programs

Although it did not originate that way, Celebrity has evolved into a cruise line that pampers kids as well as adults. Each ship has a **playroom** and **supervised activities** as well as private and group **baby-sitting.**

Activities are geared to those 3 to 17, and include treasure hunts, arts and crafts, dancing, movies, ship tours, ice-cream-sundae-making and pizza parties, karaoke, and computer games, as well as theater productions and junior Olympics contests. For teens ages 14 to 17 who don't think themselves too cool to participate, there are talent shows, karaoke, pool games, and trivia contests.

A once-weekly, complimentary parents' night out program allows mom and dad to enjoy dinner alone while the kids dine with counselors. Every evening, group slumber party–style baby-sitting in the playroom is available from 10pm to 1am for children ages 3 to 12, for $3 per child per hour or $5 per hour for two or more children from the same family. Private in-cabin baby-sitting by a crew member is available on a limited basis for $8 per hour for up to two children.

Entertainment

Although entertainment is not a prime reason to sail on a Celebrity ship, the line does offer a nice selection of varied, innovative performances. For instance, Celebrity Cruises fleetwide has introduced a **strolling a cappella group** as well as a wandering magician, who perform in lounges and public areas in the afternoons and before and after dinner. The four-man troupe of singers, sans instruments, delights passengers with well-known songs old and new, performed in a fun, entertaining style. Meanwhile, the tuxedo-clad magician dazzles guests with card tricks and disappearing acts.

Celebrity also offers the popular favorites, like **Broadway-style musicals** led by a sock-it-to-'em soloist or two and a team of lip-synching dancers in full Vegas-esque

Gourmet Experiences on Shore

Celebrity, in partnership with *Gourmet* magazine, offers a program called Gourmet Valet, where passengers can browse the menus of in-port restaurants chosen by the magazine and then make table reservations through the ship's shore excursions desk. The shore excursions team can also help arrange transportation to your restaurant of choice.

Celebrity Fleet Itineraries

Ship	Home Ports & Season	Itinerary
Millennium	14-day Scandinavia & Russia, round-trip from Amsterdam (July to Aug.); 13-day Med, Amsterdam to Genoa (Sept.); 10-day W. Med and 11-day E. Med, round-trip from Genoa (Sept., Oct.).	**14-day Scandinavia & Russia:** Oslo (Norway), Nynashamn (Sweden), Helsinki (Finland), St. Petersburg (Russia), Muuga (Estonia), Gdynia (Poland), Rostock (Germany), and Copenhagen (Denmark). **10- to 13-day Med:** port calls may include Le Havre, Villefranche (France), Vigo, Malaga, Barcelona (Spain), Lisbon (Portugal), and Civitavecchia/Rome, Naples, Livorno (Italy). **11-day E. Med**: Valletta (Malta), Katakolon, Piraeus/Athens, Santorini (Greece), Kusadasi (Turkey), Iraklion (Crete), and Civitavecchia/Rome, Livorno (Italy)

regalia. Other nights in the showroom, you'll find magicians, comedians, cabaret acts, and passenger talent shows. Showrooms aboard all Celebrity ships have excellent acoustics and sight lines praised as among the most panoramic and unobstructed at sea.

When you tire of Broadway-style entertainment, you'll find all the ships have **cozy lounges** and **piano bars** where you can retreat for a romantic nightcap. In these more intimate lounges, the music of choice is often laid-back jazz or music from the Big Band era, spiced with interpretations of contemporary hits by the likes of Celine Dion or Whitney Houston. There's also the elegant and plush **Michael's Club** for a cigar and cordial and some quiet conversation. Each ship has late-night disco dancing, usually until about 3am. You'll also find **karaoke** and **first-run movies** in the theater. Each ship has a spacious **casino.**

SERVICE

Service is polite, attentive, cheerful, and especially professional. Waiters have a poised, upscale-hotel air about them, and are able to think on their feet. On one sailing, when I mentioned to my cabin steward I was disappointed there were chairs but no deck chair on my cabin balcony, he promptly snuck one off the Pool Deck for me. There are very professional sommeliers in the dining room, and in the Lido breakfast and lunch buffet restaurants, waiters are on hand to carry passengers' trays from the buffet line to a table of their choice.

If you occupy a suite on any of the ships, you'll get a tuxedo-clad **personal butler** who serves afternoon tea and complimentary hors d'oeuvres from 6 to 8pm, bringing them right to your cabin. If you ask, he'll handle your laundry, shine your shoes, make sewing repairs, deliver messages, and do many other errands and favors. For instance, on a recent sailing our butler brought my mother a glass of juice each night, which she needed to take her medication. Your butler will serve you a full five-course dinner if you'd rather **dine in your cabin** one night, and if you're in the mood to compile a guest list and pay for the drinks and hors d'oeuvres everyone will consume, your butler will even organize a cocktail party for you and your list of cruising friends, either in your suite or in any of several suitable public areas on board the ship.

Other hedonistic treats bestowed upon suite guests include a bottle of champagne on arrival, personalized stationery, terry-cloth robes, a Celebrity tote bag, oversized bath towels, priority check-in and debarkation, express luggage delivery at embarkation, and complimentary use of the soothing thalassotherapy pool. Suite guests can even get an **in-cabin massage** daily between the hours of 7am and 8pm.

Millennium (Preview)

Debuting this year, Celebrity's newest ship will be its largest, weighing in at 91,000 tons, carrying 1,950 guests, and offering a host of onboard activity and entertainment options that expand on the line's core strengths: relaxed elegance, fine food, exceptional spa facilities, and modern flair.

The Olympic Restaurant, an alternative dining facility, will be designed around a series of original hand-carved wall panels taken from the RMS *Olympic,* sister-ship to the *Titanic.* Decorated in a rich, Edwardian style to match these panels, the room will offer guests a taste of what life was like aboard early–20th-century luxury liners. In addition to the Olympic paneling, Celebrity Cruises will display three rare bottles of 1907 Heidsieck Monopole champagne in the ship's wine cellar, adjacent to the Olympic Restaurant. The champagne was salvaged from the wreck of the *Jonkoping,* a Swedish merchant ship that was sunk by the Germans in the Baltic in 1916. The same champagne was believed to have been aboard the *Titanic* when it went down.

Other innovative features aboard the *Millennium* include the cruise industry's first music library, with thousands of digital recordings available for guests at individual listening stations; the largest spa facilities at sea; the first shipboard elevators that offer ocean views; and a sports bar themed on extreme sports (even the chairs look like Gore-Tex expedition gear).

Eighty percent of the *Millennium*'s staterooms are outside, and 75% of those have verandas. Per diems start at $238 inside, $273 outside, $428 suite.

Holland America Line

SHIPS IN EUROPE Maasdam • Noordam • Rotterdam

300 Elliott Ave. W., Seattle, WA 98119. ☎ **800/426-0327** or 206/281-3535. Fax 800/628-4855. www.hollandamerica.com.

THE LINE IN A NUTSHELL More than any other line today (except Cunard), Holland America has managed to hang on to some of its seafaring history and tradition, offering an affordable, classic, ocean liner–like cruise experience.

THE EXPERIENCE Holland America consistently delivers a worthy and solid product for a fair price, and is unique for offering mid-sized to large ships with an old-world elegance that remains appealingly low-key and not stuffy. These ships aren't boring, but they're sedate, so it's no surprise that the line attracts predominantly passengers in their 50s on up (the age range has widened a bit as the line has introduced new vessels).

The line's well-maintained ships are mid-sized, creating a cozy atmosphere, understated, and with excellent layouts to ease passenger movement. HAL's older ships, including the *Noordam* in Europe, are the most humble, with plain-ish one-level dining rooms and pleasing, but simple, public rooms. The newer ships are more lavish, but still in an understated way.

Holland America emphasizes tradition, and that's what sets it apart. In the public areas,- you'll see antiques, trophies, and memorabilia, and the very names of the vessels hark back to ships in the line's past. For example, the line's flagship, the 62,000-ton *Rotterdam,* is the sixth HAL ship to bear that name.

Pros

- **History and tradition.** The impressive collection of artifacts and artwork on the ships reflect Holland America's important place in seafaring history and lend the ships more of a traditional ocean liner ambiance than can be found on nearly any other line.
- **Private verandas.** Over 25% of all cabins on the newer ships boast private verandas.
- **Great gyms.** For their size, the ships offer some of the most attractive, roomy, and well-stocked gyms and aerobics areas at sea.

Cons

- **Sleepy nightlife.** While there's always a few stalwarts and a couple of busy-ish nights, if you're big on late-night dancing and bar hopping, you may find yourself partying mostly with the entertainment staff.
- **Homogenous passenger profile.** Although this is changing to a certain degree, passengers tend to be a pretty homogenous group of 50+, low-key North American couples who aren't overly adventurous.

Frommer's Ratings: Holland America Line

	Poor	Fair	Good	Excellent	Outstanding
Enjoyment Factor					✓
Dining				✓	
Activities				✓	
Children's Program		✓			
Entertainment			✓		
Service					✓
Overall Value					✓

HOLLAND AMERICA: GOING DUTCH

One of the most famous shipping companies in the world, Holland America Line was founded in 1873 as the Nederlandsch-Amerikaansche StoomvAart Maatschappij (Netherlands-American Steamship Company), and because the line provided service between New York City and Rotterdam, Holland, it soon became known as Holland America Line. The company's first ocean liner was the original *Rotterdam,* which took its maiden, 15-day voyage from the Netherlands to New York City in 1872.

By the turn of the century, Holland America owned a fleet of six passenger-cargo ships, and traveled between Holland and Asia (the Dutch East Indies) via the Suez Canal. In the early 1900s, Holland America was one of the major lines transporting thousands of immigrants from Europe to the United States, and continued a regular schedule of transatlantic crossings up until 1971, when the line turned to offering cruises full time.

During World War II, the company's headquarters moved from Nazi-occupied Holland to Dutch-owned Curaçao, then the site of a strategic oil refinery. Strong links were forged with North American interests after the war when Westours, a Seattle-based company, began booking large blocks of Holland America cabins. In 1973, Holland America Line changed its name to Holland America Cruises to promote its new focus on cruising; then, in 1974, Westours and HAL were linked to give the line a presence in Alaska, where it has remained one of the two biggest cruisetour players today.

The line changed its name back to Holland America Line in 1983, seeking to capitalize on its history and seafaring traditions, and began building a fleet of mid-sized ships.

In the midst of this building spree, in 1988, HAL acquired Windstar Cruises, an upscale operator (see review in chapter 8). To everyone's surprise, both companies were acquired a year later by Carnival Corporation. Carnival improved entertainment quality and quantity (the line needed both), upgraded HAL's cuisine, and provided the cash and credit to commission additional vessels.

THE FLEET

Holland America has nine ships, and growing. In Europe in 2000, it is positioning the ***Noordam,*** at age 16 among the older and plainer of the line's ships; the ***Maasdam,*** among a group of four Italian-built ships of the same well-crafted design (with just a bit of glitz here and there); and the ***Rotterdam,*** the line's impressive flagship. (In 1998, it replaced the vintage *Rotterdam V,* now operating as the *Rembrandt* for U.S.-based Premier Cruises.)

Two new ships are scheduled to launch in 2000, including the *Amsterdam,* a sister to the *Rotterdam VI,* and more new ships are planned.

PASSENGER PROFILE

Before its acquisition by Carnival in 1989, HAL passengers tended overwhelmingly to be older people in their 60s and 70s, but Carnival's influence has moved the demographics toward a somewhat younger market, although any kind of real transformation is slow as molasses in coming and far from complete (if indeed it ever will be). HAL's passenger rosters typically include some graying, 50-ish members of the baby-boom generation, mixed in with many passengers of their parents' age.

Passengers tend to be hospitable and amiable, and sensible with their money. They tend to be fairly set in their ways and not adventurous.

The line attracts many groups traveling together, from incentive groups to social clubs on a lark together. If you're a 40-something member of such a group and are worried

HAL: The Generous Line

Holland America is generous with its complimentary treats (a rarity in today's nickel-and-diming industry), serving hot canapés in some of the bar/lounges during the cocktail hour, offering freshly popped popcorn in the movie theater, doling out espresso and cappuccino at no charge in the Java Cafes, and serving lemonade on deck on all warm-weather cruises. Unlike other lines, there's no cover charge in the small, alternative restaurant on the Rotterdam. Stewards replenish a bowl of fruit in your cabin daily, and each guest is given a Holland America canvas tote bag.

about finding company aboard, don't abandon hope, particularly if you happen to be a divorcée, widow, or widower: You won't be alone.

DINING

Joining the trend, Holland America recently began offering an **alternative dinner option** in its casual buffet-style breakfast and lunch Lido restaurant, several times during every sailing.

Of course, an elegant dinner in the main dining room is still the preferred venue. As its executive chef, HAL employs the renowned Reiner Greubel, formerly of Westin Hotels, New York's Plaza Hotel, and his own Reiner's Restaurant in Seattle. Instead of daring experimentation, he recognizes that some of the world's finest cuisine comes from classics prepared with fresh and high-quality ingredients, and that some sophisticated palates still prefer traditional favorites: osso buco, cassoulet, Alaskan king crab, and Caribbean snapper, for instance. Dinner items might be as straightforward as roast prime rib of beef with baked Idaho potatoes and horseradish cream, or as esoteric as warm hazelnut-crusted brie with a compote of apples and onions. Children can enjoy tried-and-true staples like pizza, hot dogs, burgers with fries, chicken fingers, and tacos.

Greubel has also expanded the line's **light and healthy cuisine,** and he serves what he calls **fun foods,** meaning spring rolls and sushi. And he did a major league improvement in the area of desserts, moving away from grandmother's favorite cakes to things more sophisticated, including many desserts based on tropical fruit and delicate sauces.

Buffets for breakfast and lunch, with the inevitable queues, are bountiful and frequent, and include separate stations for omelets, tacos, and pasta. **Indonesian dishes** are the theme of at least one buffet a week. There are also theme dinners in Europe reflecting European regions.

Dutch influences prevail with Gouda cheese offered at breakfast and, at least once during each cruise, a **Dutch Chocolate Extravaganza,** a Holland-themed midnight buffet where the calories stack up so fast you might as well give up trying to count them.

Room service is available 24 hours a day. Mid-morning bouillon and **afternoon teas** are well-attended events. Hot canapés are served in some of the bar/lounges during the cocktail hour. The Maasdam and Rotterdam have **Java Cafes,** coffee bars that serve complimentary espresso and cappuccinos.

ACTIVITIES

Activities are varied, relatively nontaxing, and fun. The Flagship Forum lecture series, featuring knowledgeable Smithsonian Association lecturers, is particularly popular in Europe. You can learn how to dance cheek-to-cheek, be taught the fine art of vegetable carving or creative napkin folding, or play bingo or bridge. A member of the cruise will take interested passengers on **art tours,** discussing the ship's impressive art collection and giving passengers a handout about the collections.

HAL, like its competitors, has an incentive-based fitness program in which passengers are awarded points every time they take an aerobics class or do some other fitness activity. Points can be redeemed at the cruise's end for T-shirts, souvenirs, and so on.

Children's Program

Whenever demand warrants it (usually during the summer months), HAL offers supervised programs for children, called **Club HAL.** The menu of activities is not anywhere as extensive as on lines like Disney, Carnival, Celebrity, Royal Caribbean, and Princess, and HAL never pretends it is. When enough kids are on board, programs are designated for three different age brackets: 5- to 8-year-olds, 9- to 12-year-olds, and teens. However, based on the number of young people aboard, these barriers sometimes blur.

Regardless of the age of the attendees, young people are diverted with pizza and soda parties, as well as tours of the bridge, the galley, and other areas below deck. There might also be movies, ice-cream parties, arts and crafts, storytelling sessions, games, karaoke, golf lessons, disco parties, charades, bingo, and Ping-Pong. On the first night of each cruise, parents meet and mingle with staff responsible for the care, counseling, and feeding of their children. Activities are not scheduled while a ship is in port.

There are **playrooms** on all ships (on the *Noordam*, the room does double duty as a meeting or card room when there aren't many kids on board).

Baby-sitting is sometimes (but not always) available from volunteers among a ship's staff. If a staff member is available—and be warned, their availability is never guaranteed—the cost is usually around $5 per child per hour.

Entertainment

Onboard entertainment has improved since HAL's acquisition by Carnival, which really understands how cabaret shows should be presented. Each ship features small-scale glittery **Broadway-style shows** with live music, singers, dancers, and laser lights. Some of the extravagant costumes are by famous designer Bob Mackie. There are also musicians, comedians, illusionists, and the like performing in the various lounges.

Regular offerings on Europe sailings include a '50s and '60s dance party, a talent show by the crew (with Indonesian and Filipino songs and folk dancing), and first-run movies (complete with popcorn) in the movie theaters.

Pre-dinner cocktails and **dancing** are a major event of the day. And on cruises 14 nights and longer, women traveling alone or those whose escorts have two left feet need not fear for lack of dance partners: A complement of "gentlemen hosts" sail on board and are available for a whirl or two around the dance floor.

On the *Maasdam* and *Rotterdam*, the **disco** is part of the spacious Crow's Nest observation lounge. Generally a live four-piece band plays from about 9pm to midnight and a DJ takes over for the next few hours. On the *Noordam,* the disco is also in a larger lounge and sees more action than you might expect a few nights a week.

Service

Onboard service is permeated with nostalgia for the Netherlands' past and its genteel traditions. During lunch, a uniformed employee might hold open the door of a buffet, and a steward ringing a chime will formally announce the two dinner seatings.

Holland America is one of the few cruise lines that maintains a training school (a land-based facility in Indonesia dubbed in HAL circles SS *Jakarta*) for the selection and training of its staff. On the ships, the soft-spoken staff smiles more often than not as they labor to offer attentive service.

Holland America Fleet Itineraries

Ship	Home Ports & Season	Itinerary
Maasdam	7-day W. Med, round-trip from Barcelona (May); 14-day Europe Capitals, Barcelona to Stockholm (June); 7-day Scandinavia & Russia, round-trip from Stockholm (June–Aug); 12-day Scandinavia & Russia, Stockholm to Copenhagen (Aug).	**7-day W. Med:** La Goulette (Tunisia), Palermo (Italy), Rome, Monte Carlo, Marseille (France). **14-day Europe Capitals:** Málaga (Spain), Gibraltar, Lisbon, Vigo (Spain), Le Havre (France), Dover (England), Antwerp (Belgium), Oslo (Norway), and Copenhagen (Denmark). **7-day Scandinavia & Russia:** Tallinn (Estonia), St. Petersburg (Russia), Helsinki (Finland), and Visby (Sweden). **12-day Scandinavia & Russia:** St. Petersburg (Russia), Tallinn (Estonia), Helsinki (Finland), Gdansk (Poland), Rønne (Denmark), Warnemünde (Germany), and Århus (Denmark).
Noordam	10-day W. Med, Lisbon and Rome (May–Nov); 10-day E. Med, Rome and Istanbul (May–Nov).	**10-day W. Med:** Barcelona, Marseille, Ajaccio (France), Sardinia, Palermo, Livorno (Italy), La Goulette (Tunisia), Valletta (Malta), Monte Carlo (Monacco), Mallorca and Cadiz (Spain), Casablanca (Morocco), and Gibraltar. **10-day E. Med:** Naples (Italy), Heraklion (Crete), Santorini, Piraeus/Athens, Mykonos (Greece), and Kusadasi (Turkey).
Rotterdam	12-day W. Med, Rome and Lisbon (May); 12-day Europe Capitals, Lisbon to Copenhagen (May); 12-day Norway & North Cape, Copenhagen to London (June); 12-day Scandinavia & Russia, Copenhagen and London (June, July).	**12-day W. Med:** Port calls may include Casablanca (Morocco), Mallorca and Barcelona (Spain), Marseille (France), Monte Carlo (Monaco), La Goulette (Tunisia), Naples, Livorno, Palmero (Italy), Valletta (Malta), and Gibraltar. **12-day Europe Capitals:** Vigo (Spain), Dublin, Belfast (Ireland), Le Havre (France), Dover (England), Antwerp (Belgium), Rotterdam (Holland), Oslo (Norway). **12-day Norway & North Cape:** Bergen, Geiranger, Trondheim, Honningsvåg, Tromsø, Flåm, and Stavanger (Norway). **12-day Scandinavia & Russia:** Oslo (Norway), Helsingborg and Stockholm (Sweden), Warnemünde (Germany), Helsinki (Finland), St. Petersburg (Russia), and Tallinn (Estonia).*

* Also does Holy Lands cruises and 19-day cruises from Copenhagen (Russia and Scandinavia) and Dublin (W. Med, E. Med, Egypt and Israel) that can be combined for a 38-day sailing, from Aug through Sept.

Beginning in the mid-1990s, HAL hired more multilingual staff members (usually Dutch, German, Spanish, and English) to ensure that its guests enjoy their cruise experience unhampered by language barriers, although room stewards, for example, are almost always Indonesian or Filipino.

Although Holland America proudly touts its no-tipping-required policy, it's more lip service than anything else. In fact, like most other ships, tips are expected; it's just that on Holland America ships you won't be bombarded by guidelines and reminders—you can feel as though you're tipping because you truly enjoyed the service. HAL's no-tipping-required policy includes bar tabs, which, unlike on most lines, do not automatically include a 15% gratuity (if you want, you can tip a bar waiter in cash or handwrite a tip onto your tab).

Onboard services include **laundry** and **dry cleaning.** Each ship also offers a **self-service laundry.**

Maasdam

Maasdam (photo: HAL)

The Verdict

One of the more attractive mid-sized ships out there. Functional, appealing public areas are enlivened with just a dash of glitz and collections of art, artifacts, and shipping memorabilia.

Specifications

Size (in tons)	55,451	Officers	Dutch
Number of Cabins	633	Crew (Indonesian/Filipino)	588
Number of Outside Cabins	502	Passenger/Crew Ratio	2.2 to 1
Cabins with Verandas	150	Year Built	1993
Number of Passengers	1,266	Last Major Refurbishment	N/A

Frommer's Ratings (Scale of 1–5)

Cabin Comfort & Amenities	4	Pool, Fitness & Spa Facilities	5
Ship Cleanliness & Maintenance	4	Children's Facilities	3
Public Comfort/Space	5	Itineraries	4
Decor	4	Worth the Money	5

Weighing in at 55,000 tons, the *Maasdam,* one of four identical ships in the HAL fleet, was built at Fincantieri shipyard in Monfalcone, Italy, and falls somewhere between mid-sized and megaship.

The design makes good use of the space, and has an easy traffic flow. The ship has unusual squared-off sterns surrounded by windows, and the interior is designed with practicality, cost-efficiency, and easy maintenance in mind. There are eight elevators connecting each deck.

Interior components include furniture from around the world, and touches of marble, teakwood, polished brass, and around $2 million worth of artwork evoke the era of the classic ocean liners.

CABINS Cabins are roomy, unfussy, uncomplicated, and comfortable, with color schemes awash of bordering-on-drab earth tones. Minisuites are a roomy 284 square feet. Full suites are 565 square feet, and culminate at 1,126 square feet in a sprawling penthouse suite. (All square footage measurements include the cabin's veranda.)

Cabins in some cases are outfitted with floral-patterned curtains that separate the sleeping area from the sitting area. Closets and storage space are larger than the norm. Bathrooms are well designed and well lit.

All cabins have twin beds that can be converted to a queen and, in some cases, a king. About 200 cabins can accommodate a third and fourth passenger on a fold-away sofa bed and/or an upper berth.

Outside cabins have picture windows. While none have obstructed views, those on the Navigation Deck have pedestrian walkways (and, consequently, pedestrians) between you and your view of the sea. Special reflective glass prevents outsiders from seeing in during daylight hours, but to guarantee privacy at nighttime, you have to close the curtains.

Fresh flowers, gracious stewards, and bowls of fresh fruit in the cabins add a warm, hospitable touch.

Six cabins are wheelchair-accessible and specially outfitted for passengers with disabilities. That, plus spacious corridors, wide elevators, and wheelchair-accessible toilets, makes these ships popular with people with disabilities.

Cabins & Rates

Cabins	Per diems from	Bathtub	Fridge	Hair Dryer	Sitting Area	TV
Inside	$220	some	no*	yes	yes	yes
Outside	$267	yes	no*	yes	yes	yes
Suite	$381	yes	yes	yes	yes	yes

**Fridges can be requested through your travel agent and placed in cabins for a nominal fee.*

PUBLIC AREAS Joe Farcus, the designer of Carnival Cruise Lines' "Fun Ships," played a role in the interior design of these ships, albeit with considerably more reserve and subtlety than he uses with Carnival.

For the most part, public areas are subdued, consciously tasteful, and soothing. One of the most appealing areas is the top-most Sky Deck, which offers a 360-degree panorama (and the roaring wind, too). One floor below that, almost equivalent views are available from the gorgeous Crow's Nest nightclub. With floor-to-ceiling windows, this romantic venue, with its cozy clusters of seating, is perfect for pre-dinner cocktails and dancing, too, when it becomes the ship's disco and after-dinner nightclub. The three-story atrium is not very large, but is exciting in a subtle way, designed with a dose of brass and flash and "Totem," a huge green Murano glass avant-garde sculpture of marine mythology by Luciano Vistosi, as the focal point.

The showroom is stylish, and pays tribute to Rembrandt. Unlike most ships, which have rows of banquettes or theater-like seats, this showroom is configured with cozy groupings of cushy chairs and banquettes.

The ship's roomy library honors Leyden, and is a tranquil retreat. There is also a spacious card room and small video arcade. The casino is good-sized and designed with enough glamour and flashing lights to get gamblers in the mood.

POOL, FITNESS & SPA FACILITIES The *Maasdam* has a sprawling expanse of teak-covered aft deck surrounding a swimming pool. One deck above that is a spacious deck area including a second swimming pool, two hot tubs, a wading pool, plus the attractive Dolphin Bar, with its umbrellas and wicker chairs, that can all be sheltered from inclement weather with a sliding glass magrodome roof. Both pool areas are well-planned and wide open.

Fitness fanatics will like the practice tennis courts and the unobstructed track on the upper deck designed for walking or jogging. The ship's windowed Ocean Spa gym is one of the most attractive and well-equipped at sea, with a couple of dozen exercise machines, a large separate aerobics area, a juice bar, steam rooms, and saunas. The spa offers the typical menu of treatments (see chapter 4, "The Cruise Experience," for a discussion of spa options).

Noordam

Noordam (photo: HAL)

The Verdict

This mid-sized '80s ship is among the oldest and coziest in the fleet, offering a comfortable, calm, glitz-free cruise experience and a slice of the past.

Specifications

Size (in tons)	33,930	Officers	Dutch
Number of Cabins	607	Crew (Indonesian/Filipino)	530
Number of Outside Cabins	413	Passenger/Crew Ratio	2.2 to 1
Cabins with Verandas	0	Year Built	1984
Number of Passengers	1,214	Last Major Refurbishment	N/A

Frommer's Ratings (Scale of 1–5)

Cabin Comfort & Amenities	4	Pool, Fitness & Spa Facilities	3
Ship Cleanliness & Maintenance	4	Children's Facilities	2
Public Comfort/Space	3	Itineraries	3
Decor	4	Worth the Money	5

The *Noordam* provides the amenities most passengers associate with a classic ocean liner. Inside and out there are lots of nooks and crannies that create a cozy and intimate atmosphere that's much different than the wide-open, sprawling spaces on newer ships. This ship is pared down in scope and scale from its newer rivals, and consequently, cabins go at a commensurately pared-down price. It's a great ship for those looking for value.

The vessel was built at the Chantiers de l'Atlantique shipyard in St-Nazaire, France, and the basic design is classic, almost nostalgically evocative of the pre-megaship age of cruising.

Overall, passengers aboard this vessel tend to be more sedate and low-key than those aboard the line's larger ships, though they're certainly not opposed to a good time.

If you plan on traveling with children, it's wiser to opt for the larger, newer HAL ships, although the *Noordam does* have children's programs during holidays and on sailings that have a lot of kids on board. At these times, an all-purpose room is converted to a children's playroom.

Cabins & Rates

Cabins	Per diems from	Bathtub	Fridge	Hair Dryer	Sitting Area	TV
Inside	$242	no	no*	no	no	yes
Outside	$293	some	no*	no	some	yes
Suite	$418	yes	yes	no	yes	yes

**Fridges can be requested through your travel agent and placed in cabins for a nominal fee.*

CABINS Standard outside cabins are a decent size (measuring 177 square feet), while lower-end inside cabins are still comfortable at 152 square feet. All are furnished in HAL's low-key style. Mirrors make the space seem larger than it is, storage space is more than adequate, and bathrooms are compact and well designed. The highest category of cabin is the minisuite, which is about 294 square feet.

Most cabins on the Boat and Navigation Decks have views obstructed by lifeboats, and those on the Upper Promenade Deck overlook an unending stream of joggers, walkers, and passersby. Cabins near the stern are subject to more than their share of engine noise and vibration. Many cabins have bathtubs and all have TVs, music channels, and a fruit bowl. (There are no in-cabin safes, but valuables can be kept at the purser's desk.)

Four cabins in the B category—deluxe outside double rooms on the Boat Deck—are suitable for people with disabilities. Elevators are wheelchair accessible.

PUBLIC AREAS The decor is discreet and pleasant, with bouquets of fresh flowers liberally scattered through public areas. A 15-foot-wide teak-covered promenade allows plenty of room for deck chairs, strollers, joggers, and voyeurs to mingle under the open sky. Some passengers consider it the ship's most endearing feature and it's a lovely reminiscence of the classic ocean liner.

There are some other unfortunate design flaws, however. For example, the show lounge is not large enough to seat all passengers. And, in general, the ship's choppy clusters of public areas and decks can leave you disoriented at times. The one-story main-dining room, while pleasant, is rather plain when compared to the more glamorous ones on the line's newer ships (but it does boast floor-to-ceiling windows and fresh flowers on the tables).

The Crow's Nest is the best place to enjoy a pre-dinner cocktail, and the Explorer's Lounge is a nice venue for after-dinner drinks and coffee (and afternoon tea as well).

POOL, FITNESS & SPA FACILITIES There are two outside pools, a wading pool, and a hot tub. The classic aft tiered decks offer many nooks and crannies for sunbathing or a snooze in a deck chair. You can walk or jog on the broad, unobstructed Promenade Deck. The gym and spa are small, but the gym, located on one of the topmost decks, has windows and is equipped with rowing machines, weight machines, and stationary bicycles. The spa is really just a couple of treatment rooms for massages and facials, plus a steam room and sauna and a beauty salon. Aerobics classes are held on the decks or in a public room. A sports deck up top features a pair of practice tennis courts and shuffleboard.

Rotterdam

The Verdict

This gorgeous ship replaced a classic and is a modern classic in its own right. Antiques, artwork, and polished woods give it an old world charm, but the ship is also spacious, sleek, and thoroughly modern.

Rotterdam (photo: HAL)

Specifications

Size (in tons)	62,000	Officers	Dutch
Number of Cabins	658	Crew (Indonesian/Filipino)	658
Number of Outside Cabins	541	Passenger/Crew Ratio	2 to 1
Cabins with Verandas	160	Year Built	1997
Number of Passengers	1,316	Last Major Refurbishment	N/A

Frommer's Ratings (Scale of 1–5)

Cabin Comfort & Amenities	5	Pool, Fitness & Spa Facilities	5
Ship Cleanliness & Maintenance	5	Children's Facilities	3
Public Comfort/Space	5	Itineraries	5
Decor	5	Worth the Money	5

The *Rotterdam VI* replaced the classic 1959 *Rotterdam V* as HAL's flagship. So as not to upset the loyal following of its predecessor (or, "The Grand Old Lady" as HAL folks like to call her), the line incorporated a lot of features of the old ship into the new vessel's design, including a double smokestack. The new ship also borrows its basic interior layout from the line's *Statendam*-class ships, including the *Maasdam*. But the new ship is at the same time larger and wider, more airy and modern, and more technologically advanced (it can go 25 knots, faster than most other ships its size).

Almost like a mini-museum in places, the *Rotterdam* is filled with antiques to reflect HAL's seafaring tradition, and its $2 million art collection includes many works commissioned for the vessel.

The ship has many special features, including an entire deck devoted to suites, with a private lounge (for suite guests only) and concierge service (to book shore excursions, restaurant reservations, and so forth). It's also the first in the Holland America fleet to have a specialty restaurant. And as an added convenience to passengers, the *Rotterdam VI* has three staircases instead of the two found on the other ships.

To further satisfy fans of the *Rotterdam V*, Holland America brought over about half its staff to the new vessel, so if you've been on the *Rotterdam V* you might see some familiar faces.

Cabins & Rates

Cabins	Per diems from	Bathtub	Fridge	Hair Dryer	Sitting Area	TV
Inside	$238	no	no	yes	yes	yes
Outside	$288	yes*	no	yes	yes	yes
Suite	$414	yes	yes	yes	yes	yes

**With the exception of handicapped-accessible cabins, which are shower only.*

CABINS Cabins are good-sized, and all outside cabins have bathtubs and showers. All cabins have two beds that are convertible to queen-sized and good storage space, as well as air-conditioning, closed-circuit TV, music channels, phone, and hair dryer. The Navigation Deck is all suites and offers a private lounge and a Concierge Desk, located in the private Neptune Lounge (accessible with a key), which provides special services like booking shore excursions and spa appointments. Suites range from 300 square feet to 1,126 square feet, including verandas. Those aft on the Navigation Deck have particularly easy access to the outdoor pool.

The suites and minisuites come with refrigerators, minibars, VCRs, whirlpool tubs, verandas, sofa beds that can sleep an additional two, and other amenities (such as heavy terry-cloth bathrobes, high tea and hors d'oeuvres served in suite, complimentary laundry services, feather pillows, corsages and boutonnieres for the first formal night, and CD players and VCRs). The four penthouses (whoppingly sized at 1,126 square feet) have separate living, bedroom, and changing rooms; a steward's entrance; and a large dining area. Some outside cabins on the Lower Promenade Deck have obstructed views.

There are 23 wheelchair-accessible cabins, including some in the suites and minisuites categories. Hearing-impaired guests can make special arrangements in advance with their travel agent for a blinking doorbell light, closed-caption TV, and a vibrating wake-up system.

PUBLIC AREAS The La Fontaine dining room is in the stern of the vessel and is spectacular, with floor-to-ceiling windows, a Venetian glass ceiling, and a pair of grand staircases. The Odyssey, the ship's specialty restaurant (reservations are required) is designed to look like a room in a 17th-century Italian villa, and is accented by pictures in gold frames and candelabras.

The three-deck atrium features a sculpture designed to look like a Dutch clock tower (with some 14 clocks). The Ambassador Lounge, where the decor includes replicas of items from the old Holland America building in Rotterdam, doubles as both a nightclub and piano bar; the Crow's Nest as both an observation lounge and, at night, a disco; and the Club Hal children's room as a quiet retreat for coffee and snacks when there aren't many kids on board. Coffee lovers will also enjoy the ship's Java Cafe, where complimentary cappuccinos and espressos are dispensed.

The Explorer's Lounge, located outside the upper level of the dining room, has a dance floor made of crushed Italian marble.

POOL, FITNESS & SPA FACILITIES The ship has great recreation facilities. There are two swimming pools (one with a retractable roof), and the spa offers dual saunas, steam rooms, a loofah scrub room, massage rooms, and a beauty salon and barber shop. The roomy glass-walled gym is equipped with an array of exercise machines as well as a juice bar. The ship even has practice tennis and volleyball courts. And walkers will enjoy the nostalgic wraparound teak deck, which has real wooden deck chairs just like the classic liners for those who just want to sit and watch.

Norwegian Cruise Line

SHIPS IN EUROPE **Norwegian Dream**

7665 Corporate Center Dr., Miami, FL 33126. ☎ **800/327-7030** or 305/436-4000. Fax 305/436-4126. www.ncl.com.

THE LINE IN A NUTSHELL NCL offers affordable, down-to-earth cruises that attract seasoned travelers and first-timers alike. In Europe, the line's alternative dining and sports offerings set it apart.

THE EXPERIENCE NCL has a varied fleet, from new to old, mid-size to mega. The line's ship in Europe, the 1,750-passenger *Norwegian Dream,* falls somewhere in the middle. While the line strives to lure more upmarket travelers, truth is the product is very mid-market and the experience not as fine-tuned and sharp as it could be. In general, the *Norwegian Dream* draws an older crowd of passengers attracted by the ship's relatively intimate size and low prices (the line offers frequent discounts). About 90% are from North America.

Despite its shortcomings, the line is very innovative in certain areas. In Europe, there's an enrichment program with lectures on such topics as religion, ancient history, earth sciences, and astronomy. NCL also justifiably touts its sports offerings, which include basketball courts. For the more sedentary sports fan, major games and taped highlights are broadcast into passengers' cabins and onto the video monitors of each vessel's high-tech sports bar, sometimes with multiple screens broadcasting different games in different areas of the bar (all assuming the satellite link working, which it usually is).

The line is also proud of its alternative dining choices, which offer finer cuisine than what's served in the main dining rooms. The *Norwegian Dream's* reservations-only Le Bistro restaurant is smaller and more intimate than the main dining room, and serves such dishes as filet mignon, grilled salmon, mahimahi, and Caesar salad prepared at the table. NCL's midnight buffets include the always popular Chocoholic Extravaganza.

Pros

- **Sports.** NCL is a leader in this regard, and you can even watch a football game on ESPN International (on tape delay, assuming ESPN has broadcast rights) .
- **Activities.** From cha cha lessons to basketball, there's a wider range and a greater number of activities on NCL ships than on most.

Cons

- **Inconsistent service.** Across the board, service isn't always as sharp as it could be and often seems lackadaisical.
- **Unmemorable food.** Don't expect miracles in the food department. As long as you don't crave sophisticated cuisine, you'll be fine.

Frommer's Ratings: Norwegian Cruise Line

	Poor	Fair	Good	Excellent	Outstanding
Enjoyment Factor				✓	
Dining		✓			
Activities					✓
Children's Program			✓		
Entertainment				✓	
Service		✓			
Overall Value			✓		

THE NORWEGIAN WAY

Norwegian Cruise Line, which today prides itself on its sports and activities offerings and on its diverse fleet, was one of the pioneers of the North American cruise market. Its earliest roots go back to the now-defunct Kloster Cruises. In 1966, Knut Knutson, the Norwegian owner of Kloster, had a cruise ship but no marketing system, and Ted Arison, an Israeli, had a great North American marketing system but no ships. Together, they formed Norwegian Caribbean Line, launching 3- and 4-day cruises from Miami to the Bahamas. In 1972, Arison and his entourage split from the company to form Carnival Cruise Lines, now the giant of the industry.

Over the years that followed, NCL had its difficulties, financial and otherwise, but by 1997 the hardest times seemed to be past, and a major program of expansion and marketing was put in place. This included the "stretching" of three of its ships, including the *Norwegian Dream* (they were literally cut in two, and a new mid-section was inserted to increase capacity and add public space). NCL changed the name of almost all its ships to include the word "Norwegian," and started marketing itself as offering cruising "The Norwegian Way," making the most of its Norwegian heritage (which you'll be hard pressed to find any evidence of—it's more of a marketing ploy than anything based on reality).

In May, 1998, the line purchased Orient Lines and its 800-passenger M/V *Marco Polo*. The *Norwegian Crown* transfers to Orient Lines in April, and will offer cruises in Europe for that line (see Orient Lines section later in this chapter).

THE FLEET

For 2000, Norwegian has seven ships in its fleet, including the new 2,000-passenger *Norwegian Sky* launched in 1999, and plans to build more megaships. The ***Norwegian Dream*** is the line's only ship in Europe in 2000. The ship made headlines in late 1999 when it collided with a cargo vessel in the English Channel, but has since been repaired.

PASSENGER PROFILE

In Europe, NCL attracts an older crowd, with an average age of around 60. About 90% are from North America, and they tend to be more affluent than the line's crowd in the Caribbean and—as is true with American passengers on most European cruises—are more experienced: The majority have cruised before. The atmosphere aboard all NCL ships is informal and down-to-earth and well-suited to first-timer cruisers as well.

This is the cruise line for sports nuts who can't be without access to major sports events. But it's also a good choice for those looking for value who don't want to be on a big, brand-new megaship, but don't want to be on a budget ship either.

DINING

Cuisine is not Norwegian Cruise Line's strong suit, but there is a lot of choice. Meals in Europe include regional favorites, and that means the addition of Norwegian salmon, Schnitzel, and the like, along with your more standard prime rib. On the longer itineraries, the line features a different menu cycle, meaning no menus are repeated.

There is always a **light spa cuisine** choice as well as a **vegetarian entree** at lunch and dinner, and fresh fruit is often offered throughout the day. There are also **children's menus,** featuring the popular standards: burgers, hot dogs, spaghetti and meatballs, and ice cream sundaes.

Recent improvements have included greater emphasis on **alternative dining rooms.** All NCL ships have the reservations-only Le Bistro restaurants, which are smaller and more intimate than the main dining rooms and serve more gourmet fare, such as filet mignon, grilled salmon, mahimahi, and Caesar salad prepared at the table, and desserts

NCL Fleet Itineraries

Ship	Home Ports & Season	Itinerary
Norwegian Dream	12-day Scandinavia & Russia, round-trip from Dover (May–Aug); 14-day Med, Dover to Piraeus/Athens (Sept); 10-day Med, Istanbul to Barcelona (Nov); 10-day Black Sea, Athens and Istanbul (Sept, Oct).	**12-day Scandinavia & Russia:** Warnemünde (Germany), St. Petersburg (Russia), Helsinki (Finland), Stockholm (Sweden), Copenhagen (Denmark), and Oslo (Norway). **10- and 14-day Med:** Port calls may include La Coruña, Cadiz, Barcelona (Spain), Marseilles and Cannes (France), Livorno, Civitavecchia, Messina, Naples (Italy), and Santorini and Piraeus/Athens (Greece). **10-day Black Sea:** Port calls may include Mykonos, Rhodes, Santorini (Greece), Kusadasi and Dikili (Turkey), and Odessa and Yalta (Ukraine).*

*The ship also does Holy Lands itineraries from Athens and Istanbul.

like cherries jubilee, chocolate fondue, bananas Foster, and crepes Suzette. Be sure to make your reservations as soon as you get aboard. There's a suggested $5 tip.

NCL is also proud of its **midnight buffets,** which include, on the *Dream,* the always popular Chocoholic Extravaganza on each sailing. For sugar addicts, an ice-cream bar is open a few hours a day, in the afternoon you can enjoy **English high tea, a coffee bar** serves specialty coffees as well as other beverages, and there's a pizzeria. **Room service** is offered 24 hours a day.

Activities

Activities are one of the line's strongest points. You can take cha-cha lessons; play duplicate bridge, shuffleboard, or basketball; attend an art auction or spa or beauty demonstration; or listen to a band at the pool. There are galley and bridge tours, trapshooting, makeovers, talent shows, wine tasting, and trivia contests. In Europe, the line also offers an enrichment program with **guest lecturers** including university professors who present lectures on such topics as religion, ancient history, earth sciences, and astronomy. Some recent lectures have included Jewish Traditions in the First Century, Development of Christianity, Greek Civilization, The Earth's Wonders, Stone Mysteries Throughout the World, and The History of the Ukraine.

Children's Program

Although the program and playroom is not as well-stocked as those on many other lines, NCL has expanded its Kids Crew program to offer year-round **supervised activities** for children ages 3 to 17. The program divides children into four age groups: junior sailors, ages 3 to 5; first mates, ages 6 to 8; navigators, ages 9 to 12; and teens, ages 13 to 17. During the off-season, activities are offered for three age groups (3 to 5, 6 to 12, and 13 to 17 years). **Activities** may include sports competitions, dances, face painting, treasure hunts, magic shows, arts and crafts, cooking classes, and even a Circus at Sea, which provides an opportunity for the kids to learn circus acts, most of them humorous or magic (like card tricks) rather than the athletic variety, which they share with their parents in a performance towards the end of the cruise. Children get their own "Cruise News" detailing the day's events.

Group baby-sitting is offered for $4 per hour per child and $2 for each additional child. **Private, in-cabin baby-sitting** by a member of the crew is available from noon to 2am aboard all NCL's ships for $8 per hour for the first child and $2 per hour for each additional child.

Special Hotel Deal

Book your NCL Europe cruise at least 180 days in advance and you get two pre- or post-cruise nights in a first-class hotel for free.

Entertainment

NCL has found a nice balance between theme-related events and general entertainment that keeps everyone happy. In Europe, **local performers** come on board and in the past have included a Spanish flamenco group, a Portuguese folkloric troupe, and Irish dancers from the Cowhie-Ryan troupe, whose members have also been selected to perform in *Riverdance.*

The casino on the *Dream* is lively but small. There are several bars where you can slip away for a quiet rendezvous, and small tucked-away corners for more intimate entertainment, like **pianists** and **cabaret acts** that include comedy, magic, juggling, vocalists, ventriloquists, concert and classical pianists, and other instrumentalists (including the occasional banjo player). Live big-band and ballroom-style music for dancing is popular before or after the big **production shows,** which include "Crazy for You," "Sea Legs at Sea," and "On Broadway." These Vegas-style productions are expensive, lavish, and artistically ambitious.

Service

"Uneven" is the word that keeps cropping up to describe service aboard NCL vessels. However, some passengers, especially first-timers, find the service excellent. Generally, room service and bar service fleetwide are speedy and efficient, and cabin attendants win passenger approval.

If problems do occur, it's usually in the main dining rooms. The breakfast and lunch buffet restaurants often seem understaffed and hectic, especially if you're there at prime times.

The Norwegian officers are generally smooth and charming.

Norwegian Dream

Norwegian Dream (photo: NCL)

The Verdict

Despite its 1,748-passenger capacity, this ship doesn't feel like a megaship, though it offers most of the amenities and facilities of one.

Specifications

Size (in tons)	56,760	Officers	Norwegian
Number of Cabins	874	Crew	614 (International)
Number of Outside Cabins	716	Passenger/Crew Ratio	2.8 to 1
Cabins with Verandas	48	Year Built	1993
Number of Passengers	1,748	Last Major Refurbishment	1998

Frommer's Ratings (Scale of 1–5)

Cabin Comfort & Amenities	4	Pool, Fitness & Spa Facilities	4
Ship Cleanliness & Maintenance	4	Children's Facilities	3
Public Comfort/Space	3	Itineraries	4
Decor	4	Worth the Money	4

If your heart isn't dead set on a cruise aboard a brand-new megaship, you may find this modern mid-sized ship very appealing. It's a quality, moderate-cost ship known for its innovative designs (by Bjorn Storbatten, the Scandinavian designer who also designed the much more upscale Seabourn twins).

In 1998, both the *Dream* and its sister, the *Wind*, sailed into the Lloyd Werft shipyard in Bremerhaven, Germany, where they were "stretched" by grafting a 130-foot midsection into each, an operation that raised the ships' tonnage from 41,000 to 46,000 and increased their capacity from the 1,200-passenger range to over 1,700. Other improvements made possible by the stretch included the addition of a casual restaurant, another gift shop, lounges, a library, a card room, a cigar bar, and improved spas, health clubs, and children's facilities (designed to gain NCL additional market share in the families-with-children niche).

The design makes the *Dream* appear more spacious than it really is. Both forward and aft, the ship's upper decks cascade down in evenly spaced tiers, resulting in panoramic views both ahead and behind the moving ship. Walls of glass line the length of the vessel, and 85% of the contemporary cabins are outside. However, in an attempt to save money, low-grade materials were used in the passageways and stairways (and in the cabins too), so you know you're not on anything close to a luxury yacht (or even any Celebrity, Holland America, or Princess ship).

Cabins & Rates

Cabins	Per diems from	Bathtub	Fridge	Hair Dryer	Sitting Area	TV
Inside	$182	no	no	yes	no	yes
Outside	$200	no	no	yes	some	yes
Suite	$243	yes	yes	yes	yes	yes

CABINS The big draw is that nearly all cabins are outside, and about 80% of them have picture windows. Standard outside cabins measure 160 square feet, which is fairly roomy, but not large (Carnival's standard cabins, for instance, are 185 square feet). The inside cabins are small, ranging in size from 130 to 150 square feet.

The accommodations have a breezy, pastel-based decor evocative of the West Indies. Unfortunately, bathrooms are tiny and storage space is minimal. Two people can just barely manage, but when a third or fourth person shares a cabin, it can get truly cramped.

Most cabins have a separate sitting and sleeping area, but to accommodate this feature, the area around the beds was made smaller and now requires the grace of a dancer to negotiate without stubbing toes and banging knees. Most cabins have twin beds that can be converted to queen size, and cabins on the port side are for nonsmokers. Note that lifeboats block the views of the Category 4 cabins amidships on the Norway Deck, and early morning joggers might disturb late sleepers who have cabins on the Promenade Deck.

Suites are rather luxurious and decent-sized, with floor-to-ceiling windows and mini-fridges; many have private balconies. The dozen-plus Owner's Suites are the most dramatic, followed by penthouse suites with private balconies. The 10 Superior Deluxe Penthouse suites amidships on Norway Deck have partially obstructed views because of the overhang from the restaurant above. Avoid them.

All cabins have TVs showing ESPN and CNN. Nearly a dozen cabins are wheelchair accessible, and an additional dozen or so are equipped with doorbell/phone/emergency alert lights and vibrating alarm clocks for those with hearing impairments, an innovation aboard cruise ships.

PUBLIC AREAS The ship has a tiered design, making for roomier lower-level public areas, generous amounts of deck space on upper levels, and good passenger flow.

The ship has three dining rooms offering two seatings, as well as Le Bistro, an alternative restaurant. The Terraces is the most cozy and attractive of the dining rooms, rising three levels and evoking a supper club in a 1930s movie.

The casino is of the glitzy variety, but is on the small side. Lucky's Bar and the Dazzles disco on the Star Deck see the most late-night action. The sports bar, with its giant big-screen TVs, is the most popular bar on the ship (light meals are also served here).

POOL, FITNESS & SPA FACILITIES The Pool Deck is gorgeous, with dark wood and crisp blue-and-white striped canvas umbrellas making you feel like you're at some stylish beach resort on the French Riviera. The ship has two hot tubs and two pools, the more theatrical of which is on the International Deck, where semicircular rows of chaise lounges and deck chairs surround a small and almost purely decorative keyhole-shaped pool at the ships' stern. The view—whether of the ocean or of your fellow passengers—is panoramic. A larger pool lies two decks above on the Sun Deck. A great pool bar allows you to sip a drink while bobbing happily in the shallow pool.

The 24-hour fitness center is equipped with state-of-the-art exercise equipment. Aerobics and exercise classes are part of the activity-filled agenda, and a small spa offers massages and a sauna along with a whirlpool. On the Sports Deck, there are also Ping-Pong tables and a golf-driving range, while upstairs on the Sky Deck are a jogging track and basketball/volleyball court.

Orient Lines

SHIPS IN EUROPE Crown Odyssey • Marco Polo

1510 S.E. 17th St., Ste. 400, Fort Lauderdale, FL 33316. ☎ **800/333-7300** or 954/727-6660. Fax 954/527-6657. www.orientlines.com. E-mail: info@orientlines.com.

THE LINE IN A NUTSHELL A good-valued cruisetour is Orient Lines' great strength, pairing a cruise and land tour to make a more in-depth travel experience that includes air, hotel, some meals ashore, sightseeing, and transfers.

THE EXPERIENCE Orient Lines has traditionally catered to an English-speaking clientele looking for a classically styled ship, serious destinations, better-than-average food, and a fair price. Orient Lines' demographic is 50 and up, sometimes way up, though in Europe you can count on the shorter Mediterranean itineraries to attract a younger crowd than the longer Northern European cruises. Passengers on these northern trips are more likely to be experienced cruisers, and the line has also been successful in attracting British and Australian passengers along with the majority of Americans.

The *Marco Polo* has an interesting history: It was built 35 years ago and sailed as the transatlantic liner *Aleksander Pushkin,* but in the early 1990s was completely rebuilt from the ice-strengthened hull and engines up and is now a sturdy and graceful cruise liner, both modern and traditional—it's a young ship, yet able to boast the graceful profile of a classic liner. The newly acquired *Crown Odyssey* was built in 1988 and offers a roomier onboard atmosphere and only a slightly larger passenger capacity, with a more contemporary ambiance. A cruise aboard either is social and fairly low-key, without the glitz typical of much larger ships or the pulsating round of activities. The ships perform destination-oriented cruises concentrating on the ports and well-run shore excursions.

Pros

- **Great cruisetour packages.** It is easy to plan a longer vacation by combining land extensions either side of the cruise.
- **Service-oriented staff.** The ship's Filipino crew aims to please.
- **The price is right.** Orient Lines has been a value-oriented company since its inception.
- **Expanding itineraries.** For past passengers there are now additional itineraries in northern Europe and creative positioning voyages between the Mediterranean and Scandinavia thanks to the addition of the *Crown Odyssey.*

Cons

- **Very limited room service.** Continental breakfast is the only in-cabin food service openly promoted.
- **Some design quirks.** The *Marco Polo's* show lounge is awkwardly arranged, and viewing can be limited.

Frommer's Ratings: Orient Lines

	Poor	Fair	Good	Excellent	Outstanding
Enjoyment Factor					✓
Dining				✓	
Activities				✓	
Children's Program	N/A				
Entertainment			✓		
Service				✓	
Overall Value					✓

ORIENT LINES: DESTINATION-ORIENTED & A GOOD VALUE

The company got its start in 1991 when Gerry Herrod, an English entrepreneur, bought the former 1965-built Soviet liner *Alexandr Pushkin* and had it completely rebuilt as the *Marco Polo* in a Greek shipyard for long cruises to exotic parts of the world. Some years before, Herrod had started Ocean Cruise Lines, operating worldwide itineraries with small second-hand ships catering to the British, American, and Australian markets, and attracting passengers who wanted something more than a party cruise. He later sold that operation and took a hiatus before starting Orient Lines with much the same thrust, only this time, aboard a larger ship, the *Marco Polo.* Like before, most of the passengers were older and generally experienced cruisers, though the start of short Mediterranean cruise tours has broadened the base. In 1998, Herrod sold the one-ship fleet to Norwegian Cruise Line, a company looking to expand its cruising range, and soon after NCL announced that they would expand the Orient Lines' fleet and keep it a separate brand. The new ship, the *Norwegian Crown,* will be transferred in May 2000.

THE FLEET

The ***Marco Polo,*** with its black hull, pronounced sheer, and traditional lines, has a graceful ocean liner look and is one of the most handsome ships afloat today. Because she appears to reflect the past, many think she is an old ship but in fact everything but the ice-strengthened hull and engines date from the early 1990s. In today's growing fleets of megaships with lengthy passenger lists, the 850-passenger *Marco Polo* provides one of a dwindling number of mid-size ship experiences, one that is neither a high-priced all-suite vessel, nor a pulsating city at sea. While touted as an elegant liner with art deco flourishes, she is actually rather simple in decor and for some lacks a distinctive character. The outer decks are pure ocean liner style, and she is a delight to explore from stem to stern.

Her new partner is the larger, 1,050-passenger ***Crown Odyssey,*** originally built in 1988 for Royal Cruise Line, a Greek company based in California. The ship was once the pride of the Greek merchant marine until the company was sold and the fleet disbanded. With a name change to *Norwegian Crown* under the Norwegian Cruise Line banner, few changes were made to her post-war art deco style that features wood paneling, brass, smoked glass, mirrors, and chrome. Built for longer voyages, the ship has reverted to her original name of *Crown Odyssey* and her hull will get a handsome black paint job, becoming a fitting partner to the *Marco Polo.*

PASSENGER PROFILE

The shorter Mediterranean itineraries should attract the youngest passenger list, and the Northern European and positioning cruises an older crowd. Orient Lines' demographic is 50 and up, sometimes way up. Most passengers on these northern trips are more likely to be experienced cruisers, and the line has also been successful in attracting British and Australian passengers along with the majority of Americans. Repeaters are a major chunk of Orient's business, and that should continue with a new ship and a new summer program outside the Mediterranean.

DINING

Meals are at two sittings, and the festive atmosphere and low ceilings unfortunately make for a noisy room. On the bright side, dinner offers four main courses, which range along the lines of Surf & Turf (grilled tenderloin and baby rock lobster), honey-roasted Long Island duck, New Zealand lamb, and pan-fried snapper. **Vegetarian and health-oriented choices** are also available, and preparation and presentation are uniformly good, portions are sensible, and the Filipino stewards provide friendly, helpful service.

Orient Lines Fleet Itineraries

Ship	Home Ports & Season	Itinerary
Crown Odyssey	6-day Greek Isles, Piraeus/ Athens, Istanbul (May–Oct); 6- to 14-day Med, Barcelona, Istanbul, Vicitavecchia/ Rome, Piraeus/Athens (May–Oct); 8-day Black Sea, Istanbul (Aug).	**6-day Greek Isles*:** Delos/Mykonos, Santorini, Rhodes (Greece), and Kusadasi (Turkey). **6- to 8-day Med*:** Port calls may include Monte Carlo (Monaco), Civitavecchia/Rome, Sorrento, Livorno, Portofino (Italy), Cannes(France), Valletta (Malta), Mallorca (Spain), Santorini (Greece). **14-day Med*:** Visits all of the above. **8-day Black Sea:** Nesebur (Bulgaria), Odessa and Yalta (Ukraine), Kusadasi (Turkey), and Delos and Mykonos (Greece).**
Marco Polo	6- and 9-day Greek Isles, Piraeus/Athens and Venice (Apr–Oct); 6-day W. Med, Barcelona and Civitavecchia/ Rome (May–Sept); 8- to 17-day Med, Istanbul, Barcelona, Venice (Apr–Oct); 8-day Scandinavia & Russia, Copenhagen (May–Aug); 7- to 12-day Norway, Copenhagen (June–Aug); 14- to 16-day Europe Capitals, Civitavecchia/Rome and Copenhagen (May, Sept).	**6-day Greek Isles*/**:** Port calls may include Delos/ Mykonos, Santorini, Piraeus/Athens, Rhodes (Greece), Dubrovnik (Croatia), and Kuasadasi (Turkey). **6-day W. Med*:** Livorno and Portofino (Italy), Cannes (France), and Palma de Mallorca (Spain). **8 to 17-day Med*:** Port calls may include Monte Carlo (Monaco), Livorno, Civitavecchia/Rome, Sorrento (Italy), Corfu, Santorini, Delos/Mykonos (Greece), Dubovnik (Croatia), and Kusadasi (Turkey). **8-day Scandinavia & Russia*:** Stockholm (Sweden), Helsinki (Finland), St. Petersburg (Russia), Tallinn (Estonia). **7 to 12-day Norway*:** Port calls may include Flam, Gudvangen, Hellesylt, Geiranger, Bergen, Gravdal, Honningsvag, Alta, Tromso, Oslo (Norway), and Aarhus (Denmark). **13 to 15-day Europe Capitals*:** Port calls may include Cannes, Le Havre, La Rochelle (France), Barcelona (Spain), Lisbon (Portugal), Dover (England), Amsterdam (Holland), Hamburg (Germany), and Gibraltar.**

*Sold as part of a cruisetour packaged with three to nine hotel nights.
**Also does Holy Lands itineraries.

Wines are very reasonably priced, and the list encompasses far-reaching parts of the world from California to France and Chile.

Raffles, on the *Marco Polo*, located forward of the pool, serves enticing and varied breakfast and luncheons. It is especially well run, and on selected nights, it becomes a tranquil, candlelit, reservations-only restaurant with an Italian, Spanish, French, or Greek menu for a $15 charge including gratuities and wine. The outdoor grill turns out kebabs, hamburgers, and hot dogs, and machines dispense ice cream, coffee, and tea. Well over half dress on formal nights. The *Marco Polo's* Palm Court fills up quickly for a substantial afternoon tea service on days when the bulk of the passengers are not ashore. The *Crown Odyssey* will have a similar alternative restaurant when she joins the fleet in May 2000.

ACTIVITIES

The European itineraries are destination-oriented so daytime activities are fewer than on the longer cruises elsewhere. The *Marco Polo* has a smallish outdoor pool aft with a poolside bar and barbecue. Three decks above, a trio of hot tubs, with great views over the stern, is a popular meeting ground at sailing time. There are Ping-Pong, shuffleboard, bingo, and cooking demonstrations (the line prides itself on its cuisine). The card room tends to be a busy place, attracting lots of bridge players.

Children's Programs

There are no special facilities on this ship, and the line has historically carried very few children.

Entertainment

Big-time shows and revues are not a feature of the line; instead, the Ambassador Show Lounge stages more low-key performances like cabaret acts, classical concerts, the Filipino crew show, and some local entertainment brought aboard in way ports. The lounge is one gently sloping level with poor sight lines. Further, it can get crowded because of the tightly packed banquettes and moveable seating and structural columns. The Polo Lounge is a delightful setting with a pianist playing before meals and in the evening, and is a pleasant option for those not taking in the show. The small casino offers blackjack, roulette, slots, and video poker machines. Later at night, the cruise staff and passengers (usually not too many) gather in the Charleston Club for the disco and late-night carousing.

Service

The *Marco Polo* is very service-oriented in the restaurants and bars, but room service is pretty much limited to continental breakfast. Overall, the line has a loyal, hardworking staff, some who have been around since the line opened for business.

Crown Odyssey

Crown Odyssey (photo: Orient Lines)

The Verdict

The *Crown Odyssey* has a roomier onboard atmosphere and only a slightly larger passenger capacity than the *Marco Polo.*

Specifications

Size	34,242	Officers	Scandinavian/
Number of Cabins	526		European
Number of Outside Cabins	412	Crew	470 (Filipino)
Cabins with Verandas	16	Passenger/Crew Ratio	2.24 to 1
Number of Passengers	1,052	Year Built	1988
		Last Major Refurbishment	1999

Frommer's Ratings (Scale of 1–5)*

Cabin Comfort & Amenities	N/A	Pool, Fitness & Spa Facilities	N/A
Ship Cleanliness & Maintenance	N/A	Children's Facilities	N/A
Public Comfort/Space	N/A	Itineraries	N/A
Decor	N/A	Worth the Money	N/A

*As the *Crown Odyssey* had not yet been taken over by Orient Lines at press time, ratings are not yet possible.

At press time, this 34,242-ton ship was slated to be transferred from Norwegian Cruise Line to Orient Lines, , so while she had a good reputation under NCL as the *Norwegian Crown* (and an even better one with Royal Cruise Line as their flagship), she has not been tested in her present role. All commentary below describes the ship as she sailed with NCL.

Cabins & Rates*

Cabins	Per diems from	Bathtub	Fridge	Hair Dryer	Sitting Area	TV
Inside	$129	some	no	no	no	yes
Outside	$172	some	no	no	some	yes
Suite	$232	yes	yes	yes	yes	yes

**All rates include hotel stay, some sightseeing, and transfers.*

CABINS The 526 wood-trimmed cabins are larger than the *Marco Polo's* (standard cabins are 165 square feet), and come with TV, hairdryer, safe, phone, and spacious closets. Many cabins have bathtubs, though some are not full size. There are many configurations, especially at the higher levels, with differing cabin layouts, window arrangements, and verandas. Suites come in six levels. The 12 owner's suites (the top level) have floor-to-ceiling windows, a living room, veranda, VCR, walk-in closet, refrigerator, marble bath, and whirlpool tub. Some can be connected with superior deluxe penthouse suites to provide more than 1,000 square feet of space (which is apartment-sized). Some intriguing rooms have bay windows allowing a view fore and aft as well as directly out to sea.

PUBLIC AREAS The range of public rooms, which all boast lots of light, marble, and glass, is extensive. Like on the *Marco Polo*, most public rooms occupy one full deck. The main show lounge has steeply sloped seating for good views, a much better design than aboard the *Marco Polo*. The Top of the Crown lounge is a wraparound disco at night, and a quiet observation lounge with views in three directions during the day. The card room offers lots of tables, but the library is small and has very limited shelf space. The line plans to redesign the Bistro before it debuts to match the one aboard the *Marco Polo*, offering buffet dining at breakfast and lunch and intimate candlelight dinners. The main dining room, with two sittings, is arranged on two levels with a stained-glass raised ceiling in the central portion. Because of its hard stainless steel and glass surfaces, it's as noisy as that aboard the *Marco Polo*.

POOL, FITNESS & SPA FACILITIES The ship has a very good Roman Spa with a columned indoor pool that harks back to the ocean liner era. The facilities include a mirrored gym, separate men's and women's sauna and massage, two whirlpools, and a full-service beauty salon. In addition, there is an outdoor pool, and a splash pool and two whirlpools all the way aft.

Marco Polo

The Verdict

The *Marco Polo* is a comfortable ship that is well-suited to both longer itineraries and shorter, port-intensive cruises.

Marco Polo (photo: Orient Line)

Specifications

Size (in tons)	22,080	Officers	Scandinavian/
Number of Cabins	425		European
Number of Outside Cabins	294	Crew	350 (Filipino)
Cabins with Verandas	None	Passenger/Crew Ratio	2.43 to 1
Number of Passengers	850	Year Built	1993
		Last Major Refurbishment	1993

Frommer's Ratings (Scale of 1–5)

Cabin Comfort & Amenities	3	Pool, Fitness & Spa Facilities	4
Ship Cleanliness & Maintenance	4	Children's Facilities	N/A
Public Comfort/Space	3	Itineraries	5
Decor	3	Worth the Money	4

The *Marco Polo,* a former transatlantic liner, was completely rebuilt from the hull and engines up in the early '90s and is now a sturdy and graceful cruise liner, both modern and traditional. She has been Orient Lines' only ship since the line started up in 1993, calling on a vast repertoire of far-flung ports on seven continents. Now, with the addition of the *Crown Odyssey,* the ships can do an even greater variety of European itineraries beyond the Mediterranean.

Cabins & Rates*

Cabins	Per diems from	Bathtub	Fridge	Hair Dryer	Sitting Area	TV
Inside	$181	no	no	yes	no	yes
Outside	$245	some	no	yes	some	yes
Suite	$380	yes	yes	yes	yes	yes

**All rates include hotel stay, some sightseeing, and transfers.*

CABINS The 425 cabins (294 outside) are mostly average-size, twin-bedded staterooms ranging between 115 and 158 square feet, with light wood trim, TVs, three-channel radios, phones, good storage, and hair dryers. Higher-category staterooms and junior and deluxe suites have tubs. The cabins are found on all passenger decks apart from Belvedere, the level for the public rooms.

PUBLIC AREAS The forward Ambassador Lounge spotlights after-dinner shows, large parties, and lectures, but seating is tight, and sight lines are poor. The cheerful piano bar, running the full width of the ship, draws passengers for cocktails and bingo. Tea is served in the Palm Court, and the tiny bar there is a snug hideaway. The casino offers blackjack, roulette, and slot machines; and a card room, good library with limited hours, and two boutiques share an adjacent area. Aft of the buffet is an open and partly covered deck, a favorite gathering place at the end of a day ashore. One deck up is a disco, and above that are the well-equipped health club and the beauty salon. The cluster of three hot tubs looks over tiered decks aft, and below are several quiet areas to enjoy a snooze or a good book from the comfort of a deck chair. Handsome wooden deck chairs line wide teak promenades, and the Upper Deck has a wraparound walking track. Because of narrow side sections, however, most walkers prefer to stroll the promenade below.

POOL, FITNESS & SPA FACILITIES Besides the outdoor pool and three hot tubs, there is a mirrored aft-facing fitness center and spa two decks above the Lido, offering aerobics and t'ai chi classes. Fitness equipment includes rowing machines, stationary bikes, treadmills, and weight machines, and Steiner of London provides the spa's beauty treatments, facials, hydrotherapy, and massage. The layout of the decks is not conducive to unobstructed wraparound walking or jogging because of some extremely narrow sections on one level and a wide but not continuous path on the other.

Princess Cruises

SHIPS IN EUROPE Crown Princess • Grand Princess • Royal Princess

10100 Santa Monica Blvd., Los Angeles, CA 90067-4189. ☎ **800/421-0522** or 310/553-1770. Fax 310/284-2845. www.princesscruises.com.

THE LINE IN A NUTSHELL These lovely ships offer a cruise experience that's both glamorous and fun, whether it's aboard a classic ship or the line's newer huge floating resorts.

THE EXPERIENCE Owned by British firm Peninsular Oriental Steam and Navigation Company (also known as P&O), Princess achieved worldwide fame as the line portrayed in the TV series *The Love Boat.* It's a company that strives, quite successfully, to please a wide variety of passengers. It offers more choices in terms of accommodations, dining, and entertainment than nearly any other line.

The line's ships in Europe for 2000 are diverse. The *Royal Princess,* the oldest of the ships, was built in 1984 and christened by Princess Di, whose portrait hangs prominently on board. The ship was cutting-edge when built, with more veranda cabins than the industry had seen up to that time. Today it's a bit dated looking, but is still an appealing ship. The *Crown Princess* is a modern, futuristic-looking vessel with intimate indoor spaces. The *Grand Princess* is grand indeed—the second-largest passenger ship in the world, it manages to offer both massive, dramatic spaces out on deck (particularly in the stern) and remarkably cozy lounges, restaurants, and bars.

Overall, the Princess ships are one notch above mainstream competitors like Royal Caribbean. But they are not luxury vessels. They offer a consistent product, and serve the middle ground of the market in a very consistent manner. You get a well-functioning, semiformal product delivered on a large (and in the case of the *Grand Princess,* massive) scale, and a good value for your vacation dollar.

Pros

- **Verandas.** The Princess ships have a lot of them.
- **Lots of dining choices.** All the ships offer 24-hour casual dining, pizza, and 24-hour room service, and the *Grand Princess* also has three main dining rooms, two intimate alternative dining restaurants, and a Häagen-Dazs ice-cream parlor.

Cons

- **No free ice cream.** It may sound petty, but it's irritating that Princess sells only Häagen-Dazs ice cream—at $1.90 a scoop and $3.75 for a sundae—in lieu of the free frozen yogurt and soft ice cream most all other lines offer from self-serve machines in the Lido restaurant all day, or at least for a few hours each afternoon. (Princess serves the free stuff only in the dining room at mealtime.)

Frommer's Ratings: Princess Cruises

	Poor	Fair	Good	Excellent	Outstanding
Enjoyment Factor					✓
Dining			✓		
Activities				✓	
Children's Program				✓	
Entertainment				✓	
Service				✓	
Overall Value				✓	

PRINCESS: THE LUVVVVV BOATS

Few other cruise lines have managed to start so small and grow so rapidly in such a short time, starting as an obscure West Coast cruise outfit and growing into the hyper-modern upper-middle-class giant it is today.

Princess Cruises originated in 1962, when the company's founder, Stanley McDonald, chartered the long-gone *Princess Patricia* as a floating hotel for the Seattle World's Fair. He then continued to charter ships for cruises between Los Angeles, Alaska, and the Pacific coast of Mexico. Soon after, two additional ships, one of them brand-new, were leased from Costa Cruises to meet demand. In 1974, the company was snapped up by British shipping giant P&O Group, which has intensified its efforts to promote Princess vessels and Caribbean itineraries in markets on both sides of the Atlantic.

In the late 1970s, Princess benefited enormously by associating itself and its ships, *Island Princess* and *Pacific Princess,* with the multimillion-dollar Aaron Spelling TV series ***The Love Boat*** with its story lines of love on the high seas. The series helped Princess, and the cruise industry in general, shed what was mostly a white-gloved-old-lady image. The series created a flood of paying customers, and Princess made the most of the exposure by signing on actor Gavin MacLeod (Capt. Merrill Stubing) as its pitchman and adopting "The Love Boat" as its official nickname.

Even to this day, you'll still hear the theme song from the show ("the Luvvvvv Boat") played over the loud speakers as passengers embark.

THE FLEET

Princess has a diverse fleet of 10 ships. It has its largest ship in Europe this year, the 109,000-ton ***Grand Princess,*** as well as the ***Crown Princess,*** a near-mega ship, and the smaller ***Royal Princess.*** The *Royal Princess*, the older of the ships, was considered quite cutting edge when it was built in 1984, introducing more cabins with verandas than the industry had seen up to that time. The futuristic-looking *Crown* and its twin sister, *Regal Princess*, were on order for Sitmar when Princess parent P&O acquired that company in the late 1980s.

In May 1998, Princess made giant waves throughout the travel industry with the launching of what was to date the largest cruise ship in the world, the *Grand Princess.* Two sisters to the *Grand Princess* are in the works and scheduled to enter service in the spring and fall of 2001.

In addition to the ships profiled in this review, the *Pacific Princess*—one of the original Love Boats—offers 12- and 14-day Holy Land cruises from Athens that include Israel and Egypt, sailing in April, November, and December.

PASSENGER PROFILE

In the past, most Princess passengers were middle-aged middle Americans, but the new megas, including the *Grand Princess,* are attracting younger, more active 30- and 40-something cruisers and honeymooners. The *Grand Princess* has extensive kids' facilities, making it ideal for families (including several generations traveling together). The *Grand Princess* is also attracting love birds with its wedding chapel, and its captain is the only one conducting official marriage ceremonies at sea every week.

All the ships strike a nice balance between formal and informal. They draw a relatively affluent but not overly wealthy crowd that appreciates the traditional cruise experience, as well as a dose of bells and whistles.

DINING

The *Grand Princess* offers the most dining options, including three main dining rooms; two reservations-required alternative restaurants (Mexican and Italian) that have a $3.50

Getting Married at Sea

Talk about the Love Boat: Aboard the *Grand Princess,* the captain can actually marry you in a charming wedding chapel adorned with fresh flower arrangements (there are two full-time florists on board), ribbons strung along the aisle, and stained glass. There's seating for a few dozen friends and family members, and assistant pursers, decked out in their handsome dress blues, are available to escort a bride down the mini-aisle. Three different ceremony packages are offered, ranging from $1,400 to $2,400 per couple and including photography, video, music, and salon treatments for the bride. And if you've got friends and family on board, reception packages start at $70 per person, and include hors d'oeuvres, champagne, and wedding cake.

cover charge; and a Häagen-Daz ice-cream parlor (selling its sweet treats for several dollars a pop).

All the ships in Europe have 24-hour casual dining (in the Lido restaurant), pizzerias, and 24-hour room service; and the *Crown Princess* and *Grand Princess* also have outdoor grills, patisseries and wine and caviar bars.

Princess's food is on par with that of competitor Holland America, though not as good as that of competitor Celebrity. Some of the food is, frankly, mediocre; but you'll occasionally get a dish that really makes you smile. The pastas are usually the best bet.

The dining rooms offer two seatings, and are open for breakfast, lunch, and dinner. The menus include a choice of four or five entrees, featuring halibut with saffron mayonnaise, broiled lobster tail, royal pheasant in pan juices, beef Wellington, plus a pasta dish like ravioli con salsa di funghi porcini (pasta squares filled with meat in a creamy mushroom sauce). There's also always **"healthy" choices** and **vegetarian options.**

A touch I really like: On request, a bowl of fresh fruit will be delivered to your cabin.

Activities

The line that wants to be all things to all people is expert at programming activities to please a wide range of tastes. In Europe, the *Grand Princess* offers the most elaborate and extensive repertoire, and the *Crown Princess* and *Royal Princess* are much more sedate.

Activities include your typical shuffleboard and bridge tournaments, lectures, games like Passenger Feud, art auctions, and exercise classes.

The *Grand Princess* also offers golf via virtual-reality simulators, basketball and volleyball, a sprawling and well-stocked virtual-reality game room (including a motion-simulator ride), and a **9-hole miniature golf course.** And of course, you can always relax on deck or in your cabin (where you can watch *Love Boat* reruns).

If you participate in aerobics classes or other sports activities, you receive chits you can cash in for prizes, like water bottles and T-shirts, at the end of your cruise.

Princess devotes a lot of attention and space to its onboard libraries. And the ships all have movie theatres offering first-run movies.

Children's Program

Supervised activities are offered for ages 2 to 17, and are divided into two groups: "Princess Pelicans," ages 2 to 12, and teens, ages 13 to 17. The *Grand Princess* has a spacious **children's playroom** and a sizable area of fenced-in outside deck dedicated for kids only, with a shallow pool and tricycles. **Teen centers** have computers, video games, and a sound system (and the one on the *Grand Princess* even has a teen's hot tub and

Princess Fleet Itineraries*

Ship	Home Ports & Season	Itinerary
Crown Princess	10-day Scandinavia & Russia, round-trip from Copenhagen (May–July); 12-day Europe Capitals, Civitavecchia/Rome to Copenhagen (May).	**10-day Scandinavia & Russia:** Port calls may include Stockholm (Sweden), Helsinki (Finland), St. Petersburg (Russia), Tallinn (Estonia), Gdansk (Poland), Oslo (Norway), and Warnemunde (Germany). **12-day Europe Capitals:** Monte Carlo (Monaco) Barcelona and Vigo (Spain), Lisbon (Portugal), Le Havre (France), Dover (England), Amsterdam (Holland), and Gibraltar.
Grand Princess	Barcelona and Istanbul, June–Sept.	**12-day Med:** Monte Carlo (Monaco), Livorno, Naples, Venice (Italy), Piraeus/Athens (Greece), and Kusadasi (Turkey).
Royal Princess	12-day Med, Barcelona to Lisbon (Apr), Lisbon to Istanbul (May); 12-day E. Med, Istanbul to Rome (May); 12-day Med, Rome to Dover (June); 12-day Norway and 12-day Europe Capitals, round-trip from Dover (June, July); 12-day Med, Dover to Rome, Rome to Lisbon, and Lisbon to Istanbul (Sept); 12-day Black Sea, Istanbul to Venice (Oct); 12-day E. Med, Venice to Rome (Oct).	**12-day Med:** Port calls may include Valletta (Malta), Taormina, Sorrento, Civitavecchia/Rome, Livorno (Italy), Monte Carlo (Monaco), Casablanca (Morroco), Barcelona, Cadiz, Vigo (Spain), Lisbon (Portugal), Le Havre (France), Olympia, Piraeus/Athens, Santorini (Greece), Kusadasi (Turkey), and Gibraltar. **12-day E. Med:** Port calls may include Kusadasi and Istanbul (Turkey), Santorini and Piraeus/Athens (Greece), Dubrovnik (Croatia), and Venice, Taormina, Sorrento (Italy). **12-day Black Sea:** Varna (Bulgaria), Odessa and Yalta (Ukraine), Kusadasi (Turkey), and Santorini, Piraeus/Athens, Katakolon (Greece). **12-day British Isles:** Plymouth (England), Waterford and Dublin (Ireland), Hollyhead (Wales), Glasgow and Invergordon (Scotland), and Le Havre (France). **12-day Europe Capitals:** Port calls may include Bilbao (Spain), Bordeaux (France), Glasgow and Rosyth (Scotland), Dublin and Cork (Ireland), Plymouth (England), Le Havre (France), Zeebrugge and Antwerp (Belgium), Amsterdam (Holland), Oslo (Norway), Copenhagen (Denmark), and Hamburg (Germany). **12-day Norway:** Vik, Flam, Gravdal, Tromso, Honningsvag, Trondheim, Hellesylt, Geiranger, and Bergen (Norway).

*The *Pacific Princess* also does Holy Land itineraries from Rome, Istanbul, and Piraeus/Athens.

private sunbathing deck). The *Grand Princess* is clearly the top choice in Europe for families.

While in dry dock in early 1999, Princess added a playroom and teen center to the *Crown,* and there's also a children's program offered year-round. The *Royal Princess,* on the other hand, does not have a dedicated children's playroom and only offers activities when there are 15 or more kids on board.

Kids' activities include karaoke, movies, tours of the galley and bridge, scavenger hunts, arts and crafts, coloring contests, and teenage versions of *The Dating Game.*

In late 1998, Princess lowered its minimum age requirement to 6 months; previously a child had to be at least a year old to sail. Princess does not offer private in-cabin baby-sitting at all, but does provide **slumber-party-style group baby-sitting** in the playroom for $4 an hour (10pm to 1am nightly, and 9am to 5pm when in port).

ENTERTAINMENT

There's a lot going on, and the quality of the overall package ranks way up there. From glittering, well-conceived, and well-executed **Vegas-style production shows** to New

York cabaret singers on the main stage; from a wonderfully entertaining **cabaret piano/ vocalist** in the Atrium Lounge (a throwaway space for many ships) to a rocking disco, this line offers a terrific blend of musical delights, and you'll always find a cozy spot where some soft piano or jazz music is being performed. Hypnotists, puppeteers, and comedians are also part of the act. The Princess **casinos** are sprawling and exciting places, too, and are bound to keep gamblers happy for hours (or until the cash runs out).

SERVICE

Overall, service is efficient and lines miraculously aren't much of a problem (even on the *Grand Princess*). Staff and crew are friendly, well-intentioned, and generally good. (I've seen waiters deal with even the rudest of guests in an even manner.) Suites and minisuites on the *Grand Princess* come with butler service. And every cabin on all the ships gets turndown service, including chocolates, at night.

The ships offer **laundry** and **dry cleaning** services, and have their own **self-service Laundromats.**

Crown Princess

Crown Princess (photo: Princess)

The Verdict

In spite of its cramped outdoor deck space, most people will find the *Crown*'s exterior and interior design appealing, and the ship an overall winner.

Specifications

Size (in tons)	70,000	Officers	Italian
Number of Cabins	795	Crew	696 (International)
Number of Outside Cabins	624	Passenger/Crew Ratio	2.3 to 1
Cabins with Verandas	184	Year Built	1991
Number of Passengers	1,590	Last Major Refurbishment	1999

Frommer's Ratings (Scale of 1–5)

Cabin Comfort & Amenities	4	Pool, Fitness & Spa Facilities	3
Ship Cleanliness & Maintenance	4	Children's Facilities	3
Public Comfort/Space	4	Itineraries	4
Decor	4	Worth the Money	4

Between 1991 and 1995, the *Crown Princess,* along with its identical twin, the *Regal Princess,* were the company's most modern, most dramatic, and most frequently photographed vessels. Their designer, Renzo Piano, is also responsible for such high-profile designs as Paris's Pompidou Center. To create the ships, he worked from "the silhouette of a dolphin." The result was a cutting-edge exterior design that some people like and others find just downright weird.

Inside, the ship is warm and inviting, although the layout is somewhat disjointed, and boasts a multimillion-dollar art collection as well as all the amenities one would expect, including 24-hour casual dining in the Café del Sol, a good choice of bars, a coffee and pastry cafe, a wine and caviar bar, a pizzeria, cushy seating areas (including in the lobby), a decent casino, and a variety of shopping options.

The vessel's outdoor deck space is a disappointment because there's not enough of it. This means congestion at deck buffets and around swimming pools whenever the ship is full. There's also no uninterrupted Promenade Deck around the periphery of the ship, so for a bit of exercise you'll have to walk back and forth along the ship's sides or get on a treadmill in the gym.

Cabins & Rates

Cabins	Per diems from	Bathtub	Fridge	Hair Dryer	Sitting Area	TV
Inside	$203	no	yes	yes	no	yes
Outside	$222	no	yes	yes	no	yes
Suite	$345	yes	yes	yes	yes	yes

CABINS Of 795 total, 624 are outside cabins, and many have private verandas; in fact, two whole decks of cabins have them.

Standard cabins are quite spacious at 190 square feet to 210 square feet, and suites with balconies are 587 square feet (including veranda). Decor includes comfortably upholstered chairs and sofas, framed artwork, and rectangular windows for easy wave-gazing. Bathrooms are compact but comfortable.

If you're booking a standard cabin, opt for one of the four classified as category GG on the Plaza Deck, if they're available. These outside doubles with queen-sized beds are the ship's most convenient and the best of the standard lot. Note that views from some cabins on the Dolphin Deck are partially obstructed by lifeboats.

The lowest priced outside cabins are category G on the Fiesta Deck, which have bunk beds and round portholes. These cabins are good buys, especially for budget-minded friends or families traveling together.

All cabins have safes, terry-cloth robes for use during the cruise, and TVs broadcasting CNN, ESPN, Nickelodeon, BBC programming, and TNT.

About 10 cabins are wheelchair accessible.

PUBLIC AREAS The elegant interiors, studded with artwork (and lots of pillars that wind up obstructing the flow of the rooms), feel as much like a hotel as a ship.

The three-story Plaza Atrium is an oval-shaped area with a reception desk, patisserie, wine and caviar bar, and shops. The overall effect is refined elegance. The Crown Court dining room boasts two-level terracing, and there's also a two-level show lounge for nightly Vegas-style entertainment. Amidships is Kipling's, an attractive bar with a British theme. If you'd like to escape the hordes, though, seek out the relative calm and soothing premises of the Intermezzo Bar.

The forward dome on top was meant to be the observation lounge, but it was found to be far too big for that purpose, and was converted into the ship's casino and a bar. You can still use the space to view the passing scenery (an observation area is separated from the rest of the room via a glass partition) but don't expect much peace or serenity while you're doing it (unless you find jangling slots and ringing bells soothing). A better place to catch the views is on the Promenade Deck or Lido Deck aft.

POOL, FITNESS & SPA FACILITIES There are two pools on the Lido Deck, one with a waterfall and in-pool bar, and two whirlpools. There's shuffleboard, Ping-Pong, a half basketball court, and a jogging track.

The health club/spa is located very low in the ship, so there are no ocean views. But it is well-equipped and well-maintained. The spa offers massage and treatment rooms, as well as steam rooms, saunas, and a tiny beauty salon.

Grand Princess

Grand Princess (photo: Princess)

The Verdict

This smart ship is one of the biggest in the world, but somehow manages to feel uncrowded, and even cozy. Miraculously, lines are not a problem. But the ship, because of its gargantuan size, does tend to overwhelm some of the European ports it visits.

Specifications

Size (in tons)	109,000	Officers	Italian/British
Number of Cabins	1,300	Crew	1,100 (Internat'l)
Number of Outside Cabins	928	Passenger/Crew Ratio	2 to 1
Cabins with Verandas	710	Year Built	1998
Number of Passengers	2,600	Last Major Refurbishment	N/A

Frommer's Ratings (Scale of 1–5)

Cabin Comfort & Amenities	5	Pool, Fitness & Spa Facilities	4
Ship Cleanliness & Maintenance	4	Children's Facilities	4
Public Comfort/Space	5	Itineraries	3
Decor	5	Worth the Money	5

For its first year of life, the 109,000-ton, 2,600-passenger *Grand Princess* was the world's biggest and most expensive ($430 million) cruise ship. With 18 towering decks, the ship is taller than the Statue of Liberty (from pedestal to torch) and too wide to fit through the Panama Canal. In fact, it's so big that the line's *Pacific Princess,* the original Love Boat, could easily fit inside its hull and still have lots of room to spare.

Inside and out, the *Grand Princess* is a marvel of size and design. Its massive white, boxy body with its spoiler-like aft poking up into the air cuts a bizarre, space-age profile and is like nothing else at sea. It might look a bit scary, but the ship's well-laid-out interior is very easy to navigate and, amazingly, the ship never feels crowded.

The *Grand Princess* offers an amazing variety of entertainment and dining options and recreational activities. There's no question it's designed to be a floating resort. There are six restaurants (plus a pizzeria and outdoor grill), four swimming pools, and three show lounges, as well as expansive deck space.

Even the ship's medical center is grand: It boasts a high-tech "telemedicine" program that, via a live video hook-up, links the ship's doctors to the emergency room at Cedars Sinai Medical Center in Los Angeles.

Cabins & Rates

Cabins	Per diems from	Bathtub	Fridge	Hair Dryer	Sitting Area	TV
Inside	$245	no	yes	yes	no	yes
Outside	$286	no	yes	yes	no	yes
Suite	$382	yes	yes	yes	yes	yes

CABINS The *Grand Princess* has 710 cabins with verandas; only Royal Caribbean's *Voyager of the Seas* has more (757). (Be forewarned: The verandas are tiered, so passengers in levels above may be able to look down on you.) Cabins are nicely decorated and all have safes, hair dryers, refrigerators, robes (for use during the cruise), and TVs broadcasting CNN, ESPN, Nickelodeon, BBC programming, and TNT (as well as *Love Boat* reruns). Storage is adequate and features more closet shelves than drawer space.

A standard outside cabin (including veranda) ranges from 215 to 255 square feet; suites are anywhere from 515 to 800 square feet, including verandas.

The suites and minisuites (the entire Dolphin Deck is nothing but minisuites) have tubs as well as showers (suite tubs have whirlpools), separate sitting areas with sofa beds, private balconies, and two TVs (which really seems unnecessary).

A pair of Grand Suites even have fireplaces (not real wood-burning ones, of course) and hot tubs. There are two family suites that can sleep up to eight.

In addition to the room stewards, all suites and minisuites come with the services of white-gloved butlers who wear beepers so they're at passengers' beck and call to help with unpacking, deliver nightly canapés, make sure the minibar is stocked with beverages (it's stocked one time on a complimentary basis, including alcohol), arrange shore excursions, and make spa appointments.

The views from many cabins on the Emerald Deck are obstructed by lifeboats.

The ship has 28 wheelchair-accessible cabins, more than any other ship afloat. (The Skywalkers disco has a wheelchair lift up to the elevated dance floor, too.)

PUBLIC AREAS You'll wonder where everyone is. The *Grand Princess* is a huge ship with a not-so-huge-ship feeling. Thanks to its smart layout, with lots of small rooms rather than a few large rooms, passengers are dispersed rather than concentrated into one or two main areas, and you'll have no problem finding a quiet retreat.

The *Grand's* public areas have a contemporary and upscale appeal, thanks to pleasing color schemes and touches like wood, marble, and brass. Two full-time florists create and care for impressive flower arrangements and a large variety of live plants.

There are three main dining rooms, all named for famous artists—da Vinci, Botticelli, and Michelangelo—and decorated with artwork accordingly (reproductions, of course). The da Vinci even has a copy of the Mona Lisa. The rooms are purposefully not very large (the largest is actually smaller than the main dining room on the *Royal Princess*), so you don't feel you're dining with crowds (you may also feel like the ceiling is closing in on you a bit). In Europe, there are specialty theme nights including a Greek night featuring Greek music and national cuisine.

You are smartly assigned to the dining room closest to your cabin. This means women don't have to trek a mile in high heels to get to dinner.

The Horizon Terrace, open 24 hours a day, offers casual dining with clusters of buffet stations for breakfast and lunch, and table service at night (from 7:30pm to 4am).

Sabatini's Trattoria is a lively Italian cafe, open on a reservations only basis (the food here is a cut above food in the rest of the ship, but service may be slow). The Painted Desert, also reservations only, is the first Southwestern restaurant on a ship. The concept probably works great in the Caribbean, but seems a bit weird in Europe.

Entertainment on the ship is pretty hot, with three main show lounges taking center stage: The Princess Theater, with an elaborate stage setup; the Vista Lounge, which has, frankly, lousy sight lines; and my favorite, the Explorer's Club, an open room in the middle of the ship on the Promenade Deck, done up in safari decor. The performances in the latter catch your eye as you walk by (more times than not, causing you to stop and watch).

Gamblers will love the sprawling and dazzling 13,500-square-foot Atlantis Casino, one of the largest at sea. There's also a clubby, old-world Wheelhouse Lounge as well as a woody sports bar, Snookers.

The ship's most striking design feature is the disco, which juts out the back, and is suspended, scarily in my opinion, some 155 feet above the water. From this space you can literally look back at the rest of the ship, as if you were in a helicopter behind the vessel. It's really quite spectacular. Smoke machines and other high-tech gizmos add to the effect.

Kids are hardly ignored on this vessel. There are two-tiered children's and teen's centers, the latter with its own disco. The kiddies have access to computers, games, a wading pool and even a fleet of bright red tricycles. Teens get their own whirlpool.

The ship's large virtual reality center, with interactive games and a motion-based simulator "ride," is designed to please kids and adults alike (all for an extra fee, of course).

The *Grand Princess* also has a library, small writing room, card room, and business center with computers, from which e-mails can be sent and received ($7.50 for 15 minutes of use).

POOL, FITNESS & SPA FACILITIES This ship has something like 1.7 acres of open deck space, so it's not hard to find a quiet place to soak in the sun (in some of the more remote areas you may find a few women discreetly going topless). There are four great swimming pools, including one with a retractable glass roof so it can double as a sort of solarium, another touted as a swim-against-the-current pool (although truth be told, there really isn't enough room to do laps if others are in the pool), and a third, aft under the disco, that feels miles from the rest of the ship (and is the least crowded).

A large, almost separate part of the ship, on the forward Sun Deck, is reserved for pampering the body. Surrounding the lap pool and its tiered, amphitheater-style wooden benches is the large Plantation Spa, with a layout I personally find a bit weird (for instance, there are no showers in the dressing area). The complex includes a very large ocean-view beauty parlor and an ocean-view gym, which is surprisingly small and cramped for a ship of this size (although there is an unusually large aerobics floor). Unfortunately, the sports decks are just above the spa, and if you're getting a relaxing massage when someone is playing basketball, you'll hear it.

Other active diversions include a jogging track, basketball, paddle tennis, a fun nine-hole putting green, and computerized simulated golf.

Royal Princess

Royal Princess (photo: Princess)

The Verdict

This ship, christened by Princess Diana in 1984, was ahead of its time, with all ocean-view cabins and more cabins with verandas than ever before. It's still a lovely vessel, offering a traditional cruise experience.

Specifications

Size (in tons)	45,000	Crew	520 (International)
Number of Cabins	600	Passenger/Crew Ratio	2.3 to 1
Number of Outside Cabins	600	Year Built	1984
Cabins with Verandas	152	Last Major Refurbishment	1999
Number of Passengers	1,200		

Frommer's Ratings (Scale of 1–5)

Cabin Comfort & Amenities	4	Pool, Fitness & Spa Facilities	4
Ship Cleanliness & Maintenance	4	Children's Facilities	N/A
Public Comfort/Space	4	Itineraries	5
Decor	4	Worth the Money	5

Princess Cruises set standards for the industry with its classy *Royal Princess.* The ship's 152 cabins with verandas was by far the highest number of veranda cabins on any ship at the time, and Princess has reflected the success of that concept with every vessel it's built since.

Even today, the *Royal Princess* is in some ways ahead of its time. But that's not its greatest claim to fame; it's the fact this ship was christened by Princess Diana.

The interior design concept at work on this vessel was to create a simple yet elegant atmosphere. Carpets and wall coverings are in mostly neutral tones, and traditional nautical touches such as teak and brass enhance an otherwise contemporary ambiance. The sea is never far from sight, since all public areas boast floor-to-ceiling windows (the vessel has some 16,000 square feet of windows all told). The art collection (all original) reflects both British and American artists.

Cabins & Rates

Cabins	Per diems from	Bathtub	Fridge	Hair Dryer	Sitting Area	TV
Outside	$245	yes	yes	yes	no	yes
Suites	$455	yes	yes	yes	yes	yes

CABINS All cabins have large picture windows, and a quarter have private verandas. They are comfortably laid out, with a standard cabin 168 square feet, and suites 336 square feet, including verandas. Twin beds can be combined to make a queen, and in standard cabins one bed can be folded into the wall during the day to create more room to walk around. The cabins all have bathtubs and showers. The two penthouse suites are very large (more than 800 square feet) and each has a separate sitting/dining area with a sofa bed, table, and chairs, as well as a queen-sized bed, large closets, and Jacuzzi tub.

Cabins on the Baja and Caribe decks, and some on the Dolphin Deck, have obstructed or partially obstructed views. Since the cabins on Promenade Deck are located directly above the public areas, you're best off avoiding them if you're a light sleeper.

In-cabin amenities in all cabins include safes, hair dryers, refrigerators, robes for use during the cruise, and color TVs broadcasting CNN, ESPN, Nickelodeon, BBC programming, and TNT.

Ten cabins are wheelchair accessible.

PUBLIC AREAS Most of the ship's public rooms are on the Riviera Deck, including the show lounge, nightclub, theatre, and casino, and all are good-sized, creating an overall feeling of spaciousness. The Princess Court is a circular lounge amidships that overlooks The Plaza, the ship's elegant and comfortable two-story lobby. The two-level restaurant has floor-to-ceiling windows.

The Horizon Lounge on the top deck offers a panoramic view that makes it the best place to catch the passing scenery. The space is used as an observation lounge during the day and a disco at night.

The ship has lots of teak deck space, including a Promenade Deck you can walk all the way around.

POOL, FITNESS & SPA FACILITIES The ship has three pool areas, including one of the largest lap pools at sea. The pool on Lido Deck is actually a combination of several pools grouped together in a circular pattern.

The ship's small spa and ocean-view gym (with Lifecycles, an 11-station multi-gym, and two massage rooms) are on the top deck, where there are also two saunas, an indoor hot tub, and a beauty salon, as well as table tennis and shuffleboard. You can jog on the Promenade Deck.

Renaissance Cruises

SHIPS IN EUROPE: R1 • R2

250 East Las Olas Blvd., Fort Lauderdale, FL 33301. ☎ **800/525-5350.** www.RenaissanceCruises.com.

THE LINE IN A NUTSHELL Renaissance Cruises' rapidly expanding fleet of midsize ships provides one of the best values on the high seas, operating year-round European itineraries.

THE EXPERIENCE With Renaissance, you cruise in the elegance of an English country hotel that offers surprisingly good food in a wide variety of settings, on port-intensive itineraries at both ends of the Mediterranean. All cruises have pre- and post-cruise land packages with the hotel category and the length of stay dependent on the cabin category chosen.

Since Renaissance itineraries generally last more than a week, the average passenger age is 55 and up, though peak vacation periods will see a slightly younger set (but no children). Many of the mostly middle- to upper-middle-class passengers are new to cruising and aren't particularly adventurous. At present, the ships are marketed almost exclusively in North America, so you'll find few other nationalities aboard.

The *R1* debuted in August 1998 on eastern Mediterranean itineraries, while the *R2* entered service in the western Med a few months later. Two of the line's original boutique ships, *Renaissance Seven* and *Renaissance Eight,* continue to operate, at least for the time being. The ships follow a no-smoking policy.

Given that the price includes air, hotel, transfers, and the cruise, plus frequent discounted offerings, Renaissance provides an extraordinary value in all categories. The focus is the destination rather than elaborate daytime activities or evening entertainment.

Pros

- **Value.** It's truly an all-inclusive package, with air, land, and sea connections included at a very good price.
- **Varied dining options.** At dinner, there are no less than four different dining venues, and that does not count room service with dinner for two on the balcony.

Cons

- **Suggested tipping amount too high.** You are encouraged to give $15 a day per person to the wait staff and $5 a day to the cabin attendants, totaling twice the industry norm. There is a short list of others to tip as well.
- **No enrichment program aboard.** The Mediterranean world is complex and fascinating, and while the tour program ashore is great, there should be at least one lecturer aboard.

Frommer's Ratings: Renaissance Cruises

	Poor	Fair	Good	Excellent	Outstanding
Enjoyment Factor				✓	
Dining				✓	
Activities		✓			
Children's Program	N/A				
Entertainment			✓		
Service				✓	
Overall Value					✓

RENAISSANCE: A NEW VALUE-ORIENTED FORMULA

Renaissance Cruises began with a bang in 1989 when the original Norwegian owners Fearnley and Eger ordered eight similar all-suite ships, carrying just over 100 passengers to ports around the world. The concept worked for a while, but global unrest decimated interest in certain destinations, and the high cost of operating such small ships drove the company into bankruptcy.

New Italian and American owners sold or chartered off most of the original fleet and then began planning new mid-size ships. Now, with eight almost carbon-copy ships in service or on order, it's a new ball game. Renaissance has made a name for itself in more ways than one. By offering year-round cruise itineraries for most of the fleet, they wield considerable clout and can negotiate lower prices with the local agencies, tour companies, and suppliers. Also, the company emphasizes direct mail solicitations and states that by booking with the line you get a better deal than through a travel agent. Their marketing methods have not endeared them in the travel trade, but so far, the formula that they have developed seems to work for the consumer.

THE FLEET

The company's fleet falls into two categories. The original boutique fleet of eight ships now numbers just two 4,280-ton vessels taking up to 114 passengers in one-room suite accommodations. Renaissance has said that as long as there is a market for these small guys, they will remain in the fleet. Passengers who sail these ships are generally not interested in the larger new tonnage.

Built in France at Chantiers de l'Atlantique under generous financial terms (read: French government subsidies), the new series, including the ***R1*** and ***R2,*** has a gross tonnage of 30,200 and a passenger capacity of 684, based on double occupancy. While the European programs were only the start of a destination-driven, valued-oriented cruise line that had established itself in French Polynesia, with the new series, Renaissance plans to expand its itineraries into northern Europe, the Caribbean, and Alaska. While exhibiting a somewhat piled-up superstructure to maximize the interior accommodations, the new ships have a smart, bulky profile with a stylized letter 'R' on a funnel placed well aft. Two bands of tinted glass run fore and aft above three decks of veranda cabins, down to the black hull.

Within, the attractive lounges and public spaces are handsomely wood-paneled (in a medium to dark veneer) with furnishings in blues and reds with light accented patterns, Oriental-style carpets, pretty wall lamps, and marble-mantel fireplaces. The resulting atmosphere is that of an English country hotel, and the style is repeated throughout the fleet, which seems more appropriate in European waters than in the South Pacific or other planned tropical cruising areas. There are many comfortable lounges throughout the ship.

An amazing 93% of the cabins are outside and 68% have private verandas. Most are certainly roomy enough to spend lots of time in, whether reading or resting.

PASSENGER PROFILE

With itineraries that generally last more than a week, and with year-round European cruise programs, the age of the passenger is on average 55 and up, though peak vacation periods will see a slightly younger set (but no children). In fact the company policy states no one under the age of 18 is allowed aboard. The ships have a no-smoking policy, but if caught, you are asked to obey the rule rather than escorted off the ship and fined as with Carnival's *Paradise.*

Many passengers, mostly middle- to upper-middle-class couples or friends traveling together, are new to cruising and aren't particularly adventurous. As the new fleet grows, no doubt many first-timers to Renaissance will want to try out the other itineraries.

At present, the ships are marketed almost exclusively in North America, so if you hear any foreign languages at all, they'll likely be coming from bilingual Americans. On the eastern Mediterranean itineraries, religious groups may be aboard because of interest in the Holy Land.

DINING

There is great strength in the line's dining, from the number of eating venues to the quality and presentation of the menus. Apollo, the caterer used by Celebrity cruises, provides a mostly European wait staff who are as attentive and well-trained as one will find.

The largest of the four dining venues is the 354-seat Club Restaurant, a formal two-tier room with tables and banquettes accommodating from two to eight, and large view windows on three sides. A pianist plays at dinnertime next to a small dance floor. When you arrive at the entrance, you may ask the maitre d' for a table with other passengers or request to dine alone, space permitting. An adjoining bar lounge is a comfortable spot to wait if the dining room is full. The dress code for every night is referred to as country-club casual, and few men are seen in ties, although many wear jackets at dinnertime.

Entrees include well-prepared dishes like crisply roasted raspberry duck, honey-baked tenderloin of pork, and cherry strudel with cinnamon sauce. The wine list is varied enough for this moderately sophisticated crowd and is fairly priced.

Two specialty restaurants requiring reservations are very popular, so it's a good idea to be quick about reserving a spot when the bookings open each morning. The menus, while generally fixed, have several choices for each course, so many passengers will book a second and even a third time.

The handsome wood-paneled Grill, seating about 96, provides some changing entrees such as broiled lobster tails and Norwegian salmon, with pork chops, lamb, and steak available every night. Next door, the Italian Restaurant, with a pale yellow and gold decor, offers no less than nine entrees, with two excellent choices being the sage veal medallions with prosciutto and the fusilli with grilled chicken, roasted pine nuts, sun-dried tomato, and Montrachet cheese. The lemon mascarpone brulee tart with pecan flavor is an excellent dessert.

When you return tired from a day ashore, the Panorama Buffet is an informal choice for a quick meal, but this pretty space, with lemon-lime green-paneled walls depicting English country houses and scattered potted palms, comes alive at breakfast and lunch. There are additional outdoor tables, with partial cover, overlooking the wake and more under cover near the Lido pool.

At breakfast, a chef prepares omelets, and at lunch there's a choice of at least two hot entrees, a pizzeria with two daily variations, and a barbecue set up with ribs and chicken as well as hamburgers and hot dogs.

For a moderately priced, mid-sized ship, the food and the choices of venues make Renaissance an especially good value.

ACTIVITIES

Daytime activities include fairly routine games such as bingo, name that tune, trivia quizzes, fashion shows, and jewelry seminars; and black jack, roulette, and slots in the casino. Out on deck, there are shuffleboard and golf putting tournaments.

Some Special Deals

Renaissance uses direct mail and the Internet for its promotions, and there are frequent offers, even over the phone if you get on their list. Call the number at the top of the review for information.

Renaissance Fleet Itineraries

Ship	Home Ports & Season	Itinerary
R1	Piraeus/Athens and Istanbul, year-round.	**5-day Greek Isles:** Santorini and Rhodes (Greece), Kusadasi (Turkey), and Crete.
R2	Barcelona and Lisbon, year-round.	**5-day W. Med:** Seville and Malaga (Spain), and Gibraltar.

*Every cruise is bracketed by hotels stays; cruisefare usually includes some sightseeing.

The library has two computers with word processing capabilities, so guests can write out their travel journals. There are also tables for games, puzzles, and bridge as well as comfy couches and wing-back chair seating for delving into a good book. A favorite location is the sofa in front of the fireplace, beneath a painted dome ceiling depicting birds in flight.

A circular mezzanine above the Lido Deck has a track for walking and jogging, and space for deck chairs overlooking the central pool and two whirlpools. A band plays atop a bandstand at lunchtime. The Fitness Center offers a wide variety of exercise equipment in a spacious glassed-in room facing forward, and the facility offers a private lounge deck and spa pool overlooking the bow. The staff includes professional trainers, including those who conduct aerobics classes and give holistic body treatments.

As these are port intensive cruises, especially the western Mediterranean itinerary, there are not many full days or half days at sea.

Children's Programs

Children under the age of 18 are not permitted on board.

Entertainment

Evening entertainment takes place in a one-level but sufficiently tiered showroom and offers typical song and dance medleys and, for example, on some cruises, the fast-paced acts of two clever puppeteers who work a dozen of their own home-made puppets. In the attractive, partitioned forward observation lounge and bar, a duo plays for dancing after dinner; later the space becomes a disco. Also after dinner, the dining room pianist moves to the central foyer to play amongst the shops. The central interior section is a sports bar with a dozen TV screens.

Service

The hotel staff is supplied by Apollo, a catering company, and most of the staff is European, with eastern European countries predominating. Most are well seasoned, though with a new expanding line of ships, there will be some raw recruits as well. Perhaps the outrageous tipping guidelines ($20 per day per person for the wait and cabin staff) are an extra incentive to work harder, and the service levels are very high throughout the ship.

Cabin service is efficient, and if your cabin has a balcony, breakfast is a popular in-cabin meal. It comes promptly, and is convenient when you're leaving for early morning tours.

Perhaps the only frustration is reserving a table in the two alternate restaurants. The line will likely be busy and the space taken up quickly before you can get through; this is partly because many passengers dine there more than once. On a 14-day cruise, demand does taper off a bit near the end of the voyage.

R1 • R2

R1 (photo: Renaissance Cruises)

The Verdict

This identical pair offers a terrific value for middle-aged passengers who like a traditional English country-style setting, with an American country-club casual dress code.

Specifications

Size (in tons)	30,200	Officers	International
Number of Cabins	342	Crew	373 (International)
Number of Outside Cabins	317	Passenger/Crew Ratio	1.8 to 1
Cabins with Verandas	232	Year Built	1998
Number of Passengers	684	Last Major Refurbishment	N/A

Frommer's Ratings (Scale of 1–5)

Cabin Comfort & Amenities	4	Pool, Fitness & Spa Facilities	5
Ship Cleanliness & Maintenance	4	Children's Facilities	N/A
Public Comfort/Space	5	Itineraries	4
Decor	4	Worth the Money	5

Mid-size ships in the 600- to 1,000-passenger range are becoming a rare breed and smaller percentage of the world's cruising fleets, so it's welcome news that Renaissance has chosen slightly less than 700 berths for its new series. For the guests, it's much less hectic when going ashore, but the downside, for some, is less lavish entertainment aboard. However, the variety of dining venues, no less than four places for dinner, is unusual for a ship of this size. The quality of cabin accommodations is uniformly high, and the public spaces are most inviting in all types of weather.

Cabins & Rates*

Cabins	Per diems from	Bathtub	Fridge	Hair Dryer	Sitting Area	TV
Inside	$136	no	no	yes	yes	yes
Outside	$145	no	no	yes	yes	yes
Suite	$200	yes	yes	yes	yes	yes

**Rates are based on the off-season for an 11-day cruisetour, including a 5-day cruise, 2 nights in Lisbon and Barcelona, transfers, and air to and from New York/Newark.*

CABINS With 93% outside, cabins are an asset to this value-priced ship. The largest number of rooms in the C and D categories measure 216 square feet, while the bathrooms are small. All cabins have a mirrored vanity/desk, sofa, and breakfast table with complimentary room service; TVs with CNN, CNBC and Euronews broadcasts and nine different movies within 24 hours; direct dial phone; and a hair dryer. Suites have bathtubs, refrigerated minibars, robes, and slippers.

PUBLIC AREAS Public rooms are varied in size and location and include intimate, busy, and walk-through lounges and bars. Some foyers also provide additional seating, and the layout is complex enough so that guests will not get bored moving about the interiors. There are more rooms you might enjoy using than there is time to do so. The partitioned forward observation-lounge-cum-sports bar is particularly well designed to serve several different functions during the day and evening, with quiet recesses, great views forward, and both intimate and spacious interior sections that are popular after dark. The whole ship is restful, seasoned, and inviting without being stuffy.

Deck space is generous and it is easy to find unobstructed views both fore and aft.

POOL, FITNESS & SPA FACILITIES There are one outdoor pool, two adjacent whirlpools, and an airy big-windowed fitness, spa, and hair-styling center with two saunas, a Thalassotherapy spa pool, a private lounge deck all the way forward, and a "fog shower" that creates a kind of steam room effect.

Royal Caribbean International

SHIPS IN EUROPE Legend of the Seas • Splendour of the Seas

1050 Caribbean Way, Miami, FL 33132. ☎ **800/327-6700** or 305/539-6000. Fax 800/722-5329. www.royalcaribbean.com.

THE LINE IN A NUTSHELL These megaships bring to Europe the mass-market American experience that's proven so popular in the Caribbean. They're contemporary, attractive, and glamorous without being overly glitzy.

THE EXPERIENCE Royal Caribbean International is one of the most successful cruise companies in the world. It sells a big-ship cruise experience that's reasonably priced and designed to please everyone, except, perhaps, those who hate crowds. The ships are well-run and provide a consistent product, overseen by an army of service employees who pay close attention to detail.

The line is known for offering a wealth of activities, but in Europe, where ports are more the focus, they are more muted than in the Caribbean. Entertainment is varied and well-executed, and there's always enough happening to keep things exciting.

Most passengers in Europe are couples in their 40s to 60s, but you'll also find honeymoon couples, younger singles, and families. The majority of passengers are North American, although these ships also attract Europeans. Whenever there are more than 200 non-English speakers of a particular language on board, announcements are made in that language.

The company's vessels in Europe are megaships with multistory atria, mall-like shopping complexes, two-story dining rooms and show lounges, wide-open public areas, indoor (with retractable roof) and outdoor pools, and relatively small cabins.

Pros

- **Entertainment.** The line's entertainment offerings are among the best at sea, and include both flashy show productions and headliner acts.
- **Attractive public rooms.** They are witty and classy, with lots of greenery and artwork, and just the right amount of glamour. And there's lots of glass, most notably the line's trademark Viking Crown Lounges, for viewing the scenery outside.

Cons

- **Cabin categories.** These ships have 17 different cabin categories, which can be very confusing, and cabins aren't very big (but they do all offer sitting areas).
- **Crowds.** Hey, these are big ships, so there are going to be lines at times, especially in the buffet restaurants, at bars, and getting on and off the ship in port.
- **Laundry and dry cleaning.** While the services are available, the ships do not have self-service laundries, which can be an annoyance on a 12-night cruise.

Frommer's Ratings: Royal Caribbean International

	Poor	Fair	Good	Excellent	Outstanding
Enjoyment Factor					✓
Dining			✓		
Activities				✓	
Children's Program				✓	
Entertainment					✓
Service			✓		
Overall Value				✓	

ROYAL CARIBBEAN: MODERN GIANT

Royal Caribbean is a bold, brash industry innovator, second only in size to Carnival (which does not sail in Europe). The line, founded in 1969 by a consortium of Norwegian ship owners, used to specialize only in the Caribbean (hence the name). But in the late '80s, the company began expanding its horizons, offering cruises to Europe, Alaska, and the Pacific, and in the process tagging the "International" onto its name.

In 1990, the Pritzker family of Chicago (and Hyatt Hotels) bought a major stake in the company, and funds from the sale, coupled with all the credit-worthiness of Hyatt, helped finance the line's massive expansion during the 1990s. Royal Caribbean has since blossomed into an immensely profitable multinational public corporation (it went public in 1993) with a staggering volume and a flotilla of state-of-the-art megaships valued in the billions. Royal Caribbean put another plum in its pocket with the acquisition of the more upscale Celebrity Cruises in 1997.

Back in 1988, Royal Caribbean was the first line to introduce megaships. The 73,192-ton *Sovereign of the Seas* was the largest passenger ship built in the previous 50 years, and introduced features that have become industry standards, including the multistory atrium. In late 1999, Royal Caribbean grabbed headlines again by introducing the largest ship in the world, the 142,000-ton *Voyager of the Seas,* which among other innovations offers, for the first time on a cruise ship, interior cabins with views of the atrium (think Hyatt hotels).

THE FLEET

Royal Caribbean will have 15 ships in its fleet by the end of 2000, including the world's largest, the 3,114-passenger *Voyager of the Seas* and its equally mammoth sister *Adventure of the Seas.* The 1,804-passenger ***Legend of the Seas*** (1995) and ***Splendour of the Seas*** (1996) were the first of the line's highly successful six-ship Vision class. Yet another new class of megaships currently under construction (the first is due this year) is 85,000 tons.

PASSENGER PROFILE

Most passengers in Europe are couples in their 40s to 60s, but there are also honeymoon couples, younger singles, and families (including three generations—children, parents, and grandparents—traveling together). About half of the guests have cruised before; more than half will be on their first trip to Europe. The majority of passengers come from somewhere in North America, although these ships also attract Europeans. Whenever there are more than 200 non-English speakers of a particular language on board, announcements are made in that language (usually Spanish, French, German or Russian).

DINING

Royal Caribbean is in the process of changing and upgrading its menus, which in the past might have included roast prime rib of beef, grilled medallions of veal, deviled crab, and Chinese roast duck, as well as a pasta like ravioli. There's always a **ShipShape healthy menu option** (along the lines of pan-seared salmon) as well as a **vegetarian option** such as Indian spiced curry. Cuisine is often presented in different themes, with table settings, menus, and waiters' costumes reflecting the theme, including Latin Night.

The **formal dining room** on each ship offers two seatings and an alternative casual evening dining option is offered in the poolside Windjammer Cafe most nights of the cruise. You can eat breakfast and lunch in the main dining room or in the buffet-style Windjammer Cafe. Lines, unfortunately, can grow long. **Ice cream** and a couple of toppings are available throughout the day from a station in the Windjammer. There's also a **midnight buffet** nightly, and sandwiches are served throughout the night in the public lounges. Pizza is served in the afternoon and late night for those after-partying munchies.

Royal Caribbean Fleet Itineraries

Ship	Home Ports & Season	Itinerary
Legend of the Seas	7-day W. Med, round-trip from Barcelona(May–Sept); 12-day W. Med, round-trip from Barcelona (May, Sept, Oct); 10-day Greek Isles and Italy, Barcelona to Piraeus/ Athens (Nov); 14-day Greek Isles and Italy, Piraeus/ Athens to Lisbon (Apr).	**7- to 12-day W. Med:** Port calls may include Mallorca (Spain), Marseille and Villefranche (France), Livorno, Naples, Civitavecchia/Rome, Venice, Messina (Italy), and Valletta (Malta). **10- to 14-day Greek Isles and Italy:** Livorno, Civitavecchia/Rome, Naples (Italy), Heraklion (Crete), Santorini and Rhodes (Greece), Kusadasi (Turkey), Barcelona (Spain), and Gibraltar.
Splendour of the Seas	12-day Europe Capitals, Barcelona to Harwich, England (May); 12-day Scandinavia & Russia, round-trip from Harwich (June–Aug); 12-day Norway, round-trip from Harwich (June); 12-day Norway/British Isles, round-trip from Harwich (July).	**12-day Europe Capitals:** Lisbon (Portugal), Le Havre (France), Hamburg (Germany), Oslo (Norway), Copenhagen (Denmark), Gibraltar. **12-day Scandinavia & Russia:** Oslo (Norway), Stockholm (Sweden), Helsinki (Finland), St. Petersburg (Russia), Muuga (Estonia), and Copenhagen (Denmark). **12-day Norway:** Flam, Honningsvag, Tromso, Molde, Hellesylt, Geiranger, Bergen, Stavanger (Norway). **12-day British Isles/ Norway:** Le Havre (France), Plymouth (England), Cobh and Dublin (Ireland), Greenock (Scotland), Bergen, Geiranger, Hellesylt, Flam (Norway), and Amsterdam (Holland).

An extensive **kids' menu** features items like fish sticks, burritos, oven-fried lemon chicken, spaghetti and meatballs, and pizza; the standard burgers, hot dogs, and fries; plus lots of yummy desserts.

Room service is available 24 hours a day from a fairly routine, limited menu. However, during normal lunch and dinner hours, your cabin steward can bring anything being served in the restaurant to your cabin.

Activities

Daytime activities are typical cruise line fare: bingo, shuffleboard, horse racing, line-dancing lessons, craft lessons, spa and beauty demonstrations, contests and games, and art auctions. Destination-type lectures focus on the itinerary. The *Legend* and *Splendour of the Seas* even feature **miniature golf courses,** right on board!

If you participate in the line's **ShipShape fitness program,** which includes aerobics and other classes, you'll get chits you can turn in at the end of the cruise for prizes like T-shirts and baseball caps.

If **shopping** can be considered an activity, Royal Caribbean offers a particularly impressive selection of shops clustered around the atrium.

Children's Program

Year-round, Royal Caribbean offers **supervised kids' programs** fleetwide for children ages 3 to 17. Male and female youth staff all have college degrees in education, recreation, or a related field. The "Adventure Ocean" program offers fun and games for four age groups: Aquanauts, ages 3 to 5; Explorers, ages 6 to 8; Voyagers, ages 9 to 12; and Navigators, ages 13 to 17.

Each ship has a **children's playroom,** a **teen center and disco,** and a **video arcade.** The fun includes talent shows, karaoke, pizza and ice cream parties, bingo, scavenger hunts, and game shows.

Slumber-party–style **group baby-sitting** is available nightly and also when the ship is in port. The charge is $4 per child. Private, **in-cabin baby-sitting** by a crew member is available and must be booked at least 24 hours in advance through the purser's desk. The charge is $8 per hour for up to two children in the same family, and $10 per hour for a maximum of three kids in the same family.

Entertainment

The line doesn't scrimp on entertainment. There is something happening on these ships from before dinner until late at night, including lavish Las Vegas–style show productions done on sprawling high-tech stages, music acts, comedians, and sometimes even name-brand performers.

Royal Caribbean uses 12- to 16-piece bands for its main showroom, and its large-cast revues are among the best you'll find on a ship. Show bands and other lounge acts, who keep the music playing all over the ship, are all first-rate.

Service

Overall, service in the restaurants and cabins is friendly, accommodating, and efficient, despite some language barrier problems (sign language often comes in handy). You're likely to be greeted with a smile by someone polishing the brass in a stairwell, a greeting that supervisors encourage on the part of even the lowest-ranking employees. That said, big, bustling ships like Royal Caribbean's are no strangers to crowds, lines, and harried servers not able to get to you exactly when you'd like them to.

Legend of the Seas • Splendour of the Seas

Legend of the Seas (photo: RCCL)

The Verdict

These contemporary cruise ships are truly floating resorts (think Hyatt Hotels on the high seas) and offer just the right amount of glamour and excitement, without going overboard—so to speak.

Specifications

Size (in tons)	69,130	Officers	Norwegian/Int'l
Number of Cabins	902	Crew	(International) 720
Number of Outside Cabins	575	Passenger/Crew Ratio	2.5 to 1
Cabins with Verandas	231	Year Built	1995/1996
Number of Passengers	1,804		

Frommer's Ratings (Scale of 1–5)

Cabin Comfort & Amenities	4	Pool, Fitness & Spa Facilities	5
Ship Cleanliness & Maintenance	4	Children's Facilities	4
Public Comfort/Space	5	Itineraries	4
Decor	5	Worth the Money	5

These are two of the first in the Vision class, marking the beginning of a highly successful series of ships. The contemporary ships are quite spectacular, from their chrome, glass, and marble multistory atria to their dazzling casinos and high tech theatres, and will no doubt elicit a fair number of "Ahs." Glass and light are everywhere on these ships (each contains about 2 acres of glass canopies, glass windbreaks, skylights, and floor-to-ceiling windows with sweeping views). The decor is enhanced by impressive art collections and lots of greenery.

Cabins & Rates

Cabins	Per diems from	Bathtub	Fridge	Hair Dryer	Sitting Area	TV
Inside	$171/$179*	yes	no	no	no	yes
Outside	$199/$220*	no	some	no	yes	yes
Suite	$328/$374*	yes	yes	no	yes	yes

CABINS To be polite, cabins are compact. Inside cabins measure 138 square feet and outsides 153 square feet. For big, check out the Royal Suite on each of these ships—they measure a mammoth 1,150 square feet. Nearly one-fourth of the cabins aboard each ship have private verandas and about a third can accommodate third and fourth passengers. All have beds convertible to queen-sized, phone, interactive TV (with some 20 channels), safe, radio, and individually controlled air-conditioning. Bathrooms, while not the largest, have good storage space, including a multilevel built-in shelf in the shower stalls. Seventeen cabins on each ship are handicapped accessible.

PUBLIC AREAS Warm woods and brass, luxuriant fountains and foliage, glass and crystal, buttery leathers, and carefully chosen artwork and textures highlight the well laid-out public areas. A soaring seven-story "Centrum" atrium crowned by a sloped two-deck-high skylight is the focal point aboard each ship. Glass elevators, à la Hyatt, take passengers up through the Centrum into the stunning Viking Crown Lounge, a glass-sided spaceship-like area high above the waves.

There is an array of other hideaway refuges, including cocktail bars, a well-stocked library, and card rooms. The Schooner Bar is a casual piano bar, and is a great place for a pre-dinner drink or late-night unwinding. Ditto the Champagne Terrace at the foot of the atrium. The large dining rooms aboard the vessels span two decks and are interconnected with a very grand staircase. A pianist plays a massive grand piano throughout dinner service.

The ships have two-story theaters, and there's not a bad seat in the house. Casinos are Vegas-style flashy and offer hundreds of gambling stations. The ships' conference rooms can hold up to 200 people. Regrettably, there are no self-service Laundromats.

POOL, FITNESS & SPA FACILITIES The ShipShape spas on these ships are wonderful, soothing respites from the hubbub of ship life. They offer a wide selection of treatments, as well as the standard steam rooms and saunas. Adjacent to the spas on each ship are spacious solariums with a pool (with a retractable roof), lounge chairs, and floor-to-ceiling windows. These spots are peaceful places to repose before or after a spa treatment, except in the afternoon when pizza is being served (for some reason pizza draws loud people). The gyms are not particularly large, but are well equipped.

Overall, there's more than enough open deck areas, plus a jogging track, shuffleboard, Ping-Pong, and 6,000-square-foot, 18-hole miniature golf courses, complete with trees, sand traps, and water hazards. The main pool area on each ship has two whirlpools, and there are two more in the Solarium.

The European Lines

7

These mostly mid-sized ships are European-owned and operated and offer a different cruise experience than the mainstream American vessels. Most in this category are older, classic ships that hold a lot of appeal for ship buffs, though some have not been kept up as they should be (the teak deck may be covered with outdoor carpet to hide its splinters). There are also some new ships in this category, designed to continue the classic cruise tradition but with more modern amenities (see First European Cruises' *Mistral* later in this chapter).

I've included the British lines P&O and Swan Hellenic in this chapter, though the experiences on these ships are more upmarket and somewhat different than on the other lines mentioned, most of which are in the budget to moderate-price category. Similarly, the Italian line Costa Cruises offers more of a megaship, mainstream cruise experience.

The Euro lines tend to attract those looking for an affordable cruise, including older couples, families, and singles sharing a cabin. The crowd on these ships is mostly European, and that means lots of languages spoken on public address systems (because of this, announcements may seem to go on forever). It also means, especially on the non-British ships, there may be plenty of people who do not speak English (brush up on your sign language!) and lots of smokers, though some lines, like First European, now ban smoking in the dining rooms. To really enjoy these cruises, American travelers have to be really comfortable with people from other countries.

The vessels will appeal to the more adventurous American traveler who wants something different, the type who will only stay at European hotels (and not Marriotts or Hiltons) when in Europe. The moderate prices and friendly atmosphere are the big attractions. But keep in mind that these vessels tend to have lots of passengers and can feel crowded.

Onboard activities may be conducted in several languages. For shore excursions, there are usually separate buses for each language, but if there aren't enough English speakers to fill a whole bus, you might have to hear another translation as well.

Cabins tend to be smaller than what Americans are used to (just like rooms in European hotels tend to be smaller than those in American hotels) and you're best off booking a deluxe room or suite if you can afford it. Cabins are likely to have portholes rather than large windows, and few of these vessels have private verandas in any cabin categories.

A Word About SOLAS

The future of some of these older ships will depend on compliance with a set of international safety regulations known as the Safety of Life at Sea (SOLAS), which are predominantly concerned with issues like fire prevention. Ships built after 1994 automatically incorporate SOLAS safety features, such as alarm and sprinkler systems, while ships built before 1994 have been required to add them by a progressive set of deadlines. The most sweeping changes were completed by a 1997 deadline, and another series of changes must be implemented by 2000 and 2005. You may want to inquire in advance whether a ship is fully equipped for fire safety with smoke detectors, alarms, sprinklers, and low-level emergency lighting for escape pathways. The changes required could prove too costly for the lines that operate some of these old-timers and seal their fate forever—so enjoy them while you can.

These ships may be difficult for travelers with disabilities, with few wide-door cabins and, quite often, high doorway sills that would be a major roadblock to wheelchairs.

The **itineraries** of these ships tend to be port-intensive (usually a port a day), so for many people the nighttime meal will be all the entertainment they need before bed. People at the late seating may mingle till the wee hours. Discos usually quiet down early, and Europeans just aren't as casino-crazy as Americans. Entertainment tends to be much more amateurish than on the American vessels, and to appeal to a multi-language crowd, the ships may feature more magicians, singers, and dancers than, say, comedians.

DRESS CODES Like the mainstream American lines, weeklong cruises on these ships generally feature two formal nights, but you won't find too many passengers in tuxedos or fancy sequined dresses. Overall, ships in this category are somewhat more casual, with guests preferring suits or sport coats to tuxes, and pantsuits or sundresses to gowns (although it's not unheard of to see a tux and a shimmery dress). Guests are asked not to wear shorts and T-shirts in the formal dining room. Daytime is casual.

Cruise Lines Reviewed in This Chapter

- Costa Cruises
- First European Cruises (Festival Cruises)
- Fred. Olsen Cruise Lines
- Mediterranean Shipping Cruises
- Norwegian Coastal Voyage/Bergen Line Services
- P&O Cruises
- Royal Olympic Cruises
- Swan Hellenic Cruises

Costa Cruises

SHIPS CostaAllegra • CostaMarina • CostaRomantica • CostaClassica • CostaVictoria • CostaAtlantica (preview)

World Trade Center, 80 SW 8th St., Miami, FL 33130-3097 (mailing address: P.O. Box 01964, Miami, FL 33101-9865). ☎ **800/462-6782** or 305/358-7325. Fax 305/375-0676. www.costacruises.com.

THE LINE IN A NUTSHELL Fun, food, and Italian-style ambiance is what these mid- and mega-sized European ships are all about. They offer good value, too, with airfare from New York included in the cruise fare.

THE EXPERIENCE With an illustrious history stretching back almost 90 years to Genoa, Italy, Costa has managed to hold onto its heritage, and that's what sets this cruise line apart from so many others. Its officers are Italian and its ships' interiors, food, festive atmosphere, and activities are still as Italian as you can find.

Costa's Europe cruises attract a majority of Italians, but also French, Germans, British, and others. Americans are in the minority on these sailings, representing about 20% of the clientele on any given sailing, but that's part of the fun: meeting new people and trying out a few remembered words from high school language classes.

Costa does an excellent job catering to its diverse clientele, but announcements are delivered in five languages on the loudspeakers and at entertainment and activities gatherings, which can get a bit tiring. Also, because these ships cater so heavily to Europeans, Americans should be aware there may be smokers in large numbers. Some areas of the dining rooms, lounges, and bars are designated nonsmoking, but not everyone pays attention to the signs.

The onboard currency is Italian lira. Currency exchange services are offered, but it can get confusing translating your money to lira and then to the other currencies.

Pros

- **Italian flavor.** The whole onboard atmosphere shows a festive Italian flair.
- **The Pasta.** While the rest of the food is fairly standard (but tasty) the handmade pasta really shines.
- **Lots of late-night action.** Despite port-intensive itineraries, people stay up late and party on these vessels. The disco gets going at midnight.

Cons

- **Very few cabins with private verandas.** The *Victoria* has none at all. (The new *CostaAtlantica,* though, will have verandas in the majority of its cabins.)
- **Lots of lots of languages.** Activities and entertainment are geared to a five-language audience.

Frommer's Ratings: Costa Cruises

	Poor	Fair	Good	Excellent	Outstanding
Enjoyment Factor				✓	
Dining		✓			
Activities				✓	
Children's Program			✓		
Entertainment			✓		
Service			✓		
Overall Value			✓		

COSTA: CRUISING ITALIAN-STYLE

Costa's origins are as Italian as could be. In 1860, Giacomo Costa established an olive-oil refinery and packaging plant in Genoa. After his death in 1916, his sons bought a ship to transport raw materials and finished products from Sardinia through Genoa to the rest of Europe. Within 19 years, the family had acquired an additional half-dozen ships, but their fortune fell with that of their country in the years during and after World War II. At war's end, only one tiny ship remained in the family's fleet, but within 3 years they managed to acquire a dozen more, most of them carrying European passengers. Costa was the world's largest operator of passenger ships in the early 1960s, before the explosion of the U.S. cruise industry nudged it into fifth place (it's still the top line in Europe).

In 1968, the Costa family made a major commitment to the U.S. market by establishing Costa Cruises, now a subsidiary of Genoa-based Costa Crociere. The size of both the ships and the fleet grew rapidly, and today the line boasts six ships, including the 54,000-ton *CostaRomantica* and 76,000-ton *CostaVictoria,* both modern and beautiful vessels, with more on the way.

In 1997, Carnival Corporation and Airtours (a British tour operator in which Carnival has a 30% stake) each bought a 50% interest in Costa, vowing to keep the line just the way it is. And so they have, adding efficiencies, doing some upgrading, adding "American comforts," but not changing the wonderful onboard atmosphere.

THE FLEET

The Costa fleet is diverse, from gleaming megas to old, rebuilt liners from the 1960s. Of its current fleet of six, there is one megaship, the 1,928-passenger ***CostaVictoria,*** built in 1996; a pair of mid-sized 1,300-passenger ships, the ***CostaRomantica*** (built in 1993) and the ***CostaClassica*** (built in 1991); the 800-passenger ***CostaAllegra,*** built in 1969 as a container ship and rebuilt as a cruise ship in 1992; the 770-passenger ***CostaMarina,*** built in 1969 as a container ship and rebuilt in 1990; and the 972-passenger ***CostaRiviera,*** the line's oldest ship, built in 1963 and rebuilt in 1993. All the ships spend the summer in Europe.

Costa's first newbuild since the launch of the *CostaVictoria* in 1996, the 2,112-passenger, 84,000-ton ***CostaAtlantica*** is scheduled to debut in spring of 2000. In many ways, the ship represents a new chapter for Costa. The *Atlantica* will be the first Costa ship to have a substantial number of private verandas; nearly 70% of the ship's cabins will be outfitted with them.

PASSENGER PROFILE

This line attracts passengers of all ages, with a good number of couples in their 40s and 50s. Americans on board will be older, experienced travelers, many of whom deliberately avoid all-American megaships and are attracted by Costa's port-intensive itineraries. Costa passengers appreciate a sense of cultural adventure and fun, and like the atmosphere of casual, sophisticated elegance and a sense of romance at which the Italians excel.

The line is a favorite of European honeymooners, and on some sailings from Italy there may be dozens of honeymoon couples on board (an older friend who was on one of these cruises reported it was great fun watching the young couples enjoy their special vacation). Families are also attracted to these cruises, although the number of kids on board is rarely overwhelming (August cruises attract the highest numbers). In the summer, the ships that depart from Italy often fill up with the Italian equivalent of the Carnival "Fun Ship" crowd, which can lead to some lively times.

DINING

Food is well-prepared continental with an Italian slant. Most memorable are the **pastas,** prepared fresh by a team of onboard pasta-makers and served with lovely sauces that will have you saying mmmmmm.

The six-course dinners might feature appetizers like fried calamari and Parma ham and melon, as well with a vegetarian appetizer selection, along with soup, salad, and a choice of two pasta dishes such as cannelloni and spaghetti. Among the main courses are roast rack of lamb with an herb crust, salmon with dill sauce, and beef tenderloin in puff pastry. Also available on every menu is a **vegetarian entree** such as a vegetable-stuffed artichoke heart. There is also a **regional choice,** such as deer and juniper berry sauce, a Scandinavian specialty offered as a special one night on a Baltic itinerary.

Costa goes out of its way to cater to a number of international tastes and make everyone happy. Hence a table of Americans may be offered off-menu items popular in the States, such as fettucine Alfredo and Caesar salad.

The **dessert menu** is limited to a few selections, but includes such Italian delights as tiramisu, gelato, and cannelloni siciliani, as well as chocolate soufflé.

Entertainment is part of the dining experience: Much emphasis and a few theatrics are placed on head waiters tossing a pasta or energetically seasoning a salad while diners look on. And most evenings have a theme, with the waiters donning special costumes and singing or dancing. On Mediterranean night, for instance, staff members don the native dress of cultures around the Mediterranean and present a red rose to each woman passenger during dessert.

Most of the ships have a single dining room; the bigger *CostaVictoria* has two. Meals are offered in two seatings, breakfast including a choice of a buffet or menu, lunch served at noon and 1:30pm, and dinner at 7pm and 9pm or 9:15pm. (Note: Late seating on these ships is later than on American ships.) Lavish midnight buffets include a Grand Buffet that takes up half the dining room and includes a half-dozen elaborate ice sculptures and a unique galley buffet (a combination midnight buffet and galley tour).

The Lido restaurant is the venue for fairly standard **casual breakfast and lunch** each day; a few nights during each cruise an informal, buffet-style dinner is also offered in the Lido for those too exhausted from a day in port to sit through a more formal dinner in the dining room (the same menu is offered at the buffet). As a nice touch, tablecloths are put on the tables of the casual eatery for the occasion.

Between meals, Juliette's Pâtisserie serves espresso, chocolates, and pastries aboard the *CostaVictoria* and *CostaRomantica;* and **Romeo's Pizzeria** offers pizza throughout the day and night. On the other ships, pizza, sweets, and other treats are offered during afternoon tea, served in the Lido restaurant.

As on most lines, cappuccino and espresso count as bar drinks and appear on your bar tab at the end of the cruise. There is no brewed decaf coffee available (instant only). The wine list is not extensive and there are no wine stewards.

Room service is offered on a 24-hour basis, but the selection is spartan at best, and there is a charge (about $2.50) for delivery.

Late last year, Costa introduced a **gourmet alternative restaurant** as an additional dining venue on the *CostaVictoria,* and will have a similar offering on the *CostaAtlantica.* A fee of $18.75 (much higher than that of other lines with alternative dining options) is charged for the experience. The experience is styled on that offered at the famous Zeffirino restaurant in Genoa.

ACTIVITIES

Activities on the ships are overseen by a team of "animators" who don costumes like clown suits and Hawaiian shirts and try their best to get everyone involved in the action.

Special Deals

Passengers booking 90 days before the cruise receive a discount of up to $1,700 per couple, and there's also an early-booking bonus of two free post-cruise hotel nights on select sailings. All Costa fares include airfare from New York. There is an add-on airfare in some cases to get passengers to New York, but that fee (usually $100 to $350) is waived on cruises between April 16 and June 14 and September 1 and November 5.

Nights include **theme nights** such as Carnivale, when people are encouraged to make and don Venetian-style masks, and a Circus night, when passengers are given tokens and participate in fun games set up in the lounges, such as throw-the-ball-at-the-target. Popular events also include a nighttime Mr. Universe contest, musical chairs, and Samba Night (lessons are given during the day to prepare for the event). Daytime activities include Italian language and cooking classes as well as such traditional cruise staples as bingo, bridge, napkin-folding, dance classes, Ping-Pong tournaments, exercise classes, beauty demonstrations, trivia games, and fun pool-side competitions. Sports offerings include shuffleboard, paddle tennis, and Ping-Pong, and on some of the ships Foosball and pool tables. Each ship also has a library (although it may not have many English selections) and a card room.

A full-time Catholic priest conducts mass almost every day in the ship chapel.

Children's Program

Compared to other cruise lines, Costa places less emphasis on separating children from adult passengers. Only about 10% of passengers are traveling with their families, so there are not throngs of children on board (except sometimes in July and August, popular family travel times), and the kids' programs and facilities are not nearly as extensive as those available on the American mainstream lines.

There's a full-time **youth counselor** aboard each Costa ship, with additional staff pressed into service whenever more than a dozen children are on the passenger list. Costa offers three children's clubs tailored to specific age groups: The Baby Club (3 to 6), featuring a story hour, crafts, games, and ice cream parties; The Junior Club (7 to 12), with jogging and aerobics, a puppet theater, mini-Olympics, and treasure hunts; and The Teen's Club (13 to 17), offering sports and fitness programs, guitar lessons, video show productions, and a rock and roll hour. The *Victoria* has a teen disco.

Group **baby-sitting** is available, at no charge, for children ages 3 (out of diapers) and up, every night until 11:30pm (but the hours can be extended until 1am if you make arrangements at least 24 hours in advance).

Entertainment

Entertainment directors program amusements such as concerts, magic and mime acts, acrobatics, and cabaret that, although produced with an Italian bent, do not require audiences to actually know the language.

If you're not looking for Las Vegas–style glitter, you'll likely find the shows amusing. Particularly notable is the fact the dancers attempt something approaching modern ballet (with some degree of success, too). Costumes and lighting are particularly creative, and the repertoire includes everything from folk music to techno-pop (not necessarily on the same night).

The *CostaVictoria, CostaClassica,* and *CostaRomantica* have particularly notable showrooms, two-tiered affairs that evoke the half moon–shaped amphitheaters of an 18th-century opera house. The other ships have more typical showrooms with pillars blocking some sight lines.

Costa Fleet Itineraries

Ship	Home Ports & Season	Itinerary
CostaAllegra	11-day Black Sea, round-trip from Genoa (May).	**11-day Black Sea:** Naples and Catania (Italy), Istanbul (Turkey), Yalta and Odessa (Ukraine), and Santorini, Mykonos, Kithera (Greece).*
Costa Atlantica	7-day Greece and Turkey, round-trip from Venice (July–Oct); 5-day Italy and Greece, Genoa to Venice (Oct).	**7-day Greece and Turkey:** Bari (Italy), Katakolon and Piraeus/Athens (Greece), and Kusadasi and Istanbul (Turkey). **5-day Italy and Greece:** Bari and Naples (Italy), Katakolon (Greece), and Valletta (Malta).
Costa Classica	7-day Greek Isles, round-trip from Venice (May–Nov); 5-day Italy and Greece, between Venice and Genoa (May, Nov).	**7-day Greek Isles:** Bari (Italy), Katakolon, Santorini, Mykonos, Rhodes (Greece), and Dubrovnik (Croatia). **5-day Italy and Greece:** Port calls may include Bari, Catania, Naples (Italy), Corfu (Greece), Valletta (Malta), and Dubrovnik (Croatia).
CostaMarina	7-day Norwegian Fjords, round-trip from Copenhagen (June–Aug); 7-day Scandinavia and Russia, round-trip from Copenhagen (June–Sept).	**7-day Norwegian Fjords:** Flam, Vik, Hellesylt, Geiranger, Bergen Kristiansand, and Oslo (Norway). **7-day Scandinavia and Russia:** Stockholm (Sweden), Helsinki (Finland), St. Petersburg (Russia), and Tallinn (Estonia).
Costa Romantica	12- and 14-day Norway, round-trip from Amsterdam (June–Aug); 10- and 11-day Scandinavia & Russia, round-trip from Amsterdam (June, Aug, Sept); 9-day Europe Capitals, Amsterdam to Genoa (Sept).	**12- and 14-day Norway/North Cape:** Port calls may include Alesund, Honningsvag, Tromso, Trondheim, Gravdal, Hammerfest, Molde, Andalsnes, Olden, Flam, Geiranger, and Bergen (Norway). **10- and 11-day Scandinavia and Russia:** Ronne (Denmark), St. Petersburg (Russia), Helsinki (Finland), Stockholm and Visby (Sweden), and Copenhagen (Denmark). **9-day Europe Capitals:** Dover (England), St. Malo (France), Leixoes (Portugal), and Cadiz and Malaga (Spain).*
CostaVictoria	7-day W. Med, round-trip from Genoa (May to Oct).	7-day W. Med, visits Naples and Palermo (Italy), Tunis (Tunisia), Mallorca and Barcelona (Spain), Marseille (France).

*Also does Holy Lands cruises.

In addition to live shows, the theaters are used for movie screenings that include Pavarotti concerts.

The **casinos** on these ships are large by European standards, and include dozens of slot machines, roulette tables, poker, and blackjack. The **discos** are popular places, and there's always dancing into the wee hours.

SERVICE

While far from pampering, service is more than adequate in both the dining room and cabins. The crew is friendly and quick-witted, though not all speak great English. Dining-room staff is composed of charming Italian waiters, but special culinary requests sometimes get lost in translation.

So as not to offend Italian passengers, who are less used to tipping than Americans, suggested tips are incredibly low by industry standards. For a 1-week cruise, recommended tips per passenger are $10 for the cabin steward, $14 (combined) for the waiter and his assistant, and $5.50 (combined) for the maitre d'hotel and his team.

CostaAllegra • CostaMarina

CostaAllegra (photo: Costa)

The Verdict

These ships are small enough so you don't get lost, comfortable, and lively, in a special Italian way.

Specifications

Size (in tons)	30,000/25,000	Officers	Italian
Number of Cabins	410/399	Crew	450/385
Number of Outside Cabins	205/183	Passenger/Crew Ratio	2 to 1
Cabins with Verandas	10/8	Year Built	1992/1990
Number of Passengers	800/770	Last Major Refurbishment	N/A

Frommer's Ratings (Scale of 1–5)

Cabin Comfort & Amenities	3	Pool, Fitness & Spa Facilities	3
Ship Cleanliness & Maintenance	3	Children's Facilities	2
Public Comfort/Space	4	Itineraries	4
Decor	4	Worth the Money	4

Both the *CostaAllegra* and *CostaMarina* were originally built in the 1960s as container ships and were completely reconstructed in the early 90s as cruise ships with a modern, Italian decor. While not sister ships, they have been reconfigured to have nearly the same layout (though the *Allegra* is longer). The *Marina* is fun and friendly; the *Allegra* slightly more formal. Both have most of their public rooms on Deck 6, making it easy for guests to know where to head to find the action.

Both vessels offer lots of windows, including a wall of glass in the stern. The dining rooms have windows on three sides, and on the Marina, even some of the ladies rooms have large windows offering ocean views. Both ships look striking from the rear with their three-deck wall of glass, domed disco on top, and trademark Costa cluster of yellow smokestacks.

Cabins & Rates

Cabins	Per diems from	Bathtub	Fridge	Hair Dryer	Sitting Area	TV
Inside	$350/$432*	no	no	yes	no	yes
Outside	$414/$511*	no	no	yes	no	yes
Suite	$510/$647*	yes	some	yes	yes	yes

**First-listed rates are for* CostaAllegra, *second for* CostaMarina. *All rates include airfare from New York.*

CABINS Standard cabins are not particularly large (145 to 160 square feet on *Allegra,* 140 to 170 on *Marina*) but are comfortable and offer twin beds, good storage space, desk, phone, safe, TV, and hair dryer. Decor is nothing special, with plain white walls and colorful banners added for color.

The *Allegra* has three large (575 square foot) Grand Suites that can sleep five or six and have forward-facing windows. Ten minisuites have verandas. All have a whirlpool bathtub, a sitting area, and two lower or a queen-sized bed; the Grand Suites also have a wet bar.

The *Marina* has eight suites located on Deck 7, all with a private veranda, sitting area, queen-sized bed, and whirlpool tub.

The *Allegra* has eight handicapped-accessible cabins; the *Marina* has none.

PUBLIC AREAS There is one dining room on each ship, located on Deck 5 and offering glass on three sides. The best place to sit is in the rear of the room, where the windows are larger than even the large portholes on the sides.

Most public rooms are located on Deck 6, are large enough to handle the crowd, and flow easily into each other. There's a large lounge/ballroom at one end, a large showroom at the other, and a large casino (with dozens of slot machines) in between, as well as a bar area with live music. Above the lounge/ballroom, the ships offer a funky round-windowed disco with a glass dome. The *Marina*'s is designed to look like a planetarium, with twinkling stars. During the day, the discos on both ships, with their panoramic views, double as observation lounges.

Other public rooms include an ocean-view library (really just a room with one wall of books, few in English) and card room, plus a fully equipped meeting/conference room on the *Allegra.* The Murano Bar on the *Allegra* features striking walls of smoked blue Murano glass illuminated from behind.

The children's rooms on both ships are small, and the show lounges are your typical old-fashioned showrooms, with poor sight lines in the rear. If you want to see the dancers' feet, get there early and get a seat in the front, and don't sit behind a pillar.

POOL, FITNESS & SPA FACILITIES The *Allegra* has a jogging deck; the *Marina* has more limited deck space. Both ships have small but well-equipped gyms and spas, with steam rooms and sauna. On the *Marina,* the small aerobics floor is really just an aisle between the equipment, making it difficult for more than six to join an exercise class comfortably.

The *Marina* has a small pool with two Jacuzzis and a pool bar, as well as a third Jacuzzi behind the disco. As a funky design feature sure to please exhibitionists, the bottom of the pool can be seen in the casino below thanks to a glass wall, which makes the bottom of the pool, and anyone in it, part of the casino's decor. The *Allegra* has a larger swimming pool with a Jacuzzi and waterfall, as well as a pool bar, and a second Jacuzzi area aft behind the disco.

On the *Marina,* there are Foosball and Ping-Pong tables on the Pool Deck, and a small video arcade.

CostaRomantica • CostaClassica

The Verdict

Italophiles will adore these mid-sized ships that deliver an authentic slice of *la dolce vita.*

CostaRomantica (photo: Costa)

Specifications

Size (in tons)	54,000/53,000	Officers	Italian/Internat'l
Number of Cabins	678/654	Crew	610/650 (Internat'l)
Number of Outside Cabins	462/428	Passenger/Crew Ratio	2 to 1
Cabins with Verandas	10	Year Built	1993/1991
Number of Passengers	1,356/1,308	Last Major Refurbishment	N/A

Frommer's Ratings (Scale of 1–5)

Cabin Comfort & Amenities	4	Pool, Fitness & Spa Facilities	3
Ship Cleanliness & Maintenance	4	Children's Facilities	3
Public Comfort/Space	3	Itineraries	5
Decor	4	Worth the Money	4

These ultra-modern sister ships have a cool, European interior design that some people find almost clinical and that contrast sharply with the lively shipboard atmosphere. The *Classica* is so knock-you-in-the-head modern with its white marble, hip art, metal accents, and glass walls that Costa mellowed its act when building sister ship *Romantica,* adding some wood paneling and warmer colors.

The vessels were the largest and most stylish ships in the Costa armada until 1996, when they were supplanted by the larger *CostaVictoria.* Many passengers are repeat customers, drawn to these vessels for their emphasis on comfort and a contemporary Italian design accented with the best of Italy's traditions. The relatively small size means you'll begin to recognize your fellow passengers after a few days at sea. And with the public rooms located on the upper four decks, it's hard to get lost.

At press time, the *CostaClassica* was scheduled to be enlarged through midsectioning, a now-common procedure in which the ship is cut in half and a new (in this case 147-foot) midsection added. Scheduled to begin in November, the stretching should be completed in March 2001.

Cabins & Rates

Cabins	Per diems from	Bathtub	Fridge	Hair Dryer	Sitting Area	TV
Inside	$300/$432*	no	no	yes	no	yes
Outside	$372/$504*	no	no	yes	no	yes
Suite	$484/$661*	yes	yes	yes	yes	yes

**First-listed rates are for* CostaRomantica, *second are for* CostaClassica. *All rates include airfare from New York.*

CABINS In a word, big. At 200 square feet, standard outside cabins are among the largest available on any mainstream cruise line and much bigger than those on most European lines. The well-designed modern cabins are attractively paneled with polished cherry wood and done up in warm colors. Each cabin is furnished with twin beds (some convert to queens), two armchairs, a small table and desk, good-sized closets, safes, hair dryers, TV, and music channels.

Lower-end inside cabins are still large at 175 square feet. Ten suites on each ship have verandas. The *CostaRomantica* also has six suites with panoramic, forward-facing windows and 18 minisuites that measure 340 square feet. The suites can all accommodate up to six passengers and are furnished with a queen bed, single sofa bed, and Murphy bed along with sitting area, minibar, double vanity, and whirlpool bath.

Six inside cabins on the *Romantica* and five on the *Classica* are wheelchair-accessible.

PUBLIC AREAS Public areas take their names from the heritage of Italy, and sometimes sport decors to match—for instance, in the *CostaRomantica*'s Botticelli Restaurant, murals and window blinds evoke themes from the Renaissance. Classic Italian touches in different areas include chandeliers from Murano, intricate mosaics, pearwood inlays, and lots and lots of brilliant white Carrara marble, while a modern Italian design esthetic shows in an abundance of steel, mirrors, and sharp, efficient edges.

Both ships have an outdoor cafe, with access to a frequently replenished buffet that sometimes gets a bit overcrowded, as do some of the other public areas aboard the ship.

One of the most stunning public spaces is the *CostaRomantica*'s L'Opera Showroom, which resembles a Renaissance amphitheater complete with tiered seating. Rising two decks high, it contains 6 miles of fiber optics and mosaics inspired by 14th-century models.

The neat, glass-walled circular discos on each ship are high up, affording an opportunity to dance close to the stars.

FITNESS, POOL & SPA FACILITIES These are definitely not ships for fitness fanatics, as facilities consist of a small albeit pleasant gym with a wall of windows, a handful of StairMasters and treadmills, and sauna, steam, and massage rooms. Because of a lack of exercise space, it's often necessary to conduct aerobics classes in the disco. It's obvious that working out is not a top priority for most passengers, whose only trips to the fitness area, it seems, are to weigh themselves on the scale.

On both ships, the Caracalla Spa has a Turkish bath as well as treatment rooms offering a wide range of massages, wraps, facials, and hydrotherapy baths, but it pales in comparison to the *CostaVictoria*'s Roman-styled spa.

There are two outdoor pools, one with a fountain, and four hot tubs (two on the *CostaClassica*), as well as a jogging track on Deck 11.

CostaVictoria

The Verdict

A sleek megaship with a European ambiance and stunning decor, this ship is an all-around beauty.

CostaVictoria (photo: Costa)

Specifications

Size (in tons)	76,000	Officers	Italian/International
Number of Cabins	964	Crew	800 (International)
Number of Outside Cabins	573	Passenger/Crew Ratio	2.4 to 1
Cabins with Verandas	0	Year Built	1996
Number of Passengers	1,928	Last Major Refurbishment	N/A

Frommer's Ratings (Scale of 1–5)

Cabin Comfort & Amenities	4	Pool, Fitness & Spa Facilities	4
Ship Cleanliness & Maintenance	4	Children's Facilities	3
Public Comfort/Space	4	Itineraries	4
Decor	5	Worth the Money	4

The ship that launched Costa Cruises into the megaship era was built in Bremerhaven, Germany, and inaugurated in the summer of 1996. With an impressive cruising speed of between 21 and 23 knots, it has a streamlined, futuristic-looking design with four tiers of glass-fronted observation decks facing the prow. Its mammoth size allows for more spacious and dramatic interior features and more options for dining and after-dark diversions than any other Costa ship. When built, it was the largest and most technologically sophisticated ship ever launched by Costa, though this year it will be bested by the line's larger new flagship, the *CostaAtlantica.*

The interior is splashier and more colorful than those of other Costa vessels (it feels a bit more like an American ship). Signature design elements include an abundant use of stainless steel, teak, suede, leather, tile mosaics, and Italian marble in swirled patterns of blues and greens—for instance, brilliant royal blue suede covers the tops of card tables, and deep, salmon-colored suede is used on the walls of the Concorde Plaza lounge. The Bolero Buffet features teak floors, and a wraparound tile mosaic creates eye-catching walls in the Capriccio Lounge.

The sleek, seven-story Planetarium Atrium—a Costa first—features four glass elevator banks and is punctuated by a thin string of ice-blue neon subtly spiraling toward the glass ceiling dome. Also a new concept in the Costa fleet are the *Victoria*'s two dining rooms, with two seatings and an abundance of seating for couples (ideal for honeymooners).

Cabins & Rates

Cabins	Per diems from	Bathtub	Fridge	Hair Dryer	Sitting Area	TV
Inside	$454*	no	yes	yes	no	yes
Outside	$518*	no	yes	yes	no	yes
Suite	$611*	yes	yes	yes	yes	yes

**Rates include airfare from New York.*

CABINS Ironically, the cabins on this biggest of Costa ships are smaller than those on the *Romantica* and *Classica.* At 120 to 150 square feet, standard inside and outside cabins certainly won't win any awards for their size (the smallest are like walk-in closets), but their sleek, minimalist design and decor bring a delicious European touch to the cruise experience. Decorative fabric panels hang on the wall above headboards, matching the bedspreads. Bedside tables and dressers are sleek and art deco. Stainless steel is used for all bathroom sinks, and for dressers and mirrors in the minisuites. All cabins have TVs, music channels, hair dryer, minibar, and safe. Some 60% of them feature oversized round portholes opening onto sea views. None have verandas.

Especially desirable are 14 minisuites, which have separate living rooms, reading areas, and tubs with hydro-massage equipment. Each is outfitted with one queen-sized bed and two Pullman-style beds. What makes them a bargain is that they contain many of the same amenities and interior design features as the more expensive suites, and their space is very generous at 301 square feet. For those with imperial taste, six full-sized suites raise the beam on luxury, with one queen and two Pullman-style beds and generous 430-square-foot proportions that make them feel roomy even if they're bunking four passengers. Furnishings in these suites are made of pear wood, with fabrics by Laura Ashley, who is not even remotely Italian, and whose particular patterns in this case are relatively bold and not particularly frilly looking. Some of the suites have floor-to-ceiling windows.

Four of the ship's cabins are specifically outfitted for passengers with disabilities. Cabins on Deck 6A don't benefit from direct elevator access, and require that guests climb a half-flight of stairs from the nearest elevator bank.

PUBLIC AREAS Public areas throb with color and energy, especially the big and brassy Monte Carlo Casino, which is linked to the Grand Bar Orpheus one floor below by a curving stairway whose glass stair treads are illuminated in patterns that are almost psychedelic. This bar is the preferred spot aboard for sampling an espresso or cappuccino, or—if it's late enough and you feel a bit reckless—a selection of grappas.

Designed to re-create an Italian piazza, the four-story Concorde Plaza is one of the *Victoria*'s signature public areas. Seating over 300, it boasts a four-story-high waterfall on one end and a wall of windows facing the sea on the other, and is a great venue for evening dancing and music or for a relaxing drink by day.

New in the multi-function Tavernetta Lounge on Deck 12 is a gourmet restaurant inspired by the famous Zeffirino restaurant in Italy (where guests including Frank Sinatra and Pope John Paul II have dined). The cost to eat here is $18.75 per person.

Other public rooms include a play area for children, a club for teens, three conference rooms, an array of boutiques, a card room, a library, a disco, and an observation

Preview: *CostaAtlantica*

Costa officials are downright gleeful about the impending arrival of the 2,112-passenger, 84,000-ton *CostaAtlantica,* the line's first new ship since the *CostaVictoria* in 1996. The ship is being built at the Kvaerner Masa shipyard in Helsinki, Finland, to the tune of $400 million, and is scheduled to debut in July 2000.

To those who know Carnival cruise ships, there may be a note of the familiar to the vessel. It features a very similar layout to Carnival's recent ships, such as the *Destiny* and *Triumph.*

The Atlantica will add something that Costa has been lacking: lots of cabins with verandas. In fact, nearly 70% of the ship's cabins (736 of 1,057) will offer them, starting with mid-priced cabins and including three levels of suites: regular suites, Panorama suites, and Grand suites. All the suites will also come with whirlpool baths and sitting areas, and every cabin will have a phone, TV, hair dryer, safe, and minibar.

Other special features include a retractable glass roof over one of the two pools at the ship's main pool area (there's also a separate kiddie pool), allowing for swimming rain or shine. The ship's ocean-view spa and fitness center, main dining room, and disco are all two decks high. The Caruso Theater is three decks high.

The ship's 12 passenger decks are named after movies directed by the famous Italian director Frederico Fellini (such as *Fred & Ginger, 8½, Roma, La Strada, Amarcord,* and *La Dolce Vita*). The Venetian-style cafe is being modeled on the famous 18th-century Caffe Florian in Venice's St. Mark's Square, and will serve specialty coffees and drinks. Among the numerous bars and lounges, the Madame Butterfly Grand Lounge will come complete with geisha waitresses, and the Coral Lounge has coral on the walls.

There is an alternative, reservations-only restaurant in the Club Atlantica, a two-deck space on top of the ship. Dinner there will cost an extra $18.75 per person. The ship also has a pizzeria.

Per diems start at $461 inside, $501 outside, and $625 suite, including airfare from New York.

lounge that serves as a grand arena for socializing and special shipboard events and as a theater for evening entertainment.

POOL, FITNESS & SPA FACILITIES The *Victoria*'s Pompeii Spa includes its own indoor pool. It's done with richly colored mosaic tiles and Roman columns. You can release your tensions in a steam bath, a sauna, or a Turkish bath, or sit and soak in the spa's Jacuzzi, which is perched artfully within the larger waters of the heated swimming pool. The attractive but smallish workout room shares a glass wall with the spa and pool area and features over a dozen exercise machines.

Out on deck, there's a pair of swimming pools as well as a "misting pool" that cools off overheated sunbathers with fine jets of water. Further decks wrap around the pools and their sunbathing area, providing plenty of space for passengers to stretch out and soak up the rays, even when the ship is fully booked. It looks like a resort on the Italian Riviera with its bright yellow and blue deck chairs and its nautical blue-and-white-striped lounges. There are four Jacuzzis, a tennis court that does double-duty as a half-sized basketball court, and a jogging track, four circuits of which equal 1 mile. There's also a beauty salon aboard.

First European Cruises (Festival Cruises)

SHIPS IN EUROPE Azur • Flamenco • Mistral

95 Madison Ave., Ste. 1203, New York, NY 10016. ☎ **888/983-8767** or 212/779-7168. www.first-european.com.

THE LINE IN A NUTSHELL A popular line in Europe, First European operates mid-sized ships with a friendly, informal atmosphere.

THE EXPERIENCE First European's well-maintained ships offer good value, a friendly and relaxed atmosphere, and imaginative itineraries, but they can seem crowded at times, particularly in high season, when lines at disembarkation and at buffets are not uncommon. Cabins tend to be small, so if you've got the bucks you're best off booking a deluxe cabin or suite. Currently, the line caters mostly to a European audience but, especially with the new ship *Mistral*—a particularly nice entrant into the moderately priced marketplace (its designers have also worked on premium vessels like those in the Celebrity fleet)—it hopes to attract more Americans and other English-speaking guests.

Due to the pan-European clientele aboard, communication with fellow passengers can get tricky, and announcements in English, German, French, Italian, and sometimes Spanish as well are near constant, since it takes so long to get through all the languages. Onboard activities and shore excursions are also conducted in a variety of languages.

The ships offer particularly good onboard duty-free shopping opportunities, and on the *Azur* and *Flamenco* (where the spas are not yet operated by Steiner, as they are on the *Mistral*), massages and facials are a bargain, too.

Pros

- **Cuisine.** Great food, designed to please a variety of palates.
- **Public rooms.** There's a good variety for ships of this size.
- **Unusual itineraries.** Itineraries go beyond the norm. The line's Greek Isles cruises on the *Mistral,* for instance, leave from Venice and include a port call in Dubrovnik, Croatia, and in Bari, Italy, in addition to Katakolon, Santorini, Mykonos, Rhodes, and Piraeus, Greece.

Cons

- **No verandas.** No cabins on the three ships have private balconies except the suites on the *Mistral.* (Of course, this is a "con" only if you want a veranda cabin.)
- **Incessant announcements.** There's a constant babble of public address announcements in multiple languages.

Frommer's Ratings: First European Cruises

	Poor	Fair	Good	Excellent	Outstanding
Enjoyment Factor				✓	
Dining				✓	
Activities			✓		
Children's Program			✓		
Entertainment		✓			
Service		✓			
Overall Value			✓		

FIRST EUROPEAN: NEW SHIPS, NEW EURO-AMERICAN FOCUS

First European is the name adopted by Greece-based Festival Cruises in 1997 for U.S. marketing purposes. The company was established in 1992 in Piraeus by Greek entrepreneur George Poulides, who began with a trio of older, refurbished, mid-sized ships (the *Azur, Bolero,* and *Flamenco*), and whose ambitious expansion program led last year to the introduction of the *Mistral,* the line's first new ship. Additional 1,500-plus passenger new-builds are in the works, to be delivered in June 2001 and March 2002, and the company has also announced plans for two additional 2,000-passenger vessels, to be delivered in 2003 and 2004. All four will be aimed at a pan-European and American market.

THE FLEET

The ***Azur,*** the line's first ship, was built in 1971 as a ferry and later remodeled into a classic-style cruise ship. The ***Bolero,*** built in 1968, is on charter this summer to the U.K.'s First Choice. The ***Flamenco,*** built in 1972, underwent a $10 million refurbishment in 1997 and offers more in the way of amenities than the *Azur.*

The ***Mistral*** is a brand new mid-sized vessel that's very contemporary, and the line's best ship yet. Cabins include 80 suites with verandas, and there is a good variety of public rooms.

Other new ships are being built for the line at Chantiers de l'Atlantique shipyards in St. Nazaire, France, and are due in 2001 and 2002.

PASSENGER PROFILE

The passenger mix aboard is a middle-class, budget-conscious European one, and includes everyone from kids and young singles to retirees. The most-represented nationalities are Italian and German. The line draws about 15% of its passengers from the U.S., but wants to see those numbers increase. Its introduction of Caribbean cruises aboard the *Mistral* this year should help that cause.

Passengers tend to enjoy the open deck space when the ship is not in port, and the majority go to bed pretty early at night. Because we're talking Europeans, there will be lots of smokers.

DINING

The line handles well the differing food tastes of its international crowd, offering a good variety of meat, chicken, and fish dishes. Pastas are particularly tasty.

The main dining rooms on the *Flamenco* and *Azur* are large and can get noisy. The one on the *Mistral* is an improvement; the ship also boasts an **alternative dining** venue (suite guests get to eat there every night) that offers both indoor and outdoor dining.

Most people prefer to take three meals a day in the dining rooms, but there are also **deck buffets** for breakfast and lunch, as well as midnight buffets and afternoon tea.

There is 24-hour room service, but from a limited menu. Pizza is served late at night at the bars. **Vegetarian and light items** are available, but are not always on the menu. You should notify the maitre d' of your needs when you get aboard.

Smoking is not permitted in the dining rooms.

Special Deals

If you book at least 90 days in advance, you get $100 per person off the price of the cruise. The line also offers special rates for kids ages 2 to 17 and under sharing a cabin with their parents.

First European Cruises Fleet Itineraries

Ship	Home Ports & Season	Itinerary
Azur	7-day E. Med, Savona, Italy (May, June); 7-day E. Med, round-trip from Genoa (Dec).	**7-day E. Med:** Port calls may include Capri, Catania, Naples, Ischia, Civitavecchia/Rome, (Italy), Porto-Vecchio (Corsica), Valletta (Malta), Katakolon and Corfu (Greece), and Dubrovnik (Croatia).*
Flamenco	3-day Italy/Spain, (Apr), 5- and 6-day Med (May, Sept), 7-day W. Med (May), all round-trip from Genoa; 10-day W. Med, Genoa or Kiel, Germany (May, Sept); 7-day Norway and 7-day Scandinavia & Russia, round-trip from Kiel (June–Sept).	**7-day Norway:** Flam, Gudvangen, Hellesylt, Geiranger, Bergen and Oslo (Norway), and Copenhagen (Denmark). **7-day Scandinavia & Russia:** Visby and Stockholm (Sweden), Tallinn (Estonia), St. Petersburg (Russia), and Gdynia (Poland); **3-day Italy/Spain:** Mahón and Barcelona (Spain); **5-, 6-, and 7-day Med:** Port calls may include Porto Vecchio and Ajaccio (Corsica), Palermo, Civitavecchia/Rome, Naples (Italy), Sète (France), Valletta (Malta), Tunis (Tunisia), Mallorca, Ibiza, Mahón, Barcelona (Spain).
Mistral	7-day Greek Isles/Adriatic, round-trip from Venice (June–Oct); 6-day Med, Genoa to Venice (May).	**7-day Greek Isles/Adriatic:** Dubrovnik (Croatia), Bari (Italy), and Katakalan, Santorini, Mykonos, Rhodes, Piraeus/Athens (Greece); **6-day Med:** Ajaccio (Corsica), Valletta (Malta), Catania (Italy), Corfu (Greece), and Dubrovnik (Croatia).*

*Also does Holy Land itineraries.

Activities

Daytime activities include multi-language quiz games, scavenger hunts, volleyball and basketball, dance lessons, lectures, bingo, pool games, and aerobics classes, but most people are happy to just stretch out on the generously sized decks. Bargain hunters will want to give the onboard gift shops a workout (the duty-free prices are great).

The **spa** on the *Mistral* is Steiner-operated and offers that firm's well-established standard services and prices, but the spas and beauty shops on the other ships are independently operated and offer bargain prices.

One English-language film is shown in each ship's cinema each day, and on the *Flamenco* and *Mistral* there are also movie choices on TV. The *Mistral*'s interactive TVs are an activity in themselves.

The **casinos** are small by U.S. cruise ship standards (Europeans aren't as into gambling as Americans), and offer roulette, blackjack, and slots.

Children's Program

These ships are family-friendly, and kids get a variety of supervised daily activities (including crafts and games). The *Flamenco* has a kiddie pool.

Keep in mind the multi-national ambiance on these ships translates to the kids' programs as well. It can be a great experience for kids to mingle with their peers from other countries, but they should be forewarned that not everyone will speak English.

Baby-sitting is available on all the ships.

Entertainment

Entertainment includes acts that are musical or visual—for instance, dancers and magicians—and thus can appeal to people speaking a variety of languages.

These ships offer a variety of nightclubs and bars (including a cigar bar on the *Mistral*) and discos. Karaoke is a popular offering.

SERVICE

Service is warm and friendly but not very refined. The crew is well versed in English, and a good crew-to-passenger ratio means you can nearly always find a helping hand. The Greek officers can be downright charming.

Azur

Azur (photo: First European)

The Verdict

This older ship offers a friendly, informal cruise experience well suited to first-timers and those who don't care much about big-ship amenities.

Specifications

Size (in tons)	15,000	Officers	French/Greek
Number of Cabins	360	Crew	330 (International)
Number of Outside Cabins	178	Passenger/Crew Ratio	2 to 1
Cabins with Verandas	0	Year Built	1971
Number of Passengers	800	Last Major Refurbishment	1996

Frommer's Ratings (Scale of 1–5)

Cabin Comfort & Amenities	2	Pool, Fitness & Spa Facilities	3
Ship Cleanliness & Maintenance	3	Children's Facilities	3
Public Comfort/Space	3	Itineraries	4
Decor	2	Worth the Money	4

Built as a ferry in 1971 and remodeled shortly thereafter into a cruise ship, the *Azur* is a friendly ship with classical appeal. There's plenty of open deck space, spacious public rooms, several bars, and lots of activities to keep passengers happily occupied.

Cabins & Rates

Cabins	Per diems from	Bathtub	Fridge	Hair Dryer	Sitting Area	TV
Inside	$203*	no	no	no	no	no
Outside	$257*	no	no	no	no	no
Suite	$297*	yes	no	no	some	no

**Rates include round-trip air from Boston, Newark, New York, or Philadelphia.*

CABINS The cabins are well-designed but small by American standards, with bright, late-'60s-style appeal (think oranges and bright blues). The suites, at 204 square feet, have picture windows, bathtubs, and sitting areas. All cabins have two music channels and phones, but no TVs.

Two cabins are handicapped accessible.

PUBLIC AREAS Large is the word. There's a large, bright, and sometimes noisy restaurant and two large lounges. The Tahiti Disco faces one of two swimming pools, while the Pacific Lounge has picture windows on three sides for nice views. There are also a number of bars, a small casino (with blackjack, slots, and roulette), a children's playroom, a library, and a nice cinema with real theater seats and even a balcony. The ship, in general, has a nice warm feel.

POOL, FITNESS & SPA FACILITIES There are two swimming pools, one with a retractable roof. The ship has a small fitness center, sauna, and massage rooms. Deck sports include volleyball, basketball, and Ping-Pong. Aerobics classes are also offered.

Flamenco

Flamenco (photo: First European)

The Verdict

A warm and friendly yet sometimes crowded ship, the *Flamenco* is particularly well suited for first-timers and families.

Specifications

Size (in tons)	17,000	Officers	Greek
Number of Cabins	392	Crew	350 (International)
Number of Outside Cabins	262	Passenger/Crew Ratio	2 to 1
Cabins with Verandas	0	Year Built	1972
Number of Passengers	800	Last Major Refurbishment	1997

Frommer's Ratings (Scale of 1–5)

Cabin Comfort & Amenities	2	Pool, Fitness & Spa Facilities	2
Ship Cleanliness & Maintenance	3	Children's Facilities	3
Public Comfort/Space	4	Itineraries	4
Decor	3	Worth the Money	3

The *Flamenco* underwent a $10 million refurbishment before it entered the First European fleet in 1997, and offers public rooms done up in a warm and tasteful decor, and a nice relaxed atmosphere. The Greek officers and international crew keep the ambiance friendly, but there are a lot of passengers on this ship and there are occasionally crowds, like at buffet lines and disembarkation.

Cabins & Rates

Cabins	Per diems from	Bathtub	Fridge	Hair Dryer	Sitting Area	TV
Inside	$355*	no	no	no	no	yes
Outside	$454*	no	no	no	no	yes
Suite	$528*	some	no	no	some	yes

**Rates include round-trip air from Boston, Newark, New York, or Philadelphia.*

CABINS Deluxe outside cabins are on the small side at 153 square feet, and are simply furnished and rather spartan, with bright-colored fabrics and dull-colored walls, phones, music channels, and TVs. Cabins have good storage space, however, with big closets with built-in drawers. Bathrooms are compact. There are no tubs or verandas. Four good-sized suites offer sitting areas and picture windows.

Two cabins are wheelchair-accessible.

PUBLIC AREAS The public rooms on this ship are contemporary and comfortable. The Universe show lounge has okay sight lines, but for the best views you'll want to grab the seating in the raised areas on the sides. The Starlight Lounge, a favorite hangout spot at the top of the ship, is a circular room offering panoramic views and dancing at night (everything from ballroom to disco).

The casino is not very large; the health club is downright tiny. But the ship does offer a variety of bars and lounges, plus a piano bar, a cinema, a children's playroom, and a library (which attracts a lot of smokers and has few English titles), plus the large (main) Galaxy Restaurant and a small Lido restaurant on pool deck, with indoor and outdoor seating for casual breakfast and lunch buffets (most passengers prefer to eat in the dining room).

There is lots of sundeck space, but it can get crowded.

POOL, FITNESS & SPA FACILITIES The tiny (though windowed) gym has only a few treadmills and an assortment of weights. Gold's Gym it's not.

There's one outdoor pool for adults and a shallow pool for kids. The "Sports Deck," located on Galaxy Deck aft, behind the galley, and accessible via stairs from the Lounge Deck above, has only a basketball court. Beauty services and massages at the spa are offered at really low rates.

Mistral

The Verdict

This ship moves First European way up the evolutionary ladder, offering a lot of the amenities you'd only expect to find on a larger ship, but in a friendly and intimate setting.

Mistral (photo: First European)

Specifications

Size (in tons)	48,000	Officers	Greek
Number of Cabins	598	Crew	500 (International)
Number of Outside Cabins	362	Passenger/Crew Ratio	2.4 to 1
Cabins with Verandas	80	Year Built	1999
Number of Passengers	1,200	Last Major Refurbishment	N/A

Frommer's Ratings (Scale of 1–5)

Cabin Comfort & Amenities	4	Pool, Fitness & Spa Facilities	4
Ship Cleanliness & Maintenance	5	Children's Facilities	4
Public Comfort/Space	4	Itineraries	5
Decor	5	Worth the Money	4

Launched last summer, and built at Chanters de l'Atlantique in St. Nazaire, France, the $240 million *Mistral* is the largest ship to fly the French flag. Its friendly and smart interior was designed by a Greek firm that also worked on Celebrity Cruises' vessels. Each deck is named after a European city: Paris, Rome, London, Berlin, Brussels, Athens, Cannes, and Madrid.

The ship offers several dining options including an alternative restaurant, and boasts an outdoor thalassotherapy center (a sort of giant-sized whirlpool tub) and 80 large suites with verandas, both unusual offerings on a moderately priced, mid-size vessel.

Trivia Fact: All prices for drinks, shore excursions, gift shop purchases, and so forth are listed in euros, making the *Mistral* the first ship to use the new European single currency. As on most every ship, purchases are charged to your onboard account, and paid at the cruise's end. Passengers are given calculators as an amenity to translate prices into their native currency.

Cabins & Rates

Cabins	Per diems from	Bathtub	Fridge	Hair Dryer	Sitting Area	TV
Inside	$365*	no	yes	yes	no	yes
Outside	$437*	no	yes	yes	no	yes
Suite	$517*	yes	yes	yes	yes	yes

**Rates include round-trip air from Boston, Newark, New York, or Philadelphia.*

CABINS All the cabins are a comfortable 150 square feet, and the 80 minisuites with verandas are 236 square feet (including veranda). All cabins are nicely decorated and have interactive TVs, phones, radios, minibars, safes, hair dryers, and writing areas, as well as a good amount of storage space. The lowest category cabins have bunk beds, making them suitable for families or singles trying to save a buck. The suites have sitting areas, bathtubs, and VCRs.

Two cabins are wheelchair-accessible.

PUBLIC AREAS The ship was designed for Europeans, but with Americans in mind as well. For instance, there's a small casino, but when the vessel is in the Caribbean (in the winters) the casino can be expanded by using the conference room next door. The ship has a two-story atrium with a grand piano and black granite waterfall sculpture.

The main restaurant boasts an art-deco style, and the Rialto alternative restaurant is particularly lovely, done up with Portuguese tiles and offering both indoor and outdoor dining. Passengers in the ship's minisuites dine every night in the Rialto, while other passengers can book tables in the restaurant on a reservations-only basis.

There are numerous bars and lounges. The multi-deck show lounge was built without pillars for great sight lines, and there's a cigar bar and library cleverly tucked under its slope.

The vessel also has both children's and teens' playrooms, a coffee bar, and several shops, as well as a particularly well-equipped medical center with dialysis machines (as required by French regulations).

POOL, FITNESS & SPA FACILITIES This vessel boasts the rare and wonderful offering of an outdoor thalassotherapy center (a large whirlpool-style pool, a larger version of which is offered on Celebrity's *Millennium*). The center and other spa offerings—including thermal suites and an aromatic steam room, as well as sauna and massage areas and a beauty salon—are operated by Steiner.

The *Mistral* also has two swimming pools and a good-sized gym with up-to-date machines.

Fred. Olsen Cruise Lines

SHIPS IN EUROPE Black Prince • Black Watch

Fred. Olsen House, White Horse Road, Ipswich, Suffolk, England IP1 5LL. ☎ **01473/292200.** Fax 01473/292410. USA Sales Representative: EuroCruises, 33 Little West 12th St., Ste. 106, New York, NY 10014. Reservations: ☎ **800/688-3876** or 212/691-2099. Brochures: 800/661-1119. Fax 212/366-4747. www.eurocruises.com.

THE LINE IN A NUTSHELL Homeported in Dover, England, and largely catering to British passengers, the *Black Watch* and *Black Prince* offer value that's hard to beat. On *Black Watch* especially, passengers are offered an experience aboard a venerable ocean liner for a price hardly equaled for ships of this comfort and class.

THE EXPERIENCE Both the line's friendly, older, fairly priced ships cater to a professional and/or early retired class of mostly British Europeans, though the line is trying to attract Americans, as this excerpt from the "Cruising British Style" section of its promotional brochure makes clear: "The British have fabulous sea manners. All say Good Morning, are orderly on line, ask before interrupting, and are most cordial. Formal tea, between 3 and 4, includes scones and tasty biscuits. . . .You'll meet others who are generally well versed in world history, politics, and geography. And they are fun—in a contained sort of way. When you score at carpet boule [like Italian bocce ball with a nautical slant] they exclaim 'lovely' or 'brilliant.'" The last line of the little promotional item concludes: "Best of all, everybody speaks English."

It's likely North Americans who sail aboard will find themselves seated with the Brits at one of the big round dining room tables where conversations may turn on Tony Blair, the late Princess Di and the two young princes, or their favorite programmes (not "shows") on the telly. If you think you may have difficulty adjusting to Brit-speak, these ships are not for you.

Pros

- **British sensibility.** A chance to view Europe with affable British passengers and through a British sensibility.
- **The *Black Prince*'s indoor swimming pool.** A rare find in a vessel this size. The vessel's drop-down marina also makes for easy access to watersports.
- **The *Black Watch*'s public rooms.** All tastefully restored with an eye towards tradition.

Cons

- **British sensibility.** Some Americans may feel out of place among so many British passengers.
- **Some small spaces.** The *Black Prince* has small cabins and rather dark public rooms.

Frommer's Ratings: Fred. Olsen Cruise Lines

	Poor	Fair	Good	Excellent	Outstanding
Enjoyment Factor				✓	
Dining		✓			
Activities			✓		
Children's Program		✓			
Entertainment		✓			
Service		✓			
Overall Value					✓

THE FRED. OLSEN WAY

Fred. Olsen Cruise Lines is a division of a 150-year-old company that originated in Hvitsten on Oslofjord in Norway when three Olsen brothers began an international shipping company that's now diversified into tankers, ships' crewing, shipbuilding, and property development—in recent decades, it's even had the franchise for Timex watches in Scotland (go figure...). After years of seafaring experience, the company is today reportedly enthralled with its foray into the cruise passenger market and hopes to expand to three ships.

Though Fred. Olsen Cruise Lines is headquartered in Ipswich, England, Olsen's main offices remain in Norway's capital of Oslo, and both the *Black Prince* and *Black Watch* are registered in Norway. When either one ventures north up or down the fjord to Oslo, the ships give a friendly blast when they pass the Olsen estate on the eastern bank below the city. Any Olsens present come out to wave at their ship.

THE FLEET

Fred. Olsen Cruise Line's flagship vessel is the ***Black Watch.*** Built in 1972 at the Wartsila shipyard in Finland for Royal Viking Line as the *Royal Viking Star,* this fine ship, with its sister ships *Royal Viking Sky* and *Royal Viking Sea,* was acknowledged at the time to be one of the finest passenger vessels afloat. With their sleek lines, cheerful decor, and understated elegance, they brought a feeling of sophistication to cruising.

In 1996, Fred. Olsen acquired and completely retrofitted the ship, stretching it to 630 feet. At 28,492 tons, it's a medium-sized liner with classical lines, generously sized cabins, an open and airy feeling, a wide teak deck for walkers and joggers, a serious library, and expansive public rooms and lounges that were restored and decorated with taste. The ship's inaugural cruise was in November 1966 from Dover to the Canary Islands, the most popular cruise destination for British ships, especially in winter months when the Canaries are to Brits what the Caribbean is to North Americans seeking sun.

The company's other ship, the 11,209-ton, 412-passenger ***Black Prince,*** is considerably smaller and more intimate. She was built for Olsen at the Lubecker Fender Werft shipyard in Lubeck, Germany, in 1966 and served for a while as a car ferry and cargo carrier with a rear opening and an auto-truck ramp, doing heavy duty in the North Sea between England and Norway. At the ship's latest retrofit, the auto ramp was eliminated and what had formerly been a large cargo and car-carrying area was converted to an inside recreation area with a sizable indoor heated pool, rare in a vessel this size.

Neither ship shows any ostentation in service or decor.

PASSENGER PROFILE

Naturally with their home base in Dover, both vessels attract a largely British clientele, but as the ships become better known in the Americas, the passenger mix is changing slightly. On *Black Watch,* non-Europeans amount to about 10%. The figure is half that on the *Black Prince.*

The cruise line has stated outright that its target market is middle-class, aged 50+, retired professionals, self-employed small business people, and civil servants. (Demo-

Fred. Olsen Theme Cruises

A wide variety of theme cruises are offered on the *Black Watch,* including opera, gardening, food and drink, golf (with time to play on courses at the ports), archaeology, film classics, classical music, ballroom dancing, watercolor painting, bridge, and antiques. Contact the line or ask your travel agent for sailing dates and details.

Fred. Olsen Fleet Itineraries

Ship	Home Ports & Season	Itinerary
Black Prince	11- to 15-day Norway, round-trip from Leith (Scotland) or Dover (May–July); 14-day Scandinavia & Russia (July) and 14-day W. Med (Apr, Sept, Oct) round-trip from Dover.	**11- to 15-day Norway:** Port calls may include Stavanger, Gudvangen, Flam, Trondheim, Geiranger, Alesund, Hellesylt, Olden, and Bergen (Norway). **14-day Scandinavia & Russia:** Oslo (Norway), Copenhagen and Svendborg (Denmark), Visby (Sweden), Helsinki (Finland), St. Petersburg (Russia), Tallinn (Estonia), and Holtenau (Germany). **14-day W. Med:** Port calls may include Lisbon and Portimao (Portugal), Ajaccio (Corscia), Barcelona, Mallorca, La Coruna (Spain), and Gibraltar.
Black Watch	14- and 18-day Med, round-trip from Dover (July and Sept); 10-day Med, Dover or Malaga, Spain (March, Apr); 12-day Med, Civitavecchia/ Rome or Piraeus/Athens (March, Apr); 7- to 14-day Norway and 9- to 13-day Scandinavia or Scandinavia & Russia, all round-trip from Dover (June–Aug).	**10- to 18-day Med:** Port calls may include La Coruna and Cadiz (Spain), Toulon and Villefranche (France), Livorno, Civitavecchia/Rome, Sorrento, Palmero, Alghero (Italy), Katakolon, Santorini, Mykonos, Rhodes, Khios (Greece), Heraklion (Crete), and Istanbul and Kusadasi (Turkey). **7- to 14-day Norway:** Port calls may include Balestrand, Bergen, Eidfjord, Lofthus, Kristiansand, Flam, Honningsvaag, Tromso (Norway), and Amsterdam (Holland). **9- to 13-day Scandinavia or Scandinavia & Russia:** Port calls may include Oslo (Norway), Gothenburg and Stockholm (Sweden), Helsinki (Finland), St. Petersburg (Russia), Tallinn (Estonia), Copenhagen (Denmark), Holtenau, Brunsbüttel, Hamburg (Germany), and Amsterdam (Holland). **56-day Grand Europe:** Spain, France, Italy, Tunisia, Malta, Greece, Turkey, Cyprus, Egypt, Israel, Morocco, and more.

graphics differ between the two ships, with the *Black Watch* attracting a slightly younger clientele.) In other words, the line concedes the high end of cruising to other lines, but thinks of its passengers as pleasant people attracted by a reasonable price on a venerable ship far removed from the megaship experience.

Dining

While the food is not memorable, it is perfectly acceptable and sometimes served with elan. Dinner is in two seatings on both ships, and there are breakfast and lunch **buffets** as an alternative to taking all three meals in the dining rooms. Afternoon tea is served in the lounges and on deck. Both ships also offer a late-night buffet, but it is sometimes sparsely attended. **Vegetarians** are provided for at meals, but service isn't seamless: They must sometimes wait for their "special" soup or meal from the kitchen while others are served, which makes for awkwardness at a large table. And yes, as aboard so many ships, the tired last-night **Baked Alaska** routine is honored here too.

Activities

Daytime activities include deck sports (the *Black Watch* has a golf net and deck tennis), carpet boule (somewhat like Italian bocce ball), card games (including bridge), lectures, and classes in subjects like clay modeling and ceramics. The *Black Prince* has a marina from which passengers can enjoy a variety of watersports offerings. The bridge aboard both ships is often open for visits.

Children's Program

The *Black Watch* has a small children's playroom, with the plastic ball bins kids can jump around in, among other attractions. There are activities like pizza and ice cream parties.

The *Black Prince* is not geared for kids.

Entertainment

The entertainment is pleasant but many of the jokes are Brit-oriented, with references to members of Parliament, the game of snooker, or *Bridget Jones's Diary.* There is a nightly show in the show lounge with cabaret-style song and dance, headline acts, and local performers brought on at ports of call, followed by live band music for dancing. Piano music is also offered in a separate lounge area. The *Black Watch* has a cinema.

Service

Service is adequate on both ships. Waiters are not obsequious. Virtually everyone on the ship speaks English.

The *Black Watch* has a self-service laundry and ironing room. Dry cleaning is available on both.

Black Prince

The Verdict

An intimate and comfortable ship with a mostly British clientele and a nifty drop-down marina, as well as an indoor swimming pool.

Black Prince (photo: Fred. Olsen)

Specifications

Size (in Tons)	11,209	Officers	Norwegian
Number of Cabins	241	Crew	200 (British/
Number of Outside Cabins	145		Filipino/Malaysian)
Cabins with Verandas	0	Year Built	1966
Number of Passengers	451	Last Major Refurbishment	1998

Frommer's Ratings (Scale of 1–5)

Cabin Comfort & Amenities	2	Pool, Fitness & Spa Facilities	3
Ship Cleanliness & Maintenance	3	Children's Facilities	N/A
Public Comfort/Space	3	Itineraries	4
Decor	3	Worth the Money	4

A smaller ship than the *Black Watch,* this intimate, comfortable 412-passenger vessel attracts a slightly younger clientele, 90% of whom are European, largely from the U.K. Many people aboard will know the ship is named for none other than the Black Prince (Edward of Woodstock) born in the 14th century and son of Edward III of England.

The ship underwent a multimillion-dollar refurbishment in 1998, and offers a relaxed atmosphere. It's fully stabilized, with a sizable indoor pool and adjacent health fitness center in what once was a cargo and garage when, decades ago, the ship was a car ferry on the North Sea sailing from England to Norway.

Cabins & Rates

Cabins	Per diems from	Bathtub	Fridge	Hair Dryer	Sitting Area	TV
Inside	$180	no	no	yes	no	yes
Outside	$180	no	some	yes	no	yes
Suite	$360	yes	yes	yes	yes	yes

CABINS Some outside and all inside cabins come with either a Pullman bed or sofa bed that you can put away to have more space during the day. Category G outside cabins have upper and lower berths. The cabins are small, with the exception of the junior suites (the highest cabin category), which have bathtubs and fixed beds. Family cabins offer a double bed and one upper and one lower berth. All cabins have telephones, TVs, and hair dryers. The five top-level cabins are junior suites, with sitting areas, bathtubs, and refrigerators.

Special cabins for singles have a Pullman or sofa bed. Two cabins are designed for wheelchair passengers.

PUBLIC AREAS Public rooms are small, which can be a plus (more intimate) or a minus (if one is looking for large and airy spaces). The ship has three small restaurants: Fleur de Lys, the Royal Garter, and (most recently) the conservatory-style Balblom Restaurant with retractable ceiling, as well as several lounges and bars. The Aquitaine Lounge is smaller, with relaxing piano music, while the Neptune Lounge is brighter and livelier, with "Showtime" held here nightly. There is also a small casino.

POOL, FITNESS & SPA FACILITIES Few passenger vessels this size have such a formidable heated inside pool and fitness area, all made possible by the space vacated when the ship no longer ferried cars and trucks. There are also a small outdoor pool, two Jacuzzis, a sauna, and Steiner spa and beauty services. The ship has a drop-down marina from which passengers can enjoy watersports such as waterskiing and windsurfing while the ship is at anchor in calm seas.

Black Watch

The Verdict

An ocean-liner ambiance with an appeal that's decisively British.

Black Watch (photo: Fred. Olsen)

Specifications

Size (in tons)	28,492	Officers	Norwegian
Number of Cabins	427	Crew	330 (British/
Number of Outside Cabins	375		Filipino/Malaysian)
Cabins with Verandas	9	Year Built	1972
Number of Passengers	798	Last Major Refurbishment	1998

Frommer's Ratings (Scale of 1–5)

Cabin Comfort & Amenities	3	Pool, Fitness & Spa Facilities	2
Ship Cleanliness & Maintenance	4	Children's Facilities	2
Public Comfort/Space	4	Itineraries	5
Decor	4	Worth the Money	5

The larger of Fred. Olsen Cruise Lines' two vessels, the *Black Watch* is an ocean liner in the tradition of ships built in the seventies, before megaships came along. If the ship's pianist around tea time is playing some classic tunes, one can feel a bit of nostalgia and be satisfied that this once-acclaimed vessel, after its elaborate retrofit, is still sailing the seas as it was intended to, carrying cruise passengers out of Dover. Call it historic preservation. After all, cruise ships, like fine homes, can be preserved and updated to enjoy a new life.

Despite the fact that this ship entered service in 1972, there's nothing dowdy about the interior. Bright colors in good taste are employed throughout. There's nothing garish, and no kitsch.

Cabins & Rates

Cabins	Per diems from	Bathtub	Fridge	Hair Dryer	Sitting Area	TV
Inside	$186	no	no	yes	no	yes
Outside	$211	some	no	yes	no	yes
Suite	$310	yes	yes	yes	yes	yes

CABINS Cabins range from small insides to spacious suites. About 90% are outside. Cabins in the upper categories and some lower categories as well come with bathtubs. All cabins have TVs, telephones, and hair dryers, and upper categories (junior suites on up) offer refrigerators and sitting areas. Suites also offer VCRs and stereos, floor-to-ceiling windows, and verandas. All cabins have taped television programming and, when the ship is within range, live reception.

There are four categories of cabins designed for singles, and four cabins are available for wheelchair passengers.

PUBLIC AREAS Many passengers appreciate the staffed Explorers Library with its nautical motif and large stock of up-to-date books. Just off this room is a small smoking room where the smell of cigar smoke is evident, some of it drifting into the library. Adjacent to the library on the Bridge Deck is the Dalreoch Card Room for card games, bridge, Scrabble, and special presentations.

There is a small casino on the Lido Deck, along with the Star Night Club and several bars. Nightly shows are held in the Neptune Lounge, with smoking restricted to one side of the lounge, and movies are shown at the 150-seat cinema.

POOL, FITNESS & SPA FACILITIES There's a large outdoor pool, an outdoor splash pool, and Jacuzzis, as well as a spa operated by Steiner, a beauty salon, and a good-sized fitness center with saunas and some sophisticated exercise equipment. On the Sun Deck are golf nets and deck tennis court.

Mediterranean Shipping Cruises

SHIPS Melody • Monterey • Rhapsody

420 Fifth Ave., New York, NY 10018. ☎ **800/666-9333** or 212/764-4800. Fax 212/764-8593. www.mscruise.com.

THE LINE IN A NUTSHELL The ships aren't the fanciest afloat but they're all friendly and informal, and offer a decent range of amenities and activities at a low price.

THE EXPERIENCE This Swiss/Italian line offers a good bargain for passengers on three older ships in Europe. The ships—including the *Melody,* which may be familiar to some Americans because it used to be Premier Cruises' *Big Red Boat*—are all mid-sized, have been updated with modern decor that's comfortable rather than plush, and offer lots of open deck space, port-intensive itineraries, and an experience that's friendly and fun, thanks in large part to the Italian crew members. Expect a European ambiance and an experience that sometimes leans further toward creakiness than toward over-the-top elegance.

Mediterranean Shipping Cruises doesn't offer the range of activities and entertainment you'll find aboard the big new megaships, but they do offer good variety, with distractions like volleyball, Italian lessons, sunset cocktail parties with dance music, poolside contests, casinos, discos, and small spas.

MSC is an Italian entity that's relatively new to the North American market, so you'll find few Americans aboard, and many, many Italians and Germans, as well as a goodly number of Brits. Most are couples in their 40s on up. Announcements are made in multiple languages depending on the passenger manifest. Because of the line's affordable prices, these ships are particularly well suited to first-time cruisers.

Pros

- **Affordable rates.** That's what really makes these cruises attractive options.
- **Informal international flair.** The ships offer an appealing Italian flavor and an international passenger mix.
- **Well-laid-out and spacious public rooms.** There's a pretty good variety in the offerings.

Cons

- **Un-fancy dining.** The dining rooms are loud and a bit cafeteria-like.
- **Lots of passengers.** These ships are sometimes densely packed, and that means lines and crowds.

Frommer's Ratings: Mediterranean Shipping Cruises

	Poor	Fair	Good	Excellent	Outstanding
Enjoyment Factor				✓	
Dining		✓			
Activities		✓			
Children's Program		✓			
Entertainment		✓			
Service			✓		
Overall Value			✓		

MEDITERRANEAN SHIPPING: SWISS LINE, ITALIAN STYLE

This four-ship line is owned by Mediterranean Shipping Company, a large Geneva-based Swiss outfit that is the fourth largest container ship company in the world. The cruise line itself is based in Naples, Italy.

In the early 1990s, the company bought StarLauro line, infamous as the owner of the *Achille Lauro,* whose passengers in 1985 endured a much-publicized terrorist attack off the coast of Egypt. For obvious reasons, the name was later changed to Mediterranean Shipping Cruises. The famous ship is no longer in existence (it sunk off Africa).

The MSC ships are all older, classic vessels that have been updated to provide a more modern cruise experience (though not totally modern—you won't find such offerings as cabins with verandas or alternative dining venues on these ships). They have all been upgraded with sprinkler systems to meet SOLAS requirements (see explanation earlier in this chapter).

In 1998, the company expanded from its European base into the rapidly growing Caribbean market, and now offers 11-night eastern and western Caribbean itineraries from Fort Lauderdale.

The onboard currency on all the ships is the Italian lira, and the crew includes a good number of Italians, who add much to the onboard ambiance.

THE FLEET

The ***Melody,*** formerly *StarShip Atlantic,* sailed as the Big Red Boat for Premier Cruise Line. Aside from a paint job, MSC has made virtually no changes to the ship since its purchase.

The ***Monterey,*** built in 1952, and the ***Rhapsody,*** built in 1974 and formerly the *Cunard Princess,* were modernized by MSC. The *Symphony,* formerly a Costa ship, is under long-term charter to Golden Sun cruises (see "Zeus Tours and Yacht Cruises" in chapter 9).

PASSENGER PROFILE

MSC is an Italian entity that's only recently begun marketing in North America, so there will be few Americans aboard. Italians and Germans make up the largest percentage of passengers, but since the line is also popular with Brits you will find plenty of English speakers. The line's affordable prices draw from Europe's middle class, and include some families, young singles, and honeymooners, though mostly couples in their 40s on up.

These ships are particularly well suited to first-time cruisers.

DINING

The main dining room on each ship offers two seatings at lunch and dinner and one at breakfast. On the pool deck there's also buffet-style breakfast and lunch, the latter including pastas and salads.

The cuisine is primarily Italian. For the captain's dinner you can expect choices including lobster and baked Alaska, and for each meal you can choose fish, fowl, meat, vegetarian, and pasta (the latter especially good). The wine list is mostly made up of well-chosen Italian vintages.

Special diets are catered to on request. There is also 24-hour **room service** from a limited menu.

Mediterranean Shipping Fleet Itineraries		
Ship	**Home Ports & Season**	**Itinerary**
Melody	Round-trip from Genoa, May-Oct.	**7-day W. Med:** Naples and Palermo (Italy), Tunis (Tunisia), Mallorca and Barcelona (Spain), and Marseille (France).
Monterey	Round-trip from Genoa, May-Oct.	**11-day Greek Isles:** Naples and Capri (Italy), Santorini and Volos (Greece), Istanbul and Kusadasi (Turkey), and Heraklion (Crete).
Rhapsody	Round-trip from Venice, May-Sept.	**7-day Greek Isles:** Bari (Italy), Katakolon, Santorini, Rhodes (Greece), and Dubrovnik (Croatia).*

*Also does a Holy Lands itinerary.

Activities

These ships don't offer the range of amenities and state-of-the-art distractions you'll find on the big new megaships, but they do offer good variety, with table tennis, volleyball, and shuffleboard, plus activities like bridge, cards, jigsaw puzzles, Italian lessons, aperitif parties before lunch, sunset cocktail parties with dance music, poolside contests, visits to the beauty salon, stretch-and-tone aerobics classes, and movies in the cinema. Each ship also has both a **casino** and **disco.** The small **spas** are concessions and offer reasonably priced massages and beauty services.

Despite all these options, most passengers will head to the sundeck (spacious on all the ships) when their ship isn't in port (which it is, often, as these ships offer port-intensive itineraries).

Some news in English is printed out and made available every day.

Children's Program

There are children's programs on all the ships, and a **children's center** including a wading pool on the *Melody.* The *Rhapsody* also has a kiddie pool. Activities are of the low-tech, low-key variety like games, crafts, and Italian lessons.

Baby-sitting by crew members is available for a modest fee.

Entertainment

There is at least one singer and a **musical group** that trots out danceable show tunes and favorites from both sides of the Atlantic, as well as an amateurish song and dance show presented nightly.

In the Italian tradition, passengers will spend a lot of time at meals, considering that a form of nighttime entertainment.

Service

Overall, the Italian career staffers are fine examples of that country's superb tradition of attentive service. What they deliver is not all that refined, but is warm and genuine.

Laundry and dry cleaning service is offered. There are no coin-operated laundry facilities.

Melody

The Verdict

This friendly, well-laid-out ship offers lots to do and decent-sized spaces in which to do it.

Melody (photo: MSC)

Specifications

Size (in tons)	36,000	Officers	Italian
Number of Cabins	538	Crew	539 (International)
Number of Outside Cabins	371	Passenger/Crew Ratio	2 to 1
Cabins with Verandas	0	Year Built	1982
Number of Passengers	1,076	Last Major Refurbishment	1997

Frommer's Ratings (Scale of 1–5)

Cabin Comfort & Amenities	3	Pool, Fitness & Spa Facilities	3
Ship Cleanliness & Maintenance	3	Children's Facilities	2
Public Comfort/Space	3	Itineraries	3
Decor	3	Worth the Money	4

This medium-sized ship was built in the style of a classic ocean liner, with a layout of decks and public areas originally conceived for long-haul cruises. Teakwood decks and heavy doors with the traditional raised sill are commonplace. Real round portholes—an increasing rarity in these picture-window days—have been retained in many instances, and provide a nice reminder of traditional ship design.

Many thousands of nautical miles have washed beneath this ship's hull, and it experienced lots of wear and tear in its days as Premier's *Big Red Boat.* Very few cosmetic or architectural changes have been made since the ship's acquisition by MSC in 1997.

Cabins & Rates

Cabins	Per diems from	Bathtub	Fridge	Hair Dryer	Sitting Area	TV
Inside	$143*	no	no	on request	no	yes
Outside	$178*	some	no	on request	some	yes
Suite	$270*	yes	some	yes	yes	yes

**Port charges are an additional $129.*

CABINS Cabins come in many different configurations, the smallest of which tend to be somewhat cramped; the others, averaging 185 square feet, are relatively comfortable. Suites are a bit more plush and good-sized (280 to 440 square feet) and can accommodate four or five people, which is great for families. Each cabin is equipped with music channels, telephone, and TV (with a satellite feed). Hair dryers are available from the purser on request. Most outside cabins and all suites have a bathtub/shower combination.

Four cabins have been configured to allow a collapsible wheelchair to go through (the chair can be no more than 29 inches wide, though).

PUBLIC AREAS The decor is cheerful, but definitely feels like vintage early '80s, with lights twinkling along shiny metallic surfaces and bright but not jarring color schemes. The Blue Riband room is, by contrast, a deliberately darkened and artsy-looking jazz pub.

Cabaret and comedy acts are presented at Club Universe. There's also a few bars, a video arcade, and an unmemorable casino that's set amidships on the Lounge Deck. There's no library, per se, just a small collection of books. The Mercury Theater shows movies from both sides of the Atlantic, and kids get their own playroom.

POOL, FITNESS & SPA FACILITIES The *Melody* has two swimming pools (one with a retractable roof), a kids' wading pool, and two whirlpools, all of which can get quite full. The ship's tiered aft decks offer lots of prime spots for sunbathing.

There's a small gym with updated equipment, a couple of massage rooms, and a beauty salon. The Sun Deck has a jogging track, and there are setups for aerobics classes, Ping-Pong, and shuffleboard.

Monterey

Monterey (photo: MSC)

The Verdict

This one-time cargo ship works well as a classic cruise vessel, with lots of open deck space and pleasing public rooms.

Specifications

Size (in tons)	20,000	Officers	Italian
Number of Cabins	290	Crew	200 (International)
Number of Outside Cabins	163	Passenger/Crew Ratio	2.8 to 1
Cabins with Verandas	0	Year Built	1952
Number of Passengers	576	Last Major Refurbishment	1998

Frommer's Ratings (Scale of 1–5)

Cabin Comfort & Amenities	2	Pool, Fitness & Spa Facilities	2
Ship Cleanliness & Maintenance	3	Children's Facilities	N/A
Public Comfort/Space	2	Itineraries	4
Decor	2	Worth the Money	4

Built in 1952, this old workhorse of a ship (it was originally a U.S.-built cargo ship) is friendly, if not as packed with things to do as newer ships. The decor features an art deco-ish style, with some wood and brass, and there's lots of open deck space.

Cabins & Rates

Cabins	Per diems from	Bathtub	Fridge	Hair Dryer	Sitting Area	TV
Inside	$145*	no	no	on request	no	no
Outside	$182*	no	no	on request	no	no
Suite	$254*	yes	yes	yes	yes	yes

**Port charges are an additional $149.*

CABINS Cabins are comfortably furnished and come in a variety of sizes and configurations. Standard cabins vary from a tiny 100 square feet to a comfortable 180 square feet. All cabins have radios, phones, and writing areas, and some have bathtubs, sitting area, and double beds. Hair dryers are available upon request through the purser's office. The two suites and two junior suites are very large (up to 400 square feet) and have

TVs, minibars, sitting areas, and picture windows. Some of the cabins on the Boat Deck have obstructed views.

There are no cabins for travelers with disabilities.

PUBLIC ROOMS MSC recently updated the *Monterey's* decor. The two-level dining room can be noisy but is otherwise pleasant. The Palm Court has piano music for pre-dinner drinks, then cabaret and dancing. The vessel also has a disco, cinema, library, and casino (with blackjack, slots, and roulette).

The ship has a good amount of deck space, although the Promenade Deck is not of the wrap-around variety.

POOL, FITNESS & SPA FACILITIES There's one outdoor pool, one whirlpool, and a modest gym and spa with a sauna and massage rooms. Deck sports include paddle tennis, Ping-Pong, volleyball, shuffleboard, and aerobics and exercise classes. The ship does not have a children's room, but does offer both children's and teens' activities.

Rhapsody

The Verdict

The *Rhapsody* used to be a Cunard vessel, and still shows signs of elegance even though the atmosphere today is less formal. Though friendly, the vessel can sometimes feel crowded.

Rhapsody (photo: MSC)

Specifications

Size (in tons)	16,852	Officers	Italian
Number of Cabins	384	Crew	250 (Italian/int'l)
Number of Outside Cabins	257	Passenger/Crew Ratio	3 to 1
Cabins with Verandas	0	Year Built	1977
Number of Passengers	768	Last Major Refurbishment	1997

Frommer's Ratings (Scale of 1–5)

Cabin Comfort & Amenities	2	Pool, Fitness & Spa Facilities	3
Ship Cleanliness & Maintenance	3	Children's Facilities	N/A
Public Comfort/Space	3	Itineraries	3
Decor	3	Worth the Money	4

The *Rhapsody,* a sister ship to Royal Olympic's *Olympic Countess,* is a nicely laid out ship that was previously operated as the *Cunard Princess.* The vessel's cabins are small and its public rooms big (including a two-story atrium and a neat indoor/outdoor nightclub), and there's lots of open deck space.

Cabins & Rates

Cabins	Per diems from	Bathtub	Fridge	Hair Dryer	Sitting Area	TV
Inside	$171*	no	no	on request	no	no
Outside	$193*	no	no	on request	yes	no
Suite	$271*	yes	yes	yes	yes	yes

**Port charges are an additional $99.*

CABINS Standard cabins are nicely furnished but very small—the largest cabin on the ship can only hold three people, maximum. The 20 junior suites (at 160 square feet) are most appropriate for Americans. There are also two suites, each about 250 square feet. Only the suites have bathtubs, but both suites and junior suites have sitting areas. All cabins have phones, music channels, and writing areas, with hair dryers available on request.

There are no cabins for handicapped travelers.

PUBLIC AREAS The 8 Bells Nightclub is an indoor/outdoor entertainment venue that allows you to dance under the stars. The Top Sail Lounge is an observation area and nightclub on the Sun Deck and includes a piano bar.

The dining room has nice ocean views, but can be noisy. There's also a cinema, library area, and small casino with blackjack, roulette, and slots.

POOL, FITNESS & SPA FACILITIES There is no wraparound Promenade, but there is a jogging track on the Sun Deck. The ship has a good-sized swimming pool, a kiddie wading pool, and two whirlpools. There's a small gym and spa and a beauty shop, and aerobics and stretch classes are offered. There is no children's playroom. Deck sports are of your typical Ping-Pong and shuffleboard variety.

Norwegian Coastal Voyage/Bergen Line Services

SHIPS IN EUROPE Harald Jarl • Kong Harald • Lofoten • Midnatsol • Narvik • Nordkapp • Nordlys • Nordnorge • Polarlys • Richard With • Vesteralen

405 Park Ave., New York, NY 10022. ☎ **800/323-7436** or 212/319-1300. Fax 212/319-1390. www.bergenline.com.

THE LINE IN A NUTSHELL The Norwegian Coastal Voyage offers a comfortable, moderately priced way to visit normally expensive Norway and get to know its people, towns, and wonderful mountain and island scenery.

THE EXPERIENCE These relatively small working ships maintain about as regular and invariable a schedule as exists anywhere, operating year-round and offering a close-up and personal view of coastal Norway on 12-day round-trip itineraries that begin in Bergen every evening at 10:30 and call at 35 coastal ports, from tiny villages to sizable cities, en route to Kirkenes at the very top of Norway. Shorter, one-way trips are also available. These ships carry cargo and vehicles as well as passengers and are considered a daily lifeline to some coastal and island regions.

The entertainment on these voyages is the scenery, the port arrivals and departures, and your fellow passengers; there are no evening shows or casinos aboard. Open stretches of sea, some lasting up to 24 hours long and others for just a few hours, can produce swells and even quite stormy weather, especially just north of Bergen at the North Cape. Temperatures are typical of a cool maritime climate, so prepare for cool weather.

Pros

- **A thrifty way to see Norway.** The voyages are moderately priced compared to a land itinerary in this expensive country.
- **Shows you beautiful Norway up close.** As these are coastal ships, they stay near to land, and stopping frequently keeps you in touch with the country and its people.
- **Every season has its attractions.** In the late spring to early summer you see 24 hours of daylight (plus, above the Arctic Circle, the midnight sun in a narrower band of time), in the late summer and early fall you get the changing colors and few tourists, and in winter you can see the often spectacular Northern Lights.

Cons

- **Ships do not penetrate the deepest fjords.** Unlike cruise ships that visit the most famous Norwegian fjords, the coastal fleet, while navigating some narrow passages, hugs the coast and threads a route among the islands.
- **The food is somewhat repetitious.** If you take the complete 12-day voyage, the food takes on a certain sameness.

Frommer's Ratings: Norwegian Coastal Voyage

	Poor	Fair	Good	Excellent	Outstanding
Enjoyment Factor					✓
Dining			✓		
Activities	N/A				
Children's Program	N/A				
Entertainment	N/A				
Service			✓		
Overall Value				✓	

Norwegian Coastal's Older Ships: A Retro Coastal Adventure

Built in the early 1960s, the very traditional 2,600-ton *Harald Jarl* and *Lofoten* are reminiscent of old steamships. Taking less than 200 passengers, they offer the atmosphere of a small, intimate country hotel with traditional wood-paneled walls. Most passengers who book these two ships have little or no interest in the larger cruise-style ships, preferring these ships' old seagoing feel. Watching the cargo being lifted by crane into the ships' holds is like stepping back into a Humphrey Bogart movie—it's an experience you can have almost nowhere else these days. When these ships are gone, there will be nothing like them left anywhere in the world.

The 4,200-ton mid-generation ships *Midnatsol, Narvik,* and *Vesteralen* take 325 passengers in functional cabins with private facilities. These three ships have an attractive dome-style lounge on the top deck and a small forward observation lounge, plus a dining room, a cafeteria, and a small shop.

NORWEGIAN COASTAL VOYAGE: WORLD'S MOST BEAUTIFUL

The Norwegian coastal service dates back more than 100 years to the 1890s, and was for years the daily lifeline for coastal and island communities that had little or no other access to the outside world, or contact with each other. Locals could practically set their watches by the comings and goings of the northbound and southbound coastal steamers, which have maintained the same schedules for decades. In recent years, as roads, railways, and high speed ferries developed into a sophisticated interconnecting network, the coastal ships' transportation role has declined, and the service has increasingly been seen as a pleasure voyage.

Over the years, several different and occasionally changing ship owners have contributed to the 11-ship fleet. The line's mail contract was withdrawn on January 1, 1995, and the government subsidy under which the line has operated is scheduled to be completely withdrawn in a couple of years. After that, the service may not operate daily in winter, and the newer vessels may go cruising in the off-seasons.

Norwegian Coastal Voyage also markets the Silja Line, operating large overnight Scandinavian cruise ferries, some of which gross up to 50,000 and 60,000 tons, on routes between Sweden and Finland and Finland and Germany, and also books Scandinavian DFDS Seaways cruise ferries that ply between Denmark, Norway, Sweden, Germany, the Netherlands, and England. For the time being, there is also a weekly summer cruise from northern Norway to Spitsbergen.

THE FLEET

The NCV fleet is divided into three distinct groups: the new ships ***(Kong Harald, Nordkapp, Nordlys, Nordnorge, Polarlys,*** and ***Richard With),*** the mid-generation ships ***(Midnatsol, Narvik,*** and ***Vesteralen),*** and the traditional ships ***(Harald Jarl*** and ***Lofoten).*** Gradually, the small, older, traditional passenger cargo ships, which still use cranes and pallets to lift on the cargo, have been replaced by newer tonnage that rolls on the cargo and vehicles through side doors. The first of the new breed appeared in the early 1980s, and they were enlarged later in the decade when they were found to be too small.

In the 1990s, an even larger class began to arrive, until only two classic ships now remain in service. The newest ships—those I've concentrated on in this review—have almost completely changed the character of the shipboard experience, approaching cruise

Coastal Cruise Tip

The best time to make the Norwegian Coastal Voyage is just before the middle of May, when you have 24 hours of daylight, fewer crowds, and lower fares. The only drawback may be snow still blocking the road to the North Cape.

---

ship standards in the variety of public rooms and attractive decor offered. Their cabins remind one of Carnival's older ships—functional and plain. However, there is little organized entertainment, gambling, or hoopla. There is also, unfortunately, little of the rugged maritime atmosphere of the older ships, and the sheer size of the new ships translates into a more remote connection to the port activities and cargo handling. (See "Norwegian Coastal's Older Ships: A Retro Coastal Adventure," above, for details on the line's older vessels.)

Bergen Line also markets a number of North Sea and Baltic ferry services, and these overnight voyages offer something akin to a cruise with multiple dining options, dancing, and sophisticated entertainment (and, on some routes, duty-free shopping in supermarket-size facilities). In the summer, one of the former traditional Norwegian Coastal Voyage ships makes weekly cruises from northern Norway to Spitsbergen.

Passenger Profile

Coastal Voyage passengers making one-way or round-trip passages are generally 50 and up, as the trip is seen as a sedentary, scenic cruise. In summer, there will be some younger passengers. Germans are the most numerous nationality, followed by British, Norwegians, and other Scandinavians and Europeans. Most Americans book as part of a tour operator's package, but some independent travelers will be aboard in the warmer months.

As the ships do provide basic transportation between ports, you'll find Norwegians aboard as deck passengers or occupying a cabin for a night or two, and also lots of youthful backpackers during the summer holidays. The newer ships have conference facilities, and with oodles of available space in the off-season, the Norwegian meetings market is growing.

Announcements are kept to a minimum, but English is always one of the languages. In the high season, there's a courier aboard to handle shore excursions and passenger information, and he or she will likely speak many languages.

Dining

The food is geared to Norwegian and European tastes and is prepared and presented in a straightforward manner. Breakfast and lunch are buffets, and dinner is served by Norwegian women. There are two sittings when the complement is large enough, and tables are assigned at embarkation according to language.

Breakfast will offer fruits, cereals, cold meats and cheese, various breads and toast, and often boiled eggs and bacon or sausage. **Lunch** is the best meal, with several hot entrees, soup, salad fixings, cold meats, herring served about a half-dozen ways, and cakes and pies. **Dinner** is a set three-course meal with soup, main course (often fish,

Some Special Deals

There are off-season rates, and various packages combining sea, air from New York, hotels, and the scenic train ride between Oslo and Bergen.

Norwegian Coastal Voyage Fleet Itineraries

Ship	Home Ports & Season	Itinerary
Entire Fleet	Between Bergen & Kirkenes, year-round.	**6- and 7-day:** 35 coastal ports, either north- or southbound, with shore excursions offered at Geiranger, Trondheim, Ornes, Tromso, Honningsvag, and Kirkenes on northbound; at Honingsvag, Tromso, Harstad, Svolvaer, Trondheim, and Kristiansund, southbound. **12-day round-trip:** Visits the same 35 ports.*

*The northbound voyage has the much better timings for the most interesting ports such as Alesund, Bodo, Trondheim, Tromso, and Honnigsvag (for the North Cape). Passengers may join or alight at any port. Cabin berths sell out far in advance between late May and Aug.

chicken, or veal), and dessert. **Special diets** can be catered to with advance notice. After a week aboard, the food may become somewhat monotonous, but it has improved with the coming of the new ships and the need to attract cruise-type passengers.

As this is a domestic service, and taxes on alcohol are high, you can expect to pay a minimum of $6 for a bottle of beer and $25 for wine. Some passengers bring their own supplies but, of course, they are not permitted to bring them into the dining room.

All the ships have **cafeterias,** mainly catering to the shorter port-to-port passenger, while full restaurant meals are included for the full one-way or round-trippers.

Activities

The main activity while under way is viewing the passing scenery. The ships stop in their 35 ports at all hours of the day and night—at which point passengers flock ashore for a walk or to buy newspapers and souvenirs—and if you take the complete 12-day round-trip you'll eventually visit all the ports at a convenient hour. Calls may be as short as 15 minutes or as long as a few hours. There is a package of reasonably priced **shore excursions** that provide a most worthwhile way to see some of interior Norway and several fjords. They are booked through the onboard courier or in advance as a package.

There are no activities offered otherwise—you have to be self-motivated, playing a game of cards or reading.

Children's Program

Children come aboard with families making short hauls but generally not for the longer voyages. There's a video arcade on the newer ships.

Entertainment

In the summer season, there may be a band and dancing on selected evenings, but it is hit and miss. The **Arctic Circle crossing ceremony** is great fun if you enjoy being baptized with ice water, and the 180-degree turn in the tight Trollfjord basin amidst cascading waterfalls is also diverting.

Service

The crew is all Norwegian (or at least people living in Norway), and most of the hotel staff is female, from long-time employees to recent recruits in their early 20s. On the smaller ships, service can be personal and friendly, but on the larger ones it is efficient and matter-of-fact. Tips are generally left with the dining room manager and pooled among the staff.

Kong Harald • Nordkapp • Nordlys • Nordnorge • Polarlys • Richard With

Nordnorge (photo: Bergen Line)

The Verdict

These six ships, the newest members of the fleet, are attractive, comfortable, and serviceable vessels providing a moderately priced, casual, low-key cruise.

Specifications

Size (in tons)	11,200	Officers	Norwegian
Number of Cabins	230	Crew	60 (Norwegian)
Number of Outside Cabins	203	Passenger/Crew Ratio	8.2 to 1
Cabins with Verandas	None	Year Built	1993–1997
Number of Passengers	490	Last Major Refurbishment	N/A

Frommer's Ratings (Scale of 1–5)

Cabin Comfort & Amenities	3	Pool, Fitness & Spa Facilities	N/A
Ship Cleanliness & Maintenance	4	Children's Facilities	3
Public Comfort/Space	4	Itineraries	5
Decor	4	Worth the Money	5

These are attractive, comfortable, and low-key ships, but curiously, for vessels that are marketed as sightseeing-intensive, they don't provide much incentive to spend time out on deck: Space there is limited and less cozy than aboard the older ships. On the plus side, though, these ships have cheerful and comfortable public rooms, lounge TVs, and lots of activities. Those seeking peace and quiet should sail in the shoulder season, when things aren't so busy on board.

Cabins & Rates

Cabins	Per diems from	Bathtub	Fridge	Hair Dryer	Sitting Area	TV
Inside	$191	no	no	yes	no	no
Outside	$209	no	no	yes	no	no
Suite	$347	no	no	yes	yes	yes

CABINS The cabins, mostly outside, are nearly all standardized and vary mostly by location. All are plainly furnished, with bunks that become bench-type sofas during the day, and many have an upper fold-away berth. There is sufficient stowage space, plus a small shower, basin, and toilet compartment. The lowest passenger deck cabins have portholes while the rest have windows, and some facing the lifeboats will have obstructed views. Room service is limited to bed-making and cleaning.

PUBLIC AREAS The ships excel in Norwegian art, with specially commissioned sculpture and paintings depicting maritime scenes such as fishing boats, village life, and older coastal steamers in stormy seas. The furnishings feature bold colors and patterns, and there are lots of shiny surfaces in steel, brass, and glass. These offer great appeal, especially during the long, dark Norwegian winters.

The forward observation lounge is the most popular daytime spot, with comfortable seating and wraparound windows. Aft is a large bar and lounge. On the restaurant deck, the main dining room is aft with wraparound windows, and is reached by a long starboard side galley lounge. Forward are an entertainment lounge and bar, a library, and a conference room. Amidships are a 24-hour cafeteria, shops, and a game room for children.

With generally cool temperatures, deck space is limited to a large enclosed area aft on the highest deck, smaller afterdecks, and a wraparound, narrow promenade.

POOL, FITNESS & SPA FACILITIES There are a small gym and sauna on each ship, but no pool.

P&O Cruises

SHIPS IN EUROPE Arcadia • Oriana • Victoria • Aurora (preview)

77 New Oxford St., London WC1A 1PP, England; in the U.S., contact Princess Tours, 2815 Second Ave., Ste. 400, Seattle, WA 98121-1299. ☎ **800/340-7074.** Fax 206/336-6100. www.pocruises.com.

THE LINE IN A NUTSHELL P&O, the parent company of Princess Cruises, has been around since 1837 and is one of the most legendary British shipping lines. With an overwhelmingly British passenger base aboard all its ships, taking a cruise with the line is like being dipped whole into English culture—and you might not even have to bring your umbrella.

THE EXPERIENCE Since P&O caters primarily to British passengers, the line's vessel and its operations have all been designed with their tastes in mind. For an American, it's like taking two vacations: one geographical and the other sociological. Overall, you're more likely to find kippers on your breakfast plate than pancakes, *Fawlty Towers* on the TV rather than *Friends,* and a droll attitude in place of the usual cruise ship whoopee.

The ships themselves resemble those of Princess Cruises, with the same clean lines and smooth, modern feel, though public rooms in particular display a distinct British sensibility, often resembling the rooms of an Edwardian men's club, with dark wood paneling, heavy, overstuffed chairs and sofas, low lighting, portraits and paintings of old oceangoing vessels on the walls, and large wooden display cases.

Pros

- **British sensibility.** For Anglophiles or anyone who enjoys immersing in another culture, an experience with P&O is fantastic—and without the language barrier.
- **Interesting passenger mix.** P&O was one of the great shipping lines of the British Empire, and aboard its ships you're likely to encounter passengers from former British colonies like India and Singapore mixed in among the Brits. The passenger talent shows are wonderful.
- **Beautiful ships.** The three newest P&O ships mix modern ship design with an old-world sensibility, while the smaller *Victoria* is more of an old-style cruiser.

Cons

- **British sensibility.** If you're an American, you're a foreigner here—a cultural student, as it were. If that's not what you want from your vacation, sail with an American line.
- **Few totally nonsmoking areas.** As on most European ships, smoking is either not restricted to specific areas or the enforcement is lax. Nonsmokers can have a tough time finding a totally clear space.

Frommer's Ratings: P&O Cruises

	Poor	Fair	Good	Excellent	Outstanding
Enjoyment Factor				✓	
Dining				✓	
Activities				✓	
Children's Program				✓	
Entertainment					✓
Service				✓	
Overall Value				✓	

P&O: BRITISH TRADITION AT SEA

P&O, the very British parent company of very American Princess Cruises, began in 1837 as the Peninsular and Oriental Steam Navigation Company. One of the most legendary names in British shipping, the line ruled passenger travel between England, Australia, India, and the Far East for the better part of a century. Today, the line's ships sail itineraries in the Atlantic, the Mediterranean, Northern Europe, the Black Sea, and the Caribbean, primarily departing from Southampton.

THE FLEET

The ***Arcadia*** was launched in 1988 as the *Sitmar Fairmajesty* of Sitmar Cruises before P&O's buyout of that line, then sailed for a time as Princess's *Star Princess* before joining the P&O fleet under its new name in late 1997. Weighing in at 63,500 tons and carrying 1,475 passengers, the *Arcadia* has the look of a modern cruise ship but some of the posh interior feel of a classic old-time liner—a distinction shared by the 69,000-ton, 1,810-passenger ***Oriana,*** which entered service in 1995. The ***Victoria,*** on the other hand, really *is* a classic, having been launched in 1965 as the *Kungsholm* for the Swedish American Line and acquired by P&O in 1978, sailing first as the *Sea Princess,* then under its current name. Weighing in at 27,670 tons and carrying only 745 passengers, the *Victoria* is by far the line's most intimate vessel.

In May 2000, P&O will debut its newest ship, the 76,000-ton, 1,850-passenger ***Aurora.*** Though a sister ship to the *Oriana,* the vessel will have several features that put it in league with the most modern American ships, amenities-wise.

PASSENGER PROFILE

Americans tend to think the differences between ourselves and the British are minimal—which ain't necessarily so. The British have different traditions, habits, history, psychology, vocabulary, and manners, and when you're an American put down in the midst of 1,300 of them, you know it. Aboard P&O, you'll likely meet many passengers who are of an age to remember when the sun never set on the British Empire, some of whom served in World War II and a small number of whom hail from former colonies such as India and Singapore. When I sailed aboard the *Oriana* in early 1999, I noticed that these latter passengers were clearly more at home in the ship's atmosphere than I was.

DINING

Food aboard ship is, as you'd expect, extremely British, something Americans will notice first thing in the morning when they spot the kippered herring, smoked haddock in milk, and black pudding on the breakfast menu or buffet. Lunchtime might be the traditional fish and chips, followed a few hours later, naturally, by **afternoon tea.**

Dinner sees some wonderfully prepared dishes served in low-key, quietly elegant dining rooms (two each on the *Oriana* and *Aurora,* one each on the *Victoria* and *Arcadia*). In addition to British classics like beef Wellington, cream of Stilton and leek soup, and smoked Scottish salmon, you'll also find **vegetarian** and **health-conscious dishes** as well as international entrees popularized during the days of the Empire. As the line's publicity says, "We've been making and serving our famous curries since the days of the Raj." The *Oriana, Arcadia,* and *Aurora* all have a Lido-style buffet restaurant, plus other options like pizzerias and ice cream stations. The *Victoria* has only its single dining room, plus a buffet area on the Lido Deck. Sandwiches and snacks are available through room service, as well as morning coffee/tea and biscuits.

ACTIVITIES

P&O onboard activities run the gamut from bingo and bridge to some of the best **port lectures** in the business, with dances, dance lessons, arts and crafts, cricket and tennis,

P&O Fleet Itineraries

Ship	Home Ports & Season	Itinerary
Arcadia	All sailings round-trip from Southampton. 12- & 13-dayW. Med (May, July, Aug, Sept); 17-day W. Med (July–Aug); 7-day Norway (July); 13-day Norway (May–June); 4-day North Sea (June); 13-day Baltic (Aug–Sept); 7-day Atlantic Coast (Oct); 9-day Atlantic Coast (Sept).	**12- & 13-day W. Med:** Port calls may include Elba, Naples, Livorno, Santa Margherita (Italy), St. Tropez, Toulon, Cannes (France), Ciudadela (Mallorca), Cartagena, Barcelona, Cádiz (Spain), Ajaccio or Calvi (Corsica), Alghero (Sardinia), Gibraltar, and Monte Carlo; **17-day W. Med:** Málaga (Spain), Cagliari (Sardinia), Dubrovnik (Croatia), Venice and Messina (Italy), Praia Da Rocha (Portugal), Palma de Mallorca; **7-day Norway:** Stavanger, Olden, Geiranger, Bergen (Norway); **13-day Norway:** Olden, Trondheim, North Cape, Tromso, Lofoten Islands, Andalsnes, Bergen (Norway); **4-day North Sea:** Amsterdam (Netherlands), Bruges (Belgium), St. Peter Port (Guernsey); **13-day Baltic:** Amsterdam (Netherlands), Tallinn (Estonia), St. Petersburg (Russia), Helsinki (Finland), Stockholm (Sweden), Copenhagen (Denmark), Kristiansand (Norway); **7- & 9-day Atlantic Coast:** Ports calls may include Bilbao, La Coruña, Vigo (Spain), Lisbon (Portugal), La Rochelle or Lorient (France), St. Peter Port (Guernsey).
Aurora	All sailings round-trip from Southampton. 12-day W. Med (July); 14-day W. Med (May, Aug, Oct); 16-day W. Med (Oct); 18-day E. Med & Black Sea (Sept); 12-day Norway (June); 13-day Baltic (June); 5-day Atlantic Coast (Sept); 7-day Atlantic Coast (May & Aug).	**12-day W. Med:** Barcelona (Spain), Cannes (France), Livorno and Elba (Italy), Gibraltar; **14-day W. Med:** Port calls may include Lisbon (Portugal), Barcelona, Málaga, Cádiz (Spain), Messina, Livorno, Naples, Elba, Santa Margherita (Italy), Marseille and Toulon (France), Ajaccio (Corsica), La Maddelena (Sardinia), Palma de Mallorca, Gibraltar, Monte Carlo, and Malta; **16-day W. Med:** Vigo and Alicante (Spain), Cagliari (Cardinia), Dubrovnik (Croatia), Venice (Italy), Malta, Gibraltar, Palma de Mallorca; **18-day E. Med & Black Sea:** Lisbon (Portugal), Athens (Greece), Istanbul (Turkey), Yalta and Odessa (Ukraine), Palma de Mallorca; **12-day Norway:** Andalsnes, Lofoten Islands, North Cape, Trondheim, Olden, Bergen (Norway); **13-day Baltic:** Oslo (Norway), St. Petersburg (Russia), Helsinki (Finland), Stockholm (Sweden), Berlin (Germany), Copenhagen (Denmark), Bruges (Belgium); **5- & 7-day Atlantic Coast:** Port calls may include Lisbon (Portugal), Vigo, La Coruña, Gijon (Spain), La Rochelle and Brest (France), St. Peter Port (Guernsey).*

**Aurora* and *Oriana* do 18-day Holy Land/Egypt cruises in Oct–Nov; *Victoria* does 14-day Holy Land/Egypt/E. Med cruise in Sept, Nov, and Dec.

**All itineraries not running round-trip from Southampton include air transportation between the port of embarkation and/or debarkation and London or Manchester.

exercise classes, and art auctions among the other offerings. The *Arcadia, Oriana,* and *Aurora* have cinemas for showing feature films (the *Victoria* shows films in its combination show lounge/cinema), plus a **casino,** a **library,** and the usual array of bars and lounges.

Each ship has a **gym** and Steiner-managed **spa,** with the area on *Victoria* boasting an indoor spa pool (remember, this ship was designed originally for north Atlantic crossings)

Oriana	All sailings round-trip from Southampton. 12-day W. Med (June); 13-day W. Med (July & Oct); 16-day Med (May); 17-day E. Med (Aug); 4-day France (May); 4-day Netherlands (July); 14-day Norway/Iceland (July); 14-day Baltic (June); 7-day Atlantic Coast (Sept).	**12- & 13-day W. Med:** Port calls may include Ajaccio and Calvi (Corsica), Civitavecchia, Santa Margherita, Livorno, Elba (Italy), Marseille and Villefranche (France), Barcelona (Spain), Gibraltar, Monte Carlo, and Palma de Mallorca; **16-day Med:** Vigo and Cartagena (Spain), Cagliari (Sardinia), Dubrovnik (Croatia), Venice and Syracuse (Italy), Gibraltar, Palma de Mallorca; **17-day E. Med:** Lisbon (Portugal), Santorini, Mytiline, Athens (Greece), Kusadasi and Istanbul (Turkey), Gibraltar; **4-day France:** Brest and Lorient (France), St. Peter Port (Guernsey); **4-day Netherlands:** Amsterdam (Netherlands), Bruges (Belgium), St. Peter Port (Guernsey); **14-day Norway/ Iceland:** Stavanger, Bergen, Vik, Flamm, Olden, Geiranger, Trondheim (Norway), Akureyri and Reykjavik (Iceland); **14-day Baltic:** Oslo (Norway), Elsinore and Copenhagen (Denmark), Stockholm (Sweden), Helsinki (Finland), Tallinn (Estonia), St. Petersburg (Russia), Gdansk (Poland), Warnemünde (Germany), Bruges (Belgium); **7-day Atlantic Coast:** Vigo (Spain), Lisbon (Portugal), Lorient (France), St. Peter Port (Guernsey).*
Victoria	12-day Med, from Southampton to Larnaca (July); 14-day Med, Thessaloniki to Barcelona (Aug & Oct), Barcelona to Larnaca (Aug), Larnaca to Thessaloniki (Sept, Oct), Barcelona to Thessaloniki (Nov); 14-day E. Med/Black Sea, Larnaca to Thessaloniki (July); 15-dayNorway/Iceland, round trip from Southampton (June); 13-day Norway, round trip from Southampton (July); 13-day Northern Europe, round trip from Southampton (June); 13-day Baltic, Southampton (May).**	**12-day Med:** Cádiz and Cartagena (Spain), Port Mahon (Menorca), Civitavecchia (Italy), Pylos, Athens, Santorini (Greece), Antalya (Turkey), Larnaca (Cyprus); **14-day Med:** Ithaca, Monemvasia, Athens, Thessaloniki, Mykonos, Katakolon, Zakinthos, Nauplia, Volos, Corfu (Greece), Bodrum, Kusadasi, Istanbul, Dikili (Turkey), Heraklion (Crete), Dubrovnik (Croatia), Venice, Messina, Sorrento, Portovenere, Civitavecchia, Santa Margherita (Italy), Villefranche, Toulon, St. Raphael (France), Korkula (Dalmatian Islands), Propriano (Corsica), Barcelona (Spain), Larnaca (Cyprus), and Rhodes; **4-day E. Med/ Black Sea:** Port calls may include Larnaca (Cyprus), Antalya, Canakkale, Bodrum, Kusadasi, Dikili, Istanbul (Turkey), Kos, Mykonos, Athens, Mytiline, Thessaloniki (Greece), Varna (Bulgaria), Odessa and Yalta (Ukraine), Sochi (Russia), Nesebur (Bulgaria), and Rhodes; **15-day Norway/Iceland:** Dublin (Ireland), Reykjavik, Isafjorder, Akureyri (Iceland), Trondheim, Geiranger, Bergen, Stavanger, Eidfjord (Norway); **13-day Norway:** Geiranger, Tromso, North Cape, Hammerfest, Trondheim, Andalsnes, Bergen (Norway); **13-day Northern Europe:** Bruges (Belgium), Berlin (Germany), Tallinn (Estonia), St. Petersburg (Russia), Helsinki (Finland), Stockholm (Sweden), Copenhagen (Denmark), Oslo (Norway); **13-day Baltic:** Amsterdam (Netherlands), Stockholm (Sweden), Helsinki (Finland), St. Petersburg (Russia), Tallinn (Estonia), Copenhagen (Denmark), Bergen (Norway).*

and that on *Oriana* taunting passengers with one of the cruelest layouts I've ever seen: The gym is *right next to* the very fine Al Fresco Pizzeria. *Oriana,* and *Aurora* also boast wraparound promenades that get a lot of use from the British passengers, and the *Aurora* will feature a golf simulator. Cricket matches between passengers and officers are always well-attended.

Children's Activities

Each ship has a children's **playroom** and, except on the *Victoria,* a teen center and outdoor play/pool area. The new *Aurora* will also have a virtual reality center, as well as separate playrooms for kids under 5, 6 to 9, and 10 to 13. Each ship (again, aside from the small *Victoria*) offers a staffed night nursery, and kids can attend separate early dinner seatings, with or without their parents.

When there are few children aboard, some areas may be converted to other uses. On the Oriana, the door to the teen center is marked "You are about to enter outer space." I once pushed it open to find two elderly British gentlemen playing Ping-Pong.

Entertainment

Here's where the British-American cultural divide pops up again. While **production shows** are first-rate, there's only a fifty-fifty chance Americans will feel in the cultural loop, as the shows will feature either recognizable fare or British favorites that are so distinctly homegrown that Americans will be left scratching their heads.

Outside the show lounge, entertainment may feature a pianist, a big band (which sometimes provides accompaniment for ballroom dancing), and other combos, plus **comedians** who play up their British humor to the hilt. The **passenger talent shows** are a must-do, typically going far beyond the usual off-key karaoke (though you'll hear some of that, too).

Service

Staff aboard all P&O ships is generally a mixture of British, other European nationalities, and Indian, all of whom tend toward the formal, crisp, and efficient. Brits tend to predominate in the "front office" jobs.

Arcadia • Oriana

Arcadia (photo: Princess)

The Verdict

Though modern and up-to-date in every way, both these ships also boast warm, old fashioned, very British public rooms that evoke the classic steamship era.

Specifications

Size		Officers	British
Arcadia	63,524	Crew	British/Indian/Int'l
Oriana	69,153	*Arcadia*	650
Number of Cabins		*Oriana*	760
Arcadia	748	Passenger/Crew Ratio	
Oriana	914	*Arcadia*	2.25 to 1
Number of Outside Cabins		*Oriana*	2.4 to 1
Arcadia	583	Year Built	
Oriana	594	*Arcadia*	1988
Cabins with Verandas		*Oriana*	1995
Arcadia	50	Last Major Refurbishment	
Oriana	118	*Arcadia*	1997
Number of Passengers		*Oriana*	N/A
Arcadia	1,475		
Oriana	1,810		

Frommer's Ratings (Scale of 1–5)

Cabin Comfort & Amenities	4	Pool, Fitness & Spa Facilities	4
Ship Cleanliness & Maintenance	5	Children's Facilities	4
Public Comfort/Space	4	Itineraries	4
Decor	4	Worth the Money	4

The handsome *Oriana* and *Arcadia* bear more than a passing resemblance to their cousins in the Princess fleet. It's evident that both vessels were designed with British passengers in mind. While cabins are modern, with the same kind of light wood design and modern fixtures that you find aboard Princess's megaships, public rooms like the *Oriana's* Anderson's Lounge and Monte Carlo Club have the warm atmosphere of an old London club, with comfortably soft couches and high-backed chairs, oil portraits on the walls, ship models, and faux bookcases. All that's missing is the fireplace.

CABINS No old-world nostalgia furnishings here. Cabins differ in size and decor, those on the *Oriana* being far more sleek and modern, decorated in light, Scandinavian-type woods designed to make them look more spacious than they are (in reality, standard cabins are only about 150 square feet—comfortable, but not huge). By contrast, cabins on the *Arcadia* are approximately 190 square feet, though their decor is not as contemporary. All cabins on both ships offer TV and music channels, refrigerator, telephone, safe, hair dryer, and vanity table/writing desk. All bathrooms have showers.

Cabins are available with two lower twin beds convertible to king-size, and a number of cabins have third and fourth berths. Both ships also offer minisuites (approximately 220 square feet on *Oriana,* 372 square feet on *Arcadia*) and full suites (414 square feet on *Oriana,* 538 on *Arcadia*). Both suite levels have private verandas, two wardrobes, bar, and bathrooms with bathtubs (Jacuzzi bathtubs on *Oriana*). Full suites on *Oriana* have separate bedrooms and living areas; those on *Arcadia* have a small separate sitting area, though the bedroom and large main sitting area share the same space.

Accommodations aboard *Arcadia* are more spacious, but the *Oriana* offers far more cabins with balconies, as well as about twice as many single cabins—though the number on both (64 on *Arcadia,* 108 in *Oriana*) represent real rarities in such modern cruise ships, which typically have no singles at all, or very few. Eight cabins on *Oriana* and 10 on *Arcadia* are wheelchair accessible.

Cabins & Rates

Cabins	Per diems from	Bathtub	Fridge	Hair Dryer	Sitting Area	TV
Inside	$242/$255*	no	yes	yes	no	yes
Outside	$251/$288*	no	yes	yes	no	yes
Suite	$473/$555*	yes	yes	yes	yes	yes

**Rates at left for* Arcadia; *rates at right for* Oriana.

PUBLIC AREAS Public rooms aboard *Oriana* are mostly concentrated on two decks with spacious corridors. Aboard *Arcadia,* they're spread among several decks, most on Deck 7. On both ships, rooms have been designed like an idealized England in miniature. Many lounges have a clubby, dark wood ambiance, and a pub on each features some of the best draught beer selections I've seen aboard any ship. The Lord's Tavern, *Oriana's* pub, is themed on cricket, with cricket bats and wickets on the walls, a mural of a cricket field, cricket-themed photos and paintings hanging here and there, and carpeting that looks like grass. *Arcadia's* pub is the more classically styled Oval.

Both ships feature well-designed two-deck theaters, cinemas, eight to 10 bars, pizzerias serving *very* tasty pizza and garlic bread, nightclubs, discos, libraries, card rooms, and lovely traditional-looking casinos. *Arcadia* has one main dining room and a buffet restaurant, while *Oriana* has two smaller main dining rooms and a buffet that's not terribly well-designed, traffic-wise—it gets chaotic.

POOL, FITNESS & SPA FACILITIES Both ships have sizable pool decks, with Jacuzzis and twin pools (one of which, on *Arcadia,* features a swim-up bar—no need to leave the pool for that martini) and facilities for tennis or cricket, trapshooting, and more. For children, there's a "paddling pool" on an outside deck by the children's center.

Each ship has a gym, the *Arcadia*'s buried, in the old style, low down on deck 2, while the *Oriana*'s is in the more modern, accessible position, way up on the Lido Deck, just forward of the pools (and, as noted above, almost attached to the pizzeria). The spas on both ships are run by Steiner Leisure, which operates the spas on most cruise ships, offering a vast arsenal of massage and beauty therapies.

Victoria

Victoria (photo: Princess)

The Verdict

A real ocean liner of the old school, this beautiful, classic vessel carries only 745 passengers, allowing a more intimate, less crowded cruise experience.

Specifications

Size (in tons)	27,670	Crew	417 (British/Indian/ International)
Number of Cabins	379		
Number of Outside Cabins	291	Passenger/Crew Ratio	1.8 to 1
Cabins with Verandas	0	Year Built	1966
Number of Passengers	745	Last Major Refurbishment	1997
Officers	British		

Frommer's Ratings (Scale of 1–5)

Cabin Comfort & Amenities	3	Pool, Fitness & Spa Facilities	3
Ship Cleanliness & Maintenance	4	Children's Facilities	3
Public Comfort/Space	4	Itineraries	5
Decor	3	Worth the Money	4

One of a steadily decreasing number of classic ocean liners still sailing today, the *Victoria* was built as the *Kungsholm* for the now-defunct Swedish American Line, and was purchased by P&O in 1978, at which time the number of cabins aboard was increased (meaning about half the cabins today are tiny at only 126 square feet—see more on cabin size below). For a time, the ship sailed as the *Sea Princess,* partially for Princess cruises. Throughout, *Victoria* is a lovely old ship, retaining much of her fine original design and workmanship, and offers a real old liner experience in these megaship days.

CABINS As noted above, approximately half the standard cabins, both inside and outside, are very tight at 126 square feet (those are designated by the line as "two bedded cabins"); "staterooms," on the other hand, are more spacious at 180. All offer two lower beds (in the "two bedded cabins" one folds away during the day), TV and music channels, wardrobes, vanity table/writing desk, safe, and phone. Many cabins have bathrooms with bathtubs—a rarity for which we can thank the ship's vintage—while the rest have only showers. Cabins designated "two berth" are truly Lilliputian at 95 square feet, with upper and lower berths, though they otherwise offer the same amenities as the other two standard categories. Suites are relatively large at 306 square feet, with living and bedroom areas sharing the same space, and additional amenities like a king-size bed, bathroom with Jacuzzi tub, stereo system, refrigerator/bar, and two large picture windows. (Windows in other categories are generally portholes.) There are 10 cabins for singles, and eight cabins that are wheelchair accessible.

Cabins & Rates

Cabins	Per diems from	Bathtub	Fridge	Hair Dryer	Sitting Area	TV
Inside	$226	some	no	no	some	yes
Outside	$287	some	no	no	some	yes
Suite	$568	yes	yes	no	yes	yes

PUBLIC AREAS Many public areas on *Victoria,* especially the indoor pool and the lovely enclosed promenade decorated with potted plants, reveal the ship's former life sailing transatlantic voyages on the North Atlantic. Three lounges and four bars (including the very nice International Bar, attached to the show lounge) ensure variety, while a disco and nightclub join the show lounge in offering after-dinner entertainment. Other rooms include a small casino, a library/writing room, and a card room.

POOL, FITNESS & SPA FACILITIES The ship's small Lido pool is perched in a small area—a crater, almost—between the funnel and what used to be the forward funnel, which was purely decorative and was removed when P&O acquired the vessel. The pool and attached buffet area are nicely decorated and cozy. Another pool, this one with a Jacuzzi, sits farther astern on the same deck. The real news though is that *Victoria* has one of the cruise world's only remaining indoor pools, which were once common when ships regularly sailed the cold North Atlantic. The *Victoria's* is very classy and nicely tiled, with a Jacuzzi, a small gym, and massage and sauna rooms opening off the same main pool area. *Victoria* offers no other spa facilities or services aside from the massage rooms and a hairdresser/beauty salon on a different deck. Indoor and outdoor promenade decks offer lots of space for walkers.

Preview: P&O's New *Aurora*

P&O's grand new vessel, the *Aurora,* is scheduled to make its debut in May 2000, sailing a revolving sequence of itineraries that include 9-, 12-, 13-, 14-, 18-, and 21-night Mediterranean, 12-night Norwegian Fjords, 13-night Baltic Capitals, and 5- and 7-night France/Spain.

A sister ship to the line's *Oriana, Aurora* will boast several new features that should put it in a league with the very best of the mainstream ships, whether British or American. For romantic (or relaxation-minded) types, 40% of the ship's cabins will have private verandas. For families, the ships offers interconnectable cabins, extensive children's facilities (with four separate areas for ages under 5, 6 to 9, 10 to 13, and teens), and an aft pool that will be reserved for families during certain times of the year. Another pool can be covered by a sliding roof for use in inclement weather, while a third will feature a waterfall descending from the tiered decks that surround it.

In the public rooms, *Aurora* will offer a range of lounges and bars, some reminiscent of the tried-and-true British-style rooms on the other vessels, some new, including P&O's first champagne bar, chocolate bar, and coffee bar. Other rooms will include a West End–style theater, a large concert hall/cinema, a virtual reality center, a sports bar, a business center, two dining rooms (as on *Oriana*), and a number of alternative dining options, including a 24-hour bistro-style restaurant.

Royal Olympic Cruises

SHIPS IN EUROPE Odysseus • World Renaissance • Olympic Countess • Stella Solaris • Triton • Olympic Voyager (preview)

850 Third Ave., New York, NY 10022-751. ☎ **800/872-6400** or 212/688-7555. Fax 212/688-2304. www.royalolympiccruises.com.

THE LINE IN A NUTSHELL These casual, friendly, and affordable ships offer a Greek-flavored cruise like no other line out there.

THE EXPERIENCE The Royal Olympic ships are all casual, friendly, mid-sized vessels that focus on the destination as much as the shipboard experience. Passengers typically want to see as much of the islands as they can in 3, 4 or 7 days, so most of the itineraries are pretty jam-packed, some including visits to as many as two ports a day.

The ships are old (with the exception of the *Olympic Voyager,* which is the line's first new build) and low-key, staffed by very professional crews. There's no glitz or razzmatazz, no neon lights or lavish atriums. These aren't high-energy ships. For their size, though, they offer a good variety of public rooms, although they can at times (particularly in mid-summer) feel crowded. For the most part, decor is modern, bright, and cheery, with modern Greek artwork and an overall European ambiance, in an older setting. Unfortunately, due to recent financial turmoil at the line (see below), upkeep has not been what it should be, and you may see some signs of wear and tear on the ships.

As with other lines in this category, the international crowd aboard means announcements are made in many languages, which can get a bit monotonous.

Pros

- **Great Greek service.** Dining room and cabin service are delivered with a friendly, personal touch.
- **Well-organized and diversified shore excursions.** It's clear this line knows the Greek Isles.
- **Good variety of public rooms.** These ships have their fair share of quiet nooks and crannies, even though they are pretty small, high-density vessels.

Cons

- **The ships show their wrinkles.** While the crews work diligently to keep everything clean and polished, evidence of deterioration cannot be camouflaged.
- **Small gyms and spas.** On the plus side, the spas are operated by the line and reasonably priced.
- **A lack of TVs and verandas.** Only the *Olympic Voyager* has verandas (and only 12 of them). All cabins on the *Olympic Voyager* have interactive TV, but on the other ships TVs can only be found in top suites (the *Triton* has none).

Frommer's Ratings: Royal Olympic Cruises

	Poor	Fair	Good	Excellent	Outstanding
Enjoyment Factor				✓	
Dining				✓	
Activities			✓		
Children's Program		✓			
Entertainment		✓			
Service				✓	
Overall Value				✓	

ROYAL OLYMPIC: GREEK GIANT

Greek powerhouse Royal Olympic is to Greece what Carnival Cruise Line is to the Caribbean: the dominant market giant. The line was formed in 1995 by the merger of two top Greek lines: Sun Line, an upscale operation, and Epirotiki, a more casual operation. In 2000, Royal Olympic will have five ships offering Greek Island itineraries, and a sixth, the new and fast *Olympic Voyager,* offering 7-day Holy Lands itineraries from Athens.

Royal Olympic has had financial problems of late, and frequent changes in management. In the summer of 1999, the line cancelled a number of sailings, merging passengers onto other vessels in an attempt to sail only full ships. Company officials blamed the conflict in Kosovo for its problems, and even filed a multimillion-dollar suit against the European Community seeking compensation. Separately, the line sought some concessions from the strong Greek seaman's union. When those concessions weren't forthcoming, Royal Olympic said it would move the registration of its ships this year from Greece to Luxembourg.

As a result of all this trouble, the line ran at a loss in 1999, after making a small profit the year before—its stock dropped from $15 in 1998 to about $2.50 by the fall of 1999. There were rumors that the company might be sold, or might sell off some of its vessels. One ship, the *Triton,* was chartered to U.S.-based Premier Cruises for winter use in Mexico.

At press time, Royal Olympic officials were looking forward to launching the line's first new ship, the *Olympic Voyager* (see below), with hopes the new vessel—and a summer season without a Kosovo-like conflict—will help to revitalize the somewhat unsteady line. Royal Olympic received more good news when Cyprus-based Louis Cruise lines agreed to buy a majority stake in the line. Currently, Louis operates charters and short (2- and 3-day) cruises from Cyprus, geared towards a European clientele. The deal was awaiting government approval, as both firms are publicly traded.

THE FLEET

Royal Olympic's fleet is currently made up of five older, classic vessels, all built between 1953 and 1976. Shortly after going public in 1998, the line announced that for the first time it would build some new ships, the first of which, the ***Olympic Voyager,*** is scheduled to be introduced in June. A sister ship, the ***Olympic Explorer,*** is under construction in Hamburg, Germany, and due to be introduced in the spring of 2001.

The ships are a real hodgepodge. The ***Stella Solaris,*** in service since 1953, is a classic ocean liner, while the ***Countess*** and ***Triton*** are more sleek and contemporary. The ***World Renaissance*** and ***Odysseus*** are comfortable older vessels, but not classic. Both joined the fleet in 1998.

The new ships are being designed to offer a yacht-like, smaller-ship ambiance, and are exceptionally fast vessels, expected to cruise at 27 knots (which according to the line will make them the fastest ships in the Eastern Mediterranean).

PASSENGER PROFILE

The cruises are affordably priced, and unlike some of the other European lines, attract about 60% Americans and 40% Europeans and others (including Australians and Japanese). Most tend to be seasoned travelers with an intellectual interest in the places they are visiting. But these ships, with their affordable rates, are also suitable for first-timers and families. And they also attract groups (a cruise I took on the *World Renaissance* was about half filled with French doctors and their wives or husbands). The age range is across-the-board, with most in their 40s on up. Younger travelers looking for energetic nightlife may be disappointed. For the most part, passengers tend to go to bed rather early, saving their energy for exploring the ports. There's rarely more than a handful of people in the midnight disco. The *Stella Solaris* gets the oldest crowd, with many in the over-55 category. Activities for children and teens are offered on the ships based on need (if there enough kids booked, the line will put a youth counselor on board).

Dining

No one ever goes hungry on these ships and the quality and presentation of the Greek cuisine, featured as specials on the continental menu, really stand out. Offerings include *tash kebab* (chunks of tender beef simmered with tomatoes and herbs served with rice pilaf), *sfyrida all spetsiota* (baked sea bass in tomatoes with potatoes), and *spanakopita* (spinach pie).

Dinner is served in two seatings, and menus also offer three continental entrees, plus vegetarian dishes, spa cuisine (low cholesterol, reduced salt), and Pacific Rim cuisine (dishes with the flavor and spices of the Orient). Following the entree is a choice of four desserts (including homemade baklava) plus a sugar-free dessert and an assortment of domestic and international cheeses and fresh fruit.

Passengers can eat breakfast and lunch in either the dining room or on Lido Deck. Those who choose the dining room have the option of a buffet breakfast and/or ordering from a breakfast menu, while the Lido offers an extensive buffet. Similarly, a full five-course lunch is served in the dining room, whereas the Lido has a choice of several wonderful salads, cold cuts and cheeses, sandwiches, several meat and fish dishes, and various desserts. While the food at the deck buffets is plentiful, getting a seat can be a problem, so your best bet is to get there early.

On the *Olympic Voyager*, the line will introduce international theme breakfasts, with a different theme every day including Mexican, English, and German. The *Olympic Voyager* will feature a poolside pasta bar open from 11am to 2am.

The ships also offer afternoon tea either on deck or in a bar, snacks are served at midnight, and there's very limited 24-hour room service.

Activities

The ships offer pretty standard fare: exercise classes, dance lessons, deck sports (Ping-Pong and shuffleboard), arts and crafts classes, backgammon, bingo, and bridge.

What sets the line apart is its special enrichment programs, most prevalent on longer sailings. Royal Olympic boasts of having hosted more Pulitzer Prize-winning authors as guest lecturers than any other line, as well as specialists in various fields including astronomers, archaeologists, historians, and ambassadors.

On all Greek Isles sailings, a licensed guide offers lectures on the ports, as well as on topics such as archaeology, architecture, art, and mythology. A special feature on the *Olympic Voyager* will be a chance for passengers to interact on a one-on-one basis with the speakers, who will eat in the dining room, participate in shore excursions, and so forth. The *Olympic Voyager* will also offer Greek and spa cuisine cooking classes.

All the ships have a saltwater swimming pool (in some cases two), small gym, spa, and beauty parlor. (Unlike the vast majority of lines, who employ the London-based Steiner to run and staff their spas, Royal Olympic runs its own beauty services program, and the spa and beauty treatments are very reasonably priced.) Each ship in the fleet also offers expansive deck space for taking in the Greek sun, and the *Olympic Countess* offers tennis and a golf-driving range as well.

Children's Program

The *Olympic Countess* is the only ship in the fleet with a dedicated children's playroom. All the ships offer kids' activities when there are enough kids on board. The program includes pool games, disco dancing, magic tricks, contests, movies, and breakfast with the captain and his officers on the bridge.

Royal Olympic Fleet Itineraries

Ship	Home Ports & Season	Itinerary
Odysseus	Round-trip from Piraeus/ Athens (May, June, Aug–Oct).	**3- to 7-day Greek Isles:** Port calls may include Mykonos, Rhodes, Patmos, Santorini (Greece), Heraklion (Crete), and Kusadasi and Istanbul (Turkey).
Olympic Countess	Round-trip from Piraeus/ Athens (May–Oct).	**3- and 4-day Greek Isles:** Port calls may include Mykonos, Rhodes, Patmos, Santorini (Greece), Heraklion (Crete), and Kusadasi (Turkey).
Olympic Voyager	Round-trip from Piraeus/ Athens (June–Nov).	**7-day Greek Isles/Holy Lands:** Santorini, Rhodes, Mykonos (Greece), Alexandria (Egypt), Ashod (Israel), and Istanbul and Kusadasi (Turkey).
Stella Solaris	Round-trip from Piraeus/ Athens (Apr–Oct).	**7-day Greek Isles:** Heraklion (Crete), Santorini, Rhodes, Patmos, Mykonos (Greece), and Kusadasi and Istanbul (Turkey).
Triton	Round-trip from Rome (May–Oct).	**7-day Med:** Messina (Italy), Itea, Piraeus/Athens, Mykonos, Patmos, Santorini (Greece), and Kusadasi (Turkey).*
World Renaissance	Round-trip from Piraeus/ Athens (March–May, Sept–Nov).	**3- and 4-day Greek Isles:** Port calls may include Mykonos, Rhodes, Patmos, Santorini (Greece), Heraklion (Crete), and Kusadasi (Turkey).

*The *Triton* also offers a 10-day Holy Lands itinerary in Oct.

ENTERTAINMENT

The song and dance team tries its best to perform light cabaret shows on the dance floors of the main lounges. Headline performers such as Leroy Schultz, formerly of The Platters, and acts like magicians, are part of the line's repertoire. Each ship also has a disco, but don't expect too much action there.

By far, the most popular and exciting entertainment event is **Greek Night,** when the crew joins in with each ship's resident Greek musicians and other entertainers to create a lively party atmosphere. Guests are encouraged to wear blue and white (the colors of the Greek flag), and festivities begin at sunset with an ouzo party accompanied by bouzouki music, followed by a dinner featuring a five-course, all-Greek meal. The evening culminates with a gala celebration of Greek music and dance in the show lounge, with passengers invited to come on stage at the end of the show to join the crew and performers in some lively Greek folk dancing.

Nightly dancing in the show lounge is another popular activity, and many sailings feature gentlemen hosts (to dance with single ladies).

SERVICE

While many cruise lines have a rapid turnover in personnel, some of the crew on these ships have been with the company for years (especially on the *Stella Solaris*). It's not uncommon to see them greet repeat passengers like old friends—a greeting the passengers return in kind. Service aboard the ships is warm and very good, and I had a doting female cabin steward on one ship who was downright grandmotherly. The waiters take pride in their job and are very attentive to individual passenger requests. They also tend to have a great sense of humor, making mealtime a pleasure all around.

The ships do not have self-service laundry or dry cleaning, but do offer laundry and pressing services.

The crew pools tips, with a recommended contribution of $9 per person, per day.

Odysseus • World Renaissance

Odysseus (photo: Royal Olympic)

The Verdict

These are older ships, but they get the job done, transporting you to the Greek islands in friendly and comfortable surroundings.

Specifications

Size (in tons)		Officers	Greek
Odysseus	12,000	Crew	(Greek/Filipino)
World Renaissance	12,000	*Odysseus*	200
Number of Cabins		*World Renaissance*	235
Odysseus	224	Passenger/Crew Ratio	2 to 1
World Renaissance	243	Year Built	
Number of Outside Cabins		*Odysseus*	1962
Odysseus	183	*World Renaissance*	1966
World Renaissance	178	Last Major Refurbishment	
Cabins with Verandas	0	*Odysseus*	1998
Number of Passengers		*World Renaissance*	1997
Odysseus	400		
World Renaissance	457		

Frommer's Ratings (Scale of 1–5)

Cabin Comfort & Amenities	3	Pool, Fitness & Spa Facilities	2
Ship Cleanliness & Maintenance	3	Children's Facilities	N/A
Public Comfort/Space	3	Itineraries	3
Decor	3	Worth the Money	3

These ships are friendly and relaxed, but not at all fancy. The *Odysseus* was acquired by Epirotiki in 1987 after sailing as the *Aquamarine,* a privately owned ship. The *World Renaissance* was with Epirotiki (a predecessor of Royal Olympic) for a few years, then went to Awani in Indonesia, coming back to RO in 1998.

Both ships do what they are supposed to do, providing passengers with a comfortable way to see as many islands as is humanly possible in a limited amount of time. The decor has been upgraded and is tasteful, but the ships are still old-fashioned in a 1960s kind of way without being classic (maybe if you think of it as "retro" you'll be happiest).

Cabins & Rates

Cabins	Per diems from	Bathtub	Fridge	Hair Dryer	Sitting Area	TV
Inside	$212	no	no	no	no	no
Outside	$251	no	no	no	some	no
Suite	$358	some	no	no	some	some

CABINS Cabins on the *Odysseus* are on the small side (a superior is about 130 square feet), while those on the *World Renaissance* are larger (about 165 square feet). All cabins come with a writing area, phone, and 4-channel radio. Some suites on each ship have sitting areas, bathtubs, double beds, and TVs. On the *Odysseus,* some cabins offer sofa beds, allowing you to tuck away your bed and have sitting space during the day.

A handful of cabins on both are equipped with upper and lower bunks. There are no wheelchair accessible cabins nor any cabins with verandas on either ship.

PUBLIC AREAS The ships both have an old-fashioned main show lounge with raised seating on the side and a dance floor in the center, that serves as the ship's hub (it's a gathering place for shore excursions and so forth). Both ships have various other bars and lounges, most on the same deck, as well as a cinema and a small casino. One of the more lively rooms is the Taverna bar on the Odysseus, a popular social venue that sometimes features Greek musicians.

Special attention seems to have been paid to the decor in the dining rooms, which are plush, bright, and pleasant, with nice fabrics, an intimate ambiance, and glass-fronted wine display cases that make for a more upscale decor than that in the rest of the ships' public rooms. The other rooms are done up, in most cases, in cheerful colors, although the *World Renaissance* has some rooms, like the main show lounge, that are a tad dark.

POOL, FITNESS & SPA FACILITIES The *Odysseus* has one outdoor pool and the *World Renaissance* has two; neither has a hot tub. The ships also have small gyms, saunas, beauty shops, and massage rooms.

Both ships have a good amount of deck space for sunning and lounging, although the pool areas can feel crowded at times, particularly when the buffet lunches are served. The *Odysseus* also has sheltered teak-deck promenade areas for walking, though there's no unobstructed wraparound deck.

Olympic Countess

The Verdict

This lovely ship, formerly owned by Cunard, is slightly more elegant and more modern than the others.

Olympic Countess (photo: Royal Olympic)

Specifications

Size (in tons)	18,000	Officers	Greek
Number of Cabins	423	Crew	350 (Greek/Int'l)
Number of Outside Cabins	281	Passenger/Crew Ratio	2 to 1
Cabins with Verandas	0	Year Built	1976
Number of Passengers	840	Last Major Refurbishment	1996

Frommer's Ratings (Scale of 1–5)

Cabin Comfort & Amenities	2	Pool, Fitness & Spa Facilities	3
Ship Cleanliness & Maintenance	3	Children's Facilities	2
Public Comfort/Space	3	Itineraries	4
Decor	3	Worth the Money	3

The *Olympic Countess,* a sister ship to Mediterranean Shipping Cruise's *Rhapsody,* was built for Cunard, which was at the time trying to create an informal line to complement its traditional upscale cruises, a concept it later abandoned. The vessel later sailed in Indonesia as the *Awani Dream II* for now defunct Awani Dream Cruises. It's a nice, airy ship that has a more hotel-like feel than the other Royal Olympic vessels, with a larger reception area, casino, and pleasant cinema.

Cabins & Rates						
Cabins	**Per diems from**	**Bathtub**	**Fridge**	**Hair Dryer**	**Sitting Area**	**TV**
Inside	$212	no	no	no	no	no
Outside	$251	no	no	no	no	no
Suite	$358	yes	yes	no	yes	yes

CABINS Cabins are small but done up in attractive light colors like tan and peach. Windows get extra attention with fancy curtains and other window treatments. Bathrooms are rather tight. The 58 deluxe suites average 215 square feet and have windows, tubs, sitting areas, and TVs. Superior cabins are tiny at 125 square feet. Some have double beds, and some cabins have sofa beds, allowing you to tuck away your bed and have sitting space during the day. There are connecting cabins for families, and a few with upper and lower bunks. Only the suites have safes and TVs. None of the cabins is wheelchair accessible.

PUBLIC AREAS This ship has a good-sized, hotel-like reception area and a more modern feel than some of the other ships in the fleet. It's light and airy with lots of windows and a pleasant decor. Public rooms include a 487-seat restaurant, a main show lounge done up in tasteful fabrics (and featuring oval windows), and a large indoor/outdoor disco where the decor includes (bizarrely) suits of shining armor. Other public rooms include a casino, piano bar, tea room, card room, and new and larger children's playroom (added in 1998).

POOL, FITNESS & SPA FACILITIES While the *Countess* has no wraparound promenade, it does offer a good amount of open deck space, including two levels of decking surrounding the one swimming pool. There's also a kiddie pool, a hot tub, and even an outdoor practice tennis court, a rare find on a ship of this size.

The *Countess* has a larger gym than most of the other ships in the fleet (it's about the same size as the one on the *Stella Solaris*) and it has a dozen exercise machines.

Two massage rooms are located nearby. The ship also has a small beauty salon.

Stella Solaris

Stella Solaris (photo: Royal Olympic)

The Verdict

Calling all culture vultures! This warm, hospitable Greek ship offers a comfortable, old-fashioned way to see the Greek Isles.

Specifications

Size (in tons)	18,000	Officers	Greek
Number of Cabins	329	Crew (Greek/Filipino)	320
Number of Outside Cabins	250	Passenger/Crew Ratio	1.9 to 1
Cabins with Verandas	0	Year Built	1953
Number of Passengers	620	Last Major Refurbishment	1999

Frommer's Ratings (Scale of 1–5)

Cabin Comfort & Amenities	3	Pool, Fitness & Spa Facilities	3
Ship Cleanliness & Maintenance	3	Children's Facilities	N/A
Public Comfort/Space	4	Itineraries	3
Decor	3	Worth the Money	4

After almost half a century of service, the *Stella Solaris*—which began life as the French liner *Cambodge* and was extensively refitted in 1973—continues to run smoothly, although it shows obvious signs of wear in both the public spaces and cabins (something Royal Olympic officials said they planned to fix in a dry dock at the end of 1999). The ship is a true classic ocean liner, one of the oldest cruise vessels around today, and has a classic wraparound teak Promenade Deck (unfortunately rather weathered at this point), polished hardwood railings, and a traditional profile.

Most passengers who choose to sail on *the Stella Solaris* don't seem to mind any of the ship's wear and tear, and the vessel continues to sell out many of its cruises and maintains a strong, loyal following with a repeat-passenger rate averaging around 50% per cruise. Waiters remember the repeaters and warmly welcome them. It's like being part of a big, happy Greek family. When you choose this ship, you choose a vessel with heart and soul, repeaters say; something, they add, big new ships just don't seem to provide.

Cabins & Rates

Cabins	Per diems from	Bathtub	Fridge	Hair Dryer	Sitting Area	TV
Inside	$261	no	no	no	no	no
Outside	$310	yes	no	no	yes	no
Suite	$460	yes	no	no	yes	yes

CABINS Cabins are brightly colored and comfortable but not at all fancy, and come in 11 price categories. Top-of-the-line accommodations are the 34 deluxe suites located on the Boat Deck, which measure a spacious 215 square feet and offer picture windows looking out onto the classic promenade. The 100 deluxe outside cabins measure 182 square feet. The lowest-level inside cabins have bunk beds. Suites, deluxe cabins, and superior outside cabins have bathtubs, and suites alone also have walk-in closets and TVs, which screen four movies daily plus national news, weather, sports, and financial reports.

All cabins come with four music channels featuring Greek, classical, easy-listening, and American Armed Services radio news, and are also equipped with telephones and hair dryers.

There are no cabins with verandas, and none of the cabins are equipped for wheelchair users.

PUBLIC AREAS The all-purpose, 550-seat Solaris Lounge is the ship's largest public space and serves as gathering place, activity hub, and entertainment center. During the day it accommodates everything from lectures to dance classes to bingo, and in the evening it hosts before- and after-dinner dancing and cocktails, as well as nightly cabaret-style shows. Situated at one end of the lounge is the Solaris piano bar, which along with a grand piano has three gaming tables (two blackjack, one roulette); the rest of the casino is made up of 19 slot machines located in a separate room off the Solaris Foyer, near the shore-excursion desk. While there's a late-night disco, it rarely sees much action.

Just steps away from the Solaris Lounge is the dining room, an expansive, cheerful space surrounded by large picture windows. Around the corner is a richly appointed piano bar with leather chairs—it's the ship's favorite evening watering hole.

The Lido Cafe opens directly onto the Pool Deck and, weather permitting, offers passengers the option of eating inside or at one of the tables around the pool.

Other public areas include a cinema that screens daily movies and occasional documentaries and also serves as the venue for lectures. There is also a combination card room/library.

POOL, FITNESS & SPA FACILITIES The small gym has only a few exercise machines crammed into one room; the spa offers five massage/treatment rooms plus sauna and steam rooms. There's also a beauty parlor.

The wide, shaded promenade encircling the Boat Deck provides plenty of space for walkers and joggers and is one of the ship's most attractive features. On days at sea it's an ideal place to relax in a deck chair with a good book and immerse oneself in the balmy breezes. There is a single pool just aft of the Lido Bar, but no hot tubs.

Triton

Triton (photo: Royal Olympic)

The Verdict

The destination is the main objective on these cruises, not the ship, and the *Triton* does a decent job of offering a comfortable place to relax in between ports.

Specifications

Size (in tons)	14,000	Officers	Greek
Number of Cabins	353	Crew (Greek/Filipino)	315
Number of Outside Cabins	236	Passenger/Crew Ratio	2 to 1
Cabins with Verandas	0	Year Built	1971
Number of Passengers	620	Last Major Refurbishment	1992

Frommer's Ratings (Scale of 1–5)

Cabin Comfort & Amenities	2	Pool, Fitness & Spa Facilities	3
Ship Cleanliness & Maintenance	3	Children's Facilities	N/A
Public Comfort/Space	3	Itineraries	4
Decor	3	Worth the Money	3

The ship was built by Cunard for informal cruising, and later sailed for Norwegian Cruise Line as the *Sunward II.* It joined Epirotiki in 1992. The look is contemporary inside and out; the decor is bright and cheery. That said, the ship can feel crowded. The standard cabins are particularly narrow, and there are no suites on this vessel, although there are some good-sized deluxe cabins.

Cabins & Rates

Cabins	Per diems from	Bathtub	Fridge	Hair Dryer	Sitting Area	TV
Inside	$252	no	no	no	no	no
Outside	$311	some	no	no	some	no

CABINS Deluxe cabins are a generous 219 square feet, superior cabins are only 133 square feet, and there are no suites. Cabins on the Venus Deck have windows, while those on the Dionysos Deck have portholes. All cabins come with phones and radios, as well as writing desks, while some deluxe cabins have bathtubs, sitting areas, and picture windows. Some lower-end cabins have upper and lower bunks. There are no wheelchair-accessible cabins nor cabins with verandas.

PUBLIC AREAS Public rooms are located on the top four decks, with most cabins below. The dining room is light and bright, with a contemporary feel. The Nefeli Bar

Preview: Royal Olympic's *Olympic Voyager*

Royal Olympic is celebrating the millennium with the launch of its first new build, the 840-passenger, 25,000-ton *Olympic Voyager,* scheduled to debut in June. Built in Hamburg, Germany, and featuring a unique mono-hull design with a pointy bow that makes it look like a big yacht, the *Olympic Voyager* will be one of the fastest ships afloat, capable of cruising at 27 knots.

More upscale than other ships in the fleet, the ship will boast a warm, contemporary yacht-like design, although most of the public rooms will be generously sized.

Top-of-the-line accommodations will include 48 suites (ranging from 183 to 258 square feet): 12 penthouse suites with verandas, 16 deluxe suites with bay windows, and 20 junior suites. The top suites come with butler service.

Standard cabins will be on the small side at 140 square feet, but will be well-appointed. All 420 cabins will have minibars, hair dryers, and interactive TV, and four cabins will be fully accessible to passengers with disabilities.

Materials being used in the decor throughout the ship are high-quality and include plush fabrics, nice wood veneer, and brushed metals, as well as lots of original artwork and glass. There will be yacht-like stainless steel balustrades on the deck.

The dining room will boast gold-leaf walls and hand-painted crystal chandeliers from Milan. The casino is being designed, in the words of one of the vessel's designers, to be "glitzy but not disturbing."

The ship will have a cushy smoking room with a fireplace (not wood-burning, of course!), as well as a library, card room, coffee bar, piano bar, and state-of-the-art spa with beauty salon. And there will be a pool-side pasta bar.

From late June through November, the *Olympic Voyager* will offer a 7-day Three Continents itinerary from Athens that includes port calls in the Greek Isles, Turkey, Egypt, and Israel.

is located under a canopy on the top deck, next to the Nine Muses Nightclub, where panoramic windows also allow use as an observation lounge. One deck below is the Theatron cinema with theater seating, and the smallish Monte Carlo Casino.

POOL, FITNESS & SPA FACILITIES There's a large oval-shaped swimming pool, with a small fitness center adjacent. There are wide teak decks around the pool, and a wraparound Promenade a deck above, both of which mean a good choice of deck space.

Swan Hellenic Cruises

General U.S. Sales Agent, Kartagener Associates, 12 West 37th St., New York, NY 10018. ☎ **877/219-4239.** Fax 212/268-8299. www.swanhellenic.com.

SHIPS IN EUROPE **Minerva**

THE LINE IN A NUTSHELL Swan Hellenic has always been in a class by itself, where mostly British passengers, and a minority of Americans, come aboard to be as active in mind and body as they are at home, sometimes more so.

THE EXPERIENCE Swan Hellenic provides one of the strongest, if not the top, enrichment program on the high seas, with four or five lecturers from British universities or the Anglican church giving talks aboard, dining with the passengers, and accompanying them ashore. The non-repeating itineraries, generally lasting 2 weeks, attract a very loyal and generally well-educated British clientele for whom a standard cruise would never do. There is a Swan code of behavior, and good manners and a quiet approach to life reign throughout the ship. Local entertainment in port, two crew shows, and classical concerts are the extent of organized evening activities.

The *Minerva,* a small ship by today's standards, takes just 344 passengers double occupancy and usually fewer, because there are many single travelers. Most cabins are a good size, and the public-room atmosphere is like that of a genteel English country house, with both traditional clubby decor and airy rooms decorated in pale colors. Dining for all three meals is a choice between the formal and informal, and the focus is on lively conversation.

Pros

- **Well thought-out itineraries.** They're destination-oriented, yet provide enough time at sea to introduce the lecture program and catch up on reading and napping.
- **An attractively decorated ship.** It feels like an English country hotel, with a wide range of comfortable public rooms.
- **One of the best libraries afloat.** Offers a large selection of fiction, nonfiction, travel guides, and other reference books, and plenty of lounge chairs for reading.
- **An unusual dining policy.** The maitre d' seats passengers at shared tables (different ones each night), which facilitates social interaction. You can, though, often request a table for two.

Cons

- **Service varies in the formal restaurant.** Some waiters are friendly, others very matter of fact, perhaps the result of the gratuities being included in the fares.
- **It's best to play by the rules.** This is not a cruise geared for Americans who want to stick together as a group or who like to make lots of individual demands on the crew.

Frommer's Ratings: Swan Hellenic

	Poor	Fair	Good	Excellent	Outstanding
Enjoyment Factor					✓
Dining				✓	
Activities					✓
Children's Program	N/A				
Entertainment			✓		
Service			✓		
Overall Value					✓

SWAN HELLENIC: A WORLD OF ITS OWN

Swan began operating cruise tours to the Hellenic world in the 1950s and soon extended the programs to the Nile Valley. Cruise itineraries throughout the Mediterranean and Black Seas and in northern Europe became a regular staple using a chartered Turkish ship built in the United States in 1927. That ship, which had mostly bathless cabins and two single-sex dormitory-style accommodations, was replaced in 1974 by the small chartered Greek-flag *Orpheus,* with cabins for about 300 passengers. This ship, built as an Irish overnight ferry, proved to be extremely popular for the now well-established Swan passenger who came first and foremost to see the civilized world in the company of like-minded fellow travelers. The food, what the Greeks deemed should be British, was secondary to the overall travel experience.

In 1983, Peninsular and Oriental Steam Navigation of London, also owners of P&O and Princess Cruises, bought the company and happily left it alone to operate as before. Then, in 1996, taking into consideration advice from both the long-serving staff and former passengers, the company brought a brand-new ship into service designed specifically for the Swan experience. While the *Minerva* is nearly two and a half times the size of the dear old *Orpheus,* the passenger complement remains at just over 300. Hence, the *Minerva* is a far more spacious ship offering a wider range of public rooms and improved cabin accommodation. Naturally, the higher standards mean higher rates, but the philosophy of including virtually everything except drinks provides a very good value.

American presence on Swan Hellenic cruises has never exceeded about 15%, and in recent years has been much lower. At one point, the company went after alumni and museum groups, but a single outside contingent within a British passenger list of individuals did not work, so the U.S. sales agency is targeting mainly individual American bookings. The goal is to reach 30% from North America, but starting at less than 5%, that ambitious level is still a long way off.

In addition to the deep-sea cruises of the *Minerva,* which in winter sails beyond Europe to India, Southeast Asia, and the Far East, the company charters European riverboats. For the first time, in 2000, Swan will also charter Clipper Cruise Line's 120-passenger *Clipper Adventurer* and, using Swan staff, will offer cruises from Greenland to eastern Canada, the West Indies, and coastal Brazil, including the lower Amazon.

THE FLEET

The company has never operated more than a single oceangoing ship at any one time, and the latest ship was built up from the hull of an uncompleted Ukrainian nuclear submarine maintenance vessel. Completed in 1996, the ship was named by the Duchess of Gloucester in a ceremony that took place on the Thames just above London's Tower Bridge and made her first cruise in April. The ***Minerva*** sets a new high standard for Swan.

PASSENGER PROFILE

Presently, the passenger list is overwhelmingly British with a high percentage of repeat passengers on every voyage—often, the first questions asked will be "Have you cruised with Swan before? And if so, how many times and on which ships?" Once that is established, the social interaction begins. The age range is 55 and up, with many passengers in their 70s and 80s, but they tend to be as active in mind and spirit as those 20 years younger. Single women, traveling alone or with a friend, make up a significant minority. The northern European cruises will have a higher average age than the Mediterranean cruises. Most are well educated, and if not possessing university degrees or higher, then keenly interested in where they are going. Swan Hellenic has snob appeal, and many will say that they would never go on a cruise, meaning a standard cruise.

Americans will likely be Anglophiles, at least to some extent. Everything aboard ship and ashore operates to military precision, and the passengers like it that way. Children are not part of the scene.

DINING

When passengers appear at the entrance to the main restaurant, they are escorted to a table with seats available; thus, in the course of 2 weeks, a couple may meet upwards of 100 passengers. One may request a table for two, and a few do, but they will not be available at peak dining times on a full sailing. The sophisticated formal dining room requires a jacket and tie for men every evening. Service from a Filipino wait staff and Ukrainian wine stewards ranges from friendly to abrupt. Menus reflect the countries the ship is visiting, with dinner hours generally 7:30 to 9pm (most people are seated by 8pm). Breakfast and lunch are also served here.

The Bridge Cafe, one deck up, serves all three meals, and is generally full at breakfast and lunch, especially at meals before tour departures. Pale green shades predominate, and the chairs are wicker backed. The food is buffet style with separate stations for salads, cold meats, hot entrees, and desserts. Coffee and tea are waiter served. Additional seating is available around the pool on fine days. The dinner hour does not require a jacket and tie but many still do adhere to the main restaurant's policy. As there is less demand here at dinner, those who like a table for two will find one easily. The service here is more consistently friendly than in the main restaurant.

The food is not as important to Swan passengers as on comparably priced ships catering to the American market. In the beginning, the menus were disappointing, as they tried to achieve something complex and missed the boat, probably an overreaction to the Anglo-Greek food of the *Orpheus* days. Now, however, there is a nice balance between British and continental menus, with themed Scottish or Indian dinners.

At dinner, there are generally three appetizers, two soups, one salad, three main courses plus a vegetarian selection, and three desserts plus a good selection of cheeses, fresh fruit and a savoury (like a pickled fish or brandied fruit). The chef has the flexibility to buy fresh produce locally, hence there is no set rotation for the menus, and as often as possible, local dishes are prepared. Catering to upscale but not necessarily risk-taking British passengers, the menus include entrees such as roast sirloin of beef, steamed tuna, grilled swordfish, loin of venison, and guinea fowl casserole. Salads at dinner are less varied than on a ship catering to Americans.

Lunch and dinner in the Bridge Cafe generally has a pared-down menu of what is available in the main dining room. The salad selections and desserts are more extensive, especially at lunch. Breakfast offers the usual range of hot and cold selections, plus cold meats and cheeses for European tastes, and freshly prepared omelets. The croissants are fresh and light.

Wines, mostly from European countries, are moderately priced, and many passengers who regularly drink wine with dinner choose the French red or Italian white house wines priced at $12 a bottle. Bottles are marked with cabin numbers for those who wish to save the remains for the next evening.

Some Special Deals

Besides the typical advance booking discounts, special offers to past passengers, discounts for combining two cruises, special offers on slow-selling sailings, and a program of standby fares, passengers under 26 travel at half fare. In the past, notice of discounted cruises were generally not available in North America but with the new general sales agent, that is expected to change.

Swan Hellenic Fleet Itineraries

Ship	Home Ports & Season	Itinerary
Minerva	7- or 14-day Greece and Turkey from Kusadasi (Apr– May), Izmir (Sept), Istanbul (May), Piraeus/ Athens (Apr, May, Aug), Naples (Aug), Thessalonki, Greece (Sept); 14-day Italy, Venice (May); 7- to 14-day Med, Barcelona (June), Southampton (June), Funchal (Portugal) (June); 13- and 14-day Scandinavia & Russia, Stockholm (July), Southampton (June); 12-day British Isles Leith, Scotland (July); 3-day France, Southampton (July); 14-day Black Sea, Istanbul (Aug).	**7- or 14-day Greece and Turkey:** Port calls may include Gulluk, Fethiye, Kas, Dikili (Turkey), Rhodes, Delos, Naxos, Thessaloniki, Preveza, Nauplion, Gythion, Samos, Kalamata, Itea, Kos (Greece), Heraklion, Aghios Nikolaos (Crete), and Kotor, Korcula, Dubrovnik (Croatia). **14-day Italy:** Ravenna, Taranto, Porto Empedocle, Trapani, Naples, Civitavecchia/Rome, Livorno (Italy), Elba, Corsica. **7- to 14-day Med:** Port calls may include Brest, Gijon, La Pallice, Bordeaux (France), La Coruna, Bilbao, Malaga, Cadiz (Spain), Lisbon (Portugal), and Tangier (Morocco). **13- and 14-day Scandinavia, Russia, and Norway:** Port calls may include Copenhagen (Denmark), Gdynia (Poland), Riga (Latvia), Tallinn (Estonia), St. Petersburg, (Russia), Helsinki (Finland), Bergen, Flam, Gudvangen (Norway), and Stockholm (Sweden). **12-day British Isles:** Port calls may include Aberdeen, Kirkwall, Lerwick, Loch Ewe, Tobermory, Rothesay (Scotland), Dublin and Cobh (Ireland), and Hollyhead (Wales). **3-day France:** St. Peter Port (Guernsey), and St. Malo (France). **14-day Black Sea:** Sochi (Russia), Yalta, Sevastopol, Odessa (Ukraine), Varna (Bulgaria), and Thessaloniki (Greece).

ACTIVITIES

The *Minerva* is a smallish ship, so the range of activities is limited but also geared to what Swan passengers want. Lectures are an integral part of all Swan cruises, and there are usually four or five lecturers aboard covering subjects appropriate to the destination, such as archaeology, anthropology, architecture, history, politics, and religion. Most are men who hail from British universities, but there may also be a newspaper columnist on gardens, an ornithologist from the Royal Society for the Protection of Birds, and a priest or bishop from the Anglican church. Names and brief biographies are listed in the brochure. Talks are formal presentations, with and without slides, scheduled twice in the morning or afternoon on sea days. They are very well attended and last no more than 40 minutes, with questions taken after the talk in the adjacent Wheeler Bar. Guest speakers are expected to be available on the shore excursions, and may actually lead some tours in countries where this is allowed. A program of complimentary shore excursions is included for every port, with no sign-up required. Some ports will offer supplementary tours, some lasting all day with lunch, and they are generally fairly priced at about $50 to $60 per person. You're encouraged to book alternate tours (such as a ballet performance, for which you'd pay the ticket price) before the cruise, but may also be able to book on board based on availability. Swan prides itself on organization and the high quality of the tours, deservedly so. Disembarkation rotates from day to day according to deck.

The card room is popular for bridge games, and an instructor is aboard for some cruises. The large library may be considered a major activity center for reading, researching, and sharing in the ubiquitous puzzle with usually three completed each cruise. The moderate-size gym sees limited use and is taken over by the crew in the evenings. The cinema shows a film usually once a day. There are no bingo, horse racing, casino or pool games, and no one seems to mind; in fact, many would object to their presence.

Children's Programs

Children are generally not part of the scene, and if aboard, they need to enjoy adult company.

Entertainment

All entertainment, which is limited by design, takes place in the main forward lounge. In the evening, there may be dancing to a small band, a popular place after dinner for coffee and liqueurs. Shows are limited to the Filipino and Ukrainian crew performances and local folkloric groups in a few ports. Classical concerts may be a feature on several evenings.

Service

Cabin service is taken care of by Ukrainian stewardesses who are generally excellent at keeping the cabins clean and tidy. Coffee, tea, and light snacks are available free of charge, but there is a charge for cabin meals, and few passengers opt for this service. There are laundry and dry cleaning services and a small passenger laundrette with no charges. Restaurant service is by Filipino stewards and Ukrainian wine waiters, and ranges from excellent to good enough to matter-of-fact. In the Bridge Cafe waiters are on hand to help passengers with trays. Bar service is excellent. The ship carries a British doctor and there is no charge for consultations.

Minerva

The Verdict

The *Minerva* offers a high standard of comfort in an English country hotel setting for serious destination cruising.

Minerva (photo: Swan Hellenic)

Specifications

Size	12,500	Crew (mostly Filipino and Ukrainian)	155
Number of Cabins	170		
Number of Outside Cabins	136	Passenger/Crew Ratio	2.2 to 1
Cabins with Verandas	12	Year Built	1996
Officers	British and European	Last Major Refurbishment	None

Frommer's Ratings (Scale of 1–5)

Cabin Comfort & Amenities	3	Pool, Fitness & Spa Facilities	3
Ship Cleanliness & Maintenance	4	Children's Facilities	N/A
Public Comfort/Space	5	Itineraries	5
Decor	5	Worth the Money	5

Swan Hellenic was able to design the *Minerva* for its specific market of destination-oriented cruises for mostly British passengers. The ship incorporates a first-rate library, lecture facilities, a roomy variety of public rooms, and a good standard of cabin accommodation for passengers who only expect to sleep and rest there.

The interiors, designed for the British market, set new standards for Swan Hellenic, which had previously chartered first a Turkish and then a Greek ship. The public rooms combine the formal with the informal and provide a range of settings for different kinds of uses with plenty of room, even when passengers are driven inside by the weather.

Past passengers were asked to donate artwork and photographs, and the result is a potpourri collection that reflects the regions through which the ship travels as well as recalls the past. In addition, there are some very fine sets of drawings of Roman and Greek artifacts and statesmen, and maps of the Ancient World.

Cabins & Rates

Cabins	Per diems from	Bathtub	Fridge	Hair Dryer	Sitting Area	TV
Inside	$310	no	no	yes	no	yes
Outside	$352	some	some	yes	some	yes
Suite	$585	yes	yes	yes	yes	yes

Rates are based on a 15-day Mediterranean cruise including port charges, air between London and the ship, transfers, a program of shore excursions, and tips to personnel aboard and on trips ashore.

CABINS Cabin accommodations are comfortable, but not huge, with most rooms between 140 and 162 square feet, all equipped with a two-seat sofa, writing/vanity table, direct-dial telephones, TV and radio, hair dryer, binoculars, and set of company-produced reference guides. Superior grade and up categories have full tub baths. Deluxe cabins (226 square feet) and up have refrigerators, and suites have private verandas (suites measure 290 square feet, including veranda). Two Owners' Suites (360 square feet) also have verandas. Insulation is good, and four cabins are wheelchair accessible.

PUBLIC AREAS The public rooms are extensive and spacious, decorated like an English country house and spread over two decks. The main lounge, furnished with bold colors, has a large wooded dance floor, and with the furniture rearranged, serves as the main lecture hall. Walking aft from here is the Wheeler Bar, with a clubby lounge atmosphere and furnished with sofas and chairs arranged in conversational groupings. There are a sit-up bar and a pianist playing before lunch and before and after dinner. The paneled library is one of the largest on any ship and is heavily used by readers and researchers. Next door are a large card room with suede walls and a true smoking room with leather chairs. The small auditorium screens films. The bright and cheerful Orpheus Bar, a cocktail venue before meals, and a sitting lounge at other times, also takes the overflow from the Bridge Cafe next door at peak periods. The Bridge Cafe is decorated in light colors and is located right above the formal dining room, designed with dark furnishings and chandeliers.

Deck space is more than adequate, with a wide-open Funnel Deck, a teak wraparound promenade, and covered deck aft. Shaded sections are limited and the outdoor pool area is set up for drinks and meals in good weather.

POOL, FITNESS & SPA FACILITIES The outdoor swimming pool is surrounded by a Lido area on Bridge Deck. The small and spare gym on the Promenade Deck is adequate for a Swan passenger who gets most exercise taking constitutional walks on deck and going ashore.

Other Lines

The following lines cater predominantly to European passengers; Peter Dielmann to Germans, the others to Brits. I decided to include them here mostly for European readers (and for Americans looking to avoid other Americans). Upscale Dielmann did make efforts in 1999 to attract Americans to its new *Deutschland.* While the ship, which is one of the prettiest afloat, did draw a few Americans on its North America sailings, the numbers at this point still keep the vessel in the Other Ships category. (But that could all change next year.) Meanwhile, Airtours, which is partially owned by Miami-based Carnival Corporation, could, by nature of that arrangement, also have Americans in its future. One never knows.

AIRTOURS/SUN CRUISES

SHIPS IN EUROPE Carousel • Seawing • Sunbird • Sundream

Wavell House, Holcombe Road, Helmshore, Rossendale, Lancashire BB4 4NB, United Kingdom. Reservations agents ☎ **44/1706260000;** direct 44/1706 830130. www.airtours.co.uk.

Airtours offers down-to-earth cruises geared to those who have not cruised before. The average Airtours passenger is around 48 years old, 7 years below what the Passenger Shipping Association in London reports as the UK industry average, and more than one-third are repeat passengers. Overall, its product is mainstream, but it has recently introduced a premium product, the *Sunbird.*

The line's aim is to take the perceived formality out of cruising. Because the small size of the ships limits what can be done, the entertainment is mediocre and not of the standard of the big American megaships. While there are onboard activities, the cruises are geared towards the ports of call and shore excursions. Each ship has a children's club, though catering to kids is not the line's top priority.

Dining on these ships, which naturally tends to be British in taste, is better than on comparable lines, with better presentation and more inventive choices.

Being older, Airtours' ships have a traditional appeal. Three vessels are almost 30 years old while the fourth, *Sunbird,* was built in 1982. Three of the ships were bought from Royal Caribbean: *Carousel* was the *Nordic Prince, Sunbird* was the *Song of America,* and *Sundream* was the *Song of Norway. Seawing* was formerly NCL's *Southward.*

Sunbird (built in 1982; 37,580 GRTs; 1,595 passengers) has nine public decks, two outdoor swimming pools, two bars, restaurant, gymnasium/sauna, sports deck, library, beauty salon, and casino. There are TVs in all cabins and the vessel has nine penthouse suites (the first in the fleet). Cabins come in superior and standard inside and outside categories. There are elevators to each deck.

Sundream (built in 1970; 22,945 GRTs; 1,190 passengers) has seven public decks all served by elevators and all decorated in clean, bright Scandinavian style. There are an outdoor pool, a poolside bar, another deck bar and gym, a casino, and several public rooms.

Carousel (built in 1971; 23,149 GRTs; 1,160 passengers), *Sundream*'s sister, also has seven decks served by elevators. There's an outdoor pool and gym, and entertainment is offered in the Carousel lounge, the Show Boat Lounge, and the casino.

Seawing (built in 1971: 22,945 GRTs; 916 passengers) was Airtours' first ship. The vessel has seven public decks (all served by elevators), plunge pool, poolside bar, and gym. There is entertainment in the Clipper Lounge, Crows Nest nightclub, Riviera bar, Piano bar, and the casino.

Cabins on all ships have air-conditioning, telephone, music channels, power socket (U.S. adapter required), dressing table, drawers, and wardrobe space.

Seawing is based in Cyprus, and offers two different 7-day eastern Mediterranean cruises that visit the Greek islands and Turkey; the two can be combined to make a 14-day sailing. *Carousel* and *Sunbird* cruise from Mallorca, each on two western Mediterranean itineraries that can be combined. *Sundream* sails from Southampton on 14-day sailings that include the western Mediterranean, Scandinavia and Russia, and the North Cape. Per diem rates are from $102 for inside cabins ($137 on the Sunbird) and from $181 for outside cabins.

HEBRIDEAN ISLAND CRUISES

SHIPS IN EUROPE Hebridean Princess

Griffin House, Broughton Hall, Skipton, North Yorkshire, BD23 3AN England. ☎ **800/659-2648** or 011 44 1756 701338. Fax 011 44 1756 701455. www.hebridean.co.uk.

Hebridean Island Cruises' ***Hebridean Princess*** was converted in 1989 from a rugged 600-passenger Scottish ferry into a posh floating country house for a maximum of 50 mostly British passengers who consider the ship to be their territory. In 1998, the ship was acquired by new owners for whom the optimal mix is two to five North American couples in among the Brits. Anglophilia greatly enhances passengers' enjoyment of this superb 235-foot, 2,112-ton ship, whose crew is also British. The British passengers may include lords and ladies; retired army, navy, and colonial personnel; and the new rich who wish to partake of the genteel atmosphere. Children are not normally aboard, and there are no special facilities for them. Nor is there a pool.

With such a small passenger capacity, fares are very high (per diems range from $285 to $1,966, including port charges, shore excursions and gratuities, soft drinks and bottled water, and watersports equipment), but the *Hebridean Princess* is a one-of-a-kind treasure appealing to well-heeled Anglophiles, many of whom come back year after year. The ship operates 6- to 15-day cruises mostly from Oban, northwest Scotland, and explores British waters, with the Scottish coast and the Inner and Outer Hebrides the principal destinations. To keep the many repeaters happy, two cruises cross the North Sea and visit the Norwegian fjords, and one calls at Northern Ireland ports and the Isle of Man. A guide accompanies all cruises, and excursions include visits to stately homes and country gardens (some not on the normal tourist run), fishing villages, and remote islands. The season begins in early March and lasts through early November, and passengers should come prepared for Scottish mists and uncertain weather. The ship anchors or ties up at night except on a few sailings to the outer islands and passages through the Irish and North seas.

The cozy public rooms evoke the feel of comfy country inns, nowhere more so than in the forward observation lounge with its upholstered armchairs and settees and rustic brick and timber fireplace. A small bar is off to one side. The library has leather and tartan-upholstered seating. Two other lounges feature afternoon tea and cigar smoking amid wicker furniture. Passengers lounge on open and protected decks in wooden deck chairs.

The restaurant operates like a hotel dining room. Passengers have their choice of tables, but singles are seated with fellow singles. Fresh ingredients produce excellent seafood and Scottish specialties, including wild game and haggis. Presentation and service are top-notch. At breakfast and lunch, varied buffets and table service are offered. Some evenings are formal, and on warm evenings, passengers gather on deck for champagne receptions with hot hors d'oeuvres. The former vehicle deck is outfitted with a small gym, and the ship carries bicycles, fishing tackle, watersports equipment, and small boats for passengers' use.

The 30 individually designed and furnished cabins (24 outside) vary widely, but most show chintz frills above headboards and around windows that open. TVs, minibars, teamakers, irons and ironing boards, trouser presses, hair dryers, dressing tables, and ample stowage are standard throughout.

Two inside cabins on the lowest deck share a bath, and there are 11 dedicated inside and outside singles. The better staterooms are as plush as any afloat. Four staterooms have private balconies. The ship is not air conditioned, but this is seldom a problem in these northerly waters.

PETER DEILMANN EUROPEAMERICA CRUISES

SHIPS IN EUROPE Deutschland • Lili Marleen

1800 Diagonal Rd., Ste. 170, Alexandria, VA 22314. ☎ **800/348-8287** or 703/549-1741. Fax 703/549-7924. www.deilmann-cruises.com.

This German line's handsome new flag ship, ***Deutschland*** (built in 1998; 22,400 GRTs; 505 passengers) carries passengers and crew hailing largely from the German-speaking countries of Germany and Austria, though the line is looking to develop the same kind of North American following for this oceangoing cruise ship that they have for their European riverboat fleet. The firm operates eight riverboats that ply the waters of Germany, Austria, Hungary, France, and Holland (see chapter 10), as well as the 50-passenger luxury sailing yacht ***Lili Marleen*** (built in 1994; 750 GRTS; 50 passengers). The company's 420-passenger oceangoing cruise ship *Berlin* is not marketed in North America.

The $64 dollar question is, of course, will English-speaking passengers be happy cruising aboard the *Deutschland* on its world-girdling itineraries?

For a sophisticated American who is truly looking for a European ship experience, the answer would be yes, but for American guests to be well satisfied, the line needs to implement a few improvements in its English-language presentation. The English spoken by staff at the purser's desk, in cabin service, and in the restaurants, bars, and on deck is as good or even better than on some ships with international crews catering to North American passengers; however, the initial printed materials were substandard, with far too many spelling and typographical errors. Communication between Americans and the ship's German-speaking passengers is generally good, as many of the Germans speak English and enjoy putting it to use.

Within, the *Deutschland* is, without qualification, absolutely beautiful, extremely well designed and with a public room layout that suits many different occasions and moods. The decor is richly Edwardian, with art nouveau and art deco flourishes on the paneling and elevator doors and in the styles of lighting fixtures. For quiet reading, playing games, and having afternoon tea, the Lido Terrace, an observation lounge, provides a light-filled atmosphere with wicker chairs and views outside to the surrounding open decks.

For a drink before meals, the Lili Marleen Salon (dedicated to Marlene Dietrich) is a cozy space with polished medium-dark paneling, a beamed ceiling with plaster decoration, and opaque cut glass globes with additional indirect lighting from floor lamps. A trio provides music to drink to. The room looks through open colonnades to the port and starboard side galleries and out to sea.

Two lounges have specialized functions with very popular followings at different times of the day. Zum Alten Fritz replicates a dark paneled tavern with its etched-glass mirrors and button leather curved banquettes, and offers live music, hot snacks such as bratwurst (frankfurters) and weiss wurst (white veal sausage), and beer by the stein. The tiny Adlon Lounge serves as a sophisticated wine and cigar bar and smoking room, though smoking is also permitted in many more locations than is the case on North American ships.

Outside, varnished wooden deck chairs with royal blue cushions are arranged in settings that include open and protected venues forward, aft, high up, around the Lido pool, and along an old-fashioned covered promenade. "Das Traum Schiff" (The Dream Ship), written on the funnel overlooking the Lido, refers to the popular German TV show set on the *Deutschland* and copied in concept from North America's *The Love Boat.*

Dining takes place in a two-sitting main restaurant, the Berlin; in the Four Seasons with reservations but no extra charge; and in the Lido Gourmet buffet, which offers indoor and outdoor seating. Menus are continental with German specialties, and the preparation is good to excellent, with the exception being a handful of bland dishes. Some of the more interesting presentations are air-dried beef with fresh horseradish; mild French goat cheese with grape-seed oil and baguette; cream of asparagus with baby shrimps; black noodles with lobster and scallops; grilled lemon sole with lime sauce; one-half fresh Maine lobster; veal loin with morels and dates in a cream sauce; and white chocolate mousse with basil

Lunchtime buffets offer hot and cold meats, a fair variety of salad fixings, lots of cheeses, excellent desserts, and, from the grill, freshly prepared shrimp, lamb chops, rib eye steaks, and chicken. At breakfast, the menu caters to European and American tastes, but the main criticism here was finding a table with clean place settings, as the system was to reset the tables only after someone was seated. The service in the main dining room, and especially in the Four Seasons, was generally professional but very slow, with dinner sessions ranging from 2½ to 3 hours, making one nearly always late for the 10:15 show times.

For English-speaking passengers, the entertainment is more successful when the program is a singing group and a big band than one that features German-language banter. The Kaisersaal is an extraordinarily opulent cabaret lounge (one of the most stunning at sea) furnished in a 1920s bordello style with comfortable chairs, small table lamps, a huge glass chandelier, and a mezzanine with tables for two set next to the railing.

Of the 286 cabins, 224 are outside (including 17 singles) and 50 inside, and all have white wood-tone paneling, handsomely framed reproduction oil paintings, color TVs, music channels, safes, stocked refrigerators (selections are charged to your account), and good closet, storage, and counter space. Only two suites have verandas.

The *Deutschland* sails in Europe from April till early July 2000 before making a transatlantic crossing for a series of South America cruises. Its Europe itineraries include 5- to 14-night Mediterranean cruises departing from Haifa, Genoa, Venice, Piraeus, and Istanbul, and three 11-, 13-, and 16-night Baltic Sea cruises, two sailing round-trip from Keil, Germany, and one sailing between Keil and Cuxhaven. Lowest-category per diems are approximately $308 inside, $325 outside, $810 suite.

The *Lili Marleen,* a re-creation of a 19th-century sailing ship, has 25 outside cabins. The ship sails 7- to 14-day itineraries in the western Mediterranean/French Riviera from Nice, April to June and August to September, and in the eastern Mediterranean in July and August. All cabins are outside, with per diems ranging from $334 to $474.

THOMSON CRUISES

SHIPS IN EUROPE Emerald • Topaz

Greater London House, Hampstead Road, London NW1 7SD, United Kingdom. Direct bookings ☎ **44/990-502562.** www.thomson-holidays.com.

Thomson, Britain's largest holiday group, now offers mass-market cruises as an extension of its vast package tour program, particularly aiming at first-time cruisers. Prices are competitive, even allowing for discounts offered by established operators.

On these ships, cruisers should expect to share their holiday with mostly British passengers. Dining is good enough (especially considering the low-end nature of the line), but won't soon be winning any awards. The British-slanted entertainment does not compare with that of American ships. There is a full range of onboard activities, but the main focus is port calls and shore excursions. Families would not feel out of place in this environment.

As Thomson is a tour operator rather than a cruise line, they use chartered vessels. The *Emerald* and *Topaz* are both more than 40 years old and therefore traditional in character. The company also books space and actively sells other ships, including Royal Caribbean's new *Voyager of the Seas.*

The ***Emerald*** (built in 1958; 26,431 GRTs; 1,198 passengers) has two restaurants, five bars, and two lounges. There are also a discotheque, casino, swimming pool, two whirlpools, beauty salon, boutiques, children's playroom, fitness center, sauna, library, and card area in the Starlight Lounge. The ship has 10 decks, and cabins come in six grades from single inside to premier.

Topaz (built in 1956; 31,482 GRTs; 1,050 passengers) has five grades of cabins ranging from two-berth inside up to superior outside. There are three restaurants, four bars, two lounges, a discotheque, a swimming pool, a whirlpool, a hairdresser and massage parlor, a shopping arcade, a teen area, a children's playroom, a gymnasium, and laundry facilities at an extra charge. There are seven decks in all.

Topaz sails 7-day western Mediterranean itineraries from Mallorca that include ports in Spain and Italy. The *Emerald* offers the same as well as 7-day sailings that include the French Riviera, 14-day western Mediterranean/Spain itineraries, and a 16-day Holy Lands itinerary that includes ports in the western Mediterranean, eastern Mediterranean, Egypt, and Israel.

8 The Ultra-Luxury Lines

These cruise lines are the top shelf, the best (and most expensive) of the best, catering to discerning travelers who want to be pampered with fine gourmet cuisine and wines and ensconced in spacious suites with marble bathrooms, down pillows, sitting areas, minibars, and walk-in closets. Caviar is served on silver trays and chilled champagne in crystal glasses. Elegant dining rooms are dressed in the finest linens, stemware, and china, and guests dress in tuxedos and sparkling dresses and gowns on formal nights and suits and ties on informal nights. (An exception to this is Windstar Cruises, which, though luxurious and upscale, offers a much more casual kind of luxury and a more laid-back decor. Radisson Seven Seas also tends toward the casual, but not to Windstar's degree.)

Exquisite French, Italian, and Asian cuisine on these ships rivals that of the best shoreside restaurants and is served in high style by doting, gracious waiters who know how to please. A full dinner can even be served to you in your cabin, if you like.

Entertainment and organized activities are more limited as guests tend to amuse themselves, and enjoy cocktails and conversation in a piano bar more than they would flamboyant Vegas-style shows.

With the exception of Cunard's *QE2* and *Caronia* and Crystal's *Crystal Symphony,* these high-end ships are small and intimate—usually carrying just a few hundred passengers—and big on service, with almost as many staff as passengers. You're not likely to feel lost in the crowd, and staff will get to know your likes and dislikes early on. The onboard atmosphere is much like that of a private club, with guests trading traveling tales and meeting for cocktails or dinner.

Although the high-end lines are discounting more than ever, they still can cost twice as much as your typical mainstream cruise. Besides early-booking discounts, many high-end lines give discounts to repeat cruisers and those booking back-to-back cruises, and sometimes offer two-for-one deals and free airfare. Many extras are often included in the cruise rates (see box above).

Most people attracted to these types of cruises are sophisticated, wealthy, relatively social, and used to the finer things in life. While most are well traveled, they've most likely not done overly adventurous or exotic traveling, sticking instead to the five-star kind.

These lines are not geared to children except for Crystal, which does have a children's play center on its vessels. Every so often kids show up on the other ships, and baby-sitting can sometimes be arranged privately with an off-duty crew member.

Freebies for the Ultra-Luxury Set

It's a fact: The ultra-luxury ships treat passengers as though they're the Sultan of Brunei. The following shows what the lines offer their guests on a complimentary basis (or at least what they've already figured into their cruise rates).

Tips: Radisson, Seabourn, Silversea

Port Charges: Crystal, Silversea, Windstar

All Booze: Silversea

Wine with Lunch & Dinner: Radisson, Seabourn

One-Time Stocked Minibar: Radisson

Unlimited Stocked Minibar: Cunard (top suites only), Seabourn (upon request), Silversea

Unlimited Soda Water/Mineral Water: Radisson, Seabourn, Silversea

Some Shore Excursions: Seabourn, Silversea

DRESS CODES On Seabourn, Silversea, Cunard, and Crystal, bring the tux and the gown—guests dress for dinner on the two or three formal nights on these cruises. Informal nights generally call for suits and ties for men and fancy dresses or pantsuits for ladies. Sports jackets for men and casual dresses or pantsuits for women are the norm on casual nights. Windstar espouses a "no jackets required" policy during the entire cruise, so men, bring nothing but dress slacks, chinos, and nice collared shirts (short or long sleeves); women, leave the pantyhose at home—casual dresses and slacks are fine for evenings. Radisson is somewhere in between, so bring the suit and nice dresses, but no need to lug the tux or fancy full-length gown on board if it's not your style.

Cruise Lines Reviewed in This Chapter

- Crystal Cruises
- Cunard Line
- Radisson Seven Seas Cruises
- Seabourn Cruise Line
- Silversea Cruises
- Windstar Cruises

Crystal Cruises

SHIPS IN EUROPE Crystal Symphony

2121 Ave. of the Stars, Los Angeles, CA 90067. ☎ **800/446-6620** or 310/785-9300. Fax 310/785-3891. www.crystalcruises.com.

LINE IN A NUTSHELL Fine-tuned and fashionable, Crystal's dream ships offer the best of two worlds: pampering service and scrumptious cuisine on ships large enough to offer lots of outdoor deck space, generous fitness facilities, four restaurants, and over half a dozen bars and entertainment venues.

THE EXPERIENCE Crystal has the two largest truly upscale ships in the industry. Carrying 960 passengers each, they aren't huge, but they're big enough to offer much more than their high-end peers. You won't feel hemmed in, and you likely won't be twiddling your thumbs. Service is excellent, and the cuisine is very good and close to par with that of Seabourn, Silversea, and Radisson; the line's Asian food is tops.

Unlike Seabourn, which tends to be more staid, Crystal's California ethic tends to keep things mingly and chatty. Passengers are social and active, and like dressing for dinner and being seen.

Pros

- **Four restaurants.** Only the megaships offer as many options—and none so sophisticated. There are two alternative restaurants (an Italian and Asian) as well as a formal dining room and a casual Lido restaurant that puts on some of the best theme luncheon buffet spreads at sea.
- **Best Asian food at sea.** The *Symphony*'s reservations-only Asian restaurant serves up utterly delicious, authentic, fresh Japanese food, including sushi. At least once per cruise, they also hold an Asian theme buffet lunch offering an awesome spread.
- **Fitness choices.** No need to sit around and simply be pampered all day long if you'd rather get a workout in. There's a nice-sized gym, a paddle-tennis court, shuffleboard, Ping-Pong, an uninterrupted jogging circuit, golf-driving nets, and a putting green.
- **Computer learning.** No other ship has such an extensive computer lab, with over 20 computer stations, complimentary training classes during sea days, and e-mail.

Cons

- **Price.** High-end lines are, well, high-priced. Crystal is no exception, so be prepared to shell out at least $4,000 per person for a 12-night Mediterranean cruise.
- **Formality.** If you're not nuts about dressing up fit to kill nearly every night, think twice about a Crystal cruise. Some passengers even get gussied up during the day.
- **Cabin size.** While certainly not tiny or uncomfortable, accommodations are smaller compared to those of Seabourn, Radisson, and Silversea.

Frommer's Ratings: Crystal Cruises

	Poor	Fair	Good	Excellent	Outstanding
Enjoyment Factor					✓
Dining					✓
Activities					✓
Children's Program					✓
Entertainment					✓
Service				✓	
Overall Value					✓

CRYSTAL: SPARKLING & SPACIOUS

Established in 1990, Crystal Cruises has held its own in the high-stakes lottery of the super-upscale cruise market, establishing a unique place there. Its ships are the largest in the high-end sector of the industry, and while not quite as plush and dripping with luxury as its closest competitors—Seabourn, Radisson Seven Seas, and Silversea—the Crystal sisters provide a truly refined cruise for discerning guests who appreciate superb service and top-notch cuisine.

Crystal is the North American spin-off of Japan's largest container shipping enterprises, Nippon Yusen Kaisa (NYK). Based in Tokyo, NYK is responsible for hauling large quantities of raw materials and finished goods around the Pacific. Despite these origins, a passenger aboard Crystal could conceivably spend an entire week at sea and not even be aware that the ship is Japanese owned, built, and funded. More than anything else, Crystal is international, with a strong emphasis on European service. The Japanese exposure is more subtle, and you'll feel it in the excellent Asian cuisine and tasty sake served in the Kyoto alternative restaurant and in the Asian theme buffets, as well as in the handful of Japanese passengers on board many cruises. (There's a Japanese concierge on board, so don't worry about having to sit through announcements and activities being translated into Japanese.)

THE FLEET

Crystal's fleet comprises two nearly twin 960-passenger ships. The ***Crystal Harmony,*** built in 1990, weighs 49,400 tons and cruises in Alaska as well as the Caribbean/Panama Canal, South America, and the South Pacific. The ***Crystal Symphony*** was built in 1995 and is slightly bigger (at 51,044 tons), with a larger atrium and some expanded public rooms. In addition to spending May through November in the Mediterranean and Europe, the ship does Panama Canal cruises and a world cruise from Los Angeles to London, visiting the South Pacific, Asia, and Africa.

PASSENGER PROFILE

Few other cruise lines attract as loyal a crop of repeat passengers, many of whom hail from affluent areas of California and most of whom step aboard for a second, third, or fourth cruise with a definite sense of how they want to spend their time on board. There's commonly a small contingent of passengers from Japan, Australia, Europe, and South America who make up about 10% to 15% of the passenger mix. Most passengers are well-heeled couples, stylish but not particularly flamboyant, and over 55. A good number of passengers "step up" to Crystal from lines like Princess and Holland America.

Many Crystal passengers place great emphasis on the social scene before, during, and after mealtimes, and many enjoy dressing up (sometimes way up) for dinner and adorning themselves with the biggest and best diamonds they own. You'll see no shortage of big rocks and gold Rolexes. On formal nights, the majority of men wear tuxes and many women wear floor-length gowns (although your classic black cocktail dress is just fine). Passengers tend to be well traveled, although not particularly adventurous.

The onboard jewelry and clothing boutiques do a brisk business, and it's obvious that women on board have devoted much care and attention to their wardrobes and accessories, and spent lots of time in the boutiques of Rodeo Drive and the like before their arrival on board. Although, as on most ships, dress codes are much more relaxed during the day, after 6pm men are usually dressed as you'd expect conservative Fortune 500 board members would be. On formal nights, at least three of which occur during every l0- or 11-day cruise, virtually every male aboard opts to wear a dinner jacket or tux.

There are rarely kids on board except during the holidays, when you may see 20 to 40.

Dining

One of Crystal's best features is its diverse and high-quality cuisine. Its two themed, reservations-only **alternative restaurants**—Jade, a pan-Asian restaurant, and Prego, an Italian restaurant—are right up there with the best at sea.

Overall, the galleys aboard Crystal's ships feature a light-textured, thoughtful, **California-esque cuisine** with selections like roasted duck with apricot-sage stuffing served with a Grand Marnier orange sauce, broiled Black Angus sirloin steak, or seared sea scallops and jumbo shrimp served with a light lobster beurre blanc over a bed of pumpkin risotto. At lunch and dinner in the dining room there's a **low-fat selection,** such as broiled fillet of Chilean sea bass served with steamed vegetables (with calories, fat, cholesterol, sodium, carbohydrates, and protein content listed), as well as an **entree salad**—like a mixed grill salad with grilled herb-marinated chicken breast, jumbo shrimp, and filet mignon. **Vegetarian** meals are available. In the Mediterranean, the chef will often feature more seafood and local specialties, like lamb.

In a kind of homage to the California wine industry, Crystal offers one of the most sophisticated inventories of **California wines** on the high seas. Extensive **French wines** are also offered. Prices begin at as little as $18 a bottle, with many selections in the $20 to $60 range, going as high as $800. In the Mediterranean, Crystal will try to have more local wines in the inventory.

The main dining room is chic and stylish, with white Doric columns, high-backed chairs, and mirrored ceilings with lotus-flower lighting fixtures. Tables are not too close together, and there are well over 20 tables for two, mostly along the side or near the ocean-view windows.

Because of the size of the *Crystal Symphony,* **dinner is served in two seatings.** Lunches and breakfasts, however, are open seating in the dining room and the Lido buffet restaurant. Service by the team of ultra-professional, gracious European male waiters is excellent, and there seem to be more nattily attired staff than passengers. In the main dining room—and to a somewhat lesser degree in the alternative restaurants—table settings are lavish and include fine, heavy crystal and porcelain. Even in the Lido restaurant, waiters are at hand to serve you your salad from the buffet line, prepare your coffee, and then carry your tray to wherever you want to sit.

Themed luncheon buffets—Asian, Mediterranean, or a western barbecue, for instance—are excellent and are generously spread out at lunchtime by the pool and sometimes in the lobby/atrium, where the midnight buffet takes place. No expense or effort is spared to produce elaborate food fests, with heaps of jumbo shrimp, homemade sushi, Greek salads, shish kebabs, and more.

If you don't want to stroll much farther than your deck chair or if you've slept through lunch, between 11am and 6pm daily you can order something from the **Trident Grill** on the Pool Deck and have a seat, in your bathing suit if you so desire, at the counter or head back to your deck chair. The Grill serves beef, chicken, and salmon burgers; pizza; tuna melts; hot dogs; fries; fruit; and a special of the day, like a Caesar salad and chicken wrap.

Yet another place for a snack or a specialty coffee is the Bistro, open from 9:30am to 11:30am for a late continental breakfast and then between 11:30am and 6pm for complimentary grazing at the buffet-style spread of cheeses, cold cuts, fruit, cookies, and pastries. For a few dollars, you can also sip an almond mocha, hazelnut latte, espresso, or fruit shake, or a glass of pinot grigio or a nice merlot.

For **afternoon tea,** it's the ultra-chic Palm Court on one of the ship's uppermost decks. A sprawling space with floor-to-ceiling windows and pale blue-and-white leather furniture, the area gives off an overall light, soft, and ethereal ambiance.

There is, of course, **24-hour room service.** If you've booked one of the suites, room-service attendants are likely to be of the white-gloved variety.

Activities

While not overwhelming, Crystal offers an interesting selection of activities. Count on several **enrichment lectures** throughout a cruise, such as a professor of European history or geography presenting lectures on the region, or a movie critic talking to guests about Hollywood and movies. Most speakers are not celebrities, but well-known personalities do occasionally show up on Crystal cruises. In the past, some notables have included TV patriarch Walter Cronkite, glitz-meister Judith Krantz, former secretary of state and Iran-contra defendant Caspar Weinberger, Hollywood gossip enthusiast Bill Harris, *Laugh-In* regular Artie Johnson, NBC news commentator Edwin Newman, biographer David McCullough, and maritime historian Bill Miller.

Crystal also offers its **Wine & Food Festival** program during many of its cruises (some 30 in 1999), when a respected wine expert conducts two complimentary tastings, and a guest chef from a well-known restaurant conducts a pair of cooking demonstrations for guests and then presents those very entrees at dinner that night. Guests can ask questions of and mingle with these interesting personalities.

Dancing lessons are often taught by guest teachers as well, popular when offered. Learn to swing, or do the rumba and merengue. Group lessons are complimentary, and sometimes private lessons can be arranged with the instructors for about $50 per hour per couple.

Crystal is also big on organizing **bridge and paddle-tennis competitions,** game-show-style contests, and trivia games, as well as providing mid-afternoon dance music with the resident dance trio or quartet, serving tea to the accompaniment of a harpist, offering interesting arts and crafts like glass etching, and even presenting guest fashion shows. Commonly, a golf expert sails on board, too, conducting complimentary **group golf lessons** by the driving nets several times per cruise (again, private lessons can be arranged for a fee).

Kudos to the line's **Computer University**—it's really something else. Each ship has a well-stocked computer lab with over 20 computer workstations. On cruises with at least 6 days at sea, complimentary classes are offered on topics like a basic introduction to using the computer, understanding the Internet and the Web, and how to buy a computer. Cruises with fewer sea days also offer guests the opportunity to learn about using e-mail. There's no other computer program at sea that's this extensive. On all cruises, e-mail access is readily available, as well, so passengers can send and receive e-mails to a special personal address they're given when they get their cruise documents. All computer use is free of charge, though e-mail carries an initial $5 set-up fee and a charge of $3 every time you send or receive an e-mail up to about seven to eight pages long.

Children's Program

Relatively speaking, this is not a line for kids. Crystal is a sophisticated cruise line that focuses its attention on adults. That said, each ship does have a small but bright **children's playroom,** primarily used during holiday cruises when as many as 20 to 40 kids may be on board. At times like this, **counselors** are on hand to supervise activities for several hours in the morning and in the afternoon (on a recent Easter-time cruise, six counselors were on board to supervise about 35 kids). **Baby-sitting** can be arranged privately through the concierge, but Crystal is not shy about pointing out that they do not offer a day-care service and parents are responsible for well-behaved kids. Generally, though, you'll find few if any kids on board the majority of Crystal cruises.

Crystal Fleet Itineraries

Ship	Home Ports & Season	Itinerary
Crystal Symphony	11- and 12-day Med, Southampton (May), Civitavecchia/Rome (May, June, Aug, Oct), Piraeus/ Athens (May, Sept, Oct), Dover (Aug), Venice (Sept), Barcelona (Sept); 12- and 13-day Scandinavia & Russia, Dover (June–July), Stockholm (July)	**11- and 12-day Med (E. Med, W. Med, Greek Isles):** Port calls may include Lisbon (Portugal), Malaga, Cadiz/ Seville, Mallorca (Spain), Casablanca and Agadir (Morocco), Villefranche, Cannes, Bordeaux, Lorient (France), Florence/Livorno, Sicily, Venice, Taranto, Portofino, Portoferraio, Sorrento (Italy), Valletta (Malta), Kusadasi and Istanbul (Turkey), Santorini, Mykonos, Corfu (Greece), and Monte Carlo (Monaco). **12- and 13-day Scandinavia & Russia**: Port calls may include Amsterdam (Holland), Oslo (Norway), Copenhagen (Denmark), Helsinki (Finland), St. Petersburg (Russia), Warnemünde (Germany), and Göteborg and Visby (Sweden).

Entertainment

Shows in the horseshoe-shaped, rather plain Galaxy Lounge encompass everything from **classical concertos** by accomplished pianists to **comedy.** A troupe of spangle-covered, lip-synching dancers and a pair of lead singers are likely to do a **Vegas-style performance.** Onboard entertainment is good, but certainly not the high point of the cruise. There sure are lots of options, though.

In addition to the Galaxy show lounge, a second large, attractive lounge is the venue for nightly after-dinner **ballroom style dancing** to a live band. There's also the Starlight **nightclub** that doubles as the **disco** for a few late-night revelers. Nightly, there's a pianist in the dark, paneled, and romantic Avenue Saloon (my favorite room) playing popular show tunes and pop hits from "New York, New York" to "My Funny Valentine" before and after dinner. A few nights per cruise the Avenue Saloon is the venue for **karaoke.** Next door, **cigar smokers** will enjoy the cozy and genteel Connoisseurs Club. A **movie theater** shows first-run movies several times a day, and cabin TVs feature a wonderfully varied and full menu of movies each day, listed in the daily schedules under categories such as comedy, classics, arts and documentaries, concerts, and regular first-run movies. It's one of the best TV systems at sea.

Gamblers will have no problem feeling at home in the roomy **casino,** which is supervised directly by Caesar's Palace Casinos at Sea.

Service

The hallmark of a high-end cruise like Crystal is its service, so the line's staff is better-trained and more attentive than that aboard most other cruise lines, and is typically of an international cast: The dining room and restaurant staffs hail from Italy, Portugal, and other European countries, and have trained in the grand restaurants of Europe and North America; the pool attendant who brings you a fresh towel and a glass of lemonade, as well as the bartender mixing your martini, is likely to be Filipino; and the cabin stewardess who tidies your stateroom is likely to be from Scandinavia or some other European country like Hungary. Overall, the dining/bar staff is best, outshining the room stewardesses. Without a doubt, service is a high point of the Crystal cruise experience. Even the staff manning the information and concierge desks in the lobby are endlessly good-natured and very helpful—a rare find, indeed.

Children's Specials

Children 11 and under pay 50% of the minimum fare when accompanied by two guests paying full fare.

I might note, the Crystal ships are the only ones I've come across that have both a small pool and a hot tub for their crew members (located at the bow of the ship on Deck 5). It pays to keep the crew happy!

In addition to laundry and dry cleaning services, self-serve laundry rooms are available.

Crystal Symphony

Crystal Symphony (photo: Crystal)

The Verdict

This gracious ship is small enough to feel intimate and personal, yet large enough for a whole range of entertainment, dining, and fitness diversions.

Specifications

Size (in tons)	51,044	Officers	Norwegian/ Japanese/Internat'l
Number of Cabins	480		
Number of Outside Cabins	480	Crew	545 (International)
Cabins with Verandas	276	Passenger/Crew Ratio	1.7 to 1
Number of Passengers	960	Year Built	1995
		Last Major Refurbishment	N/A

Frommer's Rating (Scale of 1–5)

Cabin Comfort & Amenities	4	Pool, Fitness & Spa Facilities	4
Ship Cleanliness & Maintenance	4	Children's Facilities	3
Public Comfort/Space	5	Itineraries	4
Decor	4	Worth the Money	5

Plush, streamlined, extravagantly comfortable, and not as overwhelmingly large as the megaships being launched by less glamorous lines, the *Crystal Symphony* competes with the hyper-upscale Seabourn vessels, although Crystal's ships are almost five times as large as Seabourn's, with a broader choice of onboard diversions and distractions.

The hub of the ship is the atrium. Impressive and stylish, and less overwhelming than aboard some of the larger mainstream ships, it's where you'll find the concierge, the information and shore excursion desk, the Crystal Cove lounge, the ship's chic shops, and the site of the much-awaited midnight buffets, which are presented with fanfare every evening. The two alternative restaurants are located on the main entertainment deck.

Cabins & Rates

Cabins	Per diems from	Bathtub	Fridge	Hair Dryer	Sitting Area	TV
Outside	$349	yes	yes	yes	yes	yes
Suite	$745	yes	yes	yes	yes	yes

CABINS The smallest cabins aboard the *Symphony* are 202 square feet, a size large enough to incorporate a sofa, coffee table, and desk. Outside staterooms with verandas measure 246 square feet (including the veranda). Despite their high price tag, the majority of Crystal's cabins are smaller than the smallest aboard any of the Seabourn vessels (its smallest cabins measure 277 square feet), and are even a hair smaller than the space within the smallest cabins aboard either of Cunard's *Sea Goddesses* (205 square feet). Just over half the accommodations have small verandas, measuring about 6 by 8 feet. While drawer space is adequate, the hanging closets are smaller and tighter than you'd expect on ships of this caliber. Tiled bathrooms have double sinks and are smartly laid out.

Deck 10 holds the ships' spectacular, attractively styled penthouses; the two best measure nearly 1,000 square feet, including the balconies. The other two categories are about 491 and 367 square feet, including balconies. All have walk-in closets and Jacuzzi bathtubs, and the penthouse suites and the Crystal Penthouses have bidets.

All of the *Symphony's* cabins are outside, more than half with verandas; those without have large rectangular windows. The E category cabins on Deck 8 have views obstructed by lifeboats.

Overall, color schemes are pastels—pinks, mints, blues, and beiges—and golden-brown wood tones, and are cheerful, breezy, and light. All cabins have a sitting area; bathtub and shower; TVs broadcasting CNN, ESPN, and other channels; VCR; minibar; hair dryer; and safe.

PUBLIC AREAS Throughout the ship, you'll notice an intensely cultivated sense of craftsmanship, with marble features and brass, glass, and hardwood paneling mingling with flowers and potted plants (especially palms). In that classic California style, the color schemes are light and airy throughout with lots of white and very pastel furniture and walls. Passenger throughways are wide and easy to navigate. The atrium/lobby area is a miniature, more subdued version of the glittery megaship atria, but still the most dazzling area of the ship.

Designed with curved walls and low, vaulted ceilings, the ship's main dining room is elegant and spacious and done up in light colors. The chunky silverware and heavy crystal glassware twinkle and shine and mirror a sophisticated land-based restaurant. The Jade and Prego alternative restaurants on the *Symphony* are much more interesting and colorful than the *Harmony*'s plainer, almost ordinary decor.

There are two large entertainment lounges, one for Vegas-style material and another for ballroom dancing to a live band (and disco dancing late at night).

The ship has a hushed, somewhat academically charming library that's outfitted with comfortably upholstered chairs and a worthy collection of books, periodicals, and videos. There's also a large theater for movies and slide-lectures.

The ship has six-plus bar/entertainment lounges as well as a roaming staff that wanders the public areas throughout the day and much of the night, offering to bring drinks to wherever you happen to be sitting. The dark Avenue Saloon, where polished mahogany, well-maintained leather upholsteries, and a live pianist draw passengers in, is one of the prime before- and after-dinner cocktail spots (and my personal favorite). The adjacent Connoisseurs Club (newly created in early '99 from a part of the Avenue Saloon) offers a similar ambiance for cigar smokers and lovers of fine cognacs.

RECREATION & FITNESS FACILITIES The *Symphony* offers a lot of outdoor activities and spacious areas in which to do them. There are two outdoor swimming pools separated by a bar, ice-cream bar, and sandwich grill, as well as two hot tubs. One of the pools is refreshingly oversized, stretching almost 40 feet across one of the sundecks. The other has a swim-up bar and can be covered with a retractable glass roof. The gym and separate aerobics area are positioned for a view over the sea, and the adjacent Steiner-managed spa and beauty salon are sizable.

There's also a pair of golf driving nets, a putting green, a large paddle-tennis court, and Ping-Pong tables. Runners and walkers, note: Just under four laps equals 1 mile on the broad, uninterrupted teak Promenade Deck.

The ship's generous tiered afterdecks are gorgeous and provide quiet places for an afternoon spent dozing in a deck chair or for quiet repose leaning against the railing and allowing yourself to become entranced by the ship's wake.

Cunard Line

SHIPS IN EUROPE Caronia • Queen Elizabeth 2

6100 Blue Lagoon Dr., Ste. 400, Miami, FL 33126. ☎ **800/528-6273.** Fax 305/463-3010. www.cunardline.com.

THE LINE IN A NUTSHELL Cunard may be the last truly traditional line still afloat, and for a true transatlantic crossing, there is no competition. The two ships are lovingly looked-after treasures from the past.

THE EXPERIENCE If you want tradition, you want Cunard. In business since the mid–18th century and once the dominant British line on the north Atlantic, Cunard has had its ups and downs since the invention of the passenger aircraft, but in the past couple years it has reemerged with its very classic, very British personality intact, like an old Shakespearean actor who's finally reached the age to play King Lear after a lifetime of Hamlet.

Interestingly, it may be the line's acquisition by the incredibly American Carnival Corporation (parent of Carnival Cruise Lines) that's responsible for this new focus on the Cunard's core strengths. After the purchase, Cunard's sleeker, newer ships were transferred to Seabourn Cruises, leaving Cunard with just two vessels, the *Caronia* (formerly called the *Vistafjord*) and the *Queen Elizabeth 2,* the latter the most famous ocean liner in the world today. The atmosphere on board both ships is genteel and as formal as it gets today, and most passengers like it that way. Except on short cruises, or ones that fill up with deeply discounted fares, the passengers enjoy dressing up for dinner, creating an elegant atmosphere that lasts throughout the evening. Neither ship stages big Broadway- or Las Vegas–style shows.

Pros

- **Cruising much the way the last well-heeled generation did.** The *QE2* is today the only ship sailing a full schedule of transatlantic crossings.
- **Graceful ocean liner profiles.** This pair turns heads; they're handsome-looking ships, not apartment blocks on a squared-off hull with a blunt bow.
- **Most passengers feel at home aboard ship.** The atmosphere is social because Cunard passengers enjoy life at sea where ports often play a secondary role.

Cons

- **Neither ship is high-tech.** There are no multi-tiered show lounges.
- **Deck space is limited.** On "fun in the sun" cruises (which both ships do occasionally), the outer decks get crowded at midday.
- **The *QE2* gets mixed reports.** Some passengers who dine in the Mauretania Restaurant find the service uneven and sometimes quite slow.

Frommer's Ratings: Cunard Line

	Poor	Fair	Good	Excellent	Outstanding
Enjoyment Factor					✓
Dining				✓	
Activities				✓	
Children's Program				✓	
Entertainment				✓	
Service			✓		
Overall Value				✓	

CUNARD: A STEP BACK IN TIME

The venerable Cunard Line was founded way back in 1840 when it won the transatlantic mail contract between Britain and the U.S., first using Boston as the western port then soon switching to New York, the terminus for today's crossings from England. The line remained the dominant carrier for well over 100 years, and in the mid-1930s took over the White Star Line. As transatlantic travel went into a steep, irreversible decline in the 1960s, so did Cunard, which sold off most of its ships as they proved unsuitable for warm-weather cruising. A revival of the company's fortunes came when it took over Sea Goddess Cruises and Norwegian America Cruises, a business decision that served as a signal for other lines to begin takeovers. Cunard then stood still for a long time, passing through several owners, two of which were not particularly interested in cruise shipping. In 1998, the Carnival Corporation bought Cunard and began to make changes by first mingling Cunard and its Seabourn brand, then redividing their fleets (with Cunard's comprising classic liners and Seabourn's comprising small ultra-luxury vessels), investing in refurbishment, and announcing an ambitious plan to build the next generation transatlantic liner. Cunard's *Sea Goddess* pair and the *Royal Viking Sun* were transferred to the Seabourn fleet and given Seabourn prefixes, thus paring Cunard down to just two ships, the lowest count since back in the 1840s, but those ships are in excellent condition and should see another decade of fine service.

THE FLEET

The *Caronia* spends a large part of the year cruising northern Europe and the Mediterranean, and the *QE2* makes several cruises from Southampton, England, in addition to about a score of Atlantic crossings between Europe and New York. The two ships, while having traditional ocean liner style, are quite different in size and layout.

The 70,327-ton ***QE2*** takes up to 1,750 passengers at speeds generally not exceeding 24 knots, though she can make over 30 knots if behind schedule. Built as a semi-two-class liner, she has a wide variety of public rooms tucked around the ship and has undergone many changes to keep her up-to-date. More recently, these alterations have been very well received, especially the elegant decor, the use of burled wood veneers, and the return of a traditional ballroom. The ship has a huge variety of cabin accommodations, from tiny inside cabins with upper and lower berths to some of the finest paneled ocean liner cabins afloat and a top tier of private suites with verandas. There are also 120 single cabins—far more than aboard any other ship sailing today. Dining assignments to one of five restaurants come with the choice of cabin category.

The 24,492-ton ***Caronia,*** known as the *Vistafjord* until late 1999, takes only 675 passengers in generally roomy cabins that include 73 cabins for single occupancy. She is elegantly furnished in a British hotel style from the Garden Lounge forward through the two-deck-high ballroom aft on the same deck. A pub, card room, and library provide intimate venues. The service is European sophistication, which matches the tastes of most of the passengers, and she is an easy ship on which to spend many sea days.

The powers that be at Carnival Corporation, the new Cunard Line owners, have indicated that they intend to invest in growing the Cunard fleet in the future, first by building at least one running mate for the *QE2,* probably of a size that will exceed maximum for Panama Canal crossings. The new ship, known for now simply as Project Queen Mary, would make even more high-revenue crossings than does the *QE2* and then cruise in the very off-season, while the *QE2* would cross to Europe in the summer months and then do worldwide cruising the rest of the year.

PASSENGER PROFILE

The *Caronia*'s well-heeled passengers have a simple profile that is older and hails from the United States, Britain, and Germany for the most part, with the German element

much higher on Baltic cruises than on other itineraries. They like traditional service and enjoy dressing up at night.

The *QE2*'s mix varies considerably depending on whether you're sailing transatlantic voyages or cruising from England. On the Atlantic, there is still the traditional traveler who is visiting Europe or North America and prefers to go at least one way by sea. There are many repeaters in this group who would never consider taking the ship on a cruise. Some passengers want to do the *QE2* just once and not come back. Especially in the summer months, passengers represent the age spectrum from small children looked after by English nannies to those who crossed as small children before World War II and are back for another try. On cruises from England, the number of British passengers increases enormously, though Americans are also given incentives to take a transatlantic crossing one way and then take a connecting cruise. As the fares for cruises from England are lower, the atmosphere is less formal and passengers are, for the most part, less well heeled. (Rates are higher on the North Atlantic because the ship has no competition there.)

DINING

Dining is formal on both ships, though formal attire is not requested every night. However, the middle 4 nights of a transatlantic crossing are designated formal and most passengers comply because they like it that way. It certainly makes dining, whether on the Atlantic or a European cruise, more elegant.

On the *QE2* there are a total of **five restaurants** with reserved seating, including three grills—Queens, Princess, and Britannia—and two large dining rooms—Caronia and Mauretania, the latter with two sittings. The 225-seat Queens Grill has its own kitchen, so preparation and presentation are of a higher standard. Passengers here may order items that aren't on the menu, and many do, especially game dishes such as pheasant or guinea fowl or a specially prepared rib roast of beef sliced right at the table. Princess and Britannia Grill passengers, enjoying 100-seat side-facing and slightly tiered rooms, can also order items not appearing on the menu. Some regulars who book the highest cabin categories actually prefer to dine in one of these two grills rather than the larger, top-of-the ship Queens Grill.

The Caronia Restaurant has been completely redesigned into an elegant London hotel dining room, and now uses the grand space into which one descends to its best advantage since the ship was completed in 1969. The room benefits from big side windows and some partitioning.

The lowest priced cabin occupants eat in the Mauretania Restaurant, a very large, low-ceiling room but with attractive etched glass dividers that create more intimate spaces. A two-sitting policy operates here, and the continental menu is the same as for the Caronia restaurant. Being a quasi-British ship catering mostly to British and American passengers, the menu reflects their tastes and runs from excellent beef and veal dishes, prepared many different ways, to daily changing salads, terrific fancy desserts, and a traditional cheese tray with lots of biscuits from which to choose.

The **alternative dining** takes place in a large and somewhat noisy Lido Restaurant, located aft and with a low ceiling. Avoid the peak-hour queues and try finding a table near one of the big side windows or facing aft. In heavy, pitching seas, this room rises and falls, especially all the way aft. The buffet layout is good with separate sections for the salad bar, pizza, dessert, and ice cream (lots of toppings). Coffee and tea are also available at all times. The Lido is open at night, when it is frequented more on a European cruise than on the North Atlantic because the latter attracts a traditional crowd who prefers the main restaurant.

On the *Caronia,* there is one formal, single-seating dining room with highly polished European service that caters to a broader mix of Europeans and North Americans. The

Cruise Tip

The *QE2* often offers deep discounts for off-season transatlantic sailings.

continental menu, featuring heavier sauces to accompany the veal and game dishes than aboard the *QE2,* also caters to lighter tastes with salmon, Dover sole, and shellfish dishes. The informal Lido buffet aft is small and can be cramped for seating at lunchtime, with the spillover on a rainy day taking up residence in the adjacent ballroom. The selections are well prepared, but the variety is less because of the tight space. At night, Italian dining is available in the festive 40-seat Tivoli Restaurant, an intimate space facing aft over the afterdeck and pool. The menu is a set one, and the careful preparation takes place in a separate kitchen.

Vegetarian/spa choices are available on both ships.

Activities

On the *QE2* there is no shortage of daytime activities as the ship spends a lot of time at sea, especially when sailing to and from Europe. The *QE2*'s well-received **lecture program** features a wide range of speakers, some well known and others just very good at what they do, on diverse topics such as an author's latest book (later made available for purchase and signing at the library); producing a movie; investing in the stock market; foreign affairs; how to shop for bargains in New York; and ocean liner history. The **Computer Learning Center** has helped many overcome the fear of using this wonderful development in communication; classes are held regularly, and the facilities are available to all at other times. A staff member takes passengers on the ship's **Heritage Trail,** displaying Cunard's 160-year history in original oil paintings, trophies, and collected memorabilia, including a mesmerizing photo display of the famous passengers who have crossed on Cunard ships. Outdoors, there are a putting green, a golf range, basketball, paddle tennis, deck tennis, shuffleboard, and both indoor and outdoor pools.

On the *Caronia,* there are fewer activities because of the ship's size, but it still carries on the tradition of a good **enrichment program,** especially focusing on the destinations and cooking demonstrations by the chefs. The card room is popular for bridge players and for board games, and a proper cinema screens films.

Children's Programs

The structure of the *QE2*'s programs will depend on how many children are booked. For the young ones, there's a large children's room-cum-nursery with tiny furniture, staffed throughout the day. It's located high up, out of the way and near the pet kennels. Young children may choose from a kid's menu and have an early supper. The *QE2* has a private room for teenagers called Club 2000, with video games, Foosball, and board games. Most children from the U.S. will be aboard on the summer transatlantic trips.

The *Caronia* sees very few children and has no special programs.

Entertainment

Compared to the newest large cruise ships, Cunard does not offer lavish shows as there simply is not the room to stage them. The *Caronia* has a ballroom with only a slightly raised stage and the *QE2* uses the Grand Lounge, which has a slightly better setup for

Cunard Fleet Itineraries

Ship	Home Ports & Season	Itinerary
Caronia	15-day Norway, Southampton (May), Hamburg (July); 12-day Scandinavia & Russia, Dover (June), Copenhagen (June); 14-day W. Med, Dover (July), Barcelona (Aug), Civitavecchia/Rome (Oct); 14-day E. Med, Venice (Aug), Genoa (Sept), Istanbul (Sept); 14-day Black Sea, Istanbul (Sept).	**15-day Norway:** Port calls may include Amsterdam (Holland), Leith (Scotland), and Olden, Aalesund, Trondheim, Honningsvag, Tromso, Svolvaer, Molde, Hellesylt, Geiranger, Bergen (Norway). **12-day Scandinavia & Russia:** Copenhagen (Denmark), Tallinn (Estonia), St. Petersburg (Russia), Helsinki (Finland), and Visby and Stockholm (Sweden). **14-day W. Med*:** Port calls may include Pauillac (France), Leixoes and Lisbon (Portugal), Cadiz, Mallorca, Malaga (Spain), Cagliari (Sardinia), Ajaccio (Corsica), and Villefranche (France). **14-day E. Med*:** Port calls may include Aghios Nikolaos (Crete), Rhodes, Corfu, Santorini, Piraeus/Athens, Volos, Navplion (Greece), and Kusadasi and Bodrum (Turkey). **14-day Black Sea*:** Odessa, Yalta, Sevastopol (Ukraine), Nesebur (Bulgaria), Piraeus/Athens, Santorini, Zakinthos (Greece), Kuasadasi (Turkey), and Valletta (Malta).
Queen Elizabeth 2	Between Southampton and New York (Apr–Dec); Europe cruises, round-trip from Southampton; May–Oct.	**6- and 7-day transatlantic crossings:** Sail between New York and Southampton; may make no stops or may visit Cherbourg (France), Amsterdam (Netherlands), or Boston (Mass, USA). **12-day W. Med:** Mallorca (Spain), Naples and Palermo (Italy), Malaga and Cadiz (Spain), and Lisbon (Portugal). **7-day British Isles:** Waterford (Ireland), Liverpool (England), Invergordon (Scotland), and Le Havre (France). **10-day Norway:** Oslo, Hellesylt, Geiranger, Trondheim (Norway), and Edinburgh (Scotland).

*Can also be booked as 7-day segments.

shows. Hence the evening entertainment is cabaret acts such as singers, dancers, illusionists, and the like. However, both ships do offer ballroom dancing and provide dance lessons and male hosts. On the *QE2,* dancing takes place every night in the Queens Room to a large band, and on the *Caronia* on selected nights and before the after-dinner cabarets. In addition, the *Caronia* offers high-quality **after-dinner concerts** in the Garden Lounge. The *QE2*'s Golden Lion Pub and Yacht Club each have bands, and a pianist plays the old Queen Mary's grand piano alternating with a harpist. The *QE2* has a large **cinema** with balcony; the *Caronia*'s is smaller, and on one level.

SERVICE

Cunard offers **24-hour cabin service,** but sometimes you need to ask if you want a particular service (morning tea, ice at 6, leaving the curtains open at night so you can see the dawn, etc.), after which it's willingly performed. The dining staff may be a little harried in the two-sitting Mauretania Restaurant, but excellent otherwise (though staff turnover may turn up a raw steward on occasion). The bad old days of inconsistent service are gone forever, hopefully, and the staff is friendlier and more willing than ever before.

Caronia

The Verdict

The *Caronia* provides a traditional, sophisticated, mid-size ship experience, a rarity on the high seas today.

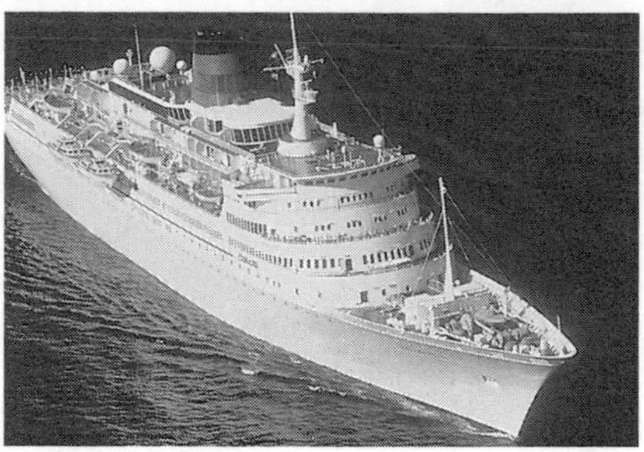

Caronia (photo: Cunard)

Specifications

Size (in tons)	24,492	Officers	British
Number of Cabins	376	Crew (Mostly European)	400
Number of Outside Cabins	324	Passenger/Crew Ratio	1.7 to 1
Cabins with Verandas	25	Year Built	1973
Number of Passengers	679	Last Major Refurbishment	1999

Frommer's Ratings (Scale of 1–5)

Cabin Comfort & Amenities	4	Pool, Fitness & Spa Facilities	.3
Ship Cleanliness & Maintenance	4	Children's Facilities	N/A
Public Comfort/Space	4	Itineraries	5
Decor	4	Worth the Money	5

The *Caronia* came on the scene just as the transatlantic trade was drying up, and while she resembled her earlier sister *Sagafjord* (now *Sage Rose*), the *Caronia,* then called *Vistafjord,* never made regular Atlantic crossings. However, she is one of the last surviving ocean liner–style ships, with unmatched traditional elegance and grace. Her recent refit is wonderful news, ensuring that she will be around for some years to come, offering the high-end market spacious European-style cruising.

Cabin & Rates

Cabins	Per Diems From	Bathtub	Fridge	Hair Dryer	Sitting Area	TV
Inside	$282	some	yes	yes	some	yes
Outside	$306	some	yes	yes	some	yes
Suite	$755	yes	yes	yes	yes	yes

CABINS Most of the 376 cabins are outside, and all are designed for longer voyages, with spacious floor plans and plentiful stowage. The detailed cabin plans are well worth studying because of the intriguing variety of arrangements. All cabins have light wood accents, TVs with VCRs, two music channels, phones, safes, minibars, robes, fresh fruit daily, and bottles of sparkling wine upon embarkation. Many cabins on Promenade Deck overlook the open side deck, but some views are obstructed by lifeboats. Some cabins in the top categories have verandas, and two Hollywood-style duplex suites are among the nautical world's best, featuring glass-enclosed lounges with treadmills and indoor-outdoor hot tubs on upper levels and bedrooms with hot tubs below.

PUBLIC AREAS *Caronia*'s public rooms are paragons of understated British hotel elegance, from the forward circular Garden Lounge for afternoon tea and concerts to the spacious ballroom for shows and dancing. Gentleman hosts provide company for ladies traveling alone. Side galleries provide intimate spaces for a newly refitted bar (now a British-style pub), card room, mahogany-paneled library, and casino. The elegant dining room serves some of the best food afloat at one unhurried sitting. Passengers dress accordingly. Tivoli, a 40-seat restaurant with an all-Italian menu and wine list, is open for dinner from 6:45 to 8:30pm. It's popular, so book early. Buffets are set up in the cafe and by the pool, and it's a bit cramped here on a fine day. Amidships is a cinema for first-run films and special-interest lectures, and the aft-facing nightclub doubles as a daytime retreat for readers, who revel in the views over the Veranda Deck pool.

POOL, FITNESS & SPA FACILITIES There is an outdoor pool aft and a second pool that lies deep within the hull in a complex that includes a gym and spa with aerobics, bikes, rowing machines, StairMasters, sauna, steam bath, thalassotherapy, and massage facility. There is a wraparound deck for jogging and walking.

Queen Elizabeth 2

QE2 (photo: Cunard)

The Verdict

For the past two decades, the *QE2* has been the only game in town for a traditional transatlantic crossing, and she seems to get better doing it with each passing year.

Specifications

Size (in tons)	70,327	Officers	British
Number of Cabins	931	Crew	1,000 (Internat'l)
Number of Outside Cabins	625	Passenger/Crew Ratio	1.74 to 1
Cabins with Verandas	33	Year Built	1969
Number of Passengers	1,740	Last Major Refurbishment	1999

Frommer's Ratings (Scale of 1–5)

Cabin Comfort & Amenities	3	Pool, Fitness & Spa Facilities	4
Ship Cleanliness & Maintenance	3	Children's Facilities	3
Public Comfort/Space	4	Itineraries	4
Decor	4	Worth the Money	5

The *Queen Elizabeth 2* is an unusual dual-purpose ship that makes both transatlantic crossings and cruises and has kept this balance for the last 3 decades. Since her re-engining and major subsequent refits, she has simply become better and better in food, service, decor, and amenities. No ship has had a greater capital investment, and it shows.

Cabins & Rates*

Cabins	Per diems from	Bathtub	Fridge	Hair Dryer	Sitting Area	TV
Inside	$239	no	no	no	no	yes
Outside	$324	some	some	some	some	yes
Suite	$1,510	yes	yes	yes	yes	yes

**Six-day transatlantic cruises start at $417 inside, $563 outside, $2,605 suite.*

CABINS Being an older ship originally designed for two classes, the *QE2* has a huge range of cabin accommodations, and even layout and decorative variations within a single category. The high-up veranda cabins were added to the ship over the years, and they are located in a separate penthouse location, effectively cut off from the rest of the ship. The amidships One and Two Deck Q3 Grades were the top accommodations when the ship was new, and they remain the preferred choice for traditionalists who want an authentic steamship cabin. They have wood paneling, satin-padded walls, a large elliptical window or three elliptical portholes, walk-in closets-cum-dressing-rooms, a corner for a standing steamer trunk, and a large marble bathroom with full-size tub and bidet. On a rough North Atlantic crossing, these well-situated, middle-of-the-ship cabins are preferred by those in the know.

The mid-priced Princess and Caronia Grade rooms are also roomy for this level, while the lowest-priced are deep in the ship and relatively tight, with many inside, including some with upper and lower berths. However, they provide moderately priced accommodations for those who could otherwise not afford the ship. During rough weather conditions, the portholes on Five Deck may be sealed by metal covers called deadlights.

PUBLIC AREAS Nearly all the public rooms range over two complete decks (Upper and Quarter Decks) and offer a great variety of venues for socializing, reading, and special functions. Every public room has been redone several times over the years, and today the decor is both traditional and up-to-date rather than dated. The Queens Room, with its tapered white columns, comes alive at a formal afternoon tea with music and again after dinner for ballroom dancing with several gentlemen hosts at the ready. The most attractive bar lounge is the Chart Room, a two-section space with a cozy interior, seats next to the starboard side windows parallel to the path of the indoor promenaders, and a pianist or harpist in attendance.

Passengers dining in the three grill rooms have exclusive access to the Queens Grill Lounge high on the Boat Deck for reading, tea, or drinks. In the afternoon and evening, the Golden Lion Pub attracts the beer set, who come for the small-band sounds, while the Yacht Club is the late-night venue where the officers and staff mingle with passengers. The theater, a two-level room with a balcony, offers films and special-interest talks. The library, often as busy as Grand Central Station, is a two-room complex with two professional librarians, 7,000 books, and ocean liner books, videos, and memorabilia for sale.

POOL, FITNESS & SPA FACILITIES Steiner runs the spa and fitness facilities (as they do on almost every other cruise ship), and while they're complete in the range of offerings, they lie deep down in the hull, with the spa on Six Deck and the gymnasium and indoor pool on Seven Deck. The Spa offers a 10-station AquaSpa and treatment rooms, sauna, and massage. The gym positioned alongside the glassed-in pool has the typical range of treadmills, cycles, and machines, plus classes and daily forced-march hikes on deck. The outdoor pool is One Deck aft.

Radisson Seven Seas Cruises

SHIPS IN EUROPE Radisson Diamond • Song of Flower

600 Corporate Dr., Ste. 410, Fort Lauderdale, FL 33334. ☎ **800/333-3333** or 954/776-6123. Fax 954/722-6763. www.rssc.com.

THE LINE IN A NUTSHELL Radisson Seven Seas Cruises offers one of the most sophisticated, nearly all-inclusive cruising styles afloat, and the line takes its destinations seriously, offering a strong enrichment program.

THE EXPERIENCE Cruising European waters with Radisson Seven Seas is sea travel at its best, a culturally rich experience shared with a couple hundred rather than a couple thousand fellow passengers. While the 354-passenger *Radisson Diamond* and the 180-passenger *Song of Flower* are quite different types of ships, they both provide many inclusive features in the overall cruise price, reducing the number of nagging extra charges at the end of the cruise. Both ships offer a wide variety of port-intensive itineraries in northern Europe and the Mediterranean.

Passengers are generally well traveled and have high incomes, some still working and some retired. The *Radisson Diamond* attracts a more luxury-seeking set with its posh accommodations and outstanding dining experience, while the *Song of Flower,* a step down in luxury, attracts less status-seeking passengers who like the ship's small size and serious destinations. Most passengers are North American, with a small percentage of Europeans and Australians in the mix.

Pros

- **A nearly all-inclusive price.** Rates include air from the U.S. East Coast, gratuities, complimentary wines with dinner, complimentary soft drinks, and a stocked minibar. Rates for the *Song of Flower* also include drinks at the bar.
- **No crowds aboard.** With just 180 passengers aboard the *Song of Flower* and 354 aboard the roomy *Radisson Diamond,* it's a low-key, relaxed cruising atmosphere.
- **Terrific menus.** Both ships pride themselves on fine dining that reflects the regions through which they are traveling. Both offer single-seating dining.

Cons

- **Awkward public rooms on the *Radisson Diamond.*** The piano bar lacks windows, and the show lounge has poor sight lines beyond the first couple of rows.
- **The *Diamond* is slow.** The ship's cruising speed is a paltry 13 knots, hence port calls have to be closely spaced.
- **The *Song of Flower* has a noisy afterdeck.** The aft engine uptakes are irritatingly noisy when you're seated between them at the outdoor buffet tables on the Sun Deck.

Frommer's Ratings: Radisson Seven Seas Cruises

	Poor	Fair	Good	Excellent	Outstanding
Enjoyment Factor					✓
Dining					✓
Activities		✓			
Children's Program	N/A				
Entertainment			✓		
Service				✓	
Overall Value				✓	

RADISSON: HIGH-END & NEARLY ALL-INCLUSIVE

Radisson Seven Seas is now a division of Carlson Hospitality Worldwide, but it got started as Diamond Cruises (which then merged with Radisson Hotels) and Seven Seas Cruises, originally owned by a Japanese businesswoman. Each cruise line owned just one ship. The fleet expanded to include chartered ships (the *Paul Gauguin* and *Seven Seas Navigator*) and the *Hanseatic,* which sails in Antarctica. The line aims to cover the world with an expanding fleet of smallish upscale ships, some managed and owned by the Vlasov Group in Monaco, offering a luxurious onboard experience while taking passengers to serious destinations. The ships' size (larger than the vessels of Seabourn and Silversea) will allow lower prices than these lines' all-suite boutique ships and place Radisson in a unique position at the upper end of the cruise market.

THE FLEET

Every Radisson ship is different in design, which is confusing to some prospective passengers, but the over-all experience maintains much in common. The 354-passenger ***Radisson Diamond*** is a futuristic, one-of-a-kind twin-hulled ship (like a huge catamaran) that's stable and especially roomy. It was originally designed for the incentive and conference markets; hence, the public rooms have a hotel feel and lack communion with the sea. The 180-passenger ***Song of Flower*** has always been best known for its terrific value rather than high level of luxury, and for the well-run onboard operation that takes passengers to exotic and out-of-the-way destinations. Its small size results in a country-club-style atmosphere. Both ships have a loyal following, and the varied itineraries give passengers an incentive to come back.

The 184-passenger *Hanseatic* is now chartered for a couple of cruises to Antarctica, where it's the most luxurious ship in the market. The 320-passenger *Paul Gauguin* is based year-round in the South Pacific, and the 490-passenger *Seven Seas Navigator* is spending next year outside European waters.

PASSENGER PROFILE

Radisson passengers are usually a well-traveled lot with high incomes, some still working and some retired. The *Radisson Diamond* gets a more status-seeking clientele because of the luxurious accommodations and outstanding dining experience. The European itineraries are a big draw, but the ship's loyal following will follow her elsewhere to less culturally rich destinations. The *Song of Flower,* a step down in luxurious accommodations, attracts passengers that are the antithesis of status seekers. For the most part they like the ship's small size, the intimate feel of a seagoing club with no pretensions, and its serious destinations, be they in Europe or elsewhere. Most passengers hail from North America, though there are likely to be some Europeans and Australians aboard.

DINING

The line prides itself on having some of the best food afloat and ever-changing menus. The *Radisson Diamond*'s dining room is one of the best settings for lunch or dinner on the high seas, and the Italian headwaiters run a very good show. Passengers in a romantic mood can usually obtain a table for two, and may also have full-service meals served in their suite or on the balcony. The *Song of Flower*'s cuisine may not be so lavishly presented but it is fine nonetheless, with great attention to selections that reflect where the ship is cruising. Both ships offer wonderful **lunchtime buffets** with a different theme each day that may feature freshly prepared Italian, Chinese, Japanese, and fish entrees. The *Radisson Diamond* has far more space to set up several stations for a greater choice, but the quality is the same on both ships. An alternative **Italian restaurant** is housed

Radisson Seven Seas Fleet Itineraries

Ship	Home Ports & Season	Itinerary
Radisson Diamond	7- to 11-day W. Med, Funchal/Madeira, Portugal (May), Civitavecchia/Rome (May, Oct), Barcelona (May), Nice (June and Sept); 7- and 11-day Scandinavia & Russia, Dover (June), Stockholm (July, Aug), Copenhagen (July); 7-day Greek Isles, Civitavecchia/Rome (Sept), Istanbul (Oct), Piraeus/Athens (Oct); 7-day Spain/France/UK, Lisbon (June); 11-day Spain/France/UK, Dover (Aug).	**7- to 11-day W. Med:** Port calls may include Malaga, Cadiz, La Cornuña, Santander, Bilbao, Barcelona (Spain), St. Tropez, Sete, Nice, St. Malo, Port Vendres (France), Livorno and Portofino (Italy), and Monte Carlo (Monaco). **7- and 11-day Scandinavia and Russia:** Port calls may include Amsterdam (Holland), Warnemünde (Germany), Visby (Sweden), Tallinn (Estonia), St. Petersburg (Russia), and Helsinki (Finland). **7-day Greek Isles:** Port calls may include Sorrento and Taormina (Italy), Santorini, Patmos, Samos, Rhodes, Mykonos, Santorini (Greece), and Kusadasi, Canakkale, Dikili (Turkey). **7- and 11-day Spain/France/UK:** Port calls may include Guernsey (UK), St. Malo (France), La Coruña, Santander, Bilbao, Barcelona, Cádiz (Spain), and Lisbon (Portugal).
Song of Flower	7-day Greek Isles, Piraeus/Athens (May, Oct), Istanbul (June, Oct), Monte Carlo (Sept); 7- and 10-day W. Med, Civitavecchia/Rome (June), Lisbon (Sept); 8- and 10-day France and Spain, Lisbon (June), London (Aug); 9-day British Isles, Rouen, France (June); 7- and 10-day Scandinavia & Russia, Edinburgh (July), Stockholm (July, Aug), Copenhagen (July), Hamburg (Aug).	**7-day Greek Isles:** Port calls may include Santorini, Mykonos, Itea, Rhodes, Patmos, Samos (Greece), Kusadasi and Dikili (Turkey), and Taormina and Sorrento (Italy). **7- and 10-day W. Med:** Port calls may include Monte Carlo (Monaco), Livorno (Italy), Sete and Cannes (France), Barcelona, Cadiz, Malaga (Spain), Casablanca (Morocco), and Portimao (Portugal). **8- and 10-day Spain and France:** Port calls may include Villagarcia, Santander, Bilbao (Spain), and Arcachon, Belle Ile, Bordeaux, Honfleur, St. Malo (France). **9-day British Isles:** Cherbourg (France), Fowey (England), Fishguard and Hollyhead (Wales), Dublin (Ireland), and Iona, Portree, Kirkwall (Scotland). **7- to 10-day Scandinavia & Russia:** Port calls may include Copenhagen (Denmark), Warnemünde (Germany), Riga (Latvia), Tallinn (Estonia), Gdynia (Poland), St.Petersburg (Russia), Amsterdam (Holland), and Helsinki (Finland).

in a private room on the *Song of Flower* and in the Grill (part of the indoor/outdoor buffet complex) on the *Radisson Diamond.* Both take reservations, offer a set multi-course menu, and have Italian waiters that burst into song near the end of the meal.

Activities

Both ships are fairly low-key in this area, with the emphasis on the destinations. The **cultural enrichment lectures** are a big draw and will include experts in the fields of European art, culture, wine and food, history, and current affairs. Both ships have outdoor pools, **golf instruction** and video swing analysis, casinos, and a good selection of free videos to take to the cabin. The *Radisson Diamond*'s spa is far more impressive than the one aboard the *Song of Flower.* The *Song of Flower* has an open bridge policy during daylight hours, a popular pastime when at sea.

Children's Programs

Neither ship has any special facilities for children, and you should only consider bringing children who enjoy adult company aboard.

ENTERTAINMENT

Entertainment includes cabaret-style acts rather than full-blown production shows, and both ships carry pianists who play during afternoon tea and at the cocktail hour. Dancing is to five-piece orchestras. Only a few passengers stay up to the wee hours on these port-intensive cruises.

SERVICE

The personnel is primarily European, with some Filipinos, and both ships are very service oriented. Service is more personal aboard the *Song of Flower* as the ship has half the *Diamond*'s passenger capacity and a higher percentage of passengers frequent the lounges and bars. On the *Diamond*, many passengers hang out in their suites and on the verandas, so the excellent **room service** is used more often.

Radisson Diamond

Radisson Diamond (photo: Radisson)

The Verdict

A great ship to tour Europe in luxury and privacy, with low passenger capacity and a terrific enrichment program.

Specifications

Size (in tons)	20,295	Officers	Scandinavian
Number of Cabins	177	Crew	200 (European)
Number of Outside Cabins	177	Passenger/Crew Ratio	1.77 to 1
Cabins with Verandas	123	Year Built	1992
Number of Passengers	354	Last Major Refurbishment	1998

Frommer's Ratings (Scale of 1–5)

Cabin Comfort & Amenities	5	Pool, Fitness & Spa Facilities	4
Ship Cleanliness & Maintenance	4	Children's Facilities	N/A
Public Comfort/Space	3	Itineraries	4
Decor	3	Worth the Money	4

The *Radisson Diamond* is the most unusual-looking cruise ship afloat, and by far the world's largest catamaran with overnight accommodations. Her cabins are roomy and meant for spending a quiet afternoon, and her dining, whether at the buffet or in one of the loveliest dining rooms afloat, is tops. However, her public rooms are an odd hotel design and lack connection to the sea.

Cabins & Rates

Cabins	Per diems from	Bathtub	Fridge	Hair Dryer	Sitting Area	TV
Outside	$642*	yes	yes	yes	yes	yes
Suite	$1,199*	yes	yes	yes	yes	yes

**Rates are based on a 7-day Baltic/Scandinavian capitals cruise and include air from the East Coast gateways, gratuities, wine with dinner, soft drinks, and in-room bar setup.*

CABINS Most staterooms have picture windows, spacious teak balconies, and solid partitions for privacy. They show honey-color woods and pale shades of mauve, blue, and green accented with white and chrome. Spacious sitting areas, TVs, VCRs, phones, stocked refrigerators, four complimentary bottles of liquor, safes, only adequate storage, queen beds, hair dryers, and combination shower baths are common to all.

PUBLIC AREAS Entry is through the impressive Deck 6 lobby, with patterned carpeting showing pink roses on a teal meadow background, brass accents, black-trimmed mirrors, and walls of bird's-eye maple. A circular staircase and two glass elevators rise through the five-story atrium. The sleek tri-level lounge on Deck 8 offers dancing and shmw but sight lines are good only from the first couple of rows, and the windowless piano bar draws few patrons at cocktail hour. The small casino contains three blackjack tables, one Caribbean stud poker table, one roulette wheel, and a sweep of slot machines. For conferences and incentive groups, there are meeting rooms, a business center, secretarial services, and computer hookups. The library has plenty of current books and videos. The stunning main dining room seats 230 in an elegant cream, gold, and silver setting with great views in three directions and a double-height center section.

POOL, FITNESS & SPA FACILITIES The spa on Deck 11 offers facials, massages, herbal wraps, saunas, steam rooms, a full-service beauty salon, and a state-of-the-art fitness center. A jogging track and driving range are also on board. The retractable marina platform astern provides in-port access to waterskiing, jet-skiing, and sailing. Passengers congregate on Deck 10 to sunbathe, read, and chat around the small pool, whirlpool, and bar. The ship boasts more deck space per passenger than any other ship afloat and deck chairs are ample, as is protection from the sun. Waiters serve free soft drinks.

Song of Flower

Song of Flower (photo: Radisson)

The Verdict

An intimate social experience, with a very low passenger capacity, a little luxury, and a great enrichment program.

Specifications

Size (in tons)	8,282	Officers	Scandinavian
Number of Cabins	100	Crew (European/Filipino)	144
Number of Outside Cabins	100	Passenger/Crew Ratio	1.39 to 1
Cabins with Verandas	10	Year Built	1986
Number of Passengers	200	Last Major Refurbishment	1998

Frommer's Ratings (Scale of 1–5)

Cabin Comfort & Amenities	4	Pool, Fitness & Spa Facilities	3
Ship Cleanliness & Maintenance	4	Children's Facilities	N/A
Public Comfort/Space	4	Itineraries	5
Decor	3	Worth the Money	5

This efficiently run ship exudes the charm and character of a seagoing club full of like-minded travelers who enjoy a relaxed air of exclusivity. The decor is luxurious, with pastels and earth tones dominating the subtle color schemes. With a small passenger complement, the ship does not intrude on small European ports.

Cabins & Rates						
Cabins	**Per diems from**	**Bathtub**	**Fridge**	**Hair Dryer**	**Sitting Area**	**TV**
Outside	$585*	some	yes	yes	yes	yes
Suites	$1,056*	yes	yes	yes	yes	yes

**Rates are based on a 7-day Mediterranean cruise and include air from East Coast gateways; gratuities; complimentary liquor, wine, and soft drinks; and a stocked refrigerated minibar.*

CABINS Cabins come in six categories, and each supplies a TV, VCR, music channels, minibar, ample stowage, and shower or half-tub. Some cabins on Decks 5 and 6 have views partly blocked by lifeboats, but these rooms are all outside and lie forward, well away from noise. (Generators switching on and off are a problem in a few cabins.) Cabins on Deck 3 have double portholes instead of the windows found in higher categories. Two-room suites have sitting rooms and two baths. Slightly smaller veranda cabins, by far the most popular category, feature sliding doors to private balconies.

PUBLIC ROOMS Most public rooms are located aft and include the roomy tiered main lounge with a bar at the rear for shows and lectures, and a more intimate nightclub one deck below, adjacent to the casino with blackjack tables and slot machines. The library has over 1,000 books and 450 videos. The forward observation lounge is a delightful retreat for reading, meeting friends, afternoon tea, or taking in the views.

POOL, FITNESS & SPA FACILITIES Deck space is generous and creatively designed for securing a chair in a quiet location. The main outdoor area is framed by twin funnels and is noisy with the ship underway. There is free use of jet skis, sailboards, snorkeling equipment, and inflatable motorboats. The 80-seat launch, *Tiny Flower,* can take passengers to the beach for dry landings. There's an outdoor pool, a sauna, and a fully equipped (though small) health club with upright and recumbent bicycles, stairclimbers, treadmills, free weights, and strength-training machines.

Seabourn Cruise Line

SHIPS Seabourn Goddess I • Seabourn Goddess II • Seabourn Legend • Seabourn Spirit • Seabourn Pride • Seabourn Sun (preview)

55 Francisco St., Ste. 710, San Francisco, CA 94133. ☎ **800/929-9595** or 415/391-7444. Fax 415/391-8518. www.seabourn.com.

LINE IN A NUTSHELL Small and intimate, these sleek modern ships are floating pleasure palaces bathing all who enter in doting service and the finest cuisine at sea.

THE EXPERIENCE This line is a genuine aristocrat, with perfect manners. Its small, luxurious ships have unprecedented amounts of onboard space and staff for each passenger, service worthy of the grand hotels of Europe, and the hushed, ever-so-polite ambiance that appeals to prosperous, usually older passengers who appreciate the emphasis on their individual pleasures.

Pros

- **Top-shelf service.** Staff seem to know what you need before you ask, and there's more staff per passenger than on most any other line afloat. They're professional, polished, and champing at the bit to please. On the *Goddesses,* you'll even be served champagne and caviar on the beach when in port.
- **Excellent cuisine.** Rivaling the best land-based restaurants, cuisine is exquisite with creative, flavorful, well-presented dishes served with an extensive wine list.
- **Uncrowded ports of call.** These ships are able to visit less-touristed ports—like Cassis and La Lavandou in France and Maddalena island in Italy—that larger ships can't or don't care to visit.
- **Large cabins.** Cabins are not mere cabins, but roomy suites, with cushy features like walk-in closets, bathtubs, quality bath amenities from Neutrogena, personalized stationery, and complimentary stocked minibars.

Cons

- **Limited activities.** If you need things to do around the clock, forget about it. The Seabourn ships have limited organized activities on board (though those they do have are good). For the most part, guests are content with socializing over cocktails and catching up on their reading.
- **Shallow drafts, rocky seas.** If you happen to be sailing through rough water, you'll know it. These small ships get tossed around more than the megas.
- **Few or no private verandas.** It's unfortunate that there are only six private balconies on the *Legend* and *Pride,* and none on the *Goddesses* (there are, though, over 100 on the *Sun*).

Frommer's Ratings: Seabourn Cruise Line

	Poor	Fair	Good	Excellent	Outstanding
Enjoyment Factor					✓
Dining					✓
Activities		✓			
Children's Program	N/A				
Entertainment			✓		
Service					✓
Overall Value				✓	

SEABOURN: THE CAVIAR OF CRUISE SHIPS

Seabourn was established in 1987 when luxury cruise patriarch Warren Titus and Norwegian shipping mogul Atle Brynestad commissioned a trio of ultra-upscale 10,000-ton vessels from a North German shipyard. Streamlined, with modern, yacht-inspired designs, the Seabourn ships manage to look both aggressive and elegant in their bright white paint jobs, and are small enough to venture safely into exotic harbors where megaships cannot go.

Although now co-owned by founder Brynestad and industry giant Carnival Corporation, the line maintains strong links with its Norwegian roots, registering each of its ships in Norway and preferring to restock many of its marine supplies there.

In mid-1998, Carnival Corporation bought Cunard Line, one of Seabourn's primary competitors in the luxury cruise market. Faced with the problem of how to market the two brands, which together account for almost 50% of the worldwide luxury cruise market, Carnival decided to go with core strengths, maintaining Seabourn's niche in the small-ship ultra-luxury market and pushing Cunard as the option for cruisers who want the traditional British ocean liner experience. As a result, three of Cunard's small ships—the *Sea Goddess I, Sea Goddess II,* and *Royal Viking Sun*—were transferred to the Seabourn fleet in early January of 2000 and renamed *Seabourn Goddess I, Seabourn Goddess II,* and *Seabourn Sun* (the *Sun* after undergoing a major refit, to the tune of $15 million). Together, Seabourn and Cunard operate under the umbrella banner of Cunard Line Limited.

THE FLEET

Officially beginning in 2000, the Seabourn fleet comprises six globe-trotting ships, its three originals and three former Cunarders. All three of its original 204-passenger, 10,000-ton trio—the ***Legend*** (built in 1992), ***Spirit*** (built in 1989), and ***Pride*** (built in 1988)—spend part of the year in the Mediterranean and/or elsewhere in Europe. Seabourn's new adoptees are the 115-passenger, 4,260-ton ***Seabourn Goddess I*** and ***II*** (built in 1984 and 1985) and the 740-passenger, 37,845-ton ***Seabourn Sun*** (built in 1988). The *Goddesses* spend half the year in the Mediterranean and the other half in the Caribbean. *Sun* splits its time between the Mediterranean, other parts of Europe, South America, the Pacific, and the Caribbean and Panama Canal.

PASSENGER PROFILE

Most have more than comfortable household incomes, usually in excess of $250,000. Many are retired (or never worked to begin with), and many have net worths in the millions, and sometimes much higher. The majority of passengers are couples, and there is always a handful of singles as well, usually widows or widowers. Few seem to come aboard with children or grandchildren in tow.

In many ways, the passenger roster looks like the membership of a posh country club, where old money judges new money. Most passengers are North American, and dress expensively though not, of course, flashily. Many passengers are not excessively chatty, giddy, or outgoing. They are likely to have sailed aboard other luxury cruise lines and stayed in five-star hotels. Passengers expect to receive good service in an atmosphere of discreet gentility.

The line's history of repeaters is among the highest in the industry, sometimes as many as 50% aboard any given cruise.

DINING

Cuisine is one of Seabourn's strongest points, matching what you'd find in a world-class European resort hotel. The line assumes that most of its passengers are used to getting what they want, usually whenever they want it, so meals are served in a manner that

Goddesses on the Beach

The pièce de résistance of your *Seabourn Goddess* cruise comes at midday near the end of the trip, as you lounge on a quiet beach. As you gaze out toward the anchored ship you'll see the captain, standing at the bow of a bright-red Zodiac and holding a huge flag, coming swiftly toward the beach, looking like George Washington crossing the Delaware, but in decidedly better weather and absolutely bluer water.

The captain's soldiers—20-something European stewards—hop out carrying a life ring that doubles as a floating serving tray for an open tin of Russian malossol caviar, encircled by other delicacies. Wade into the gentle surf up to your waist and spoon up a morsel. Stewards move about with bottles of Moët & Chandon champagne and Absolut vodka encased in orchid-filled cylinders of ice.

A buffet spread out under a lean-to features a spread of gourmet items. Passengers feast not on beach towels spread out on the sand, but under umbrellas at tables set with proper china and hotel silver brought ashore by the staff.

It doesn't get any better than this!

satisfies both appetite and the expectation of high-class service. Fleetwide, dining is offered in a single seating, and, except for the *Sun* (which assigns passengers to specific tables), the ships have an open-seating policy, allowing guests to dine whenever they choose and with whomever they want, within a window of several hours at each mealtime.

While tables seat up to 8 or 10, you'll almost never have a problem getting a table for two if that's your wish. Also, tables are spaced far enough apart so you'll never feel crowded.

Dinner service is high style and extremely formal. Men are expected to wear jackets and, on most evenings, neckties as well. Two formal evenings are held during the course of any 1-week cruise. Virtually every male present appears in a tuxedo, and the events are, indeed, very formal. Staff members almost run at a trot through the elaborate, six-course European service. It's all extremely civilized.

On the *Goddesses,* the dress code and ambiance are less formal and stuffy (no jackets are required, although many will still wear them), but the food and service are no less top-of-the-line.

Seabourn cuisine is an eclectic mix. The *Legend, Pride,* and *Spirit* feature old favorites such as beef Wellington, Dover sole, and broiled lobster; ethnic dishes reflecting the itinerary of wherever the ship happens to be at the time; and a mixture of light Pacific Rim and California cuisine. Dishes are prepared to order, **spa menus** are available at every meal, and passengers can make virtually any special request they want. On the *Goddesses,* the dinner menu includes three appetizers such as carpaccio of beef tenderloin, lobster aspic, and sautéed crab cakes; three hot or cold soups; and four entrees such as a baby lamb loin or stuffed quail; plus a Golden Door Spa menu and a **vegetarian dish.** Complimentary wines are served at lunch and dinner, and every night features a flaming dessert served in individual portions or such choices as chocolate mousse with fresh berries or coconut crème brûlée.

If your mood doesn't call for the dining room, the *Legend, Pride,* and *Spirit* have an **alternative dining option,** the Veranda Café; on the *Sun,* it's called the Venezia Restaurant. On the *Goddesses,* all meals are served in the dining room, and one night there's a festive dinner served out on deck by the pool. All the ships have a casual restaurant as well, serving bountiful breakfasts every morning, with omelets made fresh to your

Seabourn Fleet Itineraries

Ship	Home Ports & Season	Itinerary
Seabourn Goddess I	5- to 8-day W. Med, Malaga, Spain (Apr), Barcelona (May), Monte Carlo (May, Oct), Civitavecchia/Rome (Oct); 4- to 8-day Greek Isles and E. Med, Civitavecchia/Rome (May, Sept), Venice, (June, Sept) Istanbul (June–Aug), and Piraeus/Athens (July–Sept).	**4- to 8-day E. Med:** Port calls may include Mykonos, Limnos, Itea/Delphi, Galaxidhi/Delphi, Katakolon, Hydra, Skopelos, Samos, Volos, Hydra, Skiathos, Amorgos (Greece), Kusadasi, Bodrum, Fethiye (Turkey), Sorrento and Taormina (Italy), and Dubrovnik, Hvar, Korcula (Croatia). **5- to 8-day W. Med:** Port calls may include Porto Cervo, Porotferraio, Livorno, Portofino (Italy), Cannes, Nice, Cassis, Le Lavandou, St. Tropez, Port Vendres, Corsica, Porquerolles, Sanary-Sur-Mer (France), Agadir and Casablanca (Morrorco), Barcelona, Menorca, Altea, Mallorca (Spain), and Monte Carlo (Monaco).
Seabourn Goddess II	6- and 7-day E. Med, Civitavecchia/Rome (May, Sept), Istanbul (May, June), Piraeus/Athens (June), and Venice (Sept); 5- to 8-day W. Med, Barcelona (May, Aug, Oct), Civitavecchia/Rome (July, Aug, Sept), Monte Carlo (May, July-Sept), and Nice (July).	**6- and 7-day E. Med:** Port calls may include Galaxidhi/Delphi, Skiathos, Patmos, Amorgos, Molivos, Volos, Skopelos, Katakolon, Hydra, Corfu (Greece), Taormina and Sorrento (Italy), Dubrovnik, Hvar, Korcula (Croatia), Bodrum and Kusadasi (Turkey), and Sarande (Albania). **5- to 8-day W. Med:** Port calls may include Livorno/Florence, Portofino, Elba, Sardinia, Portovenere, Ischia, Giannutri (Italy), Cannes, Cassis, Le Lavandou, St. Tropez, Port Vendres, Corsica, Porquerolles, Sanary-Sur-Mer (France), Agadir and Casablanca (Morocco), Cadiz, Malaga, Menorca, Altea, Mallorca (Spain), and Monte Carlo (Monaco).
Seabourn Legend	7- to 14-day W. Med, Lisbon (May, June, Sept), Monte Carlo (May, Oct), Civitavecchia/Rome (May), Barcelona (Sept, Oct); 9- and 14-day Northern Europe, Amsterdam (July); 10-day Scandinavia & Russia, Amsterdam (July, Aug, Sept), Stockholm (July, Aug), and London (Aug).	**7- to 14-day W. Med:** Port calls may include Livorno/Florence, Isla Maddalena, Portofino, Elba (Italy), Cannes, Nice, Cassis, St. Tropez, La Croix-Valmer, Port Vendres, Sanary-Sur-Mer, Corsica, Le Lavandou (France), and Cadiz, Barcelona, Seville, Malaga, Menorca, Ceuta (Spain). **9-and 14-day Northern Europe and 10-day Scandinavia & Russia:** Port calls may include La Coruna and Bilbao (Spain), Rouen/Paris, St. Jean-de-Luz, Bordeaux, Brest, St. Malo (France), Antwerp (Belgium), Gdynia/Gdansk (Poland), Svendborg (Denmark), St. Petersburg (Russia), and Guernsey and the Isle of Wight (England).

specifications. At lunchtime, you'll find salads, sandwich makings, fresh pasta, and maybe jumbo shrimp, smoked salmon, and smoked oysters on the cold side and hot sliced roast beef, duck, and ham on the carving board. On the *Legend, Spirit,* and *Pride,* a **special of the day**—pizza with pineapple topping, chili, or corned beef—will also be available at the Sky Bar overlooking the Lido, for those who don't want to change out of their swimsuits. On these ships, dinner is served under the stars on the Lido Deck several evenings a week as well, offering a meal roughly equivalent to whatever's being whipped up in the main dining room. Dinners here are romantic candlelight affairs, and are often based on Italian, French, and seafood themes. In good weather it's a treat to eat at one of the arc of tables located aft overlooking the wake and under a protective canvas awning.

Seabourn Pride	14-day France and Spain, Lisbon to Hamburg (Apr); 11- and 14-day Scandinavia & Russia, Hamburg (May), London (June, July); 7- or 14-day British Isles, London (May, Aug), Dublin (June); 7- or 14-day Norway, Copenhagen (June, July), Bergen (July), or Tromso (July).	**14-day France and Spain:** La Coruna, Bilbao, Santander (Spain), and Bordeaux, St. Malo, Rouen (France). **11- and 14-day Scandinavia & Russia:** Port calls may include Svenborg and Ronne (Denmark), St. Petersburg (Russia), Tallinn (Estonia), Olso (Norway), Kalmar and Stockholm (Sweden), Helsinki (Sweden), and Amsterdam (Holland). **7- or 14-day British Isles:** Port calls may include St. Peter Port (Guernesy), Cobh, Dublin, Waterford, Derry (Ireland), and Invergordon and Leith (Scotland). **7- or 14-day Norway:** Port calls may include Lillesand, Stavanger, Flaam, Gudvangen, Aalesund, Bodo, Molde, Oye, Olden, Geiranger, Tromso, and Bergen (Norway).
Seabourn Spirit	7- and 14-day Greek Isles, from Piraeus/Athens (Apr–Oct) and Istanbul (May–Oct); 10- and 11-day E. Med, from Civitaveechia/ Rome (May), Nice (Aug), Istanbul (Aug), or Piraeus/ Athens (July); 7- and 14-day Black Sea, Istanbul (Aug).	**7- to 14-day Greek Isles:** Port calls may include Despotiko, Navplion, Monemvasia, Mykonos, Piraeus/ Athens, Rhodes, Santorini, Patmos, Limnos, Volos, Piraeus/Athens (Greece), Aghios Nikolaos (Crete), and Kusadasi and Istanbul (Turkey). **10-, 11-, and 13-day E. Med:** Port calls may include Sorrento, Taormina, Civitavecchia/Rome, Livorno, Venice (Italy), Dubrovnik, Hvar, Korcula (Croatia), Corfu, Volos, Navplion, Galaxidhi, Katakolon, and Galaxidhi (Greece), Monte Carlo (Monaco), and Cannes (France). **7- and 14-day Black Sea:** Port calls may include Yalta, Sevastopol, Oddessa (Ukraine), Nesebur (Bulgaria), Cannakkale and Istanbul (Turkey), Volos, Mykonos, Despotiko, Monemvasia (Greece), and Aghios Nikolaos (Crete).*
Seabourn Sun	14-day Med, Barcelona (Apr); 14-day W. Med, Genoa (May); 7- and 14-day Black Sea/Med, Istanbul (May) and Piraeus/Athens (May); 14-day Scandinavia & Russia, Southampton (June) and Copenhagen (June); 7- and 14-day British Isles, Copenhagen (June) and Dublin (June).	**14-day Med & 14-day W. Med:** Villefranche (France), Livorno, Venice, Rome (Italy), Corfu (Greece), Dubrovnik (Croatia), Kusdasi (Turkey), Barcelona, Malaga, Cadiz, Vigo (Spain), Lisbon (Portugal), Rouen (France), and St. Peter Port (Guernsey). **7- and 14-day Black Sea/Med:** Port calls may include Yalta, Sevastopol, Odessa (Ukraine), Nesebur (Bulgaria), Piraeus/Athens (Greece), Valletta (Malta), Messina (Sicily), and Sorrento and Civitavecchia/ Rome (Italy). **14-day Scandinavia & Russia:** Port calls may include Hamburg (Germany), Stockholm and Visby (Sweden), Helsinki and Mariehamn (Finland), and St. Petersburg (Russia). **7- and 14-day British Isles:** Port calls may include Leith and Ivergordon (Scotland), Derry (Northern Ireland), Dublin and Cobh (Ireland), St. Peter Port (Guernsey), and Antwerp (Belgium).

*Also sails on Holy Lands itineraries.

On the *Goddesses,* there are wonderful hors d'oeuvres, such as jumbo shrimp, smoked salmon, and the best caviar, available practically around the clock in unlimited quantities.

Room service is available 24 hours a day on all ships. During normal lunch or dinner hours, your private meal can mirror the dining room service, right down to the silver, crystal, and porcelain. After hours, the menu is more limited, with burgers, salads, sandwiches, and pastas. And whenever a cruise itinerary calls for a full-day stopover on a remote island, a lavish beach barbecue might be whipped up at midday.

Activities

These small ships don't offer much in the way of organized activities, and that's what most passengers really love about the line. With no rah-rah, in-your-face cruise directors shouting at them, passengers are just left alone to pursue their own personal peace.

You won't find the bingo, karaoke, and silly poolside contests featured by mass-market lines. The atmosphere is ever-tasteful and unobtrusive. Activities include card games and tournaments, trivia contests, tours of the ship's galley, visits to the cozy library, and watching movies in your cabin. As the biggest ship in the fleet, the *Sun* has a movie theater. You'll soon realize that many passengers are aboard to read, quietly converse with their peers, and be ushered from one stylish spot to the next.

That said, you don't have to be sedate, either. The *Legend, Pride,* and *Spirit,* and both *Goddesses* have **retractable watersports marinas** that unfold from the ships' stern, weather and sea conditions permitting, and gracefully usher passengers into the sea for waterskiing, windsurfing, sailing, snorkeling, banana-boat riding, and swimming. The *Sun,* being over three times the size of the others in the fleet, does offer more diversions, with golf driving cages, a putting green, a paddle tennis court, and a lap pool in addition to the regular pool.

There are few, if any, public announcements to disturb your solitude, which is a relief when compared to the barrage of noise broadcast aboard many other lines.

On certain cruises there are **guest lecturers,** such as noted chefs, authors, or statesmen, or maybe a wine connoisseur, composer, anthropologist, TV director, or professor, who present lectures and mingle with guests. From time to time, the line manages to bring on the likes of Patricia Neal, Walter Cronkite, or Art Buchwald. You can generally count on port lectures from resident travel experts.

Each ship has a small-scale, staid, and rather un-casino-like **casino** with a couple of blackjack tables and a handful of slots.

Children's Program

These ships are not geared to children, although they are permitted. You may see a younger child occasionally on the *Legend, Pride, Spirit,* or *Sun*—probably a very bored child, as the line provides no special programs, no special menus, and no special concessions for children.

In a pinch, you may be able to arrange baby-sitting by an available crew member.

Entertainment

Entertainment is not Seabourn's strong suit, but if you're happy with a singer, pianist, or duo doing most of the entertaining, you'll be pleased enough. On all the ships, a resident dance band or music duo performs a roster of favorites, while the mellow piano bar is always a good option. The *Sun, Legend, Spirit,* and *Pride* have small show lounges, but the *Goddesses* have none.

Service

Seabourn maintains the finest service staff of any line afloat. Most are young northern Europeans, many Norwegian, who are recruited after they've gained experience at one of the grand hotels of Europe. They are, overall, universally charming, competent, sensitive, and discreet—among Seabourn's most valuable assets.

Laundry and dry cleaning are available. There are also self-service laundry rooms on the *Sun, Legend, Spirit,* and *Pride.*

All Seabourn ships provide Neutrogena bathroom amenities as well as designer soaps from Hermés, Chanel No. 5, and Tiffany. Cabin minibars on all but the *Sun* are stocked with two bottles of wine or spirits of the guests' choice along with soft drinks (replenished only on request). Fleetwide, complimentary wine is served with lunch and dinner. In public bars and lounges soft drinks are complimentary, while wines and spirits will be charged to passengers' onboard accounts.

Across the fleet, gratuities are officially included in the cruise fare, but staff is not prohibited from accepting additional tips, and some passengers do tip.

Seabourn Goddess I • Seabourn Goddess II

Seabourn Goddess I (photo: Seabourn)

The Verdict

About as good as it gets, with highest marks for the small ship atmosphere, the attentive European service, and the creative menus. Of course, the champagne and caviar served poolside whenever you want them aren't too shabby either.

Specifications

Size (in tons)	4,250	Officers	Norwegian
Number of Cabins	58	Crew	89 (European/int'l)
Number of Outside Cabins	58	Passenger/Crew Ratio	1.3 to 1
Cabins with Verandas	0	Year Built	1984/1985
Number of Passengers	116	Last Major Refurbishment	1997

Frommer's Rating (Scale of 1–5)

Cabin Comfort & Amenities	5	Pool, Fitness & Spa Facilities	3
Ship Cleanliness & Maintenance	4	Children's Facilities	N/A
Public Comfort/Space	5	Itineraries	5
Decor	4	Worth the Money	4

These two ships espouse a casually elegant ethos similar to Windstar's, where tuxes, ties, and gowns can be left at home. For both weary workaholics or those used to doing very little, it would be hard to find a more relaxing vacation, better food, or more attentive service while enjoying a variety of small Caribbean ports. Calling at yacht harbors and anchoring off beautiful beaches, these petite ships seem to blend right in.

While the *Seabourn Goddesses* continue to provide the supreme service and yacht-like elegance they did in their Cunard days, they're now being targeted to a younger crowd in their 30s and 40s—people who want the service and top-notch amenities, but without over-the-top formality. Despite the marketing, expect the ships to continue drawing a mostly middle-aged 50- to 60-something crowd for at least a while longer.

Cabins & Rates

Cabins	Per diems from	Bathtub	Fridge	Hair Dryer	Sitting Area	TV
Suite	$598	yes	yes	yes	yes	yes

CABINS The 58 virtually identical one-room ocean-view suites average 205 square feet. Unlike the layouts on many ships, the layout positions the bedroom alongside the cabin's large window, and the sitting area is inside. The suites are located forward and amidships, and the soundproofing between cabins is good and engine noise minimal. While similar in design, they are less roomy than those aboard the larger *Legend, Spirit,* and *Pride* or the Silversea twins, and the bathrooms are relatively small.

Superb suite features and amenities include twin beds convertible to queens, several mirrors, remote control television and VCR, music channels, automated wake-up calls, international direct-dial phones, complimentary stocked minibar and refrigerator, fresh flowers, fresh fruit, terry-cloth robes, hair dryer, and bathrooms with full-sized tubs. The 24-hour room service provides a full-course meal set up in your suite at a proper table seating four.

If you can afford it, two units can be interconnected to provide a full 410 square feet of space.

These ships are not recommended for passengers with disabilities, as doorways leading to staterooms and toilets are not big enough to accommodate a wheelchair. Persons in wheelchairs also can't go ashore, because the wheelchairs can't be taken on the launches that shuttle passengers to shore in ports where the vessel must anchor offshore.

PUBLIC AREAS Upon boarding, you immediately notice the elaborate flower arrangements in all public areas and the sophisticated European atmosphere and high-quality furnishings. Public areas are awash in marble, polished hardwoods, and Oriental carpets. So posh are they, and so yacht-like the feel of the vessels, that you expect an English lord to walk through the door at any moment to suggest a cocktail.

The Main Salon and its small bar alcove are the venue for indoor socializing before dinner, and a singer and musical duo often provide light entertainment. The hot and cold hors d'oeuvres may include smoked salmon, jumbo shrimp, and an open tin of malossol caviar.

There's dancing in the Main Salon after dinner, while one deck up a popular, long-serving pianist entertains at the Club Salon piano bar, located next to the diminutive two-blackjack-table casino. There's also a small book and video library, several slot machines, and a purser's foyer with a boutique.

RECREATION & FITNESS FACILITIES The mostly open and partly shaded Lido Deck has deck chairs, pool, hot tub, and bar (order yourself some champagne, caviar, and jumbo shrimp while you lounge!). A covered deck above has additional deck chairs with more at Sun Deck level. The gym, spa, and beauty salon are high up, looking aft on Deck 5. There's also a jogging track on this level, but it's so small-scale you're likely to get dizzy if you run it at high speeds.

Seabourn Pride • Seabourn Spirit • Seabourn Legend

Seabourn Legend (photo: Seabourn)

The Verdict

Hands-down, these ships are top of the market and the cream of the crop. They're the most luxurious ships at sea, designed to let you be as social or as private as you like.

Specifications

Size (in tons)	10,000	Officers	Norwegian
Number of Cabins	100	Crew	140 (International)
Number of Outside Cabins	100	Passenger/Crew Ratio	1.5 to 1
Cabins with Verandas	6	Year Built	1988/1989/1992
Number of Passengers	204	Last Major Refurbishment	N/A

Frommer's Rating (Scale of 1–5)

Cabin Comfort & Amenities	5	Pool, Fitness & Spa Facilities	3
Ship Cleanliness & Maintenance	4	Children's Facilities	N/A
Public Comfort/Space	5	Itineraries	5
Decor	4	Worth the Money	4

These three understated, beautifully designed ships represent luxury cruising at its very best, going everywhere one would ever want to cruise. Passengers who like to be social and meet others with similar interests will find plenty of opportunities to do so at open-sitting meals, in the intimate public rooms, and out on deck. On the other hand, if you want to get away from it all, you can also be completely private in your spacious suite, at a table for two in the restaurant, or in a quiet corner of the deck.

Cabins & Rates

Cabins	Per diems from	Bathtub	Fridge	Hair Dryer	Sitting Area	TV
Suite	$384	yes*	yes	yes	yes	yes

**The four handicapped-accessible suites have showers only.*

CABINS The great majority of the accommodations are handsomely designed "Type A" 277-square-foot one-room suites (for comparison, an average cabin on Carnival is 190 square feet), varying only in location but priced at four different levels. Suites are popular for entertaining and dining, as the lounge area's coffee table rises to dining table height, and one can order hors d'oeuvres such as caviar and smoked salmon at no extra charge. Closet space is more than adequate for hanging clothes, but drawer space is more limited. The *Pride* and *Spirit* have twin sinks in the all-white marble bathrooms; *Legend* has a single sink.

The two Classic Suites measure 400 square feet, and two pairs of Owner's Suites are 530 and 575 square feet. These six have the only (small) verandas on the ships. At press time, French balconies with sliding glass doors (read: no space for sitting or standing) were to be added by year-end 2000 to 44 of the three ships' 102 suites (the 277-square-foot Type A suites on the top two decks), replacing the current bay windows

The Owner's Suites have dining rooms and guest powder rooms. As in any cabins positioned near the bow of relatively small ships such as these, these forward-facing suites can be somewhat uncomfortable during rough seas. The dark wood furnishings make the overall feeling more like a hotel room than a ship's suite. Regal Suites, at 554 square feet, are simply two combined 277-square-foot Seabourn suites with one room given completely over to a lounge.

Everything about a Seabourn cabin has the impeccably maintained feel of an upscale Scandinavian hotel. Each unit contains a stocked bar, walk-in closet, safe, hair dryer, VCR and TV broadcasting CNN and ESPN among other channels, crystal glasses for every kind of drink, terry-cloth robes, and fresh fruit daily. Videotape movies are available from the ship's library, and the purser's office broadcasts films from the ship's own collection. Color schemes are either tastefully ice-blue or champagne-colored, with lots of bleached oak or birch wooden trim, as well as mirrors and a sophisticated bank of spotlights.

Owner's Suites 05 and 06 have obstructed views. There are four wheelchair-accessible suites.

PUBLIC AREAS An attractive double open spiral staircase links the public areas, which are, overall, a bit duller than you'd expect on ships of this caliber. For the most part, they're spare and almost ordinary looking. Art and ornamentation are conspicuous by their absence. It's almost as if in its zeal to create conservative decors, management couldn't decide on the appropriate artwork and so omitted it completely. (There are a few exceptions: The *Legend* has an attractive curved ocean liner–motif mural in its stair foyers.)

Preview: The "New" *Seabourn Sun*

The last ship to carry the venerated Royal Viking name, the *Royal Viking Sun,* built in 1988 for luxurious long-distance cruising, was Cunard's most elegant ship, especially after the line spent some $11 million on a face-lift in 1995 to freshen her up. In late November of 1999, the ship was transferred to the Seabourn fleet after undergoing a dramatic $15 million conversion that completely redesigned her public rooms and refurbished her cabins, transforming her into the *Seabourn Sun.* The Midnight Sun lounge extended aft and turned into a full-sized cabaret show lounge, and the spa/gym/pool area above expanded. The Garden Cafe Lido restaurant expanded, too, and an alternative 60-seat Italian restaurant called Venezia added.

The forward-facing observation lounge on Sky Deck offers an attractive, quiet venue all day long for reading, a drink before meals, cards, and afternoon tea. A chart and compass will help you find out where the ship is currently positioned, and a computerized wall map lets you track future cruises.

The Club lounge and bar, with an aft-facing position, is the ship's principal social center, with music, a small band, a singer and/or pianist, and fancy hot hors d'oeuvres before and after dinner. Next door, behind glass, is the ship's casino, with gaming tables and a separate small room for slot machines. The semicircular and tiered formal lounge on the deck below is the venue for lectures, pianists, and the captain's parties.

The formal restaurant, located on the lowest deck, is a large low-ceilinged room with an open-seating policy. The Veranda Café, open for breakfast, lunch, and, except on formal nights, dinner, is an intimate, well-designed indoor/outdoor facility.

One of the best places for a romantic, moonlit moment is the isolated patch of deck at the far forward bow on the Magellan Deck.

RECREATION & FITNESS FACILITIES The outdoor pool, not much used, is awkwardly situated in a shadowy location aft of the open Lido Deck, between the twin engine uptakes, and is flanked by lifeboats that hang from both sides of the ship. A pair of whirlpools are located just forward of the pool. There's a third hot tub perched on the far forward bow deck. It's isolated and a perfect spot (as is the whole patch of deck here) from which to watch the landscape or a port come into sight or fade away.

A retractable, wood-planked watersports marina opens out from the stern of the ship so passengers can hop into sea kayaks or go windsurfing, waterskiing, or snorkeling right from the ship. An attached steel mesh net creates a saltwater pool when the marina is in use.

The gym and Steiner-managed spa are roomy for ships this small, and are located forward of the Lido. There is a separate aerobics area, plus two saunas, massage rooms, and a beauty salon.

Silversea Cruises

SHIPS IN EUROPE Silver Cloud • Silver Wind • Silver Shadow (preview)

110 East Broward Blvd., Fort Lauderdale, FL 33301. ☎ **800/774-9996** or 954/522-4477. Fax 954/468-3034. www.silversea.com.

THE LINE IN A NUTSHELL No arguments: The last word in quality. These all-suite ships offer an impressively high degree of comfort, ambiance, and elegance, supported by excellent, attentive service both at sea and ashore.

THE EXPERIENCE Spacious suites, complimentary beverages (alcoholic or otherwise), no tipping expected, careful baggage handling, smiles all around, and a bottle of good champagne (no cheap stuff on these ships) that greets passengers in their suites when they arrive—what could be more inclusive than that?

The company's two 296-passenger ships, *Silver Cloud* and *Silver Wind,* are small and intimate, offering all-suite accommodations that run the range from 240 square feet up to a massive 1,314 square feet—larger than some homes I've seen. Public areas are small but are consequently more intimate and more likely to lead to new friendships.

Passengers tend to include executives and wealthy retirees, all of whom want the best and can pay for it. Most will be older, and you'll see few children aboard, ever.

Dining is a joy not merely because of the quality of the food but also because of the single seating, come-down-for-dinner-any-time-between-6:30-and-9:30 system. Come alone, with a partner, or with two or three newfound friends, and the maitre d' will find you a table. There's also an alternative dining option and a theme dinner in the Terrace Cafe several nights during the cruise.

Pros

- **A surprisingly high degree of informality.** Considering the economic level of most of those on board there's very little stuffiness.
- **Golf.** The two ships offer a huge selection of golf cruises involving play at some of Europe's best courses, from Valderrama to St Andrews. (The golf packages are extra, of course.)
- **Many private verandas.** Three-quarters of the suites have balconies.

Cons

- **Limited space for entertainment.** Casino facilities are limited and, because of the space restrictions, the resident entertainers don't get a chance to really show their talents.

Frommer's Ratings: Silversea Cruises

	Poor	Fair	Good	Excellent	Outstanding
Enjoyment Factor					✓
Dining					✓
Activities			✓		
Children's Program	N/A				
Entertainment				✓	
Service					✓
Overall Value					✓

THE SILVERSEA WAY

Silversea is partly owned by the V Group, a Monte Carlo–based organization operated by the Vlasov family, which earlier owned Sitmar Cruises in the U.S. Founded in 1992 and putting its first ship, the *Silver Cloud,* into the water in the spring of 1994, Silversea's concept is ambitious. It aims to provide, at one price, all of the components that go into making a truly deluxe cruise. It succeeds admirably.

At the time of Silversea's start-up, the luxury small ship market was dominated by Seabourn Cruises, Radisson's *Song of Flower,* and Cunard's *Sea Goddesses.* But within a couple of years people who had sailed on those other lines and ships were beginning to sample Silversea's wares, and some were sufficiently impressed to switch allegiance.

THE FLEET

The company has twin, ultra-deluxe, 296-passenger, 17,000-ton ships, the ***Silver Cloud*** and ***Silver Wind,*** built in Italy in 1994. Both will be in Europe in the summer of 2000. Two bigger and still ultra-deluxe 25,000-ton, 388-passenger ships are under construction. The first of the new ships, the ***Silver Shadow,*** debuts in September 2000, with one Rome to Lisbon cruise, followed by a transatlantic crossing. The ***Silver Mirage*** is set to debut in June 2001.

PASSENGER PROFILE

On either ship, the passenger manifest is apt to include high-powered entertainment industry types, Fortune 500 executives, and wealthy retirees—people who like their cruising top drawer and can pay for the best. You are not likely to find a significant number of small children. This is not a younger crowd cruise line. One of the reasons that its show lounge, small as it is, is adequate for the purpose is that half of the passengers are bound for bed by the time the entertainment starts.

Considering the economic level of most people on board you might expect stuffiness, but that isn't generally the case. On a recent Mediterranean cruise, for example, the passenger list included a bank president and his wife (both of them dripping with gold) and an elderly, apparently very successful southern England dairy farmer and her husband, a retired British army major. These couples looked a trifle intimidating to some but were among the liveliest, most down-to-earth people on the ship.

DINING

Food is one of Silversea's strengths, and not just in the main meal services in the dining room (known, rather prosaically, as The Restaurant) but also in the breakfast and lunch buffets in the Terrace Cafe on Deck 7, and in the theme dinners served (reservations, please) in the same room. Be it an Italian, Chinese, Southwestern U.S., or any other theme meal, the quality is tops.

In The Restaurant, the mixed menu offers excellent fish, steak cooked as requested (isn't that a novel thought), a vegetarian option, and more than enough variety to satisfy any taste.

If you want a very special bottle of wine at dinner, you'll have to pay the going rate. Otherwise, the very acceptable wines served in the dining room are on the house.

You can get croissants, juice, and coffee in the lounge in the very early morning.

ACTIVITIES

Activities tend toward the sedentary. There are the usual bridge, shuffleboard, and Scrabble setups, and the cruise director conducts a daily quiz in the lounge. There's no skeet, no putting tournaments, no knobbly knees contests, and nothing organized for youngsters. These just aren't those kinds of ships.

Silversea Fleet Itineraries

Ship	Home Ports & Season	Itinerary
Silver Cloud	7- to 14-day Med, Piraeus/ Athens (May, July), Barcelona (May, Aug), Venice (June, Oct), Monte Carlo (July, Sept), Civitavecchia/Rome (June, July), Istanbul (Sept), Valletta,Malta (May); 10- and 11-day Black Sea, Istanbul (June) and Piraeus/ Athens (Aug).	**7- to 14-day Med (E. Med, W. Med, Greek Isles):** Port calls may include Kusadasi, Dikili, Kas, Marmaris (Turkey), Rhodes, Katakolon, Mykonos, Nauplion, Corfu, Volos, Kithira, Santorini (Greece), Taormina, Portoferraio, Amalfi, Portofino, Sorrento, Lipari, Naples, Genoa, Salerno, Palermo, Venice, Civitavecchia/Rome, Portovenere, Alghero, Livorno (Italy), Aghios Nikolaos (Crete), Valletta (Malta), Hvar, Korcula, Dubrovnik (Croatia), Tunis (Tunisia), Bastia, Bonifacio, Calvi, Marseille (France), Monte Carlo (Monaco), Malaga, Mallorca, Mahon, Ibiza (Spain), and Gibraltar. **10- and 11-day Black Sea:** Odessa, Sevastopol, Yalta (Ukraine), Nesebur (Bulgaria), Kusadasi, Dikili, Marmaris (Turkey), Santorini, Mykonos, Nauplion (Greece).*
Silver Wind	7- and 14-day E. Med, Piraeus/Athens (May), Istanbul (May), Venice (May); 11-day Italy, Venice (May); 10-day W. Med, Monte Carlo (May); 7- to 12-day Northern Europe, Lisbon (June), London (June–Aug), Copenhagen (July, Aug), Stockholm (Aug).	**7- to 14-day E. Med:** Port calls may include Mykonos, Rhodes, Nauplion, Katakolon, Corfu (Greece), Kas, Marmaris, Kusadasi, Istanbul (Turkey), and Dubrovnik (Croatia); **11-day Italy:** Ravenna, Taormina, Sorrento, Civitavecchia/Rome, Livorno (Italy), Vis (Croatia), and Valletta (Malta); **10-day W. Med:** St. Tropez, Marseille, Calvi (France), Cadiz (Spain), Livorno, Portofino, Portovenere, (Italy), Casablanca (Morocco), and Gibraltar. **7- to 12-day Northern Europe (Europe Capitals, Scandinavia & Russia, Norway, British Isles):** Port calls may include La Coruña and Bilbao (Spain), Bordeaux and St. Malo (France), St. Peter Port (Guernsey), Zeebrugge and Antwerp (Belgium), Stockholm and Visby (Sweden), Helsinki (Finland), Gdansk (Poland) Riga (Latvia) Lübeck (Germany), St. Petersburg (Russia), Tallinn (Estonia), Bergen, Gudvangen, Flam, Olden (Norway), Leith, Inverness, Dunvegan (Scotland), Londonderry, Belfast, Dublin (Ireland).*

*Also does Holy Lands itinerary.

Silversea throws in for free a special shore excursion called **The Silversea Experience** on every cruise. In Norway, it might be a trip to a year-round ski jump (the surface in summer is straw matting) to view an exhibition by some Olympic hopefuls. In Italy, it might include a wine-and-cheese tasting at the town hall and a welcome by the mayor. Always, it is something that nobody else offers. Other shore excursions are at the passenger's expense, although Silversea always provides a shuttle from dockside to and from the city center.

Children's Program

Silversea has no children's program whatsoever—which really says it all, doesn't it?

Entertainment

The entertainers are energetic but the size of the facilities cramps their style—they sing and dance Broadway show tunes well enough but can't be expected to do justice to the helicopters in *Miss Saigon* or the falling chandelier of *The Phantom of the Opera* considering the bandbox stage they have to deal with.

Some of Silversea's onboard **lecturers** are well worth listening to, though.

Service

Uniformly of the highest standard, and there's more than one crew member to every two passengers—a high ratio indeed. They seem forever to be not only willing, but anxious, to serve. The smiles are broad and genuine and requests are fulfilled promptly.

One surprising weakness, though, seems to be in the way the Italian officers on board interact with the passengers. They're polite and welcoming, of course, but they have a tendency to keep their own counsel.

Silver Cloud • Silver Wind

Silver Cloud (photo: Silversea)

The Verdict

A superior product, by any yardstick. Intimate, elegant, and warm, either of the Silversea ships is unquestionably among the leaders in its category.

Specifications

Size (in tons)	16,800	Officers	Italian
Number of Cabins	148	Crew	210 (International)
Outside Cabins	148	Passenger/Crew Ratio	3 to 2
Cabins with Verandas	128	Year Built	1994/1995
Number of Passengers	296	Last Major Refurbishment	N/A

Frommer's Ratings (Scale of 1–5)

Cabin Comfort & Amenities	5	Pool, Fitness & Spa Facilities	3
Ship Cleanliness & Maintenance	4	Children's Facilities	N/A
Public Comfort/Space	4	Itineraries	5
Decor	5	Worth the Money	4

Don't choose a Silversea cruise if you absolutely must have nonstop activity, acres of gambling facilities, and lavishly choreographed stage presentations. But, if you need only plush surroundings, great service, and fine food—and can afford them—*Silver Cloud* and *Silver Wind* are for you.

Cabins & Rates

Cabins	Per diems from	Bathtub	Fridge	Hair Dryer	Sitting Area	TV
Suites	\$820–\$1,160*	yes	yes	yes	yes	yes

**All rates include one free hotel night in the port of embarkation.*

CABINS All the cabins are suites and all are outside. The smallest of them, the Vista Suites on Deck 4, are a spacious 240 square feet, though they lack a private veranda. All of the other suites have verandas and range from 295 square feet to the one-bedroom Royal Suite, with 1,031 square feet, and the one-bedroom Grand Suite, with an impressive 1,314 square feet. That's bigger than some homes. Non-balcony rooms have huge picture windows.

The cabin decor is easy on the eye with lots of pastel shades and good quality artwork on the walls. Stateroom refrigerators are stocked with soft drinks and liquor. Two cabins on each ship are handicapped accessible.

PUBLIC AREAS Public areas are small, as one might expect on a ship this size, but are consequently more intimate and more likely to lead to new friendships.

Preview: Silversea's *Silver Shadow*

Picture, if you will, the *Silver Cloud* or *Silver Wind,* only slightly bigger. The newcomer will be almost 597 feet long (the other two are 514 feet) and will carry 388 passengers (the others carry 296). It will be 81 feet wide (the others are only 70 feet), and at 25,000 gross registered tons it will outweigh its fleetmates by almost 8,000 tons.

There is one other statistic that is of more than passing interest to cruise aficionados. The *Silver Shadow*'s passenger/space ratio—a measurement of the vessel's interior space divided by the number of passengers—will be a whopping 64.4, one of the highest in the industry and almost a full eight points higher than even those of the spacious *Silver Wind* and *Silver Cloud.*

Shipboard amenities will include a spa and fitness center more than half as big again as the ones on the other two ships, a cigar bar, a computer center, a wine bar, a poolside grill, and a multi-tiered show lounge. Each of the 194 suites—80% of which will have private verandas—will feature a walk-in closet, writing desk, dressing table with hair dryer, Italian marble bathroom with double vanity sinks, separate toilet, entertainment center with satellite television capability and VCR, direct dial telephone, and safe deposit box. Godiva chocolates will be left on your pillow at evening turndown, Moët & Chandon will be served as the house champagne, you'll have personalized onboard stationery, and, of course, you'll be able to enjoy the line's customary Limoges china, Christofle silverware, and Frette linens. Despite the higher passenger capacity, one-seating meal flexibility will be maintained.

In short, Silversea is trying to ensure that people accustomed to the standard of service on its first two ships will find nothing lacking in its third.

One of the great gathering places on the ships is the amidships bar, a well laid out, relaxing place to mingle and meet. The Observation Lounge, up top, is another inviting area.

POOL, FITNESS & SPA FACILITIES Not to sound like a broken record, but they're small, even though they include just about everything you would want on a cruise. The pool is modest in size, about 30 feet long, and the ships have two Jacuzzis, men's and women's saunas, massage, hydrotherapy treatments, and aerobics classes. There's also a small jogging track. The beauty salon and barber shop offer manicures, pedicures, and facials as well as hairstyling.

Windstar Cruises

SHIPS Wind Spirit • Wind Song • Wind Star • Wind Surf

300 Elliott Ave. W., Seattle, WA 98119. ☎ **800/258-7245** or 206/281-3535. Fax 206/281-0627. www.windstarcruises.com.

LINE IN A NUTSHELL The no-jackets-required policy onboard Windstar's four sleek vessels defines the line's casually elegant attitude. They really do feel like private yachts—they're down-to-earth and port-intensive, yet service and cuisine are first-class.

THE EXPERIENCE Windstar offers a truly unique cruise experience, giving passengers the delicious illusion of adventure on board its fleet of four- and five-masted sailing ships and the ever-pleasant reality of first-class cuisine, service, and itineraries. This is no barefoot, rigging-pulling, paper-plates-in-lap, sleep-on-the-deck kind of cruise, but a refined yet down-to-earth, yacht-like experience for a sophisticated, well-traveled crowd who despise big ships and throngs of tourists.

On board, fine stained teak, brass details, and lots of navy-blue fabrics and carpeting lend a traditional nautical ambiance. While the ships' proud masts and yards of white sails cut an ever-so-attractive profile, the ships are ultra-state-of-the-art and the sails can be furled or unfurled at the touch of a button. The ships are so stable that at times the bridge may actually induce a modest tilt so passengers remember they're on a sailing ship. Under full sail, the calm tranquility of the cruises is utterly blissful.

Pros

- **Cuisine.** The ambiance, service, and imaginative cuisine created by renowned Los Angeles chef Joachim Splichal is superb. Dining is an event much looked forward to each day. Seating is open, and guests can usually get a table for two.
- **Informal and unregimented days.** This line offers the most casual high-end cruise out there—an approach much loved by passengers who like fine service and cuisine but don't like the formality and stuffiness of the majority of high-end lines. It's the most unregimented experience in a class of cruising already known for its unregimented atmosphere.
- **Itineraries.** Besides 1 day at sea, these small ships visit a port every day of a weeklong cruise, and many of the ports visited are wonderfully less touristed than those visited on the megaship routes.

Cons

- **No verandas.** If they're important to you, you're out of luck.
- **Limited activities and entertainment.** This is intentional, but if you need lots of organized hoopla to keep you happy, you won't find much on these ships.

Frommer's Ratings: Windstar Cruises

	Poor	Fair	Good	Excellent	Outstanding
Enjoyment Factor					✓
Dining					✓
Activities		✓			
Children's Program	N/A				
Entertainment		✓			
Service				✓	
Overall Value				✓	

WINDSTAR: CASUAL ELEGANCE UNDER SAIL

Launched in 1986, Windstar Cruises combines the best of 19th-century clipper design with the best of modern yacht engineering. As you see a Windstar ship approaching port, each with four or five masts the height of 20-story buildings, you'll think the seafaring days of Joseph Conrad or Herman Melville have returned. The ships are beautiful, and so is the experience on board—the line's ad slogan, "180 degrees from the ordinary," is right on target.

But Captain Ahab wouldn't know what to do with a Windstar ship. Million-dollar Hewlett-Packard computers control the six triangular sails with their at least 21,489 square feet of Dacron, flying from masts that tower 204 feet above deck. These computers automatically trim the sails and control fin stabilizers, rudder tab, anti-heeling devices, and the rest. Sails can be retracted in 2 minutes to a diameter of less than a foot.

The original designs were developed by Warsila Marine Industries in Helsinki, and the ships were built at Le Havre in France. The catalyst behind the formation of the company was a flamboyant French entrepreneur, Jean Claude Potier, a native Parisian, who, in a 25-year span, was instrumental in leading the French Line, the Sun Line, and Paquet during their transition into the modern cruise age.

In the late 1980s, Windstar was acquired by Holland America Line, which is itself wholly owned by Carnival Corporation. As such, Windstar is the most adventure-oriented of Carnival's many cruise line divisions, and although not as luxurious as Carnival's most upscale branch, Seabourn, it nonetheless prides itself on a cruise experience that's much, much more upscale than the ones offered aboard any of Carnival's megaships.

THE FLEET

Today, Windstar's fleet consists of four ships, the 148-passenger ***Wind Star, Wind Song,*** and ***Wind Spirit,*** all constructed originally for Windstar and built in 1986, 1987, and 1988, and the 312-passenger ***Wind Surf,*** built in 1990 and sailed until 1997 as the *Club Med I* for Club Med Cruises. The *Wind Surf* is the only one of the Windstar ships to have a spa and to offer a substantial number of suites (31). All four spend the summer in the Mediterranean.

PASSENGER PROFILE

People who expect high-caliber service and very high-quality cuisine but detest the formality of the other high-end ships and the mass-mentality of the megaships are thrilled with Windstar. Most passengers are couples in their 30s to early 60s (pretty evenly distributed across range, with the average about 48), with a smattering of parents with adult children and the occasional single friends traveling together.

The line is not the best choice for first-timers, since it appeals to a specific sensibility, and is definitely not a good choice for singles or families with children under 15 or 16.

Overall, passengers are sophisticated, well traveled, and more down-to-earth than passengers on the other high-end lines. Most want something different from the regular cruise experience, eschew the "bigger is better" philosophy of conventional cruising, and want a somewhat more adventurous, port-intensive Caribbean cruise. These cruises are for those seeking a romantic escape, who like to visit Mediterranean ports not bombarded by regular cruise ships, including Portofino, Amalfi, and Bodrum.

About a fourth of all passengers have sailed with the line before, a figure that represents one of the best recommendations for Windstar, and about 20% are first-timers. There are often a few honeymooners on board.

Dining

A high point of the cruise, the cuisine is among the better prepared aboard any ship in Europe, although maybe not quite the caliber of Seabourn or the *Radisson Diamond.*

The line's cuisine was the creation of the renowned chef/restaurateur **Joachim Splichal,** winner of many culinary awards (including some from the James Beard Society) and owner of Los Angeles's Patina Restaurant and Pinot Bistro. At its best, Splichal's food is inventive and imaginative, as reflected by such appetizers as a corn risotto with wild mushrooms and basil or a "Farinetta" bread and Parmesan griddle cake with roasted chicken and shallots, followed by a seafood strudel of lobster, scallops, mussels, king crab, and shrimp in a lobster sauce; or an artfully presented potato-crusted fish with braised leeks and apple-smoked bacon; or a salmon tournedo with an herb crust served with stewed tomatoes and garlicky broccoli rabe. Irresistible desserts such as banana pie with raspberry sauce and French profiteroles with hot fudge sauce are beyond tempting. A very good wine list includes California and European vintages.

Called the "Sail Light Menu," **healthy choices** and **vegetarian dishes,** designed by light-cooking expert Jeanne Jones, are available for breakfast, lunch, and dinner (fat and calorie content are listed on the menu). The light choices may feature Atlantic salmon with couscous and fresh vegetables or a Thai country-style chicken with veggies and Oriental rice. The vegetarian options may feature a fresh garden stew or a savory polenta with Italian salsa.

The once-a-week **evening barbecues** on the pool deck are wonderful parties under the stars, and an ample and beautifully designed buffet spread offers more than you could possible sample in one evening. The setting is sublime, with tables set with linens and, often, live music performed by the ship's duo.

Each ship has **two dining rooms,** one casual and breezy and used during breakfast and lunch (The Veranda), and the other a more formal room (The Restaurant) that's the stage for dinner. On the *Wind Spirit,* The Veranda is a sunny, window-lined room whose tables extend from inside onto a covered deck (unfortunately, you do have to go outside on deck to get there, so if it's raining you get wet), while The Restaurant is enclosed and accented with nautical touches like teakwood trim and paneling and pillars wrapped decoratively in hemp rope.

At breakfast and lunch, meals can be ordered from a menu or selected from a buffet, so your choices are many. Made-to-taste omelets and a varied and generous spread of fruits are available at breakfast, and luncheons may feature a tasty seafood paella and a hot pasta dish of the day. There is **open seating for meals,** at tables designed for between two and eight diners. You can often get a table for two, but you might have to wait if you go during the rush.

Windstar's official dress code is "no jackets required," which is a big draw for guests. In The Restaurant, guests are asked to dress "casually elegant," which generally means trousers and a nice collared shirts for men and pantsuits or casual dresses for women.

The **24-hour room service** includes hot and cold breakfast items (cereals and breads as well as eggs and omelets) and a limited menu that includes sandwiches, fruit, pizza, salads, and other snacks.

Activities

Since these ships generally visit a port of call every single day of the cruise and guests spend the day on shore exploring, there are few organized activities offered, and the daily schedules are intentionally unregimented—the way guests prefer it. Weather and conditions permitting, the ships anchor and passengers can enjoy kayaking, sailing, windsurfing, banana-boat rides, and swimming from the **watersports platform** lowered at the stern. There will be a handful of scheduled diversions, such as gaming lessons in

Windstar Fleet Itineraries

Ship	Home Ports & Season	Itinerary
Wind Song	Between Piraeus/Athens and Istanbul (May–Oct).	**7-day Greek Isles:** Mykonos, Santorini, Rhodes (Greece), and Bodrum and Kusdasi (Turkey).
Wind Spirit	Between Piraeus/Athens and Istanbul, May–Oct	**7-day Greek Isles:** Port calls may include Mykonos, Santorini, Rhodes (Greece), and Bodrum and Kusdasi (Turkey).
Wind Star	7-day W. Med 1, Lisbon and Barcelona (May to Nov); 7-day W. Med 2, Barcelona and Nice (June–Oct).	**7-day W. Med 1:** Portimao (Portugal), Tangier (Morocco), and Marbella, Ibiza, Mahon (Spain).**7-day W. Med 2:** Palma De Mallorca (Spain), and Port Vendres, Marseille, Sanary Sur Mer, Porquerolles, Cannes (France).
Wind Surf	7-day Rivieras, Nice and Civitavecchia/Rome (Apr–Nov); 7-day Adriatic, Civitavecchia/Rome and Venice (May–Oct).	**7-day Rivieras:** Monte Carlo (Monaco), St. Tropez and Bonifacio (France), and Portofino, Portovenere, Portoferraio (Italy). **7-day Adriatic:** Amalfi and Taormina (Italy), Corfu (Greece), and Dubrovnik and Rab Island (Croatia).

the casino and walk-a-mile sessions and stretch classes on deck. Chances are there may be a vegetable carving or food decorating demonstration poolside, as well as clothing or jewelry sale items on display by the pool. Before ports, brief orientation talks are held.

The pool deck, with its hot tub, deck chairs, and open-air bar, is conducive to sunbathing, conversations with shipmates, or quiet repose. There's an extensive video library and CD collection from which passengers can borrow for use in their cabins.

The company's **organized port tours** tend to be more creative than usual, and the cruise director/shore excursions manager/jack-of-all trades person or couple are knowledgeable and able to point passengers toward good spots for independent activities.

Children's Program

As children are not encouraged to sail with Windstar, there are no activities planned for them. There are often a handful of teenagers on board who spend time sunbathing or holed up in their cabins watching movies.

Entertainment

For the most part, passengers entertain themselves. There's often a duo on board (a pianist and a vocalist) performing during cocktail hour before and after dinner in the ships' one main lounge. **Local entertainment,** such as a Turkish dance troupe, is sometimes brought aboard at a port of call. A very modest **casino** offers slots, blackjack, and "Ocean stud poker" (which is Caribbean stud poker with a different name). After dinner, passengers often go up to the pool bar for a nightcap under the stars, and sometimes after 10 or 11pm, disco/pop music is played in the lounge if guests are in the dancing mood.

Service

Windstar is a class operation, as reflected in its thoughtful service personnel. The staff smiles hello and makes every effort to learn passengers' names. Dining staff is efficient and first-rate as well, but not in that ultra-professional, military-esque, five-star-hotel, Seabourn kind of way. That's not what Windstar is all about. Officers and crew are helpful, but not gushing. It's common for several married couples to be among the crew.

The line operates under a "tipping not required" policy, although generally guests do tip staff as much as on other ships; on Windstar, like Holland America, there's just less pressure to do so.

Wind Spirit • Wind Song • Wind Star

The Verdict

Some of the most romantic, cozy, yet roomy small ships out there, these ships look chic and offer just the right combination of creature comforts and first-class cuisine, along with a casual, laid-back, unstructured ethic.

Wind Spirit (photo: Windstar)

Specifications

Size (in tons)	5,350	Officers	British/Dutch
Number of Cabins	74	Crew	89 (International)
Number of Outside Cabins	74	Passenger/Crew Ratio	1.6 to 1
Cabins with Verandas	0	Year Built	1988/1987/1986
Number of Passengers	148	Last Major Refurbishment	N/A

Frommer's Rating (Scale of 1–5)

Cabin Comfort & Amenities	5	Pool, Fitness & Spa Facilities	2
Ship Cleanliness & Maintenance	4	Children's Facilities	N/A
Public Comfort/Space	3	Itineraries	4
Decor	4	Worth the Money	5

Despite these ships' high-tech design and size—significantly larger than virtually any private yacht afloat—they nonetheless have some of the grace and lines of a clipper ship, with practically none of the associated discomforts. There's even a needle-shaped bowsprit jutting into the waves. Getting around is usually easy, except that there's no inside access to the breakfast and luncheon restaurant, so during high winds or rain, access via an external set of stairs can be moderately inconvenient.

Cabins & Rates

Cabins	Per diems from	Bathtub	Fridge	Hair Dryer	Sitting Area	TV
Outside	$423–$488	no	yes	yes	no	yes

CABINS All cabins are very similar and display a subtle nauticalness. They're roomy at 188 square feet, but nowhere near as large as your typical high-end ship suite. Beds can be adapted into either a one-queen-size or two-twin-sized format. Each cabin has a VCR and TV showing CNN and lots of movies, a CD player, a minibar, a pair of large round portholes with brass fittings, bathrobes, fresh fruit, and a compact closet. Teakwood-decked bathrooms, largish for a ship of this size, are better laid out than those aboard many luxury cruise liners, and contain a hair dryer, plenty of towels, and more than adequate storage space. Like the ship's main public rooms, cabins are based on navy-blue fabrics and carpeting, along with wood tones—attractive but simple, well constructed, and utilitarian. The large desk/bureau is white with dark brown trim, and the rest of the cabinetry is a medium wood tone.

Although all the cabins are comfortable, cabins amidships are more stable in rough seas. Note that the ship's engines, when running at full speed, can be a bit noisy.

This line is not recommended for passengers with serious disabilities or those who are wheelchair bound. There are no elevators on board, access to piers is often by tender, and there are raised doorsills.

PUBLIC AREAS There aren't a lot of public areas on these small ships, but they're more than adequate since the ships spend so much time visiting ports. The four main rooms include two restaurants, a library, and the vaguely nautical-looking Lounge, with several cozy, somewhat private partitioned-off nooks and clusters of comfy caramel-colored leather chairs surrounding a slightly sunken wooden dance floor. In the corner is a bar and, in another, a piano and music equipment for the onboard entertainment duo. Here passengers congregate for port talks, pre- and post-dinner drinks, dancing, and any local dance performances. The second bar is the one out on the pool deck, which also attracts passengers before and after dinner for drinks under the stars. There's a piano in the corner of the deck (which doesn't get much play), but mostly this is your typical casual pool bar, and the place where cigars can be purchased and smoked.

The wood-paneled library manages to be both nautical and collegiate at the same time. Guests can read, play cards, or check out one of the hundreds of videotapes (CDs are available from the purser's office nearby).

The yachtily elegant, dimly lit main restaurant is similarly styled with navy carpeting and fabrics combined with wood details and nautical touches. The Veranda breakfast and lunch restaurant is light and airy. Throughout the ship, large glass windows, which are locked into a permanently closed position, allow in plenty of light if not air.

POOL, FITNESS & SPA FACILITIES The swimming pool is tiny, as you might expect aboard such a relatively small-scale ship, and there's an adjacent hot tub. The deck chairs around the pool can get filled during sunny days, but there's always the crescent-shaped slice of deck above and more space outside the Veranda restaurant. On Deck 4, there's an unobstructed wraparound deck for walkers.

There's a cramped gym in a cabin-sized room, and an adjacent co-ed sauna. Massages and a few other types of treatments are available out of a single massage room next to the hair salon on Deck 1.

Wind Surf

The Verdict

This sleek, sexy, super-smooth sailing ship is a gem, offering an extensive spa along with an intimate yacht-like ambiance.

Wind Surf (photo: Windstar)

Specifications

Size (in tons)	14,745	Officers	English/Dutch
Number of Cabins	156	Crew	163 (International)
Number of Outside Cabins	156	Passenger/Crew Ratio	2 to 1
Cabins with Verandas	0	Year Built	1990
Number of Passengers	312	Last Major Refurbishment	1997

Frommer's Rating (Scale of 1–5)

Cabin Comfort & Amenities	5	Pool, Fitness & Spa Facilities	5
Ship Cleanliness & Maintenance	4	Children's Facilities	N/A
Public Comfort/Space	4	Itineraries	5
Decor	4	Worth the Money	5

The newest member of the Windstar fleet of deluxe motor-sailers continues the line's tradition of delivering a top-of-the line cruise experience that's as chic and sophisticated as it is easygoing and unregimented. Previously sailing under the Club Med banner (it originally entered service as the *Club Med I*), the ship was designed by the same French architect who worked on the other three Windstar vessels, and for the most part is an enlarged copy of them. Purchased for $45 million and subsequently renamed, the *Wind Surf* underwent a major $8 million renovation in early 1998, which included an overhaul of all the public areas and the addition of 30 suites, a 10,000-square-foot spa complex, an alternative restaurant, and a casino.

As part of the conversion, many areas were gutted and all the grace notes of upscale, high-end life at sea were added to make what has emerged since then as a very elegant vessel. Despite a passenger capacity more than double her sister ships (312 versus 148), the *Wind Surf* maintains the feel of a private yacht.

Cabins & Rates

Cabins	Per diems from	Bathtub	Fridge	Hair Dryer	Sitting Area	TV
Outside	$465	no	yes	yes	no	yes
Suite	$697	no	yes	yes	yes	yes

CABINS Cabins are clones of those described in the *Wind Song/Wind Spirit/Wind Star* review, above. The interiors of both suites and standard cabins feature generous use of polished woods (burled maple and teak), bedspreads and curtains in navy blue and beige color schemes (suites are maroon and beige), white laminated cabinetwork, and plentiful storage space. All cabins have ocean views, and both standard cabins (188 square feet) and suites (376 square feet) are well supplied with creature comforts, including terry-cloth robes, hair dryers, well-stocked minibars, safes, VCRs and CD players, and satellite TVs with CNN. Bathrooms have teakwood trim, and are artfully designed and more appealing than those aboard many luxury cruise ships. Extra-spacious suites have separate sleeping and living quarters and his-and-hers bathrooms (each with a shower and a toilet).

As part of *Wind Surf*'s metamorphosis in 1998, cabins were completely reconfigured for a reduced passenger capacity of 312 instead of the *Club Med*'s 386. In addition, 30 suites were added on Deck 3 (its original layout had only one), making the *Wind Surf* the only vessel in the Windstar fleet to offer suites.

The ship has two elevators (unlike the other ships in the Windstar fleet, which have none), but still is not recommended for people with serious mobility problems. Access to piers is often by tender, and ramps over doorsills are not adequate.

PUBLIC AREAS Since the *Wind Surf*'s passenger-space ratio is 30% greater than that of its sister ships, its two main public spaces—the bright and airy Wind Surf Lounge where passengers gather in the evening for cocktails and to listen to a three- to five-person band play your favorite requests, and the Compass Rose piano bar, popular for after-dinner drinks—are also roomier than comparable public spaces on the other ships. There's also the pool bar for a drink under the stars.

As on the other Windstar ships, breakfast and lunch are served in the glass-enclosed Veranda Cafe topside, but the *Wind Surf* offers an alternative dinner option that's unique—in addition to the Restaurant, the smaller, 90-seat Bistro (adjacent to the Veranda) serves dinner each night.

Also unlike the other Windstar ships, *Wind Surf* has a 2,100-square-foot conference center that lies amidships and just below the water line (a company spokesperson says about 25% of the *Wind Surf*'s total business comes from charter and corporate incentive business; sometimes the whole ship is chartered, sometimes just half or less). Suitable for between 118 and 180 occupants, depending on the arrangement of tables and chairs, it contains technical amenities such as a photocopy machine and audiovisual equipment.

Other public areas include a casino that's nestled into one edge of the Windsurf Lounge, a library (in which the line hopes to install dataport jacks for laptops), and a gift shop.

POOL, FITNESS & SPA FACILITIES The *Wind Surf* has the most elaborate fitness and spa facilities in the Windstar fleet (the line's three 148-passenger ships have no spa and a tiny gym) and, in fact, outclasses facilities on other similar-sized ships. There's a well-stocked windowed gym on the top deck, a "sports" pool for aqua-aerobics and scuba lessons (passengers can get resort certification), and an aerobics room one deck below that's also used for yoga and golf swing practice. The new Steiner-managed WindSpa offers a roster of exercise, massage, and beauty regimens that rival those available at many land-based spas. There's aromatherapy, a variety of massages and other treatments, a sauna, and a steam room. Spa packages—geared to both men and women—can be purchased in advance through your travel agent, with appointment times made once you're on board.

Besides the sports pool, there's another pool on the Main Deck as well as two hot tubs. For joggers, a full-circuit teak promenade wraps around the Bridge Deck.

9 The Alternative Lines

The ships in this chapter offer a much more personal experience than larger ships, carrying fewer passengers than the big ships and spending more time in port, which means you'll to get to know your destination much better. The ships—some sailing ships and others motorized yachts—are small and intimate, many of them offering a measure of adventure mixed in with your sea voyage. Plus, with the exception of the *Sea Cloud* and Classical's *Clelia II,* which are more upscale than the other ships, these ships are resolutely casual, meaning you can leave the jackets, ties, pumps, and pearls at home.

These ships generally visit a port every day, and because they have shallow drafts (the amount of the ship that rides below the waterline), they're able to sail adventurous itineraries to small, out-of-the-way ports that the big cruise ships would run aground trying to approach. There is generally little time spent at sea, with the emphasis on giving you the maximum amount of time possible in each port.

Passengers tend to be well-traveled people who like to learn and explore and care little about plush amenities and onboard activities of the bingo and horse-racing variety. Don't expect doting service, but do expect very personal attention, as crew and passengers get friendly fast. Also, since there are so few passengers aboard (36 to 386 rather than 1,200 to 2,600), you'll get to know your fellow shipmates better—it's not uncommon for people on these ships to make friends and plan follow-up trips together.

The ships in this chapter are more like private yachts or summer camps at sea than floating resorts. You'll have fun, make lots of new friends, and be able to let your hair down. Food will be basic, hearty, and plentiful, but don't count on room service and midnight buffets, because there may not be any. There may not be TVs in the cabins, and you won't find a casino except aboard Club Med's *Club Med 2.*

DRESS CODES Dress code? What's a dress code? Aboard most of the ships in this chapter you can get away with a shirt and shorts during the day and a polo shirt and pants at night (sundresses for ladies).

- Classical Cruises
- Clipper Cruise Line
- Club Med Cruises
- Sea Cloud Cruises
- Special Expeditions
- Star Clippers
- Zeus Tours and Yacht Cruises

Classical Cruises

SHIPS IN EUROPE Clelia II • Panorama • Halcyon

132 East 70th St., New York, NY 10021. ☎ **800/252-7745.** Fax 212/774-1545. www.classicalcruises.com.

THE LINE IN A NUTSHELL Classical Cruises focuses on educational cruises and offers some wonderfully unusual itineraries on ships that look and feel like private yachts (that's because they actually are).

THE EXPERIENCE Vasos Papagapitos, president of this company, likes to say that he handcrafts the itineraries. He spreads nautical charts across his desk and with a protractor plots times and distances, and also uses history as a guide. The results are unique cruises such as one that traces the route of Homer's Odysseus.

The cruise company's forte is its stops at exotic and sometimes little-trafficked ports; scholarly lectures focusing on history and the arts; and educational shore excursions (included in the cruise fare) that focus on museums, archaeology, architecture, and nature. The line attracts well-traveled passengers (generally over 55) who are interested in a learning experience. Members of museum and college alumni associations often sign up as a group for the sailings, which get started with an enlightening bang: an overnight hotel stay paired with a tour and lecture.

The line's three ships are diverse. The *Clelia II* (which sailed previously as Renaissance's *Renaissance IV*) is a large private yacht owned by a Greek shipping magnate who leases it to Classical for several months of each year. All its cabins are spacious outside suites, while its public spaces are roomy, with more public areas than you usually find on a ship this size. The *Halcyon* is a smaller, catamaran-style yacht with well-proportioned and well-appointed public room and a contemporary feel. The *Panorama* is a three-masted motorized sailing yacht that offers the most classic appeal of the three, with its tall masts and broad teak decks. The atmosphere onboard all three ships is casual and slightly upscale (more upscale on the *Clelia II* than on the other ships), and all the cruises are sold as cruisetours, meaning they include a hotel stay (in this case pre-cruise) and land tour. The expert lecturers start their lectures at the hotels. All shore excursions are also included in the cruise fare.

Pros

- **Lots of intellectual discussion.** On these cruises you will learn something.
- **Lots of suites.** All the cabins on the *Clelia II* are suites.

Cons

- **Few amenities.** The *Panorama* and *Halcyon* are pretty basic in the amenities they offer (the *Clelia II* offers more).
- **So-so cuisine.** The food could be improved upon, especially set dinners.

Frommer's Ratings: Classical Cruises

	Poor	Fair	Good	Excellent	Outstanding
Enjoyment Factor				✓	
Dining			✓		
Activities					✓
Children's Program	N/A				
Entertainment		✓			
Service		✓			
Overall Value				✓	

CLASSICAL CRUISES: EDUCATIONAL CRUISING

Classical Cruises is a division of Travel Dynamics, a tour company that specializes in educational itineraries. The cruise line offers educational cruises aboard small yacht-type ships, visiting unusual destinations. The ships are chartered from private owners. The *Clelia II,* for instance, is owned by a Greek shipping family (the owner purchased the ship as a gift to his daughter).

With long years of involvement in the industry, Classical does an excellent job developing unusual itineraries and shore excursions (which are included in the cruise fare). Discussions with guest lecturers begin even before the cruise, with guests staying at a hotel for a pre-cruise tour and lectures.

THE FLEET

The ***Clelia II*** is a motorized yacht and the largest ship in the fleet. The ***Halcyon*** is a smaller motorized yacht, while the ***Panorama*** is a sailing yacht (although it also operates under engine power).

PASSENGER PROFILE

Passengers are well-traveled, and most are over 55. But the line has also created a unique program to attract families, hosting young explorer's programs on one ship each year (in 2000 it's on the *Halcyon*).

Some guests travel independently, but many are part of alumni groups from universities including Yale, UCLA, and Princeton, or museum groups from the Boston Museum of Fine Arts and the like. They are mostly Americans, and they are the kind that can easily entertain themselves with a good book or intellectual discussion.

DINING

Open seating for all meals at tables of six, eight, and 10 enables passengers to quickly get acquainted with one another. Copious **buffets** with a delicious selection of hot and cold food are served in the morning and at noon.

The set menu **dinners,** served by a wait staff, aren't always as well executed. Appetizers and soups are tasty, but for the main courses the meat can be tough and the fish dry. Provisioning difficulties in places like the Black Sea may be part of the problem.

A special **room service** menu is available during the hours that the restaurant is open on the *Clelia II.* The ship also sometimes offers alfresco dining on the deck.

"Dressy" attire is suggested for the captain's welcoming and farewell dinners, but no one appears in black tie or fancy gowns. Men might want to pack a jacket, but don't need a tie; women might want to pack a dress or two or another nice outfit.

ACTIVITIES

Lecturers of the highest quality accompany each cruise and provide the main form of organized activity. They introduce each port and talk to passengers in both formal presentations and one-on-one discussions. On one typical cruise, the curator of classical art at the Boston's Museum of Fine Arts, a Princeton Near East studies professor, and a Yale history professor delivered 11 compelling talks in all. On **shore excursions** and pre-cruise tours (which are included in the cruise fare) the scholars augment the information presented by local guides. Participation in the tours is usually 100%.

Other than that, there's not much in the way of organized activities on these ships. A staff member tapes the BBC news and rebroadcasts it in the lounge once a day. And a crew member on the *Clelia II* leads an early-morning workout in the gym.

Classical Fleet Itineraries

Ship	Home Ports & Season	Itinerary
Clelia II	13-day Med, Canakkale, Turkey (Mar, Oct); 8- to 11-day Greek Isles, Piraeus/ Athens (May, June, Sept, Oct).	**13-day Med:** Trapani, Pozzuoli, Sorrento, Lipari, Taormina (Italy), Corfu, Ithaca (Greece), Tunis, and Malta. **8- to 11-day Greek Isles:** Port calls may include Delos, Serifos, Sifnos, Folegandros, Santorini, Amorgos, Andiparos, Chios, Samothraki, Gytheion, Patmos, Lesbos, Rhodes, Volos (Greece), Agios Nicolaos and Heraklion (Crete), and Kusadasi (Turkey).
Halcyon	7-day Italy, Catania, Italy (Apr, May); 6- to 9-day Greece, Piraeus (July), Nauplion (Oct, Nov), Heraklion, Crete (Mar).	**7-day Italy*:** Palermo, Porto Empedocle, Taormina, Licata, Selinunte, Reggio di Calabria, and Syracuse (Italy). **6-, 7-, and 9-day Greece*:** Port calls may include Sitia, Ierapetra, Aghia Galini, Sfakia, Gramvousa, Kastelli Kisamou, Chania, Rethimnon, Serifos, Sifnos, Andriparos, Folegandros, Santorini, Nauplion, Monemvasia, Gytheion, Koroni, Methoni, Pylos (Greece), and Heraklion (Crete).
Panorama	7- and 8-day France, Bordeaux (July), Honfleur (Aug); 7-day Greece, Piraeus (Apr, May); 9-day Med, Catania, Italy (June); 9-day Spain, Barcelona (June); 6-day Spain and Portugal, Lisbon (Sept); 7-day England (Aug).	**7-day France*:** Belle Ile, Roscoff and St.-Malo, and La Rochelle (France), and St. Peter Port (Guernsey). **7-day Greece*:** Delos, Mykonos, Naxos, Antiparos, Sifnos, Santorini, Heraklion, and Monemvasia (Greece). **9-day Med*:** Taormina, Syracuse, Porto Empedocle, Licata, Trapani, and Pallermo (Italy). **9-day Spain and Portugal*:** Polenca, Alicante, Aguilas, Motril, Heulva, Puerto Banus (Spain), and Tangier (Morocco). **6-day Spain and Portugal*:** Faro (Portugal), Cadiz, Puerto Banus, Malaga (Spain), Tangier (Morocco), and Gibraltar. **7-day England*:** Sark, Jersey, St. Peter Port, Scilly Islands, Truro, and Dartmouth (England), and St. Malo (France).

*Sold as a cruisetour with two to four hotel days.

Both the *Panorama* and *Halcyon* also have some watersports equipment available for those inclined to use it.

Children's Program

The line's annual **Young Explorers excursion** is designed for those traveling with kids (including grandparents). This year's program, July 3 to 14, visits the Greek Isles. The focus is the myths and legends associated with the ancient world. Among the activities are visits to the Parthenon in Athens and the white-marble Temple of Poseidon at Cape Sounion. The cruise includes frequent swimming stops as well. Special reduced rate fares (starting at only $149 a day when the child shares a room with two full-paying adults) are offered for the program.

Entertainment

Because of the active and exhilarating days on shore, many passengers go to bed right after dinner, though the *Clelia II* does offer after-dinner piano music.

Service

Service is well intentioned in the dining room, but sometimes amateurish. Laundry service is available. Tips are pooled among the dining room, crew, and cabin stewards, with a recommended contribution of $10 per person, per day.

Clelia II

Clelia II (photo: Classical)

The Verdict

This private yacht lets you explore unique itineraries in all-suite comfort.

Specifications

Size	4,077	Officers	European
Number of Cabins	42	Crew	55 (European and North American)
Number of Outside Cabins	42		
Cabins with Verandas	2	Passenger/Crew Ratio	1.5 to 1
Number of Passengers	84	Year Built	1992, rebuilt 1997
		Last Major Refurbishment	1997

Frommer's Ratings (Scale of 1–5)

Cabin Comfort & Amenities	5	Pool, Fitness & Spa Facilities	4
Ship Cleanliness & Maintenance	4	Children's Facilities	N/A
Public Comfort/Space	5	Itineraries	5
Decor	5	Worth the Money	5

The present owner, a wealthy Greek shipping magnate who considers *Clelia II* to be a private yacht (it is leased to Classical for several months of the year), purchased the former *Renaissance IV* as a gift for his daughter. The accommodations, as part of a total refurbishing in 1997, were reconfigured into 42 outside suites, including several penthouses and apartments on the top two decks.

Cabins & Rates

Cabins	Per diems from	Bathtub	Fridge	Hair Dryer	Sitting Area	TV
Outside	$599*	no	yes	no	yes	yes

**Rates include complimentary house wines, shore excursions, land tours, tips to drivers and guides, airport transfers, and port charges and other taxes. Rates are for cruisetour combining a 7-night cruise and 3 to 7 nights in a hotel.*

CABINS All cabins are outside suites, and even standard suites, at 225 square feet, are spacious and comfortable, with a vanity/desk, a VCR, twin beds, a nightstand, and a sitting area with a sofa, easy chair, and coffee table. The closets, shelves, and drawers are sufficient even for those who travel with large wardrobes. The two deluxe penthouses are each 520 square feet and have verandas, separate bedrooms and living rooms, and two bathrooms. None of the cabins has a bathtub.

PUBLIC AREAS The public spaces are roomy and the facilities are more than ample for a ship of this size. They include a library (stocked with many good books and videos), two large lounges which serve as the setting for lectures, cocktail parties and late-night piano music, and an outdoor cafe that is used at tea time.

The Golden Star Dining Room, with tables for six, eight, or 10 and open seating at all meals, is done in handsome blond wood and light-toned marble.

POOL, FITNESS & SPA FACILITIES There are a beauty salon, steam bath, gym, pool, and Jacuzzi.

Panorama • Halcyon

Panorama (photo: Classical Cruises)

The Verdict

These ships provide as close to a yacht-like experience as you can get without owning your own yacht.

Specifications

Size (in tons)		Crew	European and
Panorama	599		North American
Halcyon	714	*Panorama*	16
Number of Outside Cabins		*Halcyon*	10
Panorama	22	Passenger/Crew Ratio	
Halcyon	24	*Panorama*	2.75 to 1
Cabins with Verandas	0	*Halcyon*	4.8 to 1
Number of Passengers		Year Built	
Panorama	44	*Panorama*	1994
Halcyon	48	*Halcyon*	1990
Officers	Greek	Last Major Refurbishment	
		Panorama	1998
		Halcyon	1997

Frommer's Ratings (Scale of 1–5)

Cabin Comfort & Amenities	3	Pool, Fitness & Spa Facilities	N/A
Ship Cleanliness & Maintenance	4	Children's Facilities	N/A
Public Comfort/Space	3	Itineraries	5
Decor	3	Worth the Money	5

The *Panorama* is a three-masted motorized sailing yacht. The *Halcyon* is a catamaran-style yacht. Both ships are Greek-flagged. The *Panorama,* thanks to its sails, offers a more classic appeal, highlighted by its broad, teak decks. The *Halcyon* is a more contemporary vessel with well-proportioned and well-appointed public rooms.

Cabins & Rates

Cabins	Per diems from	Bathtub	Fridge	Hair Dryer	Sitting Area	TV
Panorama, Outside	$549*	no	yes	no	no	yes
Halcyon, Outside	$469*	no	no	no	no	no

**All rates include complimentary house wines, shore excursions, land tours, tips to drivers and guides, airport transfers, and port charges and other taxes. Rates are for cruisetour; Panorama rate includes 3-night hotel stay and 7 nights on the ship, Halcyon rate includes a 4-night hotel stay and 6 nights on the ship.*

CABINS The *Panorama* and *Halcyon* both feature all outside cabins with showers. Those on the *Panorama* are tiny (73 to 124 square feet) with lower beds (twin, double, or queen), refrigerators, in-cabin music, TV/VCRs, and telephones. Those on the *Halcyon* are a little bigger (110 to 180 square feet) and have lower beds (twin, double, or queen), telephones, and in-cabin music. On both ships they come in three categories, the lowest-priced with portholes, the highest-priced with picture windows, and in between with smaller windows. Three cabins on the *Panorama* have a pull-down child's berth. No cabins on either ship have bathtubs.

PUBLIC AREAS The *Halcyon* has a nice cushy lounge with picture windows. The lounge flows into the large, wood-paneled dining room. The *Panorama* has a comfortably appointed lounge/dining room, and a second bar/lounge up on the top deck near the bridge. The lounges serve as the venue for movie nights. Both ships offer a well-stocked library and have an open-bridge policy, meaning you can hang out with the captain or officers anytime you like.

POOL, FITNESS & SPA FACILITIES The *Panorama* and *Halcyon* are both equipped with snorkeling gear, and you can swim directly from either ship's stern. The *Panorama* is also equipped with windsurfing equipment and a kayak. Both ships have a good amount of open deck space for sunbathing and relaxing, but there are no swimming pools.

Clipper Cruise Line

SHIPS IN EUROPE Clipper Adventurer

7711 Bonhomme Ave., St. Louis, MO 63105. ☎ **800/325-0010** or 314/727-2929. Fax 314/727-6576. www.clippercruise.com.

THE LINE IN A NUTSHELL Clipper, an American-owned line, is highly experienced in offering expedition-style and destination-oriented cruises in an intimate seagoing setting with a top-notch enrichment program.

THE EXPERIENCE Clipper Cruise Line is an expanding small-ship operator carrying mostly American passengers who enjoy each other's company and who get along well with the ships' youngish crews. The European programs are destination-driven, with a good enrichment program that includes well-attended informal lectures. Company-wide, there are no in-cabin TVs.

A very shippy ship, the *Clipper Adventurer*—built in 1975 as the *Alla Tarasova* and converted into a cruise ship by Scandinavian craftsmen in 1997/98—has an ice-hardened hull that allows it to follow exotic itineraries in the Arctic and Antarctic as well as its European sailings. At 4,575 tons, it's still a small ship, but it offers more public areas than most and an almost astounding amount of open deck space, considering the ship carries only 122 passengers. There are quiet areas throughout where passengers can get off on their own, plus places to congregate when one feels the urge to be social.

The *Clipper Adventurer*'s shore program is more ambitious and active than aboard the company's U.S.-flag coastal vessels, and the ship's shallow draft and nimble nature allow the captain to enter some very tight harbors and include a wider range of seldom-visited ports.

Pros

- **An intimate seagoing club.** The onboard atmosphere is informal, and camaraderie between passengers, staff, and crew comes easily.
- **Cozy, small-hotel-style public rooms.** From the comfy forward observation lounge, to the bar amidships and cozy library one deck above, this is a fine ship on which to spend 2 weeks.
- **Serious enrichment program.** Clipper prides itself in hiring a good staff of guest lecturers who enjoy sharing their knowledge, experience, and time with passengers.

Cons

- **Ship bucks in choppy seas.** The ship is small and is subject to considerable movement in large swells and stormy seas, though side-to-side rolling is minimized by stabilizers.

Frommer's Ratings: Clipper Cruise Line

	Poor	Fair	Good	Excellent	Outstanding
Enjoyment Factor				✓	
Dining				✓	
Activities				✓	
Children's Program	N/A				
Entertainment			✓		
Service				✓	
Overall Value				✓	

CLIPPER CRUISE LINE: AN EXPANDING WORLD

Clipper, a St. Louis–based company, got its start in the early 1980s as a purely domestic U.S. firm, and only recently expanded into the European market with its own ship. In 1996, Clipper merged with Intrav, a high-end wholesale and retail tour operator, and while Clipper Cruise Line is marketed separately, Intrav uses the Clipper fleet and other small ships in its own programs. Kuoni, A Swiss tour operator, bought Intrav in 1999, but the company will remain a separate division.

THE FLEET

The company began operating small U.S.-flag coastal cruise ships in 1983 on itineraries in North and Central America. While for several years Clipper chartered Society Expeditions' 138-passenger *World Discoverer,* it was not until 1997 that the company bought its own expedition ship, the Russian-flag *Alla Tasasova,* which it rebuilt into a 122-passenger expedition ship with American standards and renamed ***Clipper Adventurer.*** In November 1999, Clipper took on the similar-sized *Oceanic Odyssey,* which the company renamed the *Clipper Odyssey* and deployed for cruises in Asia and Australasia. The U.S.-flag fleet of two coastal vessels (*Yorktown Clipper* and *Nantucket Clipper*) carries an American crew while the two oceangoing expedition vessels have American and international crews.

PASSENGER PROFILE

Clipper's passengers are mostly mature Americans who have traveled quite a lot but are not risk-takers and prefer the intimacy of small ships with American management. The European programs attract a wider age range and more active passengers than do the U.S.-flag coastal ships. The passengers are not status-seeking but rather easygoing types who enjoy the company of like-minded travelers. Children are generally not part of the passenger profile, though those who enjoy adult company are likely to have a good time.

DINING

All Clipper chefs have been trained at the Culinary Institute of America at Hyde Park, New York, and they cater to American passengers who like well-prepared food, attractively presented and using top ingredients, rather than overly abundant or showy displays.

As the passengers are generally aged 55 and up, the richness of sauces is kept to a minimum. In Europe, where food supplies are plentiful and varied, the menus will reflect local ingredients such as fish and fresh fruit and vegetables, but prepared in a sophisticated American style. Steaks and roast beef will be top quality, and the seafood dishes will run to Atlantic salmon, sea bass, and lobster tails. Salads change daily, and all the breads, pastries, and desserts are freshly prepared on board.

The dining room, with large picture windows, operates with a single seating for all meals, and there are tables for mostly four and six, none far from a good view. The dining staff is American and Filipino, and at peak times during dinner there can be some delays as the serving kitchen is much too small.

The **buffet offerings** for breakfast and lunch are displayed in the observation lounge, and they are limited to continental breakfast items and soup, salads, and sandwiches at lunch, with an occasional hot entree.

Clipper Fleet Itineraries

Ship	Home Ports & Season	Itinerary
Clipper Adventurer	12-day W. Med, Lisbon to Civtavecchia/Rome (May); 11-day E. Med, Civitavecchia/Rome to Piraeus/Athens (May); 14-day Med, Piraeus/Athens to Lisbon (May); 12-day W. Europe, Lisbon to Amsterdam (June); 10-day Scandinavia & Russia, Amsterdam to St. Petersburg (June); 12-day British Isles, Dover to Edinburgh (July).	**12-day W. Med:** Portimãp (Portugal), Seville, Málaga, Barcelona, Mahón (Spain), Alghero, Elba, Livorno (Italy), and Bastia (Corsica, France). **11-day E. Med:** Sorrento and Taormina (Italy), Itea, Thira, Delos, Mykonos (Greece), and Kusadasi (Turkey). **14-day Med:** Kusadasi (Turkey), Thira and Itea (Greece), Taormina and Sorrento (Italy), Ajaccio (Corsica, France), and Mahón, Barcelona, Málaga, Cadiz (Spain). **12-day W. Europe:** Leixoes (Portugal), Villagarcía (Spain), St. Jean-de-Luz, Bordeaux, Ile d'Aix, La Rochelle, Belle-Ile, St. Malo, Honfleur, Rouen (France), and Flushing (Netherlands). **12-day British Isles:** Sark and Isles of Scilly (England), Ilnacullin and Dublin (Ireland), Holyhead (Wales), and Inveraray, Isle of Skye, Inverewe, Shapinsay, Invergordon (Scotland). 10-day Scandinavia & Russia, visits Lübeck (Germany), Copenhagen (Denmark), Gdansk (Poland), Visby and Stockholm (Sweden), Tallinn (Estonia).

Vegetarians and others following special diets can be accommodated with advance notice.

Activities

Onboard activities are limited to daytime **lectures** at sea, and games and puzzles in the library. There is an excellent reference book collection and passengers display considerable interest in educating themselves. The captain has an open-bridge policy at all times, and talking with the officers is an integral part of life aboard the *Clipper Adventurer* day and night.

Children's Programs

There are no special programs for children, but if there are a few aboard, the lecture staff will see that they have a good time, especially on trips ashore. However, children really need to enjoy adult company to enjoy this ship.

Entertainment

The only entertainment would be **local groups** coming aboard in a few ports and destination-related **films** screened in the lounge after dinner. The ship does not have a casino or regular after-dinner shows.

Service

The hotel staff is American and Filipino with Americans as bar and some of the dining crew. The cabin stewardesses are Filipino. Service is polite and low-key, though some of the older passengers will bond with some of the younger crew and, at the end of the cruise, will want to adopt them.

Bar service in the main lounge, the social center, is very personal, and after a few days, the bartenders will remember what the regulars like to drink.

Clipper Adventurer

Clipper Adventurer (photo: Clipper)

The Verdict

A well-received addition to the expedition scene, the ship has rapidly gained a top reputation among cruisers who want a well-run, destination-oriented experience in their own language and with like-minded passengers.

Specifications

Size (in tons)	4,575	Crew	58 (American & Filipino)
Number of Cabins	61		
Number of Outside Cabins	61	Passenger/Crew Ratio	2.1 to 1
Cabins with Verandas	none	Year Built	1975 (rebuilt 1998)
Number of Passengers	122	Last Major Refurbishment	1998
Officers	Scandin. & Filipino		

Frommer's Ratings (Scale of 1–5)

Cabin Comfort & Amenities	4	Pool, Fitness & Spa Facilities	2
Ship Cleanliness & Maintenance	5	Children's Facilities	N/A
Public Comfort/Space	5	Itineraries	5
Decor	4	Worth the Money	5

The *Clipper Adventurer* is an ideal-size ship for exploring the smaller ports in Europe without taking the masses with you. She is comfortable in a clubby way and was designed from scratch to appeal to homey Americans who would like to visit seriously interesting places in an informal atmosphere. While the ship is relatively new to the European market, the cruise staff and officers are as experienced as those aboard any ship of the type.

Cabins & Rates

Cabins	Per diems from	Bathtub	Fridge	Hair Dryer	Sitting Area	TV
Outside	$398*	no	no	no	no	no
Suite	$672*	yes	yes	no	yes	no

**Rates are based on Castles and Gardens cruises around the British Isles, and include all excursions, port charges, airfare from New York, and transfers to and from the ship.*

CABINS All cabins are outside, and the nine on Promenade Deck look through two sets of glass to the sea, while those on A Deck have portholes. Most cabins are of average size, all with twin beds, showers, toilet, decent storage space in closets and on shelves and flat surfaces, and phones. They are designed for sleeping and resting between trips ashore, are plainly furnished with a chair and vanity-cum-desk, and have attractive wood-grain wainscoting and trim. One deluxe cabin and three suites are clustered on Boat Deck in a private section. Soundproofing throughout is good.

The cabins on the Promenade Deck, while roomy, look onto the narrow side promenade that is lighted at night, meaning that curtains must be drawn after dark and especially when sleeping. During the day there is little traffic.

PUBLIC AREAS The ship has three main public rooms, plus the bridge, which is open 24 hours a day. The forward lounge slopes upwards with the ship's shear and can seat all passengers at once. The lectures and films take place here, plus continental breakfast and light lunch buffets. Though very comfy, the room suffers from being dark unless one is seated next to a window. Aft is a clubby lounge bar that sees little use except for card players or for a brief private chat. The library is the best of the lot, a cheerful space with a lighter atmosphere and away from any through foot traffic, of which there is very little on this ship. Passengers use the library for reading, research, games, and having coffee or a cold drink.

The dining room, located well aft on Promenade Deck, is most attractive when you're seated next to a window; in the center it's slightly gloomy. The best tables are a pair with four places all the way aft. If something worth seeing suddenly appears outside, two doors allow passengers access directly onto the after deck.

Outside space includes a wide Boat Deck with deck chairs and a covered after section, but it is not possible to walk around this deck on one level. Forward of the bridge, there is a step down to an observation deck constructed as the deck roof to the extended lounge below. On the ship's more expeditionary itineraries, "Thar she blows" will bring scores to this open space, as will the sighting of an iceberg, but for most, the view forward is enjoyed from the bridge.

The very highest deck is wide open for sunning, something not much done on this ship. There is no elevator aboard, and the ship would be very awkward in general for wheelchair users. The forward staircase foyers exhibit some very attractive sculpture and artwork. The ship is entirely nonsmoking within.

POOL, FITNESS & SPA FACILITIES The tiny gym has weights, treadmill, and stationary bicycle, and adjacent is a sauna. There is no swimming pool or whirlpool.

Club Med Cruises

SHIPS IN EUROPE Club Med 2

7975 N. Hayden Rd., Ste. A-105, Scottsdale, AZ 85258-3246. ☎ **800/CLUBMED.** Fax 480/443-2085. www.clubmed.com.

THE LINE IN A NUTSHELL French-style fun in the sun is what you'll get on this floating Club Med resort, a five-masted, engine-powered sailing ship where the crowd is international and the good times are universal.

THE EXPERIENCE Club Med's one ship, the *Club Med 2,* is a stable, high-tech version of an 18th-century clipper ship, with five masts, seven computer-operated sails, and a vague and sometimes far-fetched self-image as a private yacht. While the ship's sails add a lovely grace note, that's mostly all they do—in actuality, the ship relies almost entirely on its diesel engines for propulsion.

In Europe, Club Med carries a scant few Americans (between 5 and 10%), though you can count on some Brits being aboard as well. The language on board is French and the currency is the franc. Just as at Club Med's land resorts, the ship is staffed by a cadre of *gentils organisateurs* (GOs), an army of cheerleaders who function as quasi-passengers, participating in the activities and encouraging passengers to do the same. Many guests love these GOs, but others find them irritating.

Note that the "club" in Club Med isn't just a word: You really have to join, with a one-time initiation fee of $30 per family (which includes travel insurance coverage) and an annual fee of $50 per adult and $20 for each person under 12.

Pros

- **International ambiance.** Francophiles and anyone who particularly enjoys mingling with Europeans will appreciate the *Club Med 2*'s international mix of passengers.
- **Watersports.** Retractable watersports platform lowers from the ship's stern and allows guests to conveniently windsurf, kayak, water-ski, snorkel, and swim.
- **Comfortable cabins.** For a small ship, these cabins are comfy and come stocked with a TV, a minibar, a couple of terry-cloth bathrobes, and a hair dryer.

Cons

- **International ambiance.** Overkill. For some cruisers, the entire Club Med *savoir faire* misses the mark, fostering a cliquish rowdiness that reminds them of a summer camp for adults. Potential passengers who suspect they'd feel this way would be better off sailing with Windstar.
- **Amateurish entertainment.** It's Club Med's hallmark, but you won't find anything but talent-show-caliber stuff.

Frommer's Ratings: Club Med Cruises

	Poor	Fair	Good	Excellent	Outstanding
Enjoyment Factor				✓	
Dining				✓	
Activities					✓
Children's Program	✓				
Entertainment				✓	
Service				✓	
Overall Value			✓		

CLUB MED: FRENCH-STYLE FUN AT SEA

In the late 1980s, Club Med founder and CEO Gilbert Trigano decided to test the cruise industry's waters and ordered up a pair of exotic-looking masted ships to import the Club Med holiday experience onto the high seas. Realizing that there would be no reason for the venture if it simply siphoned off business from CM's land-based resorts, Club Med Cruises targeted as its potential passengers those people who either hadn't visited its other resorts or would not, and people attracted to the more luxurious accommodations offered at sea as opposed to the stripped-down barracks of many Club Med villages.

The venture has had mixed results. Although the cruise industry is rapidly expanding, in 1997 Club Med became one of the few cruise lines to reduce the size of its fleet when it sold the *Club Med 1* to Windstar Cruises, which immediately renamed it the *Wind Surf* and facilitated a radical upgrading of its interior.

THE FLEET

The 392-passenger, 14,745-ton ***Club Med 2*** was built in 1992 and is the sole ship of the famous vacation resort company. It's outfitted with masts and sails, but these accoutrements are just that: auxiliaries to the ship's engines, aesthetic ornaments aboard a vessel that usually diesels its way between ports. On some cruises, if the wind isn't cooperative, the sails are hoisted only occasionally, perhaps during exits and entrances from harbors, or at the beginning and end of a cruise.

Unlike actual sailing ships, the *Club Med 2* heels only slightly, and then only in the strongest of winds; sometimes CM captains actually induce a slight tilt to simulate the feeling of a ship under sail. The crew seems eerily absent from the minute-to-minute trimming of sails, and that's because the lines, ropes, riggings, and sails are set and fine-tuned via computer monitors from the bridge.

Despite all this mechanization, many passengers are awed by the vessel's sheer beauty, which adds to the romance of sailing through European waters. The ship's five masts and seven sails are merely a grace note, beautiful and evocative when viewed from the decks but far too small in proportion to the bulk of the ship's hull when seen from afar.

PASSENGER PROFILE

Many passengers are alumni from Club Med villages; others like the company's concept of relaxed informality but prefer the ship's more luxurious accommodations to the bare-boned CM villages on land. Most passengers are couples over 40 years of age. Many are French-born. On its European cruises the line also attracts passengers from Italy, Belgium, Germany, and England, as well as a handful from the U.S. and Canada (on most Europe sailings, 70% of the passengers are European).

Announcements and activities are conducted in English, German, French, and Italian.

Passengers tend to be sports- and fitness-conscious, and appreciative of luxury without insisting on formality (as aboard Windstar, no jackets are ever required). They like to visit exotic ports of call, are not particularly upset by any shortcomings in cuisine, and spend a lot of time playing at watersports.

Children under 10 are not permitted to sail aboard a Club Med vessel.

DINING

Two dining areas both allow sea views, and dinners are held in a single open seating. Officers and staff dine with the passengers, contributing to the clublike ambiance. Tables for two are widely available; conversely, if you're looking for company, one of the GOs will quickly bustle you to a communal table.

Cuisine is—you guessed it—**French,** with a few hints of Italian and other continental traditions showing through occasionally. Charming touches include **cheese carts** featuring café au lait, espresso, and a selection of cheese that is very French indeed. Food

Club Med Fleet Itineraries

Ship	Home Ports & Season	Itinerary
Club Med 2	2- to 7-day W. Med, Cannes (May, June, Sept), Lisbon (Aug, Sept); 7-day Norway, Stavanger (July, Aug); 12-day Europe, Barcelona (June); 9-day Scandinavia & Russia, Stockholm (July); 10-day Europe Capitals, Copenhagen (Aug).	**2- to 7-day W. Med:** Port calls may include Portofino, Calvi, Elbe, Portovenere, Bonifacio (Italy), St.-Tropez (France), and Barcelona and Palma (Spain). **12-day Europe:** Port calls may include Malaga (Spain), Guernsey (England), Amsterdam (Holland), and Gibraltar. **7-day Norway:** Port calls may include Bergen, Oslo, Trondheim, Helleysilt, Svartisen, Bodo, Lekness, Mold, Geiranger, Alesund, Flam, and Vik (Norway). **9-day Scandinavia & Russia:** St. Petersburg (Russia), Helsinki (Finland), Tallinn (Estonia), and Gdansk (Poland). **10-day Europe Capitals:** Hamburg (Germany), Amsterdam (Holland), and Guernsey (England).

is not superlative, but is plentiful and prepared and served with style. Meals are always accompanied by **complimentary beer or red and white wine** (usually one of Club Med's private-label wines). A surcharge is imposed for more esoteric vintages.

Substantial and somewhat formal fare is served during breakfast and lunch hours in an indoor-outdoor bistro called the Odyssey. At lunchtime, both à la carte sit-down service and **buffet spreads** are featured. On some days a crew sets up a buffet, usually with lobster, on whatever beach happens to be nearby.

Dinners are more proper events capping otherwise more relatively relaxed days. As in France itself, they can last for up to 3 hours. Diners opt for meals served between 7:30 and 9:30pm in the Odyssey or the more formal Le Louisiane Restaurant. The dress code is usually casual or informal, with the exception of two gala Captain's dinners offered during the course of each 7-night cruise. At these, men can wear a blazer but don't need a tie, while women can wear a skirt, dress, or nice pants outfit.

Room service is available 24 hours a day, although some items carry a supplemental charge and the menu is limited. Continental breakfast is always available in cabins. Upon request, **special diets** such as low-calorie, nonfat, or vegetarian are accommodated.

Activities

The teakwood decks support an ongoing cross-cultural carnival that tries to be all things to all passengers. The outdoor areas invite sunbathing, although the ship's sails sometimes block the rays. **Deck games** with the GOs come with unbounded enthusiasm that can be a bit much, particularly if you don't feel as youthful as the GOs.

One benefit of the ship's relatively small size is the *Hall Nautique,* a **private marina** created by opening a massive steel hatch at the ship's stern, allowing windsurfers, sailboaters, water-skiers, and snorkelers direct access to the open sea. Gear for all of these sports is provided free. Scuba diving is reserved for certified divers, and all equipment is provided on board. A flotilla of tenders carry day-trippers to the sands of isolated beaches.

Bridge is popular aboard ship, and a GO will organize lessons and tournaments for whoever is interested. The **casino,** offering blackjack and roulette along with the inevitable slot machines, is small but generally adequate for the number of players.

There's also a gym with his-and-hers saunas and a beauty center. Aerobic, stretch, and water exercise classes are offered.

Children's Program

Only children ages 10 and over are allowed on board, and even those who make the grade are not particularly welcome. Club Med does not advertise that it accepts

Extra Charges

Single Passengers: Single occupants of double cabins pay a 30% surcharge. **Port Charges:** For most itineraries, port charges are an additional $126 per person.

children and does not encourage it, as the ship, in theory at least, is for "sophisticated adults." If teenagers make it aboard, GOs will supervise daytime activities for them, but otherwise there are no special activities.

Entertainment

By design, it's rather amateurish. GOs entertain on every cruise, lip-synching their way through the usual repertoire. Sometimes **local bands** come aboard for the evening at various ports of call. On the do-it-yourself front, the **karaoke** microphone is a popular staple.

There's a **piano bar** on board, and a **nightclub** that's staffed by GOs who may sing, dance, and tell jokes. Later, beginning around 10:30pm, the ship's **disco** swings into action. Sheathed in mirrors and chrome, it's hidden away behind an unmarked door on the vessel's bottom deck, a little too close to the engine room for anything approaching real glamour, but far from any cabins where passengers might be sleeping.

Service

Remember that Club Med really is a club in many ways, and while efforts are made to attend to your needs, the staff is much more laid-back than your typical professional waiters and other service staff. In some ways, the army of GOs function on board as reliably energetic guests rather than as hotel staffers in the traditional sense, so service relies on cooperation and cheerful coexistence. The illusion is maintained that whoever is serving you is doing so as a favor rather than as a duty. In some cases, if the staff finds a request inconvenient, you may find that they deliberately forget it.

Laundry service is available for a supplemental fee, but dry cleaning is not.

Club Med maintains a "no tipping" policy at each of its resorts and on board its ship, a policy that's consistent with the company's all-inclusive price structures. Despite that, many staff members are pleased to discreetly accept a gratuity for exemplary service.

Club Med 2

The Verdict

This sleek, five-masted, French-flavored ship offers an exotic international passenger mix and a truly unique cruise experience.

Club Med II (photo: Club Med Cruises)

Specifications

Size (in tons)	14,983	Officers	French
Number of Cabins	191	Crew	184 (International)
Number of Outside Cabins	191	Passenger/Crew Ratio	2.1 to 1
Cabins with Verandas	0	Year Built	1990
Number of Passengers	386	Last Major Refurbishment	N/A

Frommer's Ratings (Scale of 1–5)

Cabin Comfort & Amenities	4	Pool, Fitness & Spa Facilities	3
Ship Cleanliness & Maintenance	3	Children's Facilities	N/A
Public Comfort/Space	3	Itineraries	5
Decor	3	Worth the Money	4

The decor and amenities aboard *Club Med 2* are on par with the chain's finest, most stylish, and most upscale resorts. Within the Club Med subculture, this is about as good as it gets.

Every upper deck on this vessel is affected by the very masts, riggings, and sails that make it distinct—even the understated smokestacks, with funnels that pivot so as to direct smoke away from the sails.

Cabins & Rates

Cabins	Per diems from	Bathtub	Fridge	Hair Dryer	Sitting Area	TV
Outside	$289	no	yes	yes	no	yes
Suite	$394	no	yes	yes	yes	yes

CABINS A prime incentive for a cruise aboard the *Club Med 2* is the care and attention devoted to cabin accoutrements. All cabins are outside, and have their own pair of brass-trimmed portholes, climate control, music channels, minibar, safe, surprisingly generous closet, and telephone.

Significantly, regardless of the deck on which it's located, each cabin is almost exactly identical to every other one on board, with almost no variation for the height at which it sits above the waterline. None of the units has a private balcony. Most cabins measure a generous 188 square feet. There are also five suites, each with 258 square feet and a rectangular picture window. Other than the additional space, they differ little from the cabins. Cabin decor includes high-tech detailing, mahogany trim, and white walls offset by at least one other color, often navy blue. Bathrooms come equipped with a hair dryer and a pair of terry-cloth robes. Cabins have both 110- and 220-volt current, allowing appliances from Europe and North America to be used without converters or adapters.

Some cabins contain upper bunks for a third passenger. There are no single cabins, and no cabins are especially suited for passengers with disabilities.

PUBLIC AREAS Various decorative details, including the use of Burmese teak as sheathing for all decks and a mixture of high-tech lines with lots of hardwoods, maintain the illusion that the vessel is, indeed, a small-scale yacht rather than a 14,000-ton ship. Scattered over its eight decks are four bars and lounges, a nightclub, a casino, and a medical center staffed by a doctor and nurse. One large lounge serves as an all-purpose bar, lecture hall, and rendezvous point. Lounges are soothing if colorful, often done up with unusual murals and designs in a sort of postmodern interpretation of art deco. Large windows bring views of the sea indoors. Two elevators connect the eight decks.

POOL, FITNESS & SPA FACILITIES The ship contains a pair of medium-sized saltwater pools, a small gym with ocean views, a sauna, and massage facilities. Aerobics classes are offered, and for joggers and walkers there's an uninterrupted jogging circuit around the ship.

Sea Cloud Cruises

SHIPS IN EUROPE Sea Cloud

32–40 North Dean St., Englewood, NJ 07631. ☎ **888/732-2568** or 201/227-9404. Fax 201/227-9424. www.seacloud.com.

THE LINE IN A NUTSHELL A week aboard the historic, fully-rigged *Sea Cloud* is the closest most of us ever will get to sailing aboard someone's private yacht.

THE EXPERIENCE Sea Cloud Cruises exists because of its one vessel, the *Sea Cloud.* Once owned by cereal heiress Marjorie Merriweather Post, it's the most elaborate and luxurious sailing vessel ever built. A cruise aboard her is like an elegant house party where everyone has come with high expectations.

After lying unused for a number of years, the ship was bought by a group of investors who had it refit and rebuilt at the same German shipyard that had built the vessel in 1931. At this time, 26 additional cabins were added to its eight, which include Marjorie's Suite, fitted with a blue canopied bed in antique white with golf leaf ornamentation, Louis Phillippe chairs, a marble fireplace with an elaborate mantel, a plaster ceiling, and a grand Carrara marble bathroom with swan-shaped gold faucets.

As befits this elegant setting, dinners are elegant affairs served at formal tables in the wood-paneled dining room and original salon, both with beamed ceilings and handsome oil paintings. As is true aboard most cruise experiences like this, there are few activities other than those that have to do with sailing itself. In port, there are low-key shore excursions, some independent and some organized. Passengers sailing aboard *Sea Cloud* are mostly well-heeled and well-traveled Americans, plus some Europeans. Most are attracted by the classic sailing ship experience, and many own their own sailboats.

Pros

- **An authentic four-masted sailing yacht.** The *Sea Cloud* has a proud history that includes famous owners and passengers, a sterling war career, a rescue, and a complete refit by a group of investors.
- **Friendly social atmosphere.** Passengers know exactly what they're looking for in a cruise, and that's why they choose a cruise on the *Sea Cloud.* A great spirit of camaraderie soon develops.
- **Beautiful interiors.** The wood paneling, oil paintings, lighting fixtures, and plush furnishings create an opulent setting that exists on no other cruising vessel.

Cons

- **Not always under sail.** The *Sea Cloud* has an itinerary to keep, and though it is a relaxed one, the ship is subject to wind conditions, hence the need to use the engines more than passengers may expect.

Frommer's Ratings: Sea Cloud Cruises

	Poor	Fair	Good	Excellent	Outstanding
Enjoyment Factor					✓
Dining					✓
Activities			✓		
Children's Program	N/A				
Entertainment			✓		
Service				✓	
Overall Value				✓	

SEA CLOUD: CRUISES FOR TYCOON WANNABES

Sea Cloud Cruises got its start in 1978 when a group of investors took an abandoned ship, once owned by the cereal heiress Marjorie Merriweather Post and others after that, back to Germany for a refit and rebuild at the same yard that had produced her in 1931. The original eight cabins were restored and 26 new ones added to make her a paying cruise vessel for the high end of the cruise market. While the public room layout was retained as originally built, some adaptation was required to handle the increased passenger capacity, now numbering 69. The owners have been able to market the ship to individuals and to alumni, museum, and affinity groups, with some loyal organizations returning year after year.

The Fleet

The ***Sea Cloud*'s** itineraries will vary from year to year but for the most part the ship will be based in the Mediterranean for the summer and fall, and the number of cruises available for individual bookings will depend on those dates not block-booked for groups. Even then, some groups will accept individuals if there is space.

Sea Cloud Cruises has also expanded into European river cruises, where they operate two high-class riverboats (see chapter 10).

Passenger Profile

Mostly well-heeled and well-traveled Americans, and some Europeans, who have a distinct interest in sailing and an affinity with the sea. Some passengers own their own sailboats, and others come because the *Sea Cloud* is so well-known in certain circles, and they want to partake of the good life too.

Simply being aboard the *Sea Cloud* engenders good will and camaraderie amongst passengers.

Dining

Dinner is an elegant affair with open seating at formal tables set with silver napkin rings, candlelight, fresh flowers, and navy blue, gold, and white china embossed with the ship's logo. Both the wood-paneled dining room and original salon with their beamed ceilings and handsome oil paintings are set up for the evening meal. The food is **nouvelle cuisine,** with dinner starting with a soup or salad and entrees such as rack of lamb with cassoulet or sole roulade with leek and rigatoni. **Complimentary red and white wines** accompany the set menu.

Lunch is presented as a **buffet** on the Promenade Deck, and the staff will help passengers carry their trays to the Lido Lounge one deck above, where tables are set under a blue awning. The tasty fare includes assorted salads, spring rolls with sweet-and-sour sauce, carrot soup, cold poached salmon, saltimbocca with artichoke polenta, a selection of cheeses, and fresh waffles with cherry compote.

Vegetarians and others following special diets can be accommodated with advance notice.

Cruise Tip

Don't worry if you cannot afford one of the original cabins aboard the *Sea Cloud.* You will get to see them on a tour on the next to the last evening during an open house. Also, if you have a sailing date in mind and it turns out to be a charter, find out if the group has taken all the space. They may be happy to take you on, but check to see if their interests coincide with yours.

Sea Cloud Fleet Itineraries

Ship	Home Ports & Season	Itinerary
Sea Cloud	7- and 8-day W. Med, Montril, Spain (Apr, Nov), Civitavecchia/Rome (May, June), Nice (May), Monte Carlo (May), Piraeus/Athens (Oct); 4- to 9-day E. Med, Catania, Italy (June, Oct), Kusadasi (June–Oct), Piraeus/Athens (June–Sept), Istanbul (June, July, Sept), Valletta, Malta (Aug), Anatalya, Turkey (Sept).	**7- and 8-day W. Med:** Port calls may include Mallorca (Spain), Monte Carlo (Monaco), Porto Vecchio, Portofino, Naples, Palermo, Civitavecchia/Rome, Venice (Italy), Dubrovnik (Croatia), Valletta (Malta), and Gibraltar. **4- to 9-day E. Med:** Port calls may include Catania (Italy), Piraeus/Athens, Santorini, Rhodes, Kos, Patmos, Mykonos, Chios, Lesbos (Greece), and Kusadasi, Antalya, Bodrum, Dikili, Cannakkale (Turkey).

Activities

Watching the sail-handling and ship navigation is the chief pastime at sea. Few activities are organized other than **skeet shooting** or learning the ropes—just trying to remember the names of the 35 sails is an activity itself. Many passengers simply enjoy relaxing and reading, playing games, hanging out around the bridge, or staring at the sea. In port, there are low-key **shore excursions,** some independent and some organized.

Children's Programs

Children will have to be happy in the company of adults, as there are no special children's facilities.

Entertainment

The ship carries a **pianist** who plays in the Lido Lounge, and some of the crew sing salty sea chanteys. Usually the cruise director or a **lecturer** who comes with a group will talk about the history of the ship and the glory days of sailing.

Service

Service is professional and friendly, and some of the crew have been with the *Sea Cloud* for years and consider it to be a second home. The crew hails mostly from Europe.

Sea Cloud

The Verdict

The *Sea Cloud* is a one-of-a-kind, cared-for historic treasure offering an intimate sailing experience as part of an extended family of passengers who "own" the ship for a week.

Sea Cloud (photo: Sea Cloud Cruises)

Specifications

Size (in tons)	2,532	Officers	American/Polish/ European
Number of Cabins	34		
Number of Outside Cabins	34	Crew (mostly European)	60
Cabins with Verandas	None	Passenger/Crew Ratio	1.15 to 1
Number of Passengers	69	Year Built	1931
		Last Major Refurbishment	1993

Frommer's Ratings (Scale of 1–5)

Cabin Comfort & Amenities	5	Pool, Fitness & Spa Facilities	N/A
Ship Cleanliness & Maintenance	4	Children's Facilities	N/A
Public Comfort/Space	5	Itineraries	4
Decor	5	Worth the Money	5

The *Sea Cloud* is all about history: Marjorie Merriweather Post and E. F. Hutton, the first owners; the guests who came aboard, such as the Duke and Duchess of Windsor; a wartime career as the navy's first integrated ship; a floating embassy moored in Leningrad's harbor by Mr. Joseph Harris, Marjorie's third husband; ownership by Santo Domingo's dictator Rafael Trujillo; and abandonment and then rebirth as the cruise ship we see today. The varnished wood, shiny brass, organized tangle of lines, multiplicity of sails, and ship's beautiful lines cannot fail to impress.

Cabins & Rates

Cabins	Per diems from	Bathtub	Fridge	Hair Dryer	Sitting Area	TV
Outside	$486*	no	no	yes	some	no
Suite	$1,191*	yes	no	yes	yes	no

**Rates include port charges; complimentary wines, beer, and soft drinks at meals; skeet shooting; and sports facilities.*

CABINS There are eight original cabins and 26 added when the ship was converted from a yacht to a cruise vessel in 1979. Marjorie's Suite (No.1) is fitted with a blue canopied bed in antique white with gold leaf ornamentation, Louis Phillippe chairs, a marble fireplace with an elaborate mantel, a plaster ceiling, and a grand Carrara marble bathroom with swan-shaped gold faucets. E. F. Hutton's Suite (No.2) is dark paneled with deep red furnishings and a large mahogany secretary and high-backed chairs. French country fabrics decorate the twin beds in daughter Dina Merrill's room. The cabins added in 1979 are nautically styled with wood paneling, brass fittings, and marble bathrooms with shower. All cabins have telephone, safe, hair dryer, music channel, and bathrobes. The original cabins have portholes and the added cabins have windows.

PUBLIC AREAS The decor of the dining room and lounge is marked by dark paneling, oil paintings, and fireplaces. There are a library corner, VCR, tables for playing cards and board games, and a small souvenir and gift shop. The wide promenade runs fore and aft outside this pair of rooms, and on the deck above there's an awning-covered lounge with bar. There are wooden deck chairs and isolated outdoor areas for reading and communing with the sea.

POOL, FITNESS & SPA FACILITIES The *Sea Cloud* provides free use of the snorkeling, windsurfing, and waterskiing equipment. Zodiacs take passengers to beaches for snorkeling and swimming.

Special Expeditions (a.k.a. Lindblad Special Expeditions)

SHIPS IN EUROPE Caledonian Star

720 Fifth Ave., New York, NY 10019. ☎ **800/EXPEDITION.** Fax 212/265-3770. www.expeditions.com.

THE LINE IN A NUTSHELL Special Expeditions offers soft-adventure/educational cruises that transport passengers to places of natural beauty and compelling history away from the crowded tourist stops.

THE EXPERIENCE Company founder Sven Olof Lindblad, son of legendary expedition travel pioneer Lars Erik Lindblad, is a long-time advocate of environmentally responsible tourism, and Special Expeditions' crew and staff emphasize respect for the local ecosystem in their talks with cruise passengers. A Special Expeditions cruise is built around frequent excursions off the ship on Zodiac landing craft that enable passengers to get off almost anywhere at a moment's notice. Flexibility and spontaneity are keys to the experience as the route may be altered at any time to follow a pod of whales or school of dolphins. There are usually two or three excursions every day.

Camaraderie develops between passengers through participation in excursions and through sharing their experiences at lively recap sessions every evening before dinner. These sessions feature presentations by expert naturalists and historians who greatly enhance the cruise experience by sharing their knowledge of a particular region as well as acting as guides on shore excursions.

Pros

- **Great expedition feeling.** Innovative, flexible itineraries, outstanding lecturers/guides, casual dress policy, and a friendly, accommodating staff help make the *Caledonian Star* one of the top expedition vessels sailing today.
- **Excursions included.** While per diem rates are high, all shore excursions are included.
- **Few passengers.** Due to the small number of passengers, everyone can get on and off the Zodiacs with minimal waiting.

Cons

- **Small cabins.** While most passengers don't seem to mind their cramped quarters, the spartan, no-frills cabins are far from the most comfortable at sea.
- **Few onboard activities.** There is little to do in the evenings, as most passengers turn in after dinner to rest up for the next day's explorations.
- **Not good for passengers with disabilities.** There are no elevators, so passengers have to walk up and down stairs several times a day. The ship is not wheelchair accessible.

Frommer's Ratings: Special Expeditions

	Poor	Fair	Good	Excellent	Outstanding
Enjoyment Factor				✓	
Dining			✓		
Activities				✓	
Children's Program	N/A				
Entertainment	N/A				
Service			✓		
Overall Value				✓	

Special Expeditions Fleet Itineraries

Ship	Home Ports & Season	Itinerary
Caledonian Star	14-day British Isles, between Leith, Scotland, and Dover (June); 16-day France and Spain, between Lisbon and Dover (May, Aug); 19-day North Cape, between Leith and Oslo (July, Aug); 11-day Norway, Oslo (July); 15-day W. Med, between Lisbon and Valletta, Malta (Sept, Oct); 16-day E. Med, between Valletta and Izmir, Turkey (Sept).	**14-day British Isles:** Fair Isle, Orkney Islands, Ullapool, Outer Hebrides, Isle of Skye, Isle of Rum, Iona, Staffa, Isle of Scilly, Dartmouth (UK), and Donegal, Aran Islands, Skellig Islands (Ireland). **16-day France and Spain:** Leixoes (Portugal), Islas Cies, Santiago de Compostela, and the Contabrian Coast (Spain), St-Jean-de-Luz, Bordeaux, Ile d'Aix, La Rochelle, Belle-Ile, Britanny, St-Malo (France), Sark, Alderney, Dartmouth (UK). **19-day North Cape*:** Orkney Islands, Fair Isle, Mousa Island, and Shetland Islands (UK), and Geirangerfjord, Rost, Lofoten Islands, Tromso, Fugloya, Bear Island, Spitsbergen, Longyearbyen (Norway). **11-day Norway*:** Longyearbyen and Spitsbergen, plus several days exploring the fjords (Norway). **15-day W. Med*:** Portimao (Portugal), Granada and Menorca (Spain), Sardinia, Trapani, Erice (Italy), Corsica (France), Gozo (Malta), and Gibraltar. **16-day E. Med*:** Lipari, Siracusa, Taormina (Italy), Olympia, Delphi, Skiros, Delos, Santorini (Greece), and Simena and Bodrum (Turkey).

*Includes overnight at a hotel.

SPECIAL EXPEDITIONS: EDUCATIONAL ADVENTURE

In 1984, Sven-Olof Lindblad, son of adventure-travel pioneer Lars-Eric Lindblad, followed in his father's footsteps by forming Special Expeditions, a company that specializes in environmentally sensitive, soft-adventure vacations to remote places in the world. The trips are explorative and informal in nature, designed to appeal to the intellectually curious traveler seeking a vacation that's educational as well as relaxing. Days aboard are spent learning about the outdoors from high-caliber expedition leaders trained in botany, anthropology, biology, and geology, and observing the world around you either from the ship or on shore excursions, which are included in the cruise package.

THE FLEET

The largest ship in the Special Expeditions fleet, the 110-passenger ***Caledonian Star,*** is a former North Sea trawler that was completely rebuilt for expedition cruising in 1990. It is the only Special Expeditions ship with stabilizers. In 1998, its cabins and public areas were treated to a $3 million renovation. The *Swedish Islander,* Special Expeditions' smallest capacity vessel, also sails European itineraries, carrying a maximum of 49 passengers.

PASSENGER PROFILE

Special Expeditions tends to attract well traveled and well-educated professional couples 55+ who have "been there, done that" and are looking for something completely different in a cruise experience. The passenger mix may also include some singles, a few honeymooners, and a smattering of younger couples. There is often a substantial contingent of British passengers on European itineraries. While not necessarily frequent cruisers, many passengers are likely to have been on other Special Expeditions programs (land and/or cruise). They tend to share common interest in wildlife (whale watching, bird watching) and are also intellectually curious about the culture and history of the regions they're visiting.

A Special Expeditions cruise will not appeal to couch potatoes and other sedentary types expecting a big ship lineup of fun and games.

Dining

Hearty buffet breakfasts and lunches and sit-down dinners feature a good choice of both hot and cold dishes with plenty of fresh fruits and vegetables. Many of the fresh ingredients are obtained from ports along the way, and meals may reflect regional tastes. Another plus is the selection of freshly baked breads, pastries, and cakes.

While far from haute cuisine, dinners are well prepared and presented; varied menus feature primarily continental cuisine with a choice of fish and meat entrees. All meals are served at single open seatings that allow passengers to get to know each other by moving around to different tables. Lecturers and other staff members also dine with passengers.

Activities

During the day most activity takes place off the ship on either Zodiac and/or land excursions. While on board, passengers entertain themselves with a good book or a game of bridge, Scrabble, or Trivial Pursuit (the ships carry a good selection of board games).

Children's Program

There are no organized programs, as there are few children aboard.

Entertainment

Lectures and slide presentations are scheduled throughout the cruise and documentaries or movies may be screened in the evening in the main lounge. Extensive reading material is available in each ship's well-stocked library.

Service

Dining room staff and room stewards are affable and efficient and seem to enjoy their work. Tips (recommended $7 per person per day) are pooled and divided among the staff.

There's no room service unless you are ill and unable to make it to the dining room.

Caledonian Star

Caledonian Star (photo: Lindblad Special Exp.)

The Verdict

Well-run expedition ship with terrific staff and unique itineraries provides one of the richest overall cruise experiences available today.

Specifications

Size (in tons)	3,132	Officers	Scandinavian
Number of Cabins	62	Crew	International
Number of Outside Cabins	62	Passenger/Crew Ratio	2 to 1
Cabins with Verandas	0	Year Built	1966 (rebuilt 1990)
Number of Passengers	110	Last Major Renovation	1998

Frommer's Ratings (Scale of 1–5)

Cabin Comfort & Amenities	3	Pool, Fitness & Spa Facilities	2
Ship Cleanliness & Maintenance	3	Children's Facilities	N/A
Public Comfort/Space	3	Itineraries	5
Decor	2	Worth the Money	4

While far from a luxury liner, the *Caledonian Star* is a solid, sturdy, fully stabilized vessel with a long track record of success as a pacesetter in expedition cruising. After a recent renovation which included reinforcing the hull, the *Star* is more shipshape than ever before as it sails year-round on an ambitious schedule of itineraries from the North Cape of Norway to the British Isles and the Mediterranean (Europe) to the fjords of Chile and the white continent of Antarctica.

Cabins & Rates

Cabins	Per diems from	Bathtub	Fridge	Hair Dryer	Sitting Area	TV
Outside	$435*	no	no	yes	no	no
Suites	$762*	no	yes	yes	yes	yes

**Rates include all shore excursions.*

CABINS All cabins are outside and located above the waterline with a total of 46 double cabins, 14 single cabins, and two suites. There are five price categories ranging from Category 1 cabins on the lower deck to two suites on the upper deck. Cabins in categories 1 to 4 are simply furnished with two lower beds, a writing desk with chair, toilet/shower, and either a porthole or windows for outside lighting. Single cabins have one lower bed. The suites are the only accommodations with separate sitting and sleeping areas and large view windows.

Pack judiciously as there is minimal storage space except in the two suites.

PUBLIC AREAS The two largest public spaces are the main lounge/bar and the spacious dining room. There are also a small swimming pool and fitness room plus a library, gift shop, hair salon, laundry, and small medical facility with full-time doctor. The navigation bridge is open to passengers.

POOL, FITNESS & SPA FACILITIES There are no spa facilities and only a tiny, postage-stamp-size pool and small exercise room.

Star Clippers

SHIPS IN EUROPE Star Clipper • Star Flyer • Royal Clipper (preview)

4101 Salzedo Ave., Coral Gables, FL 33146. ☎ **800/442-0553** or 305/442-0550. Fax 305/442-1611. www.star-clippers.com.

THE LINE IN A NUTSHELL With the sails and rigging of classic clipper ships and some of the cushy amenities of modern megas, a cruise on this line's 170-passenger ships offers adventure with comfort.

THE EXPERIENCE On Star Clippers, you'll have the best of two worlds. On one hand, these cruises espouse an unstructured, let-your-hair-down, hands-on ethic—you can climb the masts (with a harness, of course), pull in the sails, crawl into the bow netting, or chat with the captain on the bridge. On the other hand, the ship offers comfortable, almost cushy, public rooms and cabins.

On board, ducking under booms, stepping over coils of rope, leaning against railings just feet above the sea, and watching sailors work the winches or climb the masts and the captain and his mates navigate from the open-air bridge, are constant reminders that you're on a real working ship. Furthermore, listening to the captain's daily talk about the next port of call, the history of sailing, or some other nautical subject from his forward perch on the Sun Deck, you'll feel like you're exploring Europe's seas and ports in a ship that belongs there. In today's world of look-alike megaships, the *Star Clipper* and *Star Flyer* stand out, recalling a romantic, swashbuckling era of ship travel.

Pros

- **Hands-on experience.** While you don't have to do a darned thing if you don't want to, you're free to help pull in the sails or even climb the masts.
- **Comfortable amenities.** A pair of pools, a piano bar and deck bar, a bright and pleasant dining room serving tasty food, and a clubby, wood-paneled library balance out the adventurous spirit.
- **Rich in atmosphere.** On these wood-bound clipper ships, it's a real treat to just wallow in the ambiance.
- **Off-beat itineraries.** In concert with popular, must-see ports, the ships visit more offbeat places like Giglio, Italy, and Patmos, Greece.

Cons

- **Rolling.** Even though the ships have stabilizers and ballast tanks to reduce rolling, you'll feel the motion if you run into rough seas, as is the case with any small ship.
- **No fitness equipment.** Like most ships of this kind and size, if you like to work out, you're out of luck. You'll have to do your exercising in port.

Frommer's Ratings: Star Clippers

	Poor	Fair	Good	Excellent	Outstanding
Enjoyment Factor					✓
Dining					✓
Activities				✓	
Children's Program	N/A				
Entertainment					✓
Service					✓
Overall Value					✓

STAR CLIPPERS: COMFORTABLE ADVENTURE

Clipper ships—full-sailed, built for speed, and undeniably romantic—reigned for only a brief time on the high seas before being driven out by steam-driven engines, iron and then steel hulls, and the philosophy that bigger is better. During their heyday, however, these vessels engendered more romantic sea myths than any before or since. They helped open the Pacific Coast of California during the Gold Rush of 1849, carrying much-needed supplies around the tip of South America from Boston and New York. Even after the opening of the Suez Canal in 1869, names like *Cutty Sark, Ariel,* and *Flying Cloud* remained prestigious, and no sailing ship has ever surpassed the record of *Sea Witch,* a vessel that once sailed from Canton, China, to New York in 74 days.

By the early 1990s, despite the nostalgia and sense of reverence that had surrounded every aspect of the clippers' maritime history, nothing that could be technically classified as a clipper ship had been built since the *Cutty Sark* in 1869. In fact, their return to the high seas as viable commercial ventures could only have been realized by a nautical visionary with a passion for ship design and almost unlimited funds. The right combination of these factors emerged in Mikael Krafft, a Swedish-born industrialist and real-estate developer who invested vast amounts of personal energy and more than $80 million in the construction of two modern-day clippers at a Belgian shipyard in 1990 and 1991.

Before this venture, Krafft had sailed a series of high-tech yachts, including a particularly spectacular version 128 feet long. To construct his clippers, he procured the original drawings and specifications of Scottish-born Donald McKay (a leading naval architect of 19th-century clipper-ship technology) and employed his own team of naval architects to solve such engineering problems as adapting the square-rigged, four-masted clipper design to modern materials and construction.

In its short history, the line's *Star Flyer* has assembled quite a list of firsts: the first commercial sail-driven vessel to cross the Atlantic in 90 years; the first ship ever to pass full U.S. Coast Guard certification and safety exams on the first try; and one of the only ships to ever enter the Port of Miami under full sail—a daunting feat, considering the motorized traffic barreling through on all sides. Also impressive is the fact that both the *Star Clipper* and *Star Flyer* received the highest rating available by Lloyd's Register—the "+100 A-1-a" rating, which hadn't been awarded to a sailing vessel since 1911. On Star Clippers, you'll be sailing aboard vessels where safety and nautical logistics are more visible and more all-encompassing than aboard most other lines, whose operations are kept safely hidden away.

How do their prices and amenities compare to Windstar Cruises, another company that runs original (if modernized) sailing ships? In a nutshell, Star Clippers is less formal and less expensive than Windstar, and its onboard atmosphere is quite casual. During the day, shorts with polo shirts and topsiders are standard issue, and for dinner many passengers simply change into cleaner and better-pressed versions of the same, with perhaps a change from shorts to slacks for most men. Overall, the experience is salty enough to make you feel like a fisherman keeling off the coast of Maine, without the physical hardship of actually being one.

THE FLEET

The ***Star Clipper,*** built in 1992, spends its summers in the French and Italian Rivieras and winters in the Caribbean, and the ***Star Flyer,*** built in 1991, operates in the Aegean summers and the Far East during the winter. The twin vessels are at once traditional and radical. They're the tallest and among the fastest clipper ships ever built, and with dimensions about 100 feet longer than the average 19th-century clipper, they're so beautiful that even at full stop they seem to soar.

Part of the ships' success derives from a skillful blend of traditional aesthetics and newfangled materials and technology. The configuration of the vessels' sails is not quite traditional, having been adapted to include a higher percentage of triangular sails and fewer of the square-rigged sails usually associated with clippers. Also, sails are made of lightweight Dacron rather than canvas, which rots easily and is so heavy that the amount of sail each of Krafft's ships flies (36,000 square feet) would probably have capsized an original clipper. Further innovations include masts crafted from steel and aluminum alloys instead of tree trunks and a network of electric winches that eliminates the back-breaking labor historically involved in the sails' raising and lowering. Fewer than 10 deckhands can manipulate the ships' sails, as contrasted to the 40 to 55 that were needed to control and maintain sails aboard the 19th-century ships. Concessions to modern design include a bow thruster and a single propeller that's used to navigate in and out of tricky harbors or during dead calms. When used together, they can spin each craft around on a very tight axis. Star Clippers almost never use their bow thrusters for such basic tasks as coming about into the wind—both crew and ships are simply too proud for that.

One of the great challenges owner Mikael Krafft and his designers faced was taking a type of ship originally intended to haul tea, wool, and opium and adapting it to carry vacationing passengers. The new clippers needed the amenities of a private yacht and also the space—both for provisions and passenger comfort. I'm happy to report that they got it right.

As opposed to the *Club Med 1,* a bulkier cruise ship that just happens to be outfitted with sails, Star Clipper's ships look like they should sail under wind power, and generally rely on sails for about 25% to 35% of their propulsion, and on engines for the rest. Still, whether engines are running or not, sails are up nearly the entire trip, creating a beautiful effect.

Each ship performs superlatively, and can reach a speed of 17 knots. During the *Star Clipper's* maiden sail in 1992 off the coast of Corsica, it sustained speeds of 19.4 knots, thrilling its owner and designers, who had predicted maximum speeds of 17 knots. During most cruises, however, the crew tries to keep passengers comfortable and decks relatively horizontal, and so the vessels are kept to speeds of 9 to 14 knots.

At press time, the line plans to launch its newest ship, the 228-passenger, five-masted, fully-rigged ***Royal Clipper,*** in April of 2000. At 439 feet in length, the ship will be one of the largest sailing ships ever built.

PASSENGER PROFILE

While you're likely to find a handful of late-20-something honeymoon-type couples, the majority of passengers are well-traveled couples in their late 40s to 60s, all active and intellectually curious professionals such as executives, lawyers, and doctors.

With only 170 passengers aboard, each cruise seems like a triumph of individuality and intimacy. The line's unusual niche appeals to passengers who might recoil at the lethargy and/or sometimes forced enthusiasm of cruises aboard larger, more typical vessels. About 20% of any passenger roster is composed of people who have never cruised before, perhaps for this very reason. On the flip side, according to a company spokesperson, 80% of passengers have cruised before on big ships, like Holland America or Princess, and appreciate a "premium" soft-adventure cruise like Star Clippers.

As the line has matured and increased both its stature and its prestige, many passengers have tended to be repeaters (overall, repeaters make up a whopping 60% of passengers, according to the company). About half are European, the remainder North American. All tend to be active, sports-conscious, and curious—and, as you might expect, many come from boating or yachting backgrounds. Many are devoted conservationists who appreciate a vessel that relies heavily on wind power rather than diesel fuel, and many have traveled extensively.

Mikael Krafft himself may even be on board, in many cases with his wife and children, traveling as a low-key, highly accessible guest.

DINING

Overall, food is good and presented well, with breakfast and lunch **buffets** being the best meals of the day. Star Clippers' cuisine has evolved and improved through the years as the line has poured more time and effort into it. In fact, in the spring of 1999, an executive chef was hired to enhance the overall quality of meals fleetwide, shifting from ship to ship to implement an enhanced menu. All meals are open seating and served in the restaurant at tables of four, six, and eight, and the dress code is always casual. Catering to European as well as North American clienteles, all buffets included a better-than-average selection of cheeses, like brie and smoked Gouda, several types of salad, cold cuts, and fish. At breakfast, in addition to a cold and hot buffet spread, there's an **omelet station** where a staff member will make your eggs the way you like them. Late afternoon snacks served at the Tropical Bar include items like tacos, spring rolls, or ice-cream sundaes with fresh coconut and pistachio toppings.

At dinner, four main entrees (seafood, meat, vegetarian, and a light dish), appetizers, and dessert courses are offered as well as a soup and salad. Choices include, for example, lobster and shrimp with rice pilaf, beef curry, and pasta dishes. Dinners are sometimes sit-down and sometimes buffet, and can be somewhat chaotic and rushed. When the ship is at full capacity, things can feel a bit frenetic (breakfast and lunch don't get as crowded as passengers tend to eat at staggered times). The booths along the sides, seating six, are awkward when couples who don't know each are forever getting up and down to let the others in and out (sources tell me the new *Royal Clipper* will avoid this layout). The dining room has mahogany trim and a series of thin steel columns that pierce the center of many of the dining tables. While from an engineering standpoint the columns were the best way to solve the structural problem inherent in such a large open space, they sometimes slightly block sight lines across the tables.

Waiters and bartenders are efficient and friendly, and dress in costume for several theme nights each week.

There's a worthwhile selection of **wines** on board, with a heavy emphasis on medium-priced French, German, and California selections. Coffee and tea are available from a 24-hour coffee station in the piano bar.

Room service is available only for guests who are sick and can't make it to the dining room.

ACTIVITIES

If you're looking for action, shopping, and dozens of organized tours, you won't find much on these ships and itineraries. For the most part, socializing among passengers and with the crew is the main activity (as it is on most any ship of this size). In fact, the friendliness starts the moment you board, with the captain and hotel director personally greeting passengers and inviting them to have a complimentary cocktail and some hors d'oeuvres.

You won't find the typical cruise ship onboard pastimes, and that's a big part of the line's allure. Many activities involve simply exploring these extraordinary ships. The captain gives **informal talks** on maritime themes, and at least once a day the cruise director speaks about the upcoming ports and shipboard events. Knot-tying might be the topic of the day, or you might get to participate in a man-overboard drill. Within reason, passengers can lend a hand with **deck-side duties,** observe the mechanics of

Star Clippers Fleet Itineraries

Ship	Home Ports & Season	Itinerary
Star Clipper	Round-trip from Cannes, France, May–Sept.	**7-day W. Med:** Port calls may include Costa Smeralda, Portoferraio, Porto Rotondo, Porto Cervo, Giglio, Portovenere, Portofino (Italy), St. Tropez (France) Calvi, Bonifacio, Ile Rousse, Ajaccio (Corsica), and Monte Carlo (Monaco).
Star Flyer	Round-trip from Piraeus/ Athens, May–Oct.	**7-day Greek Isles and Turkey:** Port calls may include Bodrum, Kusadasi, Cesme (Turkey), and Patmos, Delos/ Mykonos, Astipalaia, Santorini, Serifos (Greece).

navigation, and have a token try at handling the wheel or pulling in the ropes when circumstances and calm weather permit.

Each ship maintains an **open-bridge policy,** allowing passengers to wander up to the humble-looking navigation center at any hour of the day or night.

Other activities may include a brief engine-room tour and a **scuba lesson** in the pool, and **massages** are available too (a great deal at $28 an hour), doled out in a spare cabin or a small cabana on deck. Of course, sunbathing is a sport in and of itself, and crawling in the bowsprit netting to do so is a thrill and an effective way to try and spot sea creatures just feet below you.

Port activities are a big part of these cruises. Sailing from one port to another and tending to arrive sometime after 9am (but usually before around 11am and usually after a brisk early-morning sail), the ship anchors offshore and passengers are shuttled back and forth by tender (in certain cases, you may have to walk a few feet in shallow water between the tender and the beach).

Activities in port of course revolve around exploring the historic and romantic ports that cling to the Mediterranean's shores. And, wherever possible (usually more often in the Aegean than the French or Italian Rivieras), activities will also include beaches and watersports, which are all complimentary. **Snorkeling** equipment is issued at the beginning of the week for anyone who wants it, and for waterskiing and banana boat rides the young surfer-boy sports staff operates four Zodiacs that are carried on the ship. Being that everything is so laid-back, there are no sign-up sheets, so guests merely hang out and congregate by the gangway or on the beach until it's their turn.

Ships tend to depart from their ports of call early enough so they can be under full sail during sunset. Trust me on this one: Position yourself at the ship's rail or dawdle over a drink at the deck bar to watch the sun melt into the horizon behind the silhouette of the ships' masts and ropes. It's something you won't forget.

Children's Program

This is not a line for young children, and there are no supervised activities. That said, an experience aboard a sailing ship can be a wonderful educational and adventurous experience, especially for children at least 10.

No baby-sitting is available, unless a well-intentioned crew member agrees to volunteer his or her off-duty hours.

Entertainment

Some sort of featured entertainment takes place each night after dinner by the Tropical Bar, which is the main hub of activity. There's a **crew talent show** one night, and on others a trivia contest and a dance or music performance by **local entertainers** on

Port Charges Not Included

Port charges are about $145 per person in addition to the cruise rates for 7-day French and Italian Rivieras or Greek Isles and Turkey cruises with Star Clippers.

board for the night. A keyboard player is on hand to sing pop songs before and after dinner, and a pianist plays jazzy tunes in the Piano Bar each evening. Some nights, disco music is put on the sound system and the deck between the deck bar and library becomes a dance floor.

A couple of **movies** a day are available on cabin TVs, if you feel like vegging. Besides this, it's just you, the sea, and the conversation of your fellow passengers.

SERVICE

Service is congenial, low-key, unpretentious, cheerful, and reasonably attentive. Expect efficient but sometimes slightly distracted service in the cramped dining room, and realize that you'll have to fetch your own ice, bar drinks, and whatever else you might need during your time on deck.

The crew is international, hailing from places like Poland, Switzerland, Russia, Germany, Romania, Indonesia, and the Philippines, and their presence creates a wonderful international flavor on board. Crew members are friendly and indulgent and usually good-natured about clients who want to tie knots, raise and lower sails, and keep the deck shipshape. As English is not the mother language of some crew members, though, certain details might get lost in the translation.

Officers typically dine with guests at every meal, and if you'd like to have dinner with the captain, just go up to the bridge one day and ask him.

Star Clipper • Star Flyer

The Verdict

With the sails and rigging of classic clipper ships and the creature comforts of modern megas, cruises on the 170-passenger *Star Clipper* and *Star Flyer* offer the best of two worlds and a wonderful way to do explore the Mediterranean.

Star Clipper (photo: Star Clippers)

Specifications

Size (in tons)	2,298	Crew	70 (International)
Number of Cabins	84	Passenger/Crew Ratio	2.5 to 1
Number of Outside Cabins	78	Year Built	
Cabins with Verandas	0	*Star Clipper*	1992
Number of Passengers	172	*Star Flyer*	1991
Officers	Internat'l	Last Major Refurbishment	N/A

Frommer's Rating (Scale of 1–5)

Cabin Comfort & Amenities	3	Pool, Fitness & Spa Facilities	3
Ship Cleanliness & Maintenance	4	Children's Facilities	N/A
Public Comfort/Space	3	Itineraries	4
Decor	3	Worth the Money	5

Life aboard the *Star Clipper* and *Star Flyer* means life on deck. Since there are few other hideaways, that's where most passengers spend their days. Made from teakwood, these decks were planned with lots of passenger space, although much of it is somewhat cluttered with the winches, ropes, and other equipment of these working ships. There are lots of nooks and crannies on deck, and even with a full load the ship rarely feels overly crowded (except at dinner). More sail-trimming activity occurs amidships and near the bow, so if you're looking to avoid all bustle, take yourself off to the stern.

Cabins & Rates

Cabins	Per diems from	Bathtub	Fridge	Hair Dryer	Sitting Area	TV
Inside	$239*	no	no	yes	no	no
Outside	$267*	no	no	yes	no	yes
Suite	$299*	yes	yes	yes	no	yes

**Port charges at an extra $145 per person to the 7-day cruise price.*

CABINS Cabins feel roomy for ships of this size and were designed with a pleasant nautical motif—blue fabrics and carpeting, portholes, brass-toned lighting fixtures, and a dark wood trim framing the off-white furniture and walls. The majority of cabins are outside and measure from about 120 to 130 square feet. They have two twin beds that can be converted into doubles, a small desk/vanity with stool, and an upholstered seat fitted into the corner. Storage space is more than adequate for a 7-night casual cruise in a warm climate, with both a slim floor-to-ceiling closet and a double-width closet of shelves; there is also storage below the beds, desk, nightstand, and chair. Each cabin has a telephone, hair dryer, and safe, and all but the four smallest inside cabins (measuring a compact 95 square feet) have a color television showing news and a selection of popular movies.

Standard bathrooms are small but functional, with marble walls, a nice mirrored storage cabinet that actually stays closed, and a narrow shower divided from the rest of the bathroom by only the curtain (surprisingly, the rest of the bathroom stays dry when the shower is being used). The sink and shower are fitted with annoying push valves, which release water only when they're compressed. The only real difference between the cabins in categories two and three is about a square foot of space. The eight deluxe cabins measure about 150 square feet, open right out onto the main deck, and have minibars and whirlpool bathtubs. Because of their location near the Tropical Bar, though, noise can be a problem.

None of the units is a suite, except for one carefully guarded (and oddly configured) owner's suite in the aft of the Clipper Deck that's available to the public only when it's not being set aside for special purposes.

Take note: The ship's generator tends to drone on through the night; cabins near the stern on lower decks are the most susceptible to this.

No cabins were designed for wheelchair accessibility. These ships are not recommended for passengers with mobility problems.

PUBLIC AREAS The handful of public rooms include the dining room, a comfy piano bar, the outside Tropical Bar (sheltered from the sun and rain by a canopy), and a cozy, paneled library with a decorative, nonfunctioning fireplace and a good stock of coffee-table books, tracts on naval history and naval architecture, and a cross-section of general titles.

The roomy yet cozy piano bar has comfy banquette seating. That area and the outdoor Tropical Bar are the ship's hubs of activity.

Preview: Star Clippers' *Royal Clipper*

Clipper's biggest and plushest ship is on the way. The fully-rigged, 439-foot, 228-passenger *Royal Clipper* will be launched in April 2000 (not in fall of 1999 as originally planned) and be one of the biggest sailing ships ever built, with five masts flying 42 sails that together stretch to 56,000 square feet. It will be able to hit 13 knots under engine power and 20 knots under sail power only. Size and power aside, the ship will also be extremely well-accoutered, with a windowed disco, a three-story glass atrium, a two-deck restaurant, 14 suites with private deck patios, a retractable watersports platform, three pools, and a massage and fitness center. In the winter, the ship will do alternating 7-night Caribbean cruises round-trip from Barbados, and in summers will sail 7-night alternating Mediterranean cruises.

Throughout, the interior decor is pleasant but unmemorable, mostly white with touches of brass and mahogany or teakwood trim—not as upscale-looking as vessels operated by Windstar, but cozy, appealing, well designed, and shipshape.

POOL, FITNESS & SPA FACILITIES Each ship has two small pools, meant more for dipping than swimming, one with glass portholes peering from its depths into the piano bar (and vice versa). The pool near the stern tends to be more languid, the favorite of sunbathers, whereas the one at amidships is more active, with more noise and splashing and central to the action. At both, the ship's billowing and moving sails might occasionally block the sun's rays, although this happens amidships much more frequently than it does at the stern.

While there's no gym of any sort, aerobics and stretch classes are frequently held on deck between the library and Tropical Bar. Partly because Mikael Krafft is an avid scuba diver and partly because itineraries try to focus on waters that teem with marine life, each ship offers (for an extra charge) the option of PADI-approved scuba diving. There are more scuba and snorkeling opportunities in the Aegean on the *Star Flyer* than there are in the French and Italian Rivieras on the *Clipper.* Certified divers will find all the equipment they'll need on board. Even uncertified/inexperienced divers can pay a token fee for training that will grant them resort certification and allow them to make a number of relatively simple dives. There's also snorkeling (complimentary equipment is distributed at the start of the cruise), waterskiing, windsurfing, and banana boat rides offered by the ship's watersports team in all ports (the ships carry along Zodiac motorboats for this purpose).

Zeus Tours and Yacht Cruises

SHIPS IN EUROPE Galileo Sun • Zeus II • Zeus III

551 5th Ave., Ste. 1001, New York, NY 10176. ☎ **800/447-5667** or 212/221-0006. Fax 212/764-7912. www.zeustours.com.

THE LINE IN A NUTSHELL These casual cruises let you get more than your feet wet in Greece. You'll see the country, make new friends, and have a good time doing it.

THE EXPERIENCE These ships all offer Greece in a casual manner: no formal nights, no need to pack a tie. The pricing is attractive (though the *Galileo Sun* and *Harmony G,* which are the more upmarket of the ships, are priced higher than the *Zeus* ships) and cruises can be paired with a 3-night hotel stay in Athens. (You get a better deal if you take both the cruise and hotel package.) Itineraries visits small, out-of-the-way ports in addition to popular favorites like Mykonos and Santorini, with the ships sailing only late at night or in the morning, allowing you plenty of time in port to explore, shop, taste the local cuisine, and even enjoy the nightlife. In some cases, the vessels overnight in the ports. On board, the ambiance is very laid-back, with no set regime or activities schedule.

A few caveats, though. Since you're on a small ship, the time in port is somewhat dictated by the weather, which is nearly always sunny from May to October, but can get quite windy (particularly in August). This can lead both to missing a port or two and to choppy seas (if you can't handle some pitch and toss, don't book these ships). If winds do hit, dinner may be rushed so the crew can tie everything down, and you may be urged to go to bed early.

The ships attract an international passenger mix, with many English-speaking guests. Generally, you'll find half Americans and half Europeans (including Brits), plus a handful of Australians. Most tend to be adventuresome types, and run the age range from the 20s to the 70s.

Pros

- **Offers Greece up-close and personal.** You get plenty of time in port and get to visit out-of-the-way ports as well as popular favorites.
- **Very casual ambiance.** You don't have to pack a tie.

Cons

- **Tight quarters.** There's very little public space and cabins are small (especially on the *Zeus* ships).
- **Few organized activities.** No one will plan out your fun for you here.
- **The sails.** They are there on several of the ships, but are rarely, if ever, used.

Frommer's Ratings: Zeus Tours and Yacht Cruises

	Poor	Fair	Good	Excellent	Outstanding
Enjoyment Factor				✓	
Dining			✓		
Activities		✓			
Children's Program	N/A				
Entertainment	N/A				
Service		✓			
Overall Value			✓		

Zeus Fleet Itineraries

Ship	Home Ports & Season	Itinerary
Galileo Sun	7-day Greek Isles, round-trip from Piraeus/Athens (Apr–Oct).	**7-day Greek Isles:** Sounion, Santorini, Rhodes, Astypalea, Paros, Delos, and Mykonos (Greece).
Zeus II and III	7-day Greek Isles 1 round-trip from Rhodes (Apr–Oct); 7-day Greek Isles 2 round-trip from Piraeus/Athens (Mar–Oct); 7-day Greek Isles 3 round-trip from Corfu (May–Sept)	**7-day Greek Isles 1:** Kalymnos, Kos, Patmos, Lipsi, Leros, and Simi (Greece). **7-day Greek Isles 2:** Naxos, Santorini, Ios, Paros, Delos, Mykonos, Tinos, Kea, and Sounion (Greece). **7-day Greek Isles 3:** Parga, Paxi, Lefkas, Kefalonia, Zakynthos, and Ithaki (Greece).

ZEUS TOURS: CASUAL GREECE

This 52-year old firm, one of the oldest tour operators in Greece, has its own fleet of motorized and sailing yachts known as Zeus Cruises, and represents the sailing yachts *Galileo Sun* and brand new *Harmony G.* Beyond Greece, the company also offers tours in Italy, Egypt, Israel, Turkey, and South America.

Zeus is also among U.S. tour operators representing **Golden Sun/Dolphin Hella**'s ships (which are mostly sold through tour operators), including the *Aegean I* (built in 1973; 570 passengers, 13,000 GRTs) and *Arcadia* (built in 1968; 278 passengers; 5,200 GRTs), both older budget ships with numerous public rooms and a casual ambiance. They do 3-, 4- and 7-day cruises round-trip from Athens, March to November, with per diem rates from $89 for an inside cabin and $122 for an outside (there are no suites on these ships). Also new to the Golden Sun fleet is Mediterranean Shipping Cruises' *Symphony,* which Golden Sun is leasing on a long-term basis. The 17,900-ton ship, built in 1950 as Costa Cruises' *EnricoCosta,* operates for Golden Sun as the *Aegean Spirit,* also on 3-, 4- and 7-day itineraries around the Greek Isles.

Zeus also handles packages including cruises on **Royal Olympic** and **Star Clippers** ships, Mediterranean diving cruises with Atlantis Diving, sightseeing excursions, and private yacht charters.

Zeus was acquired last year by Miami-based Far & Wide Travel Corp, a leading South and Central America operator.

THE FLEET

Zeus II and ***III*** look different from the outside (*Zeus III* has sails, which are rarely used, while *Zeus II* does not), but all have the same basic configuration and amenities. All were built in 1995. The ***Galileo Sun*** also has sails, but they are rarely used. The *Harmony G,* a more deluxe vessel than the *Galileo Sun,* is being chartered by Zeus this year and marketed under the line name Harmony Cruises. The 498-ton yacht accommodates 50 passengers in 22 cabins.

PASSENGER PROFILE

The ships attract passengers from around the world, a good number of whom are English speaking and most of whom tend to be the adventuresome type. On any given sailing there will be about half Americans and half Europeans (including Brits), as well as a handful of Australians. The age range runs from young honeymooners up to people in their 70s. These ships are not appropriate for families with young children. The ships are available full charter.

Dining

Dining is at long, family-style tables, and food is served either in buffet form or in individual servings. The tasty cuisine is Greek/international and includes lamb, beef, fish, and vegetable dishes, cheese, and fresh fruit.

Unlike other lines, Zeus offers only two meals a day—a buffet breakfast and either lunch or dinner—a system designed to encourage passengers to try local cuisine on the islands. There are a Captain's Dinner, a beach barbecue (weather permitting), and **Greek night** on every sailing.

Wine and ouzo are complimentary on all the ships. Other bar drinks are available for a charge.

On the *Galileo Sun,* fresh fruit and sweets are always available.

Activities

Each ship has an English-speaking cruise director who offers briefings on each island and sometimes accompanies shore excursions. There is a Jacuzzi on the *Galileo,* but no other recreational facilities on the ships. Snorkeling and other watersports equipment are available.

Children's Program

There is no children's program at all.

Entertainment

You will have a chance, during Greek night, to dance like Zorba, but don't expect anything even near professional. The crew tries to sing, and the experience can be painful.

Service

The friendly Greek crew on these ships adds much to the ambiance, and nothing is too much to ask. Each ship has an English-speaking cruise director.

The recommended tip for the crew is 5% of your cruise fare, which you give to the captain, who divvies it up later.

Galileo Sun

The Verdict

This sailing yacht offers an experience its owners describe as deluxe, though it's really just comfortable.

Galileo Sun (photo: Zeus)

Specifications

Size (in tons)	N/A*	Officers	Greek
Number of Cabins	18	Crew	11 (Greek)
Number of Outside Cabins	18	Passenger/Crew Ratio	3.3 to 1
Cabins with Verandas	0	Year Built	1994
Number of Passengers	36	Last Major Refurbishment	N/A

*Size not available.

Frommer's Ratings (Scale of 1–5)

Cabin Comfort & Amenities	3	Pool, Fitness & Spa Facilities	2
Ship Cleanliness & Maintenance	4	Children's Facilities	N/A
Public Comfort/Space	4	Itineraries	4
Decor	4	Worth the Money	5

This pretty and comfortable yacht offers casual cruises that are pleasant if not very upscale (it's no *Sea Cloud* or Windstar). The ship is well-suited to the Greek Isles, which are laid-back.

Cabins & Rates

Cabins	Per diems from	Bathtub	Fridge	Hair Dryer	Sitting Area	TV
Outside	$252*	no	no	no	no	no

**Port charges are an additional $80 per week.*

CABINS The 18 cabins come in three categories, and all have windows or portholes, lower beds (either twin or double), decent-sized showers, and phones. Some of the upper-category cabins have a sofa bed. Some cabins can handle three or four passengers. Storage space is minimal.

PUBLIC AREAS The wood-paneled dining room/bar/lounge area is good-sized and nicely decorated. There is plenty of open and covered lounging space on the deck and a deck chair for everyone on board, plus a library area with a good collection of travel books and maps.

POOL, FITNESS & SPA FACILITIES There's a Jacuzzi but no swimming pool or other recreational facilities.

Zeus II • Zeus III

The Verdict

These ships offer a very casual cruise experience. Some people may find it *too* casual, but its dedicated passengers love it.

Zeus II (photo: Zeus)

Specifications

Size (in tons)		Cabins with Verandas	0
Zeus II	N/A*	Number of Passengers	
Zeus III	N/A*	*Zeus II*	34
Number of Cabins		*Zeus III*	42
Zeus II	17	Officers	Greek
Zeus III	21	Crew	7 to 10 (Greek)
Number of Outside Cabins		Passenger/Crew Ratio	3 to 1
Zeus II	17	Year Built	1995
Zeus III	21	Last Major Refurbishment	N/A

*Sizes not available. Suffice to say, they're small.

Frommer's Ratings (Scale of 1–5)

Cabin Comfort & Amenities	2	Pool, Fitness & Spa Facilities	N/A
Ship Cleanliness & Maintenance	3	Children's Facilities	N/A
Public Comfort/Space	2	Itineraries	5
Decor	2	Worth the Money	5

Zeus III is a sailing yacht, but the sails are not often up. *Zeus II* is a motorized yacht. When you book a cruise on these vessels, the company decides which one to put you on.

The yachts are all pretty much the same inside: very basic. The experience is described as "casual," but in this case that means fairly spartan. That said, you don't come on these ships to spend a lot of time on board. Rather, you come to see and experience the Greek Isles, something the vessels give you in spades. And the price is certainly right.

Cabins & Rates

Cabins	Per diems from	Bathtub	Fridge	Hair Dryer	Sitting Area	TV
Outside	$155*	no	no	no	no	no

**Port charges are an additional $30 per week.*

CABINS All cabins are outside, and are clean, white, and very basic. They come with a private shower and closet. Bathrooms are small. The upper category cabins have picture windows. Some of the lower category cabins have upper and lower bunks.

PUBLIC AREAS The only public room is a dining room/bar/lounge, and the deck space is rather narrow. The decor is unimaginative—walls are painted white, for instance.

POOL, FITNESS & SPA FACILITIES None, though in port you can swim in the ocean.

10 River Cruises

Cruising on Europe's rivers, canals, and lakes affords a pleasant alternative to inland bus tours or car treks and allows you to see a good deal of each country you visit. Whether aboard **river ships** or small converted commercial **barges,** the pace is leisurely, the ambiance generally informal and, just like on an oceangoing cruise ship, you only have to unpack once and meals and accommodations (and sometimes shore excursions) are included in the cruise fare. Also a river cruise is perfect for those worried about getting seasick on an oceangoing vessel, as the waters are calm.

RIVER SHIPS

River ships are popular in Europe, especially with European travelers, although increasing numbers of Americans are discovering their virtues as well, leading the ship companies to add more English-speaking crew members (if you are cruising in Russia, it's a good rule of thumb to make sure the hotel and food service is also overseen by a non-Russian firm), plus amenities like suites and even some cabins with balconies.

On these long, low (usually no more than three or four decks) vessels, you and 100 to 250 fellow passengers will comfortably enjoy the passing scenery from a famous waterway like the Danube, Seine, or Rhine, visiting ports such as Budapest, Hungary; Vienna, Austria; and beautiful venues like Speyer and Koblenz, Germany. The vessels may cruise during the day or night, and some spend the night in key cities so you can get off and enjoy the local nightlife.

These floating hotels typically offer comfortable (though small) **cabins,** usually with a window. On the newer ships, the cabins have TVs and minibars. **Cuisine** is hearty and in some cases gourmet, as aboard the Peter Deilmann ships and KD River Cruises' *Deutschland* and *Britannia.* **Public rooms** are limited, since these are small vessels, but they will include a nice lounge and dining room, and some ships have a separate bar, large viewing decks, and sometimes small splash pools, spas, and gyms. Light entertainment may be provided by a piano player or cabaret singer or trio.

Most passengers on these ships will be adults, ages 55 and up. Itineraries range from 2 nights to more than 2 weeks. The season is March to November. Some lines also offer pre- and post-cruise land options. The rates for some are under $100 per day, making them an affordable way to visit several countries on one trip.

The Danube: A Caution

During the 1999 conflict in Kosovo, NATO planes destroyed three bridges over the Danube. At press time the collapsed structures were still disrupting commerce from Austria to Romania, including river cruises. The timetable for reopening the route was unclear as the European Union and the Yugoslav government had yet to agree on a method of clearing the rubble.

BARGES

Barges are tiny vessels, many carrying fewer than 12 passengers, and are pretty much the floating equivalent of a stay at a New England B&B—even to the extent that some barges are crewed by the families that own them. Americans are drawn to these products in particular because they're one of the most relaxing and pampered vacation experiences you can find. Intimate surroundings, gourmet food, and fine wine are what barge cruising is all about. Also, because the vessels are small, some people opt to rent the entire barge with a group of family and/or friends.

The barges move very slowly through the countryside—so slowly you can, if you choose, grab one of the bikes the barge will carry and pedal alongside. They move on historic canals that are navigated using a series of locks. When you stop at a town or city, you will be whisked away in a van for a private tour. The barges dock at night, allowing you additional opportunity to explore.

The passenger mix on board is all-important, as you'll get to know everyone very well during the course of a week, dining together, touring together, and relaxing together. **Meals** are a big part of the barge experience and are worth lingering over. Lunch and dinner will include complimentary wine, often from the region you are visiting.

Most barges have had an earlier life as supply vessels. Many are antiques and have been rebuilt to accommodate passengers. **Public rooms** typically include a dining room/lounge with a bar area, and the barges are configured to allow for a good amount of deck space. Some have tiny swimming pools and gyms. **Cabins** will be on the small side but comfortable, and some barges have larger suites available. Most cabins, but not all, have private bathrooms and windows or portholes.

Passengers will mostly be adults, although a few barges specialize in hosting families. A fun option for families are self-drive barges (see sidebar below). **Shore excursions** are usually included in the cruise fare, with the exception of the popular option of hot air ballooning, available for an extra charge.

Barges are most popular in France, but you can also cruise in Holland, Ireland, England, and elsewhere, as noted below. The season is spring to fall (reduced rates are offered in April and October/November), and most itineraries are 6-night.

BOOKING A RIVER CRUISE

Both river ships and barges are typically represented in the U.S. by **brokers** who market a number of different vessels (it's these companies I've included in this chapter). Sometimes the same vessel may be booked by several different companies. A few also operate their own vessels, as noted. All rates listed are the lowest available per diems (multiply them by the number of days covered on the itinerary), are per person, are based on double occupancy, and vary by itinerary. You can book through a travel agent, or contact the numbers listed.

Abercrombie & Kent. 1520 Kensington Rd., Oak Brook, IL 60523. ☎ **800/323-7308.** www.abercrombiekent.com.

Piloting Your Own Barge

The British **Crown Blue Line** is among a number of companies offering self-skippered barges. The easy-to-handle boats allow you the freedom to go where you want and eat where you want, with whoever you want. No previous boating experience is required. The barges, which accommodate two to 12 passengers, can be rented for as little as $71 per person, per day for a 1-week outing. You can book the product through Abercrombie & Kent, Le Boat, MaupinWaterways, and Premier Selections (see below).

Upscale tour operator A&K offers barge cruises on a fleet of 18 vessels in England, France, Belgium, and Holland, and on Continental Waterways' vessels *l'Abercrombie* and *Lafayette.* The company also offers the Crown Blue Line self-skippered product (see "Piloting Your Own Barge," above), plus Danube River cruises on ships including Sea Cloud's 90-passenger *River Cloud* and cruises through Russia aboard the 180-passenger *Viking Peterhof.* The barge cruises are 6-day, river cruises are 7-day. Per diem rates for both run from $331. Self-skippered cruises are 7-day, with per diems from $228.

B&V Waterways. 140 East 56th St., New York, NY 10022. ☎ **800/546-4777.** www.bvassociates.com.

B&V books cruises aboard over 25 privately owned barges sailing in Ireland, Holland, Belgium, England, and France (including Burgundy, Provence, the Armagnac, and the upper Loire and Loire Valley regions). Special theme cruises include golf, gardens, bicycling, wine, bird watching, and photography. Cruises are 6-day, with per diem rates from $248.

The Barge Lady. 101 West Grand Ave., Ste. 200, Chicago, IL 60610. ☎ **800/880-0071.** www.bargelady.com.

The Barge Lady represents more than 50 4- to 24-passenger barges, two 50-passenger barges, and four 90- to 207-passenger river ships (including *River Cloud*) that cruise throughout France (including from Paris), Belgium, Holland, Scotland, England, Ireland, Italy, and Austria. Cruises are 6-day, with per diem rates from $281.

Continental Waterways. c/o Abercrombie & Kent ☎ **800/323-7308;** B&V Waterways ☎ **800/546-477;** Barge Lady ☎ **800/880-0071;** or Premier Selections ☎ **800/234-4000.**

This firm, which is bookable through other companies mentioned in this chapter (as noted above) was co-founded by a British journalist working on a story in France for Reuters in 1966, and helped pioneer the concept of hotel barges on European waterways. Its dozen barges (including the *Abercrombie* and *Lafayette,* operated exclusively for Abercrombie & Kent) carry 20 to 51 passengers each. New this year is the 47-passenger *Chardonnay,* Europe's first all-suite river vessel, and *Princess Royale,* carrying 22 passengers.

Cruising areas include the Alsace, Burgundy, Champagne, Franche-Comte, Ile de France, and eastern and upper Loire. All cruises are 6 days, with per diem rates from $248.

Peter Deilmann EuropeAmerica Cruises. 1800 Diagonal Rd., Ste. 170, Alexandria, VA 22314. ☎ **800/348-8287.** www.deilmann-cruises.com.

This German firm, which also operates oceangoing vessels (see chapter 7), has eight deluxe riverships (the *Cezanne, Mozart, Danube Princess, Prussian Princess, Princess de Provence, Dresden, Konigstein,* and new *Katharina*) on the Danube, Rhine, Moselle, Seine and Elbe rivers, as well as on Belgian and Dutch canals. Each carries 58 to 148 passengers. The company markets extensively in the U.S., and about 50% of the passengers on Danube cruises (40% on the others) are American. Itineraries are 6 to 16 days, with per diem rates from $199.

Europe Cruise Line. 1010 University Ave., Ste. C201, San Diego, CA 92103. ☎ **800/290-2812.** www.europecruiseline.com.

The company's *Blue Danube I, II, and III* and *Rhine Princess* are 120- to 144-passenger river ships cruising the Danube and Rhine on itineraries that include cruises from Regensburg, Germany, to Budapest, Hungary, and from Basel, Switzerland, to Amsterdam, Holland. New in 2000 are tulip- and wine-themed cruises. All vessels have suites available. Itineraries are 4- to 14-days, with per diem rates from $156.

EuroCruises. 303 West 13th St., New York, NY 10014. ☎ **800/688-3876.** www.eurocruises.com.

EuroCruises represents the river ships *GI.A., Delphin Queen, Arlene, Rhine Princess, Viking Peterhof, Viking Normandie, Viking Arlene, Venezia, Viking Rhone,* and *Viking Bordeaux,* plus the vintage steamers *Diana, Wilhelm Tham,* and *Juno.* Carrying from 60 to 180 passengers, they operate throughout Europe, with cruises on the Danube, Rhine, Moselle, Seine, and Po rivers; on Dutch canals; on Russian waterways; and elsewhere. The *Delphin Queen,* a new, 196-passenger upscale catamaran, operates on the Danube, offering large (173 square feet) cabins with balconies on two of its three decks, and four cabins equipped for the physically challenged (rare on other river ships). Itineraries range from 3 to 12 days, but most are week-long. Per diem rates range upward from $105. EuroCruises also represents Fred. Olsen Cruise Lines (see chapter 7).

French Country Waterways. P.O. Box 2195, Duxbury, MA 02331. ☎ **800/222-1236.**

This firm owns and operates the luxury barges *Espirit, Horizon II, Liberte, Nenuphar,* and *Princess,* accommodating eight to 18 passengers. The company's seven mostly French itineraries include Burgundy, the Upper Loire Valley, the Champagne region, Alsace/Lorraine, plus Mosel River cruises in Germany. Cruises are 6-day, with per diem rates from $499.

Global Quest (formerly OdessAmerica). 170 Old Country Rd., Ste. 608, Mineola, NY 11501. ☎ **800/221-3254.** www.globalquesttravel.com.

Global Quest operates the 130- to 270-passenger river ships *Andropov, Lenin, Litvinov, Demjan Bedny, Lev Tolstoy, Novikov Priboy,* and *V. Glushkov* on the waterways of Russia, including cruises between Moscow and St. Petersburg. More unusual offerings include a cruise in Siberia down the Lena River to the Arctic Sea. The company also offers cruises on the Danube. Itineraries are from 11 to 14 days, with per diem rates from $85.

Intrav. 7711 Bonhomme Ave., St. Louis, MO 63105-1961. ☎ **800/456-8100.** www.INTRAV.com.

Intrav, parent company of Clipper Cruise Line (see chapter 9), also charters the 75- to 242-passenger river ships *Amadeus, Kirov, Switzerland II,* and *Eurostar,* and two large barges, the *Vincent Van Gogh* and *Chardonnay,* offering cruises on the Danube, Main, and Rhine as well as in Russia, Holland, France, and Switzerland. Intrav cruise directors and local experts in history and culture accompany the sailings. The *Switzerland II* sailings feature chefs from Clipper. Cruisetours (including a land stay), are 10- to 13-day, with per diem rates from $291.

KD River Cruises. 2500 Westchester Ave., Purchase, NY 10577. ☎ **800/346-6525** (east); 800/858-8587 (west); or 914/696-3600. www.rivercruises.com.

The German KD River Cruises is the oldest and largest river cruise line in Europe, having begun offering cruises on the Rhine in 1857. The company operates a dozen river ships—including the 102- to 192-passenger *Austria, Britannia, Clara Schumann, Deutschland, Heinrich Heie, Helvetia, Italia, Theodor Fontane,* and *Wilhelm Tell*—on the Rhine, Main, Danube, Moselle, Elbe, and Seine rivers in Germany, France, Switzerland, Hungary, Holland, Austria, and the Czech Republic. All cruises offer English-speaking crew members. Sister ships *Deutschland* and *Britannia* are the most luxurious in the fleet, offering gourmet food and elegant public rooms (although rather small cabins). Several of the ships (including the *Deutschland* and *Britannia*) have small pools. Sailings are 2 to 7 days, with most departures from Germany. Per diem rates are from $175.

Le Boat. 10 South Franklin Tpke., Ste. 204B, Ramsey, NJ 07446. ☎ **800/992-0291.** www.leboat.com.

Le Boat represents six self-drive barge companies, 32 independent barges, and Continental Waterways, operating in France, England, Ireland, Holland, Germany, Belgium, and Scotland from April to October, with some barges operating into December. All self-skippered trips are 7-day; crewed trips are 6-day. Per diem rates are from $281 per person for crewed barges and from $71 for self-skippered barges.

MaupinWaterways. 1421 Research Park Dr., Ste. 300, Lawrence, KS 66049. ☎ **800/255-4266.** www.maupintour.com.

Operated by tour operator Maupintour, this firm offers cruises on 32 barges and river ships carrying 6 to 150 passengers in France, England, Ireland, Holland, and Italy. Cruises are 6-day, with per diem rates from $316.

Premier Selections. 105 Calvert St., Harrison, NY 10528. ☎ **800/234-4000.** www.premierselections.com.

This firm represents more than 40 barges and two river ships in France, Belgium, Holland, Italy, England, Scotland, and Ireland. Cruises are 6-day, with per diem rates from $331.

Uniworld. 16000 Ventura Blvd., Encino, CA 91436. ☎ **800/733-7820.**

Uniworld is a California-based firm that offers 39 river cruise itineraries in Russia and other European destinations aboard the 75- to 140-passenger river ships *Amadeus II, River Queen, Swiss Pearl, Blue Danube, Prussian Princess, Rügen, Douro Princess, Arlène, Venezia, Princess de Provence, Viking Bordeaux, Mozart, Rhine Princess,* and *Normandie.* The company designs itineraries for American tastes, and the crew is English-speaking. Sailing areas include the Douro River in Portugal; the Po River in Italy; the Rhone, Saone, and Seine in France; assorted Dutch waterways; the Rhine and Moselle (Amsterdam to Basel); the Danube; and assorted waterways in Russia. A 14-day European Grand Cruise goes from Amsterdam to Vienna. Some cruises are packaged as cruisetours (including a hotel stay). The cruises range from 7 to 14 days, with per diem rates from $145.

Part 3

The Ports of Call

With information and advice on things you can see and do in 43 ports of call, whether on your own or as part of an organized tour.

11

The Port Experience: An Introduction

The ports are likely the reason you've chosen to cruise in Europe. Nearly all offer historical attractions, in some cases truly ancient historical attractions (it's amazing how young 1776 is in the scheme of things!). In addition, the ports offer cultural attractions, shopping opportunities, and, in many cases, beaches. And some of them allow you access to famous cities like London, Rome, Amsterdam, and Paris.

In the next two chapters I describe the ports in the Mediterranean and Northern Europe on a country-by-country basis. In each I've noted distances of attractions from the port as well as the availability of transportation to help you decide whether to take a shore excursion or tour on your own. Admission charges to attractions are in U.S. dollars so you can compare the rates with those offered by the cruise lines in their packaged tours.

For more detailed information on each port, consult the appropriate Frommer's guide, a listing of which appears at the back of this book.

1 Debarkation in Port

Generally, ships on European itineraries stop at a port a day, with some spending 1 day at sea (without stopping at a port). On longer cruises you will have more than 1 day at sea, during which the emphasis will be on smooth sailing and providing you with pretty views of the coastline while you relax and enjoy the onboard facilities.

Coming into port, ships generally arrive right after breakfast, allowing you the morning and afternoon to take a shore excursion (see below) or explore on your own. Your ship will either dock right at the pier or tie-up slightly offshore, in which case the ship will tender passengers ashore in small boats. In either case, there is a fair amount of time (sometimes as much as 2 hours) between when the ship stops and when you can actually get off. That's because local authorities have to board and clear the ship, a process that allows you to leave the vessel without going through Customs. Despite the logic of it, it can be frustrating to see a city laid out in front of you and have to wait to be told when you can step off the ship.

If you're on a large ship, the process may be further delayed because thousands of passengers will want to get off at the same time. In these cases, you may be assigned to a specific group and be requested to wait to leave the ship until your group is called. Those on shore excursions usually get to disembark first. Ship officials will keep you well-informed of the process.

Remember, whether on a shore excursion or touring on your own, to bring your **boarding pass** when you leave the ship, since you won't be able to get back aboard without it. Remember also to bring **money**—after a few days in the cashless atmosphere of a ship, it's remarkably easy to forget. Some ships offer currency exchange services on board. You can also usually find an ATM machine, bank, or other money exchange within walking distance of the pier where you can exchange a few dollars (though don't exchange too much or you'll end up having to change it back).

I also advise you to wear **comfortable shoes** (cobblestones and uneven surfaces are common in Europe) and bring along some **bottled water** (available on the ship), a hat, and sunscreen, especially in the summer months. If you are visiting churches or other religious sites, women may be required to cover their arms and legs. Your ship tour director should be able to offer you advice in this regard.

Currency Conversion Chart

	U.S. $1	Canada $1	British £1	Australia $1	NZ $1
Belgium (franc)	38.5	26	63	24.75	19.75
Croatia (kuna)	7.25	4.95	12	4.65	3.75
Denmark (krona)	7.10	4.75	11.65	4.55	3.60
England (pound)	.60	.40	1	.40	.30
Estonia (kroon)	14.90	10.15	24.50	9.50	7.60
Euro	.95	.65	1.55	.60	.50
Finland (markka)	5.65	3.85	9.30	3.65	2.90
France (franc)	6.25	4.25	10.30	4	3.20
Germany (deutschmark)	1.85	1.25	3.05	1.20	.95
Greece (drachma)	313	215	515	202	160
Ireland (punt)	.75	.50	1.25	.50	.40
Italy (lira)	1,845	1,260	3,035	1,190	945
Malta (lira)	.40	.25	.65	.25	.20
Netherlands (guilder)	2.10	1.45	3.45	1.35	1.05
Norway (krone)	7.9	5.35	12.95	5.05	4.05
Portugal (escudo)	191	130	315	125	100
Russia (ruble)	26	18	43	16.90	13.45
Spain (peseta)	160	110	260	100	80
Sweden (krona)	8.25	5.65	13.60	5.30	4.25
Turkey (lira)	486,000	331,000	799,000	313,000	249,000

REBOARDING

Whether you do go off to explore on your own or are just puttering around in the port after your excursion, you'll need to carefully pay attention to the ship's **departure time** and be back at least a half-hour before that time. If your shore excursion runs late, the ship will be held, but if you're off on your own and miss the boat you will be responsible for paying your way to the next port. (If you do miss the boat, immediately contact the ship's representative at the pier.)

Ships usually depart in the early evening, giving you an hour or two to rest up before dinner. Small ships may even stay in port each evening to offer you a chance to sample the local nightlife, and some large ships will overnight in major ports such as Venice, Istanbul, or Monaco.

2 Shore Excursions

The cruise lines offer shore excursions to various sites of historical or cultural value or natural or artistic beauty, all designed to help you make the most of your limited time at each port of call. In general, excursions that take you well beyond the port area are the ones most worth taking—you'll get professional commentary and avoid hassling with local transportation. In ports that have attractions within walking distance of the pier, however, you may be best off touring on your own. If you are not a good walker, look for a shore excursion that does not involve much footwork (most lines have offerings in this regard).

Shore excursions typically involve buses, with a guide assigned to each bus. Even when you are on a European ship, you will have an English-speaking guide. However, if there are not enough English speakers to fill a whole bus, you may have to hear the commentary repeated in another language as well. Some of the more upscale and educational lines have expert lecturers who accompany shore excursions, and some offer tours in limos and minivans rather than in big buses.

Tours include entrance fees to attractions, and some include lunch or local folklore performances, as well as time for shopping either on your own or at a local crafts center (where you may be not so subtly encouraged to buy souvenirs). In some cases, you may have the option of lingering in a town and returning to the ship on your own.

The tours are usually conducted by local outside contractors and not by the cruise lines themselves. In some countries, including Greece and Turkey, the guides are required to be licensed and are thus very knowledgeable about their subject matter. Elsewhere, I have also generally been impressed with the level of the tours offered, with a few notable exceptions: I had a guide in Monaco, for instance, who tried to entertain us on our way to St-Paul-de-Vence with a combination of inane commentary on the scenery ("Oh, look at the sea, isn't it blue?") and gossip about Monaco's royal family, and who dropped us off telling us she would offer a historical walking tour if we wanted, but she knew we would all rather go shopping instead. All told, though, such lack of performance by guides in Europe is rare.

Shore excursion rates listed in chapters 12 and 13 are for 1999, and may be slightly higher in 2000. **Tipping** of the guides after the tour is at your discretion, but as a general rule of thumb, you should tip $1 per person for a half-day tour and $2 per person for a full-day tour.

BOOKING SHORE EXCURSIONS

The cruise lines detail their excursions in brochures you'll likely receive in the mail with your cruise documents, to allow you to preselect excursions that appeal to you; however, in all but a few cases you must book the tours aboard ship (preferably on the first day, since some will sell out). Excursions are sold on a nonrefundable first-come, first-served basis (some have capacity restrictions). Some lines allow bookings in advance on European cruises, and some include shore excursions in their cruise fares. If you want to learn more about the shore excursions, the excursions staff will give talks aboard ship

Going Nowhere

At all the ports your ship will visit, you have the option of staying on the ship and relaxing. The restaurants usually remain open (even if you do get off, you can come back to eat, although I highly recommend in Europe that you try the local cuisine), and limited onboard activities may be offered.

to fill you in. Honestly, they're sometimes more like sales pitches (the cruise lines do, after all, make money off the tours), but they do give more background than the one- or two-paragraph summations in the brochures.

3 Touring the Ports on Your Own

If you're an independent-minded traveler and/or hate bus tours, skip the organized shore excursions and head off on your own—though bear in mind that some ports (such as Civitavecchia in Italy and Le Havre in France) are not much to look at in and of themselves, and serve primarily as seaports for large and sometimes distant cities (Rome and Paris, respectively, in this instance). Where this is the case, you're probably best off taking the organized excursions, since they're already structured to maximize your limited time.

Walking is, or course, the most enlightening way to see a port, but when you want to visit a distant site you'll have to find transportation. In most ports it's both a hassle and expensive to rent a car on your own, so you're better off either taking a taxi or public transportation such as buses or subways, or arranging to hire a car and driver—if you get together a small group to do this you can split the price and save money. Your ship's tour office should be able to offer recommendations.

Mediterranean Ports of Call

12

The ports in the Mediterranean include Lisbon and Barcelona in the west and Athens and Turkey in the east, and everything in between. Here you'll find history from B.C. on up, folk culture, high culture (think French Riviera), beaches, shopping, and above anything else, great diversity: the riches of Venice and Rome; the glistening beaches of the French Riviera (populated by chic, equally glistening bodies); tiny Monte Carlo with its famous casino; the unbelievably scenic Italian Riviera; Dubrovnik, with its medieval ramparts and role in modern history; and the Greek Isles, with their incredible archaeological and local cultural offerings.

In the Med, you can follow the path of ancient mariners and find history around every corner, or you can just sit back in the sun to admire the incredibly blue sea and fabulous scenery. There's something for everyone.

1 Croatia

Heavily damaged during the shelling of 1991–92 by Serbs and Montenegrins, the beautiful city of **Dubrovnik** has been restored—thanks in good part to donations made to the Rebuild Dubvrovnik Fund—and cruise passengers name it as one of their favorites. Unfortunately, because of its geographic location on the same side of the Adriatic as Kosovo, most lines dropped Dubrovnik from their schedules for much of the 1999 season, though some returned after the war there ended.

The Croatian city is a jewel to be sure (it's even classified as a world heritage treasure by UNESCO), encircled by medieval ramparts, with ancient streets, historic buildings and stone houses, and a rich cultural heritage, not to mention a fine position on the blue sea. The surrounding countryside provides glimpses of life the way it used to be.

ESSENTIALS

LANGUAGE Croatian.

CURRENCY The basic Croatian currency unit is the kuna. It is made up of 100 lipa. The exchange rate at press time was $1 = 7.25 kuna.

FROMMER'S FAVORITE DUBROVNIK EXPERIENCES

- **Walking the Placa (also called Stradun) and the side streets of Old Town.** Enter at the 16th-century Pile Gate and go exploring in this area, which has remained virtually unchanged since the 13th century.

- **Taking a ride in the country.** Shore excursions are offered to the pretty Konavle valley.

COMING ASHORE & GETTING AROUND

Ships dock about 10 minutes by car or bus from the Old Town. Taxis are usually available at the pier. There are also buses to Old Town.

THE BEST SHORE EXCURSIONS

Half-Day Historic Dubrovnik (3–4 hours, $31–$39): Travel by motorcoach from Gruz Harbor to Pile Gate, one of the entrances to the old town. Visit the Sponza Palace, Dominican church and monastery, Rector's Palace, Church of St. Blaise, Dubrovnik Cathedral, and 14th-century Franciscan Monastery. Walk the centuries-old streets of the Platka (Stradun).

Dubrovnik, Konavle Valley & Konavoski Dvori (5–6 hours, $129–$138): Visit the Konavle region, 30 minutes south of Dubrovnik, to spend time in a natural setting. Enjoy a welcome of brandy and dried figs at the Konavoski Dvori restaurant, situated in an old water mill next to the Ljuta River, and enjoy a lunch of traditional food including grilled roast lamb, veal, and trout. It also includes a tour of historic Dubrovnik.

Dubrovnik, Konavle Valley, Artist's Studio & Glavic House (5–6 hours, $127–$138): Travel 30 minutes south of Dubrovnik to the Konavle region and the village of Mihanici. Visit the studio of local painter Mijo Sisa Konavljanin, who paints themes of daily life in Konavle. Stop at Glavic House, a traditional family home. The family produces brandy, wine, and olive oil. Lunch is served here, featuring Croatian specialties. It also includes a tour of Dubrovnik's Old Town.

THE TOP ATTRACTIONS

Dominican Monastery. Sveti Dominika 4. Open daily 9am–5pm.

Construction began on this monastery and church complex in 1228, but it wasn't completed till some 200 years later. Some of the city's most renowned citizens are buried here, and the treasury is worth a look.

Franciscan Monastery. Placa 2. Open daily 9am–5pm.

Dating from the 14th century, the monastery has an impressive cloister, a rich library with a beautiful reading room, and a pharmacy that dates back to 1317.

The Rector's Palace. Pred Dvorom 3. Open Mon–Sat 9am–1pm.

The rector of Dubrovnik lived here, but the palace, constructed beginning in 1435, was also a seat of government. The rector was not allowed to leave the palace during his short, 1-month term unless he was engaged in state business. The architecture combines Gothic and early Renaissance styles, and the palace today houses a museum with furnished rooms, historical exhibits, and baroque paintings.

Factoid

The **Orlando Column,** which dates back to the 15th century, is considered the most significant symbol of Dubrovnik's freedom. Located in the center of the city, the column, since 1990, has been flying a white flag inscribed simply with the word "libertas."

Sponza Palace. Luža Square.

This is one of the most beautiful buildings in the city, featuring a mix of late Gothic and early Renaissance styles, with impressive stone carvings. Construction started in 1516, and the luxurious building was used as a sort of customhouse. The atrium, with its arched galley, was said to have been the most lively commercial center and meeting place for businessmen in the city. One wing of the palace housed the state mint. And intellectuals gathered here as "The Academy of the Learned."

Cathedral of the Assumption of the Virgin. Poljana M. Držića. Treasury open daily 9am–noon and 3–6pm.

The Dubrovnik cathedral was built by an Italian architect in a Roman baroque style, and was completed in 1713. Inside, the treasury offers a collection of art objects and Renaissance paintings.

STOPPING FOR A BITE

Local favorites include scampi and other seafood dishes, *manistra od bobica* (a bean soup), and *strukle* (rolls made with cottage cheese). And wash your meal down with a local Croatian wine (they're pretty good).

BEST SHOPPING BUYS

Shop here for lace, embroidery, wood carvings, carpets, ceramics, tapestries, jewelry, and leather and woolen products. There are also a number of art galleries throughout the city. Stores generally close for lunch.

2 The French Riviera & Monte Carlo

The French Riviera is less than 125 miles long and is located between the Mediterranean and a trio of mountain ranges. **Cannes, Nice, Villefranche, St-Tropez,** and **Monte Carlo** are all so close together geographically they offer nearly the same shore excursions, although each port has its own special flavor and charms. They are all located on the scenic Côte d'Azur, where the natural beauty includes coastal mountains and a very blue sea, and the man-made beauty includes yachts, diamonds, and other reminders that the French Riviera is a playground of the rich and famous. Artists who have captured the glorious landscape here include Matisse, Cocteau, Picasso, Léger, Renoir, and Bonnard. Their works can be found at numerous museums throughout the area.

All the ports are crowded with tourists in the summer months, particularly in July and August. The scenic drive between the ports is gorgeous but can be slow, depending on the traffic.

Cannes is a bustling commercial center. The grand hotels made famous during the International Film Festival can be found on the seafront boulevards, but it's Coco Chanel, not the festival, who's credited with putting the city on the map when she came, got a suntan, then went back to Paris and started a trend. Cannes beaches today continue to be more for exhibitionism and voyeurism than swimming.

The city offers great shopping opportunities, including outlets of major Paris brands such as Saint Laurent, Rykiel, and Hermés, which be found on La Croisette. More reasonable shopping can be found a few blocks inland on rue d'Antibes.

The 370-acre principality of **Monaco** became the property of the Grimaldi clan, a Genoese family, in 1297, and has maintained something resembling independence every since. Its capital, **Monte Carlo,** has for a century symbolized glamour—and the 1956 marriage of Prince Rainier and the American actress Grace Kelly after their meeting at the Cannes film festival only enhanced that status. Their children, Caroline, Albert, and Stephanie, have lived their entire lives in the spotlight, and the bachelor status of Albert, the heir, has the entire principality concerned.

Princess Grace, who was killed in a car accident in 1982, is still mourned by Monégasques. Otherwise, they are known to be a fairly happy lot with a very high standard of living. The residents do not pay taxes, something Prince Rainier has staunchly defended.

Visitors are always surprised at how small Monaco is. The second smallest state in Europe (Vatican City is smaller), Monaco consists of four tightly packed (we're talking prime real estate here) parts: the old town, setting for the royal palace (where a small changing of the guard ceremony is held daily at 11:55am) and the Monaco Cathedral (where the tomb of Princess Grace is located); La Condamine, the residential area; Monte Carlo, where the fancy hotels and famous casino are located; and Fontvieille, the commercial area.

When exploring the city, you can walk up hills or use Monaco's somewhat bizarre system of public elevators that take you, for instance, from the harbor to the casino.

Nice, while once a Victorian playground of the aristocracy, is today a big middle-class city. It's the capital of the Riviera and the largest city between Genoa and Marseille. It's also one of the most ancient cities in the region, founded by the Greeks, who called it Nike, or Victory.

Artists and writers have long been attracted to the city, including Dumas, Nietzsche, Flaubert, Hugo, Sand, and Stendahl. Henri Matisse made his home here.

The French Riviera

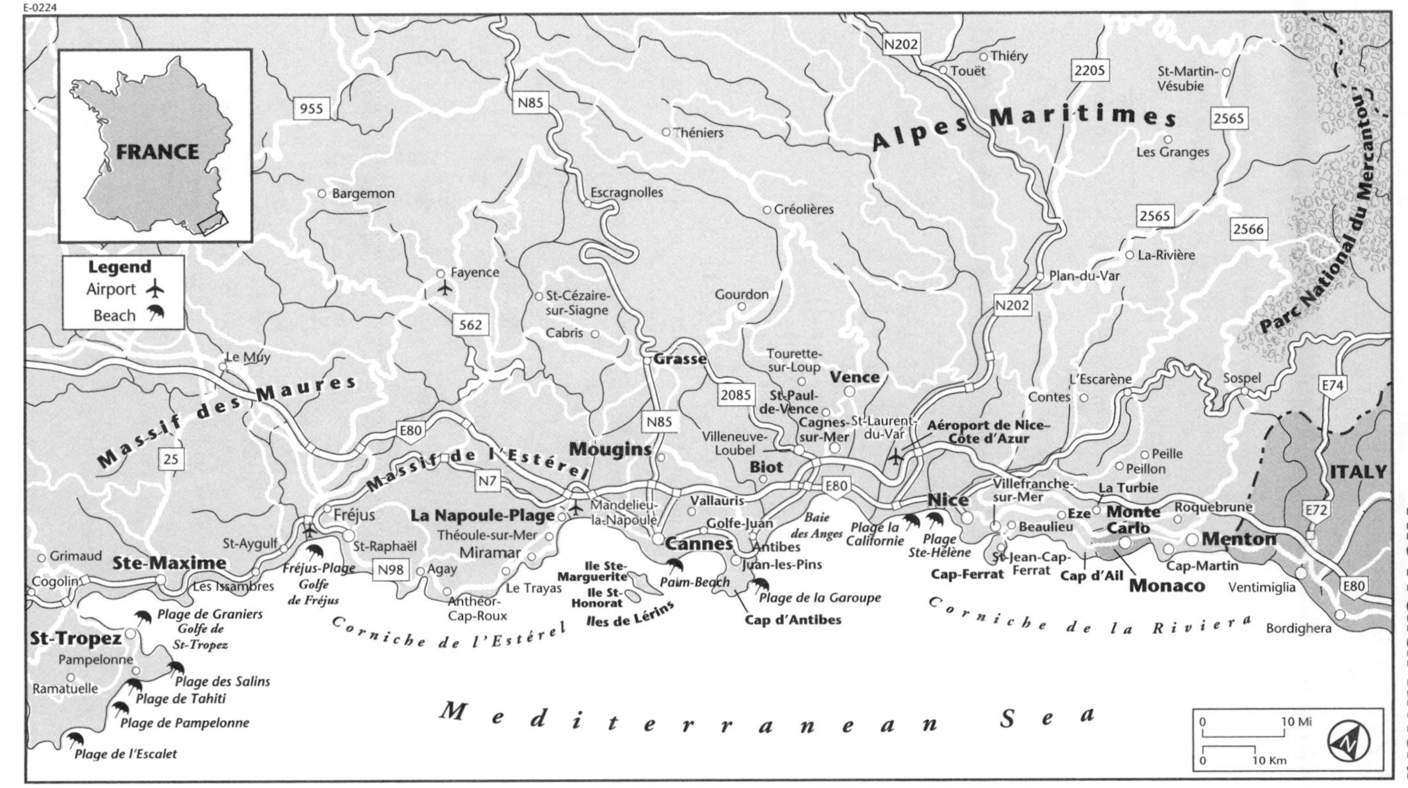

Monte Carlo Factoid

Legends surrounding the **Monte Carlo Casino** abound. A favorite is that Mata Hari shot a tsarist colonel with a jewel-encrusted revolver after he tried to slip his hand inside her bra, looking to discover military secrets.

My favorite activity here is museum-hopping, especially in nearby Cimiez, home of the Musée National Message Biblique Marc-Chagall and the Musée Matisse. It's also fun to explore Nice's old town, with its colorful houses and narrow streets. The area around the Flower Market is full of outdoor cafes and a great place to people-watch. As bizarre as it may seem, it's also worth a trek uphill to the old graveyard of Nice, where great views and an interesting setting can be found, including lavishly sculpted monuments.

The promenade des Anglais is a wide boulevard on the bay, stretching several miles, and is a lovely walking spot past cafes and historic buildings (some decaying), and, on the beaches, bronzed bodies in teeny weeny bikinis.

Brigitte Bardot made the St-Tropez resort famous when she was filmed here by husband Roger Vadim in *And God Created Woman* in 1957, and fun-in-the-sun is still the word in this thriving artists' colony. While the reputation is for hedonism (and you will see topless and even bottomless sunbathers on the beach), there is also some quaint mixed in. Among the recent celebrities spotted here are Oprah Winfrey, Don Johnson, Quincy Jones, Barbara Streisand, Jack Nicholson, Robert De Niro, Sly Stallone, and Elton John.

The town was destroyed by the Germans in 1944, but the local residents, working from old plans and photos, rebuilt it to look exactly as it had before, basically a little village. In addition to the beaches, St-Tropez offers good shopping opportunities, including a wealth of antique dealers and art galleries in old town.

Villefranche-sur-Mer is a lovely little port town, located only 4 miles from Nice. According to legend, Hercules opened his arms and Villefranche was born. But it is also home to the U.S. Sixth Fleet, and when the fleet's in, the quiet town takes on a decidedly different flavor, turning into a bustling Mediterranean port.

The town is a haven for artists (many of whom take over the houses on the hillside in summer), and provides a nice setting for a quiet day of walking and exploring. But Villefranche is also a good starting-off point for shore excursions to Nice, Eze, St-Paul-de-Vence, and Monaco.

One artist who came to Villefranche was Jean Cocteau, who left a legacy in the form of frescoes on the 14th-century walls of the Romanesque Chapelle St. Pierre.

Also of particular interest is the Rue Obscure, a vaulted street.

Away from the coast, **St-Paul-de-Vence,** visitable by shore excursion, is the best known of the region's perched villages, a feudal hamlet growing on a bastion of rock, almost blending into it. Its ramparts overlook a peaceful setting of flowers and olive and orange trees. Outside the walls is the Foundation Maeght, donated by Aimé and Marguerite Maeght as a gift "to the people" and considered the best art museum in the Riviera by lovers of modern art. The architecture is avant-garde and the collection is contemporary. A stark Calder rises on the grassy lawns; a Giacometti creates a surreal state in the courtyard; there are mosaics by Chagall and ceramics by Miró; and Bonnard, Kandinsky, Léger, Matisse, Barbara Hepworth, Ubac, and Braque are among others represented.

Some people visit St-Paul de Vence solely to dine at **La Colombe d'Or** (**☎ 04/93-32-77-78**), once the stomping ground of some of the most important artists of the 20th century. They would trade art for meals and rooms, and the walls and gardens contain works by Picasso, Braque, Miró, Matisse, Léger, Calder, Chagall and others. Unfortunately, you can't view the collection unless you spring for a meal here. Main courses are $21.60 to $32.40. Reservations are required.

For the port of **Le Havre,** see chapter 13, "Ports of Call in Northern Europe & the British Isles."

ESSENTIALS

LANGUAGE French

CURRENCY The French franc is divided into 100 centimes. Bills come in 20, 50, 100, 200, and 500 franc denominations. The exchange rate at press time was $1 = 6.25 francs.

FROMMER'S FAVORITE FRENCH RIVIERA EXPERIENCES

- **Shopping for high fashion in Cannes.** Look for famous Paris brands on La Croisette, and more affordable shopping on rue d'Antibes and the streets in between.
- **Heading to the beach in Cannes.** Free public beaches include Plage du Midi and Plage Gazagnaire. There are also private beaches where you pay a fee (usually between $16 and $18), for which you get a mattress and a sun umbrella.
- **Visiting the Aquarium in Monte Carlo.** I went to the Oceanographic Museum just to kill some time one day, and discovered a fascinating place with exhibits that include leafy sea dragons (this is the only aquarium where you can see them) and other endangered species. See description below for more info.
- **Playing James Bond at the Monte Carlo Casino.** Put on your tux and indulge in the opulence.
- **Exploring Nice's Old Town.** You'll find a maze of streets teeming with local life, inexpensive restaurants, and boutiques.
- **Climbing up to the cemetery in Nice.** It's a fascinating and scenic place and well worth a visit. Really!
- **Checking out the beaches in St-Tropez.** They're the Riviera's finest. The most daring are the Plage des Salins, Plage de Pampellone, and Plage de Tahiti. If you ever wanted to go topless or bottomless (or just want to gawk at people who are), this is the place.
- **Take a shore excursion** or spend quiet time in sleepy Villefranche. Close by are Nice, St-Paul-de-Vence, and Eze.

COMING ASHORE & GETTING AROUND

Small ships can dock at Monte Carlo, St-Tropez, or Nice. Large ships at the French Riviera ports usually tender passengers ashore.

Taxis are available at the pier, but are expensive (you may want to double up with other passengers if you're planning to go any distance). You can walk from all the ports to many local attractions. There is also great train service from Nice to other locations on the Côte d'Azur.

THE BEST SHORE EXCURSIONS

The best way to explore the French Riviera ports is on foot. You needn't book a shore excursion unless walking is a problem, or you wish to travel to a port other than the one your ship is visiting. If you're looking for something different, you may want to try one of the following.

St-Paul-de-Vence (4 hours, $41–$58): This medieval walled city offers art galleries and shops, cobblestoned streets, cafes, and gorgeous country views. The town has long attracted celebrities, and Gene Wilder and Gilda Radner were married here. The trip may be combined with a visit to Grasse, birthplace of the French perfume industry, and a stop at a perfume factory.

Medieval Eze (3–4 hours, $45): Eze literally clings to the rocks above the sea, and is a medieval village worth exploring. This tour includes a guided walk through the narrow streets, with their lovely restored houses and stunning views. Time is allowed for shopping in the town's boutiques and artists' studios.

THE TOP ATTRACTIONS

CANNES

Musée de la Castre. In Château de la Castre, Le Suquet. ☎ **04/93-38-55-26.** Admission $1.80 adults, free for students and children. Open Wed–Mon: Apr–June 10am–noon and 2–6pm; July–Sept 10am–noon and 3–7pm; Oct 10am–noon and 2–5pm.

The collection here includes 19th-century paintings, sculptures, decorative arts, and ethnography, including a gallery devoted to relics of ancient Mediterranean civilizations.

MONTE CARLO

Musée de l'Océanographie. Av. St-Martin. ☎ **93/15-36-00.** Admission $1.80 adults, $5.40 children 6–18, free for children 5 and under. July–Aug daily 9am–8pm; Apr–June and Sept daily 9am–7pm; Oct daily 9:30am–7pm.

Founded by Prince Albert I in 1910 and formerly administered by the late Jacques Cousteau, the museum is one of the best aquariums in Europe, displaying rare and unusual sea creatures. The upper floor offers a history of underwater exploration, complete with early scuba gear, a submarine mockup from the 1700s, and articles recovered from the sea such as large strips of whale baleen. On the main floor is an aquarium that offers more than 90 tanks containing such endangered species as the fascinating leafy sea dragon. The museum building is an impressive structure in itself.

Monte Carlo Casino. Place du Casino. ☎ **92/16-21-21.** Admission $9–$18, depending on where in the casino you go. Opens daily at noon. No one under 21 is permitted inside. A passport is required to get in, and at night men must wear a jacket and tie.

The Casino was built in 1878 by Charles Garnier, the architect who also created the Paris Opera House. It is a very ornate building, but those used to Las Vegas casinos will be surprised at its small size. The atrium is surrounded by 28 Ionic columns made of onyx. The gaming rooms, one leading into the next (you pay more for admission the deeper into the casino you go), feature equally elaborate decor, including gilt, frescoes, and bas-reliefs. Games offered include baccarat, roulette, craps, and blackjack, as well as slot machines (in Salle Américaine). One of the best places to people-watch is outside, where it's not uncommon to see very old and wealthy men getting into fancy cars with very young, jewel-encrusted women.

NICE

Musée des Beaux-Arts. 33 av. Des Baumettes. ☎ **04/92-15-28-28.** Admission $4.50 adults, $2.70 children. Tues–Sun 10am–noon and 2–6pm.

Housed in the former residence of the Ukrainian princess Kotchubey, this important gallery is devoted to the masters of the Second Empire and the belle époque, with an extensive collection of 19th-century French artists. Sculptures include works by Rodin. There are also works by Renoir and Monet.

Cathédrale Orthodoxe Russe St-Nicolas á Nice. Av. Nicolas-II. ☎ **04/93-96-88-02.** Admission $2.15. June–Sept, daily 9am–noon and 2:30–6pm; Oct and May, daily 9:30am–noon and 2:30–5pm.

Tsar Nicholas II himself ordered this impressive religious edifice to be built. The cathedral is richly ornamented and decorated with lots of icons.

Musée Matisse. In Cimiez. Villa des Arénes-de-Cimiez. 164 av. Des Arénes-de-Cimiez. ☎ **04/93-81-08-08.** Admission $4.50 adults, $2.70 children. Wed–Mon 10am–6pm.

Matisse spent the last years of his life in Nice, and the museum offers works donated by the artist and his heirs. Included is *Nude in an Armchair with a Green Plant, Nymph in the Forest,* and *Portrait of Madame Matisse,* as well as practice sketches and designs, and items from the artist's own collection and home.

Musée National Message Biblique Marc-Chagall. In Cimiez. Av. Du Dr.-Ménard. ☎ **04/93-53-87-20.** Admission $5.40 adults, $3.60 ages 18–24, free for children. Rates may be higher for special exhibitions. July–Sept, Wed–Mon 10am–6pm; Oct and Apr–June Wed–Mon 10am–5pm.

Located in the hills above Nice, this museum is dedicated to the artist's treatment of biblical themes. Chagall and his wife donated the works, which include oils, gouaches, drawings, pastels, lithographs, and sculptures, as well as a mosaic and stained-glass windows. A brochure is available in English to help you understand the biblical themes.

St-Tropez

L'Annonciade Musée St-Tropez. Place Georges-Grammont. ☎ **04/94-97-04-01.** Admission $5 adults, $2.50 children. Open June–Sept, Wed–Mon 10am–noon and 3–7pm; Oct, Apr, and May, Wed–Mon, 10am–noon and 2–6pm (closed in Nov).

This museum in a former chapel has one of the best modern art collections on the Riviera, including Van Dongen's *Women of the Balustrade* and paintings and sculpture by Bonnard, Matisse, Braque, Utrillo, Seurat, Derain, and Maillol.

Villefranche

Romanesque Chapelle St-Pierre. Quai de la Douane/rue des Mariniéres. ☎ **04/93-76-90-70.** Admission $2.15. Open Tues–Sun, July–Sept 10am–noon and 4–8:30pm; Oct 9:30am–noon and 2–5pm; Apr–June 9:30am–noon and 3–7pm.

Jean Cocteau left his mark here in the form of frescoes paying tribute to gypsies, St. Peter, and the young women of Villefranche.

Stopping for a Bite

Definitely try bouillabaisse, fish stew, and salade Niçoise. Other local specialties include pizza served with onions or olives. Make sure to wash your meal down with French wine. If you have very big bucks (we're talking main courses ranging from $35.10 to $135.90), you may want to eat at **Le Louis XV** in the **Hôtel de Paris** in Monte Carlo (☎ **92/16-30-01**), where Alain Ducasse does his six-star magic (both this and his restaurant in Paris received three stars from Michelin). Make reservations way in advance, and expect a snooty wait staff.

A fun, inexpensive place to dine in Nice is **Le Safari** (☎ **04/93-80-18-44**), overlooking the Flower Market. Reservations are highly recommended.

Best Shopping Buys

Shop at these ports for high-fashion items, artwork, antiques, and items made of colorful Provençal fabrics.

3 Greece

Greece is a spectacular country where ancient sites and architectural treasures join forces with the sun, scenery, and food to make one of the best vacation spots on Earth. It's a feast for the mind and the senses, a place that is exotic but at the same time friendly and familiar, and where there is always something to remind visitors of the past.

ESSENTIALS

LANGUAGE Greek is the official language, but English and French are widely spoken.

CURRENCY Drachma (DR) notes are issued in 100-, 500-, 1,000-, 5,000- and 10,000 denominations. The rate of exchange at press time was $1 = 313 drachmas. Bills are all the same size but come in different colors.

ATHENS

This fabled metropolis is a delightful mix of modern and ancient. The Parthenon and the treasures on display at the National Archaeological Museum best personify the image most of us have of ancient Greece, but interspersed among the ancient monuments, tavernas, and neoclassical buildings are high-rises, fast-food outlets, and plenty of souvenir shops. Modern Athens is crowded, teeming with inhabitants, traffic, and taxis (although getting one can be a challenge). The city is also polluted and grows unbelievably hot during the summer. To appreciate both sides of Athens, explore it slowly, and get resigned to the fact that you won't have time to see everything. Climb to the Parthenon, enjoy a leisurely lunch at an outside cafe, get caught in the hustle and bustle of the streets, and savor the moments spent in the birthplace of western civilization.

FROMMER'S FAVORITE ATHENS EXPERIENCES

- **Strolling around the Plaka.** The Plaka is the oldest neighborhood in Athens. As you wander its narrow streets you will come upon quaint single-story homes, neoclassical buildings, tavernas, nightclubs, and souvenir shops. It's easy to get lost in the maze of streets here, but along the way you may spot an ancient monument or a fascinating neighborhood church.
- **Going Museum-Hopping.** The National Archaeological Museum is enormous and can easily occupy a few hours. There are also several small museums worth a look (see below).
- **Visiting the National Gardens.** Located next to the Parliament House is the former royal family's palace garden. Visitors will find a park, a small zoo, shady trees, benches, a cafe, and small lakes and ponds with ducks, swans, and even peacocks. The garden is open daily from 7am to 10pm, but don't linger here alone at night.

COMING ASHORE & GETTING AROUND

Cruise ships dock at the port city of **Piraeus,** about 7 miles southwest of Athens. There's not much to do in Piraeus, so you'll want to head into Athens. You can take a metro train or taxi into the city, and most cruise lines also offer a bus service (for a fee). I recommend the train, which you can walk to from the pier. It costs about a quarter. If you're taking a taxi, try to bargain with the driver. The average fare from Piraeus to Syntagma Square in Athens should be about $7, but many drivers will quote a flat rate, which can be as high as $17. You can pay it or try to find another taxi driver willing to turn on the meter. The trip can take a while if there's bad traffic (which there often is here).

Note that drivers here will not always accept you as a fare. They will ask where you are going and are free to decline if they are not going your way. Consequently, it sometimes takes a fair amount of time to find a cab (so plan accordingly). It is also not uncommon for a driver to stop and pick up two or three different parties to fill the cab. If this happens, you are only responsible for your leg of the journey.

THE BEST SHORE EXCURSIONS

Athens City Tour (3½–4 hours, $38–$42): Includes a guided tour of the Acropolis; a drive past other Athens highlights, including Constitution Square, the Parliament, the Temple of Zeus, Hadrian's Arch, and Olympic Stadium; and time for souvenir shopping. A full-day city tour ($8^1/_2$ hours, $92) also includes a visit to the National Archaeological Museum, time to shop in the Plaka, and lunch.

A Day Tour of Delphi ($9^1/_2$ hours, $109): If you've been to Athens before or just aren't into big cities and crowds, you may want to try this day trip to one of the great sights of antiquity. The tour visits the ruins of the Temple of Apollo, located in a stunning setting on the slope of Mount Parnassus. Lunch is included.

The Top Attractions

The Acropolis. Enter on the west end of the site, accessible from a path off Dioskouon and Theorias sts. ☎ **01/321-0219.** Admission about $7 adults, $5 seniors, $3.35 students with ID (admission also covers entrance to the Acropolis Museum). Open daily in the summer and winter. Summer 8am–6pm; winter 8am–2:30pm.

For many centuries, the Acropolis—the heights above Athens—was the religious center of Athens, and in various times it's served as the seat of a king and the home of gods and goddesses. The most striking structures are the Parthenon (the most recognized Greek monument, dedicated to Athena), the Propylaea (the gateway to the Acropolis), the Temple of Athena Nike (built in the 5th century B.C. and restored in the 1930s), and the Erechtheion (honored by Athenians as the tomb of Erechtheus, a legendary king of Athens, and noteworthy for its delicate carving). Visitors may be disappointed to find that they cannot enter the Parthenon due to preservation and restoration reasons. However, leave plenty of time to explore the Acropolis and the museum. In the summer, it is best to start out, if possible, early in the morning, when the sun is not at its strongest and the crowds are not as overwhelming.

Ancient Agora. Below the Acropolis on the edge of Monastiraki. ☎ **01/321-0185.** Admission $4 adults, $3 seniors, $2 students. Tues–Sun 8:30am–3pm. Closed Mon.

The Agora, a jumble of ancient buildings, inscriptions, and fragments of sculpture, served as a political and commercial center of Athens. The two best ruins are the Hephaisteion (a temple to Hephaisos built in the 5th century B.C.) and the reconstructed Stoa of Attalos, which serves as a museum.

The National Archaeological Museum. Odos Pattision 44. ☎ **01/821-7717.** Admission $7 adults, $3.35 students. Mon 12:30–5pm; Tues–Fri 8am–5pm; Sat–Sun and holidays 8:30am–3pm.

This large museum takes time to navigate and is quite popular, so it's best to get there early so you'll be able to see the exhibits rather than the backs of fellow museum-goers. The museum contains collections from prehistoric times, pottery and Minoan art, sculpture, bronzes, and Egyptian art.

N. P. Goulandris Foundation Museum of Cycladic Art. Odos Neofytou Douka 4. ☎ **01/722-8321.** Admission $3.25 adults, $1.25 students. Mon, Wed–Fri 10am–4pm; Sat 10am–3pm. Closed Tues and Sun.

This attractive museum is the home of the second largest collection of art from the Cyclades, a group of about 200 islands in the Aegean, between the years 3200 and 2000 B.C. The Greek artifact collection includes jewelry, glass and metal ware, pottery, and figurines from the 3rd millennium B.C. to the 4th century A.D. A new acquisition (reached through the courtyard) is the 19th-century neoclassical Stathatos House, featuring some original furnishings.

The Museum of Greek Folk Art. Odos Kidathineon 17, Plaka. ☎ **01/322-9031.** Admission $1.65 adults, $1.35 seniors, $1 students. Tues–Sun 10am–2pm. Closed Mon.

This small museum showcases pieces dating from A.D. 1650 to the present, including embroidery, costumes, silver and metal works, pottery, and wood and stone carvings, as well as paintings by Theophilos Hatzimichail.

Athens

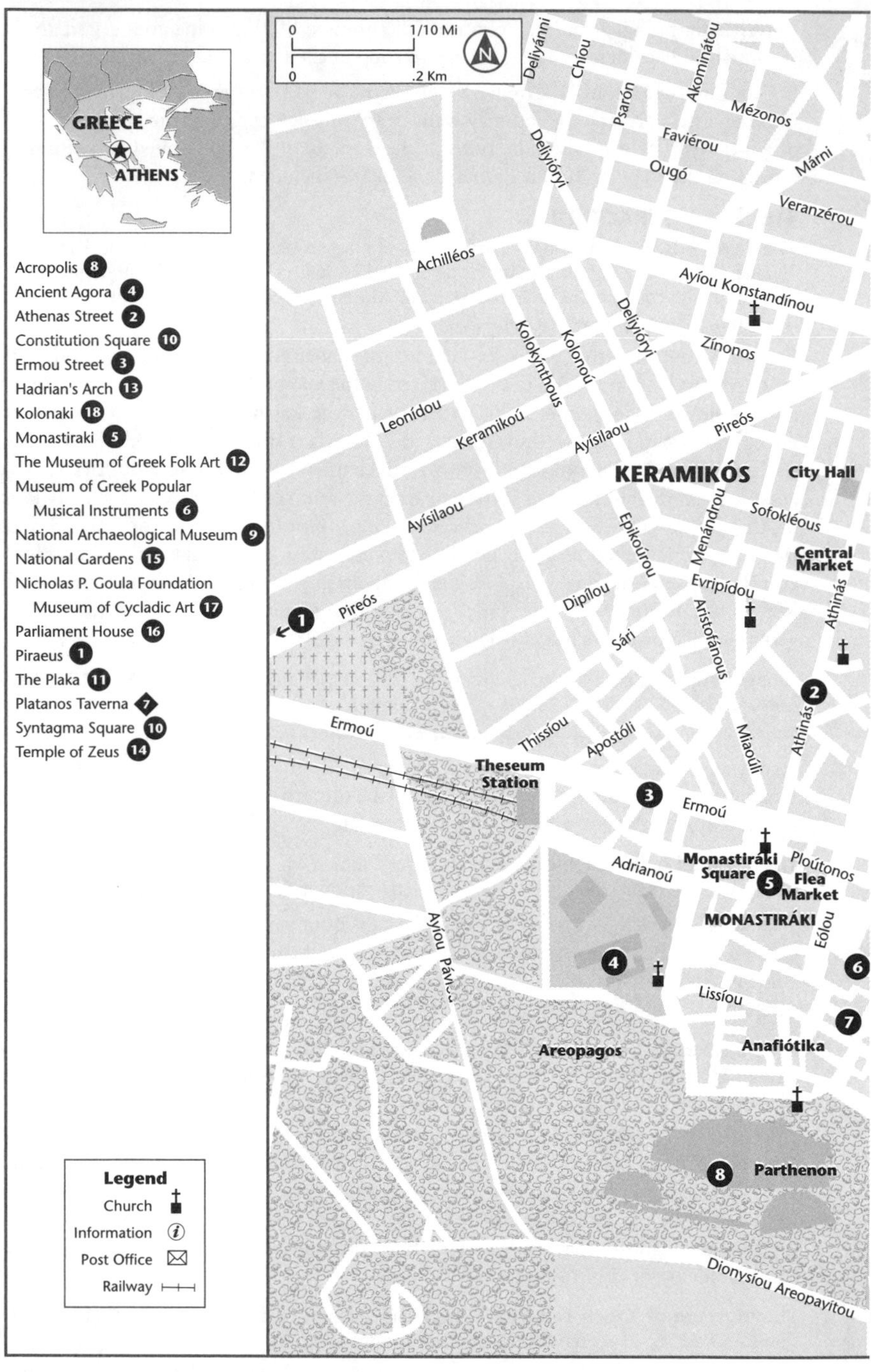
0 1/10 Mi
0 .2 Km
N
GREECE
ATHENS
Acropolis 8
Ancient Agora 4
Athenas Street 2
Constitution Square 10
Ermou Street 3
Hadrian's Arch 13
Kolonaki 18
Monastiraki 5
The Museum of Greek Folk Art 12
Museum of Greek Popular Musical Instruments 6
National Archaeological Museum 9
National Gardens 15
Nicholas P. Goula Foundation Museum of Cycladic Art 17
Parliament House 16
Piraeus 1
The Plaka 11
Platanos Taverna 7
Syntagma Square 10
Temple of Zeus 14
Legend
Church
Information
Post Office
Railway
3-0512
Deliyánni
Chíou
Psarón
Akominátou
Mézonos
Faviérou
Ougó
Márni
Veranzérou
Deliyióryi
Achilléos
Ayíou Konstandínou
Kolokýnthous
Kolonoú
Zínonos
Leonídou
Keramikoú
Ayísilaou
Pireós
KERAMIKÓS
City Hall
Sofokléous
Epikoúrou
Menándrou
Central Market
Evripídou
Dipílou
Athinás
Aristofánous
Sári
Thissíou
Apostóli
Miaoúli
Ermoú
Theseum Station
Adrianoú
Monastiráki Square
Ploútonos
Flea Market
MONASTIRÁKI
Eólou
Ayíou Pávlou
Lissíou
Areopagos
Anafiótika
Parthenon
Dionysíou Areopayítou

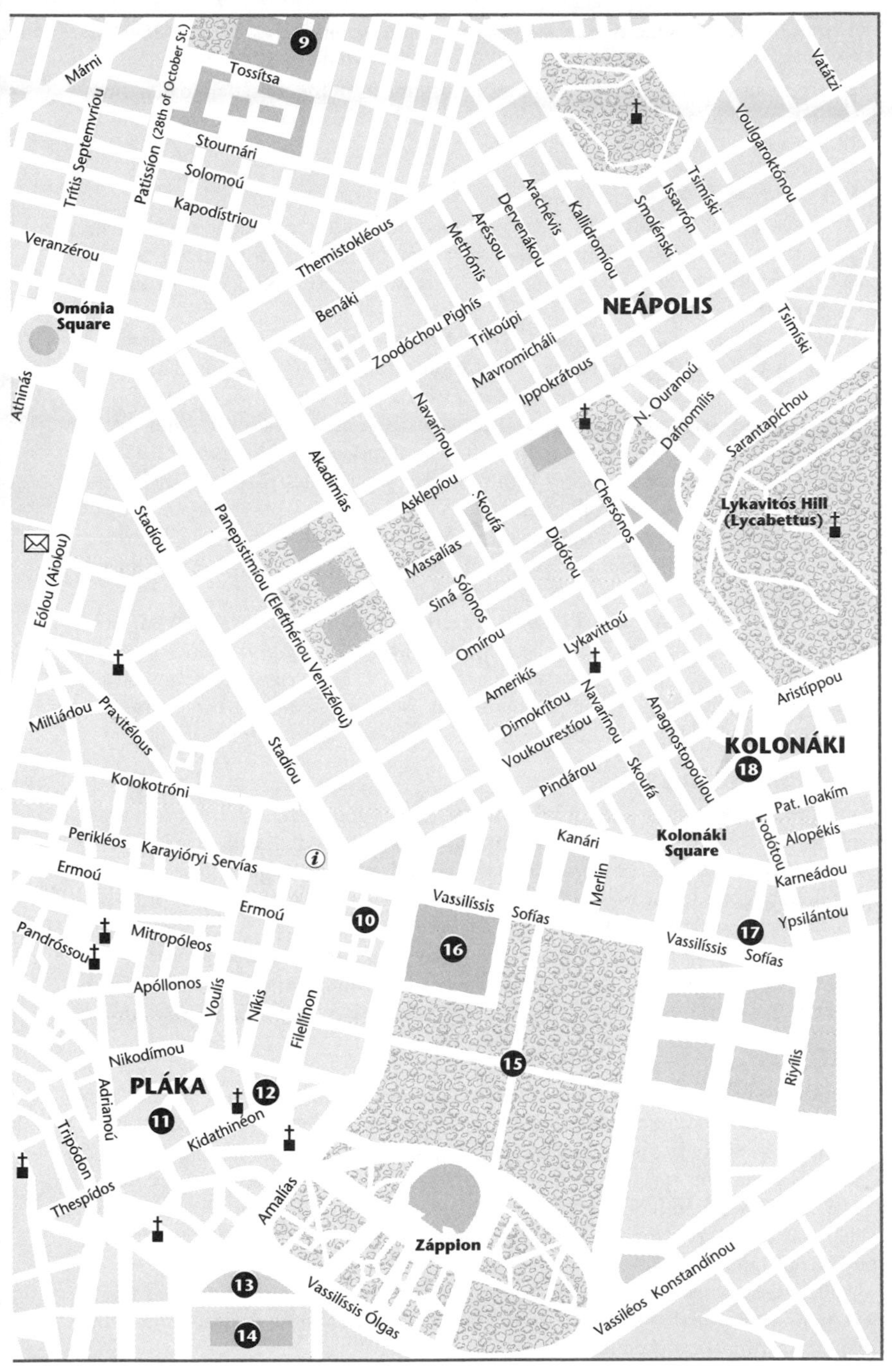
Márni
Trítis Septemvríou
Patissíon (28th of October St.)
Tossítsa
Stournári
Solomoú
Kapodístriou
Veranzérou
Omónia Square
Athinás
Themistokléous
Benáki
Zoodóchou Pighís
Methónis
Aréssou
Dervenákou
Arachévis
Kallidromíou
Smolénski
Issavrón
Tsimíski
Voulgaroktónou
Vatátzi
NEÁPOLIS
Trikoúpi
Mavromicháli
Ippokrátous
N. Ouranoú
Dafnomilis
Sarantapíchou
Navarínou
Akadimías
Asklepíou
Skoufá
Chersónos
Lykavitós Hill (Lycabettus)
Stadíou
Panepistimíou (Elefthériou Venizélou)
Massalías
Didótou
Eólou (Aiolou)
Sólonos
Siná
Omírou
Lykavittoú
Amerikís
Dimokrítou
Navarínou
Voukourestíou
Anagnostopoúlou
Aristíppou
KOLONÁKI
Miltiádou
Praxitélous
Stadíou
Pindárou
Skoufá
Kolokotróni
Pat. Ioakím
Perikléos
Karayióryi Servías
Kanári
Kolonáki Square
Loukianoú
Alopékis
Ermoú
Merlin
Karneádou
Vassilíssis
Sofías
Ermoú
Ypsilántou
Pandróssou
Mitropóleos
Vassilíssis
Sofías
Apóllonos
Voulís
Níkis
Filellínon
Nikodímou
Riyílis
PLÁKA
Adrianoú
Kidathinéon
Tripódon
Thespídos
Amalías
Záppion
Vassilíssis Ólgas
Vassiléos Konstandínou
9
10
11
12
13
14
15
16
17
18

Museum of Greek Popular Musical Instruments. Odos Dioyenous 1–3. ☎ **01/325-0198.** Free admission. Tues and Thurs–Sun 10am–2pm; Wed noon–6pm. Closed Mon.

There are about 1,200 popular Greek musical instruments in the collection (dating from the 18th century to present). The museum is housed in the Lassanis Mansion, built in 1842. Recitals are held in the museum's garden.

Stopping for a Bite

Most Greek meals start off with *mezedes* (appetizers). Items can range from grilled *oktapodi* (octopus) to *keftedes* (meatballs) to *tzatziki* (yogurt dip with cucumber and garlic). Other items include *kalamaraki* (squid), feta (white goat cheese), and *spanakopita* (spinach pies).

Typical main dishes are *moussaka* (layers of eggplant, minced meat, and potatoes topped with a cheese sauce and baked), *pastitsio* (macaroni baked with minced meat and bechamel sauce), *gemista* (either tomatoes or green peppers stuffed with minced meat or rice), *dolmades* (cabbage or vine leaves stuffed with minced meat or rice and served with an egg and lemon sauce), and *souvlaki* (pieces of meat on small skewers).

Baklava, a honey-drenched pastry with nuts, is a popular dessert that is sticky and sweet. Ouzo is a traditional Greek liquor.

Some of the most quaint restaurants in the city can be found in the Plaka, but there are also some real tourist traps in that area. Don't frequent a place where waiters are standing outside to pull you in. Also avoid places with floor shows.

A good traditional taverna is **Platanos Taverna,** Odos Dioyenous 4 (☎ **01/322-0666**), which is open for both lunch and dinner and offers outdoor tables in good weather. "Home cooking" has been served here since 1932. Especially great are the artichokes or spinach with lamb, and the house wine is pretty good too. Main courses are about $8 to $12.

Best Shopping Buys

Shop Athens for gold and silver jewelry, icons, leather goods, ceramics, kitchenware, komboloi (worry beads), and blue-and-white amulets that ward off evil spirits.

Ermou Street is the place for women's fashion. **Kolonaki** is the place to head for designer boutiques and shoe stores. Kitchenware and household items can be found on **Athenas Street,** while **Monastraki,** the area adjacent to the Plaka, is known for its flea market, most lively on Sundays (but open every day). Keep in mind that not everything sold as an antique is genuine. Also, it's illegal to take antiquities and icons more than 100 years old out of the country without an export license (which is hard to obtain).

MYKONOS

The landscape of this island's main town, **Hora,** dazzles with whitewashed homes, their doors and window frames painted brightly, and a harbor lined with fishing boats. Pelicans, the mascots of Mykonos, greet passengers at the pier.

There is a charming quality here despite the large numbers of sun-seekers, party town reputation (especially in July and August), and inevitable souvenir shops. Navigating the cobblestone streets, you will stumble upon windmills, small churches with blue domes, and outdoor cafes.

Unlike other Greek islands visited by cruise ships, Mykonos is not a setting for ancient ruins. Those starving for sacred sights of note can catch a shore excursion to nearby **Delos,** the birthplace of Apollo.

Mykonos's second town is **Ano Mera,** about 4 miles east of Hora, where you'll find a more traditional ambiance and some religious sites of note. The **Monastery of Panayia Tourliani** dates to 1580 and has a handsomely carved steeple, as well as a small

The Greek Isles

religious museum inside. Nearby is the 12th-century **Monastery of Paleokastro,** one of the greenest spots on the island.

Frommer's Favorite Mykonos Experiences

- **Hitting the beach.** Paradise, the island's original nude beach, is its most famous. Other notable stretches include Kalafatis and Ayios Sostis.
- **Having an undersea adventure.** Mykonos is the place for diving in the Aegean, especially in September. The most well-established diving center is at **Psarou Beach** (☎ and fax **0289/24-808;** e-mail: diving_center_psarou@myk.forthnet.gr).

Coming Ashore & Getting Around

Ships tender passengers to the main harbor area along the Esplanade in Hora. The best way to get around town is to walk. Much of the rest of the island is served by a good **bus** system. The central bus station is located off the left of the harbor. Bus routes go to all the beaches from Hora. There are also two types of **taxis.** The standard cab, which you can find at Taxi (Mavro) Square, can take you outside of town. There's a notice board at the square with rates. Small motor scooter taxis also zip through the narrow streets of Hora, which by government decree is an architectural landmark where cars are not allowed. These can be found at the pier.

The Best Shore Excursions

Delos Apollo Sanctuary (3–4½ hours, $37–$55): Travel by small boat from Mykonos harbor to Delos for a 2-hour guided walking tour of the tiny island that was once the

Hora (Mykonos Town)

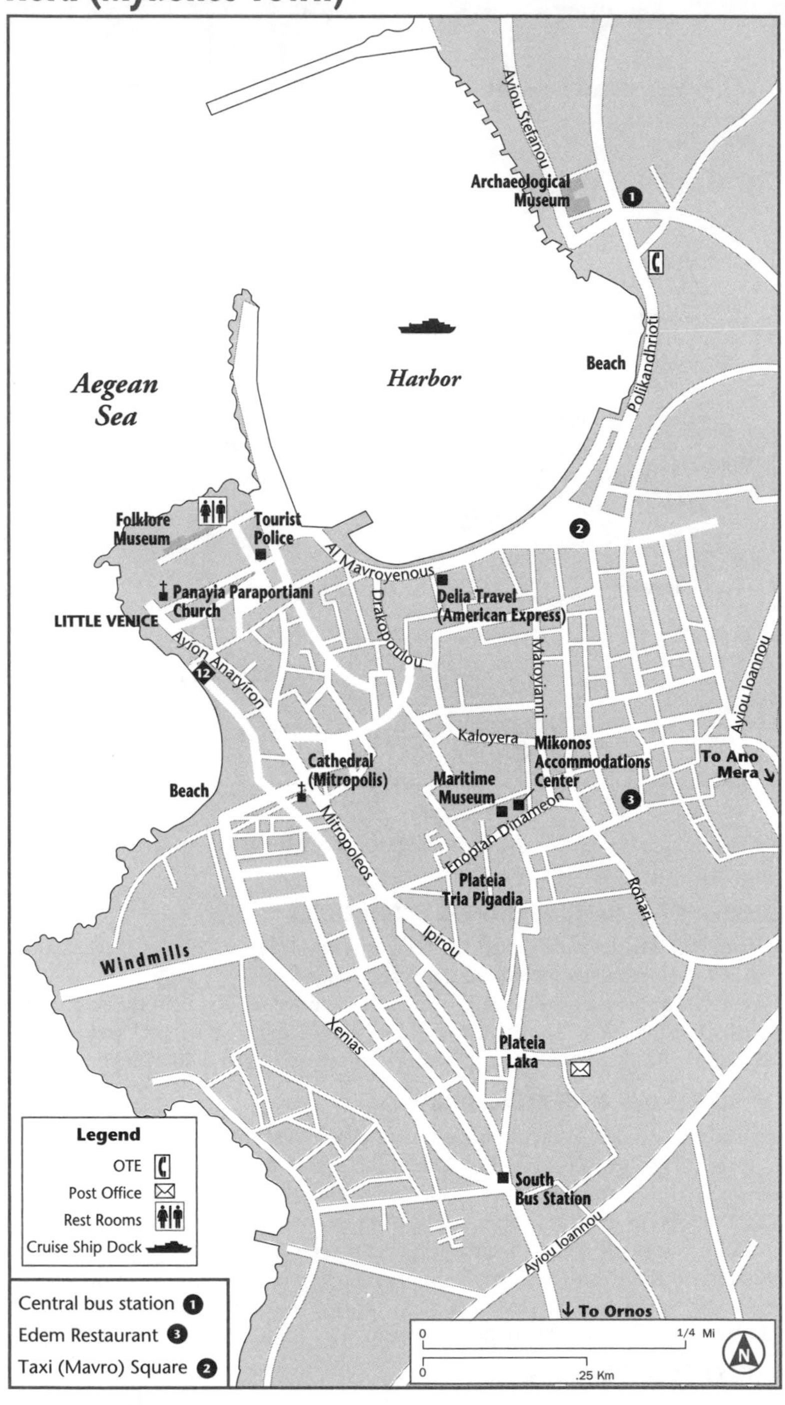

Ayiou Stefanou
Archaeological Museum
Polikandhrioti
Beach
Harbor
Aegean Sea
Folklore Museum
Tourist Police
Al Mavroyenous
Delia Travel (American Express)
Panayia Paraportiani Church
LITTLE VENICE
Ayion Anaryiron
Drakopoulou
Matoyianni
Ayiou Ioannou
Kaloyera
Mikonos Accommodations Center
To Ano Mera
Cathedral (Mitropolis)
Maritime Museum
Beach
Enoplan Dinameon
Mitropoleos
Plateia Tria Pigadia
Rohari
Ipirou
Windmills
Xenias
Plateia Laka
South Bus Station
Ayiou Ioannou
To Ornos
Legend
OTE
Post Office
Rest Rooms
Cruise Ship Dock
Central bus station 1
Edem Restaurant 3
Taxi (Mavro) Square 2
0
1/4 Mi
0
.25 Km
N

religious and commercial hub of the Aegean, but now is home only to ancient ruins and their caretakers. View the Agora; the Sacred Way, which leads to the Temple of Apollo; and the Avenue of Lions, where five marble beasts from the 7th century B.C. guard the now-dry Sacred Lake. View the remains of the Hellenistic Quarter with its harbors, waterhouses, and villas, including the House of Cleopatra, and the renowned mosaic floors in the House of the Dolphin, the House of the Masks, and the House of Dionysos. Also visit the Archaeological Museum.

The Top Attractions

The town of Hora itself, with its quaint houses, churches, and labyrinth of alleys, is the main attraction here. The best thing to do is simply wander, heading inland from the pier and wandering the labyrinth of streets, getting lost in the alleys, looking at the art galleries, jewelry, and other gift shops, or stopping at a cafe or bar. The town is like a picture postcard.

Stopping for a Bite

There are many quaint cafes and charming restaurants. Worth visiting is **Edem Restaurant** in Hora (☎ **0289/22-855**). It is known both for its meat dishes and great service, and is located above Panahrandou church—walk up Matoyianni, turn left on Kaloyera, and follow the signs up and to the left.

Best Shopping Buys

Mykonos boasts a large community of artists, with many galleries selling their work. Gold jewelry can be found throughout the island.

RHODES

The island of Rhodes is rich in history, and its landscape is dotted with beautiful beaches, mountain villages, and fertile plains. Its most famous inhabitants were the Knights of St. John, who came in 1291 after fleeing Jerusalem. They reigned for more than 2 centuries, and their legacy lives on in **Rhodes Town.** The city is now made up of the New Town and the Old Town; within the medieval walls of the Old Town are treasures from the Knights, while the New Town boasts a happening nighttime scene with its bars, discos, and tavernas.

Lindos, a picturesque village about 50 minutes from Rhodes Town, boasts the Acropolis at Lindos, which rises about 400 feet above the town on a beautiful bay.

Frommer's Favorite Rhodes Experiences

- **Exploring Old Town.** This section of the city is home to medieval treasures, charming rooftop cafes, and plenty of shops. To appreciate its many offerings, visitors must walk though its maze of streets. Along the way, you will discover historic sites, browse through a never-ending collection of souvenir shops, and be dazzled by the swirl of activity that surrounds you. Its main attractions include the Hospital of the Knights, the Streets of the Knights, and the Palace of the Grand Masters.
- **Visiting Lindos.** This picturesque village boasts the island's top archaeological site (the Acropolis) as well as traditional white-walled homes and cobblestone streets.
- **Soaking up the sun.** The island is known for its great beaches. Some of the best are located on the east coast. Faliaraki, about 20 minutes from Rhodes Town, is one of the island's most popular (admission is $3.50).

Coming Ashore & Getting Around

Ships dock at the commercial harbor, which is within walking distance of Rhodes Town's old section. The New Town is also within walking distance, but there is more to see in the Old Town.

To explore the island of Rhodes, transportation is required. Buses, rental cars, or motor scooters are available near the harbor. **Taxis** wait at the end of the pier. Negotiate fares with taxi drivers for sightseeing; the hourly rate is $25 to $35.

The Best Shore Excursions

Rhodes & Lindos (4–4$^1/_2$ hours, $47–$56): Travel by bus through the scenic countryside to Lindos, an important city in ancient times. At Lindos, view the medieval walls, which were constructed by the Knights of St. John in the 14th century. Walk or take a donkey up to the ancient Acropolis, where there are ruins and great views (you'll pass souvenir shops on the way). The trip may include a walking tour of Old Town Rhodes (see description above), a stop at a workshop selling Rhodian ceramics, and/or a visit to Mount Smith to view the ruins of ancient Rhodes, the Temple of Apollo, and Diagoras Stadium.

Lindos with Lunch by the Beach (8 hours, $65): Drive to Lindos and explore the city (see above). Continue on to a secluded beach for some swimming and sunning. Changing facilities, rest rooms, and showers are available. Enjoy lunch at a beachfront restaurant. Return to Rhodes, driving along the walls of the medieval city and stopping at Port d'Amboise for a walk through Old Town. View the Palace of the Knights and the medieval houses, as well as the Hospital of the Knights of St. John. The tour may stop at a ceramics workshop to view how Rhodian ceramics are made.

The Top Attractions

The Hospital of the Knights. Old Town. ☎ **02/41-276-57.** Admission $3. Open daily. Summer 8:30am–6pm; winter 8:30am–3pm.

The 15th-century Hospital of the Knights is now the home of the Archaeological Museum, whose collection features fine works from the Mycenaean and Roman eras.

The Street of the Knights. Old Town.

The cobblestoned street (noted on maps as "Ippoton") leads to the Palace of the Grand Masters and is where the inns of the various nations of the Knights of St. John were located. The inns served as clubs and meeting places for the knights, and their facades mirror the architectural styles of the various countries.

The Palace of the Grand Masters. Old Town. ☎ **02/41-233-59.** Admission $4. Tues–Sun, summer 8am–6pm; winter 8:30am–3pm.

This is the palace and fortress that dominates the Old Town. The floors are covered with mosaics from the island of Kos, and the palace features two permanent exhibitions about Rhodes.

Mandraki Harbor. New Town.

The Colossus of Rhodes, a 100-foot-tall bronze statue of the sun god Helios that's considered one of the Seven Wonders of the Ancient World, was erected somewhere here. (Legend has it that the statue straddled the harbor, but more likely it was erected off to one side.)

Stopping for a Bite

There are plenty of places in the Old Town and New Town to enjoy a meal, and the best bet at any of the restaurants is seafood. One of the best is **Alexis Taverna,** Odos Sokratous 18, in Old Town (☎ **0241/29-347**). Among those who have dined here are Winston Churchill and Jacqueline Kennedy, as well as assorted royalty. Reservations are recommended. Main courses run about $13 to $24.

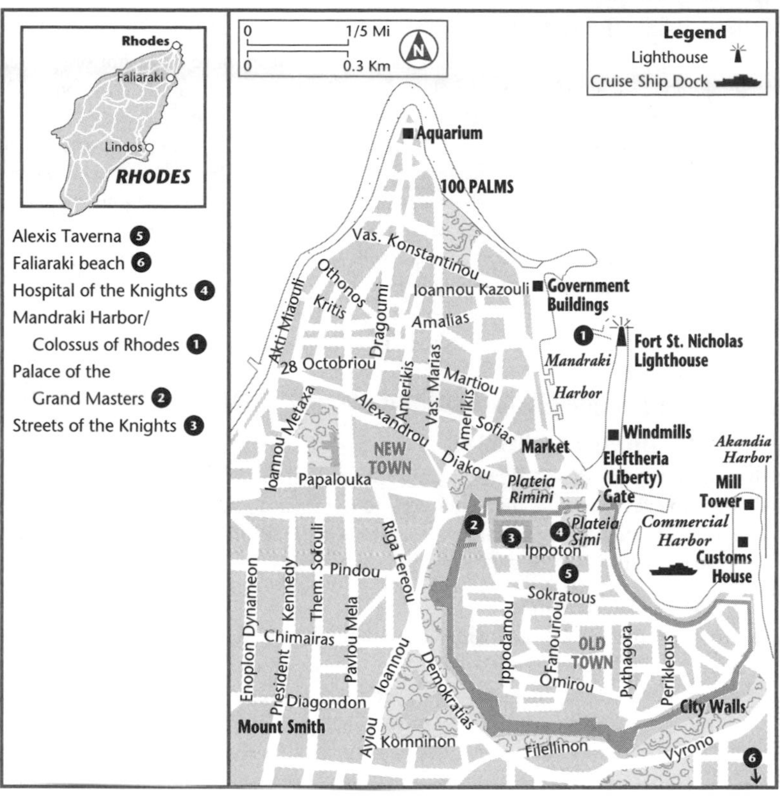

Best Shopping Buys

Shoppers should head to the Old Town for good buys on gold and silver jewelry, leather goods and furs, sea sponges, lace, and carpets and kilims.

SANTORINI

Dotted with whitewashed homes, black-pebble beaches, rich vineyards, and ancient ruins, Santorini is one of the most breathtaking islands in the world, and approaching it by ship is a dramatic experience. Ships enter **the caldera,** a central crater that was formed when a volcano erupted in 1500 B.C. Ash fell on the remaining land, burying the cosmopolitan city of **Akrotiri,** an event that some believe sparked the legend of the lost continent of Atlantis.

Fira, the capital of Santorini, lives up to its picture postcard reputation. The city is about 1,000 feet above sea level. Along its winding streets are shops, cafes, and art galleries.

Ia, about 10 to 15 minutes from Fira, is an artist's colony. The city is quite picturesque, with charming homes and galleries showcasing modern and folk art and traditional handicrafts.

Frommer's Favorite Santorini Experiences

- **Watching the sunset.** The best spots are from the ramparts of Lontza Castle in Ia, the volta (stroll) in Fira, or the footpath between Fira and Ia (see below).
- **Walking from Fira to Ia.** If you're a hiker, there's a 6.2-mile pedestrian path that follows the edge of the caldera and offers stunning views. Along the way, you pass several churches and climb two substantial hills.

Coming Ashore & Getting Around

Ships tender passengers to the port of Skala, and visitors have three options to reach town: donkey, cable car, or by foot. The **donkey and cable car rides** cost about $2.50 each way. The walk up the 587 steps is the same route the donkeys take. Word to the wise: Donkeys are fed at the bottom of the hill, so they tend to run down whether they are carrying someone or not. They are also very smelly. Cable cars run every 20 minutes; walking takes about 30 minutes (depending on the individual). Donkey rides take about 20 to 30 minutes depending on traffic and availability.

The city of Fira can be easily explored by foot. **Taxis** and **buses** are available to take you to other parts of the island. A cab ride to Ia takes about 10 to 15 minutes and costs $10 to $12 one-way; a cab ride to the ruins of Akrotiri is about 30 minutes (make sure you make return arrangements with the driver). Buses cost $1.50 to $3 each way. You can also rent a **moped** ($10 to $20 a day), but it is not the safest way of getting around (the roads on this island are notoriously treacherous).

The Best Shore Excursions

Akrotiri Excavations & Fira Town (3 hours, $47–$57): This tour takes you to Akrotiri, an excavation site that dates back to the second millennium B.C. You are then dropped off in Fira, where you'll have time to shop or stroll through town before catching a cable car ride or mule back down the slope to the ship.

The Top Attractions

Ancient Akrotiri. Akrotiri. ☎ **0286/81-366.** Admission about $4 adults, $3 seniors, $2 students. Tues–Sun 8:30am–3pm; closed Mon.

Excavations at Akrotiri, an ancient city that was preserved under a layer of volcanic ash 3,600 years ago, began in 1967 and are ongoing, giving visitors a glimpse of urban life in the Minoan period. Archaeologists have uncovered streets, houses, art, and magnificent frescoes, which are now on display at the National Archaeological Museum in Athens. It's best to take a guided tour here (as offered by the cruise lines) to fully appreciate what has been uncovered, but you can also purchase guidebooks at the site. The excavation is best explored in the morning, since the Akrotiri excavation is enclosed by a metal shed that magnifies the afternoon heat.

Ancient Thira. Kamari, 84700. ☎ **0286/31-66.** Admission $4 adults, $2 students. Tues–Sun 8:30am–3pm; closed Mon.

The extensive Hellenic, Roman, and Byzantine ruins of Ancient Thira stand on Mesa Vouna, and can be brought to life with the assistance of a good tour guide. From this perch, you get incredible views of Santorini and its neighbor islands. Two popular beaches, Kamari and Perissa, lie on either side of the mesa.

Stopping for a Bite

Watching the sunset from a cafe is a popular pastime in Santorini. **Kafe Kastro,** near Lontza Castle in Ia, offers great views from its outdoor terrace. The food is tasty and the prices are reasonable. To get a good seat outside, arrive early, have a drink, and wait for the show to begin.

In Fira, prices are higher at restaurants near the cable car station. Some of the city's finer establishments are located near the cathedral on Odos Ipapantis.

Best Shopping Buys

Jewelry prices in Fira are a tad higher than those in Athens, but there is a good selection. One of the better-known jewelers is **Kostas Antoniou** on Odos Ayiou Ioannou, north of the cable car station (☎ **0286/22-633**).

4 Italy

If you ask 10 people what their favorite country is in Europe, my guess is eight of them will say Italy, a beautiful and diverse country with an incredible cultural heritage. You can eat great food, talk to friendly people, and shop for the latest fashions; see some of the ancient world's most famous ruins, like the Forum in Rome and the ancient city of Pompeii; immerse yourself in the Renaissance in Florence; and be part of living history in Venice.

This is the land of Leonardo and Michelangelo, of Caesar and the Popes. And whether you are drawn by the treasure trove of artwork, the incredible architecture, the religious significance, the gorgeous scenery, the wonderful pasta, or all of the above, Italy, with its sense of *la dolce vita,* is bound to deliver.

ESSENTIALS

LANGUAGE Italian.

CURRENCY The Italian lira (plural lire). Bills come in 1,000L, 2,000L, 5,000L, 10,000L, 50,000L, 100,000L, and 500,000L denominations. The rate of exchange at press time was $1 = 1,845 lire.

CIVITAVECCHIA/ROME

The name of this port city probably has you shaking your head, going *Civita-who?* But Civitavecchia has served as the port of Rome since Emperor Trajan declared it such in A.D. 108.

Rome

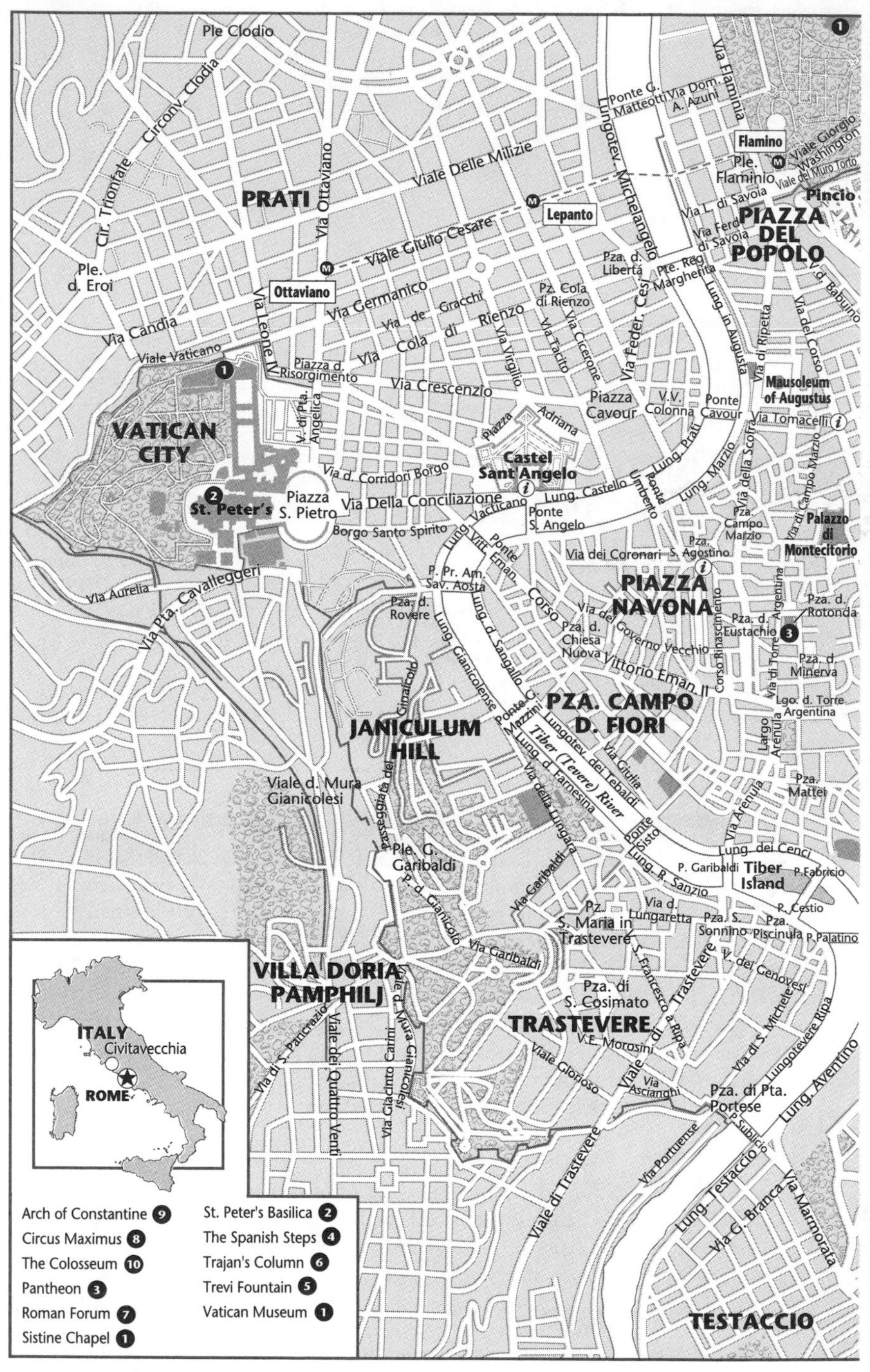

Arch of Constantine 9
Circus Maximus 8
The Colosseum 10
Pantheon 3
Roman Forum 7
Sistine Chapel 1
St. Peter's Basilica 2
The Spanish Steps 4
Trajan's Column 6
Trevi Fountain 5
Vatican Museum 1

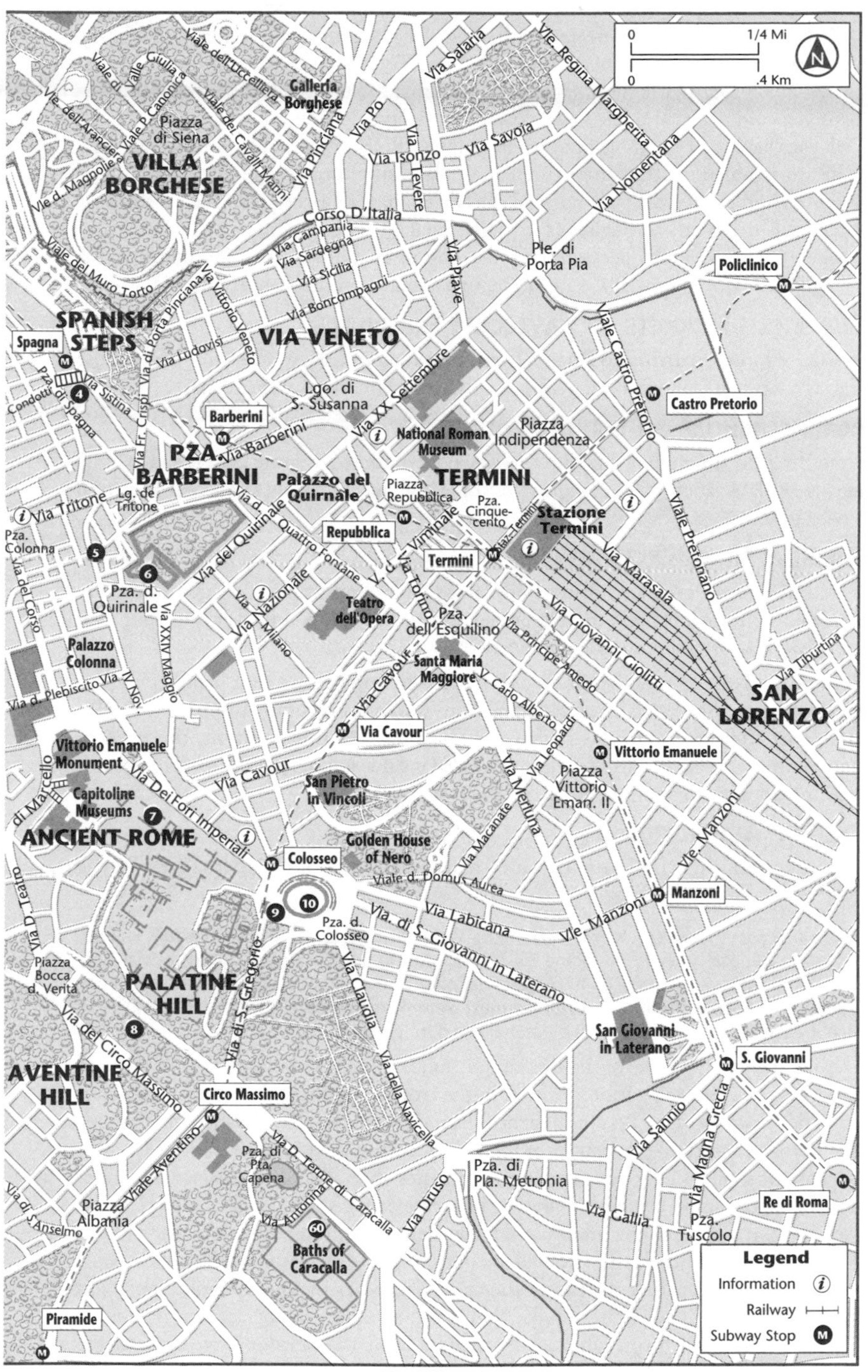

0
1/4 Mi
0
.4 Km
N
Galleria Borghese
VILLA BORGHESE
Piazza di Siena
SPANISH STEPS
Spagna
VIA VENETO
Barberini
PZA. BARBERINI
Palazzo del Quirinale
National Roman Museum
TERMINI
Piazza Indipendenza
Piazza Repubblica
Pza. Cinque-cento
Stazione Termini
Repubblica
Termini
Castro Pretorio
Policlinico
Ple. di Porta Pia
Corso D'Italia
Lgo. di S. Susanna
Lg. de Tritone
Pza. Colonna
Pza. d. Quirinale
Palazzo Colonna
Teatro dell'Opera
Pza. dell'Esquilino
Santa Maria Maggiore
SAN LORENZO
Vittorio Emanuele
Piazza Vittorio Eman. II
Via Cavour
Vittorio Emanuele Monument
Capitoline Museums
ANCIENT ROME
San Pietro in Vincoli
Golden House of Nero
Colosseo
Pza. d. Colosseo
Manzoni
PALATINE HILL
Piazza Bocca d. Verità
AVENTINE HILL
Circo Massimo
San Giovanni in Laterano
S. Giovanni
Pza. di Pta. Capena
Pza. di Pla. Metronia
Piazza Albania
Baths of Caracalla
Re di Roma
Pza. Tuscolo
Piramide
Legend
Information
Railway
Subway Stop

Cruise ships shuttle passengers from here to Rome, about an hour and a half away by bus. Civitavecchia itself, with its mostly post–World War II architecture, hasn't attracted much tourist attention. However, given that 2000 is the Jubilee Year, with numerous special events and religious celebrations planned in Rome and throughout Italy, Civitavecchia has invested big bucks in its cruise facilities and decided to make the most of its few landmarks. Renovations are taking place on fountains and ancient walls, for instance. And the Renaissance Forte Michelangelo has been designated as a setting for special cultural events throughout the Jubilee Year.

There is also shopping in town (keep in mind most shops close in the afternoon for a long lunch period) as well as some decent restaurants on the waterfront.

Frommer's Favorite Civitavecchia Experiences

- **Take a shore excursion to Rome.** There is nothing in Civitavecchia that comes close to the Roman Colosseum, the Vatican, and other amazing landmarks.

Coming Ashore & Getting Around

From the pier, it's about a 15-minute walk to town, or a 5-minute cab ride. **Taxis** are usually available at the pier. The drive to Rome is about 90 minutes. There is also **train** service to Rome.

The Best Shore Excursions

In addition to the excursion below, most ships offer a bus transfer so you can explore Rome on your own for $55 to $69. Some offer the option of a half-day on your own and a half-day of group touring for $75 to $92.

Rome City Tour (9½ hours, $125–$156): This comprehensive tour includes visits to the Colosseum, St. Peter's Basilica, the Vatican Museum, and the Sistine Chapel. Also drive past such landmarks as the Roman Forum, Trajan's Column, the Arch of Constantine, and the Circus Maximus. May also include a short walk to see Trevi Fountain. Includes lunch and time to shop for souvenirs.

The Top Attractions

There's not really much to see in Civitavecchia; all the attractions listed here are in Rome itself.

Basilica di San Pietro (St. Peter's Basilica). Piazza San Pietro. ☎ **06/69884466.** Free admission to basilica; stairs to the dome $3; elevator to the dome $3.60. Open daily Mar–Sept 7am–7pm, Oct and Nov 7am–6pm. Grottoes daily 7am–5pm. Dome daily Mar–Sept 8am–6pm, Oct and Nov 8am–4:30pm. Note: Women must wear skirts that cover the knees or pants. Men cannot wear shorts. Sleeveless tops are not allowed for either gender.

This famous earthly locus of the Roman Catholic Church is amazing, both inside and out; truly the most magnificent church in the world, and located on one of the most magnificent squares (the Bernini-designed Piazza San Pietro). Renaissance and baroque in design and measuring the length of about two football fields, the church is filled with the work of some of Italy's greatest artists, and enough marble, gilt, mosaics, and other grandeur to be almost overwhelming. The immense dome is the design of Michelangelo; over the altar is the notable bronze canopy by Bernini; and in the nave on the right in the first chapel is Michelangelo's famous statue *Pietá.* On the floor, in the center, you'll find markings comparing the size of the church to other famous Catholic cathedrals around the world. The sacristy is filled with jewel-studded religious objects. From the 375-foot dome, which you can reach by walking or by the elevator (I recommend the latter), you are treated to a panoramic view of Rome and the Vatican. The church is said to have been built over the tomb of the crucified saint.

Vatican Museum and the Sistine Chapel. Viale Vaticano, Vatican City. ☎ **06/69883333.** Admission $9 adults, $6 children. Final Sun of each month free, but there are big crowds. Mid-Mar to late Oct, Mon–Sat and the final Sun of each month 8:45am–4pm. Other times, Mon–Sat 8:45am–1:45pm. Last admission 1 hour before closing. Closed religious holidays.

This is where the independent state that is the Vatican displays its gigantic collection of treasures. The museum is massive, so you'll have to choose a route based on the museum's four color-coded itineraries, which range from 1 1/2 to 5 hours. All four itineraries culminate in the Sistine Chapel. Otherwise, you can pick based on your areas of interest. There's much to choose from, including a picture gallery with paintings from the 11th to the 19th century, an Egyptian collection, the Etruscan museum, Greek and Roman sculptures, and, of course, the Sistine Chapel, where Michelangelo labored for 4 years (1509–12) to paint ceiling frescoes taken from the pages of Genesis. The work on the nine panels, now controversially restored to their original glory, was so physically taxing to create it was said to have permanently damaged the artist's eyesight. Also worth checking out is the Stanze di Raphael, rooms decorated by the artist Raphael. *Tip:* The best way to view the Sistine Chapel's ceiling is to bring along binoculars.

Foro Romano (Roman Forum). Via dei Fori Imperiali. ☎ **06/6990110.** Admission $7.20 adults, free for children 17 and under and seniors 60 and over. Open Apr–Sept, Mon–Sat 9am–6pm, Sun 9am–1pm; Oct, Nov, and Mar, Mon–Sat 9am–3pm, Sun 9am–1pm. Last admission 1 hour before closing.

The forum was the center of Roman life in the days of the Republic, though it later lost prestige to the Imperial Forum. The remains—ruins, fragments, an arch or two, and lots of overturned boulders—are hard to put into context unless you purchase a detailed plan (available at the gate). A long walk up the hill leads to the Palatine Hill, one of the seven hills of Rome and the spot where the first settlers, under the direction of Romulus, are believed to have built their huts. It's worth the climb for the sweeping view of the Roman and Imperial forums and Colosseum.

Colosseo (Colosseum). Piazzale del Colosseo, Via dei Fori Imperiali. ☎ **06/7004261.** Free admission to the street level; upper levels $4.80. Apr–Sept, Mon–Tues and Thurs–Sat 9am–6pm (until 7pm June–Aug), Wed and Sun 9am–1pm. Oct, Nov and Mar, Mon–Tues and Thurs–Sat 9am–3pm, Wed and Sun 9am–1pm.

While a mere shell, the colosseum remains the greatest architectural remnant of ancient Rome. Construction of the amphitheater was ordered by Vespasian in the year 72, and the colosseum was inaugurated by Titus in the year 80. Here the combat involved gladiators and wild beasts; at its peak, 50,000 people could view the spectacle. Battles were staged, including naval battles (the Colosseum could be flooded), and the defeated combatants might have their lives spared for putting up a good fight. Many historians now dispute the legend, however, that Christians were fed to the lions here. Next to the colosseum, the Arch of Constantine was erected to honor Constantine on his defeat of the pagan Maxentius in the year 306.

Pantheon. Piazza della Rotonda. ☎ **06/68300230.** Free admission. July–Sept, daily 9am–6pm; other months, Mon–Sat 9am–4:30pm, Sun 9am–1pm.

The Pantheon is the only great building of ancient Rome that remains intact today. It was built in 27 B.C. by Marcus Agrippa, and later reconstructed by the emperor Hadrian in the first part of the 2nd century. The remarkable structure is among the architectural wonders of the world. Animals were once sacrificed and burned in the center, with the smoke escaping from the 27-foot-diameter opening at the top. Michelangelo studied the dome before designing the cupola of St. Peter's (where the dome is only 2 feet smaller than at the Pantheon).

Trevi Fountain. Piazza di Trevi.

Legend has it that if you toss a coin in the fountain you will return to Rome. If you can make your way through the summertime crowds you can drop a coin and take a moment to appreciate the fountain's lavish baroque design, which features the figure of Neptunus Rex, standing on a shell chariot drawn by winged horse, led by a pair of tritons. The fountain was completed in 1762.

The Spanish Steps (Scalinata della Trinitá dei Monti). Piazza di Spagna.

The famous steps take their name from the Spanish Embassy, which used to be headquartered at the site. They were designed by Italian architect Francesco de Sanctis and built between 1723 and 1725. The 136 steps and the piazza below are always packed with crowds people-watching and browsing the carts of the flower and jewelry vendors.

Stopping for a Bite

There are restaurants and trattorias on Civitavecchia's waterfront, serving pasta, seafood, and pizza.

Best Shopping Buys

Shop here for shoes and other leather goods. There are a number of good stores on the main street (though not as good as what you'll find in Rome). In the morning, it's also fun to poke around the market, located behind the main street.

LIVORNO

This major port city is the gateway to Florence, the birthplace of the Italian Renaissance, about a 2-hour drive away. It is also a port of choice for cruise lines because of its close proximity to Pisa and the leaning tower thereof, and as an entry to the Tuscany region with its famous Chianti vineyards, cypress trees, and olive groves.

There's not much happening in the way of tourist attractions in Livorno itself, but you can shop here for olive oil and Chianti and enjoy a typical Tuscan meal.

Frommer's Favorite Livorno Experiences

- **Book the shore excursion to Florence.** Or you can take the shuttle and explore Florence on your own.

Coming Ashore & Getting Around

Ships dock about a mile from the center of town. **Taxis** are usually available at the pier. Florence is a 2-hour drive. Pisa is only 12 miles away.

The Best Shore Excursions

Florence City Tour (9 hours, $103–$136): It's a 2-hour drive to the edge of the city center, where buses have to park, with the rest of the tour on foot. Visit the Galleria dell'Accademia, Europe's first drawing school, to view Michelangelo's sculptures, including *David;* the Duomo, the tremendous cathedral (it's the fourth largest church in the world); the Campanile, the 15th-century bell tower; Piazza della Signoria, the city's main square; and the 13th-century Church of Santa Croce. Lunch and shopping time are included. Some tours also make a photo stop at Pisa. (Ships usually also offer bus transfers for $66 to $69, so you can explore Florence on your own.)

The Leaning Tower of Pisa (3 hours, $42): Only 12 miles from Livorno is Pisa, home of the famous Leaning Tower. Galileo is said to have used the 180-foot tower for his gravitational experiments. On this tour you'll also explore the Baptistery and Campo Santo. Time is also allowed for souvenir shopping.

STOPPING FOR A BITE

You can try the excellent Tuscan cuisine in Livorno, either at one of the trattorias or at the fancier hotels. The food is hearty—pastas, cheeses, and simply prepared meat and fish, a main ingredient being the region's wonderful olive oil. Wash your meal down with Chianti, especially the highly regarded Chianti Classico, or other Tuscan wines.

BEST SHOPPING BUYS

There are shops along the Via Grande, Livorno's main street. Most close from 12:30 to 3:30pm. In addition to Chianti, best buys include the locally produced amber-colored olive oil.

SORRENTO

Known as the City of Sirens (those lovely mermaids who lured seamen to death with their pretty songs), Sorrento has for centuries been a favorite resort of wealthy Romans. It's dramatically located on top of a cliff overlooking the ocean. It's a charming town with great shops and quaint streets, although it can get very crowded and snarled with traffic in the summer high season.

Though most ships stop here more for the easy access Sorrento provides to the ancient city of Pompeii, the scenic Amalfi Coast, and the nearby romantic isle of Capri, Sorrento itself is a pleasant place to stroll around (there are some pretty areas of lemon groves) and a good place to do some shopping or sit in an outdoor cafe to people-watch.

FROMMER'S FAVORITE SORRENTO EXPERIENCES

- **Take the shore excursion to Pompeii or to Capri.** That's really why your ship has stopped here.
- **Stroll around town and have a coffee in an outdoor cafe.** The shops are worth a look (especially those featuring inlaid wood and other local crafts) and this is a great place to people-watch.

COMING ASHORE & GETTING AROUND

Ships tender passengers to the pier, where you'll usually find **taxis.** The center of town is about a 15-minute uphill walk. **Minibuses** operated by the city also make the uphill climb.

THE BEST SHORE EXCURSIONS

The Ruins of Pompeii (4½ hours, $48–$51): Tour this once prosperous ancient city of 20,000, which was buried when Vesuvius erupted in A.D. 79. Today, nearly two-thirds of the city has been excavated and the ruins are amazing. On your guided walk through the rocky ruins you'll visit the baths and theaters, the wrestling ground and the restored villas. During the drive you can view Vesuvius, the still-active volcano.

Capri (5 hours, $55–$79): Board a hydrofoil for a cruise to Capri. Transfer by bus to Anacapri for magnificent views and a tour of Villa San Michele, with its collection of antiquities. Return to town for a walking tour of Capri to visit the Gardens of Augustus park and explore the town's narrow streets and central square. The tour includes time to shop or visit a cafe.

Amalfi Coast (5–7 hours, $66–$85): Drive about 2 hours along the scenic Amalfi Coast to Amalfi town, a romantic little town that was a major shipping port during the Middle Ages. Take a guided tour of the town's center, including the Cathedral of St. Andrea, built in a combination of Moorish and early Gothic design. Time is allowed for souvenir shopping. From the bus, you'll see Positano with its white houses, terraced gardens, and fishing fleet, and other scenic coastal sights.

Sorrento

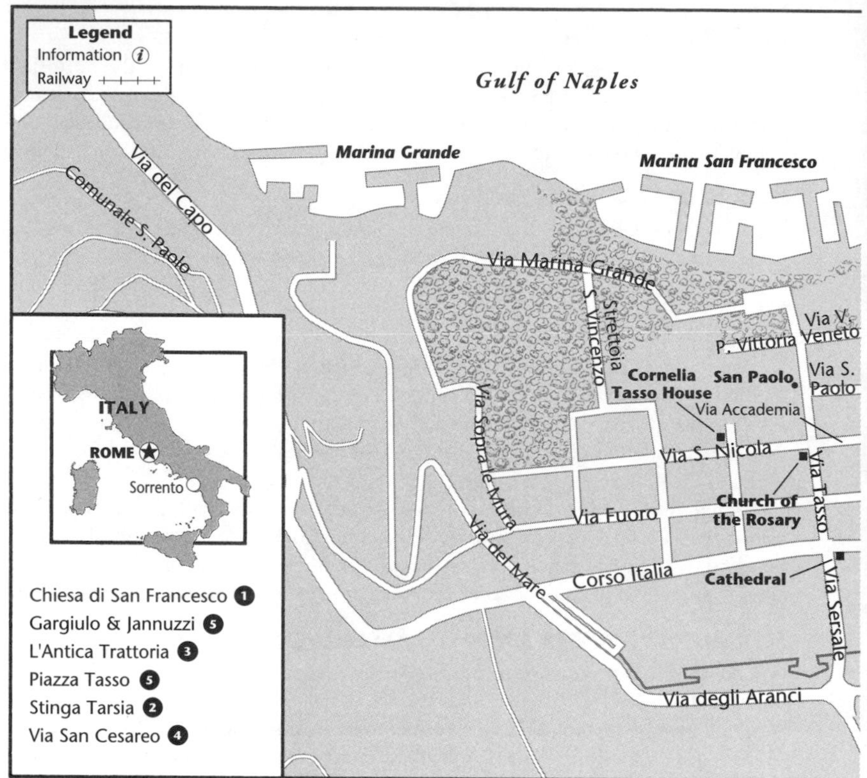

The Top Attractions

Chiesa di San Francesco (The Cloister of St. Francis). Via San Francesco. ☎ **081/878-1269.** Open daily 9am–6pm. Free admission.

While few people come here to look at churches, this one is worth a peek. It dates from the 14th century, and offers pretty archways and a lovely garden. The convent is also an art school that regularly offers exhibits.

Stopping for a Bite

Pasta with seafood and fish cooked in salt crust are popular selections here. One of the best places to sample the local cuisine is the 200-year-old **L'Antica Trattoria,** Via P.R. Giuliani 33 (☎ **081/807-1082**). Reservations are recommended. The restaurant's specialty is its antipasti.

Best Shopping Buys

The best areas for strolling and window-shopping are **Piazza Tasso** and **Via San Cesareo.** Locally made wooden inlaid items make a great souvenir, although prices are steep. The region's best-known maker of inlaid furniture is **Gargiulo & Jannuzzi,** Piazza Tasso (☎ **081/878-1041**), which opened in 1863. Employees demonstrate the technique to tourists in the shop's basement. Smaller shops—including **Stinga Tarsia,** Via L. De Maio, which has been in business since 1890—can be found nearby.

Other popular items here include linens, lace, coral jewelry, and lemon liquor (called limoncello).

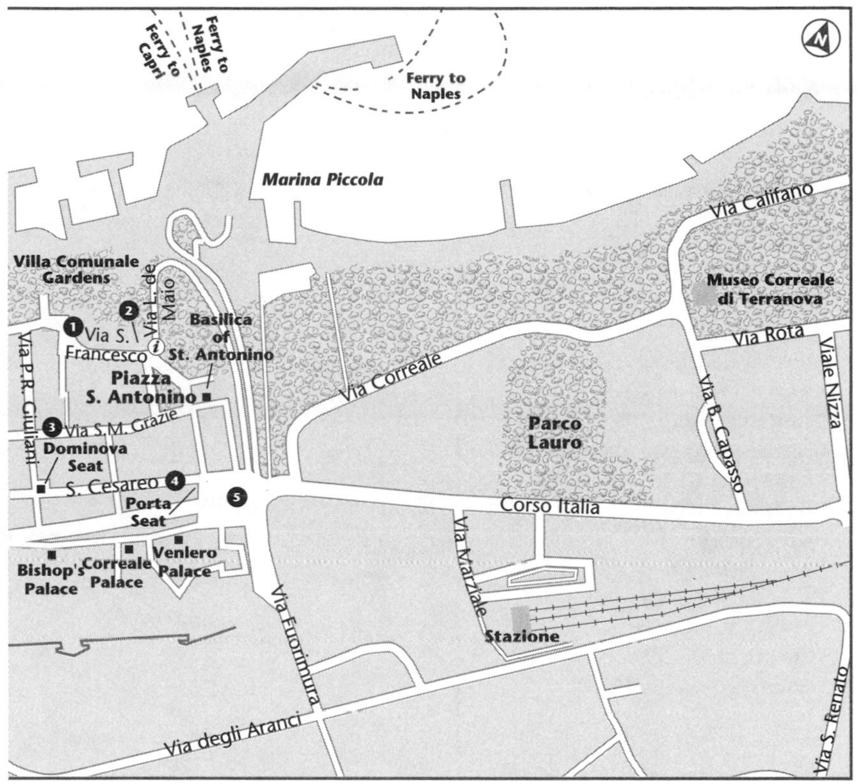

VENICE

My mom advised me on my first adult trip to Venice that you don't really have to go into a museum here because the whole city is a museum. And she was so right. Everywhere you look in Venice there's something worth seeing, whether it's the Gothic and Renaissance structures this city seems to have grown like trees, or the construction efforts aimed at stopping said buildings from sinking.

My favorite activity here is simply exploring the maze of canals and side streets, crossing the medieval bridges, people-watching, and getting lost (and finding my way back home again). That activity, in summer, helps me avoid some of the hordes of other visitors who crowd together at St. Mark's Square. (You can't get too lost anyway since there are yellow arrows all over pointing you back to main landmarks such as Piazzo San Marco or the Rialto Bridge.)

Getting out on the **Grand Canal,** a water version of a main city boulevard, is a must-do, whether you go the touristy route on a gondola (negotiate upfront with the driver and expect to pay through your teeth) or on equally overpriced water taxis, or if you go like most Venetians do on a vaporetto (water bus). The S-shaped canal curves for 2 miles past historic buildings, ornate bridges, and palaces. And as you check out the sights, you'll share the main waterway with ambulances, delivery barges, and other vessels going about the tasks of ordinary life here.

Everywhere you look there will be something artistic or otherwise fascinating to see. Like Florence, Venice has a treasure trove of paintings, statues, and frescoes in its

Venice

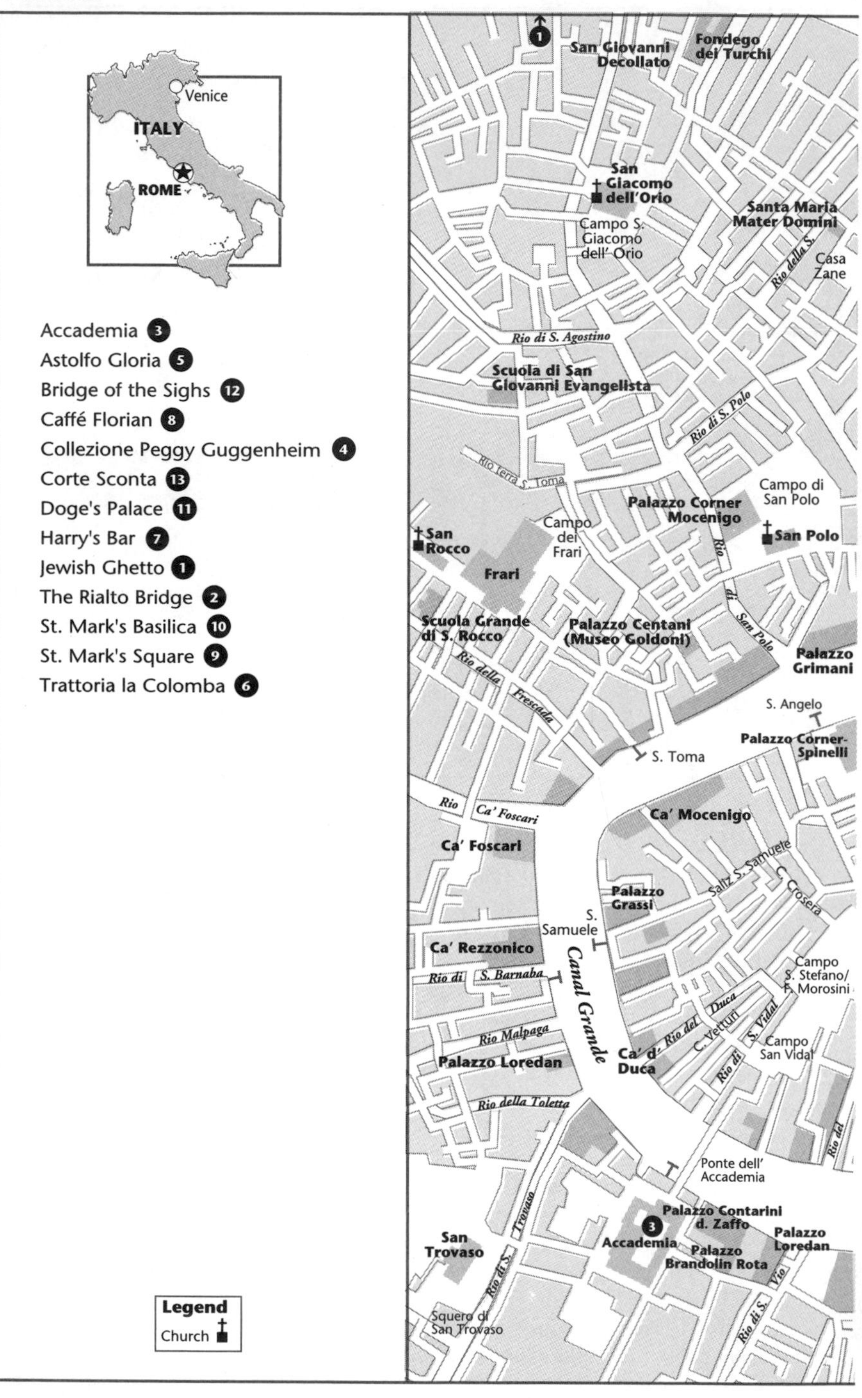
Venice
ITALY
ROME
Accademia 3
Astolfo Gloria 5
Bridge of the Sighs 12
Caffé Florian 8
Collezione Peggy Guggenheim 4
Corte Sconta 13
Doge's Palace 11
Harry's Bar 7
Jewish Ghetto 1
The Rialto Bridge 2
St. Mark's Basilica 10
St. Mark's Square 9
Trattoria la Colomba 6
Legend
Church
E-0262
San Giovanni Decollato
Fondego dei Turchi
San Giacomo dell'Orio
Campo S. Giacomo dell' Orio
Santa Maria Mater Domini
Rio della S.
Casa Zane
Rio di S. Agostino
Scuola di San Giovanni Evangelista
Rio di S. Polo
Rio terra S. Toma
Campo di San Polo
Palazzo Corner Mocenigo
San Polo
San Rocco
Campo dei Frari
Frari
Rio di San Polo
Scuola Grande di S. Rocco
Palazzo Centani (Museo Goldoni)
Palazzo Grimani
Rio della Frescada
S. Angelo
Palazzo Corner-Spinelli
S. Toma
Rio Ca' Foscari
Ca' Mocenigo
Ca' Foscari
Saliz. S. Samuele
C. Crosera
Palazzo Grassi
S. Samuele
Ca' Rezzonico
Canal Grande
Campo S. Stefano/ F. Morosini
Rio di S. Barnaba
Rio del Duca
C. Vetturi
Rio di S. Vidal
Campo San Vidal
Rio Malpaga
Ca' d. Duca
Palazzo Loredan
Rio della Toletta
Rio del
Ponte dell' Accademia
Trovaso
Palazzo Contarini d. Zaffo
Palazzo Loredan
San Trovaso
Accademia
Palazzo Brandolin Rota
Rio di S.
Rio di S. Vio
Squero di San Trovaso

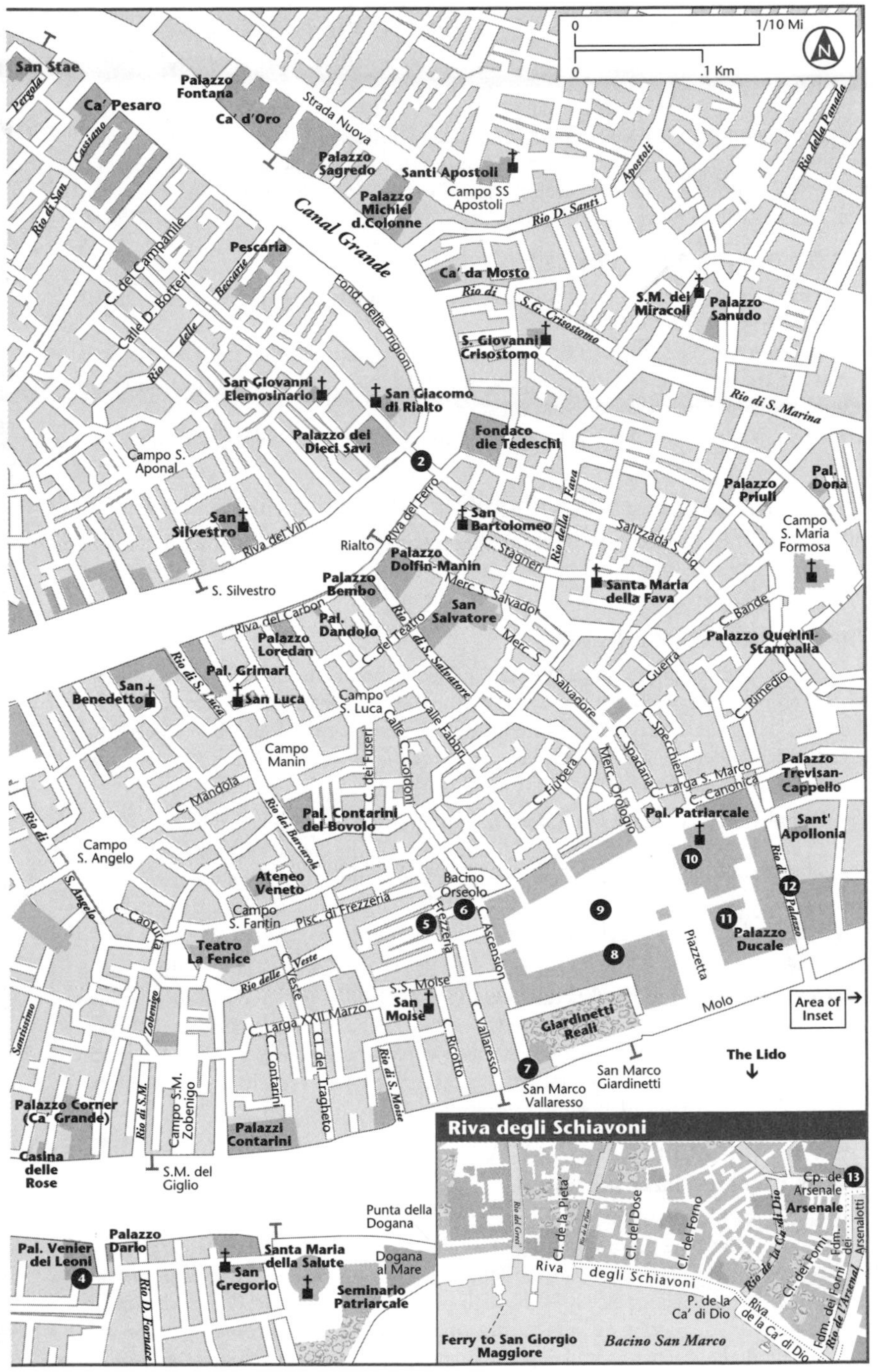
0
1/10 Mi
0
.1 Km
N
San Stae
Ca' Pesaro
Palazzo Fontana
Ca' d'Oro
Strada Nuova
Palazzo Sagredo
Santi Apostoli
Campo SS Apostoli
Palazzo Michiel d.Colonne
Canal Grande
Pescaria
Ca' da Mosto
S.M. dei Miracoli
Palazzo Sanudo
S. Giovanni Crisostomo
San Giovanni Elemosinario
San Giacomo di Rialto
Palazzo dei Dieci Savi
Fondaco die Tedeschi
Campo S. Aponal
San Silvestro
San Bartolomeo
Palazzo Priuli
Pal. Donà
Campo S. Maria Formosa
Rialto
Palazzo Dolfin-Manin
S. Silvestro
Palazzo Bembo
San Salvatore
Santa Maria della Fava
Pal. Dandolo
Palazzo Loredan
Palazzo Querini-Stampalia
Pal. Grimari
San Benedetto
San Luca
Campo S. Luca
Campo Manin
Pal. Contarini del Bovolo
Palazzo Trevisan-Cappello
Pal. Patriarcale
Sant' Apollonia
Campo S. Angelo
Ateneo Veneto
Bacino Orseolo
Campo S. Fantin
Teatro La Fenice
Palazzo Ducale
Piazzetta
S.S. Moise
San Moisè
Giardinetti Reali
Molo
Area of Inset
The Lido
San Marco Giardinetti
San Marco Vallaresso
Palazzo Corner (Ca' Grande)
Palazzi Contarini
Casina delle Rose
S.M. del Giglio
Campo S.M. Zobenigo
Punta della Dogana
Palazzo Dario
Pal. Venier dei Leoni
Santa Maria della Salute
San Gregorio
Dogana al Mare
Seminario Patriarcale
Riva degli Schiavoni
Cp. de Arsenale
Arsenale
Riva degli Schiavoni
P. de la Ca' di Dio
Riva de la Ca' di Dio
Ferry to San Giorgio Maggiore
Bacino San Marco
2
4
5
6
7
8
9
10
11
12
13

churches (including the famous St. Mark's) and in its palaces. And the Peggy Guggenheim museum houses one of the best collections of 20th-century art in the Western world.

Check out the shops and cafes in and around **St. Mark's Square.** Enjoy the fact there are no cars, and ignore the fact there are too many other tourists (especially if you visit in July or August). Also ignore the fact that the prices for food and souvenirs have gotten rather ridiculously high. Have a meal, the favorite Italian pastime; grab a coffee or gelato in a cafe; or have an overpriced Bloody Mary at Harry's Bar.

Frommer's Favorite Venice Experiences

- **Go exploring.** The maze of historic streets and canals offers fascinating sights at nearly every turn.
- **Go Shopping.** The selection of locally produced glass and other crafts is amazing, and the Italian designer shops tempting, even if the prices can be steep. And Prada is less expensive here than in New York.
- **Mangia.** Venetian cuisine, especially the seafood, is excellent, and well worth indulging in.

Coming Ashore & Getting Around

Ships generally dock about 15 to 20 minutes by boat from St. Mark's Square. Travel here is on the water, with your choice being either a water taxi (which will be pricey) or the water buses called vaporetti (which are cheap).

The Best Shore Excursions

Venice City Sightseeing (3 hours, $48–$72): Take a motor launch to St. Mark's Square for a guided walking tour of St. Mark's Cathedral, one of the world's most famous churches. Tour the Doge's Palace, the former residence of the Duke of Venice. Also includes the Golden Staircase, where you can enjoy the views of St. Mark's Basin. Cross the famous Bridge of Sighs. Stop at the small workshops of glass manufacturers.

The Grand Canal & the Inside Canal ($2^1/_2$ hours, $83–$118): Travel by motorboat with a guide and 10 to 12 other people and see the way the city works—the police, fire brigade, even wedding and funeral processions travel by boat. From the water you'll get a wonderful view of St. Mark's Square and other sights, including palaces and the Guggenheim Museum. You'll also go under the famous Rialto Bridge.

The Historic Jewish Ghetto ($3^1/_2$ hours, $41–$61): In the 16th century, the Jews of Venice were restricted to the Ghetto unless they were doctors. They had to wear distinctive clothing and could not own land. The Ghetto has been preserved and offers a fascinating glimpse of what life was like for the people who lived there, and of the modern Jewish culture in Venice (several synagogues in the Ghetto still have active congregations). You take a motor launch to the entrance and tour on foot.

The Top Attractions

St. Mark's Square (Piazza San Marco).

This square is the cultural hub of the city. You can easily spend hours here, watching people and feeding the pigeons, sitting at a cafe, visiting the Basilica and Doge's Palace (see below), and shopping. But the square is also a tourist hub which can be very crowded during the day, especially in the high summer tourist season. To see the square with fewer crowds, go very early in the morning (watch the sun come up) or in the evening. At night, there are music performances by chamber orchestras and other groups.

St. Mark's Basilica (Basillica di San Marco). Piazza San Marco. ☎ **041/522-5205.** Basilica free; treasury about $2.30; presbytery about $1.75; Marciano Museum $1.75. Basilica, Apr–Sept, Mon–Sat 9:30am–5:30pm, Sun 2–5:30pm; Oct–Mar, Mon–Sat 9:30am–5pm, Sun 1:30pm–4:30pm. Note: Men and women are barred from wearing shorts or exposing bare arms and shoulders, and women may not wear skirts above the knee in the basilica. Silence is required, and you may not take photos.

The "Church of Gold" is one of the greatest and most elaborate churches in the world, built in a conglomeration of styles, though Byzantine predominates (it looks like it would be just as at home in Istanbul). The basilica is capped by a dome that can be seen as your ship moves down the Grand Canal. On the facade are replicas of the four famous St. Mark's horses (see more below). One mosaic depicts the entry of the evangelist's body into Venice, hidden in a pork barrel (the body was smuggled out of Alexandria in 828).

In the atrium are six cupolas with mosaics depicting scenes from the Old Testament, including the story of the Tower of Babel. The basilica's interior, once used as the private chapel of the doges, is stunning, with marbles, alabaster, pillars, and an ocean of mosaics.

The **treasury** contains skulls and bones of ecclesiastical authorities as well as goblets, chalices, and Gothic candelabra. In the presbytery rests the alleged sarcophagus of St. Mark.

The **Marciano Museum** upstairs contains the Triumphal Quadriga, the four famous horses looted from Constantinople by Venetian crusaders in 1204. The horses used to be outside, but were moved indoors because of pollution damage and subsequently restored. They're the only quartet of yoked horses to have survived from the classical era. It is believed they were cast in the 4th century. Napoléon once carted these horses off to Paris, but they were returned to Venice in 1815. From the museum, which also contains mosaics and tapestries, you can walk out onto the loggia for a view of Piazza San Marco.

Palazzo Ducale (Doge's Palace) & the Bridge of Sighs. Piazzetta San Marco. ☎ **041/522-4951.** Admission $10 adults, $6 students with ID, $3.50 children 6–13, under 5 free. Apr–Oct, daily 9am–7pm.

This Venetian Gothic palazzo is Italy's grandest civic structure. And it literally gleams. While it dates back to 1309, most was destroyed by a fire and rebuilt in the 16th century. Many of the greatest Venetian painters of that century helped with the restoration. After climbing the Sansovino stairway of gold, proceed to the Anti-Collegio salon to view Veronese's *Rape of Europe* and Tintoretto's *Three Graces* and *Bacchus and Adriadne.* Downstairs you can visit the apartments of the Doges and the grand Maggior Consiglio, with its allegorical *Triumph of Venice* by Veronese on the ceiling. Tintoretto's *Paradise* over the Grand Council chamber is said to be the largest oil painting in the world.

Follow the arrows to the Bridge of Sighs, which links the Doge's Palace with the Palazzo delle Prigioni, where you'll find cell blocks—the sighs refer to the laments of those tortured here.

Climbing the Bell Tower

For about $4.65 you can climb to the top of the bell tower of St. Mark's, and you don't even have to brave a dark, steep, winding staircase to do it—there's an elevator. From the top you can get a bird's-eye view of the city, and a nice view as well of the basilica's cupolas.

Portofino

For quaint fishing villages you can't beat Portofino, known as the "Pearl of the Riviera," even if the harbor is almost overrun with luxury yachts in the summer. The village offers frescoed houses and lush vegetation and is absolutely picture postcard perfect.

Ships tender passengers right into town (some offer Portofino as a shore excursion from Genoa). The town is tiny, and you can easily explore the narrow streets on foot. There are wonderful waterfront cafes, art galleries, and jewelry shops (be aware that prices can be hefty), but I highly recommend a hike up the hill above the harbor (you can also take a cab) for lunch on the terrace at the **Hotel Albergo Splendido,** Viale Baratta 13 (☎ **800/237-1236** in the U.S. or 0185/269-551; reservations recommended). It may be the most expensive lunch you've ever eaten, but the splendid food, service, and views are worth every penny (or make that every C-note). Illustrious guests at the hotel have included the duke and duchess of Windsor, Ernest Hemingway, Greta Garbo, Ingrid Bergman, Aristotle Onassis, Clark Gable, John Wayne, and even J. R. himself, Larry Hagman.

Accademia. Campo della Caritá, Dorsoduro. ☎ **041/5222-2247.** Admission $7.20 adults, free for children 17 and under and seniors 60 and over. Mon–Sat 9am–7pm, Sun 9am–2pm.

The glory of old Venice lives on in this museum, with its remarkable collection of paintings from the 14th to the 18th century.

Collezione Peggy Guggenheim. Ca' Venier dei Leoni, Dorsoduro 701, Calle San Cristoforo. ☎ **041/520-6288.** Admission $7.20 adults, $4.80 students and children 16 and under. Wed–Mon 11am–6pm.

This impressive palazzo on the Grand Canal, which was Ms. Guggenheim's home, houses a comprehensive and brilliant modern art collection. In the tradition of her family, Guggenheim, who died in 1979, was a lifelong patron of contemporary painters and sculptors. Displayed are works by Pollack, Ernst, Picasso, Braque, Magritte, Duchamp, Chagall, Mondrian, Brancusi, Dalí, Giacometti, and Moore, as well as lesser known artists. Some ships offer the opportunity to tour the museum on a private basis, on special shore excursions.

Stopping for a Bite

Papa Hemingway liked **Harry's Bar,** Calle Vallaresso, San Marco (☎ **041/528-5777**), but the fame has made the prices here downright shocking (main courses run $46 to $55), especially given the rather simple food. Still, those wishing to pay tribute to Hemingway should at least order a Bloody Mary at the bar.

A more reasonable choice is **Trattoria la Colomba,** Piscina Frezzeria, San Marco 1665 (☎ **041/522-1175;** reservations recommended). The history of this restaurant is linked to some of Venice's leading painters, who traded art for meals. Modern paintings adorn the walls today (they change seasonally and are for sale). You can also dine outside. The cuisine is Venetian and includes wonderful seafood and pasta dishes and locally grown vegetables; main courses run from $23 to $44. For a more casual restaurant with excellent seafood, try **Corte Sconta,** Calle del Pestrin, Castello 3886 (☎ **041/522-7024;** reservations required). Main courses are in the $12 to $20 range.

One of the most famous cafes for a light lunch, coffee, or sweet snack is **Caffé Florian** in St. Mark's Square, built in 1720 and romantically decorated with plush red banquettes and elaborate murals. Casanova is on the list of famous customers.

Best Shopping Buys

Venice is a shopper's delight, as long as you don't mind the steep prices, and it's fun exploring the winding streets of shops around St. Mark's Square and the Rialto Bridge. Generally, the farther away from the square you go, the more reasonable the prices become.

You'll find plenty of locally produced items including glassware, lace, linens, masks, leather goods (including shoes), and knitwear. Shops in tourist areas stay open long hours (many close for lunch, however), and some are even open on Sundays. One of my favorite shops is the tiny **Astolfo Gloria,** Frezzeria, San Marco (☎ **041/520-6827**), which features reasonably-priced jewelry made of Venetian glass beads.

5 Malta

The former home of the Knights of St. John, the island nation of Malta, located on the southernmost tip of Europe (about 60 miles from Sicily and 180 miles from North Africa) has at one time or another been dominated by all its neighbors, including the British and the French.

Visitors to its bustling capital, **Valletta,** will find cathedrals, palazzos, and fortifications, mostly from the period of the knights, which started in the 16th century and ended when they were driven off the island by Napoleon Bonaparte in 1798. It is said that the city was built "by gentlemen, for gentlemen."

Malta became part of the British Empire in 1800, was granted independence in 1964, and became a republic in 1974. A must-see in Valletta for those interested in the island's history is The Malta Experience audiovisual presentation (see "Frommer's Favorite Malta Experiences," below).

Valletta is quite compact and easy to explore on foot. In addition to historic sights, the city offers a wealth of museums, restaurants, and shopping opportunities. Other parts of the island offer quaint towns, ancient sites (including the oldest known free-standing prehistoric temple structures in the world), and historic churches, all easily accessible.

The sea offers excellent opportunities for divers. For sun worshippers, there are a number of sandy beaches, the best of which, including Mellieha Bay, Golden Sands, and Armier, can be found in the north of the island.

Valletta's Grand Harbour is very impressive; you'll want to be on deck as the massive fortifications come into view.

Oh, and in case you were wondering, yes, Malta is where the legendary Hollywood Maltese Falcon was supposed to be from. There actually were falcons here, of the real rather than sculpted kind, but they are now extinct.

ESSENTIALS

LANGUAGE Maltese and English (Malta is a former British colony and English is widely spoken).

CURRENCY The official unit of currency is the Maltese lira. The rate of exchange at press time was $1 = .40 lira.

FROMMER'S FAVORITE MALTA EXPERIENCES

- **Seeing The Malta Experience.** This audiovisual presentation offers a look at the island's fascinating history. (Mediterranean Conference Center, Old Hospital Street. Admission is about $2.50. The 40-minute presentation is offered on the hour, Monday to Friday 11am to 4pm; Saturday and Sunday 11am and noon.)

Diving in Malta

There are great diving opportunities in Malta and numerous watersports and diving centers that hire equipment. For more information, contact the Malta National Tourism Organization in Valletta, ☎ **22-44-44.**

- **Exploring Mdina.** The island's medieval capital, about a 30-minute drive from Valletta, is a quaint, pedestrians-only walled city perched atop a plateau.
- **Visiting a museum.** You have numerous choices here, including museums of fine arts, archaeology, war, folklore, maritime (in Fort St. Angelo), science, and even toys.
- **Strolling Republic Street.** This is the place to be seen and to meet Malta's friendly populace. You can also view historically interesting buildings.

COMING ASHORE & GETTING AROUND

Ships dock close to the center of town. It's about a 15-minute walk or a 5-minute ride. Taxis are available at the pier. Malta's public transportation system is cheap and efficient. **Buses** cost less than 50¢, with the longest bus journey taking only 50 minutes.

THE BEST SHORE EXCURSIONS

Malta's Capital (4 hours, $36–$42): This bus and walking tour of Valletta (stopping at City Gate) visits St. John's Co-Cathedral, Palace of the Grand Masters, after which you drive by bus to the medieval fortified city of Mdina, where you'll find quaint winding streets and beautiful homes as well as a cathedral dedicated to St. Peter and St. Paul.

Full-Day Tour of Malta (7–7½ hours, $69–$76): A look at the island's history from the Bronze Age to the reign of the Order of the Knights of St. John. Visit Mdina; stop at the nearby town of Rabat, famous for its catacombs and Roman ruins; visit a parish church completed in 1860, and boasting the fourth largest unsupported dome in the world; visit the prehistoric Tarxien Temples; and visit Valletta, with a stop at the Palace of the Grand Masters with its Tapestry Room and Throne Room. Includes lunch and a stop at a crafts center (to watch glassblowers and traditional lacemaking, weaving, and silver filigree art).

Tour of the Temples (4 hours, $42): This tour includes some of the world's most impressive prehistoric temples, driving by bus to the Cottonera region; visiting the Malta Maritime Museum, which houses relics of Malta's history; visiting the temples of Hagar Qim with its decorated pillar and two altars, all constructed in the late megalithic period on a slope facing the tiny island of Filfla; then visiting Tarxien Temples, where the archaeological remains date back to 2,500 B.C.

THE TOP ATTRACTIONS

Palace of the Grand Master. Republic Street. ☎ **56/22-12-21.** Admission about $2.50, free for seniors and students under age 19. June 16–Sept 30 Mon–Fri 8am–2:45pm; at other times, Mon, Tues and Wed 8:30am–3:45pm, Thurs and Fri 8:30am–4pm.

This grand 500-year-old residence was completed in 1574 and today is the seat of the President and Parliament of the Republic of Malta. Inside are portraits of European monarchs and the Grand Masters of the Order of St. John, a furniture collection, Gobelin tapestries, frescoes, friezes, and other works of art.

St. John's Co-Cathedral. St. John's Square. ☎ **56/22-05-36.** Admission about $1.50. Mon–Fri 9:30am–12:30pm and 1:30–4:30pm; Sat 9:30am–12:30pm; closed Sun.

The outside of this church, built between 1573 and 1577, is rather austere, but the interior is gorgeous and holds art treasures that include the Caravaggio masterpiece *The*

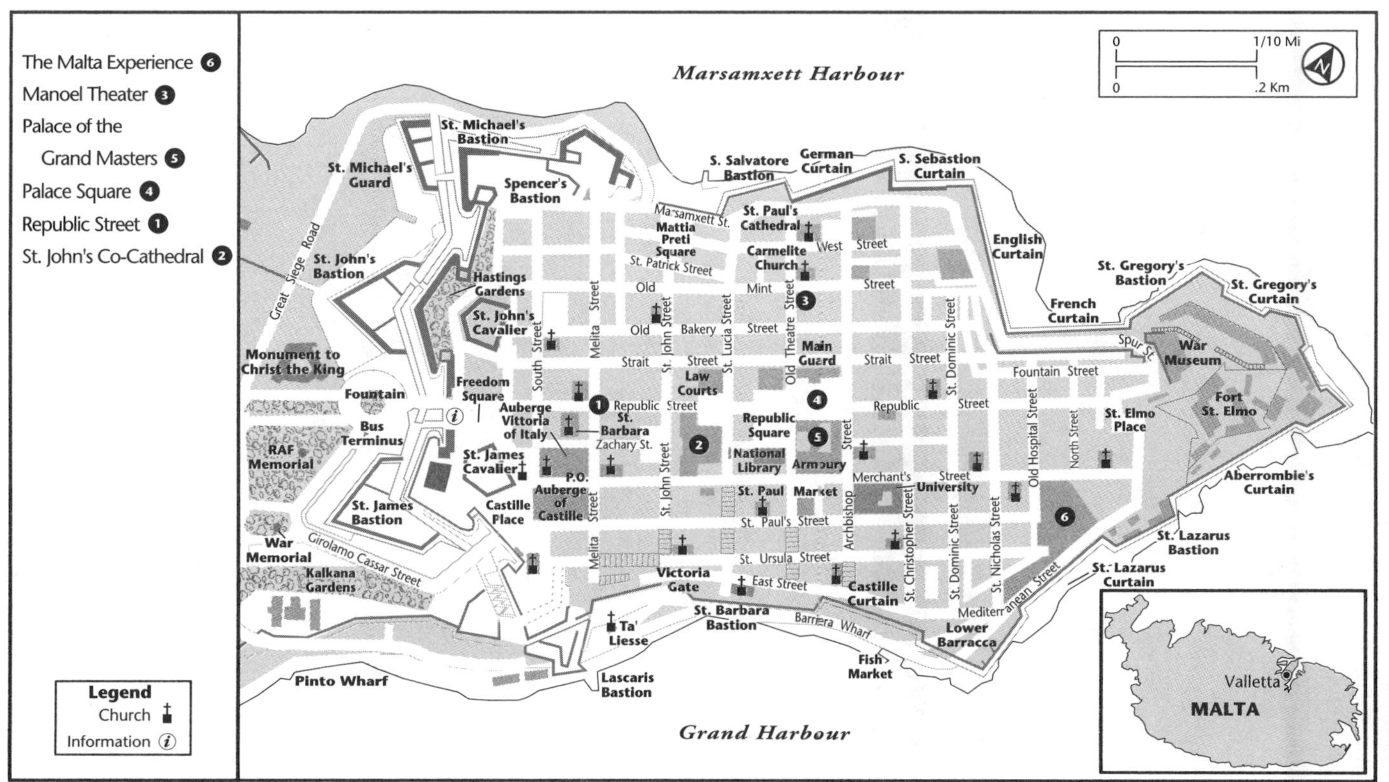

The Malta Experience 6
Manoel Theater 3
Palace of the Grand Masters 5
Palace Square 4
Republic Street 1
St. John's Co-Cathedral 2
Legend
Church
Information
Marsamxett Harbour
Grand Harbour
0 1/10 Mi
0 .2 Km
MALTA
Valletta
St. Michael's Bastion
St. Michael's Guard
Spencer's Bastion
St. John's Bastion
Great Siege Road
Hastings Gardens
St. John's Cavalier
Monument to Christ the King
Fountain
Freedom Square
Bus Terminus
RAF Memorial
Auberge Vittoria of Italy
St. Barbara
Zachary St.
St. James Cavalier
P.O.
Auberge of Castille
Castille Place
St. James Bastion
War Memorial
Girolamo Cassar Street
Kalkana Gardens
Pinto Wharf
Ta' Liesse
Lascaris Bastion
Victoria Gate
St. Barbara Bastion
Barriera Wharf
Fish Market
Castille Curtain
Lower Barracca
Mediterranean Street
S. Salvatore Bastion
German Curtain
S. Sebastion Curtain
Marsamxett St.
Mattia Preti Square
St. Patrick Street
St. Paul's Cathedral
Carmelite Church
West Street
Mint Street
Old Theatre Street
Old Street
Bakery Street
Strait Street
Melita Street
South Street
St. John Street
St. Lucia Street
Law Courts
Republic Street
Main Guard
Republic Square
National Library
Armoury
St. Paul
Market
St. Paul's Street
St. Ursula Street
East Street
Archbishop Street
Merchant's Street
University
St. Christopher Street
St. Dominic Street
St. Nicholas Street
Old Hospital Street
North Street
Fountain Street
St. Elmo Place
English Curtain
French Curtain
St. Gregory's Bastion
St. Gregory's Curtain
Spur St.
War Museum
Fort St. Elmo
Aberrombie's Curtain
St. Lazarus Bastion
St. Lazarus Curtain

Beheading of St John. The museum houses a collection of Flemish tapestries, silver objects, and church vestments.

Manoel Theater. Old Theatre Street. ☎ **56/22-26-18.** Admission about $3.75. Tours Mon–Fri at 10:30am and 11:30am; Sat 11:30am; no tours Sun.

This is one of the oldest theatres in Europe still in operation. It was built by the Grand Master in 1731.

STOPPING FOR A BITE

The food here is close to Italian, with a liberal use of garlic and olive oil. Fish is a favorite, as is rabbit.

BEST SHOPPING BUYS

Best buys here are traditional crafts including hand-blown glass and lace, ceramics, silver and gold jewelry, metalwork, pottery, and tiles. Shops can be found on Republic Street and the small streets near Palace Square.

6 Portugal

Lisbon is Europe's smallest capital but this city of seven hills is also a cosmopolitan place offering a pleasing combination of history, cultural arts, modern amenities, and visual treats. Some areas might remind visitors of Paris, with street painters and the like; others of hilly San Francisco.

The city is alternately believed to have been founded by Ulysses and the Phoenicians, and was inhabited by Romans and later the Moors. In 1755, a great earthquake destroyed much of the city, killing some 40,000 people. The rebuilding was carefully planned based on a neoclassical grid. Areas untouched by the earthquake include Belém, on the banks of the Tagus River, and Alfama.

Lisbon offers historical sights, museums, and, thanks to the city's hosting of Expo '98, new attractions such as the Lisbon Oceanarium, billed as Europe's largest aquarium.

ESSENTIALS

LANGUAGE Portuguese. Young people may also speak Spanish, English, or German.

CURRENCY The escudo is the Portuguese unit of currency, and is written with the number of escudos appearing before a dollar sign and the number of centavos (the "cents") appearing after. (For example, 1 escudo and 50 centavos would be written 1$50.) The exchange rate at press time was $1 = 191 escudos.

FROMMER'S FAVORITE PORTUGAL EXPERIENCES

- **Exploring the Alfama.** Houses in the alleys are so close together you can't stretch your arms in some places to their full length. Visit the 12th-century Sé (cathedral), check out the goods at the markets, and climb up to the Castelo Saño Jorge (St. George's Castle) to enjoy the views.
- **Shopping for handicrafts.** Although prices aren't as good as they used to be, look for colorful ceramics, embroidery, silver, porcelain, crystal, tiles, handwoven rugs, leather goods, and hand-knit sweaters.
- **Feeling like an explorer.** Belém, where the River Tagus meets the sea, is where Portuguese explorers like Magellan launched their missions. Check out Belém Tower and Jerónimos Monastery. Also explore the National Coach Museum.
- **Listening to Fado.** Singers accompanied by 12-stringed Portuguese guitars can be heard nightly performing these melancholy songs in the little houses of the Bairro Alto.
- **Spending quiet time in Sintra.** Byron called this delightful village "glorious Eden."

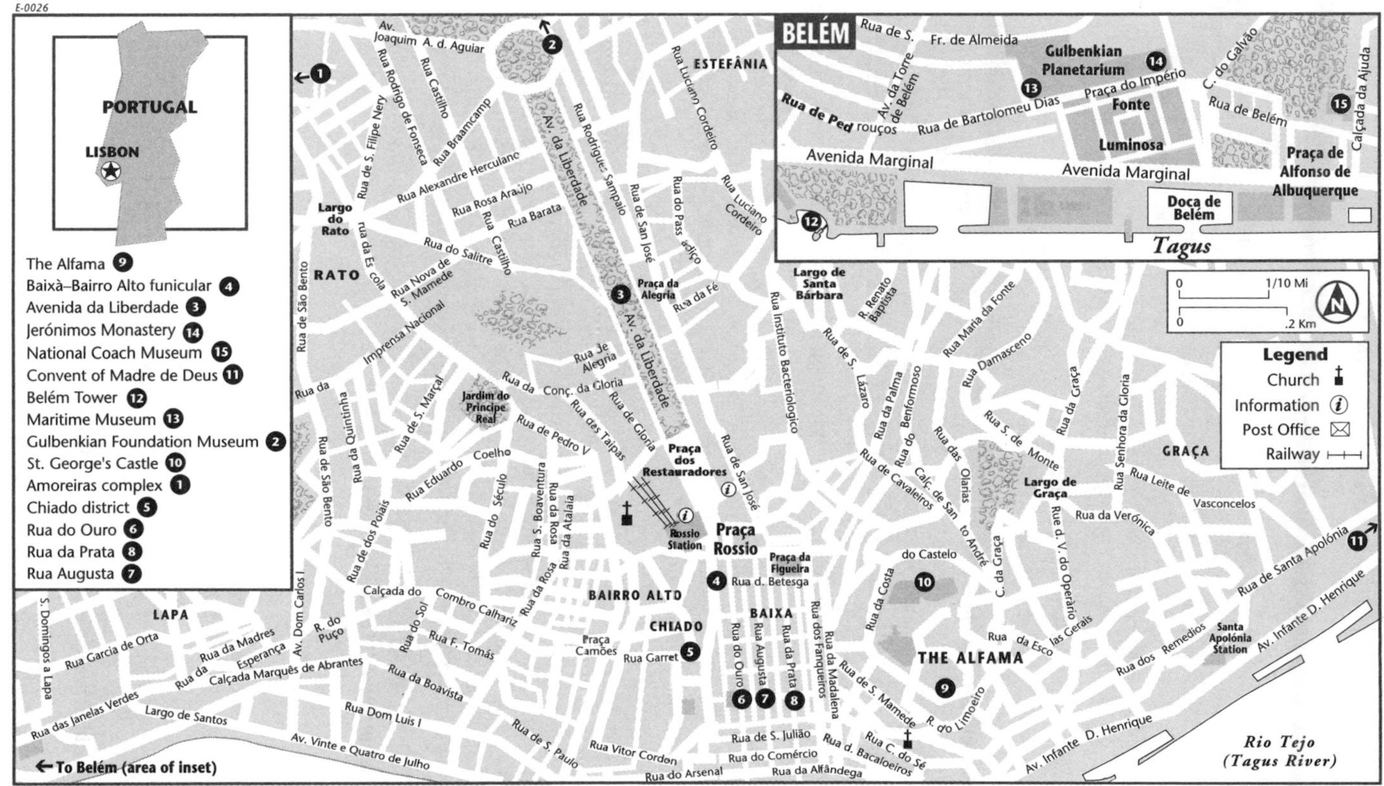
E-0026
PORTUGAL
LISBON
The Alfama 9
Baixà–Bairro Alto funicular 4
Avenida da Liberdade 3
Jerónimos Monastery 14
National Coach Museum 15
Convent of Madre de Deus 11
Belém Tower 12
Maritime Museum 13
Gulbenkian Foundation Museum 2
St. George's Castle 10
Amoreiras complex 1
Chiado district 5
Rua do Ouro 6
Rua da Prata 8
Rua Augusta 7
BELÉM
Gulbenkian Planetarium
Praça do Império
Fonte
Luminosa
Avenida Marginal
Praça de Alfonso de Albuquerque
Doca de Belém
Tagus
0 1/10 Mi
0 .2 Km
Legend
Church
Information
Post Office
Railway
ESTEFÂNIA
Largo do Rato
RATO
Av. da Liberdade
Praça da Alegria
Largo de Santa Bárbara
Jardim do Principe Real
Praça dos Restauradores
Rossio Station
Praça Rossio
Praça da Figueira
BAIRRO ALTO
CHIADO
BAIXA
Praça Camões
GRAÇA
Largo de Graça
THE ALFAMA
Santa Apolónia Station
LAPA
Rio Tejo (Tagus River)
To Belém (area of inset)

COMING ASHORE & GETTING AROUND

Cruise ships dock at the Port of Lisbon, about 15 minutes by car from the city center (2 mi/3km to the Alcantara district; 3 mi/5km to Belém Tower).

Lisbon itself is a walking city, and is easy to get around, although the hills may prove challenging to some. **Taxis** are among the cheapest in Europe and are generally available outside the terminal building. They are usually diesel Mercedes. The ride to the central sightseeing and shopping districts is between $8 and $12. Traffic can be congested, so allow extra time. The city also has a good **bus and tram service** as well as Metro **subway** to get around. There's a **funicular** (elevator) connecting the Baixa area (where you'll find shopping) with the Bairro Alto (where you'll find nightlife).

THE BEST SHORE EXCURSIONS

Lisbon City Tour (3½ hours, $38–$41): Go by bus around Lisbon to see a number of city highlights, including Avenida da Liberdade with its mosaic-lined sidewalks and the magnificent views at Black Horse Square of the River Tagus. Tour the impressive Jerónimos Monastery. Also visit the National Coach Museum, or the Convent of Madre de Deus, founded in 1509 and containing samples of religious architecture.

Sintra & Estoril (4 hours, $42–$47): This tour along the famous and scenic Estoril coast includes such memorable highlights as Sintra, a serene, historic resort nestled in the forested hills of Serra de Sintra. Here you'll find stately homes and palaces with walled gardens (the town was a royal residence in days gone by), narrow cobbled streets, and handicraft shops. The tour continues inland to Queluz, to visit the magnificent 18th-century palace built in the style of Versailles. The Throne Room features heavily gilded ceilings and walls, and the garden hedges are carved in geometric shapes. Some tours also include the well-known seaside resort of Cascais.

Fatima & Batalha (8–9 hours, $106–$110): Located 100 miles from Lisbon is the place known to Roman Catholics as the "Lourdes of Portugal." Here, according to legend, three shepherds in 1917 claimed they saw the Virgin Mary in an oak tree. The town has since become a center of the Christian faith and of world pilgrimage. You will have time here to explore the imposing modern basilica, and on some tours you'll also visit the homes, just outside Fatima, where the three shepherds lived (their remains are kept inside the basilica). Lunch will be served at a local restaurant or hotel. Afterwards, continue on to Batalha for a visit to the impressive Gothic church of Santa Maria da Victoria.

THE TOP ATTRACTIONS

Belém Tower (Torre de Belém). Praca do Imperio, Belém district. Admission $2.30 adults, $1.15 children and seniors.

Scenically located on the banks of the Tagus River, the 16th-century tower is a monument to Portugal's age of discovery and its famous explorers.

Jerónimos Monastery (Mosteiro dos Jerónimos). Praca do Imperio, Belém district. Free admission to church; to cloisters $2.30 for adults, free for children and seniors.

Built in 1502, the monastery is a masterpiece of Manueline architecture, built in the 16th century to commemorate the discoveries of Portuguese navigators, and one of the finest sights in the city.

The Maritime Museum (Museu de Marinha). Praca do Imperio, Belém district. Admission $2.30 adults, $1.15 students, free for children under 10 and seniors.

Located in the Jerónimos Monastery's west wing, this museum is one of the most important of its kind in Europe, and contains hundreds of ship models, from 15th-century sailing ships to 20th-century warships.

National Coach Museum (Museu Nacional dos Coches). Praca Afonso de Albuquerque, Belém district. Admission $2.50 adults, $1.30 students, free under 14.

Located in a former riding academy, the museum houses a collection of hundreds of royal and state coaches, including some that are opulently gilded.

Gulbenkian Foundation Museum (Museu de Fundacao Calouste Gulbenkian). Av. De Berna 45, Saldana district. Admission $1.15 adults, free for children 9 and under and seniors.

Deeded by Armenian oil tycoon Calouste Gulbenkian, who died in 1955, this museum houses one of the world's finest private art collections, including Egyptian, Greek, and Roman antiquities; Islamic art; and vases, prints, and lacquerwork from China and Japan. There are also European manuscripts, 15th- to 19th-century paintings and sculptures, and important collections of 18th-century French decorative works, French impressionist paintings, Lalique jewelry, and glassware. Notable are two Rembrandts, Rubens's *Portrait of Hélène Foourment,* and *Portrait of Madame Claude Monet* by Pierre-August Renoir.

St. George's Castle (Castelo Saño Jorge). Rua Costa do Castelo, Alfama district. Free admission.

This hilltop fortress is believed to have predated the Romans. Many of the walls still standing were erected by the Moors. The finest view of the Tagus and the Alfama can be had from the castle's esplanades and ramparts. On the grounds you'll also find olive, pine, and cork trees, and may encounter swans and rare white peacocks.

STOPPING FOR A BITE

Fresh seafood is a best bet. Typical dishes include fresh *bacalhau* (codfish), steamed mussels with ham and sausages cooked in white wine, and *acorda de marisco,* a spicy seafood soup. Meat-eaters will want to try the roasted lamb. Try your meal with a Portuguese wine. The cafes (such as those around the Rossio, the city's main square) are great places to people-watch.

BEST SHOPPING BETS

Handicrafts, ceramics, and embroidered linens are good buys. Also look for gold filigree and silver jewelry, knitwear, leather goods, colorful Portuguese wall tiles, and items made out of cork. Many smaller shops close from 12:30pm to 3pm. There are more than 200 shops in the modern **Amoreiras complex,** located in the Amoreiras district (take a taxi), and upscale shopping can be found downtown on Rua Garrett in the **Chiado district.** Other shopping districts include **Baixa** (between the Rossio and the Tagus), **Rua do Ouro, Rua da Prata,** and **Rua Augusta.** The new shopping complex Colombo is located in the Benfica district and is the largest shopping mall on Iberian Peninsula.

7 Spain

Spain offers fascinating history, pretty beaches, Moorish palaces, quaint villages, and, of course, Picasso, but the country is also full of modern-day vitality. Things began to change with the death of Generalissimo Francisco Franco and the country's 1986 entry into the European Union, and today the nation is undergoing a cultural renaissance that visitors will delight in, with cities like Barcelona, home of the 1992 Olympics, getting used to a new-found prosperity.

ESSENTIALS

LANGUAGE Spanish; Spanish and Catalan in Barcelona; Castilian Spanish and Catalan in Palma de Mallorca. Many young people also speak English or German.

CURRENCY The unit of Spanish currency is the peseta. Notes are issued in 1,000, 2,000, 5,000, and 10,000-peseta denominations. The rate of exchange at press time was $1 = 160 pesetas.

BARCELONA

Barcelona, Spain's second largest city and the capital of Catalonia, was developed as a port by the Romans and has long been a Mediterranean center of commerce. Recently it's been discovered by the cruise lines, which are attracted by the city's prime location on the Iberian Peninsula and by its wealth of historical, cultural, and artistic offerings. Nearly every major cruise line visits here today, and many use the Port of Barcelona as a turnaround point.

Once home to Picasso, Miró, Dalí and Casals, Barcelona mixes medieval architecture with Modernism, a style for which the city is world-renowned. Roman ruins, the narrow streets of the Gothic Quarter, buildings from the 13th and 15th centuries, and a Bohemian atmosphere exist side by side with I. M. Pei designs and the whimsical creations of Gaudí. In addition to beautiful architecture, the city boasts great museums, friendly people, pleasant cafes, and a very active nightlife, with bars and late-night clubs.

Barcelona even has sandy beaches thanks to a recently reclaimed waterfront.

FROMMER'S FAVORITE BARCELONA EXPERIENCES

- **Walking through the Barri Gótic (Gothic Quarter).** You can wander for hours getting lost—that's part of the fun—and seeing the great cathedral, fountains, vintage stores, cobblestones, and cafes. Exercise caution here at night, however.
- **Strolling along the Ramblas.** Victor Hugo called the Ramblas "the most beautiful street in the world." It runs from Placa de Catalunya to the sea, and is a tree-lined boulevard boasting 24-hour performers, flower vendors, birds in cages, cafes, and shops.
- **Checking the views from Montjuïc or Tibidabo.** Both of these mountain parks are accessible by funicular.
- **Exploring the Museu Picasso.** Two converted palaces on a medieval street hold an impressive collection of the artist's works.
- **Enjoy the fantastical work of Antoni Gaudí.** The designer's creations in Barcelona include his masterpiece apartment building on Paseo de Gracia and the Templo Expiatorio de la Sagrada Familia.

COMING ASHORE & GETTING AROUND

Your ship may dock close enough to the Old Port area to walk to shopping and restaurants, but getting from the port, which is on a long peninsula, requires a circuitous route and can be tricky. The city's notorious pickpockets make the task a bit risky, too. A new bridge is set to open that will shorten the distance for walkers, but for now it's recommended that you take a cab or the shuttle service provided by the cruise line. **Taxis** are available outside the terminal. The rate begins at about $1.85, and there's a charge of about 85¢ per kilometer after that. There is a special supplement if the taxi is taken inside the pier area.

The city also has a good **Metro** and **bus system.** During the summer, there is also **Bus Turistic,** which passes by a dozen of the most popular sights. You can get on and off as you please and also ride the **Tibidabo funicular** and the **Montjuïc cable car** and funicular (both for panoramic city views) for the price of a single ticket. Tickets can be purchased on the bus or at the transportation booth at Placa de Catalunya, for about $9.80 for the day.

La Rambla is about 1 to 2 miles from the pier, depending on where your ship docks.

The Best Shore Excursions

City Highlights ($3^1/_2$ hours, \$29–\$53): This bus and walking tour includes the Gothic Quarter, a stop at Montjuïc for the views, the Olympic Stadium, Gaudí's whimsical Sagrada Familia, La Rambla, and Catalunya Square.

Museums Tour ($3^1/_2$–4 hours, \$34–\$45): Includes a visit to the Picasso Museum and the medieval "Ribera" quarter and/or a drive to Montjuïc for the impressive views, and/or the Miró Foundation, and/or a drive past buildings created by Antoni Gaudí.

Pilgrimage to Montserrat (5–6 hours, \$38–\$69): This tour heads north of Barcelona 36 miles to the sacred Mountain of Montserrat, one of Spain's natural wonders. The highest peak of this jagged mountain range reaches 4,072 feet. Approximately halfway up the mountain stands the famous Montserrat Monastery, built by Philip II between 1563 and 1592. It is world-famous for its shrine of the Virgin Mary, Our Lady of Montserrat. The shrine was dedicated to the image of the virgin and has been considered for many years one of Spain's most significant places of pilgrimage. You will visit the 16th-century basilica, the cloisters, and the Black Virgin, a statue from the 12th or 13th century. Afterward, listen to the famous Escolania choir from the monastery's School of Music. After returning to Barcelona, enjoy a brief tour of the city before returning to the ship. Lunch is included.

The Top Attractions

La Sagrada Familia. Majora, 401. ☎ **93/455-02-47.** Admission \$5.60; \$1.40 extra for the elevator to the top. Apr–Aug, daily 9am–8pm; Sept–Oct, daily 9am–7pm; Nov daily 9am–6pm.

Antoni Gaudí's creation was begun in 1882 and has never been finished, but the Church of the Holy Family is a bizarre wonder, and should be at the top of everyone's list of landmarks to visit. The designer's style has been described as art nouveau run wild, and it is on full display here. Some predict it will be completed by the mid–21st century.

Cathedral de Barcelona. Placa de la Seu. ☎ **93/315-15-54.** Free admission to the church; to the museum 70¢. Cathedral open daily 8am–1:30pm and 4–7:30pm; museum daily 10am–1pm.

Barcelona's cathedral is Gothic in style. The basilica, except for the 19th-century western facade, was begun at the end of the 13th century and completed in the 15th century. The cloister offers a museum of medieval art. The three naves have wonderful Gothic details.

Museu Picasso. Montcada 15–19. ☎ **93/319-63-10.** Admission \$5.25 adults, \$2.10 students, free 17 and under. Tues–Sat 10am–8pm, Sun 10am–3pm.

This museum, one of the city's most popular attractions, is housed in two Gothic palaces and spans the famous artist's career from his blue period to cubism and more. Pablo Picasso himself donated some 2,500 of his paintings to the collection. Included is a painting the artist did at the age of 9.

Miró Foundation (Fundación Joan Miró). ☎ **93/329-19-08.** Placa de Neptú, Parc de Montjuïc. Admission \$4.90 adults, free for children 14 and under. June–Sept, Tues–Wed and Fri–Sat 10am–8pm, Thurs 10am–9:30pm, Sun 10am–2:30pm; Nov–May the museum opens at 11am, Tues–Wed and Fri–Sat.

This museum, located in Montjuïc park, pays tribute to one of Spain's greatest artists, and contains some 10,000 of the surrealist's works. Included are paintings, graphics, and sculptures.

Barcelona

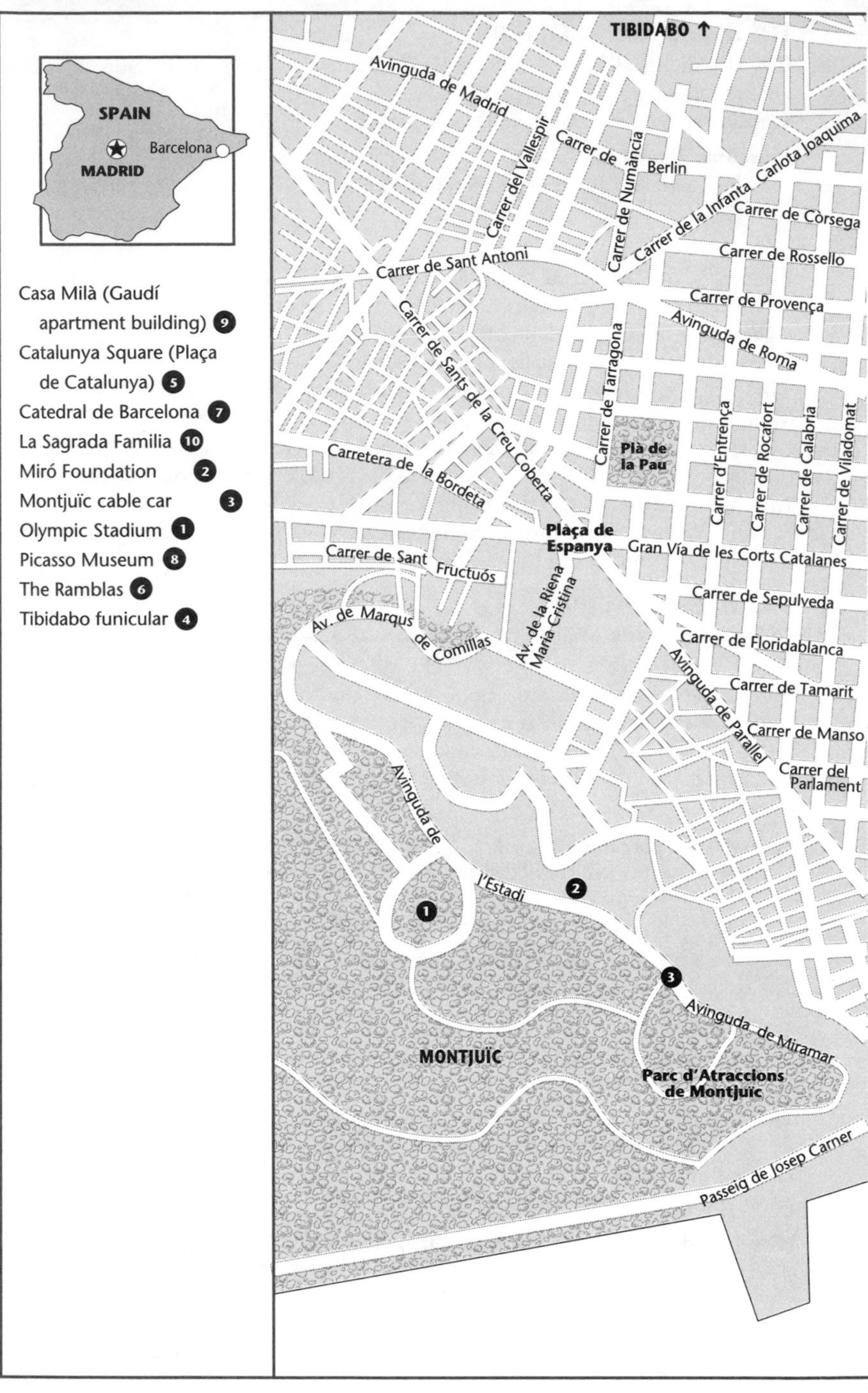

SPAIN
MADRID
Barcelona
Casa Milà (Gaudí apartment building) 9
Catalunya Square (Plaça de Catalunya) 5
Catedral de Barcelona 7
La Sagrada Familia 10
Miró Foundation 2
Montjuïc cable car 3
Olympic Stadium 1
Picasso Museum 8
The Ramblas 6
Tibidabo funicular 4
TIBIDABO ↑
Avinguda de Madrid
Carrer del Vallespir
Carrer de Berlin
Carrer de Numància
Carrer de la Infanta Carlota Joaquima
Carrer de Còrsega
Carrer de Rossello
Carrer de Sant Antoni
Carrer de Provença
Avinguda de Roma
Carrer de Sants de la Creu Coberta
Carrer de Tarragona
Pià de la Pau
Carrer d'Entrença
Carrer de Rocafort
Carrer de Calabria
Carrer de Viladomat
Carretera de la Bordeta
Plaça de Espanya
Gran Vía de les Corts Catalanes
Carrer de Sant Fructuós
Carrer de Sepulveda
Av. de Marqus de Comillas
Av. de la Riena María Cristina
Carrer de Floridablanca
Avinguda de Parallel
Carrer de Tamarit
Carrer de Manso
Carrer del Parlament
Avinguda de l'Estadi
Avinguda de Miramar
MONTJUÏC
Parc d'Atraccions de Montjuïc
Passeig de Josep Carner

Plaça de Francesc Macia
0 1/4 Mi
0 .3 Km
N
Travessera de Gràcia
Carrer de Buenos Aires
Carrer de Londres
Travessera de Gràcia
Avinguda Diagonal
Carrer de Paris
Av. de Sant Antoni Maria Claret
Carrer de Còrsega
Carrer de la Industria
EIXAMPLE
Carrer de Rossello
Carrer de Provença
Carrer de Roger de Flor
Avinguda Diagonal
Carrer de Mallorca
Carrer de Valencia
Carrer d'Aragó
Carrer de Comte Borrell
Carrer del Comte d'Urgell
Carrer de Villarroel
Carrer de Casanova
Carrer de Muntaner
Carrer d'Aribau
Carrer de Balmes
Ramble de Catalunya
Passeig de Gracia
Carrer de Pau Claris
Carrer del Consell de Cent
Passeig de Sant Joan
Carrer de Girona
Carrer de Bailèn
Carrer de Napols
Carrer de Sicilia
Carrer de la Diputació
Carrer de R. de Llúcia
Carrer del Bruc
Gran Vía de les Corts Catalanes
Plaça de Tetuan
Ronda de Sant Antoni
Carrer de Pelai
Ronda Universitat
Carrer de Casp
Plaça Urquinaona
Carrer d'Ausias Marc
Carrer de Sardenya
RAVAL
Ronda de Sant Pere
Carrer d'Ali Bei
Carrer de Ribes
Ronda Sant Pau
La Rambla
Av. Portal de l'Angel
Via Laietana
Passeig de Carles I
Carrer de Hospital
Avinguda de la Catedral
Passeig de Lluís Companys
BARRI GÒTIC
Carrer de Sant Pau
Carrer de Comerç
Carrer de Ferran
Carrer de la Princesa
Passeig de Pujades
Carrer Nou de la Rambla
Passeig de Picasso
LA RIBERA
Parc de la Ciutadella
Avinguda de les Drassanes
La Rambla
Carrer Ample
Carrer de Wellington
Plaça Portal de la Pau
Passeig de Colom
Moll de la Fusta
Avinguda d'Icàvia
BARCELONETA
Villa Olímpica→
Port Nou
4
5
6
7
8
9
10

Stopping for a Bite

The big meal of the day here is lunch *(comida),* and is served at mid-afternoon. Fresh seafood is a best bet. Cocktail hour in the late afternoon or early evening is a good time to try tapas. Dinner is served late. Bean stew, fish soup, and rice dishes are local specialties, including *zarzuela de mariscos,* or opera of seafood. Try the local wines, including cava, the Barcelona version of bubbly (the kind marked "brut" is sweeter than the one marked "brut nature").

Best Shopping Buys

Shop in Barcelona for leather goods including shoes, jewelry, high fashion, artworks, and straw products. The main shopping area surrounds the **Placa de Catalunya.** Upscale shopping can be found on **Passeig de Gracia** from the Avinguda Dagonal to the Placa de Catalunya (upper Rambla). Traditional shopping can be found between the Rambla and Via Laietana. Dozens of galleries are located in the **Gothic Quarter** (Barri Gótic) and near the Picasso museum. Most shops, with the exception of some large department stores, close from 1:30 to 4pm.

CÁDIZ

Cádiz is 3,000 years old, making it the Western world's oldest continuously inhabited city. It's a venerable seaport, where thousands of ships embarked for the New World. Christopher Columbus started his second and fourth voyages here.

Today, as in years past, it's a bustling port. The city is geographically divided into two, one side the modern city, lying on the isthmus, with its busy commercial area, the other with the historic districts of El Populo and Santa Maria, with narrow streets and ancient stone walls, and plenty of local characters.

Despite the city's age, there are few remnants of antiquity here, although you'll find an impressive cathedral and some good museums. The Oratorio de San Felipe Neri, where the first Spanish constitution was drafted in 1812, has the painting *Immaculate Conception* by Murillo, and the Santa Cruz Chapel has three frescoes by Goya.

Cádiz also has nice beaches and two world-class golf courses, Montecastillo (designed by Jack Nicklaus) and Novo Sancti Petri (designed by Steve Ballasteros).

Despite all this, the cruise lines view Cádiz as more of a jumping-off point to explore **Seville,** one of Spain's prettiest cities and also, thanks to Don Juan and Carmen (aided by Mozart and Bizet), one of its most romantic. It's located about 75 miles from Cádiz. Shore excursions are also offered to **Jerez,** home of Spanish sherry and Andalusian horses.

Frommer's Favorite Cádiz Experiences

- **Sit at a sidewalk cafe and people-watch.** The best spot in Cádiz is the Plaza de San Juan de Dios.
- **Stroll through Old Cádiz.** Explore the narrow streets of this pedestrian zone. You might also want to check out the city's parks, such as Parque Genoves, which looks onto the Atlantic.
- **Take a shore excursion** to Seville or Jerez. (See below.)

The Best Shore Excursions

Cádiz and Puerto de Santa Maria ($3^1/_2$ hours, $49): This city-highlights tour includes a visit to a local winery. From the bus, you'll see the monument to the Constitution of 1810, the city's ramparts, the historic Castle of San Sebastian, the Cathedral of Cádiz, and other city highlights. Cross the harbor to Puerto Santa Maria to visit an elegant estate and renowned winery.

Romantic Seville (8 hours, $99–$124): A full-day excursion takes you to this historic and beautiful city. Travel by bus for 2 hours through the countryside. In Seville, visit the Cathedral de Sevilla, the world's third largest cathedral, where you can see the tombs of King Fernando III and Christopher Columbus. Also visit Seville's Alcazar, a 14th-century Mudéjar palace, and the Jewish quarter. Time is allowed to stroll Seville's charming streets. Enjoy lunch at a local restaurant or hotel.

Cádiz, Jerez, & the Royal School of Equestrian Art (7½ hours, $89; or the horse farm separately, 4½ hours, $63; or Jerez separately, 4½ hours, $42). After a brief drive past the highlights of Cádiz, travel for about 1 hour to the old town of Jerez, where white mansions are guarded by historic walls and towers. Stop at a local cellar for a taste of brandy and sherry. Visit the equestrian school to see the Andalusian horses put through their training. Includes lunch.

COMING ASHORE & GETTING AROUND

It's about a 10-minute walk from the pier to the city center. **Taxis** are available at the pier. **Buses** and **trains** run regularly to Seville, about 2 hours away.

THE TOP ATTRACTIONS

Catedral de Cádiz. Plaza Catedral. ☎ **956/28-61-54.** Free admission to cathedral; museum admission about $2.80 adults, $1.40 children. Tues–Sat 10am–12:30pm.

This magnificent 18th-century baroque building has a neoclassical interior. Music lovers come here to pay respects at the tomb of Cádiz-born Manuel de Falla. The cathedral's treasury/museum offers a collection of Spanish silver, embroidery, and paintings.

Museo de Cádiz. Plaza de Mini. ☎ **956/21-22-81.** Admission about $1.75. Tues–Sun 9:30am–2:30pm.

This museum contains one of Spain's most important Zurbaran collections, as well as paintings by Rubens and Murillo. The archaeology section displays Roman, Carthaginian, and Phoenician finds. There are also exhibits of pottery, baskets, textiles, and leatherwork.

Oratorio de San Felipe Neri. Santa Ines. ☎ **956/21-16-12.** Free admission. Daily 8:30am–10am and 7:30–9:45pm. Closed in July.

The Cortes (Parliament) met here in 1812 to proclaim its constitution. There's a history museum, and Murillo's *Immaculate Conception* is on display.

STOPPING FOR A BITE

Seafood is big here and sardines are a favorite local treat. Try them with local wine.

BEST SHOPPING BUYS

Best buys are wine of the Jerez region, Andalusian handicrafts, leather, and ceramics. The main shopping area is on Columela and San Francisco streets.

MÁLAGA

Málaga is the Costa del Sol region's historic capital, and is today a bustling commercial and residential center. The city's most famous citizen was none other than Pablo Picasso, born here in 1881 at Plaza de la Merced, in the city center. Unfortunately, Picasso left little of his spirit and only a small selection of his work in his birthplace. The city does offer some interesting historical sights, however, including a 16th-century cathedral and the Moorish Alcazaba Fortress, and is a pleasant place to explore on your own, although the town can be quite crowded with tourists in the summer.

Málaga is also the port for nearby Granada, the famed Alhambra, and other inland sights.

Coming Ashore & Getting Around

Ships dock at a pier close to town, or at another short distance away that requires a taxi ride. Taxis are usually available pier-side. Watch out for purse-snatchers as you walk around the town, since Málaga has one of the highest crime rates in Spain. It's not recommended you walk alone around the area of the Castillo de Gibralfaro in particular.

Frommer's Favorite Málaga Experiences

- **Checking out the Alcazaba.** Ferdinand and Isabella slept at this Moorish palace, the remains of which are within easy walking distance of the city center.
- **Trying some local wine.** Sweet dessert wines are a Málaga specialty.
- **Taking a bus or cab to the beach.** Depending on how much time you have in port, you can head to Torremolinos, about 9 miles west of Málaga, or other resort areas on Costa del Sol.
- **Heading inland to Granada.** (See below.)

The Best Shore Excursions

Málaga City Tour (4 hours, $29–$39): On this tour you will see the Alcazaba and the Gibralfaro. Also visit the city's Renaissance-style cathedral. Drive past the Roman theater, the facade of the bullring, and the 19th-century post office and City Hall. The tour may include a stop at a local tavern to taste the region's sweet wine, or a side trip to Mijas.

Mijas & Countryside (4½ hours, $27): This tour highlights Spanish country life and visits Mijas, a classical village with beautiful views of the coast. Visit San Sebastian church in the old part of town and the Barrio Santa Ana, with its whitewashed houses. Also check out the bullring, built in 1920. You can, if you want, take a donkey ride through the streets. Or you can visit a local cafe or souvenir and handicraft shops.

Mijas & Ronda (9 hours, $109): Combines the tour above with a drive along the Costa del Sol to Ronda, a historic city divided by a natural 500-foot gorge spanned by a Roman stone bridge. Take a guided walk on the town's narrow alleys past white houses with ironwork balconies, and/or drive past sights that include some from the town's Arab occupation. Includes lunch.

Granada & the Alhambra (8½ hours, $112–$126): This tour highlights historic Granada and includes a number of interesting sights along the 2-hour drive, such as the town of Casabermeja, with its white houses, and Las Pedrizas, a scenic mountain pass. In Granada, visit the Muslim-Hispano complex known as the Alhambra, a spectacular example of Moorish architecture encircled by walls and towers. Also visit the nearby Generalife, the royal residence surrounded by water gardens, and El Vino Gate, commissioned by Carlos V in the 16th century. Includes lunch.

Granada Transfer (8½ hours, $64): A 2-hour bus ride to Granada, where you will have free time to explore on your own and still be guaranteed to get back to the ship on time.

The Top Attractions

Málaga Cathedral. Plaza Obispo. ☎ **95/221-59-17.** Admission $1.40. Mon–Sat 10am–12:45pm and 4–6:30pm.

This vast and impressive 16th-century Renaissance cathedral, located in the city center, has been declared a national monument. Its most notable interior feature are the richly ornamented choir stalls.

Cádiz/Málaga Region

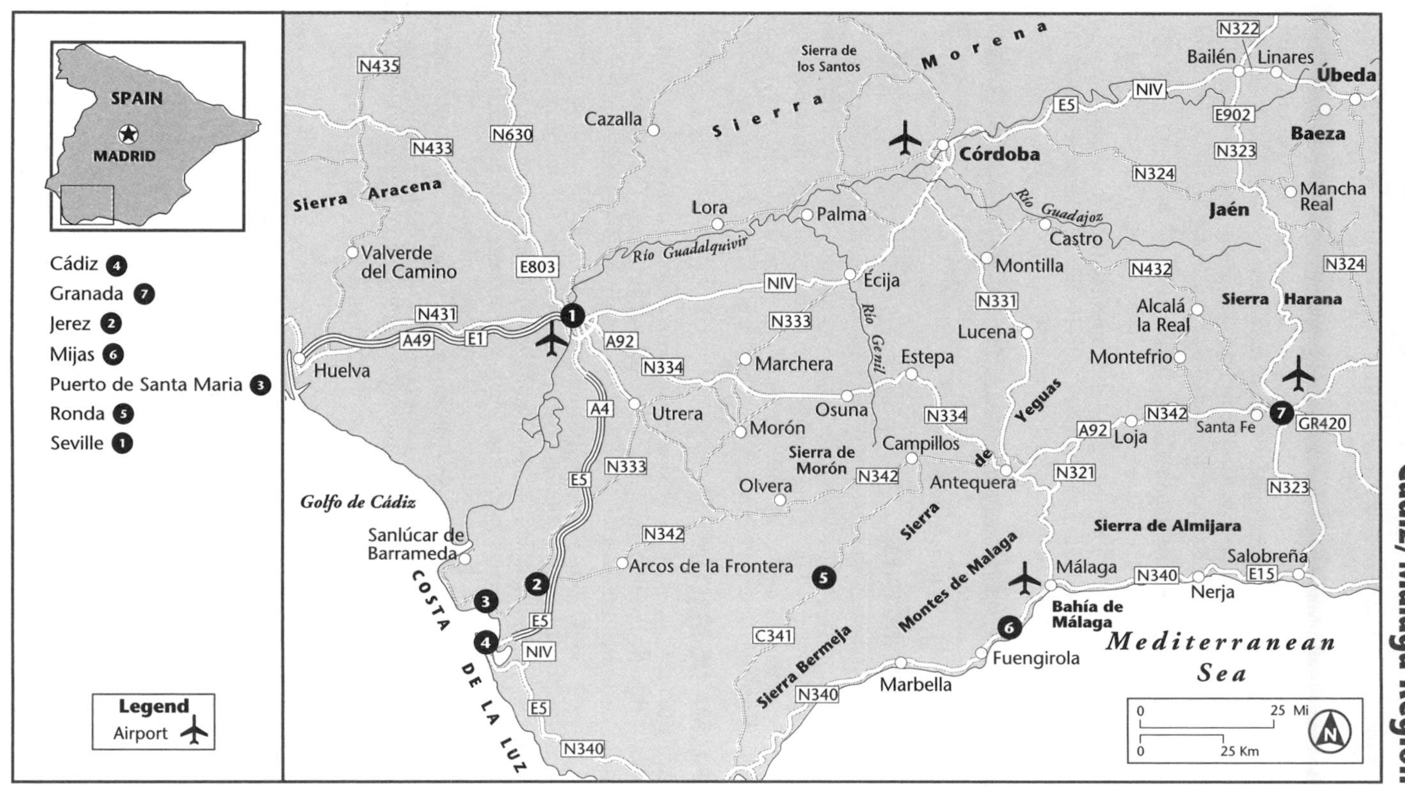

Alcazaba. Plaza de la Aduana, Alcazabilla. ☎ **95/221-60-05.** Admission to the museum about 20¢. Tues–Fri 9:30am–1:30pm and 5–8pm, Sat 10am–1pm, Sun 10am–2pm.

The remains of a Moorish palace are within easy walking distance of the city center (look for the signs pointing the way up the hill). The fortress was erected mostly in the 9th or 10th century, and among those who have stayed here were Ferdinand and Isabella. The Alcazaba now houses an archaeological museum. The grounds are beautiful, offering orange trees, purple bougainvillea, and some of the best views on the Costa del Sol.

Museo de Bellas Artes (Málaga Fine Arts Museum). Calle San Agustín, 8. ☎ **95/221-83-82.** Admission about $1.75. Tues–Fri 10am–1:30pm and 5–8pm, Sat–Sun 10am–1:30pm.

A former Moorish palace located behind the cathedral, this art museum has a gallery devoted to native son Pablo Picasso, as well as works by Murillo, Ribera, and Morales, and Andalusian antiques, mosaics, and sculptures.

Stopping for a Bite

Tapas are served here at typical tapas bars. Other local favorites include seafood dishes and gazpacho, a cold tomato-based soup.

Best Shopping Buys

Shop here for the region's rustic pottery, leather goods, silver and gold jewelry, and local wine. Most shops close between 1 and 5pm. An exception is **El Corte Ingles** department store. Small mall shops and boutiques can be found along **Calle Larios.** Outside the town limits, the most comprehensive collection of ceramics and pottery can be found at **La Vistillas,** Carretera Mijas, Km 2 (about 1¼ miles from the center of Málaga).

PALMA DE MALLORCA

Mallorca (also spelled Majorca), known as "the Island of Tranquility," is the largest of the 16 Balearic Islands, offering some 310 miles of coastline. The other main islands in the chain are Ibiza (which is also visited by some cruise ships) and Menorca.

Lying about 60 miles from the Spanish mainland and 130 miles from Barcelona, Mallorca offers a lush (some trees are more than 1,000 years old) and rugged landscape, and picturesque villages (and also some big high-rise hotels). It is a popular resort area, particularly with northern Europeans. Millions of tourists come here each year. Juan Carlos, king of Spain, has a residence in Marivent in Cala Mayor.

Palma, the capital, is a cosmopolitan city with a population of 300,000, and relies on tourism for its economy. There are big hotels and fast food joints, but there are also sights of historical interest left by the Romans, the Arabs, and later Spanish kings who at one time occupied the island. The Gothic Quarter of Palma offers a maze of narrow alleys and cobblestone streets.

Outside the city are mountains, lush valleys, fine beaches, and little fishing villages where life is still simple. It's not surprising that writers, painters, and musicians have found inspiration here.

Arrival by sea here is particularly impressive, with the skyline characterized by the Bellver Castle and the city's Gothic cathedral. Plan to be on deck so you can catch the view.

Frommer's Favorite Mallorca Experiences

- **Renting a car and heading to the mountains.** Drive west on C-719, then north on C-710, and back on C-711 (at Sóller) to pass through some of the most beautiful coastal and mountain scenery on the island.
- **Heading to the beach.** The best are Ca'n Pastilla and El Arenal, although they can get crowded. Another good bet is Cala Mayor.

Mallorca

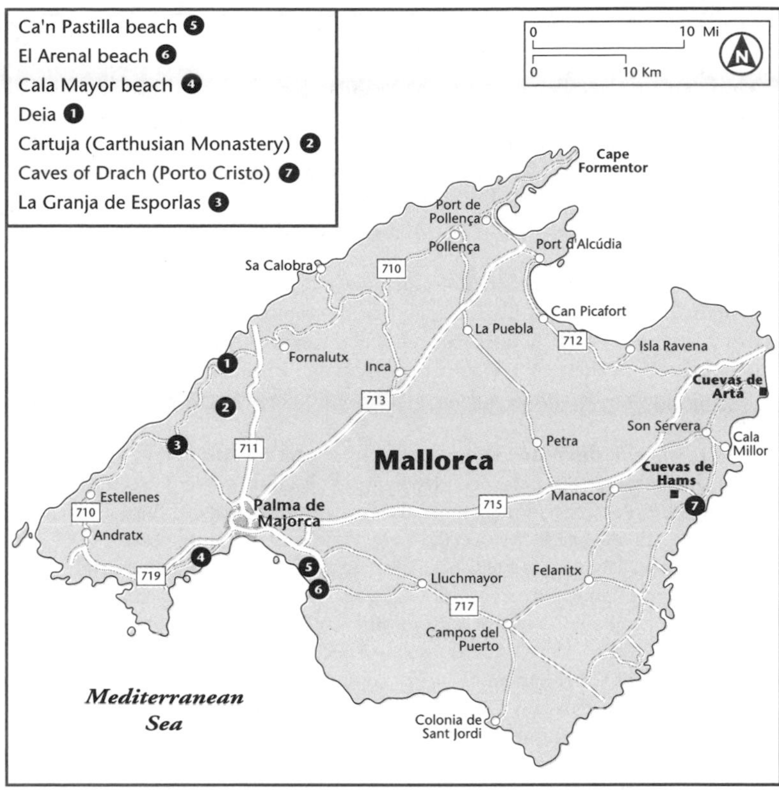

- **Exploring the Gothic Quarter.** Palma's Gothic Quarter offers narrow streets and cobblestones and interesting sights such as the Moorish baths (**Banys Arabs,** Carrer Serra, 7).
- **Spending some quiet time in Deia.** This serene little Mallorcan village is located about 17 miles from Palma (it's accessible by bus) and offers mountain and sea views, stone houses, olive trees, and creeping bougainvillea. It's long been an artist's retreat, and notables who have lived here include Robert Graves, the English poet and novelist *(I, Claudius)*, who is buried in a local cemetery.
- **Visiting the Carthusian Monastery in Valldemossa.** Chopin and George Sand wintered here. See "Valldemossa & Chopin" under "The Best Shore Excursions," below.

Coming Ashore & Getting Around

Ships dock about 15 minutes (by vehicle) from the center of town. **Taxis** are generally available at the pier. **Buses** run from Palma to popular destinations that include Valldemossa, Deia, and Sóller. There are also **trains** to Sóller. **Rental cars** are available from **Atesa** at Passeig Marítim (☎ **971/45-66-02**) and range from about $35 to $85 per day. **Avis** at Passeig Marítim (☎ **971/73-07-20**) offers cars from $66.50 to $343 per day. Reservations for either are strongly recommended.

The Best Shore Excursions

Valldemossa & Chopin ($3^1/_2$–4 hours, $34–$44): This tour explores the west side of the island. Drive 45 minutes to the quaint village of Valldemossa, located at the foot

Gibraltar

The famous rock at the entrance to the Mediterranean is visited by some ships and simply pointed out by others (as in, "We do a daylight passing of the Rock of Gibraltar"). The Rock's history dates back some 3,000 years. The name Gibraltar is derived from Jebel al Tarik, the name Arabs gave the place when they landed here in 711, under General Tarik. Spain took possession of the territory in 1462, but lost it to the British in 1713 (to this day there's tension over the Rock between Britain and Spain).

If you do set foot on the limestone rock—which is technically a peninsula rather than an island—you will find a small British colony from which you can view Africa on a clear day. In addition to spectacular views, Gibraltar offers a small town (also called Gibraltar) with Victorian architecture, natural caves, historical sights, museums, lovely botanical gardens, and the famous Barbary apes, as well as beautiful beaches.

In town, the **duty-free shops** are a big attraction. Best buys here include English china, crystal, Lladro and Nao figurines, English woolens, electronics, jewelry, watches, cosmetics, and perfume. And you can stop at one of the pubs on Main Street for fish and chips or steak-and-kidney pie, and a pint of ale.

The official language is English and the currency is the Gibraltar pound, which is equivalent to pound sterling. But U.S. dollars are also readily accepted.

Ships dock about 1 mile, or a 20-minute walk, from the center of town. And taxis and a shuttle service are both usually available at the pier.

The **Rock of Gibraltar tour** (2 to 2½ hours, $37–$51) offered by many cruise lines includes a scenic drive, with a stop at **St. Michael's Cave,** a natural grotto with spectacular stalagmites (you have to climb a lot of steps to see them), and the **Apes' Den,** inhabited by some 20 semi-wild Barbary apes (there are some 140 others in a pack in the Great Siege area). The apes were introduced as pets on the island by the British more than 200 years ago, and, according to legend, Gibraltar stays British as long as the apes remain here. The tour also includes time to shop in town. Some tours add a ride on the **Gibraltar Cable Car,** which takes you up the face of the Rock to the very top, and some include a visit to the **Great Siege Tunnels,** an ingenious defense system dating back to the 18th century.

of the Northern Mountain Range, where the history dates back to the 14th century. Visit **Cartuja,** a former royal residence turned monastery in the Middle Ages. In 1838, both George Sand and Frederic Chopin came to live at the monastery. Sand later wrote a book titled *A Winter in Majorca* about that time, and Chopin composed "Raindrop Prelude" and other works here. The tour includes a short piano recital.

Caves of Drach (5 hours, $49): This tour travels to the eastern half of the island past the tiny fishing village of Porto Cristo to the Caves of Drach, a series of mysterious caverns that hide the world's largest underground lake. The excursion also includes a stop in Manacor, known for its inlaid furniture industry. The return trip passes scenic countryside.

Palma de Mallora City Tour (4 hours, $33–$46): Explore the capital of the Balearic Islands, including the Bellver Castle, Spanish Village, Almudaina Palace, cathedral, and Gothic Quarter. The drive back to the ship passes La Rambla, Paseo Mallorca, and the Maritime Promenade.

La Granja (4½ hours, $35–$46): This tour follows a scenic route past lovely villages and popular resort areas, and includes a visit to La Granja de Esporlas, a 17th-century manor house set on what is considered one of the most idyllic spots on the island. There are beautiful fountains and formal gardens, and the house offers a museum of daily life and a wine cellar. The tour may also include a visit to Puerto Andraitx, a quaint fishing port. A tasting of regional specialties is included.

The Top Attractions

Catedral (Le Seu). Carrer Palau Reial. ☎ **971/72-31-30.** Free admission to cathedral; museum and treasury about $2.80. Mon–Fri 10am–6:30pm, Sat 10am–2pm. Museum and cathedral hours are often subject to change.

The Gothic cathedral is located in old town, and overlooks the sea. It was started during the reign of Jaume II (1276–1311) and completed in 1610. Of note is the scalloped-edged, wrought-iron canopy by Gaudí over the main altar. The treasury contains pieces of the True Cross and relics of St. Sebastián.

Castell de Bellver. Between Palma and Illetas. ☎ **971/73-06-57.** Admission $1.80 adults; $1.05 children, students, and seniors. Daily 8:30am–5:30pm. Museum closed Sun.

Erected in 1309, this hilltop castle with its double moat was once a summer palace of kings and now houses the Museu Municipal, which offers a collection of archaeological objects and coins. But it's the view that attracts visitors. In fact, *Bellver* means beautiful view.

Collecció Juan March, Art Espanyol Contemporani. Carrer Sant Miquel 11. ☎ **971/71-26-01.** Admission about $2.10. Mon–Fri 10am–6:30pm, Sat 10am–1:30pm.

This art museum features Picasso, Miró, Dalí, and Juan Gris in its collection, along with other 20th-century Spanish artists. The best known work here is Picasso's *Head of a Woman.*

Palau de l'Almudaina. Carrer Palau Reial. ☎ **971/72-91-45.** Admission about $3.15 adults, $1.75 children; free on Wed. Apr–Oct, Mon–Sat 10am–2pm and 4–6:30pm; Nov 10:30am–2pm and 4–6pm.

This fortress is a reminder that the island was once ruled by Muslims, and was used as a royal residence by Mallorcan kings. Inside is a museum with antiques, arts, suits of armor, and Gobelin tapestries. The grounds offer Moorish-style gardens and fountains, as well as panoramic views of the harbor of Palma.

Stopping for a Bite

Meat-eaters will want to try the Mallorcan specialty, pork loin *(lomo),* or sausage *(sabrasada).* Other favorites include fish pie. Finish your meal with a *café carajillo* (coffee with cognac).

Best Shopping Buys

Shop here for Mallorca pearls, inlaid wood products, needlework, pottery, hand-blown glass, olive wood carvings, and leather goods (including shoes). The upscale shops are located along **Avenida Jaume III** and the **Paseo del Borne.** Good shopping opportunities can also be found on San Miguel, carrer Sindicato, Jaume II, carrer Platería, and Via Roman. Most shops close between 1:30pm and 4:30pm, as well as on Sundays.

8 Turkey

Turkey is literally where East meets West (Istanbul sits where Europe and Asia touch) and is probably the most exotic country you'll visit on your European cruise. It's a land of mosques and minarets, sultans' treasures and crowded bazaars, unmatched Greek and Roman archaeological sites and holy Christian landmarks. While its cities teem with the energy of a modern nation looking to the West, its villages remain much as they've been for the past several hundred years.

ESSENTIALS

LANGUAGE Turkish and Kurdish are spoken here as well as English, French, and German.

CURRENCY Turkish lira (TL) notes are issued in 10,000-, 50,000-, 100,000-, 250,000-, 500,000-, 1 million, and 5 million denominations. The rate of exchange at press time was $1 = 486,0000 TL. Because of the wide fluctuation of Turkish currency, it is best to only exchange what you intend to spend.

ISTANBUL

The city where the continents of Asia and Europe meet is chaotic and congested, yet bold and exciting. A diverse mix of architectural styles, religions, and people form the backdrop and backbone of this cosmopolitan city, where modern cars careen through the streets past historic monuments that reveal a rich and ancient history. The senses spring to life here—the smell of the spice market, the sound of prayer, the taste of traditional Turkish dishes, the feel of a Turkish carpet, and the sight of awe-inspiring treasures at every turn. Istanbul served as the capital of three successive empires—the Roman, Byzantine, and Ottoman—and this legacy lives on. Everywhere you look, museums, churches, palaces, grand mosques, and bazaars attest to the city's glorious history.

FROMMER'S FAVORITE ISTANBUL EXPERIENCES

- **Exploring the old section.** Most of the major attractions are located in this area and are within walking distance of each other.
- **Shopping at the Grand Bazaar.** It's a sight to behold as 4,000 shopkeepers hawk their wares and patrons browse and bargain through a labyrinth of passageways.

COMING ASHORE & GETTING AROUND

Ships drop anchor on the Bosphorus on the European side of the city. **Taxis**—yellow, metered, and relatively inexpensive—wait to pick up passengers, and you'll also find plenty of them traveling throughout the city. The starting rate is about $1, and there is a surcharge after midnight. Tip drivers to the nearest lira. **Bus and tram service** are also available, and cruise lines usually provide shuttle buses to downtown (which usually drop you off near the expensive rug shops).

The best way to explore the old section of the city is by foot. All of the monuments are within walking distance of each other. It's a healthy walk from the pier to the Blue Mosque, and with all the crazy drivers and the generally hectic pace, you're best off taking the shuttle offered by the cruise line, or a cab.

THE BEST SHORE EXCURSIONS

Highlights of Istanbul (7–9 hours, $79–$97): Includes the Hippodrome, once the largest chariot race grounds of the Byzantine Empire; Sultan Ahmet Mosque, also known as the Blue Mosque for its 21,000 blue Iznik tiles; the famous St. Sophia, once the largest church of the Christian world; and Topkapi Palace, the official residence of the Ottoman Sultans and home to treasures that include Spoonmaker's Diamond, one of the biggest in the world. Also visit the Grand Bazaar, with its 4,000 shops. Some tours bring you back to the ship for lunch while others include lunch in a first-class restaurant. (Shorter tours are also available that include some, but not all, of the above.)

Factoid

Visitors to religious sites should dress respectfully. It is best not to visit mosques during prayer times or on Friday, the holy day.

Old Istanbul

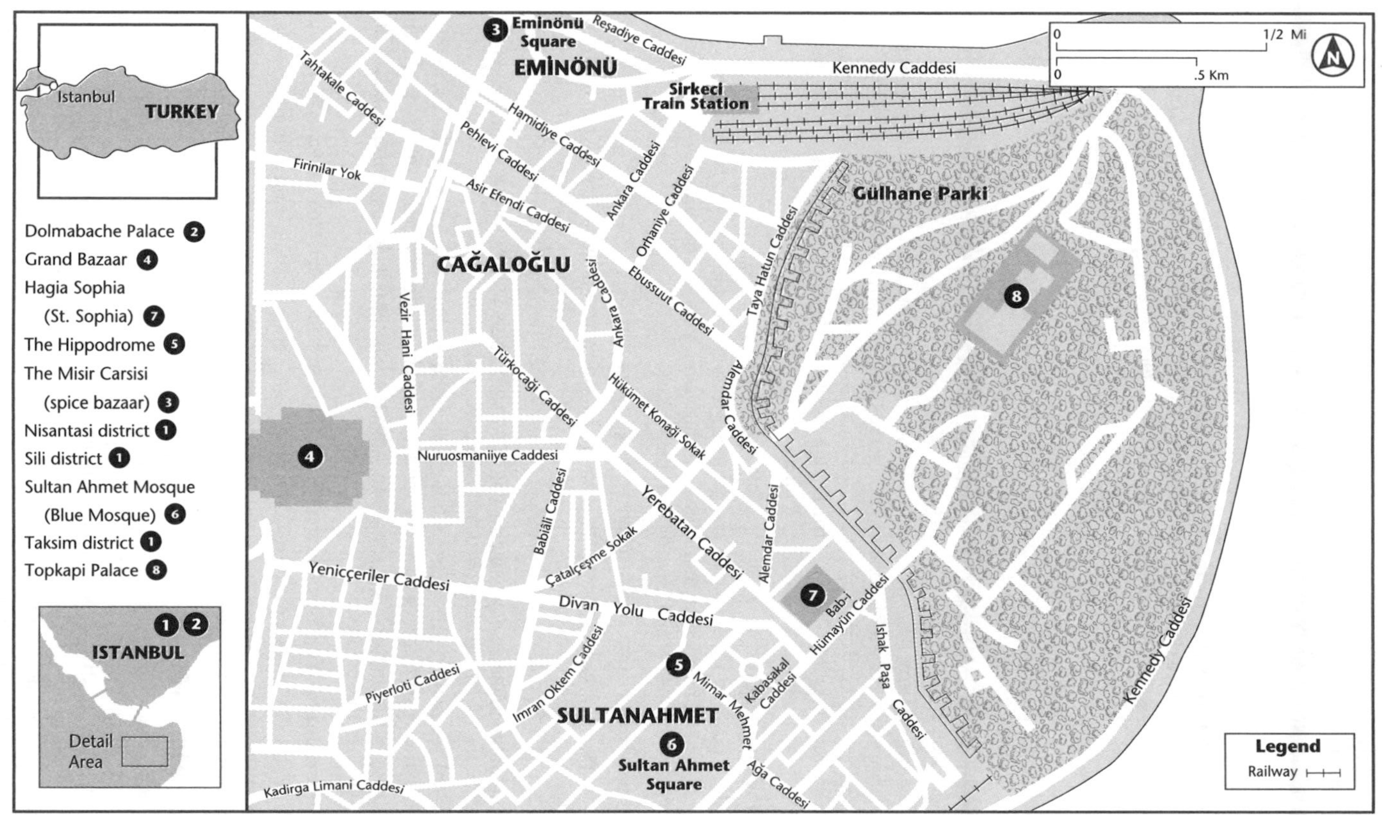

Factoid

Most museums are closed on Mondays, except Topkapi Palace, which is closed on Tuesdays.

The Top Attractions

Topkapi Palace. Kennedy Cad. Sultanahment. ☎ **212/512-0480.** Mon and Wed–Sun 9:30am–4:30pm. Admission $5; the guided harem tour costs $3.

Topkapi Palace served as the residence of sultans from the 15th century to the mid–19th century. The Ottoman complex includes the chamber of the Sacred Mantle, harem quarters, crown jewels, holy relics, the throne room, and other treasures. From the verandas of the palace, guests get panoramic views of the city. In the summer it's wise to get a ticket to the harem tour after arriving at the palace. Tours are conducted every half hour.

Hagia Sophia. Yerebatan Cad. Sultanahmet. ☎ **212/522-1750.** Tues–Sun 9:30am–5pm. Admission $5.

The 6th-century basilica is famous for its gigantic domes and magnificent mosaics. St. Sophia was commissioned by Emperor Justinian, who was looking to restore the greatness of the Roman empire. It was later converted to a mosque by the Ottomans. Also known as the Church of the Divine Wisdom, Hagia Sophia is regarded as one of the best examples of Byzantine architecture.

The Blue Mosque. Mon–Sun 9am–5pm. Free admission.

Also known as the Imperial Sultanahmet Mosque, the mosque was built in the 17th century and features dazzling blue and white Iznik tiles and six minarets. Guests must remove their shoes and leave them at the entrance.

Hippodrome. Sultanahmet (in front of the Blue Mosque).

This park was once the site of great chariot races and Byzantine civic life. What remains from those times are three monuments, the Obelisk of Theodosius, the bronze serpentine column, and the column of Constantine. Nearby is the Museum of Turkish and Islamic Arts.

Dolmabache Palace. Dolmabache Cad. ☎ **212/258-5544.** Admission $10 for a long tour; $5.50 for a short tour. Tues, Wed, and Fri–Sun 9am–5pm.

The 19th-century palace is sometimes referred to as the Ottoman Versailles because of its extravagant pieces, such as a 4-ton Baccarat chandelier that was a gift from Queen Victoria. The palace boasts a mix of architectural designs, including European, Hindu, and Turkish elements.

Grand Bazaar. Yeniceriler Cad and Fuatpasa Cad. Free admission. Mon–Sat 9am–7pm.

The Kapali Carsi (Grand Bazaar) contains 4,000 vendors selling carpets, leather goods, jewelry, antique reproductions, and other items. The oldest part of the market is Cevahir Bedesteni, which specializes in gold and silver works.

Stopping for a Bite

Turkish meals generally start with *meze* (hors d'oeuvres) that might include *borek* (pastry filled with cheese or puff pastry filled with meat), *dolma* (stuffed vine leaves), or *cig kofte* (spicy raw meatballs). Main courses usually feature fish, beef, and lamb dishes. One of the most popular items here is the kebab (either lamb or beef, skewered and grilled on a spit). The most common dessert is fresh fruit. Other desserts include *bulbul yuvasi* (pastry with pistachio and walnuts), *tel kadayif* (shredded wheat stuffed with nuts in syrup), *sutlac* (creamy cold rice pudding), and baklava (a honey-drenched pasty with nuts). The national drink is raki, which is flavored with anise.

Kusadasi/Ephesus Region

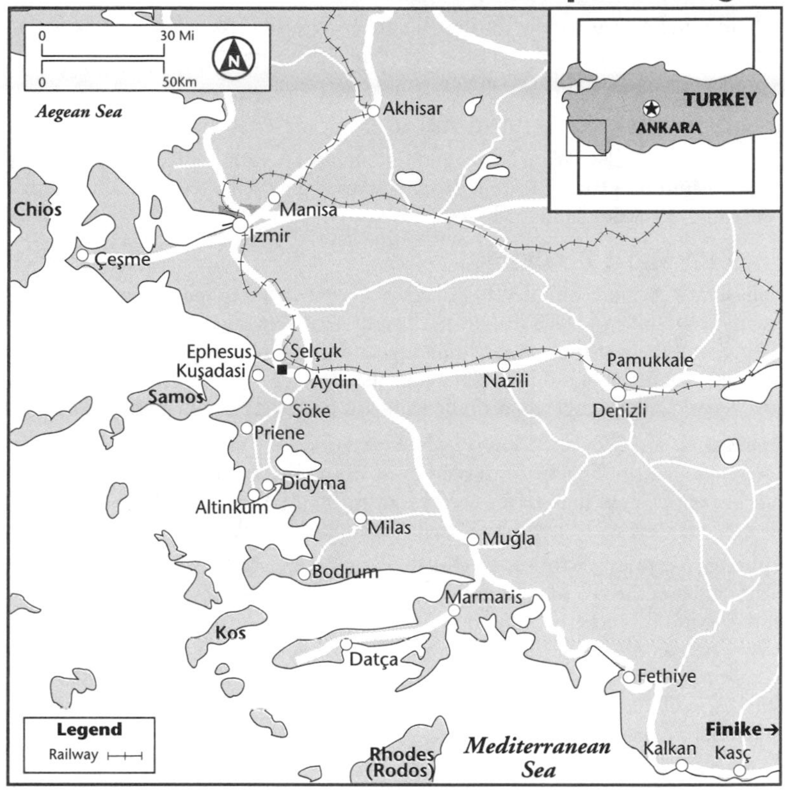

Best Shopping Buys

Shop here for carpets and kilims, onyx, leather goods, meerschaum pipes, and jewelry—and be ready to bargain. While browsing or bargaining, a shopkeeper may offer a cup of tea or a cold drink. This is part of the Turkish hospitality, so don't feel obliged to make a purchase. Bargaining is a serious business here, and it is considered bad form to start bargaining if you are not serious about buying the item.

Istanbul's legendary Grand Bazaar (see above) boasts 4,000 shops selling everything from copperware to carpets to cologne. Tucked in the bazaar's narrow alleys and passageways are cafes and restaurants.

The **Taksim, Nisantasi,** and **Sili districts** boast the most fashionable shops. Flea markets are open daily in the **Topkapi** district. The Misir Carsisi or **spice bazaar** is located next to Yeni Mosque at Eminouno.

KUSADASI

Once a sleepy port town, Kusadasi (which means "bird island" in Turkish) has become a bustling seaside resort. The city is used as a starting-off point for excursions to archaeological sites in Ephesus, Priene, Didyma, and Miletus as well as trips to beaches and Dilek National Park.

Frommer's Favorite Kusadasi Experiences

- **Visiting Ephesus.** An excursion to one of the best-preserved ancient cities in the world is a must.

- **Shopping.** As you wander through the streets, shopkeepers will try to lure you into their stores by promising you the best deal. It's fun to peruse, bargain, and buy, whether it is a small trinket or an expensive carpet.

Coming Ashore & Getting Around

Ships dock right downtown. Stores and restaurants are within walking distance of the harbor. **Minibuses** (available from the town center) and **taxis** (yellow and metered) can take you to attractions and the beach.

The Best Shore Excursions

Ephesus (3–4 hours, $27–$42): Visit one of the best preserved ancient cities in the world. Your guide will take you down the city's actual marble streets to the Baths, the theater, and the incredible library building, and along the way you will pass columns, mosaics, monuments, and ruins. The tour may include a stop at a shop for a demonstration on Turkish carpets—with the emphasis on getting you to buy.

Ephesus & The House of The Virgin Mary (3½–4½ hours, $47–$52): This tour combines a visit to Ephesus with the House of the Virgin Mary, a humble chapel located in the valley of Bulbuldagi, on the spot where the Virgin Mary is believed to have spent her last days. The site was officially sanctioned for pilgrimage in 1892.

Ephesus, St. John's Basilica, & House of the Virgin Mary (4½ hours, $52): This tour combines the two tours above with a visit to St. John's Basilica, another holy pilgrimage site. It is believed to be the site where St. John wrote the fourth book of the New Testament. A church at the site, which is now in ruins, was built by Justinian over a 2nd-century tomb believed to contain St. John the apostle. This tour may also be offered as a full-day excursion, including lunch at a local restaurant, and a visit to the museum of Ephesus (7½ hours, $75).

Three Ancient Cities (6–7 hours, $69–$85): This tour takes in the ruins that surround the region of Ephesus, including Priene, known for its Athena Temple (bankrolled by Alexander the Great); Didyma, known for the Temple of Apollo; and Miletus, which includes a stadium built by the Greeks and expanded by the Romans to hold 15,000 spectators. A light lunch at a restaurant in Didyma is included.

The Top Attractions

Ephesus. ☎ 232/892-6402. Admission $6 adults, $3 students, free for seniors over 65. Open daily 8:30am–6pm during the summer; 8:30am–5pm in the winter.

The city of Ephesus was built in the 11th century B.C. by the Ionians. The region thrived as a powerful trading port until silt accumulation over the course of centuries destroyed its harbor. Today, what remains of the city (and there's an amazing amount that remains) lies 3 miles from the sea. During its heyday, Ephesus also served as a center of worship. Its Temple of Diana was considered one of the Seven Wonders of the Ancient World. When touring the site (and I recommend you see Ephesus on a shore excursion, with a licensed guide, as you'll get more out of the experience), visitors walk down a street paved in marble to agoras, a theater, public toilets (a real must-see!), and Ephesus's most striking monument, the two-story Celsus Library. Temples, baths, columns, and a 25,000-seat amphitheater—which is still used today for concerts and other theatrical productions—are among the other attractions.

Factoid

It is best to explore sites around Kusadasi early in the day, when the sun is not at its strongest.

Basilica of St. John and the House of the Virgin Mary. Near Ephesus.

It's said that the grave of St. John the Divine is located under the ruins of the church, which was one of the largest Byzantine churches in Turkey. It is believed that Mary spent the last days of her life on a nearby hillside. A chapel is located on the site.

Kadinlar Denizi. About 5 miles from the port, via taxi.

Kusadasi's most popular beach is also goes by the name of Ladies Beach. The small stretch attracts a large crowd.

Stopping for a Bite

During the summer, restaurant prices tend to climb. The best place to eat is along the waterfront, where many establishments offer great views. Seafood dishes are particularly good in this area as well as fresh fruits like apricots, cherries, and figs.

Best Shopping Buys

There are plenty of places to shop and haggle both in town and immediately outside Ephesus. You will find Turkish carpets, brass, leather goods, copper, jewelry, meerschaum pipes, and onyx. Prices are generally bumped up when cruise ships are in port. It is a common practice for shopkeepers to offer tea or soft drinks to customers. This is part of Turkish hospitality, so don't feel obligated to make a purchase.

13 Ports of Call in Northern Europe & the British Isles

A northern European cruise is a different animal than a Mediterranean cruise, offering you the opportunity to explore the stunning fjords of Scandinavia; the windswept shores of the British Isles; historic port cities like Amsterdam, Copenhagen, and Stockholm; and even such lovely capital cities as London, Paris, and Berlin, accessible via shore excursions from the nearest ports. Some itineraries will also visit cities like St. Petersburg, Russia, with its Czarist treasures, and Tallin, in the former Soviet bloc country of Estonia, where you can see firsthand a country attempting to modernize while also preserving tradition.

All the big cities offer history, museums (including some of the best art museums in the world), and great shopping and dining opportunities, and if it's scenery you're after, you'll find it in droves, especially in Norway, the land of the Midnight Sun, whose fjords are unbelievably gorgeous and where, on some itineraries, you can even go all the way up to the Arctic Sea.

1 Belgium

The medieval city of **Antwerp** is the world's fifth largest port and comes complete with all the liveliness, sophistication, and occasional seediness one would expects to find in any large port. Coming into Antwerp, ships cruise the Scheldt River from the North Sea, a distance of about 60 miles, passing a 20 kilometer–long stretch of port activity.

Shoppers will know Antwerp is the "Diamond Center of the World"—it's the leading market for cut diamonds and second only to London for raw and industrial diamonds. A visit to a diamond factory is an obligatory tourist attraction. Antwerp also offers a fine arts museum with Flemish masterpieces—the city was the home town of Rubens and other famous artists—a stunning cathedral, and a maze of medieval streets to explore.

The cruise lines use Antwerp as a starting-off point for shore excursions into Brussels, about 30 miles away; Bruges, about 65 miles away; and Ghent, about 31 miles away.

ESSENTIALS

LANGUAGE The official languages are French, Dutch, and (in one small area of eastern Belgium) German. Many Belgians speak English.

CURRENCY The Belgian franc (BF) is made up of 100 centimes. Notes are issued in 100-, 200-, 500-, 1,000-, 2,000-, 5,000- and 10,000-franc denominations. The rate of exchange at press time was $1 = 38.5 francs.

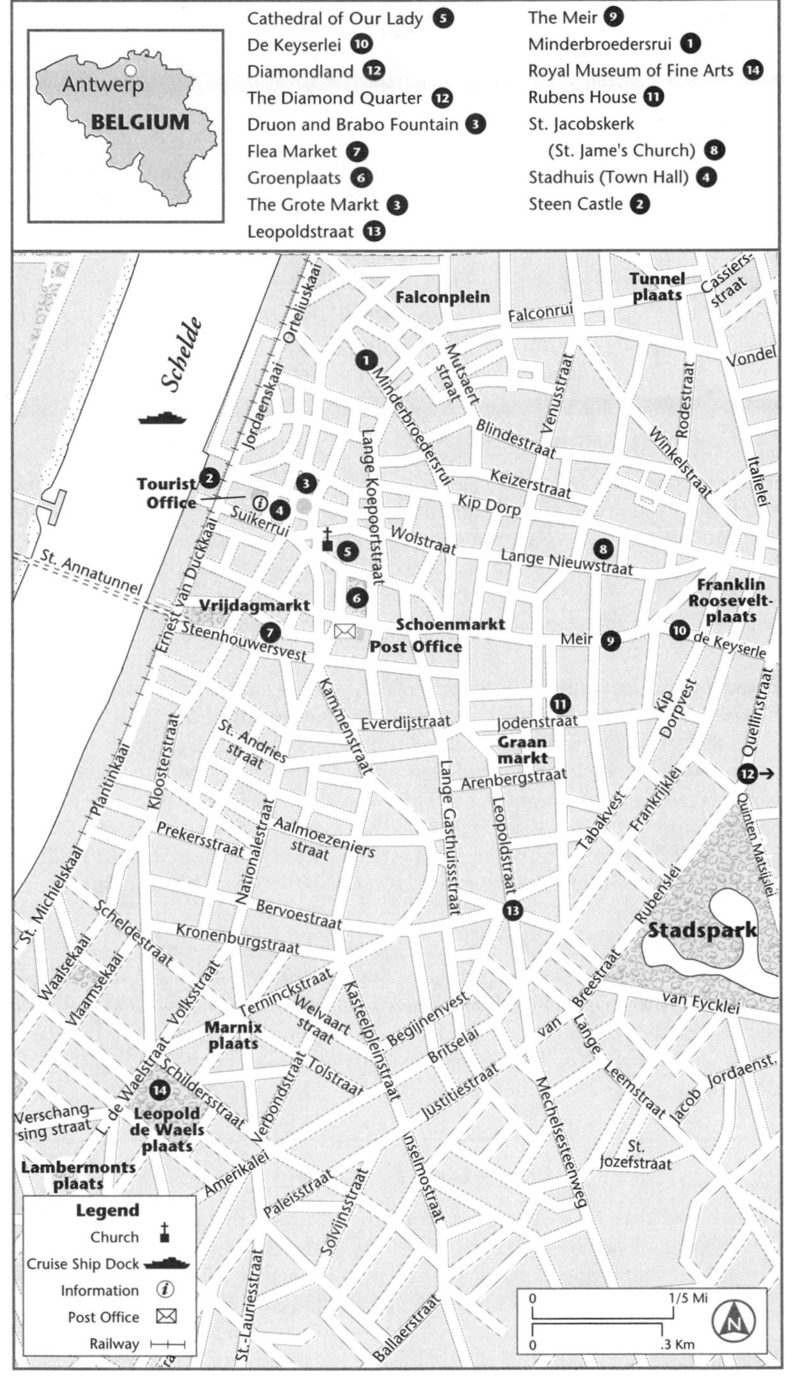
Antwerp
BELGIUM
Cathedral of Our Lady 5
De Keyserlei 10
Diamondland 12
The Diamond Quarter 12
Druon and Brabo Fountain 3
Flea Market 7
Groenplaats 6
The Grote Markt 3
Leopoldstraat 13
The Meir 9
Minderbroedersrui 1
Royal Museum of Fine Arts 14
Rubens House 11
St. Jacobskerk
(St. Jame's Church) 8
Stadhuis (Town Hall) 4
Steen Castle 2
Schelde
Falconplein
Tunnel plaats
Tourist Office
Vrijdagmarkt
Schoenmarkt
Post Office
Franklin Roosevelt-plaats
Graan markt
Stadspark
Marnix plaats
Leopold de Waels plaats
Lambermonts plaats
Legend
Church
Cruise Ship Dock
Information
Post Office
Railway
0
1/5 Mi
0
.3 Km
N

FROMMER'S FAVORITE ANTWERP EXPERIENCES

- **Eating Belgian chocolate.** Favorite handmade brands include Wittamer, Nihoul, Godiva, Leonidas, and Neuhaus.
- **Visiting a diamond factory.** The cutters in the Diamond Quarter are renowned worldwide for their skills.
- **Explore Antwerp's medieval town center.** This is the most colorful part of the city, and the warren of winding streets fans out from the Grote Markt, a lively 16th-century square right near the ship pier.

COMING ASHORE & GETTING AROUND

You can walk to the city center from the pier. It's only about 100 yards to the marketplace, 16th-century city hall, and Gothic cathedral. **Taxis** cannot be hailed on the street, but can be found at stands throughout the city. Antwerp also has a user-friendly network of **trams.** A single fare is about $1.25.

THE BEST SHORE EXCURSIONS

Antwerp City Tour (4 hours, $64): Take a 15-minute bus ride to the pedestrian center of the city for a guided walking tour through the old town section and Grote Market, including Town Hall, the gabled guild houses, cafes, and more. Visit the Vlaaikensgang alley, Our Lady's Cathedral, and Groenplaats, to see the statue of Rubens. Back in the bus, stop outside the house where Rubens lived. Visit Diamondland, a showroom where you can see diamond cutters do their thing and buy a special souvenir.

Brussels Sightseeing (5½ hours, $57): About an hour's bus ride takes you to Belgium's capital city, visiting Heysel Stadium and the site of the 1958 World's Fair. Walk through the city's historic center to see the St. Hubert Gallery, the world-famous Grand Place with its decorated guild houses and the statue of the little Manneken Pis, which is exactly what you think it is (who says this translation business is difficult?). Shopping time at Grand Place is included. Also pass by the Royal Palace, the Court House, and the European parliament, as well as the NATO headquarters building. If you want to tour Brussels on your own, you can get a bus transfer through the cruise lines for about $63.

Bruges (8½ hours, $127): After about a 2-hour bus ride from Antwerp, you will walk with a guide along the cobbled streets of this city's beautiful historic section. See the Town Hall, the Chapel of the Holy Blood, and the Market Place with its guild houses and belfry tower. At the boat dock, take a 30-minute trip on the canals for the best view of this medieval city. You'll have some free time to shop at the chocolate and lace shops at Market Place. Tour includes lunch.

A Girl's Best Friend

There are more than 12,000 expert diamond cutters and polishers at work in Antwerp's Diamond Quarter. Most belong to the Orthodox Jewish community that has traditionally handled the trade. To learn about the process, stop in at **Diamondland,** Appelmansstraat 33A (☎ **03/234-36-12**), which offers a guided tour and glittering souvenirs that you can buy to take home (at prices considerably lower than you will pay elsewhere). The workrooms are open Monday to Saturday, 9am to 6pm. Admission is free.

The Legend of Druon and Brabo

The fountain in the center of Antwerp's Grote Market recalls the legend of Druon and Brabo. According to the story, there was an evil giant named Druon who cut off the head of any Scheldt River boatman who refused to pay him a pricey toll. Brabo, a Roman centurion, eventually slew Duon and tossed his hand into the river. The Flemish word *handwerpen* (throwing of the hand) is where the name Antwerp derives from (or at least that's what they say).

Medieval Ghent & Belgian Chocolate (4 hours, $67): Take a guided walk through this historic city, visiting St. Nicholas Church, St. Bavo's Cathedral, and the Belfry Tower, a 14th-century belfry with a 54-bell carillon, located across from St. Bavo's. Learn the fine art of making chocolates through a video presentation and a visit to a Belgian chocolate factory.

THE TOP ATTRACTIONS

Rubens House. Wapper 9–11. ☎ **03/232-47-51.** Admission about $3.10 adults, $1.55 students. Tues–Sun 10am–5pm.

Rubens built this mansion in 1610 with the tidy fortune he amassed by selling his paintings (no starving artist, he). There are examples of his works throughout the house, as well as works by his contemporaries, some master painters in their own right.

Stadhuis (Town Hall). Grote Markt. ☎ **03/220-82-11.** Admission about 95¢, including a guided tour. Mon–Wed and Fri 9am–3pm.

The town hall, which dominates the Grote Markt square, contains frescoes by Hendriks Leys, an important 19th-century painter; interesting murals; and, in the burgomaster's room, an impressive 16th-century fireplace.

St. Jacobskerk (St. James's Church). Lange Nieuwstraat 73. ☎ **03/232-10-32.** Admission about $1.55 adults, 95¢ children. Mon–Sat 9am–noon.

Rubens is buried in this majestic church, and several of the painter's works are here, as well as some by Van Dyck (also an Antwerp native) and other prominent artists.

Cathedral of Our Lady. Handschoenmarkt. Admission about $1.85. Mon–Fri 10am–5pm, Sat 1–4pm, Sun 1–9pm.

This magnificent church was begun in 1352. The architecture includes seven naves and 125 pillars, making it the largest church in Belgium. In addition to a splendid interior architecture, the cathedral houses three Rubens masterpieces: *Raising the Cross, The Descent From the Cross,* and *The Resurrection.* There's also an impressive stained-glass window by Rombout, dating from 1503.

Steen Castle. Steenplein 1. ☎ **03/232-08-50.** Admission about $3.10 adults, $1.55 students. Tues–Sun 10am–5pm.

Antwerp's oldest building is built on the banks of the River Scheldt and dates back to the 13th century. The fortress houses the National Maritime Museum, which offers models of clipper ships and an extensive library on nautical subjects.

Royal Museum of Fine Arts. Leopold de Waelplaats 2. ☎ **03/238-78-09.** Admission about $4.70. Tues–Sun 10am–5pm.

This neoclassical building houses a collection of works by Flemish masters (Rubens included) that is second to none, as well as paintings by more modern artists.

STOPPING FOR A BITE

Belgian cuisine is much like French (some people actually like it better). Mussels and eel are specialties; other favorite dishes include steak and French fries, *tomates aux crevettes* (tomatoes stuffed with tiny shrimp and homemade mayonnaise), and Belgian endive (known here as *witloof*). Wash it all down with Belgian beer. There are some 400 brands, but I particularly like the dark, monk-brewed Trappist ales. Trendy bars and restaurants (and art galleries too) can be found south of the town center, around Vlaamsekaai and Waalsekaai streets.

BEST SHOPPING BUYS

Shop here for high fashion, lace, chocolate, Belgian beer, and diamonds. Expensive shops, boutiques, and department stores can be found on De Keyserlei and the Meir. For haute couture try Leopoldstraat; for lace, the streets surrounding the cathedral; for antiques, Minderbroedersrui; and for diamonds, Applemans-straat and other streets near Centraal Station. Bargain-hunters should head to the **Flea Market,** held on Wednesday and Friday mornings on Vrijfdagmarkt, facing the Plantin-Morteus Museum, for deals on household goods, especially.

2 Denmark

The Royal City of **Copenhagen** was founded in 1167 and is the capital of the oldest kingdom in the world. It's the largest city in Scandinavia, with a population of more than 1.5 million, and offers history and culture, lots of green city parks, and much charm, reflected as much in its friendly, fun-loving people as in its antique architecture.

This is a lively city where people like to have fun and the good times roll, especially at **Tivoli Gardens,** an extraordinary amusement park that's a must-visit attraction. In the summer, Copenhageners come outdoors (the winters are long), and that means lots of **outdoor cafes,** and people sunbathing (sometimes topless) in the city's parks.

The city's most famous resident was Hans Christian Andersen, whose memory still lives on here. All visitors seem to want to see **The Little Mermaid statue.** It's considered an almost obligatory stop.

You can easily cover Old Copenhagen, with its narrow cobbled streets and old houses, on foot. Especially pedestrian-friendly is the Strø, Europe's longest and oldest walking street.

The name Copenhagen comes from the word *københavn,* meaning "merchants' harbor," and this is a city where you're often on the water, be it the sea or canals. The cruise pier is just a few minutes away from the city center. The entrance to the city through The Sound (the Øresund) that separates Denmark and Sweden is worth a view.

ESSENTIALS

LANGUAGE Danish. English is commonly spoken, especially by young people.

CURRENCY The Danish krone (crown), or Kr in its plural form, is made up of 100 øre. Banknotes are issued in 50, 100, 500, and 1,000 Kr. The rate of exchange at press time was 7.10 Kr.

FROMMER'S FAVORITE COPENHAGEN EXPERIENCES

- **Spending a day (and a night, too) at Tivoli.** These 150-year-old gardens offer a unique brand of fun.
- **Strolling the Strøget.** Europe's oldest and longest pedestrian street is a shopper's paradise.

Copenhagen

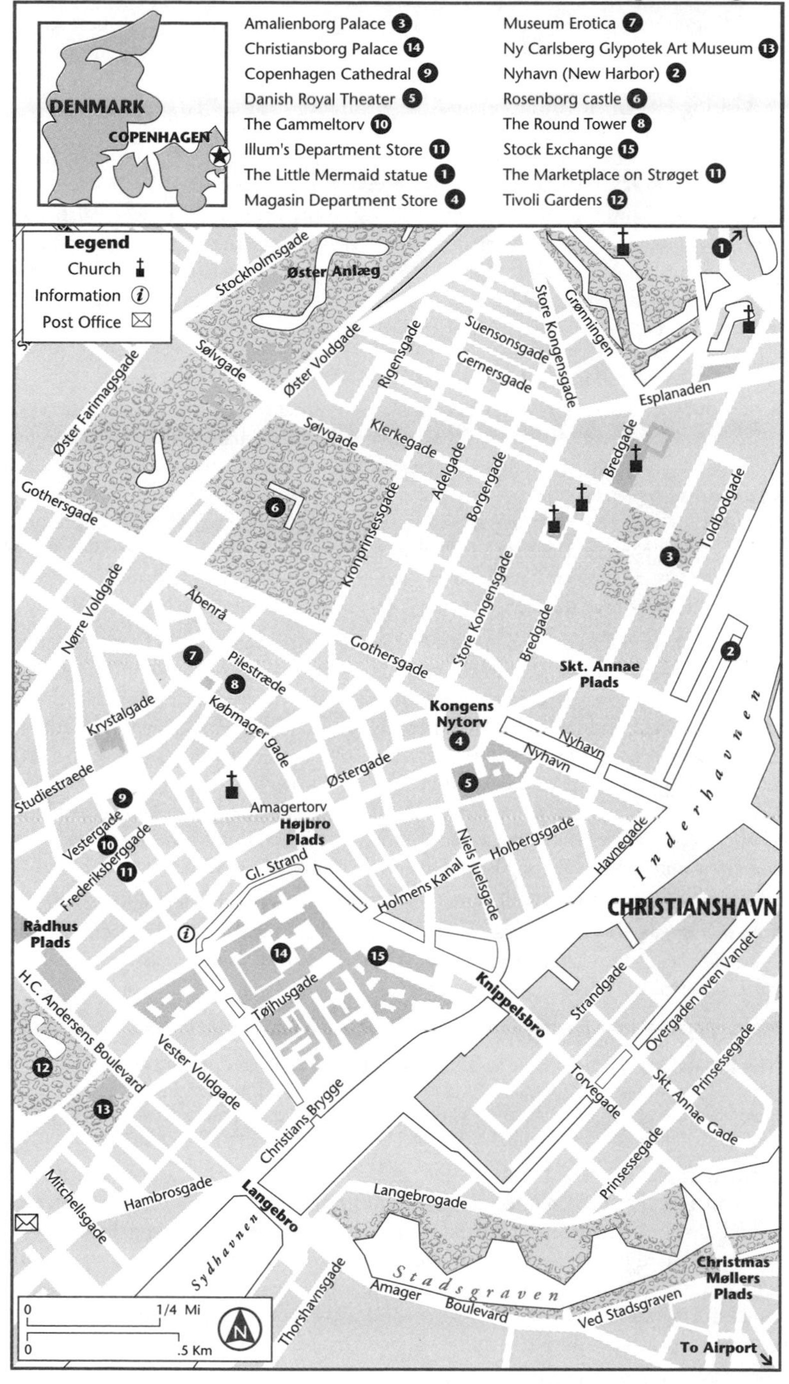

Amalienborg Palace 3
Christiansborg Palace 14
Copenhagen Cathedral 9
Danish Royal Theater 5
The Gammeltorv 10
Illum's Department Store 11
The Little Mermaid statue 1
Magasin Department Store 4
Museum Erotica 7
Ny Carlsberg Glypotek Art Museum 13
Nyhavn (New Harbor) 2
Rosenborg castle 6
The Round Tower 8
Stock Exchange 15
The Marketplace on Strøget 11
Tivoli Gardens 12
DENMARK
COPENHAGEN
Legend
Church
Information
Post Office
Øster Anlæg
Stockholmsgade
Sølvgade
Øster Voldgade
Rigensgade
Suensonsgade
Gernersgade
Store Kongensgade
Grønningen
Esplanaden
Øster Farimagsgade
Klerkegade
Adelgade
Borgergade
Bredgade
Toldbodgade
Gothersgade
Kronprinsessgade
Nørre Voldgade
Åbenrå
Pilestræde
Købmager gade
Krystalgade
Studiestraede
Vestergade
Frederiksberggade
Skt. Annae Plads
Kongens Nytorv
Nyhavn
Østergade
Amagertorv
Højbro Plads
Gl. Strand
Holmens Kanal
Niels Juelsgade
Holbergsgade
Havnegade
Inderhavnen
CHRISTIANSHAVN
Rådhus Plads
Knippelsbro
Strandgade
Overgaden oven Vandet
Tøjhusgade
H.C. Andersens Boulevard
Vester Voldgade
Torvegade
Prinsessegade
Skt. Annae Gade
Christians Brygge
Langebro
Langebrogade
Mitchellsgade
Hambrosgade
Sydhavnen
Thorshavnsgade
Stadsgraven
Amager Boulevard
Ved Stadsgraven
Christmas Møllers Plads
0 1/4 Mi
0 .5 Km
N
To Airport

- **Sitting at an outdoor cafe.** Have a beer and watch the scenery. The best spot is at Nyhavn (New Harbor), beginning at Kongens Nytorv, where the scenery includes tall ships.
- **Visiting Helsingør (Elsinore) and the Kronborg Castle.** "To be, or not to be. . . ." Shakespeare set his *Hamlet* here.

COMING ASHORE & GETTING AROUND

It's about a 20-minute walk from the pier to the city center. **Taxis** are available at the pier. Make sure the cab is metered. Tips are included in the metered rate, which begins at about $3.30 and adds about $1.15 for each kilometer thereafter. The city also has an excellent **bus** system. It is easy to get from Copenhagen to sights in North Zealand by train.

THE BEST SHORE EXCURSIONS

City Tour (3 hours, $39): Visit Christiansborg, the seat of Denmark's government since 1918, and Christiansborg Palace. Drive past the Stock Exchange with its stunning spire of entwining dragons' tails, built by King Christian IV; the Danish Royal Theater, home of the Royal Ballet Troupe, built in 1824; and Nyhavn, the sailor's district. Stop briefly outside the Amalienborg Palace to photograph the Queen's guards. Then check out the famous Little Mermaid statue. You'll also pass Tivoli Gardens, the Glyptotek Art Museum, the Round Tower, Copenhagen Cathedral, and the Gammeltorv, a marketplace and the oldest part of the city.

North Zealand & Helsingør (7 hours, $135): After a brief city tour of Copenhagen, travel by bus through the lush Danish countryside to Frederiksborg Castle in Hillerod. This magnificent Renaissance castle is now the National Museum of History. In the small chapel, you will find the oldest organ in the world, still in use today. Next stop is the Fredensborg Palace, summer residence of the Royal Family. Continue north to the town of Helsingør (Elsinore) where you'll explore the courtyard and ramparts of Kronborg Castle, which dates back to the 16th century. The castle is better known as Hamlet's Castle, immortalized when Shakespeare chose it as the setting for his play (even though Hamlet would have lived long before the castle was built). Return to Copenhagen along the coast, known as the Danish Riviera. Lunch featuring Danish specialties is included.

Copenhagen's Royal Palaces (4 hours, $52): This tour includes Rosenborg castle, home of the Danish crown jewels; and Christiansborg Palace, a massive 12th-century fortress surrounded by canals on three sides; followed by a brief city tour.

THE TOP ATTRACTIONS

Tivoli Gardens. Vesterbrogade 3. ☎ **33/15-10-01.** Admission 11am–1pm, about $4.50 for adults, $3 children; 1–9:30pm, $5.85 adults, $3 children; 9:30pm–midnight, $4.50 adults, $3 children. Rides are $2.25 each; or an all-day wristband allows unlimited access to rides for about $22.20. Sun–Thurs 11am–midnight, Fri–Sat 11am–2am. Closed mid-Sept to May.

Since it opened in 1843, this garden and amusement park has been a must-do in Copenhagen. The garden offers thousands of flowers, and the fun includes a merry-go-round of tiny Viking ships, pinball arcades, slot machines, shooting galleries, bumper cars (populated at night mostly by business men and women out for a night of fun), and a Ferris wheel of hot air balloons. There are more than two dozen restaurants located in an Arabian-style fantasy palace, and a lake with ducks, swans, and boats. Entertainment includes parades, regimental band concerts, and pantomime performances.

The Little Mermaid Statue. Langelinie.

The one thing every visitor to Copenhagen wants to see. The famous statue is a life-size bronze of the character in Hans Christian Andersen's fairy tale of the same name.

Erotic Factoid

For a little something different, visit the **Museum Erotica,** the only museum in the world where you can learn about the sex lives of such luminaries as Freud, Nietzsche, and even Duke Ellington. The collection surveys erotica through the ages, and includes Etruscan drawings, Chinese paintings, and Greek vases, all depicting sexual activity. The museum is within walking distance of Tivoli, at Købmagergade 24. ☎ **33/12-03-11.** Admission is about $9.75. May to September, daily 10am to 11pm.

It was unveiled in 1913, and is located on rocks right offshore. The statue has been attacked more than once, losing an arm in one misadventure, and beheaded in another. The statue is near the cruise ship docks, no more than a 10-minute walk.

Ny Carlsberg Glypotek. Dantes Plads 7. ☎ **33/41-81-41.** Admission about $2.25 adults, free for children under 16. Free admission Wed and Sun. Tues–Sun 10am–4pm.

The Glypotek, located near Tivoli Gardens, was founded in the 19th century by Carl Jacobsen, also founder of the Carlsberg Brewing Company. It is one of Scandinavia's most important museums. The collection includes French and Danish art, mostly from the 19th century. Sculptures by Rodin can be found on the ground floor, and works of the Impressionists, including Van Gogh's *Landscape from St. Rémy,* on the upper floors. There are also Greek, Roman, Etruscan, and Egyptian collections.

Rosenborg Castle. Øster Voldgade 4A. ☎ **33/15-32-86.** Admission about $6 adults, $4.50 seniors and students, $1.50 children under 15. Jun–Aug, daily 10am–4pm; Easter week, May, Sept to mid-Oct, daily 11am–3pm.

The red-brick Renaissance castle, built in 1607 by King Christian IV as a summer residence, was converted into a museum in the 19th century. It houses the Danish crown jewels, costumes, and other impressive royal memorabilia.

Christiansborg Palace. Christiansborg Slotsplads, Prins Jørgens Gård 1. ☎ **33/92-64-92.** Admission to the Royal Reception Rooms, about $4.95 adults, $1.50 children; parliament free; castle ruins $3 adults, 75¢ children. Reception rooms, English-language tours given mid-June to late Sept, Tues, Thurs, Sat, Sun 10am–4pm; ruins, May–Sept daily 9:30am–3:30pm.

The queen officially receives guests in the Royal Reception Chamber at the palace, located on the island of Slotsholmen (you go over a bridge to get there). Housing the Parliament House and the Supreme Court, the baroque structure is impressive, even by European standards, and you can tour the richly decorated rooms, including the Throne Room, Queen's Library, and banqueting hall. Before entering, you'll be asked to put on slippers to protect the floors. Under the palace, you can visit the well-preserved ruins of the 1167 castle of Bishop Absalon, the founder of Copenhagen.

Louisiana Museum of Modern Art. About a 40-minute train ride outside the city. Admission about $7.95 adults, $2.25 for children 4 to 16, and free for children under 4. Open Thurs–Tues 10am–5pm and Wed 10am–10pm. Take the train to Humlebaek, on the Copenhagen-Helsingør train line. The trains leave every half hour. From the train stop in Humlebaek it's about a 10- or 15-min. walk (the direction is well marked), or take a shuttle bus.

A personal favorite, the museum offers a collection that includes Giacometti and Henry Moore, located in an idyllic setting on the Danish Riviera. The museum is located about 20 miles north of Copenhagen and easily accessible by train.

STOPPING FOR A BITE

The favorite dish at lunch is smørrebrød, meaning open-faced sandwiches, and it's practically a national institution. My favorite is piled with tiny Danish shrimp, but other popular favorites are sliced pork loin, roast beef, and liver paste. Danes typically eat dinner at 6:30pm. Popular dishes include liver and onions, beef dishes, roast lamb, and roast pork with red cabbage. Cheese is often eaten with meals, and the Danish varieties, including Danish Blue and Havarti, will likely be familiar.

And what about those famous Danish pastries? They are called wienerbrød here, and they are very rich and delicious, and mostly served at breakfast time (but you can get them anytime at bakeries). Beer is Denmark's national beverage, so it's a must-do to wash down your meal with Carlsberg or Tuborg.

BEST SHOPPING BUYS

Best buys here include stainless steel items, porcelain, china, glassware, toys, textiles, and jewelry (decorative, silver, and semi-precious stones). The Strøget provides the most shopping opportunities. In addition to numerous boutiques, there are two main department stores, Illum's and Magasin.

3 England

London is the largest city in Europe and one of the best tourist cities in the world. Known for pageantry and tradition, the city offers numerous monuments to its elaborate past, but it's also a hip and lively city, very up on the latest fashion, food, and music trends, and culturally and economically diverse.There is something for everyone here—history, magnificent palaces, medieval churches, literary shrines, culture, nightlife, parks and gardens, great museums (more than 300 of them), the best theater scene in the world, and fabulous shopping (a stop at Harrods is obligatory).

It's difficult to see everything in this sprawling city, but pick a few neighborhoods and walk around. Sightseeing from a double-decker bus is also a good choice. And the city's Underground (subway) is very user-friendly and easy to negotiate.

Take a picture of **Big Ben** (at the Houses of Parliament, Westminster Palace, Old Place Yard, SW1), and while you're in the neighborhood, check out **Westminster Abbey** and **10 Downing Street** (home of the prime minister). **Buckingham Palace,** home to the Queen, is now open in the summer, and even when the gates are closed, the spectacle of the Changing of the Guard is worth fighting the crowds for. And for something different, listen to the speeches at the **Speaker's Corner** in Hyde Park (anyone can stand up and speak here), down a pint at a traditional pub, eat some fish and chips wrapped in paper, and make sure to experience afternoon tea.

There are restaurants everywhere, and even some good ones—it may be time to stop picking on British cuisine!

ESSENTIALS

LANGUAGE English.

CURRENCY The British unit of currency is the pound sterling (£), which is divided into 100 pence (p). Banknotes are issued in 1, 5, 10, 20, and 50 pound denominations. The rate of exchange at press time was $1 = 60p.

FROMMER'S FAVORITE LONDON EXPERIENCES

- **Enjoying a traditional tea.** If you've never experienced scones with clotted cream, now is your chance—they're downright heavenly!
- **Attending a play at a West End theater.** London is the theater capital of the world, with more plays produced here than anywhere else.
- **Going museum-hopping.** This is certainly the place. You have hundreds to choose from, including the Tate, National Gallery, Victoria & Albert, and British Museum, and many offer free admission.

- **Visiting a pub.** The traditional ones in central London have long mahogany bars, dark-wood paneling, and Victorian accessories, and are a great place to meet the locals.
- **Going shopping at Harrods.** Harrods in Knightsbridge is spread across 15 acres and proudly proclaims its motto *Omnia Omnibus Ubique* (or "everything for everyone"). Someone who didn't believe that claim in 1975 called the store at midnight and ordered a baby elephant to be sent to the home of the governor of California. The gift arrived safely, and Nancy Reagan sent a thank you note on behalf of herself and her husband, Ronald.

COMING ASHORE & GETTING AROUND

Some small ships, like those operated by Seabourn, Silversea, and Radisson, actually sail up the Thames and dock adjacent to Tower Bridge (opposite the Tower of London). Other ships dock at further-out ports including Southampton, Dover, and Harwich, and bus passengers into London.

Getting around London is not difficult at all. There are **taxis** everywhere. There's also a great **underground** (subway) system, referred to here as the "tube." Or, you can ride on one of the famous red **double-decker buses.**

THE BEST SHORE EXCURSIONS

My recommendation is for you to take the transfer to London offered by the cruise line and then go it on your own.

THE TOP ATTRACTIONS

Tower of London. Tower Hill (on the north bank of the Thames). ☎ **0171/709-0765.** Admission about $14 adults, $10.55 students and seniors, $9.25 children, $41.90 for a family ticket for 2 adults and 3 children. Apr–Oct, Mon–Sat 9am–5pm, Sun 10am–5pm.

Exhibits at this ancient fortress include the Armouries, which date back to the time of Henry VIII (check out his suit of armor!); a display of instruments of torture recalling some of the more gruesome moments in the tower's history; and the Jewel House, where the crown jewels are kept. Go early, as the Tower is extremely popular with Brits and tourists alike, and you're likely to encounter long lines.

Westminster Abbey. Broad Sanctuary, SW1. ☎ **0171/222-7110.** Free admission to cloisters. Abbey, about $8.25 adults, $4.95 students, $2.45 children 11–18, free for 10 and under. Mon–Fri 9am–3:45pm, Sat 9:15am–1:45pm and 4–4:45pm.

An abbey was founded on this spot in 1065 by the Saxon king, Edward the Confessor. The first English king crowned in the abbey was Harold in 1066. William the Conqueror followed, and the coronation tradition has continued to the present day, broken only twice (Edward V and Edward VIII). Today's structure owes most to Henry VIII's plans, but many architects, including Christopher Wren, contributed. Noted spots include the shrine of Edward the Confessor (who was canonized in the 12th century) and the Poet's Corner, where you'll find monuments to Chaucer, Shakespeare, Ben Jonson, Samuel Johnson, the Brontë sisters, Thackeray, Dickens, Tennyson, Kipling, and even American Longfellow.

Buckingham Palace. At the end of The Mall (the street running from Trafalgar Square). ☎ **0171/930-9625.** Palace tours, about $14.85 adults to age 60, $10.75 seniors, $8.25 children under 17. Changing of the guard free. Tours are only offered in the summer, usually Aug and Sept, when the Royal Family is not in residence. For tour hours check with your ship's shore excursions desk or consult the local tourist publications when you arrive in London. Do the same for the Changing of the Guard which, when it takes place, is offered at 11:30am.

Central London

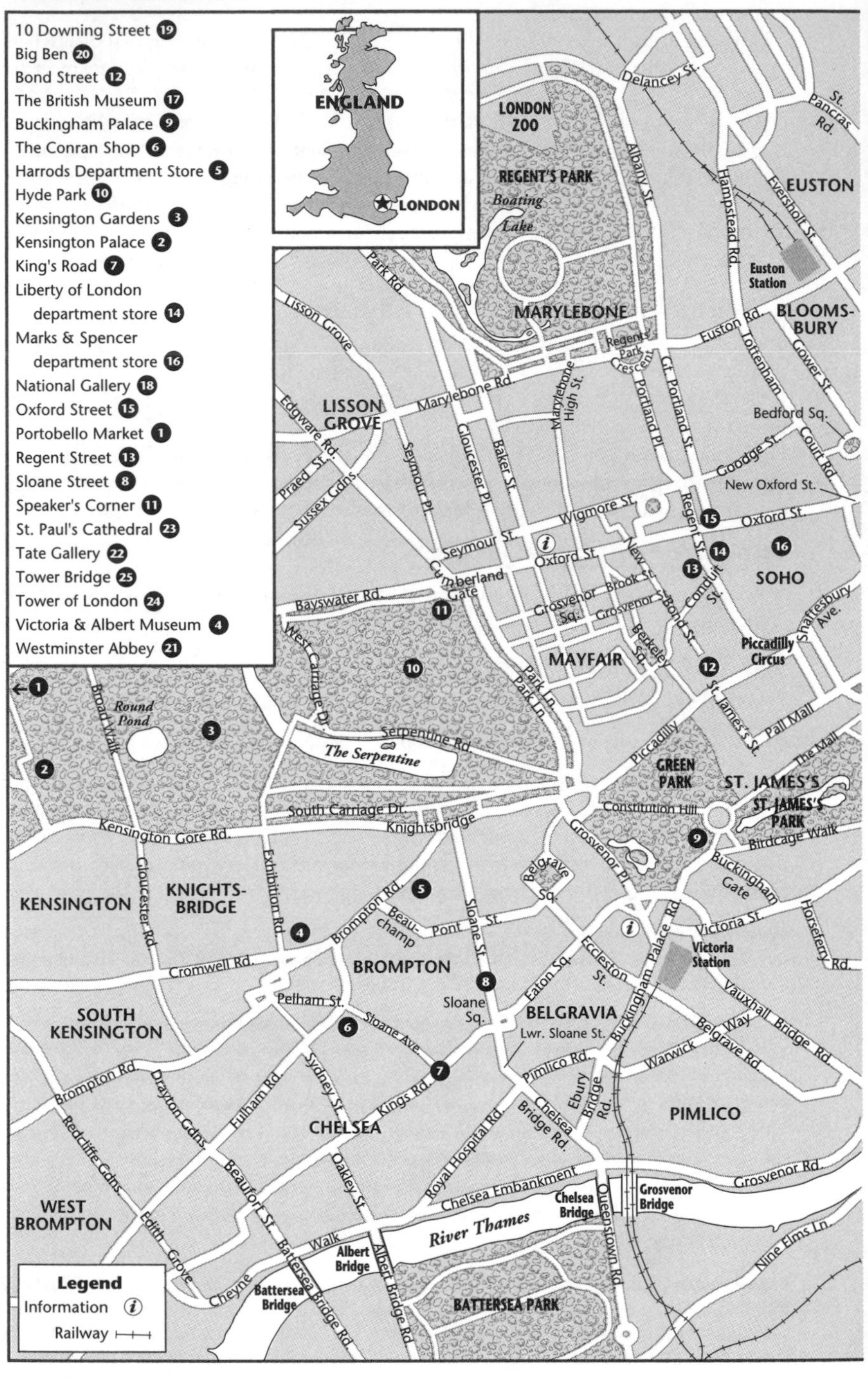

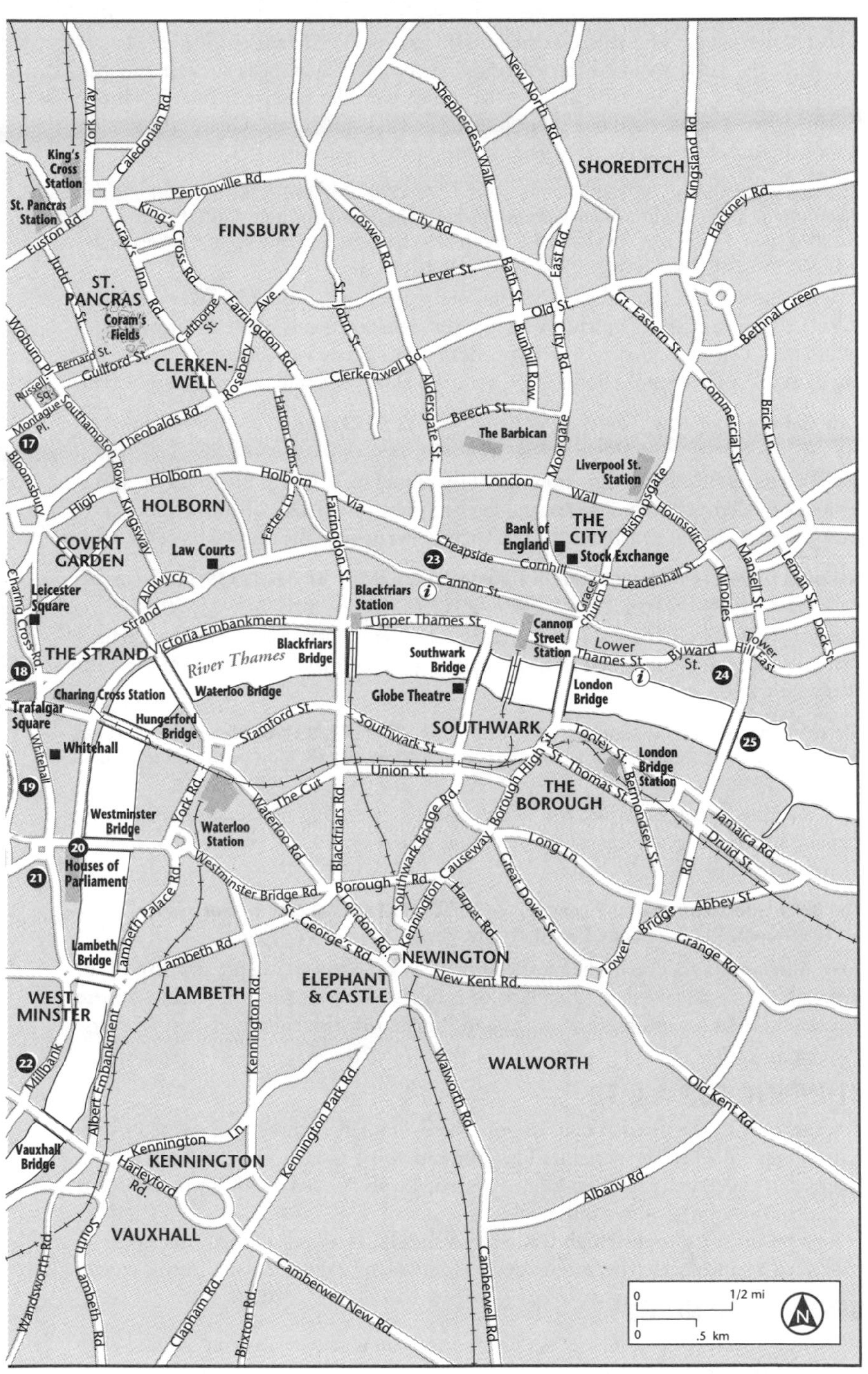
SHOREDITCH
FINSBURY
ST. PANCRAS
CLERKEN-WELL
HOLBORN
COVENT GARDEN
THE STRAND
THE CITY
SOUTHWARK
THE BOROUGH
NEWINGTON
ELEPHANT & CASTLE
LAMBETH
WEST-MINSTER
WALWORTH
KENNINGTON
VAUXHALL
King's Cross Station
St. Pancras Station
Coram's Fields
The Barbican
Liverpool St. Station
Bank of England
Stock Exchange
Law Courts
Leicester Square
Blackfriars Station
Cannon Street Station
River Thames
Blackfriars Bridge
Southwark Bridge
Waterloo Bridge
Globe Theatre
London Bridge
Charing Cross Station
Trafalgar Square
Hungerford Bridge
Whitehall
London Bridge Station
Westminster Bridge
Waterloo Station
Houses of Parliament
Lambeth Bridge
Vauxhall Bridge
0 1/2 mi
0 .5 km
N

This massive yet graceful palace is the official residence of the queen. If Her Majesty is at home the Royal Standard flag will be flying outside. When she is not at home, visitors are allowed to tour parts of the palace, including the state apartments, Throne Room, grand staircase, and picture galleries. The Changing of the Guard, the world's most famous military ritual, takes place in the palace's forecourt.

St. Paul's Cathedral. St. Paul's Churchyard, EC4. ☎ **0171/248-8348.** Cathedral about $6.60 adults, $3.30 children 6–16. Galleries $5.75 adults, $1.65 children. Guided tours $5.75, recorded tours $4.95. Free for children 5 and under. Mon–Sat 8:30am–4pm; galleries, Mon–Sat 10am–4:15pm. No sightseeing Sun (services only).

After the great fire of 1666, the old St. Paul's was razed, and Christopher Wren designed this impressive Renaissance structure with its massive classical dome. Inside are many monuments, including a memorial chapel to American service personnel who lost their lives during World War II. Wren lies in the crypt, as do the Duke of Wellington and Lord Nelson.

Tate Gallery. Beside the Thames on Millbank, SW1. ☎ **0171/887-8725.** Free admission except for special exhibitions. Daily 10am–5:30pm.

The Tate offers British paintings from the 16th century on as well as England's finest collection of modern art, both domestic and foreign. The Clore Gallery offerings paintings by M.W. Turner, who lived and died on the Thames and painted the many sides of the river.

National Gallery. On the north side of Trafalgar Square, WC2. ☎ **0171/839-3321.** Free admission. Mon–Tues 10am–6pm, Wed 10am–8pm, Thurs–Sat 10am–6pm, Sun noon–6pm.

The neoclassical building itself is impressive, and the collection houses a comprehensive collection of Western paintings representing all the major schools from the 13th to the early 20th century.

Victoria and Albert Museum. Cromwell Rd., Swy. ☎ **0171/938-8500.** Admission about $8.25 adults, $4.95 students and seniors, free for children under 18. Mon noon–5:30pm, Tues–Sun 10am–5:30pm.

This museum features the fine and decorative arts, including medieval items, Islamic carpets, and the largest Renaissance sculpture collection outside of Italy, including a Donatello marble relief.

The British Museum. Great Russell St., WC1. ☎ **0171/323-8299.** Free admission. Mon–Sat 10am–5pm, Sun 2:30–6pm. Closed in early May.

This museum houses one of the most comprehensive collections of art and artifacts in the world. It would take days to explore, so I suggest you start with the Asian, Chinese porcelain, Indian sculpture, Prehistoric, and Romano-British collections (on your first visit, anyway).

STOPPING FOR A BITE

You can find all the international favorites here—Indian is cheap and favored by locals—along with British specialties like **fish and chips** (which you can buy take-out wrapped in paper) and steak-and-kidney pie. Food is also served in pubs, where you can wash down your meal with a pint of ale.

If you want to experience **high tea,** head to a tea house or one of the better hotels. A traditional tea includes a choice of sandwiches and cakes, and scones with clotted cream.

BEST SHOPPING BUYS

You name it, you can buy it here, but prices usually aren't a bargain. You can find deals on some fashion items, British and Scottish woolens, and china. Food items make great gifts, especially English biscuits (cookies).

Remembering Diana

A sea of flowers and other tributes were left at the beautiful Kensington Gardens (which adjoin Hyde Park at Kensington Palace) after the death of Princess Diana. Even today, mourners leave flowers at the gates of the palace, where Diana resided when she was in London. The palace is open to visitors from 10am to 6pm daily, by guided tour. Admission is $11.20 adults, $7.50 children, $9.20 students and seniors (☎ **0171/937-9561**). Princess Diana is buried on a picturesque island on the Oval Lake at Althorp, the Spencer family estate in Northamptonshire, about 75 miles from London. The grounds are open to visitors on a limited basis. Advance reservations are required. Call ☎ **01604/592-020.**

Major West End shopping streets include **Oxford Street** for affordable items (the flagship brand of the **Marks & Spencer** department store is here); **Regent Street** for more upscale shopping (including the famed **Liberty of London** department store, worth seeing even if you're not in a buying mood); and **Bond Street,** for luxury designer shopping.

In Knightsbridge, you'll find the world-famous **Harrods** department store and lots of other shopping opportunities as well, including designer shops on **Sloane Street.** Harrods is a must-do stop (check out, especially, the food hall on the lower levels).

King's Road, the main street of Chelsea, was hip in the '60s, and even today is frequented by young people. Shops including **The Conran Shop,** which sells household goods, can be found nearby at **Brompton Cross.**

For a fun, typically London experience, head on Saturdays to the **Portobello Market** in Notting Hill. You'll find a little bit of everything for sale there, including antiques.

4 Estonia

Located on the Baltic Sea, only about 37 miles (60km) across the Gulf of Finland from Helsinki, Estonia spent 2 centuries as one of Russia's Baltic Provinces before becoming an independent republic in 1918. Little over 2 decades later, it fell back under Russian control when Soviet troops rolled in and incorporated the country into the Soviet Union. It became independent once again in 1991. Separated from the west for 50 years, the capitol city of **Tallinn** is now visited frequently by tourists sailing aboard hydrofoils and other vessels from Helsinki and Stockholm.

Tallin, a UNESCO world heritage site, was founded in the 12th century and has been under the rule of Denmark, Sweden, and Germany as well as Russia, and all left their mark on the city's architecture. It is one of the best preserved medieval towns in northern Europe, and makes a beautiful impression from the sea, with its ancient city walls, church spires, and red-tile roofed homes. At the old town, you pass beneath the arches of Tallinn's ancient stone walls and enter a world of cobblestones, narrow alleys, and medieval buildings. It's a fun place to explore on foot.

While under German occupation in 1944, the city was bombed and 1,100 people were killed or wounded. Also at that time, about 11% of the old town was destroyed, and was replaced afterward by bleak Soviet architecture. Today, the city is growing rapidly, with modern buildings joining the old.

ESSENTIALS

LANGUAGE Estonian.

CURRENCY The national currency is called the kroon, abbreviated as EEK, and is made up of 100 sents. The kroon is pegged to the German mark, 1DEM = 8EEK. The rate of exchange at press time was $1 = 14.90 kroons.

FROMMER'S FAVORITE TALLINN EXPERIENCES

- **Explore Old Town.** Start at the Tall Herman Tower and explore the medieval world behind the old stone walls. Views to catch include the Baroque Toompea Castle, now the residence of the Estonian Parliament; Town Hall Square and Tallinn's Gothic Town Hall; and the Holy Ghost Church, which dates to the 14th century.

COMING ASHORE & GETTING AROUND

The pier in Tallinn is 0.5 to 1 mile (1 to 2km) from the city center, depending on where the ship berths, and you can walk or take a **taxi,** which you'll find waiting at the pier. However, some ships dock in Muuga, which is about a 35-minute drive from Tallinn. You can explore Old Town on foot.

THE BEST SHORE EXCURSIONS

Historic Walking Tour (4 hours, $32–$35): Visit Old Town, including Toompea Castle, the Russian Orthodox Church of Alexander Nevsky, the Holy Ghost Church, the Gothic Town Hall, and the partly ruined historic Dominican Monastery, where you'll hear a concert of medieval music before a final walk. Time is allowed for shopping in shops and from local vendors.

Full-Day City Tour (7½ hours, $75–$85): Combines the above with a visit to Rocca al Mare, and a performance by a folkloric group in traditional costume. Includes lunch at an Old Town restaurant and time to browse the shops.

THE TOP ATTRACTIONS

Rocca al Mare. Vabaõhumuuseumitee 12. ☎ **65/49-117.** Daily 10am–8pm.

This open-air museum features Estonian village architecture from the 18th and 19th centuries. The country buildings include windmills, churches, and farms, all situated in a pleasantly wooded park. A folkloric show troupe performs traditional dances here.

Alexander Nevsky Cathedral. Lossiplats 10. ☎ **64/43-34-84.** Daily 8am–7pm.

This lovely Russian Orthodox church is a dominating feature of Upper Town's city skyline. Inside are numerous golden icons and mosaics.

The Dome Church (also known as St. Mary's). Toom-Kooli 6. ☎ **64/44-140.** Tues–Sat 9–4:30pm, Sun noon–4:30pm.

This church is of Gothic design. Inside are more than 100 medieval coats of arms.

STOPPING FOR A BITE

Estonian food is pretty plain. Local favorites include trout (smoked, pickled, or salted).

BEST SHOPPING BUYS

Shop here for handicrafts, hand-knit woolen sweaters, ceramics, leather goods, amber jewelry, and artwork. Small shops can be found in the center of town.

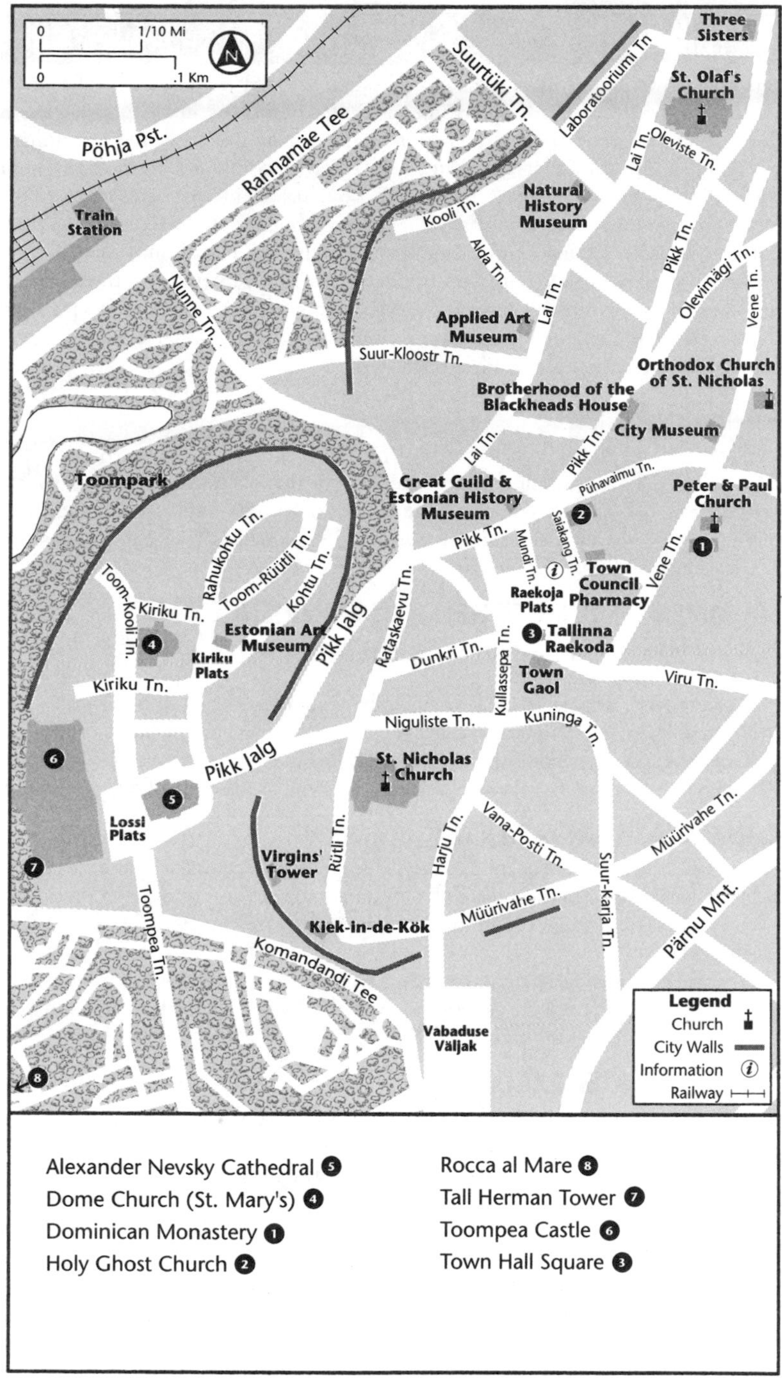

Alexander Nevsky Cathedral 5
Dome Church (St. Mary's) 4
Dominican Monastery 1
Holy Ghost Church 2
Rocca al Mare 8
Tall Herman Tower 7
Toompea Castle 6
Town Hall Square 3

5 Finland

Although not technically in Scandinavia, **Helsinki** acts very Scandinavian. The city was founded by Swedes in 1550 and became the capital of Finland in 1812, acting as such during Finland's time as an autonomous Grand Duchy of Russia and remaining so when Finland became independent in 1917. Today, Helsinki is a business and industrial center, but is also an intellectual town with a major university and many cultural institutions. Locals still refer to it as "a big village," but the city is actually a pretty sophisticated place, offering tourists a clean environment with great museums, nice harbor views, and lots of shopping opportunities. Surrounded by water on three sides and including in its territory a number of islands, it's notable for its parks and squares and for its neoclassical city buildings, dating from the 19th century and planned out by German-born architect Carl Ludvig Engel.

ESSENTIALS

LANGUAGE Finnish. English is also commonly spoken.

CURRENCY The Finnish unit of currency is the markka (plural: markkaa) which is divided into 100 pennia. Banknotes are issued in 20-, 50-, 100-, 500-, and 1,000-markkaa denominations, and coins in 10p and 50p, as well as 1-, 5-, and 10-markkaa. The exchange rate at press time was $1 = 5.65 markkaa.

FROMMER'S FAVORITE HELSINKI EXPERIENCES

- **Take a boat to the Suomenlinna Fortress.** Fortresses and parks here are located on five inter-connecting islands.
- **Go shopping.** The department store Stockmann offers the latest in Finnish design. Market Square is a fun market scene.
- **Remember Sibelius.** Visit the composer's home in the country, or view the tribute to him in Sibelius Park, where there's a monument constructed of 527 steel pipes.

COMING ASHORE & GETTING AROUND

Ships dock near Market Square. It's easy to walk around central Helsinki to see such sights as Senate Square, where there's a monument to the Russian tsar Alexander II; the 19th-century Lutheran Cathedral; Parliament House; and Alvar Aalto–designed Finlandia Hall.

Helsinki has an efficient transportation network that includes buses, trams, subway (metro), and ferries. **Taxis** are available at the pier. The fare begins at $2.95. Surcharges are imposed in the evening and on Sunday.

THE BEST SHORE EXCURSIONS

City Tour (3 hours, $42): Pass the famous Uspenski Orthodox Cathedral with its brilliant gold onion domes en route to the Senate Square, site of several important buildings attributed to the neoclassic architect Carl Ludwig Engel. On Mannerheim Street, view the Parliament House, the National Museum, and Finlandia Hall, designed by the famous architect Alvar Aalto. Continue through lovely residential districts to the Olympic Stadium, site of the 1952 Olympic Games. You'll also pass the opera house, completed in 1993; stop at the Temppeliaukio Rock Church, a unique house of worship blasted into solid rock and topped by a copper dome; then make a photo stop at Sibelius Park, where you can photograph a monument constructed of 527 steel pipes honoring the great Finnish composer Jean Sibelius. The tour includes shopping time.

Porvoo & Highlights (6½ hours, $115): Drive 45 minutes along the picturesque, shipyard-lined coastal road to Porvoo, a popular artistic center that's the second-oldest town in Finland, dating back to 1346. Here you will visit the majestic 1418 medieval cathedral and walk along the cobblestone streets of the Old Quarter, with its ancient, multicolored wooden houses. Time is allowed for some shopping. The tour also stops at Haikko Manor, one of the country's leading spas and a place of history, elegance, and romance, overlooking the Gulf of Finland and dating back to 1362 and the Royal era. Lunch and a brief city tour of Helsinki are included.

Art & Architecture (4 hours, $72): This tour combines a city tour with a visit to the charming Finnish countryside, including the coastal road, woodlands, and lake country. Visit Hvittrask, once the home of the famous Finnish architects Eliel Saarinen, Armas Lindgren, and Herman Gesellius. Built in 1902 of natural stone and logs, situated on a hill overlooking a lake and surrounded by woods, Hvittrask is an outstanding example of Finnish residential architecture, and is now an exhibition center for Finnish art and handicrafts. Tour Saarinen's magnificent home before continuing on to Tarvaspaa, the former home and studio of Finland's national painter, Akseli Gallen-Kallela. The house was built around 1912 and designed by the artist himself, and the park-like setting is on the sea. Gallen-Kallela's works and the story of his colorful life are on display here, as are exhibits by other famous artists depicting the Finnish way of life.

Suomenlinna Island Fortress (3½ hours, $48): Travel by boat for 15 minutes to the island of Suomenlinna, the Gibraltar of the North, reputed to be the largest sea fortress in the world and one of Finland's most remarkable sights (it's included on UNESCO's list of World Heritage Treasures). See "The Top Attractions," below, for details. Time is allowed to explore the museum or visit one of the island cafes. Also includes a stop at the colorful market in Helsinki.

THE TOP ATTRACTIONS

Mannerheim Museum. Kallionlinnantie 14. ☎ **09/635-443.** Admission, including a guided tour, is about $6.30 adults, $3.15 children 12–16, free for children 11 and under. Fri–Sun 11am–4pm.

Once the home of Baron Carl Gustaf Mannerheim, marshal of Finland and president of the republic from 1944 to 1946, this museum houses his collection of European furniture, Asian art, and personal items including swords and decorations.

Ainoia. Ainolantie, in Järvenpää. ☎ **09/287-322.** Admission about $4.20 adults, $1.05 children. June–Aug, Tues–Sun 11am–5pm; May and Sept, Wed–Sun 11am–5pm. Closed in Oct and Apr. Buses and trains run from Helsinki to Järvenpää, about 24 miles away.

The Finns are very proud of composer Jean Sibelius, who lived here from 1904 until his death in 1957. He and his wife, Aino, for whom the house is named, are buried on the property.

Suomenlinna Fortress. Suomenlinna. ☎ **09/668-154.** Tours offered during the peak summer months (June–Sept) are $4.20 adults, $1.70 children. At other times, tours are conducted for groups on a private basis. Accessible by ferry from Market Square, with boats running about once an hour. The round-trip ferry ride costs about $3.35 for adults, $1.90 for children.

Known as the Gibraltar of the North, the fortress dates back to 1748, when Finland was part of Sweden, and lies on five interconnected islands that guard maritime approaches to Helsinki. The main attractions include a well-preserved bastioned fort on

Factoid

The Egyptian-inspired **Helsinki Railway Station,** designed by Eliel Saarinen in 1916, has been oft-copied by avant-garde set designers for plays and films, including *Batman.*

Helsinki

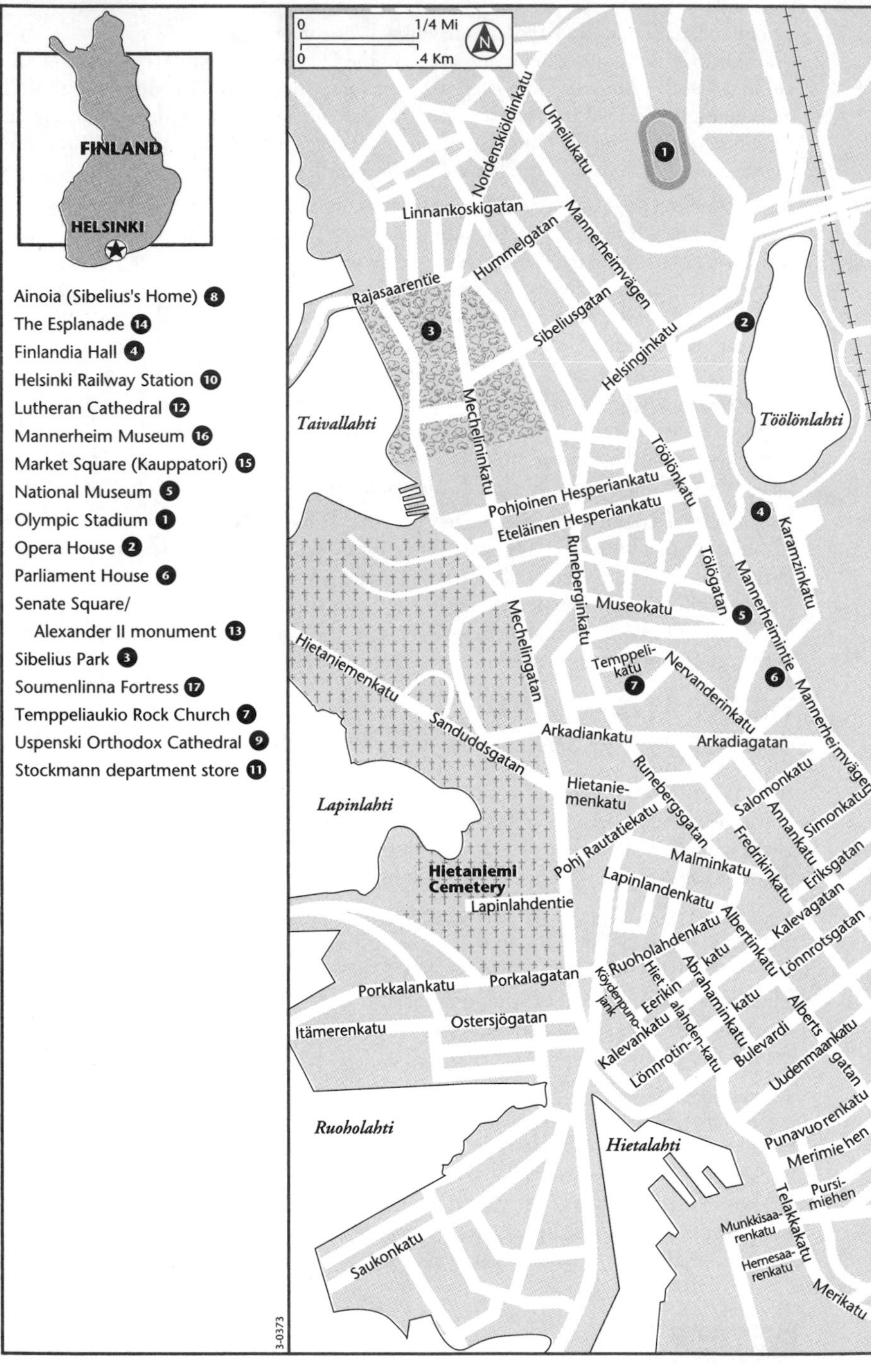

FINLAND
HELSINKI
Ainoia (Sibelius's Home) 8
The Esplanade 14
Finlandia Hall 4
Helsinki Railway Station 10
Lutheran Cathedral 12
Mannerheim Museum 16
Market Square (Kauppatori) 15
National Museum 5
Olympic Stadium 1
Opera House 2
Parliament House 6
Senate Square/
Alexander II monument 13
Sibelius Park 3
Soumenlinna Fortress 17
Temppeliaukio Rock Church 7
Uspenski Orthodox Cathedral 9
Stockmann department store 11
0 1/4 Mi
0 .4 Km
N
Nordenskiöldinkatu
Urheilukatu
Linnankoskigatan
Mannerheimvägen
Hummelgatan
Rajasaarentie
Sibeliusgatan
Helsinginkatu
Taivallahti
Töölönlahti
Mechelininkatu
Töölönkatu
Pohjoinen Hesperiankatu
Eteläinen Hesperiankatu
Karamzinkatu
Runeberginkatu
Tölögatan
Mannerheimintie
Museokatu
Mechelingatan
Hietaniemenkatu
Temppeli-
katu
Nervanderinkatu
Sanduddsgatan
Arkadiankatu
Arkadiagatan
Mannerheimvägen
Runebergsgatan
Hietanie-
menkatu
Salomonkatu
Lapinlahti
Pohj Rautatiekatu
Annankatu
Simonkatu
Malminkatu
Fredrikinkatu
Eriksgatan
Hietaniemi
Cemetery
Lapinlandenkatu
Lapinlahdentie
Albertinkatu
Kalevagatan
Ruoholahdenkatu
Lönnrotsgatan
Köydenpuno-
jank
Hiet
Eerikin
katu
Abrahaminkatu
Porkkalankatu
Porkalagatan
Alberts
gatan
Itämerenkatu
Ostersjögatan
Kalevankatu
Lönnrotin-
alahden-katu
katu
Bulevardi
Uudenmaankatu
Ruoholahti
Hietalahti
Punavuo renkatu
Merimie hen
Pursi-
miehen
Telakkakatu
Munkkisaa-
renkatu
Hernesaa-
renkatu
Saukonkatu
Merikatu
3-0373

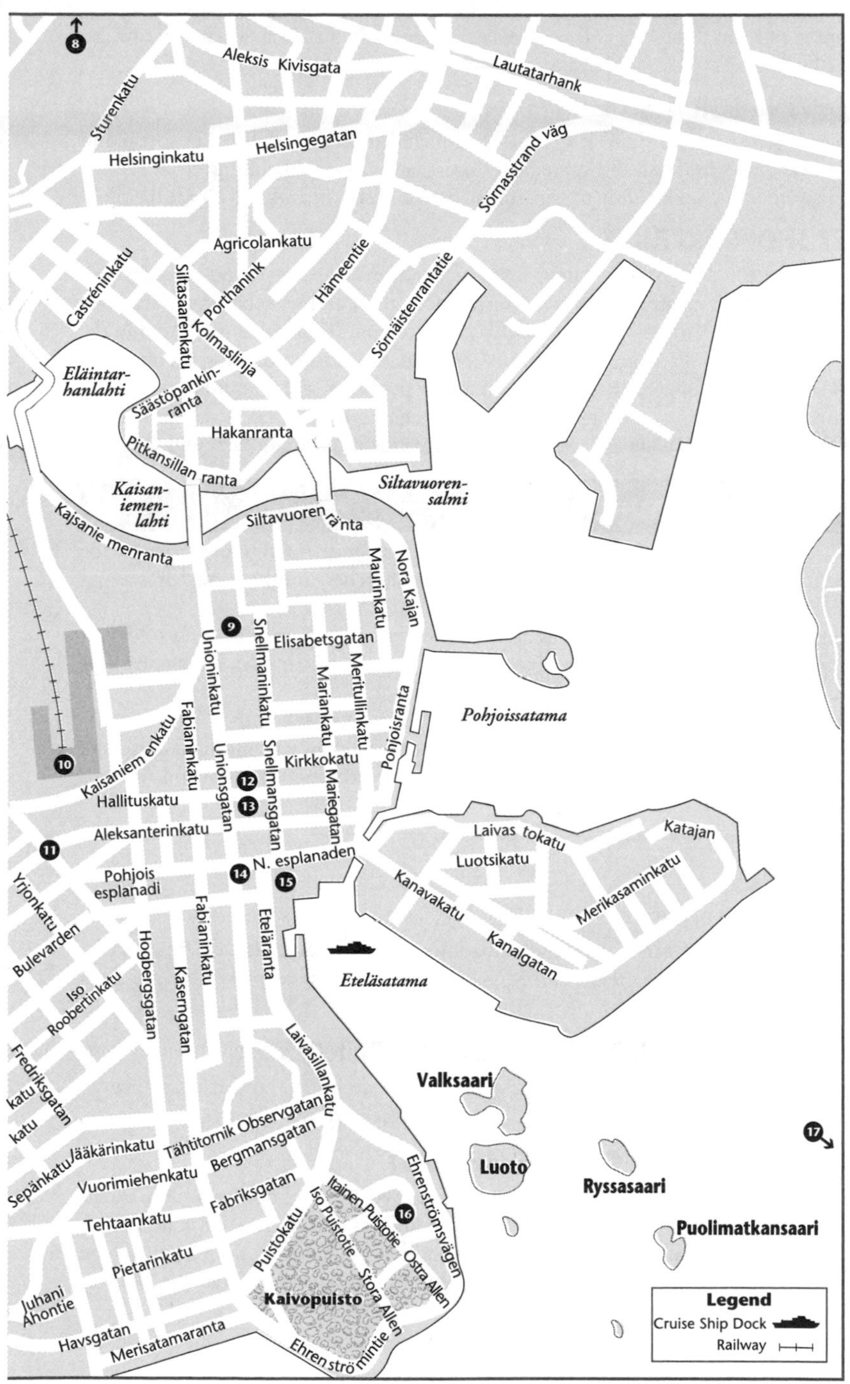
Aleksis Kivisgata
Lautatarhank
Sturenkatu
Helsinginkatu
Helsingegatan
Sörnasstrand väg
Agricolankatu
Castréninkatu
Siltasaarenkatu
Porthanink
Hämeentie
Sörnäistenrantatie
Kolmaslinja
Eläintarhanlahti
Säästöpankinranta
Hakanranta
Pitkansillan ranta
Kaisaniemenlahti
Siltavuorensalmi
Kajsanie menranta
Siltavuoren ranta
Maurinkatu
Nora Kajan
Elisabetsgatan
Unioninkatu
Snellmaninkatu
Meritullinkatu
Mariankatu
Pohjoisranta
Pohjoissatama
Fabianinkatu
Kaisaniem enkatu
Unionsgatan
Snellmansgatan
Kirkkokatu
Mariegatan
Hallituskatu
Aleksanterinkatu
Laivas tokatu
Katajan
Luotsikatu
N. esplanaden
Pohjois esplanadi
Kanavakatu
Merikasaminkatu
Yrjonkatu
Bulevarden
Fabianinkatu
Eteläranta
Kanalgatan
Hogbergsgatan
Kaserngatan
Eteläsatama
Iso Roobertinkatu
Fredriksgatan
Laivasillankatu
Valksaari
Jääkärinkatu
Tähtitornik Observgatan
Bergmansgatan
Sepänkatu
Vuorimiehenkatu
Ehrenströmsvägen
Luoto
Ryssasaari
Fabriksgatan
Itainen Puistotie
Iso Puistotie
Tehtaankatu
Puistokatu
Puolimatkansaari
Pietarinkatu
Ostra Allen
Stora Allen
Juhani Ahontie
Kaivopuisto
Havsgatan
Merisatamaranta
Ehrenströmintie
Legend
Cruise Ship Dock
Railway

the island of Kustaanmiekka, and another larger fortress on Susisaari, where you can also find a number of parks, squares, and gardens.

STOPPING FOR A BITE

Typical ingredients of a Finnish smörgåsbord included herring, lightly salted fish and roe, smoked and cold fish dishes, reindeer meat, and desserts including fresh berries. Crayfish are in season late July to September (you'll need a bib when you eat them).

BEST SHOPPING BUYS

Best buys here include ceramics and glassware, handwoven articles, hand-carved wood, fashions (I bought a nifty pair of boots here once), rugs, and jewelry. Stores are open Monday to Friday 9am to 5pm and Saturday 9am to 2pm (sometimes until 4pm in the summer). The best places to shop include the **Esplanade,** for more upscale offerings; **Market Square** (Kauppatori), an open-air market open Monday to Saturday, where you can find food, souvenirs, and gift items; and, extending to the famous Helsinki Railway Station, **Central,** where the Stockmann Department Store can be found.

6 Le Havre, France

This is the leading port on France's west coast, and is popular with cruise lines for the access it offers to the rest of Normandy, the D-Day Beaches, and Paris, which is about a 3-hour drive away.

The city itself is a modern (it was almost completely destroyed during World War II) and bustling town, and is not really worth hanging around, Instead, book one of the shore excursions listed below.

Le Havre has been an important port since at least 1066, when the Normans conquered England. In the earlier part of the 20th century, ocean liners—including those operated by the French Line, United States Line, Cunard Line, and Holland America Line—linked La Havre with New York.

For France's Mediterranean ports, see chapter 12.

ESSENTIALS

LANGUAGE French.

CURRENCY The French franc is divided into 100 centimes. Bills come in 20-, 50-, 100-, 200-, and 500-franc denominations. The exchange rate at press time was $1 = 6.25 francs.

FROMMER'S FAVORITE LE HAVRE EXPERIENCES

- **Take a shore excursion.** There's not a lot to see or do in Le Havre itself, so plan to take one of the shore excursions that leaves from the port. See below.

COMING ASHORE & GETTING AROUND

The port is about 1 mile from the center of town. If you're not booking a shore excursion, take the **transfer** offered by the cruise line to Paris and explore on your own. If you want to stay closer by, take a **taxi** to Honfleur, the quaint nearby fishing port (about 13 miles from Le Havre). You can also take a boat from Le Havre to Deauville, the chic beach resort.

THE BEST SHORE EXCURSIONS

Note: Similar tours may be offered from Honfleur, France.

Paris Highlights (10½–11 hours, $160–$165): Spend the day in the magnificent city of Paris, a 3-hour drive away. View the Arc de Triomphe, Champs Elysees, Place de la

Le Havre Area

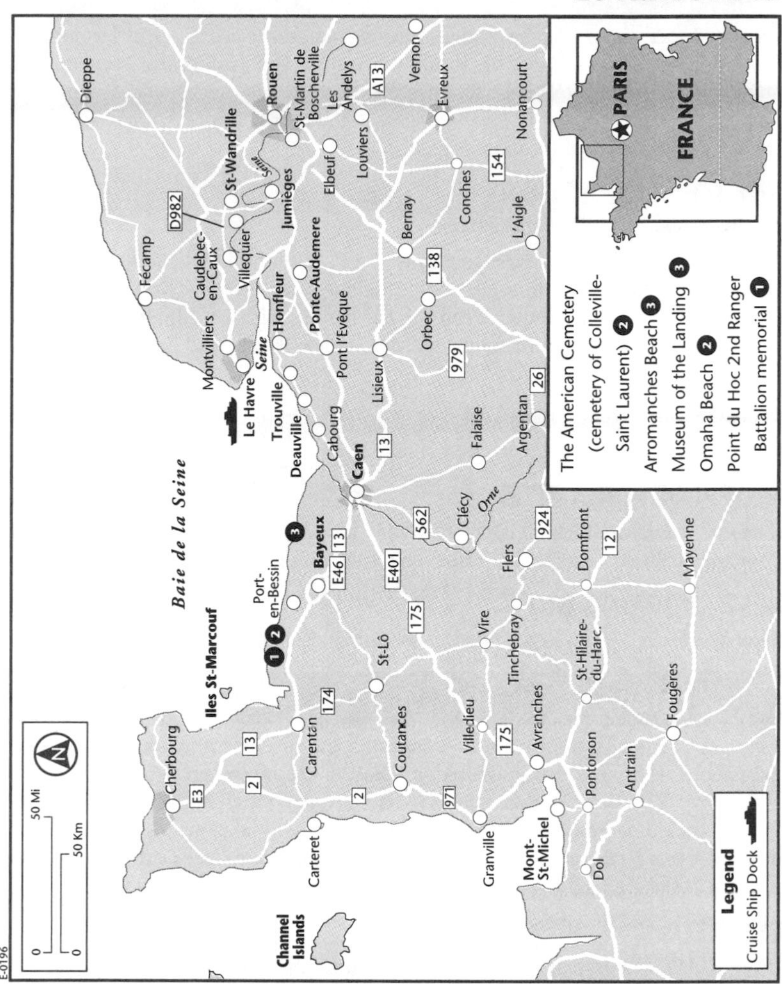

Concorde, Obelisk of Luxor, and Eiffel Tower, and visit the Cathedral de Notre Dame. Also includes lunch, and in some cases a boat ride on the Seine. (Transfers are also offered to Paris for those who want to explore on their own; 10 hours, \$85–\$99.)

Landing Beaches of Normandy (9–10 hours, \$119–\$166): On June 6, 1944, the 50th British Division towed a massive prefabricated port across the English Channel as part of the D-day invasion, and installed it at the small fishing port of Arromanches-les-Baines, enabling supplies to be brought in for the Allied forces. The wreckage of the artificial harbor lies just off Arromanches Beach, which you'll visit on this tour, along with the Museum of the Landing, also in town. Also included are visits to Omaha Beach and the American Cemetery (cemetery of Colleville-Saint Laurent); Point du Hoc, site of a memorial to the three companies of the 2nd Ranger Battalion who climbed the 100-foot cliffs on D-Day to capture the strategic position; and a drive past Sword, Juno, and Gold beaches.

The Sights of Rouen (4½–5 hours, \$52–\$76): Take a guided walking tour of historic Rouen, including the imposing Gothic cathedral, dating from 1201, made famous by

Claude Monet's impressionist studies of its facade. Also view the Gros Horloge clock tower; Rue du Gros Horloge, where you'll find 15th and 16th century timber-framed houses; and Vieux Marchae, the area in which Joan of Arc was sentenced to death and burned at the stake in 1431. You will also see the nearby 15th-century Saint Maclou church. Time is allowed for shopping.

THE TOP ATTRACTIONS

Honfleur. About 13 miles from Le Havre.

This old Norman fishing village dates from the 11th century. Early in the 17th century, colonists set out from here for Quebec. The town was later popular with artists including Daubigny, Corot, and Monet. Stroll the old harbor, with its fishing boats and slate-roofed narrow houses, stop for a bite to eat at a sidewalk cafe, and browse in the art galleries and craft shops.

Deauville. On the coast, just east of Honfleur.

This chic resort is where beach-lovers should head for a day of fun-in-the-sun.

STOPPING FOR A BITE

Regional specialties include cider, Calvados brandy, and Camembert cheese. Sauce normande is a rich white sauce. Tripe is a popular dish.

BEST SHOPPING BUYS

Shop here for ceramic ware, antiques (especially in Rouen), Calvados, and Camembert.

7 Germany

Germany is one of Europe's most complicated and diverse countries, wealthy and industrial but at the same time possessed of beautiful natural scenery. Though World War II took its toll on many of the nation's older buildings, much remains and has been restored—including much of Berlin, which has been essentially one big construction site over the past several years as the city geared up to once again become the capital of Germany in 2000, after a 50-year hiatus.

ESSENTIALS

LANGUAGE German. English is also commonly spoken, particularly by young people.

CURRENCY The unit of German currency is the deutschmark (DM), which is divided into pfennig (pf). Bills are issued in denominations of 5, 10, 20, 50, 100, 200, 500, and 1,000 marks. The rate of exchange at press time was $1 = 1.85DM.

HAMBURG

Hamburg, located on the River Elbe, is known as both "the Venice of the North" for its numerous bridges (2,100 of them) and as "Sin City" for its famous Red Light district, St. Pauli. The Port of Hamburg, stretching nearly 25 miles, is the world's fifth-largest harbor and has been one of the busiest centers of trade on the Continent since 1189. Today, more than 1,500 ships from all over the world call here each month—including cruise ships, which visit mostly to give passengers an opportunity to see Berlin, 177 miles away. If you choose not to make that trek, though, there's still plenty to see in Hamburg itself.

The 1,200-year old city was nearly destroyed during World War II. Old Hamburg still has buildings that date back to medieval times, but a new city with parks (it's the

0
50 mi
0
50 km
North Sea
Baltic Sea
Sylt
Westerland
DENMARK
Flensburg
North Frisian Is.
Schleswig
Kiel Bay
A210
Kiel
Kiel Canal
Hiddensee
Rügen
Stralsund
Pomeranian Bay
Warnemünde
Mecklenburg Bay
Rostock
Greifswald
East Frisian Is.
West Frisian Is.
Cuxhaven
Brunsbüttel
Lübeck
Wismar
Stettin Bay
Wilhelmshaven
Bremerhaven
Elbe
Neubrandenburg
Emden
Hamburg
Schwerin
Lake Mürit (Müritz)
Lüneburg
Oldenburg
Weser
Bremen
Elbe
Oder
Havel
THE NETHERLANDS
Celle
Aller
Brandenburg
BERLIN
POLAND
Osnabrück
Minden
Hannover
Braunschweig
Havel
Potsdam
Frankfurt an der Oder
Münster
Hildesheim
Bielefeld
Hameln
Magdeburg
Oder
Detmold
Weser
Bad Pyrmont
Goslar
Harz
Dessau
Wittenburg
Lippe
Lübbenau
Rhine
Essen
Dortmund
Göttingen
Ruhr
Elbe
Spree
Cottbus
Düsseldorf
E22
E26
E28
E30
E31
E35
E36
E37
E41
E45
E51
E55
E234
E331
A29
A43

greenest city in Europe) and impressive buildings grew out of the rubble. Sights worth seeing include the neo-Renaissance Rathaus (town hall), which dominates Hamburg's main square, and the baroque St. Michael's Church.

Frommer's Favorite Hamburg Experiences

- **Take the shore excursion to Berlin,** or head to Berlin on your own on the high-speed train. With its fascinating history, Berlin is one city you really shouldn't miss.

Coming Ashore & Getting Around

Ships dock in Hamburg, about 0.5 mile (1km) from the city center. The most convenient way to get to Berlin is to book the shore excursion offered by the cruise line. There is also high-speed train service that takes about 150 minutes; by bus, it's about 3 hours.

For those who want to stay in Hamburg, the city has a **subway** system (the U-Bahn), which is one of the best in Germany. **Buses** offer a good alternative, and **taxis** are available at the pier, with metered fares that begin at about $2.30.

The Best Shore Excursions

Berlin City Tour (13 hours, $219–$265): The Berlin tour includes the fascinating Checkpoint Charlie Museum, which provides an overview of how the Wall divided East and West Berlin for more than 40 years. The display here includes descriptions of how people tried to escape from East Berlin (many didn't make it). Other highlights include a visit to the impressive 19th-century Berlin Cathedral; a photo stop at the famous Brandenburg Gate; and a tour of the lavish Charlottenburg Palace, built as a summer palace in 1695 for the first Prussian king (it was heavily damaged during World War II but rebuilt in the 1950s). The tour includes lunch and shopping time.

Your cruise line may offer special-interest shore excursions in Berlin as well. The Berlin Jewish Heritage Tour (12 hours, $275) combines a Berlin city tour with a drive through the former East Berlin to visit the New Synagogue/Centrum Judaicum, which offers a look at historic and modern Jewish life in the city. The tour also passes the Jewish school and the Jewish cemetery, a reminder of the violent times of the Nazi regime in Berlin. Also visited are several memorials and a train station used by the Nazis for deportation purposes. Berlin's Allied Life (12 hours, $275) offers a city tour with a special emphasis on the 45 years of Allied presence in Berlin. Included is the Glienicker Bridge, where American and Russian spies were exchanged; the former American residential areas of Berlin; and a stop at the new Allied Museum, where displays show the city from the Allied point of view. Lunch is served at Schoneberg Town Hall, where John F. Kennedy made his famous Berlin speech.

Hamburg City Tour (3 hours, $48): This tour takes in the town hall, St. Michael's Church, and other sights including scenic Alster Lake.

The Top Attractions

Hauptkirche St. Michaelis (St. Michael's Church). Krayenkamp 4C, Michaeliskirchplatz. ☎ **040/3767-8100.** April–Sept, 9am–6pm (until 10pm Thurs). Entrance to the church is free, but to use the stairs or elevator costs about $2.30. A combined ticket to the tower, show, and crypt costs about $5.15.

Baroque St. Michaelis church is Hamburg's favorite landmark. Take the elevator or climb the 449 steps to the top of the hammered-copper tower for a sweeping view. The crypt, one of the largest in Europe, contains the tombs of famous citizens including Carl Philipp Emanuel Bach. There's also an audiovisual show that tells the history of the city.

Rathaus. Rathausplatz. ☎ **040/36-81-24-70.** Guided tours are offered in English Mon–Thurs hourly 10:15am–3:15pm. No tours are offered during official functions. Admission about $1.15.

Alster Lake Boat Tour

A boat trip on Alster Lake affords views of villas and sailing boats set against a panorama of towers and church spires, and of the beautiful **Alsterpark,** on the northwest banks of Alster Lake and encompassing 175 manicured acres of shade trees and gardens. **ATG-Alster-Touristik,** Am Anleger Jungfernstieg (☎ **040/3-57-42-40**), has departures about every 30 minutes from 10am to 6pm. The trip lasts about 50 minutes. Cassettes are available with a description of the sights in English, and a brochure in four languages (including English) is available from the captain. Offered April to October, the trip costs about $8.55 for adults, $6.85 for children under 16.

Hamburg's 647-room town hall is a Renaissance-style structure built in the late 19th century (modern compared to many of Germany's town halls). Its clock tower overlooks the city's largest canal.

St. Pauli. About a half-mile from the Elbe, and split by the Reeperbahn.

The Red Light district is the nightlife center of Hamburg. The most famous street in the district is Reeperbahn. In addition to erotica in many forms (including sex shows) the district boasts cafes, bars, discos, and music halls.

Stopping for a Bite

Seafood is a best bet, including lobster from Helgoland; shrimp from Büsum; turbot, plaice, and sole from the North Sea; and fresh oysters. For those interested in trying traditional local cuisine, a favorite is the sailor's dish, ***Labskaus,*** made with beer, onions, cured meat, potatoes, herring, and pickle. If you're adventurous, try the eel soup, another local favorite.

Among the leading restaurants is **Peter Lembcke,** Holzdamm 49 (☎ **040/24-32-90**), which has been in operation since 1910. You can get both *Labskaus* and eel soup here. The restaurant also serves excellent steaks. Reservations are recommended. Another good bet is the **Old Commercial Room,** Englische Planke 10 (☎ **040/36-63-19**), in St. Pauli. The restaurant was founded in 1643, and is considered a premier sailors' stopover. The Labskaus here is considered the best in the city, and those ordering it get a numbered certificate proclaiming you are a genuine Labskaus-eater.

Best Shopping Buys

Clocks, cutlery (especially **J. A. Henckels**), and fashion items are good buys here. Two of the major shopping streets are **Grosse Bleichen** and **Neuer Wall.** Big department stores, including Horton and Karstadt, can be found on **Mönckebergstrasse.** The more upscale (think Bloomingdales) **Alsterhaus** can be found on **Jungfernsteig,** Hamburg's main artery and shopping district.

WARNEMÜNDE & ROSTOCK

Like Hamburg, the seaside resort of **Warnemünde** in the former East Germany is visited by the cruise lines because it is fairly close to Berlin (about 3 hours by bus). Since there's not much to do in Warnemünde, I recommend if you're not making the trek to Berlin that you take a cab (you may have to phone for one), train, or shore excursion to Rostock, which is about 5 miles away.

Rostock was founded in 1218. During the Cold War period it was East Germany's major seaport. The town still bustles with maritime activity, and there's a good maritime museum. St. Mary's Church has a famous astrological clock, which dates back to the 1400s. You can also climb to the tower for a panoramic city view. Other sights worth seeing include Kröpeliner-Strasse, a pedestrian-only walkway lined with shops and restored historic buildings.

FROMMER'S FAVORITE WARNEMÜNDE EXPERIENCES

- **Take a shore excursion to Berlin,** or head to Berlin on your own. It's a city that shouldn't be missed.

COMING ASHORE & GETTING AROUND

Ships usually dock within walking distance to town. **Taxis** can be found at the taxi stand at the train station; your ship's shore excursions desk can also advise on taxis and may be able to make arrangements for you in advance of arrival. Take a taxi or train (there's frequent service) to Rostock, about 5 miles from Warnemünde, and then explore Old Town on foot.

THE BEST SHORE EXCURSIONS

Berlin City Tour: See description under Hamburg shore excursions, above.

Rostock City Tour (3½ hours, $49–$55): The tour includes Old Town, St. Mary's Church, and City Hall. Some tours also visit a local brewery that makes German Pilsner, or include a boat ride up the River Warnow.

THE TOP ATTRACTIONS

St-Marien-Kirche (St. Mary's Church). Am Ziegenmarkt. ☎ **0381/4-92-33-96.** Admission $1.15. Hours are Mon–Sat 10am–5pm, Sun worship at 10am.

This church has a famous clock that dates back to the 1400s, with astrological figures on its face. You can also climb the tower for a panoramic city view.

Schiffahrtsmuseum (Navigational Museum). August-Bebel-Strasse 1. ☎ **0381/4-92-26-97.** Admission $2.30 adults, $1.15 children. Open Tues–Sun 10am–6pm.

This museum contains exhibits related to the town's nautical history, from the Vikings on up to the early 20th century.

STOPPING FOR A BITE

The oldest sailor's pub in Rostock is **Zur Kogge,** where the decor includes all kinds of nautical items. Fish is the chef's specialty. Located at Wokrenterstrasse 27, on the harbor (☎ **0381/4-93-44-93**).

BEST SHOPPING BUYS

There are small shops in Warnemünde offering maritime souvenirs. In Rostock (to which you'll have to take a taxi), head to the pedestrian zone for a larger selection of stores, both traditional and modern.

THE KIEL CANAL

On some itineraries, ships visit Germany without even stopping, by cruising on the Kiel Canal. Built in 1895 and stretching more than 60 miles, the canal connects the Baltic Sea with the North Sea (and Western trade), and is one of the busiest artificial waterways in the world, allowing ships to avoid the 400 nautical miles they'd clock if they had to go around Denmark.

Your ship will enter the canal at either Brunsbüttel or the port city of Kiel (depending on which way you are going). At both ends of the waterway are locks, and it's fascinating to watch as the water level is adjusted so the ship can move through. It's worth being on deck to observe as the ship passes the countryside as well. Since the canal is only 528 feet wide in places, you'll get a very close-up view of houses, parks, and meadows along the waterway, and also pass some interesting bridges.

8 Ireland

Ireland is a mass of contradictions. It's ancient, filled with Bronze-age forts, Viking walls, and Norman castles, but is an adolescent in terms of its nationhood, having only severed its last constitutional ties to Britain in 1948; it's the land of poets and priests, but has been embroiled in factional struggle over the fate of the North for the better part of a century; it's a land from which the best and brightest fled for decades due to limited opportunities, but it's now the possessor of a massively booming "Celtic Tiger" economy.

And it really is green. Remarkably green, in hues you hardly see elsewhere. In the countryside you can still see whitewashed thatch-roof houses sitting among verdant fields and cozy pubs warmed by turf fires, where the Guinness on tap was delivered fresh that morning from the brewery. In the cities, especially Dublin, you can find a mix of Georgian architecture and new development, and even some places (like Dublin's Temple Bar district) that are considered among the trendiest in Europe.

ESSENTIALS

LANGUAGE English. Irish Gaelic is spoken as well in some rural areas.

CURRENCY The basic unit of currency is the Irish pound (or *punt*), which is made up of 100 pence. Notes are printed in 5-, 10-, 20-, 50-, and 100-pound denominations. The rate of exchange at press time was $1 = 75 pence.

COBH

The port city of Cobh (pronounced "Cove"), formerly known as Queenstown, was once a regular stop for famous liners like the *Queen Mary,* and was the last port of call for the ill-fated *Titanic.*

Today, Cobh is used mostly as a jumping-off point for various excursions around Ireland's southeast, including Cork, the second largest city in the Irish Republic, offering period buildings and churches and plenty of shopping opportunities; County Waterford, known for producing Waterford Crystal; Blarney Castle, home of the famous Blarney Stone; and the scenic environs of Killarney.

Outside of Cobh, Ballymaloe House is famed throughout Ireland for its fine cuisine, as is the picturesque town of Kinsale. And the East Cork town of Youghal (pronounced "yawl") is a leading beach resort and fishing port.

In the days before airline travel, Cobh was Ireland's chief port of entry and departure, and hosted about three or four transatlantic liners each week. More than 2 1/2 million emigrants departed Ireland here for new lives in the U.S., Canada, and Australia, most in the post-famine years of the early 20th century. A new visitor center called **Cobh: The Queenstown Story,** tells the city's history as an emigration port. Photos of some of the early ocean liners that visited here can be found around town.

FROMMER'S FAVORITE COBH EXPERIENCES

- **Visiting picturesque Kinsale.** The town is picture-perfect, with a gorgeous harbor and narrow hilly streets dropping to the sea. Kinsale also has the largest concentration of fine restaurants outside of Dublin, and a nifty fort to explore.
- **Golfing at Old Head Links in Kinsale.** This is Ireland's youngest world-class golf course, opened 3 years ago and already becoming a legend. (Greens fees are about $93, and the caddy fee is $31.)

Kiss and Tell: The Legend of the Blarney Stone

Here's the real deal with the Blarney Stone kissing tradition. Back in the 1830s, one Father Prout wrote: "There's a stone there / That whoever kisses / Oh! he never misses / To grow eloquent." From that line, a tourist attraction was instantly created. The stone is wedged underneath the battlements of Blarney Castle. It's kind of hard to reach—you have to lie on your back and slide your head under the wall—but that doesn't stop countless tourists from coming up for a smooch.

- **Kissing the Blarney Stone.** Oh come on, you know you want to!
- **Dining at Ballymaloe House.** The dining at this Georgian farmhouse (Ballycotton Road, Shanagarry, County Cork; ☎ **021/646785**) is so good it has its own cooking school. Only the finest ingredients are used to produce what is arguably the finest Irish fare.

Coming Ashore & Getting Around

You can walk into Cobh from the pier, but it's about 15 miles to Cork city. **Taxis** are available at the pier.

The Best Shore Excursions

Cork & Blarney Castle (4 1/2 hours, $45–$58): Drive by bus to Cork, passing St. Anne's Cathedral, noted for its Shandon bells hung in 1752, and visiting St. Finbarr's Cathedral, located near the site where St. Finbarr founded his famous monastic school around 650. Then drive to Blarney, home of the magical Blarney Stone (which you can kiss if you're willing to walk up 100-plus steps to do so). Time is allowed to enjoy the formal gardens around the castle or to visit the Blarney Woolen Mills, where you can buy something to bring home.

A Visit to Cork, Kinsale, & Charles Fort (4 hours, $58): A quick tour of Cork is followed by a bus trip through the countryside to Kinsale, known as the gourmet capital of Ireland. Enjoy a sample of "good taste" at a quaint waterfront cafe. Also at Kinsale's harbor, enjoy the views at the 17th-century Charles Fort, named for King Charles II. The views are breathtaking.

Whiskey Heritage Center & Youghal (3 1/2 hours, $42): Drive by bus to Midleton, a small market town best known as the home of the Jameson Irish Whiskey Heritage Center. Although the Midleton distillery is one of the most modern in Europe, relics of its 19th-century origins remain, including the old waterwheel and a gleaming 30,000-gallon copper pot, said to be the largest in the world. On the way back, visit Youghal (pronounced "yawl"), a historic seaport where Sir Walter Raleigh was once mayor (and where he purportedly first tried tobacco). A whiskey tasting is included in the distillery tour.

A Day in Killarney (8 1/2 hours, $109): Drive past the highlights in Cork then continue on to Killarney, in County Kerry. The unrivaled beauty of Killarney's lakes and mountains make this region one of the most celebrated attractions in Ireland. The tour here includes a visit to the restored Victorian Muckross Manor House and Gardens, located in a magnificent setting in Killarney National Park. Lunch at the Killarney Park Hotel is included, and time is allowed for exploring the beautiful town.

Waterford & Waterford Crystal (9 hours, $109–$115): From Cobh, cross the agricultural plains of east Cork to Youghal, an old fishing port with fine sandy beaches, that

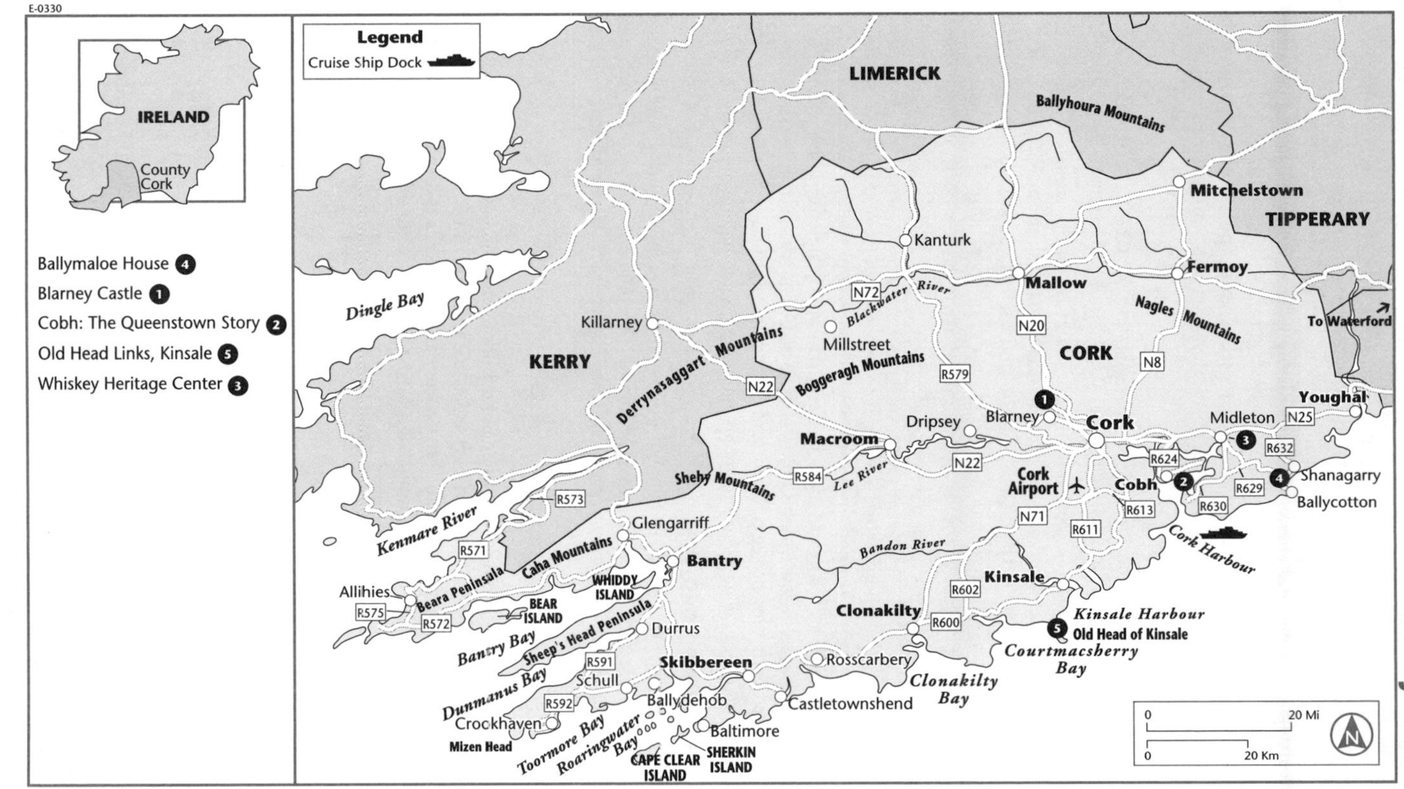

E-0330
IRELAND
County Cork
Ballymaloe House 4
Blarney Castle 1
Cobh: The Queenstown Story 2
Old Head Links, Kinsale 5
Whiskey Heritage Center 3
Legend
Cruise Ship Dock
LIMERICK
TIPPERARY
CORK
KERRY
Ballyhoura Mountains
Mitchelstown
Kanturk
Mallow
Fermoy
Nagles Mountains
To Waterford
Dingle Bay
Killarney
Millstreet
Blackwater River
Derrynasaggart Mountains
Boggeragh Mountains
N72
N20
N8
N22
R579
Youghal
Midleton
N25
Blarney
Cork
Dripsey
Macroom
R632
R624
Shanagarry
Ballycotton
R629
R630
Cobh
Cork Airport
R613
R584
Lee River
Shehy Mountains
R573
Kenmare River
Glengarriff
R571
Caha Mountains
Bantry
N71
R611
Cork Harbour
Bandon River
Kinsale
R602
Allihies
Beara Peninsula
WHIDDY ISLAND
BEAR ISLAND
R575
R572
Bantry Bay
Sheep's Head Peninsula
Durrus
Clonakilty
R600
Kinsale Harbour
Old Head of Kinsale
Courtmacsherry Bay
Dunmanus Bay
R591
Schull
Skibbereen
Rosscarbery
Clonakilty Bay
R592
Ballydehob
Castletownshend
Crockhaven
Mizen Head
Toormore Bay
Roaringwater Bay
Baltimore
CAPE CLEAR ISLAND
SHERKIN ISLAND
0
20 Mi
0
20 Km
N

somewhat resembles a New England seaport (it was so chosen as the setting for the 1950s film of *Moby Dick*). Cross the Blackwater River into scenic County Waterford. At the Waterford Crystal Works, watch master craftspeople demonstrate glassblowing, cutting, polishing, and engraving. Also visit the gallery, where the largest collection of Waterford crystal in the world is displayed. The tour may also include the 12th-century Waterford Castle or a stop at a typical country pub in the heritage town of Lismore. The excursion includes lunch and shopping opportunities.

The Top Attractions

Cobh: The Queenstown Story. Cobh Railway Station. ☎ **021/813591.** Admission about $5.45 adults, $4.65 seniors and students, $3.10 children, $15.50 families. Daily 10am–6pm.

This new heritage center, located in a former railway station, commemorates the days when Cobh, then known as Queenstown, was a vital link in transatlantic traffic. The center tells the story of the city, the harbor, and the Irish exodus in a series of displays with an audiovisual presentation. The center also offers exhibits that re-create the age of luxury-liner travel. A genealogical referral service is in the works.

Stopping for a Bite

It's not just meat and potatoes, although Irish beef is quite popular. The star of most menus these days is seafood, including wild Irish salmon, Dublin Bay prawns, Galway oysters, Kinsale and Wexford mussels, Kerry scallops, Dingle Bay lobster, and Donegal crab. Wash it all down with a Guinness or two. If you try an Irish breakfast, you'll be presented with a feast of eggs, bacon and other pork products, traditional brown bread, and more.

Best Shopping Buys

Shop here for Waterford crystal, Irish linens, crafts, woolens, pottery, and whiskey. In Cork, try **Patrick Street,** the main shopping thoroughfare, or look for antiques on **Paul's Lane.** The legendary department store **Cashs** at 18 Patrick St. dates back to the 1830s.

DUBLIN

Divided into north and south by the River Liffey, Ireland's capital offers noble public buildings, superb museums and art galleries, magnificent St. Patrick's Cathedral, lovely Trinity College (where the 8th-century Book of Kells is displayed), and tempting shopping. Once barely passable as a European capital, Dublin is on the fast track these days, quickly becoming the hub of computer software development and booming with the roar of Ireland's "Celtic Tiger" economy—in 1997, *Fortune* magazine named it as the number-one city in Europe in which to do business. With such prominence comes the key components to any major city: money, young people, and flair. So, to the last generation's surprise, Dublin is now a hip, young place with excellent international cuisine, five-star hotels, and posh nightclubs. The Dublin of old—struggling and dilapidated even just 10 years ago—has become one of the hottest up-and-coming places to live in Europe, and is now home to about 1,024,400 souls.

The city retains its original charm and history in the middle of all this modernizing, though. In fact, it's the booming economy that has allowed Dublin to clean up its act and drop money into restoring public buildings and historical exhibits. You can still find remnants of Georgian splendor, medieval churches and imposing castles, broad boulevards and picturesque parks. Worth exploring on foot are the Temple Bar area (Dublin's self-proclaimed Left Bank) and the Trinity College and St. Stephen's Green/Grafton Street areas.

Frommer's Favorite Dublin Experiences

- **Pub crawling.** The pub has for centuries been the mainstay of Irish social life, and there are more than 1,000 of them in the city, literally on every street and at every turn. See "Stopping for a Bite (or a Drink)," below, for suggestions of a few of the city's best.
- **Exploring.** Don't forget Grafton Street for great shopping, St. Stephen's Green for a bucolic moment, Trinity College for historical splendor, and Temple Bar for one of the hippest scenes in Europe.
- **Playing golf.** A quarter of Ireland's top courses are within an hour's drive of the city, including the **Portmarnock Golf Club** (**☎ 01/846-2968**) and the **Royal Dublin Golf Club** (**☎ 01/833-6346**).
- **Taking a scenic shore excursion** to Glendalough and Powerscourt or Malahide Castle. (See below.)

Coming Ashore & Getting Around

Ships dock about 1.5 miles (2.4km) from the city center at the Dublin Port. Smaller ships may come right up the River Liffey into the city center. **Taxis** are available at the pier. Double-decker **buses,** single-deck buses, and minibuses operate throughout the city and suburbs.

The Best Shore Excursions

In addition to the excursions listed below, several private companies offer escorted walking tours of note in Dublin. One of the best is the **Jameson Literary Pub Crawl** (**☎ 01/670-5603;** tickets about $9.60 per person; June to September daily at 3pm and 7:30pm), which follows in the footsteps of Joyce, Behan, Beckett, Kavanagh, and other Irish literary greats, visiting a number of pubs with literary connections. Actors provide appropriate performances and commentary at the stops. The tour assembles at the Duke Pub on Duke Street (off Grafton).

Dublin Highlights (4 hours, $48): Accomplished mostly by bus, this tour takes you past the Customs House, one of James Gandon's architectural triumphs (he also designed the Parliament House, which now houses the Bank of Ireland), Trinity College, Merrion Square and Fitzwilliam Square, the National Gallery, St. Stephen's Green and Dawson Street, City Hall and Dublin Castle, St. Patrick's Cathedral, the Guinness Brewery, the homes of the president of Ireland and the American ambassador, Ireland's Courts of Justice (Four Courts), and the General Post Office, headquarters of the 1916 uprising and birthplace of the Irish nation.

Glendalough & Powerscourt (9 hours, $112): Drive past Dublin's highlights (see above) into County Wicklow, known as the Garden of Ireland. Visit the ruins of the Glendalough monastery, founded by St. Kevin in the 6th century and located in an idyllically secluded lake setting. Then travel to Enniskerry, one of Ireland's prettiest villages, and the gardens of Powerscourt Estate. The 34,000 acres of this majestic estate extend along both shores of the River Dargle. The house at Powerscourt has recently been refurbished to include both an exhibition of the history of the estate and a shop for quality Irish goods, such as crystal and linen. The tour includes lunch and shopping time.

Coastal Drive & Malahide Castle (3½ hours, $48): Drive along the coast to Malahide, about 8 miles north of Dublin, to visit one of Ireland's oldest castles. Malahide Castle was occupied by the aristocratic Anglo-Irish Talbot family from 1185 to 1973. Fully restored, the interior offers one of the finest collections of Irish period furniture, dating from the 17th through the 19th centuries, and one-of-a-kind historic portraits on loan from the National Gallery. After touring the house, you can explore the 250-acre estate, which includes 20 acres of prized gardens with 5,000 varieties of plants and flowers. Also includes a stop at the quaint fishing port of Howth.

Dublin

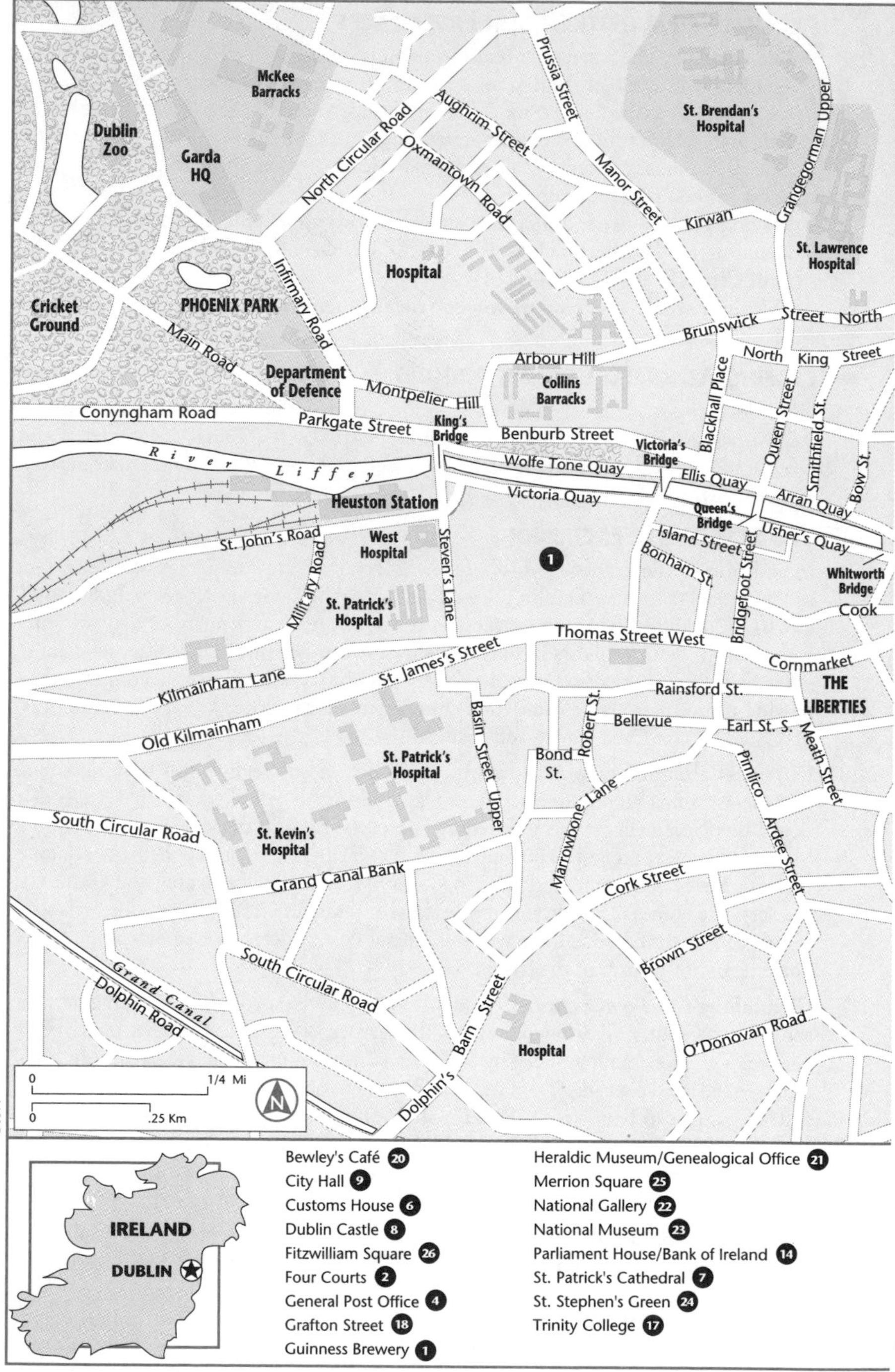
McKee Barracks
Dublin Zoo
Garda HQ
Cricket Ground
PHOENIX PARK
Main Road
Department of Defence
Infirmary Road
North Circular Road
Aughrim Street
Oxmantown Road
Prussia Street
Manor Street
St. Brendan's Hospital
Grangegorman Upper
Kirwan
St. Lawrence Hospital
Hospital
Brunswick Street North
Arbour Hill
Collins Barracks
North King Street
Blackhall Place
Queen Street
Smithfield St.
Bow St.
Montpelier Hill
Conyngham Road
Parkgate Street
King's Bridge
Benburb Street
Victoria's Bridge
River Liffey
Wolfe Tone Quay
Ellis Quay
Arran Quay
Victoria Quay
Queen's Bridge
Usher's Quay
Heuston Station
St. John's Road
West Hospital
Steven's Lane
Island Street
Bonham St.
Bridgefoot Street
Whitworth Bridge
Cook
Military Road
St. Patrick's Hospital
Thomas Street West
Cornmarket
THE LIBERTIES
Kilmainham Lane
St. James's Street
Rainsford St.
Robert St.
Bellevue
Earl St. S.
Old Kilmainham
Basin Street Upper
Bond St.
Meath Street
Pimlico
St. Patrick's Hospital
Marrowbone Lane
South Circular Road
St. Kevin's Hospital
Ardee Street
Grand Canal Bank
Cork Street
Brown Street
South Circular Road
Grand Canal
Dolphin Road
Barn Street
Hospital
O'Donovan Road
Dolphin's
0 1/4 Mi
0 .25 Km
N
E-0314
IRELAND
DUBLIN
Bewley's Café 20
City Hall 9
Customs House 6
Dublin Castle 8
Fitzwilliam Square 26
Four Courts 2
General Post Office 4
Grafton Street 18
Guinness Brewery 1
Heraldic Museum/Genealogical Office 21
Merrion Square 25
National Gallery 22
National Museum 23
Parliament House/Bank of Ireland 14
St. Patrick's Cathedral 7
St. Stephen's Green 24
Trinity College 17

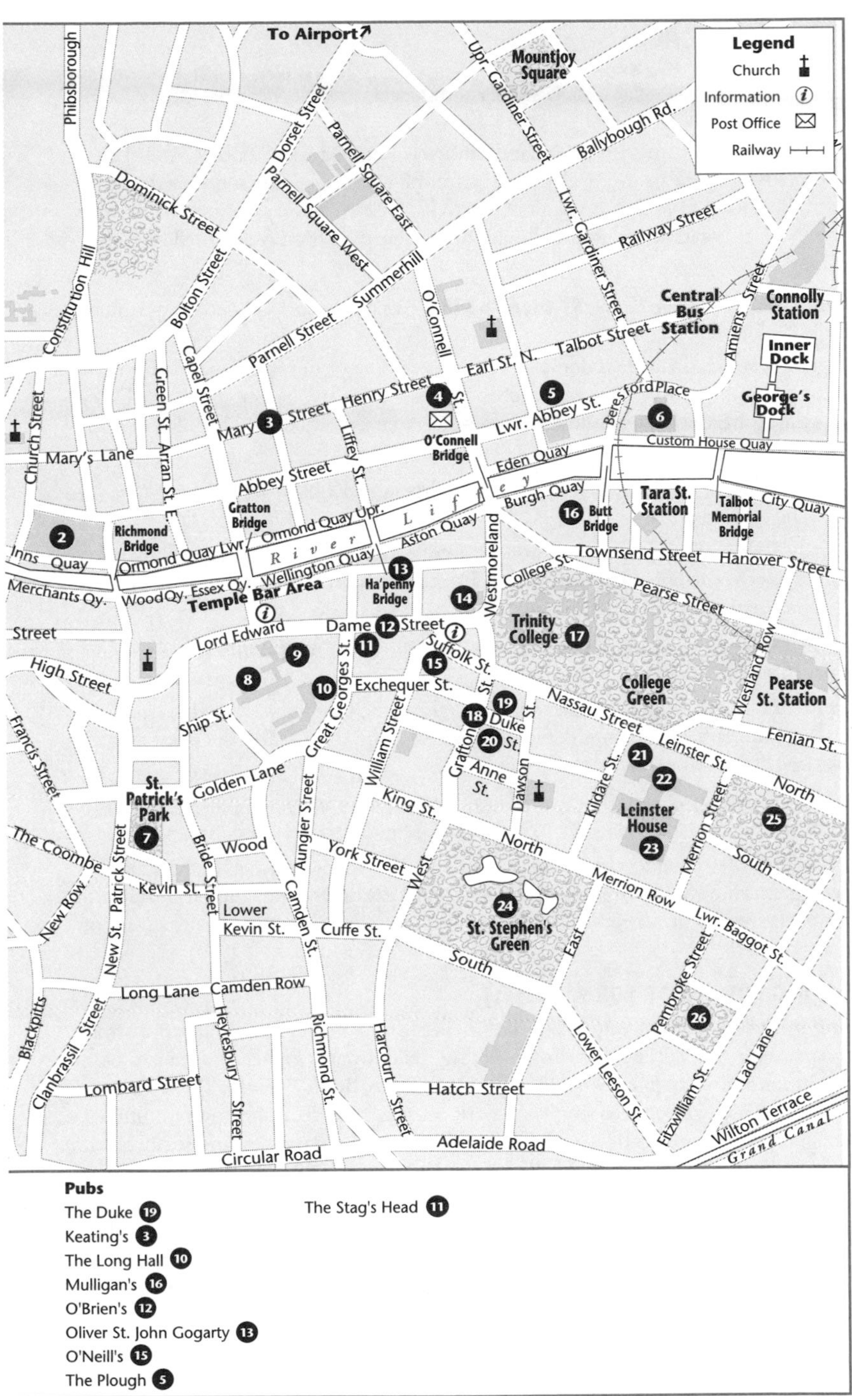
To Airport
Legend
Church
Information
Post Office
Railway
Mountjoy Square
Upr. Gardiner Street
Ballybough Rd.
Phibsborough
Dominick Street
Dorset Street
Parnell Square East
Parnell Square West
Lwr. Gardiner Street
Railway Street
Constitution Hill
Bolton Street
Summerhill
O'Connell St.
Central Bus Station
Connolly Station
Amiens Street
Inner Dock
George's Dock
Parnell Street
Talbot Street
Earl St. N.
Capel Street
Green St.
Henry Street
Mary Street
Beresford Place
Lwr. Abbey St.
Church Street
Mary's Lane
Arran St. E.
Liffey St.
O'Connell Bridge
Custom House Quay
Eden Quay
Abbey Street
Gratton Bridge
Burgh Quay
Butt Bridge
Tara St. Station
Talbot Memorial Bridge
City Quay
Richmond Bridge
Ormond Quay Upr.
Ormond Quay Lwr.
River Liffey
Aston Quay
Westmoreland
Inns Quay
Wellington Quay
Townsend Street
Hanover Street
Merchants Qy.
Wood Qy.
Essex Qy.
Temple Bar Area
Ha'penny Bridge
College St.
Pearse Street
Street
Lord Edward
Dame Street
Suffolk St.
Trinity College
High Street
Exchequer St.
Great Georges St.
Ship St.
William Street
Grafton St.
Duke St.
Nassau Street
College Green
Westland Row
Pearse St. Station
Fenian St.
Leinster St.
Francis Street
St. Patrick's Park
Golden Lane
Anne St.
Dawson St.
Kildare St.
North
Leinster House
King St.
Aungier Street
The Coombe
New St. Patrick Street
Bride Street
Wood
York Street
West
North
Merrion Street
South
New Row
Kevin St.
Lower Kevin St.
Camden St.
Cuffe St.
Merrion Row
Lwr. Baggot St.
St. Stephen's Green
East
South
Pembroke Street
Long Lane
Camden Row
Blackpitts
Clanbrassil Street
Heytesbury Street
Richmond St.
Harcourt Street
Lower Leeson St.
Lad Lane
Lombard Street
Hatch Street
Fitzwilliam St.
Wilton Terrace
Grand Canal
Adelaide Road
Circular Road
Pubs
The Duke 19
Keating's 3
The Long Hall 10
Mulligan's 16
O'Brien's 12
Oliver St. John Gogarty 13
O'Neill's 15
The Plough 5
The Stag's Head 11

The Top Attractions

Trinity College and the Book of Kells. College Green. ☎ **01/608-1688.** Admission to see the book about $5.40 adults, $4.65 seniors and students, free for children under 12. Mon–Sat 9:30am–5pm, Sun (June–Sept) 9:30am–4:30pm.

Trinity is the oldest university in Ireland, and was founded in 1592 by Queen Elizabeth I. It sits in the heart of the city on a beautiful 40-acre site just south of the River Liffey. The college is home to the Book of Kells, an 8th-century version of the four Gospels with elaborate scripting and illumination. One page per day is turned for public viewing.

National Gallery. Merrion Sq. W. ☎ **01/661-5133.** Free admission. Mon–Sat 10am–5:30pm; Sun 2–5pm.

This gallery, which opened its doors in 1864, offers one of Europe's finest collections including paintings, drawings, miniatures, prints, sculpture, and objets d'art. Every major school of European painting is represented. A new extension is scheduled to open this year.

National Museum. Kildare St. and Merrion St. ☎ **01/677-7444.** Free admission. Tues–Sat 10am–5pm; Sun 2–5pm.

Established in 1890, this museum houses a collection of Irish heritage items from 2000 B.C. to the present. Included in The Treasury exhibit, which toured the U.S. in the 1970s, are the Ardagh Chalice, Tara Brooch, and Cross of Cong.

Heraldic Museum/Genealogical Office. 2 Kildare St. ☎ **01/603-0200.** Free admission. Mon–Fri 10am–12:30pm and 2–4:30pm.

The museum boasts a unique collection of heraldry, including shields, banners, coins, paintings, porcelain, and stamps depicting coats of arms. This is also the place to start tracing your Irish roots (for a fee of about $31).

St. Patrick's Cathedral. Patrick's Close, Patrick St. ☎ **01/475-4817.** Admission about $3.10 adults, $2.70 students and seniors, $7.75 for families. Mon–Sat 9am–6pm; Sun 9am–4:30pm.

Founded in 1190 (though a church has actually stood at the site since 450), St. Patrick's is the largest cathedral in Dublin and the national cathedral of the Church of Ireland. The most famous of St. Patrick's many renowned deans was Jonathan Swift, author of *Gulliver's Travels.*

Stopping for a Bite (or a Drink)

Dining in Dublin offers great variety that includes Old World hotels, casual bistros, wine bars, and ethnic cuisine. Non-Irish offerings tend towards French and Italian. One place you can enjoy a quintessential Dublin experience is **Bewley's Café,** 78/79 Grafton St. (☎ **01/677-6761**), a three-story landmark opened in 1840, done up in traditional decor, and specializing in coffees and teas, home-baked scones, pastries, and sticky buns.

Some of the best pubs include **Mulligan's,** 8 Poolbeg St. (☎ 01/677-5582); **Oliver St. John Gogarty,** 58–59 Fleet St., Temple Bar (☎ 01/671-1822); **The Plough,** 28 Lower Abbey St. (☎ 01/874-0971); **The Duke,** 8 and 9 Duke St., off Grafton (☎ 01/679-9553); **O'Brien's,** 26 Dame St. (☎ 01/679-8497); **The Stag's Head,** 1 Dame Ct., off Dame St. (☎ 01/679-3701); **O'Neill's,** 2 Suffolk St. (☎ 01/679-3614); **The Long Hall,** 51 S. Great George's St. (☎ 01/475-1590); and **Keating's,** 14 Mary St. (☎ 01/873-1567).

Best Shopping Buys

Grafton Street, which is open to pedestrians only, offers a parade of boutiques, department stores, and specialty shops, as well as a festive atmosphere complete with street performers and sidewalk artists. In nearby **Temple Bar** are interesting boutiques as well as art and music shops. (See Cobh for the best Irish products.)

9 The Netherlands (Holland)

Is it Holland or the Netherlands? Actually, it's both, and before that it was Batavia. But whatever you call it, this small country offers a lot more than wooden shoes, tulips, and windmills. There's incredible art for one—this is the home country of Van Gogh, not to mention the Dutch masters. It's also the home of dikes and canals, of historic towns, of beautiful and raucous Amsterdam, of the Hague and the International Court of Justice, and of a cultured populace that appreciates history and the outdoors and also knows how to have a good time.

ESSENTIALS

LANGUAGE Dutch. English is also commonly spoken.

CURRENCY The national currency is the guilder or NLG (Netherlands guilder), which, like the U.S. dollar, is worth 100 cents. The exchange rate at press time was $1 = 2.10 NLG.

AMSTERDAM

Amsterdam is spread out over 70 islands and boasts 60 miles of canals, 1,000 bridges, and the largest Old Town in Europe. It's a city with a history—boats have sailed from here since the 13th century, and its 17th-century town houses and Floating Flower Market are full of old-world charm—but Amsterdam is also a young and exciting place offering a little bit for every taste, from the erotic sights of the Red Light District, to a plethora of shopping and nightlife options, to world-renowned art museums—it's been a big art city since the time of Rembrandt. Anne Frank and her family hid in a house here for 2 years, and visitors can tour the attic where she wrote her famous diary before being discovered by the Nazis. It's a very moving experience.

On the outskirts of the city are quaint villages worth exploring, including Delft, a historic town where the famous blue and white pottery is made.

COMING ASHORE & GETTING AROUND

Your ship will dock at one of the three terminals: Amsterdam Passenger Terminal (APT), about a 15-minute walk to the city center; Felison Terminal, a 30-minute drive; or Scandia Terminal, a 15-minute drive. In any case, Centraal Station, near Dam Square, is a good start-off point.

Amsterdam is an easy city to explore, either by foot or boat. **Biking** is another option. It's the mode popular with the Dutch, but you need to exercise caution if you go this route: Riding on cobblestones can be particularly tricky. You can rent bikes for about $6.25 a day (with a deposit required) from **Mac Bike,** Mr. Visserplein 2 (☎ **020/620-09-85**); **Mac Bike Too,** Marnixstraat 220 (☎ **020/626-69-64**); and **Bike City,** Bloemgracht 70 (☎ **020/626-37-21**).

Or if you really want something to talk about, rent a **water bike** to pedal along the canals. A two-seater goes for about $12.50 per hour; a four-seater for about $5 per person, per hour. Moorings are at Centraal Station, Leidseplein, Westerkerk (near the Anne Frank house), Stadhouderskade (between the Rijksmuseum and Heineken Brewery Museum), and Toronto Bridge on the Keizersgracht, near Leidsestraat.

Taxis are available at the pier. Officially, you are not supposed to hail a cab on the street (although they may stop for you anyway) but should instead call **Taxi Centrale** (☎ **020/677-77-77**). The city also has an extensive **bus** and **tram** network, as well as two **subway** lines.

Central Amsterdam

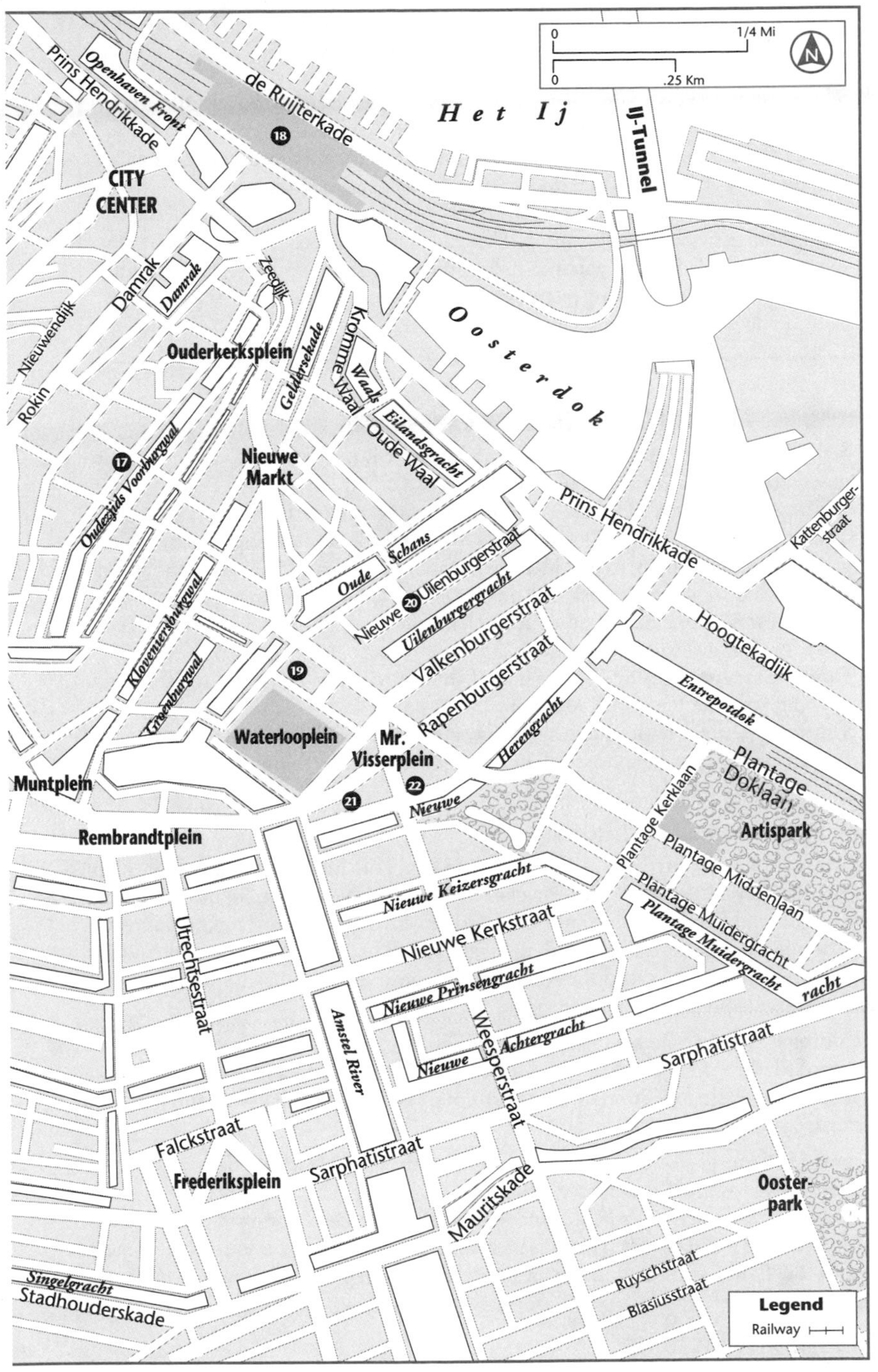

0
1/4 Mi
0
.25 Km
N
Het Ij
IJ-Tunnel
Openhaven Front
Prins Hendrikkade
de Ruijterkade
18
CITY CENTER
Damrak
Damrak
Zeedijk
Nieuwendijk
Ouderkerksplein
Geldersekade
Kromme Waal
Waals
Oosterdok
Eilandsgracht
Oude Waal
Rokin
17
Oudezijds Voorburgwal
Nieuwe Markt
Prins Hendrikkade
Kattenburger-straat
Schans
Oude
Nieuwe Uilenburgerstraat
20
Uilenburgergracht
Valkenburgerstraat
Hoogtekadijk
Kloveniersburgwal
Groenburgwal
19
Rapenburgerstraat
Entrepotdok
Herengracht
Waterlooplein
Mr. Visserplein
Plantage Doklaan
Muntplein
22
21
Nieuwe
Plantage Kerklaan
Artispark
Rembrandtplein
Plantage Middenlaan
Nieuwe Keizersgracht
Plantage Muidergracht
Plantage Muidergracht
Utrechtsestraat
Nieuwe Kerkstraat
Nieuwe Prinsengracht
racht
Amstel River
Weesperstraat
Achtergracht
Nieuwe
Sarphatistraat
Falckstraat
Sarphatistraat
Frederiksplein
Mauritskade
Ooster-park
Singelgracht
Stadhouderskade
Ruyschstraat
Blasiusstraat
Legend
Railway

The Ladies of the Night

The Walletjes (Red Light District), the warren of streets around Oudezijds Achterburgwal and Oudezijds Voorburgwal by the Oude Kerk, is one of the city's major tourist attractions. The district's ladies represent a cross-section of nationalities, displayed in windows and doorways in various stages of undress.

There's plenty to see during the day, but if you choose to tour this area at night, you should exercise extreme caution. Watch out for pickpockets and don't let the more aggressive ladies pull you into their rooms (unless you want to be so pulled). Also keep in mind that taking pictures here is a no-no—if you violate the rule your camera may be grabbed from you and broken.

Frommer's Favorite Amsterdam Experiences

- **Strolling the Red Light District.** The architecture is neat and the ladies in the windows rather fascinating (from the outside, anyway).
- **Visiting Anne Frank's House.** You'll find it a moving experience.
- **Taking a canal boat trip.** The boat's-eye view is the best for seeing the city's famed gabled houses and numerous bridges (you can catch a boat at key locations around town, including along Damrak or Prins Hendrikkade near Centraal Station, on the Rokin near Muntplein, and near Liedseplein; the cost is $5 to $7.50 for adults, $4 to $5 for children, for a 1-hour ride).
- **Going museum-hopping.** This is one of the best cities in the world for this activity. Start with the Van Gogh Museum.
- **Taking a picture at the Floating Flower Market.** The market on the Singel at Muntplein is a photographer's delight, with rows of barges selling fresh-cut flowers, plants, and tulip bulbs.

The Best Shore Excursions

Amsterdam City Tour (3½–4 hours, $32–$42): This highlights tour passes Dam Square, the Royal Palace, the 550-year-old Nieuwe Kerk (New Church), the Portuguese Synagogue, and Rembrandt's House. Then you board a glass-topped motor launch for a canal ride past historic sights including the narrowest house in Amsterdam, the skinny bridge over Amstel River, and the Anne Frank House. Some tours also include a visit to the Rijksmuseum.

Traditional Fishing Villages (4 hours, $40): This bus and walking tour visits the quaint towns of Marken, Monnikendam, and Volendam. Highlights include views of the lush countryside, cobblestone streets with colorful homes, boat-filled harbors, and a visit to a cheese factory.

Grand Holland (7–8 hours, $85–$98): This tour visits Holland's Royal City, the Hague. Drive past the Royal Palace, Houses of Parliament, and Peace Palace. Also visit Delft, one of the oldest cities in Holland and home of the Delft pottery factory, famous for its blue and white pottery. Lunch is included. Some tours include a stop at Aalsmeer to view the flower auction, or a stop at Madurodam, a reproduction in miniature of a typical Dutch city.

The Top Attractions

Anne Frankhuis (Anne Frank House). Prinsengracht 263 (just below Westermarkt). ☎ **020/556-71-00.** Admission about $5 adults, $2.50 children 10–17. Apr–Aug daily 9am–9pm; Sept daily 9am–5pm.

No one should miss this moving experience. The young Jewish girl Anne Frank wrote her diary here while hiding from the Nazis from 1942 to 1944. There's a small exhibit on the Holocaust, and you can view the famous attic where Anne and her family lived. The house is so small groups are not allowed, so you can only visit on your own (and not on shore excursions).

Stedelijk Museum of Modern Art. Paulus Potterstraat 13 (at Museumplein). ☎ **020/573-29-11.** Admission about $4.50 adults, $2.25 children 7–16. Apr–Sept 11am–7pm.

This museum offers a collection of contemporary art that includes such modern Dutch painters as Karel Appel, Willem de Kooning, and Piet Mondrian, as well as works by Chagall, Cézanne, Picasso, Renoir, Monet, and Manet, and Americans Calder, Oldenburg, Rosenquist, and Warhol.

Vincent Van Gogh Museum. Paulus Potterstraat 7–11 (at Museumplein). ☎ **020/570-52-00.** Admission about $6.25 adults, $2.50 children 18 and under. Daily 10am–5pm.

This museum houses the largest collection of Vincent Van Gogh's work in the world: The permanent collection includes more than 200 paintings and 600 drawings. Notable parts of the collection include *The Potato Eaters, Self Portrait as a Painter, Still Life with Sun Flowers,* and *Cornfield with Rows.* The museum's collection also includes works by other notable Dutch artists and paintings by Van Gogh's contemporaries, including Gauguin, Monet, and Toulouse-Lautrec.

Rijksmuseum. Stadhouderskade 42 (at Museumplein). ☎ **020/673-21-21.** Admission about $7.50 adults, $3.25 children 6–18. Daily 10am–5pm.

This major art museum houses the largest art collection in the Netherlands, with paintings from the 15th century to the 19th century, including 22 Rembrandts (*Night Watch* is the most famous), Vermeer, Frans Hals, Alvert Cuyp, and Jan Steen. The print room houses one million prints and drawings.

Koninklijk Paleis (Royal Palace). Dam Square. ☎ **020/624-86-98.** Admission about $3.50 adults, $1.50 children 12 and under. Mid-June to the first week in Sept daily 12:30–5pm; at other times, Tues–Thurs 1–4pm.

Built in the 17th century as the City Hall, the building was turned into the palace in 1808 by Napoleon when he came to Amsterdam. It's decorated in Empire Style, and is still used for receptions and official ceremonies by her majesty the queen.

Joods Historisch Museum (Jewish Historical Museum). Jonas daniël Meijerplein 204 (near Waterlooplein). ☎ **020/626-99-45.** Admission about $4 adults, $1 children 10–16. Daily 11am–5pm.

This museum, located in the city's old Jewish Quarter, in a renovated Ashkenazi synagogue, offers a view of the social and cultural history of the Jewish community in the Netherlands, including both good times and bad.

Stopping for a Bite

The restaurant choices here go across the international spectrum. A favorite is the **Indonesian rijstafel** (a sampling of various dishes). Distinctive Dutch dishes include white asparagus (in season in May), raw herring (in May or early June), and Zeeland oysters and mussels (in September). You can enjoy your meal with the local brew, Heineken. You'll see people on the street (in shopping areas) eating French fries and mayonnaise. It's a local treat that sounds gross but is really very good—just make sure you spend some time in your ship's gym afterward to work off the calories.

Best Shopping Buys

Best buys here include Delft pottery, wooden shoes, cheese, antiques, and diamonds. Main shopping streets (many pedestrian-only) are **Kalverstraat** near Dam Square (for inexpensive items), **Rokin,** parallel to the above (for quality fashions, art, and antiques), **Leidsestraat** (for upscale clothing, china, and gifts), **P. C. Hooftstraat** and **Van Baerlestraat,** near Museumplein (for hip fashion and gifts), and **Nieuwe Spiegelstraat,** near the Rijksmuseum (for antiques). **De Bijenkorf,** at Dam Square, is a top department store. If you're flying out of Holland, keep in mind the Amsterdam airport has some of the best duty-free shopping you'll find anywhere.

If you're in the market for diamonds, the following are members of the Amsterdam Diamond Foundation, and offer both showrooms and diamond-cutting and polishing demonstrations: **Amsterdam Diamond Center,** Rokin 1 (☎ 020/624-5787); **Coster Diamonds,** Paulus Potterstraat 204 (☎ 020/676-2222); **Gassan Diamonds,** Nieuwe Uilenburgerstraat 173–175 (☎ 020/622-5333); **Reuter Diamonds,** Kalverstraat 165 or Singel 526 (☎ 020/623-35-00); and **Van Moppes Diamonds,** Albert Cuypstraat 2–6 (☎ 020/676-12-42).

ROTTERDAM

Rotterdam is a bustling metropolis and a major port city, sometimes referred to as "the gateway to Europe." It's located only a half hour from the Hague and 1 hour from Amsterdam.

The city is one of contrasts, with only one tiny area, historic Delfshaven, retaining its historic structures (as well as museums and art galleries). Elsewhere in the city, big, well-designed modern buildings have taken the place of those destroyed during World War II.

Of special interest to Americans in Delfshaven is the old church in which the Pilgrims said their last prayers before boarding the *Speedwell* to the New World in 1620. When the ship did not prove seaworthy, they switched to the *Mayflower* at Southampton.

The city's museums include Boymans–Van Beuningen, an outstanding museum with a collection of ancient and modern art and design work. The old Holland America Line passenger terminal on Wilhelmina Quay has been completely renovated and serves as the city's cruise terminal. Located in the heart of the city near the new Erasmus Bridge and only a 10-minute walk from the city center, it's a tourist destination all its own.

Rotterdam is only a half hour away from major Holland tourist attractions including the historic cheese town of Gouda, which you can visit on a shore excursion.

FROMMER'S FAVORITE ROTTERDAM EXPERIENCES

- **Taking a harbor boat ride.** Spido Havenrondvaarten, on Willemsplein (☎ **010/413-5400**), offers 1-hour cruises with fascinating narration for about $8.40 per person.
- **Stopping by the Pilgrim Fathers Church.** This church (on Voorhaven) is where the pilgrims said goodbye to the Old World before heading off to the New.
- **Going museum hopping.** The Maritime Museum and Museum Boymans–Van Beuningen art museum are both worth a look.

COMING ASHORE & GETTING AROUND

It's about a 10-minute walk to the city center. **Taxis** are available at the pier, but are expensive. Rotterdam also has an extensive public transportation network of **buses, trams,** and subways (Metro).

THE BEST SHORE EXCURSIONS

Ships that dock in Rotterdam do so as an alternative to Amsterdam, so shore excursions are also offered to Amsterdam, the Hague, Delft, and other locations described in the Amsterdam section, above.

Rotterdam City & Harbor Tour (3 hours, $45): View from the bus the city's acclaimed modern architecture, and pass historic landmarks. Then take a harbor cruise of the busy port.

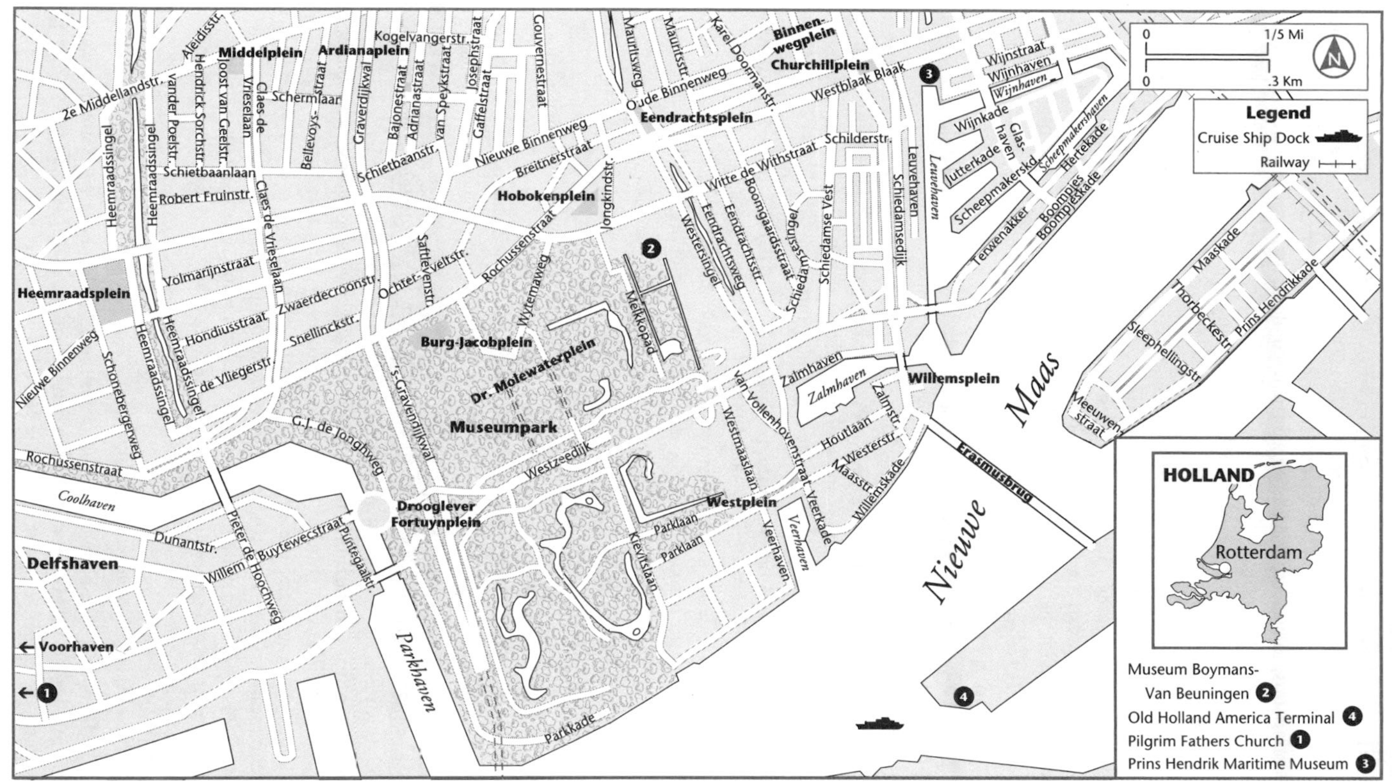
0
1/5 Mi
0
.3 Km
N
Legend
Cruise Ship Dock
Railway
HOLLAND
Rotterdam
Museum Boymans-
Van Beuningen 2
Old Holland America Terminal 4
Pilgrim Fathers Church 1
Prins Hendrik Maritime Museum 3
Nieuwe
Maas
Erasmusbrug
Willemsplein
Leuvehaven
Wijnhaven
Glas-
haven
Scheepmakershaven
Zalmhaven
Veerhaven
Parkhaven
Coolhaven
Churchillplein
Binnen-
wegplein
Eendrachtsplein
Hobokenplein
Burg-Jacobplein
Dr. Molewaterplein
Museumpark
Westplein
Droogleever
Fortuynplein
Middelplein
Ardianaplein
Heemraadsplein
Delfshaven
← Voorhaven
← 1

Zeeland & The Delta (5 hours, $54): In 1953, the Province of Zeeland was the scene of a major flood that covered more than 260,000 acres, killing nearly 1,900 people. As a result of the disaster, water management techniques were developed to reclaim the land. Dams, canals, and dykes were constructed along with a storm surge barrier. The massive project actually shortened Holland's shoreline by more than 300 miles. Visit the Delta Expo for an explanation of the fascinating hydro-engineering project. On the way, you'll pass scenic countryside and the historic city of Zierrikzee.

Gouda & Oudewater (5 hours, $39): Gouda, about half an hour from Rotterdam, is best known for producing cheese. This tour brings you to town for a walking tour that visits the market, the Gothic town hall (the oldest in the Netherlands), and the weighing house, which dates back to the 17th century. You then reboard the bus to travel to Oudewater, where you'll visit the Witches Weighing House, the only remaining such place in Holland. Last used in 1729, this is where people were weighed to determine if they were witches.

THE TOP ATTRACTIONS

Museum Boymans–Van Beuningen. Museumpark 20. ☎ **010/441-9400.** Admission about $4.35. Tues–Sat 10am–5pm, Sun and holidays 11am–5pm.

Dutch and Flemish artists from the 16th and 17th centuries are featured here, including Rubens, Hals, Rembrandt, and Steen. Separate galleries boast international modern art, applied arts, ceramics, and sculpture. There are also regular exhibitions of the museum's extensive collection of drawings and prints.

Prins Hendrik Maritime Museum. Leuvehaven 1. ☎ **010/413-2680.** Admission about $3.50 adults, $1.75 children. Tues–Sat 10am–5pm, Sun 11am–5pm.

This museum is devoted to the history of Rotterdam harbor and is full of nautical lore. It's located in the harbor area, and consists of a main building and *De Buffel,* a beautifully restored 1868 warship.

STOPPING FOR A BITE

Favorites here include raw herring and *genever* (Dutch gin).

BEST SHOPPING BUYS

Head to Delfshaven for galleries and craft shops. The central shopping area is called the Beurstraverse.

10 Norway

Norway offers visitors an embarrassment of riches, from majestic glacier-born fjords and mountain views, to charming and remote towns and villages, to summer's Midnight Sun. Both seafaring and tradition are important parts of what this natural frontier is all about—Norway's name is even nautical, deriving from *Norvegr,* a 1,000-year-old Viking term meaning "the way north," describing the shipping route along the Norwegian coast. But Norway is also a modern and technologically advanced nation with a well-educated and amazingly athletic populace—where else does nearly every child learn to ski?

ESSENTIALS

LANGUAGE Norwegian. English is also widely spoken.

CURRENCY The Norwegian currency is the krone (plural *kroner*), and there are 100 øre in 1 krone. Banknotes are issued in denominations of 50, 100, 200, 500, and 1,000 kroner. the exchange rate at press time was $1 = 7.9 kroner.

BERGEN

Bergen is the capital of Norway's fjord district, and the largest city on the west coast, an area known for its awesome natural beauty. The city is an ancient one, nearly 1,000

Bergen Art Museum 5
Det Hanseatiske Museum 2
Fløibanen funicular 1
Galleriet shopping complex 4
Torget Marketplace 3

Legend
Railway

years old, squeezed between mountain ranges and bounded by water. Until the 14th century it was the seat of the medieval kingdom of Norway. Today, it's a commercial capital, but it's also a town with important traditions, including in shipping. Besides being a starting-off point for exploration, Bergen has its own sightseeing attractions, including the historic medieval district of **Bryggen,** which is on UNESCO's list of World Heritage sites.

Frommer's Favorite Bergen Experiences

- **Visit Bryggen.** This quarter of historic timbered houses, rebuilt on the waterfront after a disastrous fire in 1702, is what remains of medieval Bergen. The buildings (some open to the public) now house workshops of painters, weavers, and craftspeople. Bryggen is on UNESCO's World Heritage List as one of the world's most significant cultural and historical re-creations of a medieval settlement.
- Take the Fløibanen funicular to Fløien. The view is worth every øre.

Coming Ashore & Getting Around

Ships dock within walking distance of the city center. **Taxis** are available at the pier, but you can easily explore the city on foot.

The Best Shore Excursions

Bergen City Highlights & Troldhaugen (3 hours, $37–$39): Drive past the historic row houses and other city sights, then visit Troldhaugen, a Victorian house in rural surroundings outside of Bergen that was the home of Norway's famous composer Edvard Grieg. The house contains Grieg's own furniture, paintings, and other mementos, and it was here that he composed many of his famous works. The tour may also include a piano recital at the nearby turf-roofed Concert Hall.

The Top Attractions

Det Hanseatiske Museum. Finnegårdsgaten 1A, Bryggen. ☎ **55-31-41-89.** Admission about $5.40 adults, free for children. June–Aug, daily 9am–5pm; May–Sept, daily 11am–2pm.

This museum, housed in one of the best-preserved wooden buildings at Bryggen, illustrates what life was like on the wharf centuries ago. The museum is furnished with authentic articles dating from 1704.

Bergen Art Museum. Rasmus Meyers Allé 3–7. ☎ **55-56-80-00.** Admission May 15–Sept 15 about $5.40 adults, free for children; the rest of year free for everyone. May 15–Sept 15, Mon–Sat 11am–4pm, Sun noon–3pm; Sept 16–May 14, Tues–Sun noon–3pm.

The works of Norwegian and international artists—among them Picasso, Braque, Miró, Kandinsky, and Paul Klee—are displayed at this museum in the city center. The museum also contains some of Edvard Munch's most important works.

Fløibanen funicular. Vetrlidsalm 23A. ☎ **55/31-48-00.** The round-trip ride about $4.60 adults, $2.15 children and seniors. May 25 to Aug, Mon–Fri 7:30am–midnight, Sat 8am–midnight, Sun 9am–midnight; May and Sept, Mon–Thurs 7:30am–11pm, Fri 7:30am–11:30pm, Sat 8am–11:30pm, Sun 9am–11pm.

A short walk from the fish market, the funicular heads up Fløien, the most famous of Bergen's seven hills, from which you can view the city, the neighboring hills, and the harbor.

Stopping for a Bite

Traditional favorites include fish and game dishes (including reindeer). Smoked salmon *(laks)* is a local delicacy. Nice cafes can be found near the harbor.

0 93 Mi
0 150 Km
N
Arctic Ocean
North Cape
Honningsvåg
Vardø
Vadsø
Hammerfest
Kirkenes
Lakselv
Norwegian Sea
Vesterålen Islands
Alta
E6
Karasjok
Tromsø
Kautokeino
Atlantic Ocean
Lofoten Islands
Harstad
Narvik
Svolvær
Abisko
Kiruna
Skutvik
FINLAND
Bodø
Fauske
ARCTIC CIRCLE
Mo I Rana
E6
Luleå
NORWAY
SWEDEN
Umea
Gulf of Bothnia
E6
Kristiansund N
Trondheim
Sundsvall
Røros
Molde
Åndalsnes
Oppdal
Geiranger
E6
Ålesund
Beitostølen
Lillehammer
Gävle
Balestrand
E68
Gjøvik
Hamar
Flåm
Uppsala
Voss
Ulvik
Lofthus
Bergen
Utne
Eidfjord
Geilo
Oslo
Stockholm
Kinsarvik
Karlstad
Skien
Baltic Sea
Haugesund
Fredrikstad
Skara
Sandefjord
E6
Stavanger
Arendal
Gotland
North Sea
E18
Kristiansand S
Gothenburg
3-0358

Best Shopping Buys

Head to the **Marketplace** (Torget) for bargains on local handicrafts from the western fjord district, including rugs and handmade tablecloths. The best time to visit is between 8am and noon. Bargaining is welcomed. The most important shopping complex in the city is **Galleriet** (Torgalmenningen 8), located near the fish market. Here you'll find 70-some stores offering tax-free shopping.

THE NORWEGIAN FJORDS

On a North Cape cruise, as you explore the Norwegian fjords, you will make several port calls, including some or all of the following.

Honningsvag

This is the world's northernmost village, and gateway to the North Cape. It is a completely modern fishing harbor (only the chapel withstood the German destruction of 1944) and has a museum called **Nordkappmuseet,** in the Nordkapphuset, Fergeveien 4 (☎ **78/47-28-33**), right at the harbor and town center, that offers exhibits relating to the cultural history of the North Cape. (Admission is about $3.10 adults, 75¢ children. Hours are June 15 to August 15, Monday to Saturday 9am to 8pm, Sunday 1 to 8pm. At other times, Monday to Friday 11am to 4pm.)

The Best Shore Excursions

The North Cape (3½ hours, $57): Drive about 45 minutes to the Nordkapp, the northernmost point in Europe. Visit North Cape Hall for a video presentation, and stop by the post office for a Nordkapp postmark. Also check out a cave offering a panoramic window facing the Arctic Ocean.

Trondheim

Founded by the Viking king Olaf I Tryggvason in the 10th century, Trondheim is Norway's third largest city and was the country's capital until the early 1200s. It's scenic, pleasant, and an active university town, noted for its timbered architecture and links to its medieval past, which include the Gothic-style **Nidaros Cathedral** and **Archbishop's Palace,** Bispegaten 5 (tel] **73/50-12-12**). Admission to both about $3.20 adults, $1.25 children. Cathedral, Monday to Friday 9am to 5:30pm, Saturday 9am to 2pm, and Sunday 1 to 4pm June 20 to August 18 (closes earlier other times of the year). Palace, June to mid-August only, Monday to Friday 9am to 3pm, Saturday 9am to 2pm, Sunday noon to 3pm.

The Best Shore Excursions

City Tour with Open-Air Folk Museum (3 hours, $39): This tour visits the Nidaros Cathedral as well as the Trøndelag Folk Museum, one of Norway's major folk-culture complexes. The collection includes farmhouses, churches (including the northernmost stave church in Norway), and town buildings, surrounded by a nature park.

Tromsø

This "Gateway to the Arctic" island has been a starting-off point for exploration of the North Pole. It's the capital of Norwegian Lapland, and a popular sight with tourists who come in summer to celebrate the midnight sun. Local sights include the **Arctic Cathedral,** built in the shape of an iceberg. The city also boasts historic buildings including the 19th-century **Tromsø Cathedral,** one of Norway's largest wooden churches.

The Best Shore Excursions

Tromsø City Tour (3 hours, $45): This tour includes the Tromsø Museum, which offers zoology, geology, and botany displays and an exhibit on the Same, the region's original inhabitants. Also visited are the Tromsdalen Church (also known as the Arctic Cathedral) and Polaria, a film presentation about Arctic life.

OSLO

Oslo is one of the oldest Scandinavia capitals, founded in the mid-11th century by a Viking king and named as the nation's capital around 1300. Though it's never been on the mainstream tourism circuit, Oslo is a growing city permeated by a kind of Nordic joie de vivre, and offers a wealth of sights and activities and numerous new restaurants, cafes, and shopping options. It's also a starting point for easy excursions along the 60-mile-long Oslofjord or to nearby towns and villages.

Oslo residents love nature and are proud of the nearby forests and fjords. It takes only a half-hour by tram to get from the Royal Palace, at Drammensveien 1, to **Tryvannstårnet Lookout Tower,** where you can enjoy the lushness of Oslo Marka, the giant forest, and look down, from the 390-foot tower, on hundreds of sailboats, motorboats, and windsurfers among the numerous islands of the Oslo archipelago. For information, phone ☎ **22/14-67-11.** Admission is about $4.60 adults, $2.30 children. Hours are May and September, daily 10am to 5pm; June, 10am to 7pm; July, 9am to 10pm; August, 9am to 8pm. Nearby is the **Holmenkollen Ski Jump,** the site of Olympic competitions in 1952.

FROMMER'S FAVORITE OSLO EXPERIENCES

- **Taking a ferry to the Bygdøy peninsula.** This is where some of Oslo's major attractions, including the Viking Ship Museum, polar ship *Fram,* and Norwegian Folk Museum are located.
- **Admiring outdoor sculptures** at the Vigeland Sculpture Park.
- **Exploring the Edvard Munch Museum.** But don't Scream!
- **Enjoying the street musicians.** They flock here by the hundreds in the summer, and can be found along Karl Johans Gate or at the marketplace.
- **Eating a bag of shrimp on the harbor.** See "Stopping for a Bite," below.

COMING ASHORE & GETTING AROUND

Ships dock right in the city center, which is small, compact, and easy to walk around. **Taxis** may be difficult to come by. The city, however, has an efficient system of **buses, trams** (streetcars), and **subways.**

THE BEST SHORE EXCURSIONS

Oslo Highlights (3 hours, $38): Drive through the capital, passing Akershus Castle, the Parliament building, the National Theater, the university, the Royal Castle, and Karl Johan Street, Oslo's main thoroughfare. Continue on through Oslo's beautiful residential areas to Holmenkollen Ski Jump. Continue on to Vigeland Sculpture Park for a walking tour, then to Bygdøy Peninsula, a former royal preserve, now the site of some of Oslo's most important museums, including the Viking Ship Museum.

Maritime Oslo & Vigeland Park (4 hours, $39): A city tour with stops at the Fram Museum, featuring a polar ship; the Maritime Museum, offering a video presentation with spectacular views of Norway's coastline and a depiction of life on the high seas; and the Viking Ship Museum. Includes a visit to the Vigeland Sculpture Park (see "The Top Attractions," below).

Oslo Countryside (7 hours, $115): Drive 1½ hours through Oslo's suburbs, farm country, and woodlands to Blaafarvevaerket, and The Cobalt Works, once Norway's largest industrial company and now a cultural museum. The annual art exhibitions here are among the most important in Scandinavia. The Cobalt Works was founded in 1776

Oslo

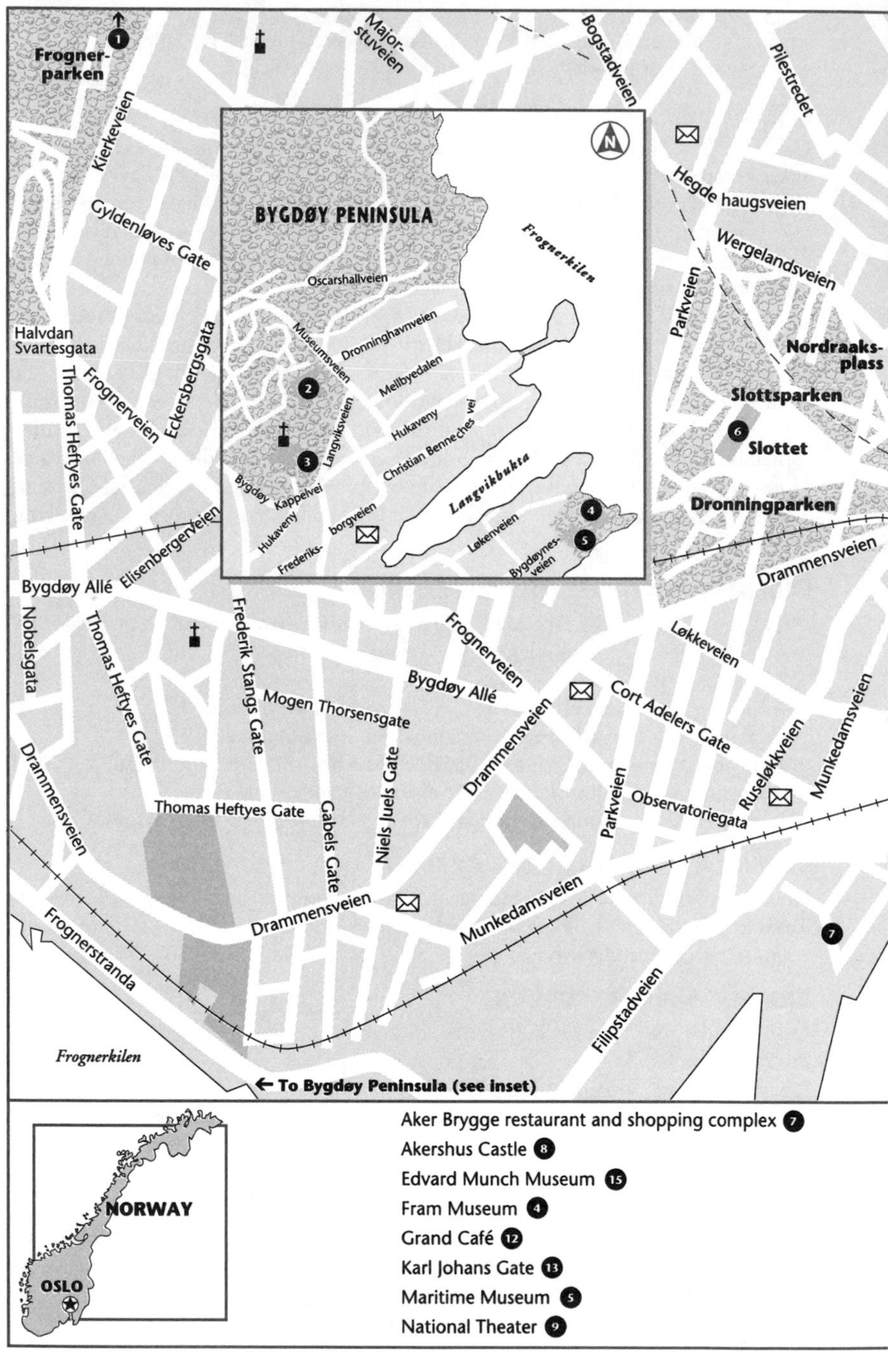
Frogner-
parken
Major-
stuveien
Bogstadveien
Pilestredet
Kierkeveien
Gyldenløves Gate
Hegde haugsveien
Wergelandsveien
Parkveien
Nordraaks-
plass
Slottsparken
Slottet
Dronningparken
Halvdan
Svartesgata
Thomas Heftyes Gate
Frognerveien
Eckersbergsgata
BYGDØY PENINSULA
Frognerkilen
Oscarshallveien
Museumsveien
Dronninghavnveien
Mellbyedalen
Hukaveny
Christian Benneches vei
Langviksveien
Bygdøy
Kappelvei
Hukaveny
Frederiks-
borgveien
Langvikbukta
Løkenveien
Bygdøynes-
veien
Elisenbergerveien
Bygdøy Allé
Drammensveien
Nobelsgata
Thomas Heftyes Gate
Frederik Stangs Gate
Mogen Thorsensgate
Frognerveien
Bygdøy Allé
Løkkeveien
Cort Adelers Gate
Drammensveien
Munkedamsveien
Ruseløkkveien
Observatoriegata
Parkveien
Niels Juels Gate
Gabels Gate
Thomas Heftyes Gate
Drammensveien
Drammensveien
Munkedamsveien
Frognerstranda
Filipstadveien
Frognerkilen
← To Bygdøy Peninsula (see inset)
NORWAY
OSLO
Aker Brygge restaurant and shopping complex 7
Akershus Castle 8
Edvard Munch Museum 15
Fram Museum 4
Grand Café 12
Karl Johans Gate 13
Maritime Museum 5
National Theater 9

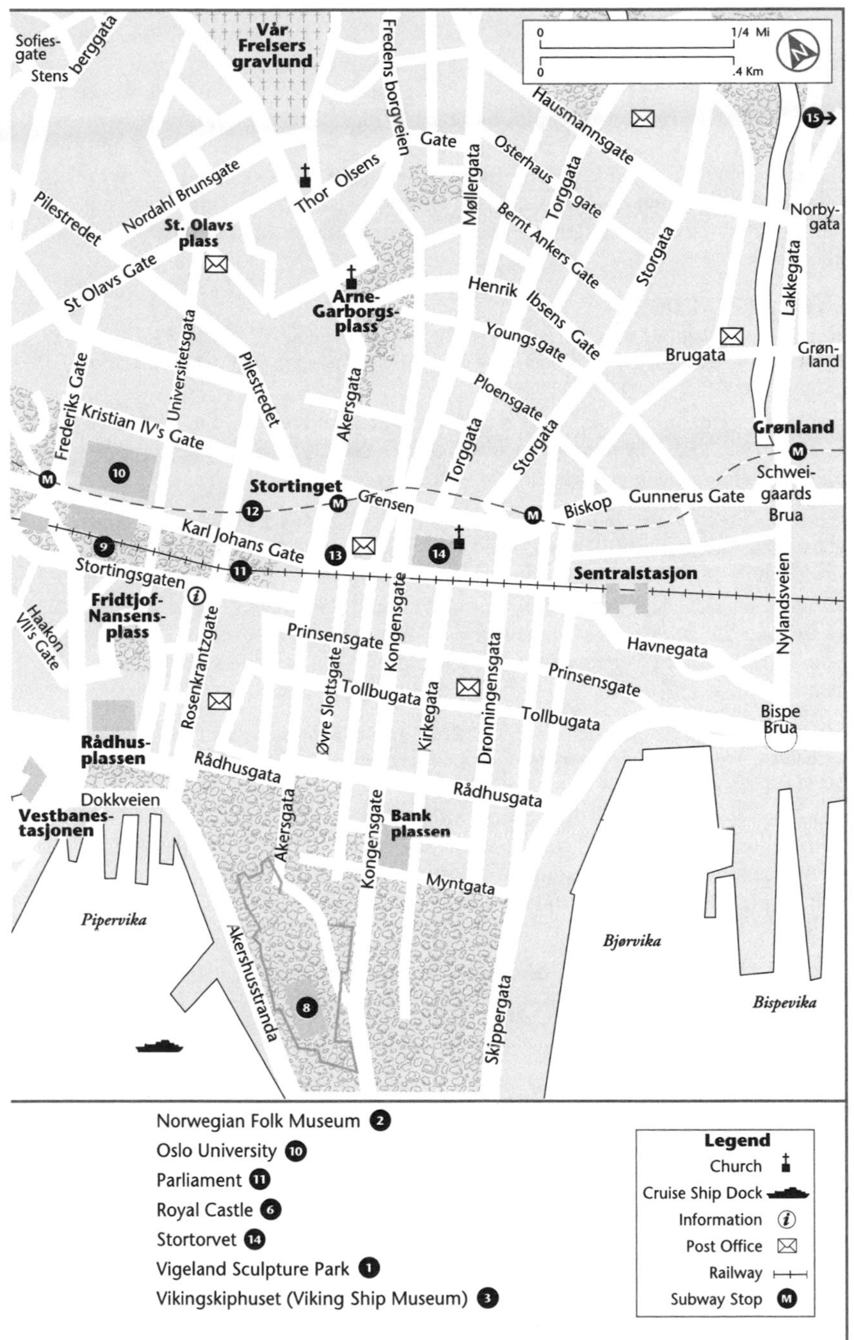
0 1/4 Mi
0 .4 Km
Sofies-gate
Stensberggata
Vår Frelsers gravlund
Fredens borgveien
Hausmannsgate
Gate
Thor Olsens
Møllergata
Osterhaus gate
Torggata
Nordahl Brunsgate
Pilestredet
St. Olavs plass
St Olavs Gate
Bernt Ankers Gate
Storgata
Norby-gata
Lakkegata
Arne-Garborgs-plass
Henrik Ibsens Gate
Youngsgate
Brugata
Grøn-land
Universitetsgata
Pilestredet
Frederiks Gate
Kristian IV's Gate
Akersgata
Ploensgate
Torggata
Storgata
Grønland
Schwei-gaards Brua
Stortinget
Grensen
Biskop Gunnerus Gate
Karl Johans Gate
Stortingsgaten
Sentralstasjon
Fridtjof-Nansens-plass
Haakon VII's Gate
Rosenkrantzgate
Prinsensgate
Kongensgate
Øvre Slottsgate
Tollbugata
Kirkegata
Dronningensgata
Havnegata
Prinsensgate
Tollbugata
Nylandsveien
Bispe Brua
Rådhus-plassen
Rådhusgata
Rådhusgata
Dokkveien
Vestbanes-tasjonen
Akersgata
Kongensgate
Bank plassen
Myntgata
Pipervika
Akershusstranda
Bjørvika
Skippergata
Bispevika
Norwegian Folk Museum 2
Oslo University 10
Parliament 11
Royal Castle 6
Stortorvet 14
Vigeland Sculpture Park 1
Vikingskiphuset (Viking Ship Museum) 3
Legend
Church
Cruise Ship Dock
Information
Post Office
Railway
Subway Stop

to extract cobalt from the Modum mines. The mineral was used to make dyes for the world's glass and porcelain industries. You'll get to tour the Works, visit the mill with its cobalt-colored displays (you can shop here for glassware), and see the latest art exhibition. Time is allowed to explore the park-like grounds. Before leaving Blaafarvevaerket, you'll stop briefly to admire the Haugfossen waterfall and visit an old-fashioned country store, then stop at Nyfossum to see the popular exhibition "A Treasure of Culture," featuring patchwork quilts in all shapes and sizes. The tour then visits a beautifully restored house built in the 1820s, with herb garden and fish ponds. Tour includes lunch.

The Top Attractions

Vikingskiphuset (Viking Ship Museum). Huk Aveny 25, Bygdøy. ☎ **22/43-83-79.** Admission about $4.60 adults, $1.55 children. May–Aug, daily 10am–6pm; Sept daily 11am–5pm. Take a ferry from Pier 3, facing the Rådhuset.

On display here are three Viking burial vessels that were found preserved in clay on the shores of the Oslofjord. The most spectacular is the 9th-century dragon ship, which features a wealth of ornaments and was the burial chamber of a Viking queen and her slave.

Vigeland Sculpture Park. Frogner Park. Nobelsgate 32. ☎ **22/44-23-06.** Free admission to the park; museum, about $3.10 adults, $1.55 children. Park, daily 24 hours. Museum May–Sept, Tues–Sat 10am–6pm, Sun noon–7pm.

This 75-acre park displays the work of Gustav Vigeland, Norway's greatest sculptor. There are some 211 sculptures of humans and animals in stone, bronze, and iron. The museum is the sculptor's former studio, and contains more of his works, sketches, and woodcuts.

Edvard Munch Museum. Tøyengate 53. ☎ **22/67-37-74.** Admission about $6.15 adults, $2.30 children. June to mid-Sept, daily 10am–6pm; May, Tues, Wed, Fri, and Sat 10am–4pm, Thurs and Sun 10am–6pm.

This museum is devoted exclusively to the works of Edvard Munch (1863–1944), Scandinavia's leading painter and creator of *The Scream.* The artist's gift to the city, the collection contains some 1,100 paintings, 4,500 drawings, and 18,000 prints, numerous graphic plates, six sculptures, and documentary material. Exhibits are changed periodically.

Henie-Onstad Kunstsenter (Henie-Onstad Art Center). Høkvikodden, Baerum. ☎ **67/54-3050.** Admission about $6.15 adults, $3.10 children 16 and under. June–Aug, Mon 11am–5pm, Tues–Fri 9am–9pm, Sat–Sun 11am–7pm; May and Sept, Tues 9am–9pm, Sat–Mon 11am–5pm. Take a bus to Høvikodden.

This museum on the Oslofjord, about 7 miles west of Oslo, displays the art collection of skating champion Sonja Henie and her husband, Niels Onstad, a shipping tycoon. There are some 1,800 works by Munch, Picasso, Matisse, Léger, Bonnard, and Miró. Also on display are Miss Henie's three Olympic gold medals and other trophies. There's also a top-notch, partly self-service grill restaurant, The Piruetten, on the premises.

Norwegian Folk Museum. Museumsveien 10. ☎ **22/12-37-00.** Admission about $7.70 adults, $1.55 children 16 and under. June–Aug, daily 9am–6pm; May and Sept, daily 10am–5pm. Take a ferry from Pier 3, facing the Rådhuset.

This open-air folk museum features 140 original buildings, transported here from all over Norway. Included are medieval dwellings, a stave church, and rural buildings grouped together by region of origin. Inside, the museum has exhibits capturing every imaginable facet of Norwegian life, past and present. There's a particularly outstanding exhibit on Norway's Lapp population.

Stopping for a Bite

At the harbor, in front of the Rådhuset, you can buy a bag of freshly caught and cooked **shrimp** from a shrimp fisherman and shell your meal as you check out the harbor scenery. Those looking for smart restaurants serving Norwegian food and foreign food (especially American) should also head to the waterfront, in particular **Aker Brygge,** the former shipbuilding yard, now a restaurant and shopping complex. The **Grand Café** in the Grand Hotel, Karl Johans Gate 31 (**☎ 22/42-93-90**) is where Edvard Munch and Henrik Ibsen used to hang out (reservations are recommended).

Best Shopping Buys

Though Oslo is one of the most expensive cities in Europe, best buys here include sportswear, silver, enamelware, traditional handicrafts, pewter, glassware, teak furniture, and products made of stainless steel. Oslo has many pedestrian streets for shoppers. A good place to start is the **Stortorvet.** Another large cluster of stores can be found along **Karl Johans Gate.**

11 Russia

Fascinating **St. Petersburg,** founded in 1703 and named for Peter the Great, had a tough 20th century, with much trauma and bloodshed. The 1917 Russian Revolution that ushered in the Soviet era also ushered in a new name for the city: Leningrad, in honor of Vladimir Lenin. In the early 1940s, Nazi troops seized Leningrad for 900 days during World War II, leaving approximately a million dead and the city badly battered.

In 1991, the city, under the new non-communist Russian government, returned to its original name, and today the one-time capital of Imperial Russia is a cosmopolitan city of five million that's both an industrial and a cultural center. It's the second largest city in Russia and the country's largest port.

The Neva River cuts through the city, which was once swampland, and there are some 360 bridges crossing the river and canals, a layout that's earned the city the nickname "Venice of the North." The canals are lined with opulent baroque and neoclassical palaces, cathedrals, and monuments. The city's ongoing restoration project requires that all existing facades in the downtown area be retained.

Top sights in St. Petersburg include the Hermitage museum, which has one of the richest art collections in the world; the Peter and Paul fortress, the burial place of the Romanov dynasty; and St. Isaac's Cathedral, the fourth largest cathedral in the world. Outside the city, you can visit the lavish summer homes of the tsars.

Cruise lines also typically offer nighttime shore excursions here to see ballet, opera, folk performers, or a circus.

ESSENTIALS

LANGUAGE Russian.

CURRENCY Rubles, but street vendors will readily accept dollars. The rate of exchange at press time was $1 = 26 rubles.

FROMMER'S FAVORITE ST. PETERSBURG EXPERIENCES

- **Strolling the Nevsky Prospekt.** St. Petersburg's main thoroughfare (and the most famous street in Russia) offers historic squares, bridges, buildings, shopping, cafes, crowds, and even the occasional scam artist and black marketeer (don't buy anything from someone who starts the conversation with "Pssst . . .").
- **Visiting a summer palace.** These historic estates of the tsars are lavish and memorable.

Important Visa Information

Passengers who participate in St. Petersburg shore excursions or arrange for private transportation through the ship's shore excursions desk (see "Coming Ashore & Getting Around," below) do not need to obtain a visa.

Those who wish to go ashore on their own, however, do have to obtain a tourist visa prior to departure. To receive a Russian visa, you must have a valid passport which remains valid at least 30 days past the last day of the cruise. Visa application forms are available from the Russian consulates in Washington, New York, San Francisco, or Seattle, or from travel agencies or visa services. The visa processing fee is $70 for not less than 2 weeks' processing time. Additional fees are charged for quicker processing.

For information, contact the Embassy of the Russian Federation in the United States (☎ **202/939-8913** or 202/939-8918; http://russianembassy.org.), open Monday through Friday, 9am to 1pm and 2:30 to 6pm.

COMING ASHORE & GETTING AROUND

The main cruise terminal is about a 20-minute drive from the city center. Small ships can come right into town up the Neva River, but you are still best off taking a **taxi,** especially at night. Official taxis are usually four-door Volvo sedans. In Russia, they also have what are known as "private" taxis. "Private," in this case, means virtually anyone can stop and pick you up, and you enter these cabs at your own risk (there have been incidents of robberies). If you want to tour the city without having to join a shore excursion, you are best off hiring a car, limo, or van with a **private guide.** Your cruise line shore excursion desk will be able to arrange this for you. The line may also provide **shuttle bus** service to the center of town.

THE BEST SHORE EXCURSIONS

City Tour (3–3½ hours, $37–$49): This introductory tour includes a view of the Peter and Paul Fortress with its gilded spire; the cruiser *Aurora,* the ship that fired a blank round in 1917 that signaled the start of the October Revolution; and the Winter Palace, which houses the Hermitage. You will see the famous Bronze Horseman statue depicting the city's founder, Peter the Great; the exquisitely decorated Church of the Spilled Blood; and the magnificent St. Isaac's Cathedral, one of the world's largest domed structures (it took 40 years to construct and was used as a museum under the Soviet regime; it's now an active church again). Some tours include a stop at 18th-century Smolny Convent, a crowning achievement of the renowned architect Rastrelli. Others include a stop at the Summer Palace, a beautiful example of 18th-century architecture.

The Hermitage (3½–4 hours, $39–$66): Take a short drive to the Winter Palace, along the banks of the Neva River, for a guided tour through parts of the vast Hermitage Art Museum. The former home of the imperial family, this 18th-century baroque palace and four adjacent buildings now house one of the most outstanding art collections in the world.

Peterhof (4 hours, $50–$60): Drive 22 miles through the suburbs of St. Petersburg to Peterhof, the former summer home of Peter the Great, built to rival Versailles. Construction began 300 years ago and spanned 2 centuries. The massive estate encompasses seven parks and more than 20 smaller palaces and pavilions. Your guided tour will

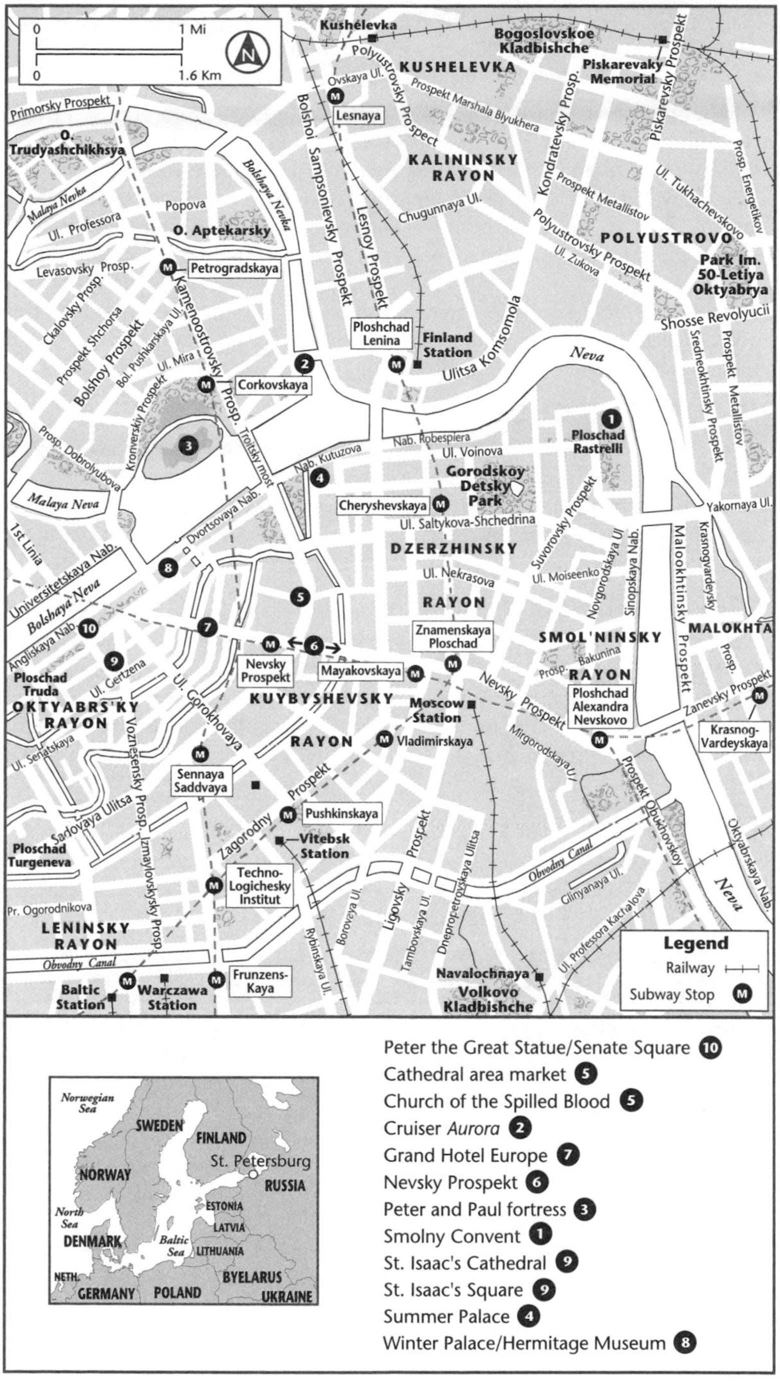
0
1 Mi
0
1.6 Km
N
Kushelevka
Bogoslovskoe Kladbishche
Piskarevaky Memorial
Piskarevsky Prospekt
KUSHELEVKA
Polyustrovsky Prospect
Ovskaya Ul.
Lesnaya
Prospekt Marshala Blyukhera
KALININSKY RAYON
Kondratevsky Prosp.
Prosp. Energetikov
Ul. Tukhachevskovo
Prospekt Metallistov
POLYUSTROVO
Park Im. 50-Letiya Oktyabrya
Polyustrovsky Prospekt
Ul. Zukova
Shosse Revolyucii
Chugunnaya Ul.
Bolshoi Sampsonievsky Prospekt
Lesnoy Prospekt
Primorsky Prospekt
O. Trudyashchikhsya
Bolshaya Nevka
Malaya Nevka
Popova
Ul. Professora
O. Aptekarsky
Levasovsky Prosp.
Petrogradskaya
Ckalovsky Prosp.
Prospekt Shchorsa
Bolshoy Prospekt
Bol. Pushkarskaya Ul.
Ul. Mira
Kamenoostrovsky Prosp.
Corkovskaya
Ploshchad Lenina
Finland Station
Ulitsa Komsomola
Neva
Sredneokhtinsky Prospekt
Prospekt Metallistov
Kronversky Prospekt
Prosp. Dobrolyubova
Troitsky most
Nab. Kutuzova
Nab. Robespiera
Ul. Voinova
Gorodskoy Detsky Park
Ploschad Rastrelli
Malaya Neva
Cheryshevskaya
Ul. Saltykova-Shchedrina
Suvorovsky Prospekt
Yakornaya Ul.
1st Linia
Dvortsovaya Nab.
Universitetskaya Nab.
DZERZHINSKY RAYON
Ul. Nekrasova
Ul. Moiseenko
Novgorodskaya Ul.
Sinopskaya Nab.
Malookhtinsky Prospekt
Krasnogvardeysky Prosp.
Bolshaya Neva
Angliskaya Nab.
Znamenskaya Ploschad
SMOL'NINSKY RAYON
MALOKHTA
Nevsky Prospekt
Mayakovskaya
Prosp. Bakunina
Ploschad Truda
Ul. Gertzena
OKTYABRS'KY RAYON
Ul. Gorokhovaya
KUYBYSHEVSKY RAYON
Moscow Station
Nevsky Prospekt
Ploshchad Alexandra Nevskovo
Zanevsky Prospekt
Krasnog-Vardeyskaya
Ul. Senatskaya
Voznesensky Prosp.
Vladimirskaya
Mirgorodskaya Ul.
Sennaya Saddvaya
Prospekt Obukhovskoy
Sadovaya Ulitsa
Zagorodny Prospekt
Pushkinskaya
Ploschad Turgeneva
Izmaylovskyky Prosp.
Vitebsk Station
Ligovsky Prospekt
Dnepropetrovskaya Ulitsa
Obvodny Canal
Oktyabrskaya Nab.
Techno-Logichesky Institut
Glinyanaya Ul.
Pr. Ogorodnikova
Borovaya Ul.
Tambovskaya Ul.
Rybinskaya Ul.
Ul. Professora Kachalova
LENINSKY RAYON
Obvodny Canal
Navalochnaya
Volkovo Kladbishche
Baltic Station
Warczawa Station
Frunzens-Kaya
Legend
Railway
Subway Stop
Norwegian Sea
SWEDEN
FINLAND
St. Petersburg
NORWAY
RUSSIA
North Sea
ESTONIA
LATVIA
DENMARK
Baltic Sea
LITHUANIA
NETH.
BYELARUS
GERMANY
POLAND
UKRAINE
Peter the Great Statue/Senate Square 10
Cathedral area market 5
Church of the Spilled Blood 5
Cruiser *Aurora* 2
Grand Hotel Europe 7
Nevsky Prospekt 6
Peter and Paul fortress 3
Smolny Convent 1
St. Isaac's Cathedral 9
St. Isaac's Square 9
Summer Palace 4
Winter Palace/Hermitage Museum 8

include the grand staircase and a walk through some of the palace's lavish rooms, as well as the palace's grounds. The 300-acre park and spectacular fountains, some 129 in total, were designed by Peter himself.

Pushkin (Tsarskoye Selo) (4 hours, $33–$52): Drive 17 miles south of St. Petersburg to Pushkin (the village of Tsarskoye Selo was renamed Pushkin in 1937 after Russia's favorite poet, Alexander Pushkin) for a visit to the opulent summer residence of Catherine the Great. The estate was presented as a gift from Peter the Great to his wife Catherine in 1710 and was the main summer residence of the imperial family from Peter's reign until the fall of the monarchy in 1917. The palace was almost totally destroyed during World War II, but has been magnificently restored to its former splendor. You'll take a guided tour of several lavish rooms, including the Great Blue Room, Picture Gallery, and Amber Room. The surrounding park features Italian-designed grounds with numerous marble statues.

THE TOP ATTRACTIONS

Due to odd museum opening hours, long lines, and a lack of English translations (you can literally get lost in the Hermitage) it is best to see the top attractions here as part of shore excursions, or in a hired car—in both cases you get an experienced guide. Cruise lines offer a particularly large selection of shore excursions here, with something suited to nearly everyone's taste.

STOPPING FOR A BITE

Restaurants in St. Petersburg are expensive and not all that great, although you may be surprised to find Chinese and Indian food in addition to the traditional Russian meat-and-potato offerings. Still, if you must try chicken Kiev and blinis and caviar, and you don't mind paying top dollar (we're talking Paris prices), you're best off heading to a top hotel, such as the **Grand Hotel Europe,** Mikhailovskaya ul. 1/7 (☎ **329-60-00**).

BEST SHOPPING BUYS

Shop here for matreoshka dolls, hand-painted lacquer boxes, caviar, fur hats, vodka, and amber jewelry. Good places to hunt for souvenirs are around **St. Isaac's Square** and the **market** near Spilled Blood Cathedral.

12 Scotland

Edinburgh, the administrative, cultural, and educational capital of Scotland, is sometimes referred to as "the Athens of the North," and is the second most visited city in Great Britain after London. And no wonder. It's a beautiful, hip city, built in hills and valleys with parks and much greenery, and offers sights associated with such notables as Mary Queen of Scots and Bonnie Prince Charles. You can visit castles and other historic buildings (some from the 11th century), stroll around medieval Old Town and Georgian New Town, check out the museums and galleries, shop, then stop off at a pub.

If you're lucky enough to visit at the end of August, you can partake of the Edinburgh International (Arts) Festival, which attracts performers from around the world. During the festival, the Military Tattoo held on the esplanade in front of Edinburgh Castle features Scottish Regiments complete with bagpipes and drums, and other international military bands. Golfers may want to check out one of the six courses run by the city, or one of the 28 within the city's boundaries.

ESSENTIALS

LANGUAGE English

CURRENCY The basic unit of currency is the pound sterling (£), which is divided into 100 pence (p). Banknotes are issued in £1, £5, £10, £20, and £50 denominations. The exchange rate at press time was $1 = 60 pence.

FROMMER'S FAVORITE EDINBURGH EXPERIENCES

- **Walking the Royal Mile.** This is where Edinburgh began, the backbone of Old Town being this medieval thoroughfare stretching about a mile from Edinburgh Castle downhill to the Palace of Holyroodhouse. It's well worth a stroll.
- **Wandering around New Town.** By new, we're talking 1766 to 1840. On the streets, squares, and circles (called "circuses") of this area you'll find one of the largest concentrations of Georgian-style buildings in the world.
- **Downing a pint at a pub.** Follow in the footsteps of such figures as Robert Lewis Stevenson and Arthur Conan Doyle, who downed a pint or two themselves when they were students at the University of Edinburgh.

COMING ASHORE & GETTING AROUND

Cruise ships generally dock in Leith, the city's port and industrial center, about 3 miles (or a 5- to 10-minute cab ride) from downtown Edinburgh. Some ships dock in Ayr, near Glasgow, about 1 1/2 hours from Edinburgh, and offer shore excursions into the city that are similar, although lengthier and pricier, to those described below.

Taxis are usually available at the pier. Walking is the best way to explore the city, particularly Old Town. The city also has an efficient bus system.

THE BEST SHORE EXCURSIONS

Edinburgh Castle & City Tour (3 hours, $48): Visit Edinburgh Castle and drive past the city's major attractions, including Princes Street, the Royal Mile, and Holyroodhouse.

Stirling Castle & Glenturret (6 hours, $92): Take in the Scottish countryside as you head to the Glenturret Distillery to learn about the malt whiskey–making process, and then to Stirling Castle, one of the finest examples of Renaissance architecture in the country and a place with a fascinating history: William Wallace (of *Braveheart* fame), Robert the Bruce, and Mary Queen of Scots all left their mark here.

THE TOP ATTRACTIONS

In addition to the attractions below, fans of malt whiskey will want to visit the **Scotch Malt Whiskey Society** in Leith (where cruise ships dock). It's on the second floor of a 16th-century warehouse at 87 Giles St. (☎ **0131/554-3451**). The only thing served is single-malt whiskey, neat, usually in a dram (unless you want yours watered down with branch water). You can choose among selections from more than 100 Scottish distilleries.

Edinburgh Castle. Castlehill. ☎ **0131/225-1012.** Admission about $9.90 adults, $2.45 children 15 and under. Apr–Oct daily 9:30am–5:15pm.

The city's dramatic landmark was built on what's believed to be a dead volcano, known as Castle Rock. Inside, you can visit the State Apartments, including Queen Mary's bedroom, where she gave birth to James VI of Scotland (later James I of England). But the highlight of a tour is the Crown Chamber, which houses the Scottish Crown Jewels. St. Margaret's Chapel is the oldest part of the castle, dating principally from the 12th century. The castle's gorgeous gardens are also worth a look.

Edinburgh

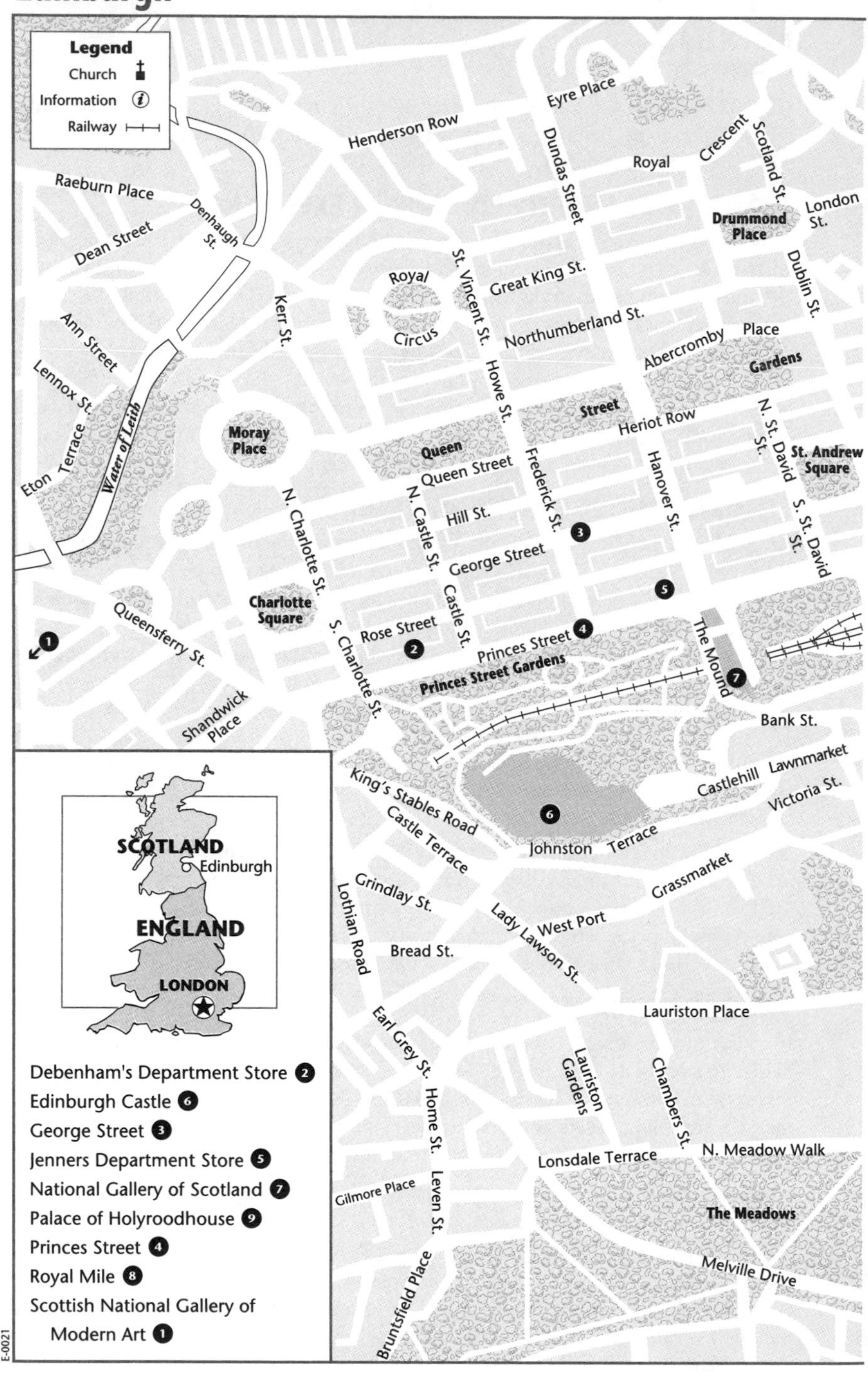

Legend
Church
Information
Railway
Henderson Row
Eyre Place
Dundas Street
Royal
Crescent
Scotland St.
London St.
Drummond Place
Raeburn Place
Denhaugh St.
Dean Street
Royal Circus
St. Vincent St.
Great King St.
Dublin St.
Kerr St.
Northumberland St.
Abercromby Place
Gardens
Ann Street
Lennox St.
Howe St.
Street
Heriot Row
Water of Leith
Moray Place
Queen
Queen Street
Frederick St.
Hanover St.
N. St. David St.
St. Andrew Square
Eton Terrace
N. Charlotte St.
N. Castle St.
Hill St.
S. St. David St.
George Street
Charlotte Square
Castle St.
Queensferry St.
Rose Street
S. Charlotte St.
Princes Street
Princes Street Gardens
The Mound
Shandwick Place
Bank St.
King's Stables Road
Castlehill
Lawnmarket
Victoria St.
Castle Terrace
Johnston Terrace
SCOTLAND
Edinburgh
ENGLAND
LONDON
Grindlay St.
Lothian Road
Grassmarket
Lady Lawson St.
West Port
Bread St.
Lauriston Place
Earl Grey St.
Lauriston Gardens
Chambers St.
Home St.
N. Meadow Walk
Lonsdale Terrace
Gilmore Place
Leven St.
The Meadows
Bruntsfield Place
Melville Drive
Debenham's Department Store 2
Edinburgh Castle 6
George Street 3
Jenners Department Store 5
National Gallery of Scotland 7
Palace of Holyroodhouse 9
Princes Street 4
Royal Mile 8
Scottish National Gallery of Modern Art 1
E-0021

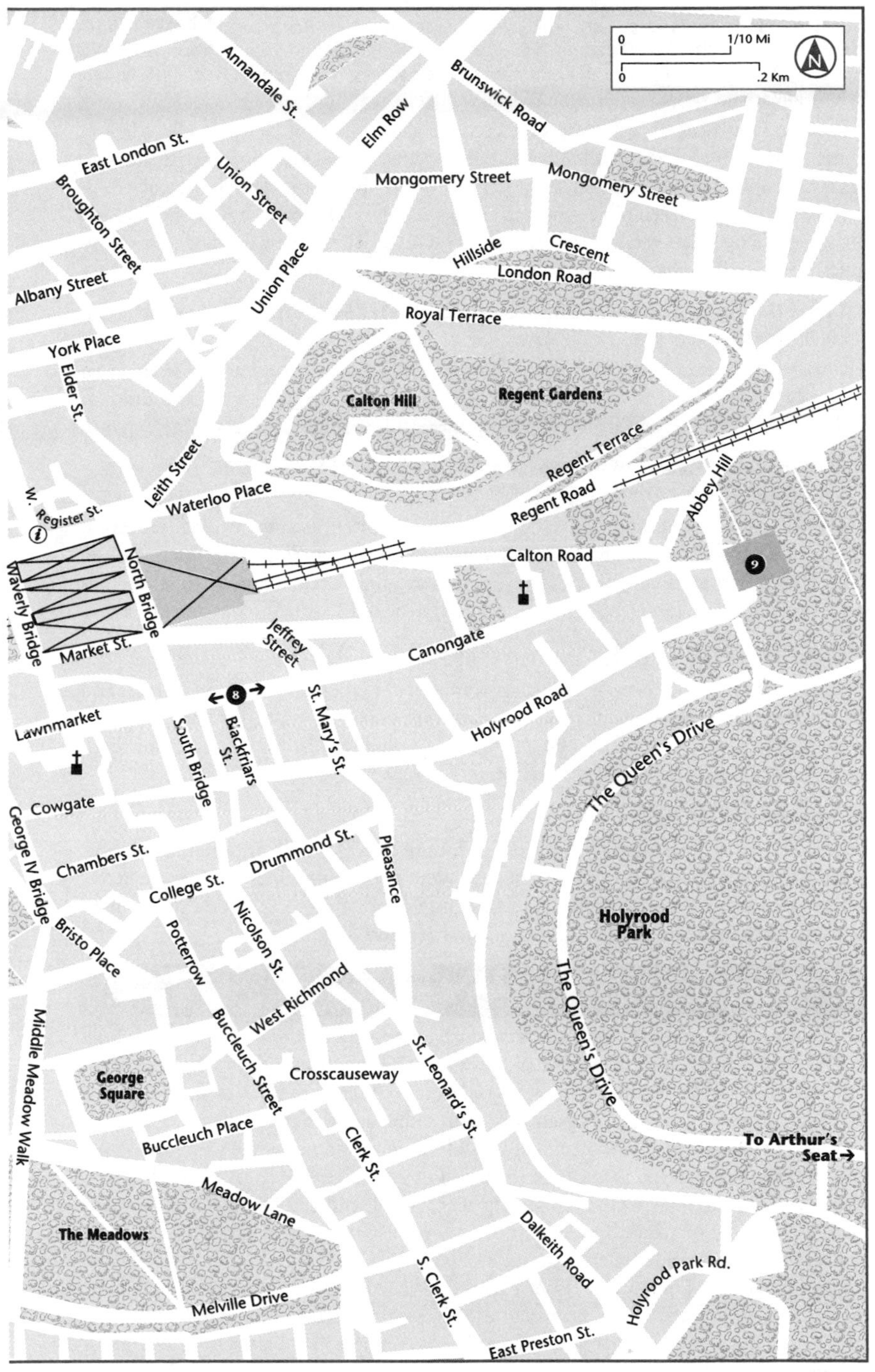

0
1/10 Mi
0
.2 Km
N
Annandale St.
Brunswick Road
Elm Row
East London St.
Union Street
Mongomery Street
Mongomery Street
Broughton Street
Union Place
Hillside
Crescent
London Road
Albany Street
Royal Terrace
York Place
Elder St.
Calton Hill
Regent Gardens
Leith Street
Regent Terrace
Abbey Hill
W. Register St.
Waterloo Place
Regent Road
Calton Road
9
North Bridge
Waverly Bridge
Jeffrey Street
Market St.
Canongate
8
St. Mary's St.
Holyrood Road
Lawnmarket
South Bridge
Blackfriars St.
The Queen's Drive
Cowgate
George IV Bridge
Chambers St.
Drummond St.
Pleasance
College St.
Nicolson St.
Holyrood Park
Bristo Place
Potterrow
West Richmond
The Queen's Drive
Middle Meadow Walk
Buccleuch Street
St. Leonard's St.
George Square
Crosscauseway
Buccleuch Place
Clerk St.
To Arthur's Seat
Meadow Lane
The Meadows
Dalkeith Road
S. Clerk St.
Holyrood Park Rd.
Melville Drive
East Preston St.

Palace of Holyroodhouse. Canongate, at the east end of the Royal Mile. ☎ **0131/556-1096.** Admission about $9.05 adults, $6.10 seniors, $4.30 children 15 and under. Mon–Sat 9:30am–5:15pm, Sun 10:30am–4:30pm. Closed last 2 weeks in May and 3 weeks in late June to early July (dates vary).

This palace has been an official residence since the early 16th century. Her Majesty Queen Elizabeth and Prince Phillip live here whenever they visit Edinburgh (the palace is closed when they are in residence). The most dramatic incident at the palace occurred when Mary Queen of Scots was in residence. Mary's husband, Lord Darnley, and his accomplices, murdered her Italian secretary, David Rizzio (he was stabbed some 56 times). Bonnie Prince Charles was also among the residents here.

National Gallery of Scotland. 2 The Mound. ☎ **0131/556-8921.** Free admission. Mon–Sat 10am–5pm, Sun 2–5pm.

The gallery is rather small, but the collection includes two Raphaels, Titian's two Diana canvases, and his *Venus Rising from the Sea,* all on loan from the duke of Sutherland. Scottish, English, and Spanish masters are represented as well.

Scottish National Gallery of Modern Art. Belford Rd. ☎ **0131/6246200.** Free admission except for some temporary exhibits. Mon–Sat 10am–5pm, Sun 2–5pm.

This former school building, which dates from 1828, offers an international collection that includes Henry Moore and Barbara Hepworth sculptures, Picasso, Braque, Matisse, Miró, Ernst, Lichtenstein, and Hockney, as well as English and Scottish artists including William Turner, John Constable, Henry Raeburn, and David Wilkie, to name a few.

STOPPING FOR A BITE

Local favorites include cock-a-leekie soup (a mixture of chicken, leeks, and prunes) and various seafood preparations. If you're adventurous, you may want to try **haggis** (made of sheep's innards). A stop at a pub is a must-do, whether just for drinks or for food. Favorite brews include McEwan's real ale or Tennent's lager.

BEST SHOPPING BUYS

Best buys here include Scottish woolens (including kilts), crystal, antiques, and crafts. **Princes Street** is the Edinburgh equivalent to New York's Fifth Avenue. **George Street** and the **Royal Mile** also offer plenty of shopping opportunities. The best department stores are **Debenham's,** at 109 Princes St., and **Jenners,** 48 Princes St.

13 Sweden

Stockholm, a city of Renaissance splendor mixed with very modern skyscrapers, is built on 14 bridge-connected islands in Lake Mälaren, which marks the beginning of an archipelago of 24,000 islands, skerries, and islets stretching all the way to the Baltic Sea. Definitely plan to be on deck as your ship cruises through the archipelago.

While the medieval walls of Stockholm's Old Town are no more, the winding cobblestone streets, dating to the 13th century, are well preserved and a real treat to visit. Here, within walking distance of the cruise ship pier, you'll find the Royal Palace, ancient churches, historic merchant houses, and dozens of restaurants and shopping opportunities (including art galleries and antique stores).

Another must is Djurgården (Deer Park), the site of many of the city's popular attractions, including the open-air museums of Skansen and the *Vasa* man-of-war. You can get there easily by ferry. If you want to further explore the archipelago, or are just looking for some quiet time, boats leave frequently in the summer from the harbor for the bathing resort of **Vaxholm** and other scenic islands.

ESSENTIALS

LANGUAGE Swedish. English is also commonly spoken.

CURRENCY Sweden's basic unit of currency is the krona (plural *kronor*). One krona is divided into 100 öre. Banknotes are issued in denominations of 20, 50, 100, 500, 1,000, and 10,000 kronor. The rate of exchange at press time was $1 = 8.25 kronor.

FROMMER'S FAVORITE STOCKHOLM EXPERIENCES

- **Exploring Gamla Stan (Old Town), especially at night.** The narrow cobblestone streets are specially lit. It's like going back in time.
- **Taking a ferry to Djurgården.** Here you'll find the Vasa Ship Museum and other popular attractions.
- **Watching the summer dawn.** If you can get yourself out of bed at 3am in midsummer, you're in for a treat.
- **Fishing.** You can even fish in downtown Stockholm, casting a line within view of the king's palace for some of the finest salmon in the world.

COMING ASHORE & GETTING AROUND

Cruise ships dock about 1 mile (1.5km) from the city center, and within easy walking distance of the Royal Palace and Gamla Stan (Old Town). You can get around by **bus, subway** (T-bana), and **tram** (streetcar). **Taxis** are available at the pier, but are expensive. The meter starts at $3.45. A short ride can easily cost more than $11.

THE BEST SHORE EXCURSIONS

City Tour (3 hours, $40): This comprehensive city tour includes districts of Gamla Stan, Normalm, Östermalm, Djurgården and Södermalm, each with its own special character. Begin with a short drive up to Fjällgatan, for a panoramic view of the city, then head through Gamla Stan, the medieval Old Town, and pass the Royal Palace.

Proceed past the Royal Dramatic Theater along Strandvägen to the island of Djurgården for a tour that includes the Vasa Museum. Continue through Diplomatic town to Östermalm, a fashionable neighborhood of stately apartment buildings, then on to Hamngatan and Sergel's Torg, the focal point of modern Stockholm. Proceed south past the Parliament Building, past the House of Nobility, and via the narrow canal at Slussen to Södermalm, the large island on Stockholm's south side, where you'll find a number of small, closely integrated neighborhoods. An alternative tour substitutes a visit to Stadshuset, Stockholm's imposing, red-brick city hall (where they hold the Nobel Prize Banquet) in place of the Vasa Museum.

Historic Stockholm & Sigtuna (6½ hours, $115): This tour offers a driving tour of the city, a walk through Old Town, a stop at the Vasa Museum, and a drive through the scenic countryside to visit Sigtuna on Lake Mälaren. This religious village was founded approximately 1,000 years ago by the first Christian king of Sweden, and even today is a bastion of religion and education. Includes lunch and shopping time.

THE TOP ATTRACTIONS

Royal Flagship *Vasa*. Galärvarvet, Djurgården. ☎ **08/666-48-00.** Admission about $6.75 adults, $4.50 seniors and students, $1.50 children. June 10–Aug 20, daily 9:30am–7pm. At other times, Wed 10am–8pm, Thurs–Tues 10am–5pm. Take ferry from Slussen.

This 17th-century man-of-war is the world's oldest identified and complete ship and the biggest tourist attraction in Stockholm. It capsized and sank on its maiden voyage in 1628. The ship was salvaged in 1961 and has been carefully restored. Some 97% of its original sculptures were also retrieved.

Stockholm

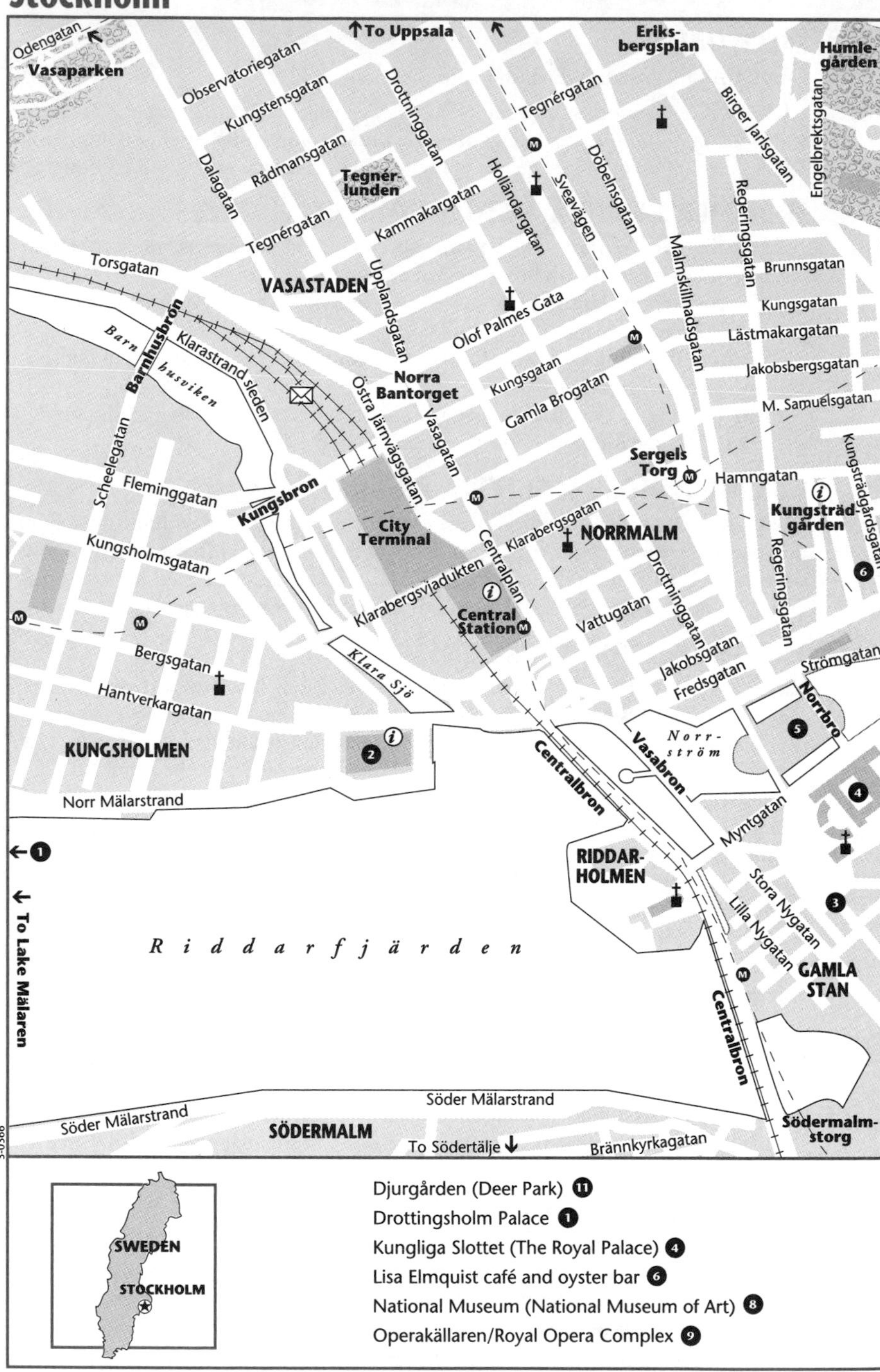

To Uppsala
Odengatan
Vasaparken
Eriks-bergsplan
Humle-gården
Observatoriegatan
Kungstensgatan
Drottninggatan
Tegnérgatan
Birger Jarlsgatan
Engelbrektsgatan
Rådmansgatan
Dalagatan
Tegnér-lunden
Holländargatan
Sveavägen
Döbelnsgatan
Regeringsgatan
Kammakargatan
Tegnérgatan
Malmskillnadsgatan
Brunnsgatan
Torsgatan
VASASTADEN
Upplandsgatan
Kungsgatan
Olof Palmes Gata
Lästmakargatan
Barnhusbron
Barn husviken
Klarastrand sleden
Jakobsbergsgatan
Norra Bantorget
Östra Järnvägsgatan
Kungsgatan
M. Samuelsgatan
Vasagatan
Gamla Brogatan
Scheelegatan
Kungsträdgårdsgatan
Sergels Torg
Hamngatan
Fleminggatan
Kungsbron
Kungsträd-gården
City Terminal
Klarabergsgatan
NORRMALM
Kungsholmsgatan
Centralplan
Drottninggatan
Klarabergsviadukten
Regeringsgatan
Central Station
Vattugatan
Bergsgatan
Klara Sjö
Jakobsgatan
Strömgatan
Fredsgatan
Hantverkargatan
Norrbro
Norr-ström
KUNGSHOLMEN
Vasabron
Centralbron
Norr Mälarstrand
Myntgatan
RIDDAR-HOLMEN
To Lake Mälaren
Stora Nygatan
Lilla Nygatan
Riddarfjärden
GAMLA STAN
Centralbron
Söder Mälarstrand
Söder Mälarstrand
Södermalm-storg
SÖDERMALM
To Södertälje
Brännkyrkagatan
3-0366
SWEDEN
STOCKHOLM
Djurgården (Deer Park) 11
Drottingsholm Palace 1
Kungliga Slottet (The Royal Palace) 4
Lisa Elmquist café and oyster bar 6
National Museum (National Museum of Art) 8
Operakällaren/Royal Opera Complex 9

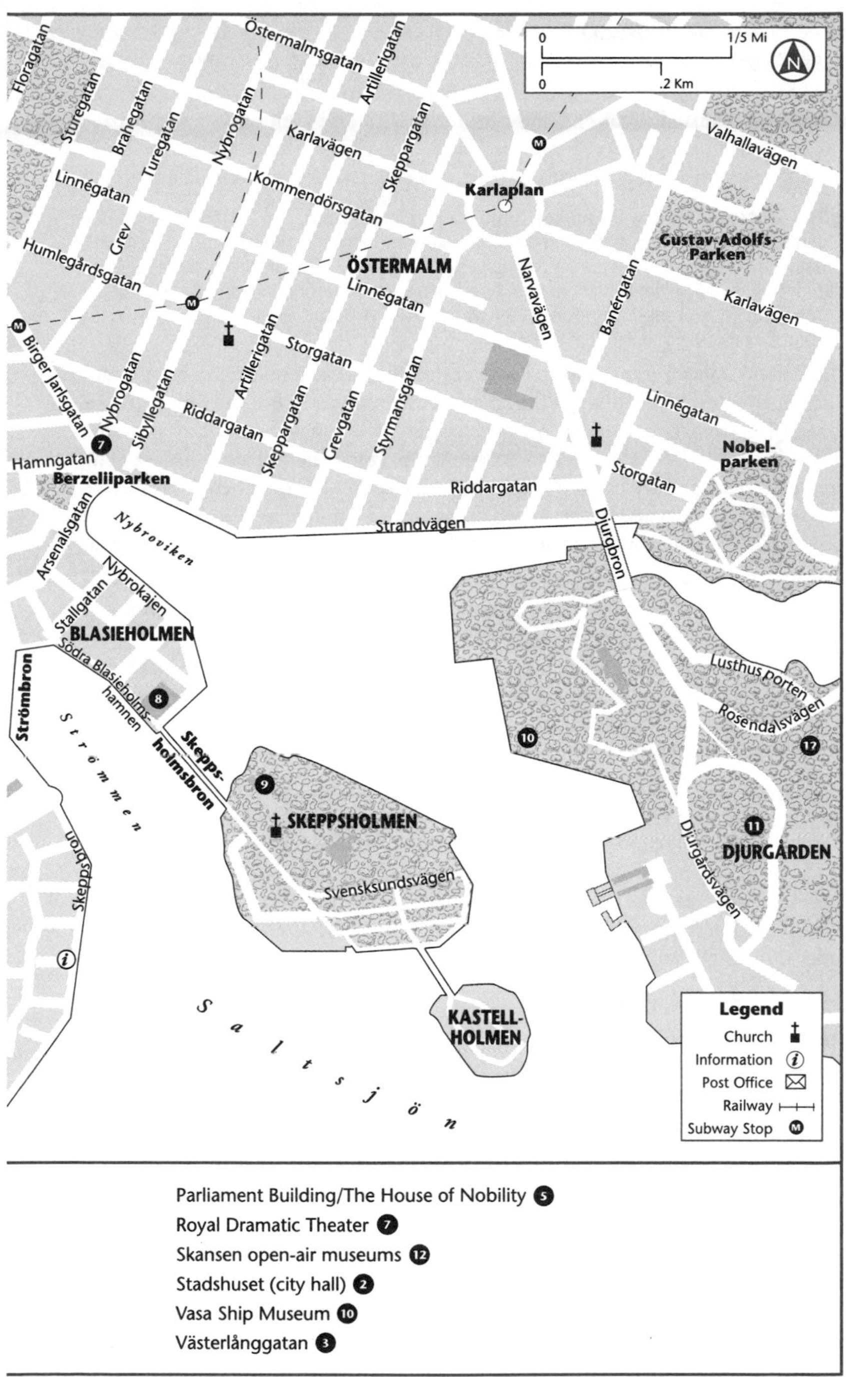

0
1/5 Mi
0
.2 Km
N
Floragatan
Sturegatan
Brahegatan
Turegatan
Nybrogatan
Östermalmsgatan
Artillerigatan
Karlavägen
Skeppargatan
Valhallavägen
Linnégatan
Kommendörsgatan
Karlaplan
Grev
Humlegårdsgatan
ÖSTERMALM
Narvavägen
Banérgatan
Gustav-Adolfs-Parken
Karlavägen
Linnégatan
Storgatan
Birger Jarlsgatan
Nybrogatan
Sibyllegatan
Artillerigatan
Riddargatan
Skeppargatan
Grevgatan
Styrmansgatan
Linnégatan
Nobel-parken
Hamngatan
Berzeliiparken
Riddargatan
Storgatan
Strandvägen
Djurgbron
Nybroviken
Arsenalsgatan
Nybrokajen
Stallgatan
BLASIEHOLMEN
Södra Blasieholmshamnen
Strömbron
Strömmen
Skeppsholmsbron
Lusthusporten
Rosendalsvägen
SKEPPSHOLMEN
Svensksundsvägen
Skeppsbron
DJURGÅRDEN
Djurgårdsvägen
KASTELL-HOLMEN
Saltsjön
Legend
Church
Information
Post Office
Railway
Subway Stop
Parliament Building/The House of Nobility 5
Royal Dramatic Theater 7
Skansen open-air museums 12
Stadshuset (city hall) 2
Vasa Ship Museum 10
Västerlånggatan 3

Skansen. Djurgården. ☎ **08/442-80-00.** Admission $4.50–$8.25 adults, $1.50 children 14 and under. May–Aug, daily 11am–5pm; Apr and Sept, daily 9am–5pm. Take ferry from Slussen.

Referred to as "Old Sweden in a nutshell," this open-air museum offers more than 150 dwellings from Lapland to Skaøne, most from the 18th and 19th centuries, that have been reassembled on about 75 acres of parkland. The exhibits range from a windmill to a manor house to a complete town quarter, plus folk dancing and open-air concerts.

Kungliga Slottet (The Royal Palace). Kungliga Husgerådskammaren. ☎ **08/402-61-30.** Admission to apartments about $6.75 adults, $3 seniors and students; Royal Armory, $6 adults, $4.50 seniors and students; Museum of Antiquities, $3.75 adults, $3 seniors and students; Treasury, $6 adults, $3.75 seniors and students. Apartments and treasury, June–Aug, daily 10am–4pm; Sept and May, Tues–Sun noon–3pm. Museum of Antiquities, June–Aug only, daily noon–4pm. Royal Armory, daily 11am–4pm.

This 608-room Italian baroque palace is one of the few official residences of a European monarch open to the public (though the king and queen prefer to live and bring up their children at Drottningholm—see below). A changing-of-the-guard ceremony is offered here Monday to Saturday at noon and on Sunday at 1pm. You can also tour the State Apartments. The Treasury exhibits a celebrated collection of crown jewels, while the Royal Armory has weapons, armor, gilded coaches, and coronation costumes from the 16th century. The Museum of Antiquities has Gustav III's Roman sculpture collection.

Drottningholm Palace. Drottningholm. ☎ **08/402-62-80.** Admission about $6 adults, $1.50 children. May–Aug, daily 11am–4:30pm; Sept Mon–Fri 1–3:30pm, Sat–Sun noon–3:30pm. Catch the ferry from City Hall (also reachable by bus or subway).

Modeled on Versailles, this palace, built on an island about 7 miles from Stockholm, is the actual home of Sweden's Royal Family. Inside are courtly art, royal furnishings, and Gobelin tapestries; outside fountains and parks. Nearby is Drottningholm Court Theater (☎ **08/759-04-06**) the best preserved 18th century theater in the world.

National Museum (National Museum of Art). Södra Blasieholmshamnen. ☎ **08/666-44-10.** Admission about $9 adults, $6 seniors and students, free for children 15 and under. Tues 11am–8pm, Wed–Sun 11am–5pm. The museum is located a short walk from the Royal Opera House.

One of the oldest museums in the world (it celebrated its 200th birthday in 1992), the collection here offers a treasure trove of rare paintings and sculpture, from Rembrandt to Rubens, Bellini to van Gogh.

STOPPING FOR A BITE

The best place to sample Sweden's legendary smörgåsbord is **Operakällaren** (☎ **08/676-58-00**), which is part of the Royal Opera Complex on Kungsträdgården and dates from 1787. The emphasis is on fresh fish, but you'll also find smoked eel, reindeer, Swedish red caviar, and grouse. There's a regular menu as well. The price tag for the smörgåsbord is around $38.25, and reservations are required. For a different kind of experience, try **Lisa Elmquist** (☎ **08/660-92-32,** reservations recommended), a cafe and oyster bar located in the produce market (Östermalms Saluhall). A favorite here is shrimp with bread and butter ($12.75 to $17.25).

BEST SHOPPING BUYS

It seems like anything of Swedish design is gorgeous, including housewares, hand-blown glass, wood items, and handicrafts, but they can all be pricey. Items to watch for include kids' clothes, silver jewelry, reindeer gloves, stainless-steel utensils, Swedish clogs, handwoven items, and woolens. Everybody's favorite shopping area is **Gamla Stan** (Old Town). The main street for browsing is **Västerlånggatan.**

Part 4

Appendixes

With information on end-of-cruise concerns such as tipping, debarking, and retrieving your luggage, plus lists of airline and car-rental toll-free numbers and Web sites.

Appendix A: Wrapping Up Your Cruise—Debarkation Concerns

Hardly anybody likes to get off the ship at the end of their cruise, but it's part of the deal. To make it easier, here are a few matters you'll have to take care of before heading back to home sweet home.

1 The Debarkation Talk

On the last full day of your cruise, the cruise director will offer a debarkation talk covering areas such as tipping, settling your onboard account, packing, dealing with Customs and Immigration, and debarkation procedures, all as they apply to your specific ship. You or a member of your party should attend the talk, particularly if you are a first-time cruiser. You might also be able to catch a broadcast of the session on your in-room TV, and procedures will also be printed in your daily bulletin, but the talk is your chance to ask any questions you might have. Some lines even offer a prize drawing to encourage your attendance at the session.

2 Tips on Tipping

Tipping is an area that some people find confusing. First, let's establish that on almost all lines (the exceptions being the ritzy Seabourn and Radisson), you are expected to tip the crew—in particular your cabin steward, waiter, and busboy—and to not do so is bad form, since these people rely on tips for the better part of their income. How much you tip is totally up to you, though the cruise line will make suggestions in the daily bulletin and in the cruise director's debarkation briefing. Keep in mind that these are just suggestions. Generally speaking, each passenger should tip his or her cabin steward and waiter a minimum of about $3 to $3.50 per day each, and the busboy $1.50 to $2. In practice, many people nudge it up a bit more so the total tips are $10 to $12 a day per person. (On some European lines, suggested amounts will be lower.) On some ships you are also encouraged to tip the waiter and maitre d'; also your butler, if you have one.

Tips to the crew are paid at the end of the cruise. Occasionally, tips are pooled and distributed among the crew after the cruise.

You may have to pay tips in cash (U.S. dollars are okay), although some lines let you put the tips on your charge account.

Bar bills automatically include a 15% tip, but if a bartender or wine steward has served you exceptionally well you can slip him or her a bill too.

Tip-Free Cruising

A few lines—for example, HAL and Windstar, have a no-tipping-required policy, meaning you're under no obligation, though staff on these ships will gladly accept tips if proffered. Some other lines, however, have a no-tipping-allowed policy that is strictly enforced.

Don't tip the captain or other officers, since they're salaried employees, and tipping them is gauche, if not embarrassing.

If a porter carries your bags at the pier, he'll likely expect a tip.

3 Disembarkation

SETTLING UP

Your shipboard account will close in the wee hours before departure, but prior to that time you will receive a preliminary bill in your cabin. If you are settling your account with your credit card, you don't have to do anything but make sure all the charges are correct. If there is a problem, you will have to report to the purser's office, where you will likely encounter long lines.

If you are paying by cash or traveler's check you will be asked to settle your account during either the day or night before you leave the ship. This will require that you report to the purser's office.

A final invoice will be delivered to your room before departure.

Keeping receipts for shipboard purchases during your cruise will help you with your tallying efforts, and also ensure you're not surprised when the bill arrives.

PACKING UP

With thousands of suitcases to deal with, big ships have established the routine of requiring guests to pack the night before departure. You will be asked to leave your bags in the hallway before you retire for the night (or usually by midnight). The bags will be picked up overnight and removed from the ship before passengers are allowed to disembark. (If you end up partying late and end up putting your bags out after other bags on your deck have already been collected, advise the purser's office so they can send someone to get your bags; if you don't leave your bags in the hall you will have to carry them off the ship yourself). You'll see them again in the cruise terminal, where they'll most likely be arranged by deck number.

It's important to make sure your bags are tagged with the **luggage tags** given to you by the cruise line. These tags are color-coded to indicate deck number and disembarkation order. If you need more tags, alert your cabin steward.

A good rule of thumb is to begin packing before dinner. Usually the last night of your cruise will be a casual night to make things easier. When packing, remember to leave out any clothes and toiletries you will need the next day, and don't pack your valuables, breakables, travel documents, or medication. Make sure everything you keep out fits in your overnight bag.

Pack all your purchases made during the trip in one suitcase. This way you can easily retrieve them if you are stopped at Customs (see below).

DEBARKATION ORDER

You'll know it's the day you have to get off the ship because loudspeaker announcements will start blaring particularly early in the morning.

You won't be able to get off the ship until it is cleared by Customs and other authorities, a process that usually takes 90 minutes.

Even so, in most cases you will be asked to vacate your cabin early in the morning (as early as 8am) to give the crew time to prepare the space for the next load of passengers. Before you leave the cabin, check all the drawers to make sure you don't leave anything behind.

On disembarkation day, breakfast may be served earlier than usual, and there may be limited room service or no room service at all. Check your daily bulletin for details.

It takes about 2 hours to get everyone off the ship, and people will be given departure numbers. Those with earlier flights will be allowed to leave first. Everyone will want to leave the ship at the same time, but unless you have an early number, you don't have to rush. Grab a book and head up to the deck, catch a movie or other ship offering, or find another way to occupy yourself. Clogging the hallways doesn't help anyone get off faster.

If things drag on and you're concerned about missing your flight, tell a crew member.

MORE BAGGAGE

If you booked your air through the cruise line and are heading right home, you will collect your bags—there should be porters to help—and proceed to the bus to the airport.

If you booked your own air, you're on your own. You can retrieve your bags—again, there should be porters to help—and catch a cab to the airport or your next destination.

If you're on a post-cruise tour, special instructions will be given by the cruise line.

4 Customs

CLEARING CUSTOMS & IMMIGRATION

Make sure you allow enough time at the European airport to check in, collect any Value-Added Tax refunds owed you on the purchases you have made (see chapter 3 for more on VAT) and clear Immigration (you'll need to show your passport).

You may also want to allow time to check out the airport's duty-free offerings.

When you return to the U.S., you will again have to show your passport at Immigration, collect your bags, and clear Customs. You will be handed a Customs form on the plane to fill out.

CUSTOMS For U.S. citizens, standard Customs allowances are $400 in goods duty-free, including 1 liter of alcohol per person over age 21 and 1 carton of cigarettes. The same goes for green card holders and non–U.S. residents staying more than 72 hours in the U.S.

On the first $1,000 worth of goods over $400 you pay a flat 10% duty. Beyond that, duty is charged on an item-by-item basis.

You don't have to pay duty on fine works of art, antiques more than 100 years old, and some other luxury items. And you do not have to pay duty on items you mail home.

If you do go over your limit, you will have to report to a Customs official. If you are in doubt about whether you have gone over the limit, you can ask a Customs officer for help in filling out the form.

If you go over your allowance, fail to declare it, and get caught, you can get in a heap of trouble, and you might have to pay stiff fines.

Remember that fruits, seeds, animals, plants, and meat are not allowed ashore (this is a Customs rule rather than a ship rule). This includes any leftovers from the fruit basket in your cabin.

Is the Earth Moving, or Is It Me?

When you get off the ship, and especially when you close your eyes, you might experience a feeling of rocking, as if you're still on the water. Don't worry—this is perfectly normal and should go away by the next day.

For more information and to help you understand the rules, which are really quite complicated, check out the U.S. Customs Service Web site (www.customs.ustreas.gov) or write for the department's booklet, "Know Before You Go," P.O. Box 7407, Washington, DC 20044.

FOR BRITISH CITIZENS You can bring home almost as much as you like of any goods from any EU country (there are limits, in theory at least, of 90 liters of wine). If you are returning home from a non-EU country or if you buy goods in a duty-free shop, you're restricted to 200 cigarettes, 2 liters of table wine, plus 1 liter of spirits or 2 liters of fortified wine. For more information, contact **Her Majesty's Customs and Excise Office,** New King's Beam House, 22 Upper Ground, London SE1 9PJ (☎ **0171/620-1313**).

FOR CANADIAN CITIZENS Canada allows a $500 exemption, and you're allowed to bring back 200 cigarettes, 2.2 pounds of tobacco, 40 imperial ounces of liquor, and 50 cigars. In addition, you're allowed to mail gifts to Canada (with some restrictions). *Note:* The $500 exemption can only be used once a year and only after an absence of 7 days. For more information, write for the booklet "I Declare," issued by **Revenue Canada,** 2265 St. Laurent Blvd., Ottawa, ONT K1G 4KE (☎ **800/461-9999** or 613/993-0534).

FOR AUSTRALIAN CITIZENS The duty-free allowance is A$400, or, for those under 18, A$200. Citizens can also bring in 250 cigarettes or 250 grams of loose tobacco, and 1125ml of alcohol. A helpful brochure, "Know Before You Go," is available from Australian consulates and Customs offices. For more information, contact the **Australian Customs Services,** GPO Box 8, Sydney, NSW 2001 (☎ **02/9213-2000**).

FOR NEW ZEALAND CITIZENS The duty-free allowance is NZ$700. Citizens over 17 years of age can bring in 200 cigarettes or 50 cigars, or 250 grams of tobacco, plus 4.5 liters of wine and beer or 1.125 liters of liquor. Most questions are answered in a free pamphlet, "New Zealand Customs Guide for Travellers," which is available at New Zealand consulates and Customs offices. For more information, contact **New Zealand Customs,** 50 Anzac Ave., P.O. Box 29, Auckland (☎ **09/359-6655**).

Appendix B: Airline & Car-Rental Toll-Free Numbers & Web Sites

AIRLINES

Aer Lingus
☎ 800/474-7424 in the U.S.
☎ 01/886-8888 in Ireland
www.aerlingus.ie

Air Canada
☎ 800/776-3000
www.aircanada.ca

Air New Zealand
☎ 800/262-2468 in the U.S.
☎ 800/663-5494 in Canada
☎ 0800/737-767 in New Zealand

American Airlines
☎ 800/433-7300
www.americanair.com

British Airways
☎ 800/247-9297
☎ 0345/222-111 in Britain
www.british-airways.com

Canadian Airlines International
☎ 800/426-7000
www.cdnair.ca

Continental Airlines
☎ 800/525-0280
www.continental.com

Delta Air Lines
☎ 800/221-1212
www.delta-air.com

Northwest Airlines
☎ 800/225-2525
www.nwa.com

Qantas
☎ 800/474-7424 in the U.S.
☎ 612/9691-3636 in Australia
www.qantas.com

Tower Air
☎ 800/34-TOWER (800/348-6937)
☎ 718/553-8500 New York
www.towerair.com

Trans World Airlines (TWA)
☎ 800/221-2000
www.twa.com

United Airlines
☎ 800/241-6522
www.ual.com

US Airways
☎ 800/428-4322
www.usairways.com

Virgin Atlantic Airways
☎ 800/862-8621 in Continental U.S.
☎ 0293/747-747 in Britain
www.fly.virgin.com

CAR-RENTAL AGENCIES

Auto Europe
☎ 800/223-5555
www.autoeurope.com

Avis
☎ 800/331-1212 in Continental U.S.
☎ 800/TRY-AVIS in Canada
www.avis.com

Budget
☎ 800/527-0700
www.budgetrentacar.com

Dollar
☎ 800/800-4000
www.dollarcar.com

Hertz
☎ 800/654-3131
www.hertz.com

Kemwel Holiday Auto (KHA)
☎ 800/678-0678
www.kemwel.com

National
☎ 800/CAR-RENT
www.nationalcar.com

Index by Ship Name

continues

Ship	Cruise Line	Page
Mistral	First European	137
Monterey	Mediterranean Shipping	149
Noordam	Holland America Line	82
Nordkapp	Norwegian Coastal Voyage	156
Nordlys	Norwegian Coastal Voyage	156
Nordnorge	Norwegian Coastal Voyage	156
Norwegian Dream	Norwegian Cruise Line	89
Odysseus	Royal Olympic	170
Olympic Countess	Royal Olympic	171
Olympic Voyager	Royal Olympic	175
Oriana	P & O	162
Panorama	Classical	239
Polarlys	Norwegian Coastal Voyage	156
Queen Elizabeth 2	Cunard Line	203
R1	Renaissance	112
R2	Renaissance	112
Radisson Diamond	Radisson Seven Seas	208
Rhapsody	Mediterranean Shipping	150
Richard With	Norwegian Coastal Voyage	156
Rotterdam	Holland America Line	83
Royal Clipper	Star Clippers	266
Royal Princess	Princess	106
Sea Cloud	Sea Cloud	253
Seabourn Goddess I	Seabourn	217
Seabourn Goddess II	Seabourn	217
Seabourn Legend	Seabourn	218
Seabourn Pride	Seabourn	218
Seabourn Spirit	Seabourn	218
Seabourn Sun	Seabourn	220
Seawing	Airtours/Sun Cruises	182
Silver Cloud	Silversea	224
Silver Shadow	Silversea	225
Silver Wind	Silversea	224
Song of Flower	Radisson Seven Seas	209
Splendour of the Seas	Royal Caribbean	117
Star Clipper	Star Clippers	264
Star Flyer	Star Clippers	264
Stella Solaris	Royal Olympic	172
Sunbird	Airtours/Sun Cruises	182
Sundream	Airtours/Sun Cruises	182

Ship	Cruise Line	Page
Topaz	Thomson	185
Triton	Royal Olympic	174
Victoria	P & O	164
Wind Song	Windstar	230
Wind Spirit	Windstar	230
Wind Star	Windstar	230
Wind Surf	Windstar	231
World Renaissance	Royal Olympic	170
Zeus II	Zeus Tours	270
Zeus III	Zeus Tours	270

FROMMER'S® COMPLETE TRAVEL GUIDES

Alaska
Amsterdam
Arizona
Atlanta
Australia
Austria
Bahamas
Barcelona, Madrid & Seville
Beijing
Belgium, Holland & Luxembourg
Bermuda
Boston
Budapest & the Best of Hungary
California
Canada
Cancún, Cozumel & the Yucatán
Cape Cod, Nantucket & Martha's Vineyard
Caribbean
Caribbean Cruises & Ports of Call
Caribbean Ports of Call
Carolinas & Georgia
Chicago
China
Colorado
Costa Rica
Denmark
Denver, Boulder & Colorado Springs
England
Europe
Florida
France
Germany
Greece
Greek Islands
Hawaii
Hong Kong
Honolulu, Waikiki & Oahu
Ireland
Israel
Italy
Jamaica & Barbados
Japan
Las Vegas
London
Los Angeles
Maryland & Delaware
Maui
Mexico
Miami & the Keys
Montana & Wyoming
Montréal & Québec City
Munich & the Bavarian Alps
Nashville & Memphis
Nepal
New England
New Mexico
New Orleans
New York City
Nova Scotia, New Brunswick & Prince Edward Island
Oregon
Paris
Philadelphia & the Amish Country
Portugal
Prague & the Best of the Czech Republic
Provence & the Riviera
Puerto Rico
Rome
San Antonio & Austin
San Diego
San Francisco
Santa Fe, Taos & Albuquerque
Scandinavia
Scotland
Seattle & Portland
Singapore & Malaysia
South Africa
Southeast Asia
South Pacific
Spain
Sweden
Switzerland
Thailand
Tokyo
Toronto
Tuscany & Umbria
USA
Utah
Vancouver & Victoria
Vermont, New Hampshire & Maine
Vienna & the Danube Valley
Virgin Islands
Virginia
Walt Disney World & Orlando
Washington, D.C.
Washington State

Frommer's® Dollar-a-Day Guides

Australia from $50 a Day
California from $60 a Day
Caribbean from $70 a Day
England from $70 a Day
Europe from $60 a Day
Florida from $60 a Day
Hawaii from $70 a Day
Ireland from $50 a Day
Israel from $45 a Day
Italy from $70 a Day
London from $85 a Day
New York from $80 a Day
New Zealand from $50 a Day
Paris from $85 a Day
San Francisco from $60 a Day
Washington, D.C., from $60 a Day

Frommer's® Portable Guides

Acapulco, Ixtapa & Zihuatanejo
Alaska Cruises & Ports of Call
Bahamas
Baja & Los Cabos
Berlin
California Wine Country
Charleston & Savannah
Chicago
Dublin
Hawaii: The Big Island
Las Vegas
London
Maine Coast
Maui
New Orleans
New York City
Paris
Puerto Vallarta, Manzanillo & Guadalajara
San Diego
San Francisco
Sydney
Tampa & St. Petersburg
Venice
Washington, D.C.

Frommer's® National Park Guides

Family Vacations in the National Parks
Grand Canyon
National Parks of the American West
Rocky Mountain
Yellowstone & Grand Teton
Yosemite & Sequoia/Kings Canyon
Zion & Bryce Canyon

Frommer's® Great Outdoor Guides

New England
Northern California
Southern California & Baja
Washington & Oregon

Frommer's® Memorable Walks

Chicago
London
New York
Paris
San Francisco
Washington D.C.

Frommer's® Irreverent Guides

Amsterdam
Boston
Chicago
Las Vegas
London
Los Angeles
Manhattan
New Orleans
Paris
San Francisco
Seattle & Portland
Vancouver
Walt Disney World
Washington, D.C.

Frommer's® Best-Loved Driving Tours

America
Britain
California
Florida
France
Germany
Ireland
Italy
New England
Scotland
Spain
Western Europe

The Unofficial Guides®

Bed & Breakfast in New England
Bed & Breakfast in the Northwest
Beyond Disney
Branson, Missouri
California with Kids
Chicago
Cruises
Disneyland
Florida with Kids
The Great Smoky & Blue Ridge Mountains
Inside Disney
Las Vegas
London
Miami & the Keys
Mini Las Vegas
Mini-Mickey
New Orleans
New York City
Paris
San Francisco
Skiing in the West
Walt Disney World
Walt Disney World for Grown-ups
Walt Disney World for Kids
Washington, D.C.

Special-Interest Titles

Born to Shop: France
Born to Shop: Hong Kong
Born to Shop: Italy
Born to Shop: New York
Born to Shop: Paris
Frommer's Britain's Best Bike Rides
The Civil War Trust's Official Guide to the Civil War Discovery Trail
Frommer's Caribbean Hideaways
Frommer's Europe's Greatest Driving Tours
Frommer's Food Lover's Companion to France
Frommer's Food Lover's Companion to Italy
Frommer's Gay & Lesbian Europe
Israel Past & Present
Monks' Guide to California
Monks' Guide to New York City
The Moon
New York City with Kids
Unforgettable Weekends
Outside Magazine's Guide to Family Vacations
Places Rated Almanac
Retirement Places Rated
Road Atlas Britain
Road Atlas Europe
Washington, D.C., with Kids
Wonderful Weekends from Boston
Wonderful Weekends from New York City
Wonderful Weekends from San Francisco
Wonderful Weekends from Los Angeles